PRINCIPLES OF EVIDENCE

PRINCIPLES

OF

EVIDENCE

PJ Schwikkard
BA (Wits) LLM (Natal)
Senior Lecturer in Law, University of Natal, Pietermaritzburg
Attorney of the Supreme Court of South Africa

A St Q Skeen
BA (Hons) (Rhodes) BL (Hons) LLB (Rhodesia) MPhil (Cantab)
Professor of Law, University of the Witwatersrand; Legal Practitioner, Zimbabwe

S E van der Merwe
BIuris (UPE) LLB (Unisa) LLD (Cape Town)
Professor of Law, University of Stellenbosch; Advocate of the Supreme Court of South Africa

in collaboration with

W L de Vos
BA LLM LLD (RAU)
Professor of Law, University of Stellenbosch; Advocate of the Supreme Court of South Africa

S S Terblanche
BIuris (PU vir CHO) LLD (Unisa)
Associate Professor of Law, University of South Africa; Advocate of the Supreme Court of South Africa

E van der Berg
BIuris LLB (UPE)
Senior Lecturer in Law, University of Port Elizabeth; Attorney of the Supreme Court of South Africa

and assisted by

H Rademeyer
BA LLM (Stell)
Candidate Attorney

JUTA & CO, LTD
1997

ACKNOWLEDGEMENTS

Parts of this work contain articles written by S E van der Merwe and previously published in 1985 *De Rebus* 445, 1991 *Stell LR* 62, 1992 *Stell LR* 175, 1995 *Obiter* 194 and 1996 *Obiter* 246. The publishers and editors are thanked for their permission to reprint.

First published 1997

© Juta & Co, Ltd
PO Box 14373
Kenwyn
7790

ISBN 0 7021 3897 5

Cover: Comet Design, Cape Town
Copy-editing and typesetting: Wyvern Publications CC, Cape Town
Printed and bound by Creda Press, Cape Town

PREFACE

Constitutional supremacy not only has significant implications for our law of evidence but also carries in its wake an unavoidable (and, we should like to suggest, exciting) period of relative uncertainty. We have endeavoured to indicate what the essential impact of constitutional provisions has been — or may or will be — on some of our common-law and statutory rules of evidence. We have tried, wherever possible, to weave constitutional provisions and issues into our discussions of the conventional areas of the law of evidence; but in two instances constitutional provisions justified independent chapters: Chapter 12 deals with the admissibility of unconstitutionally obtained evidence, and Chapter 29 addresses the constitutionality of presumptions.

We have attempted to strike a balance between the theory of the law of evidence and its practical application, and we did so in the context of our constitutionalized legal system. Our primary aim was to cater for the needs of students, but we trust that the text will also assist candidate attorneys, pupils at the bar and practitioners — steeped in the traditional Anglo-South African law of evidence — to familiarize themselves with constitutional issues arising in the law of evidence.

At the time of writing there was considerable uncertainty as to the date on which the Constitution of the Republic of South Africa, Act 108 of 1996 ("the final Constitution") would come into operation. It was therefore decided to use Chapter 3 "Fundamental Rights" of the Constitution of the Republic of South Africa, Act 200 of 1993 (in this work referred to as "the interim Constitution") as our text in preparing the manuscript, but to include Chapter 2 "Bill of Rights" of the final Constitution as Appendix A to this work. For comparative purposes and for the sake of convenience, Chapter 3 of the interim Constitution is reflected as Appendix B. It should be noted that the final, unlike the interim, Constitution deals specifically with the vexed question concerning the admissibility of unconstitutionally obtained evidence — a matter which is discussed in Chapter 12 of this work.

We should like to thank the following:
— Professors Wouter de Vos and Stephan Terblanche and Messrs Eugene van der Berg and Henk Rademeyer for their valuable contributions and punctuality;
— Ms Lindsay Norman of Juta for her efficiency in overseeing the production of this book;
— Mr Rod Prodgers of Wyvern Publications for editing and typesetting, and for compiling the tables of cases and statutes;
— Mrs Elra Smit, secretary of the Department of Public Law, University of

Stellenbosch, who cheerfully and accurately typed large parts of the manuscript;
— Mr Barry van der Merwe, Regional Court Magistrate, Pretoria, for his useful suggestions.

An attempt was made to state the law as at August 1996.

PJ SCHWIKKARD
Pietermaritzburg
ANDREW ST Q SKEEN
Johannesburg
STEPH E VAN DER MERWE
Durbanville

30 October 1996

CONTENTS

SECTION A
AN INTRODUCTION TO THE LAW OF EVIDENCE

SECTION B
THE ADMISSIBILITY OF RELEVANT EVIDENCE

SECTION E
THE ADMISSIBILITY AND PROOF OF THE
CONTENTS OF RELEVANT DETRIMENTAL STATEMENTS

SECTION F
KINDS OF EVIDENCE AND THE PRESENTATION THEREOF

SECTION G
WITNESSES

SECTION H
PROOF WITHOUT EVIDENCE

SECTION I
WEIGHT OF EVIDENCE AND STANDARDS AND BURDENS OF PROOF

Mode of Citation of Principal Works and Sources

ASSAL . . . . *Annual Survey of South African Law*

CPA . . . . Criminal Procedure Act 51 of 1977

CPEA . . . . Civil Proceedings Evidence Act 25 of 1965

Du Toit et al *Commentary* E du Toit, F J de Jager, A P Paizes, A St Q Skeen,
  S E van der Merwe Commentary on the Criminal
  Procedure Act (1987, as revised bi-annually)

Hoffmann & Zeffertt . . L H Hoffmann & D T Zeffertt *The South African Law
  of Evidence* 4 ed (1988)

Lansdown & Campbell . A V Lansdown & J Campbell *South African Criminal
  Law and Procedure* vol V *Criminal Procedure and
  Evidence* (1982)

LAWSA . . . . W A Joubert (ed), C W H Schmidt, D T Zeffertt, and
  revised by D P van der Merwe *The Law of South
  Africa* vol 9 *Evidence* First Reissue (1996)

Schmidt . . . . C W H Schmidt *Bewysreg* 3 ed (1989)

Wigmore . . . . H J Wigmore *A Treatise on the Anglo-American System
  of Evidence in Trials at Common Law* (1940) and
  revised editions (1961)

TABLE OF SOUTH AFRICAN STATUTES AND CONSTITUTIONS

TABLE OF CASES

L

M

SECTION A

AN INTRODUCTION TO THE LAW OF EVIDENCE

CHAPTER 1

An Introduction to the History and Theory of the Law of Evidence

S E van der Merwe

1 1   INTRODUCTION

Courts normally have to make a finding concerning the existence or non-existence of certain facts before pronouncing on the rights, duties and liabilities of the parties engaged in a dispute.[1] In this process of litigation and adjudication the proof of facts is regulated by the law of evidence, which is a branch of the law of procedure. However, the rights, duties and liabilities of the litigants are determined by substantive law, for example the law of contract.

It should be borne in mind, however, that there are also certain procedural rights and duties which stem from the law of evidence, for example the right to cross-examine and the duty to adduce evidence. These rights and duties are of a procedural nature in the sense that they form part of or emanate from the body of rules governing the proof of facts in a court of law. The right to cross-examine and the duty to adduce evidence relate to the law of evidence, which in turn forms part of the law of procedure in its widest sense.

The law of evidence is closely linked to criminal and civil procedure and forms part of that branch of the law commonly referred to as "adjective law"

---

[1] *S v Thomo* 1961 1 SA 385 (A) 394C–D (emphasis added): "It is . . . of importance . . . first to determine . . . what conduct . . . was established . . . Having thus determined the proper factual basis, the court can then proceed to consider what crime (if any) . . . has [been] committed. *The former enquiry is one of fact, the latter essentially one of law.*"

or "adjectival law". Some common-law and statutory procedural rights have hardened into constitutional guarantees.[2] The general impact of the interim Constitution on the law of evidence is examined in § 3 9 below.

It will later become evident that in some instances it is not always easy to draw the line of demarcation between substantive law and the law of evidence as a branch of the law of procedure.[3] However, this demarcation cannot be ignored:[4] the substantive-law rights and duties of the parties to an action are determined by rules and principles which largely stem from Roman-Dutch law, whereas the English law of evidence serves as the common law of the South African law of evidence.[5]

1 2   SCOPE AND FUNCTIONS OF THE LAW OF EVIDENCE

Procedural law gives practical meaning and effect to the rules of substantive law. It has often been said that substantive law might just as well not exist if there were no procedural machinery which could constantly transform the rules of substantive law into court orders and actual enforcements.

The law of evidence governs the proof of facts in a court of law and therefore forms part of the procedural machinery that makes substantive law effective.

The general scope of the law of evidence can be determined with reference to its specific functions. The main function of the law of evidence is to determine what facts are legally receivable (i e admissible) to prove the facts in issue. The law of evidence, however, also determines in what manner evidence should or may be adduced; what evidence may lawfully be withheld from a court of law; what rules should be taken into account in assessing the weight or cogency of evidence; and, further, what standard of proof should, in a given situation, be satisfied before a party bearing the burden of proof can be successful.

1 3   EARLY HISTORY AND DEVELOPMENT OF THE ENGLISH LAW OF EVIDENCE

The early history and evolution of the English law of evidence can be divided into three basic, successive stages:[6] the religious (primitive) stage, during which it was thought that one man should not sit in judgment upon another; the formal stage, during which the oath was the primary mode of proof and mistakes in form were fatal; and, finally, the rational stage, during which the tribunal no longer merely verified procedural formalities but was required to employ its reasoning powers in the fact-finding process.

1 3 1 The religious (primitive) stage During this stage "trial by ordeal" was considered an almost perfect aid in truth-finding. The ordeal was popular in

---

[2] See s 25(3) of the interim Constitution as well as ch 3 below.
[3] See ch 4 below.
[4] See generally *Botes v Van Deventer* 1966 3 SA 182 (A) 197. This case is discussed in § 16 4 below.
[5] See ch 3 below.
[6] See generally Esmein (transl by Simpson) *A History of Continental Criminal Procedure with Special Reference to France: Continental Legal History Series* vol V (1968) 617–19; Joubert 1982 *TSAR* 261.

England[7] and on the Continent.[8] It was really an appeal to God[9] (or the gods or the supernatural) to "decide" the factual dispute.[10] The Anglo-Saxons employed several different kinds of ordeals. In the "ordeal of the accursed morsel" (also known as the *corsnaed*) the accused was required to swallow a dry morsel of bread, accompanied by a prayer that he should choke if he were guilty.[11] In 1053 Godwin, the powerful Earl of Kent — whom Edward the Confessor had accused of murder — attempted to swallow his piece of bread, but choked and died (probably to the astonishment of all those who had attended the "trial"). This ordeal — and probably all other ordeals — might appear irrational[12] and even absurd to the modern mind.[13] But Paton and Derham maintain that there is a possible logical explanation in respect of the *corsnaed*: fear, brought about by feelings of guilt, dries the mouth and renders it more difficult to swallow a dry piece of bread![14] Would it be too far-fetched to suggest that the *corsnaed* was perhaps the early source of the modern rule that the demeanour of a witness may be taken into account as a factor affecting credibility?[15]

Trial by battle — a Norman novelty introduced after William the Conqueror's invasion in 1066 — was a further ordeal in terms of which a dispute could be settled by a duel. Holdsworth says that trial by battle was not merely an appeal to physical force:[16] "[I]t was accompanied by a belief that Providence will give victory to the right . . . The trial by battle is the *judicium Dei par excellence*." It has been suggested that the early roots of the present accusatorial (adversarial) trial system can be traced to trial by battle:[17] physical confrontation gradually developed into verbal confrontation.[18] And it will later be shown that the right to confront witnesses by cross-examining them is not only a marked characteristic of the accusatorial trial system but also gave rise to, inter alia, the hearsay rule.[19]

---

[7] See generally Nokes *An Introduction to Evidence* 4 ed (1967) 18; Thayer *A Preliminary Treatise on Evidence at the Common Law* (1898) 24–34, 67 and 81; Elton (ed) *The Law Courts of Medieval England* (1972) 25; Plucknett *A Concise History of the Common Law* (1956) 113–18; Kempin *Historical Introduction to Anglo-American Law* (1973) 54–7; Devlin *Trial by Jury* (1978) 6–7; Wakeling *Corroboration in Canadian Law* (1977) 8–9; Levy *Origins of the Fifth Amendment: The Right against Self-incrimination* (1968) 5–7.

[8] Diamond *Primitive Law Past and Present* (1971) 47, 297–312, 318, 386–7 and 390–1; Langbein *Torture and the Law of Proof* (1977) 6; Esmein (transl by Simpson) *A History of Continental Criminal Procedure with Special Reference to France: Continental Legal History Series* vol V (1968) 618; Hartland *Primitive Law* (1924) 191.

[9] Stein *Legal Institutions: The Development of Dispute Settlement* (1984) 25: "[I]n an age of faith, when there is a general belief in the direct intervention of divine providence in human affairs, it is not irrational to think that God knows what happened better than any human and that He will indicate which party was in the right."

[10] Nokes *An Introduction to Evidence* 4 ed (1967) 18.

[11] Forsyth (transl by Morgan) *History of Trial by Jury* (1878) 68. See also § 18 17 2 below.

[12] Damaska "Evidentiary Barriers to Conviction and Two Models of Criminal Procedure" 1973 121 *U Pa LR* 556n110: "By irrational I mean procedural devices such as trial by ordeal, which rests on religious imaginings, especially the belief that the deity can be summoned to intervene in the screening of the guilty from the innocent."

[13] Wigmore para 8.

[14] Paton & Derham *A Text-book of Jurisprudence* (1972) 597.

[15] See also § 30 4 below.

[16] Holdsworth in Goodhart & Hanbury (eds) *A History of English Law* vol 1 (1956) 308.

[17] Re "Oral v Written Evidence: The Myth of the Impressive Witness" 1983 57 *Australian LR* 679; Delisle *Evidence: Principles and Problems* (1984) 3.

[18] Van der Merwe 1991 *Stell LR* 281 290.

[19] See ch 13 below.

1 3 2 The formal stage The twelfth century witnessed an increase in human reason and "in the field of evidence . . . people were turning their backs on age old irrational methods".[20] In 1215 Pope Innocent III in the Fourth Lateran Council forbade priests to administer ordeals,[21] thereby destroying the validity of an entire system of proof. Langbein explains that the attempt "to make God the fact finder for human disputes was being abandoned. Henceforth, humans were going to replace God in deciding guilt or innocence . . .."[22]

In England the use of oath-helpers (later called "compurgators") became very popular. The compurgators were not eye-witnesses but merely people who were prepared to state under oath that the oath of one of the parties should be believed.[23] The party who was able to summon the largest number of compurgators "won" the case. Trial by compurgation was a formal procedure in the sense that the tribunal was still not required to weigh evidence.

In virtually every age the oath has been thought to provide the strongest hold on the consciences of men.[24] And even today the oath — however abused — plays an important role in the law of evidence.[25]

1 3 3 The rational stage (and development of the jury)[26] It was soon realized that the compurgators could make a more meaningful contribution. The compurgators were no longer called upon to express a mere belief in the veracity of a party's oath but were also expected to act as adjudicators, largely because of their knowledge of the events. A crude form of trial by jury developed, despite the personal knowledge that the "jurors" had. White describes the next development as follows:[27] "As population increased and everyday activities grew more complex, it developed that neighbours knew little or nothing of the facts in dispute. It was then that witnesses who did know some facts were called in to supply the requisite information . . . [T]he jury laid aside its old character . . . The very thing . . . [i e personal knowledge] . . . that qualified a man for jury service in the olden times, at a much later date disqualified him." In the seventeenth century it was finally decided that a witness "swears but to what he

---

[20] Van Caenegem in Kuttner & Ryan (eds) *Proceedings of the Second International Congress of Medieval Canon Law: Boston College 12–16 August 1963: Monumenta Juris Canonic* Series C vol 1 (1965) 304.
[21] Thayer *A Preliminary Treatise on Evidence at the Common Law* (1898) 37; Kempin *Historical Introduction to Anglo-American Law* (1973) 55.
[22] Langbein *Torture and the Law of Proof* (1977) 6.
[23] Forsyth (transl by Morgan) *History of Trial by Jury* (1878) 63 gives an example of the use of compurgators. Accused A had to take the following oath: "By the Lord, I am guiltless, both in deed and counsel of the charge which B accuses me." The compurgators then had to reply: "By the Lord, the oath is clear and unperjured which A has sworn."
[24] Best *A Treatise on the Principles of Evidence and Practice as to Proofs in Courts of Common Law* (1849) para 55.
[25] *S v Munn* 1973 3 SA 734 (NC) 736H. See also generally *S v Bothma* 1971 1 SA 332 (C) and *S v Ndlela* 1984 1 SA 223 (N). See further s 162 of the CPA (as read with s 163) and s 39 of the CPEA (as read with ss 40 and 41).
[26] See Kahn 1991 *SALJ* 672 and 1992 *SALJ* 87, 307 and 666 and 1993 *SALJ* 322 for a general discussion and evaluation of the jury system, as well as the history of the jury in South Africa.
[27] White "Origin and Development of Trial by Jury" 1961 29 *Tennessee LR* 8 15.

hath heard or seen . . . to what hath fallen under his senses. But a jury-man swears to what he can infer and conclude from the testimony of such witnesses . . .."[28]

This distinction between a witness's function (to testify) and a juror's function (to determine facts on the basis of testimony presented by witnesses) had the important result that "jurors now were assumed to enter the box with a cognitive *tabula rasa* so that facts could be writ upon their minds through, for example, the medium of witnesses giving oral testimony . . .."[29] The general receipt of oral testimony established the principle of orality, and personal knowledge of the event in dispute led to disqualification of a juror. The central notion of an impartial adjudicator was accepted.

During the formative period of trial by jury the relative functions of judge and jury were also settled: the jurors determined the facts and the judges determined the law.[30] This procedural distinction between the functions of judge and jury had important results: the judges (who had to decide matters of law) thought that the jury (who had to decide matters of fact) might be misled or distracted by, or might be inclined to attach undue weight to, certain categories or types of evidence which, according to the judges, were notoriously untrustworthy. The judges therefore considered the admissibility of evidence a matter of law. They then ruled, as a matter of law, that certain evidence was inadmissible, most notably character and hearsay evidence. These decisions to exclude certain evidence were decisions of law and fell within the ambit of the doctrine of precedent: *stare decisis*.

The nineteenth and twentieth centuries witnessed a large number of statutory reforms in England as well as in South Africa. The South African legislature has in the past been inclined to base its own legislation on principles contained in English legislation. Statutory reform has to a large extent been aimed at relaxing the strict evidential rules which owe their existence to trial by jury.

The exact *extent* of the jury's influence on the historical development and modern rules of the Anglo-South African law of evidence is debatable. At the same time, however, it is equally true that a proper appreciation of some of the rules of evidence is only possible if these rules are constantly seen and evaluated within the context of trial by jury — despite the fact that trial by jury no longer exists. Trial by jury in civil and criminal cases was respectively (and finally) abolished in South Africa in 1927[31] and 1969.[32] But we have retained an evidentiary system designed for jury trials. Most of our exclusionary rules — and even some of our rules pertaining to the evaluation of evidence — can be attributed directly to trial by jury. It may be said that the jury was perhaps the single most significant factor in shaping the law of evidence. But the adversarial method of trial, the principle of orality,[33] the oath, the doctrine of precedent and the

---

[28] *Bushell's Case* 124 ER 1006 1009.

[29] Forkosch "The Nature of Legal Evidence" 1971 59 *California LR* 1356 1373.

[30] Nokes *An Introduction to the Law of Evidence* 4 ed (1967) 35. See further § 1 6 below as regards the function of assessors in our system of adjudication.

[31] Section 3 of the Administration of Justice (Further Amendment) Act 11 of 1927.

[32] Abolition of Juries Act 34 of 1969.

[33] Van der Merwe 1991 *Stell LR* 281.

so-called best evidence rule[34] collectively contributed to our present intricate system in terms of which facts should be proved in a court of law.

The steady decline and gentle disappearance of the jury in South Africa theoretically opened the door for a more liberal and robust approach with regard to the admission of evidence normally excluded in a jury trial. But our courts are for various reasons[35] obliged to follow the so-called strict system of evidence which emphasizes the *admissibility* of evidence. Developments in our law of evidence have been and are largely brought about by legislative action, one example being the Law of Evidence Amendment Act 45 of 1988, which came into operation on 3 October 1988. This Act mainly changed rules relating to hearsay (see § 13 2 below), judicial notice (see § 27 6 3 below) and the competence and compellability of spouses (see § 22 11 2 below).

1 4   PROCEDURAL AND EVIDENTIAL SYSTEMS AND SOME UNIVERSAL
       PRINCIPLES OF FACT-FINDING

There are basically two systems of evidence: the Anglo-American (or so-called strict or common-law) system and the Continental (or so-called free or civil-law system). The South African law of evidence belongs to the Anglo-American "family". Most of the principles of the Anglo-American law of evidence stem from the English system of adversarial (accusatorial) trials before a lay jury as opposed to the Continental inquisitorial trials by professional judges adjudicating without the assistance of a true jury.[36] It can be said that the Anglo-American procedural method of proving or ascertaining facts in a court of law is based upon adversarial principles and a strict system of evidence, whereas the Continental method is based upon inquisitorial principles and a free system of evidence. These procedural and evidential differences — which should be understood in a broad historical and evolutionary context — really emphasize the simple truth that there is more than one solution to the problem of fact-finding.[37]

It is probably correct to say that all enlightened and refined procedural and evidential systems are honest attempts to discover and protect the truth. And in this respect there is much common ground despite the peculiar historical origins and ideological preferences that each system might have. Consider the following. *First*, it is a universal principle that protection of the truth cannot be sacrificed for the sake of mere simplicity, speed and convenience.[38] *Secondly*, presentation of facts and adjudication of disputes must of necessity proceed in an orderly fashion: a lawsuit is "essentially a proceeding for the orderly settlement of a

---

[34] The so-called best evidence rule is presently only of importance as regards documentary evidence. See § 20 3 below.

[35] See ch 3 below.

[36] Heydon *Evidence: Cases and Materials* 3 ed (1991) 3. Most of the rest of this chapter is based on an article previously published by Van der Merwe 1985 *De Rebus* 445–51.

[37] Van der Merwe "Accusatorial and Inquisitorial Procedures and Restricted and Free Systems of Evidence" in Sanders (ed) *Southern Africa in Need of Law Reform* (1981) 141.

[38] Mueller & Le Poole-Griffiths *Comparative Criminal Procedure* (1969) 50.

dispute between litigants".[39] *Thirdly*, resolution of legal disputes must be done in such a way that reasonable litigants leave court with the feeling that they were given a proper opportunity to state their respective cases, that their cases were presented in the best possible light and manner, and, further, that the issues were decided by an impartial trier. *Fourthly*, the law of procedure and evidence must at all times maintain a certain level of efficiency and effectiveness in order to ensure that the rules of substantive law — however impressive and all-embracing they may be — are not for all practical purposes relegated to the ranks of unenforceable norms.

The procedural and evidential innovations which the South African legislature has introduced in respect of small claims courts[40] should be assessed in the light of the above remarks — as well as the fact that small claims courts are seen as a proper and acceptable solution to the problem of legal costs which a litigant may encounter in enforcing a modest civil claim.

1 5 ORDINARY COURTS AND SMALL CLAIMS COURTS: AN EXAMINATION OF PROCEDURAL AND EVIDENTIAL DIFFERENCES

The fundamental differences which exist between the Anglo-American and Continental systems can — from a theoretical and practical point of view and within the context of South African courts — perhaps be best explained by comparing the procedural and evidential system of our ordinary courts with that which exists in our small claims courts.

South African small claims courts function along inquisitorial lines. Section 26(3) of the Small Claims Courts Act 61 of 1984 (hereafter "the Act") provides that a party shall neither question nor cross-examine any other party to the proceedings (or a witness called by the latter party). The same section provides that the presiding commissioner "shall proceed inquisitorially to ascertain the relevant facts, and to that end he may question any party or witness at any stage of the proceedings". But there is a proviso in terms of which the presiding commissioner may in his discretion permit any party to put a question to any other party or any witness.[41] The procedure in our ordinary courts is totally different.[42]

South African small claims courts are not bound by the ordinary Anglo-South African rules of evidence. They are not required to follow the strict system of evidence which is applied in the ordinary South African courts and which can also be referred to as the Anglo-American or common-law system. Section 26(1) of the Act provides that — subject to the provisions of chapter 5 of the Act — the rules of the law of evidence shall not apply in respect of the proceedings in a small claims court and that such a court "may ascertain any relevant fact in such manner as it may deem fit".

---

[39] Morgan "Suggested Remedy for Obstructions to Expert Testimony by Rules of Evidence" 1943 10 *Univ of Chicago LR* 285.
[40] See the Small Claims Courts Act 61 of 1984 (especially ss 26, 27 and 28).
[41] See the proviso to s 26(3) of Act 61 of 1984.
[42] See ch 18 below.

The adoption of an inquisitorial procedure and a free system of evidence in small claims courts might appear to be far-reaching and even somewhat radical — especially to the South African lawyer who is, in a procedural context, steeped in Anglo-American tradition, practice, rules and principles. But the procedural measures taken by the legislature in respect of small claims courts should be seen in the light of the peculiar characteristics and unique nature and purpose of small claims courts, namely accessibility and the promotion of procedural simplicity.

Legal representation is not permitted in small claims courts.[43] There are various valid reasons for such exclusion.[44] For purposes of the present discussion, it is necessary only to refer to the following remarks and conclusions of the Hoexter Commission:[45]

(a) Legal representation "must inevitably tend to infuse into the proceedings that air of formality and technicality which is fundamentally alien to the real spirit of small claims procedures."[46]

(b) One of the most obvious objections to legal representation "is the increased cost to the litigants . . . This is the very problem which small claims courts were designed to solve."[47]

(c) If "the adjudicator maintains an actively inquisitorial role in the proceedings, the absence of legal representation results in an easier and speedier fact-finding process."[48]

It is fairly evident from the above that procedural innovations were necessary in order to attain and maintain the advantages of small claims courts. And in principle there is certainly nothing wrong or sinister in procedural innovations which are brought about to meet new and valid demands. After all, small claims courts were created for the benefit of the public and the procedure in small claims courts had to be structured accordingly: "Die prosesreg dien die gemeenskap — nie die omgekeerde nie."[49] Other countries have taken similar steps in order to establish the viability and accessibility of small claims courts. For example, the New York small claims courts — which were established in 1918 — dispensed with traditional rules of practice, procedure, pleading and evidence and accepted the principle that decisions could be made with the aid of an informal fact-finding process.[50]

---

[43] Section 7(2) of Act 61 of 1984.

[44] See generally Ervine "Small Claims: The Central Research Unit Report and Beyond" 1984 *Journal of the Law Society of Scotland* 66 68.

[45] Hoexter JA was the chairman of the *Commission of Inquiry into the Structure and Functioning of the Courts* (hereinafter referred to as the "Hoexter Commission").

[46] Paragraph 13 11 of the 4th interim report (RP 52/1982) of the Hoexter Commission.

[47] Paragraph 13 9 of the 4th interim report (RP 52/1982) of the Hoexter Commission.

[48] Paragraph 13 10 of the 4th interim report (RP 52/1982) of the Hoexter Commission.

[49] Van Niekerk, Van der Merwe & Van Wyk *Privilegies in die Bewysreg* (1984) 8.

[50] Purdum "The Early History of Small Claims Courts" 1981 65 *Judicature: The Journal of the American Judicature Society* 31 32.

1 5 1 Small claims courts and the inquisitorial procedure and free system of evidence In the Anglo-American world small claims courts have forced the adjudicator into a new procedural role. As early as 1913 Pound concluded that the adjudicator in a small claims court should not be a mere umpire, but should represent "both parties and the law" while actively seeking the truth — largely if not wholly unaided.[51] The Hoexter Commission took a similar view. The success or failure of the small claims courts largely depends on whether the commissioners, who are all trained in the tradition of the adversary system, are able to handle the inquisitorial characteristics of the small claims courts satisfactorily. And in this context it should also be borne in mind that the strict system of evidence is — historically and practically speaking — a concomitant of the adversarial model of fact-finding. The free system of evidence is to a large extent also a necessary novelty to the commissioner in a small claims court. A free system of evidence promotes procedural simplicity and avoids that air of procedural formality and sophistication which can create psychological barriers for litigants. Involved rules of evidence — and these are the true features of the strict system of evidence — make a trial "more complicated than is necessary, and . . . might well cause a gap between the courts and the people, and this will not increase faith in the administration of justice".[52] The principles of a free system of evidence are dealt with in greater detail in § 1 5 3 below.

1 5 2 Accusatorial versus inquisitorial procedure[53] The accusatorial (adversarial) trial procedure — which finds its symbolic roots in the early ritual of trial by battle — has three leading features: the parties are in principle responsible for the presentation of evidence in support of their respective cases; the adjudicator is required to play a passive role; and much emphasis is placed upon oral presentation of evidence and cross-examination of witnesses. The adversarial model proceeds from the premiss that greater approximation of the truth is possible if litigants are allowed to present their own evidence in a process which guarantees not only cross-examination of an opponent who testifies but also all witnesses called by such opponent. This explains the emphasis upon "orality". And cross-examination — which has somewhat smugly, but in obvious hyperbolical terms, been referred to as "the greatest legal engine ever invented for the discovery of truth"[54] — is a vital procedural right in a system which makes it technically possible for a party to present only evidence which is favourable to his case. The right of parties to cross-examine explains why the adversarial trial model can to some extent afford and maintain the relative inactivity of the adjudicator.

But the adversarial trial system certainly is not beyond criticism. *First,* it "presupposes for success some equality between the parties; when this is lacking

---

[51] Pound "The Administration of Justice in the Modern City" 1913 26 *Harvard LR* 302 319.
[52] Den Hollander 1975 *Acta Juridica* 332 349.
[53] See the sources referred to by Van der Merwe in 1991 *Stell LR* 281 284n18.
[54] Wigmore para 1367.

the 'truth' becomes too often simply the view of the powerful".[55] *Secondly*, its very essence — the notion of opponents engaged in a forensic duel — can generate unnecessary conflict which is not necessarily conducive to the resolution or settlement of a dispute. *Thirdly*, much of the outcome of a case depends upon the ability, wit, energy, ruthlessness and even permissible rudeness which the cross-examiner might display. *Fourthly*, the "selfish" and partial[56] manner in which parties are allowed to present evidence and the fact that the adjudicator may only in limited circumstances call witnesses may inevitably lead to a situation where the "procedural" or "formal truth" can be promoted at the expense of the "material truth". Brett makes the following remarks in respect of the adversarial method of fact-finding:[57]

" . . . [O]bserve the practice of scientists and historians in carrying out their investigations . . . [A] lengthy search will fail to reveal one competent practitioner in either discipline who will willingly and in advance confine himself, in deciding any question involving factual data, to a choice between two sets of existing data proffered to him by rival claimants. In short, the inquisitorial method is the one used by every genuine seeker of the truth in every walk of life (not merely scientific and historical investigations) with only one exception . . . the trial system in the common-law world."

In contradistinction to the adversarial model, the inquisitorial model is judge-centred. It proceeds from the premiss that a trial is not a contest between two opposing parties but essentially an inquiry to establish the material truth. Judicial examination is accepted as the pivotal mechanism in the process of fact-finding. The emphasis is upon an inquiry conducted with the aid of such evidence as the inquirer deems fit. The absence of a right to cross-examine also explains why the inquisitorial procedure puts the written word — as a means of receiving evidence — to greater use than the adversarial system. The commissioner in the small claims court may in his discretion receive written or oral evidence,[58] and may actively call for such evidence.

Devlin remarks as follows:[59]

"The essential difference between the [adversarial and inquisitorial] systems . . . is apparent from their names: the one is a trial of strength and the other is an inquiry. The question in the first is: are the shoulders of the party upon whom is laid the burden of proof . . . strong enough to carry and discharge it? In the second the question is: what is the truth of the matter? In the first the judge or jury are arbiters; they do not pose questions and seek answers; they weigh such material as is put before them, but they have no responsibility for seeing that it is complete. In the second the judge is in charge of the inquiry from the start; he will of course permit the parties to make out their cases and may rely on them to do so, but it is for him to say what it is that he wants to know."

And Devlin continues:[60]

"The English say that the best way of getting at the truth is to have each party dig for the facts that help it; between them they will bring all to light. The inquisitor works on his own

---

[55] Delisle *Evidence: Principles and Problems* (1984) 2.

[56] Frank *Courts on Trial* (1949) 85.

[57] Brett "Legal Decision Making and Bias: A Critique of an Experiment" 1973 45 *Univ of Colorada LR* 1 23.

[58] Section 26(2) of Act 61 of 1984.

[59] Devlin *The Judge* (1979) 54.

[60] Devlin *The Judge* (1979) 54.

but has in the end to say who wins and who loses. Lord Denning denies that the English judge is 'a mere umpire' and says that 'his object' above all, is to find out the truth'. The real difference is, I think, that in the adversary system the judge in his quest for the truth is restricted to the material presented by the parties . . . while in the inquisitorial system the judge can find out what he wants to know. Put in a nutshell, the arbiter is confined and the inquisitor is not."

It may be said — at the risk of over-simplification — that the inquisitorial procedure is a natural system of fact-finding in the sense that it dispenses with technical rules and is applied in our everyday activities. For example, a father inquiring into a dispute between his children acts inquisitorially in the sense that he will not merely rely upon information which the "parties" are prepared to submit; nor, for that matter, will he follow or adopt evidential rules which tell him in advance that he may not even receive certain "evidence".

Bentham (1748–1832) considered this "domestic or natural system" an acceptable "mode of searching out the truth";[61] and he accepted the "domestic forum" as the most nearly perfect tribunal,[62] providing some basic scale model in terms of which English procedural law could be recast. Were it not for the fact that Bentham has been trapped for more than a century and a half in a state of mummification in a glass case at the University College of London,[63] he probably would have taken great delight in observing a commissioner at work in a twentieth-century small claims court. "Hear" said Bentham "everybody who is likely to know anything about the matter, hear everybody but most attentively of all, and first of all those who are most likely to know most about it — that is the parties."[64] His approach to the law of evidence was also founded upon the hypothesis that the tribunal possesses the ability to weigh the various kinds of evidence — even where the tribunal consists of judge and jury.[65] It has rightly been said that the changes which he had advocated would have brought English procedure and evidence closer to the Continental practice.[66]

1 5 3 Strict versus free system of evidence[67] The strict system of evidence is to a large extent a concomitant of the adversarial system, whereas the inquisitorial trial is generally accompanied by a free system of evidence. This almost universal phenomenon can be explained on the basis that those countries which never experienced an extensive period of lay participation in the adjudication of disputes developed and accepted the idea of adjudication by a professional or "career" adjudicator who should not — and need not — be hampered by

---

[61] Hart *Essays on Bentham: Jurisprudence and Political Theory* (1982) 31–2.

[62] Keeton & Marshall "Bentham's Influence on the Law of Evidence" in Keeton & Shwarzenberger (eds) *Jeremy Bentham and the Law: A Symposium* (1948, reprint 1970) 86–7.

[63] Van der Westhuizen 1982 *DR* 477 478.

[64] Quoted by Hart *Essays on Bentham: Jurisprudence and Political Theory* 32.

[65] Further theories of Bentham are discussed by Twining *Theories of Evidence: Bentham and Wigmore* (1985) 19–100.

[66] Keeton & Marshall "Bentham's Influence on the Law of Evidence" in Keeton & Schwarzenberger (eds) *Jeremy Bentham and the Law: A Symposium* 86.

[67] See generally Van der Merwe "Accusatorial and Inquisitorial Procedures and Restricted and Free Systems of Evidence" in Sanders (ed) *Southern Africa in Need of Law Reform* (1981) 141 144–6.

artificial rules relating to the exclusion of evidence.[68] The central idea was — and still is — that in the adjudication of facts a professional judge need not be guided by rules of admissibility: the true issue in the process of adjudication is not one of admissibility, but weight; and the determination of weight is something which can and must be left to the professional judge. Sanders explains as follows:[69]

> "Related to the inquisitorial method of procedure and the concomitant emphasis on utility is the principle of the free evaluation of evidence. Except for matters of privilege and personal incompetence to testify on grounds such as kinship, tender age or prior felony convictions, the civil law acknowledges no exclusionary rules of evidence, particularly no hearsay or opinion rule. In the eyes of civil lawyers most of the grounds which under the common law serve to preclude the admission of evidence merely affect the weight to be attached to a particular item of evidence, which, according to them, should be a matter for the judge's free evaluation."

To the Anglo-American lawyer admissibility is largely a matter of law, whilst weight is a question of fact. But even in this context the Anglo-American approach is to make admissibility dependent upon the potential weight of the evidence.[70]

Seen from this angle, it is but a small step for an Anglo-American lawyer — or any other lawyer — to disregard the first question (*admissibility*) and answer only the second and final one (*weight*). It may be argued that in small claims courts the general absence of formal preliminary findings as regards the admissibility of evidence might lead to a proliferation of evidence and a multiplicity of collateral issues. But it should be borne in mind that a commissioner in a small claims court "shall proceed inquisitorially to ascertain the relevant facts".[71] It is upon this basis that he controls the volume of evidence — not upon the basis of artificial rules originally designed for jury trials, where it was feared that the evidence in dispute might distract or mislead the jury. Obviously, in both free and strict systems the adjudicators should always bear in mind that it "is one thing to say that a factor is relevant and an entirely different thing to say that it is cogent or persuasive".[72]

The discretionary admission of hearsay in small claims courts apparently does not present any problems. In a paper delivered at the South African Law

---

[68] See generally Capelletti & Perillo *Civil Procedure in Italy* (1965) 189. Many continental courts were originally bound by strict rules which regulated the evaluation of evidence. See generally Millar *Civil Procedure of the Trial Court in Historical Perspective* (1964) 22–3. These rules largely consisted of presumptions which were supposed to furnish "half proof" (*semi probatio*) or "full proof" (*plena probatio*). According to Kralik *Introduction to the Continental Judicial Organization and Civil Procedure* (1963) 8, the acceptance of a free system of evidence was a reaction to these strict rules. At 6–7 it is stated: "The principle of free . . . evaluation of evidence means that the court is not fettered by any formal rules of evidence . . . Behind this principle is a familiar history of dissatisfaction with a system of weighing evidence by artificial scales and tables . . . So the principle of free appreciation of evidence is now one of the most characteristic aspects of modern continental procedure. As compared with English and American law, continental law is less strict in regard to the admissibility of evidence and the procedure of prooftaking . . . ." See further Van der Merwe 1991 *Stell LR* 281 294.

[69] Sanders 1981 *CILSA* 196 206–7.

[70] See ch 5 below.

[71] Section 26(3) of Act 61 of 1984.

[72] *S v Fourie* 1973 1 SA 100 (D) 102H–103A.

Conference in 1970 Mr Justice H C Nicholas remarked as follows with reference to the hearsay rule as it was then applied in our ordinary courts:[73]

> "In South Africa, jury trials in civil cases were finally abolished many years ago. With the disappearance of the occasion for the hearsay rule, what necessity remains for its retention? The strongest reason which can be advanced is that hearsay evidence may be unreliable. That, however, is an objection which goes only to the weight of the evidence, which is a matter which can and should be determined by the Court. What advantage has a rule of exclusion, subject to certain arbitrary exceptions none of which have as their basis any real guarantee of the truth, over a rule of inclusion, which would admit all relevant evidence, and leave the assessment of its value to the Court? The answer is plainly that there is no advantage discernible."

The area of acute conflict between strict and free systems of evidence relates to hearsay. Continental countries, which never experienced an extensive period of lay participation in the form of a jury in the adjudication of disputes, see no reason for the general exclusion of hearsay.

Anglo-American lawyers generally take great pride in their procedural and evidential system — and rightly so. But at the same time it would certainly be arrogant to look upon the combination of an inquisitorial procedure and a free system of evidence as an inferior fact-finding mechanism, especially in the context of small claims courts and in view of the fact that the "functional test to which all procedural rules should be subjected is their practical efficiency in providing machinery for the prompt and reasonably cheap settlement of disputes on lines that do justice to both parties".[74]

1 6   JURORS AND ASSESSORS: SOME BRIEF COMPARATIVE REMARKS

In § 1 3 3 above it was pointed out that trial by jury has been abolished in South Africa. We have, nevertheless, retained the essential structure of a system designed for trial by jury. This can perhaps be justified in view of the increased use of lay assessors in lower courts.[75] Assessors[76] in lower courts[77] and in the Supreme Court[78] can to some extent be compared with jurors[79] as they are all finders of fact and do not decide legal issues.[80] But our system of adjudication differs materially from trial by jury. The role of jurors can briefly be summarized as follows: jurors are lay people and sole finders of fact. They listen to the evidence and hear arguments, and they receive a summing-up and instructions from the

---

[73] See the addendum to the report (RP 78/1971) of the Commission of Inquiry into Criminal Procedure and Evidence 46.
[74] Paton & Derham *A Text-book of Jurisprudence* (1972) 593.
[75] See generally Van der Merwe 1991 *Stell LR* 281 306.
[76] On assessors, see generally Richings "Assessors in South African Criminal Trials" 1976 *Crim LR* 107; Van Zyl Smit & Isakow 1985 *SAJHR* 218; Van Zyl Smit 1979 SALJ 173 and 1984 *SALJ* 212; Geldenhuys & Joubert *Criminal Procedure Handbook* (1996) 166–7; Swanepoel 1990 *SACJ* 174.
[77] See s 93*ter* of the Magistrates' Courts Act 32 of 1944 and Watney 1992 *THRHR* 465.
[78] See s 145 of the CPA and Bekker "Assessore in Suid-Afrikaanse Strafsake" in Strauss (ed) *Huldigingsbundel vir W A Joubert* (1988) 32.
[79] *R v Solomons* 1959 2 SA 352 (A) 363–4.
[80] Two assessors can overrule a judge or magistrate on the facts.

presiding judicial officer. They are then called upon in their capacity as sole finders of fact to consider and reach their verdict in the absence of the presiding judicial officer. And they are not required to advance reasons in support of their verdict. But in our system the judge or magistrate is at all times either a sole finder of fact or, where assessors are involved, a co-finder of fact.[81] A judge must give reasons for his verdict.[82] Magistrates almost invariably do give reasons for their verdict[83] and, failing which, they may in certain circumstances be legally required to do so.[84] It is true that the function of assessors can be compared with the function of jurors, because the function of assessors is — with one exception[85] — also limited to fact-finding. But assessors — unlike a jury — must give reasons for their verdict.[86] They either agree or disagree with the presiding judicial officer's reasons and finding, and in the event of a disagreement must furnish their own reasons in a separate judgment which is read out in court by the presiding judicial officer. And assessors — unlike jurors — are under constant and immediate judicial guidance in the sense that a judge (or magistrate) and the assessors involved in the trial have joint deliberations in reaching their respective verdicts. During these deliberations the presiding judicial officer can and must draw the attention of assessors — who of course may be lay people — to certain rules which govern the evaluation of evidence, for example, the cautionary rule, the rules governing inferences drawn from circumstantial evidence, and those rules which determine the effect of an accused's silence on the evaluation of the prosecution's *prima facie* case.

It has been suggested[87] that our law of evidence can with ease accommodate lay persons as finders of fact because the basic infrastructure exists, namely, the concentrated trial,[88] the principle of orality and the use of exclusionary rules.

---

[81] See generally s 145(4)(a) of the CPA and s 93*ter*(3)(e) of the Magistrates' Courts Act 32 of 1944.

[82] See s 146(b) of the CPA.

[83] See generally Ferreira *Strafproses in die Laer Howe* 2 ed (1979) 500.

[84] See, e g, rule 67(3) of the rules of the magistrates' courts.

[85] See s 93*ter*(1)(b) of the Magistrates' Courts Act 42 of 1944.

[86] See s 146(d) of the CPA and s 93*ter*(3)(e) of the Magistrates' Courts Act 32 of 1944.

[87] Van der Merwe 1991 *Stell LR* 281 306–7.

[88] See generally Erasmus 1990 *Stell LR* 348 355; Kötz 1987 *TSAR* 35 40.

CHAPTER 2

BASIC CONCEPTS AND DISTINCTIONS

S E van der Merwe

2 1   INTRODUCTION

This chapter is of a preliminary nature and most of the concepts explained here will be encountered again in the rest of this work.

2 2   FACTS IN ISSUE AND FACTS RELEVANT TO THE FACTS IN ISSUE

The facts in issue (*facta probanda*) are those facts which a party must prove in order to succeed; the facts relevant[1] to the facts in issue (*facta probantia*) are those facts which tend to prove or disprove the facts in issue. For example, in a paternity case the identity of the father will be a *factum probandum*[2] (that is, a fact in issue); sexual intercourse with the alleged father will be a *factum probans*[3] (that is, a fact relevant to the fact in issue). Schmidt makes a further distinction between primary and secondary *facta probanda*.[4] According to him, primary *facta probanda* would refer to those facts placed in issue by the pleadings (in civil proceedings) and the plea (in criminal proceedings). Secondary *facta probanda* would refer to *facta probantia* which are in issue; for example, in a paternity suit it may be disputed that sexual intercourse took place at the material time. This is then a *factum probans* which is in dispute.

    The facts in issue are, generally speaking, determined by substantive law,

---

[1] Four definitions of the concept "relevance" are furnished in § 5 3 below.
[2] "*Factum probandum*" is the singular of "*facta probanda*".
[3] "*Factum probans*" is the singular of "*facta probantia*".
[4] Schmidt 5.

whereas the rules of procedure — and in particular the law of evidence — determine the facts relevant to the facts in issue.

In both criminal and civil matters the number of facts in issue at the initial stage of the case may be reduced by means of formal admissions.[5] For example, where an accused is charged with murder it is necessary for the state to prove that the accused unlawfully and intentionally killed another person. Substantive law requires that these elements must be proved. During his explanation of plea in terms of s 115 of the CPA the accused may, however, admit that he killed a human being. At the same time he may dispute that the killing was unlawful. He may, for example, claim that the killing was justified by reason of self-defence. The fact that the accused killed the deceased may (with the consent of the accused) be recorded as a formal admission.[6] The state need then prove only unlawfulness. In this way the rules of procedure and substantive law determine the facts in issue.

2 3   EVIDENCE AND ARGUMENT

The meaning of evidence is discussed in §§ 2 4 and 2 5 below. Argument ("betoog") is not presented through evidence, but is merely persuasive comment made by the parties or their legal representatives with regard to questions of fact or law. Before judgment is delivered the parties or their legal representatives have, for example, a right to address the court on the cogency (or otherwise) of the evidence received during the course of the trial. Their comment, however, does not amount to evidence. During the course of a trial parties also have the right to object to and deliver argument with regard to the admissibility of certain evidence. The court is then required to make a ruling on the issue of admissibility. But here, too, the comments of the parties do not constitute evidence.

2 4   EVIDENCE AND PROBATIVE MATERIAL

There is a distinction between evidence ("getuienis") and probative material ("bewysmateriaal"). Our courts are not entirely consistent in distinguishing between the two.[7] What follows is a simplified overview.

"Evidence" essentially consists of oral statements made in court under oath or affirmation or warning (*oral evidence*).[8] But it also includes documents (*documentary evidence*)[9] and objects (*real evidence*)[10] produced and received in court.

Evidence, however, is not the only means of furnishing proof. In *S v Mjoli*[11] it was pointed out that even though an accused's admission made during the

---

[5] See ch 26 below.
[6] Section 115(2) *(b)* as read with s 220 of the CPA.
[7] See Van Wyk (1986) 21:1 *The Magistrate* 26 for an accurate and critical analysis of the confusion in this regard.
[8] See ch 18 below.
[9] See ch 20 below.
[10] See ch 19 below.
[11] 1981 3 SA 1233 (A) 1247–8.

explanation of plea in terms of s 115 of the CPA is not evidence by the accused, it still is "probative material" and there is therefore no impediment in the way of a trial court to use against the accused material furnished during such procedure. An explanation of plea is not given under oath or affirmation or warning and therefore cannot be classified as evidence.[12]

In *S v Mokgeledi*[13] it was held that formal admissions do not constitute evidence. Formal admissions dispense with the need to adduce evidence to prove facts in issue, and must be classified as probative material.

Judicial notice,[14] similarly, cannot be classified as evidence.

In *S v AR Wholesalers (Pty) Ltd*[15] it was confirmed that presumptions[16] also do not constitute evidence.

It is submitted that the term "probative material" is a convenient term to include not only oral, documentary and real evidence but also formal admissions, judicial notice, presumptions and — in terms of *Mjoli* supra — also those statements made in terms of s 115 of the CPA and which do not amount to formal admissions. Probative material therefore refers to more than oral, documentary and real evidence.

2 5 EVIDENCE AND PROOF [17]

Proof of a fact means that the court has received probative material with regard to such fact *and* has accepted such fact as being the truth for purposes of the specific case. Evidence of a fact is not yet proof of such fact: the court must still decide whether or not such fact has been *proved*. This involves a process of evaluation.[18] The court will only act upon facts found proved in accordance with certain standards. In a criminal case the standard of proof is proof beyond a reasonable doubt.[19] In a civil case the standard of proof is proof upon a balance of probability[20] — a lower standard than proof beyond reasonable doubt.

2 6 CONCLUSIVE PROOF AND *PRIMA FACIE* PROOF

Conclusive proof means that rebuttal is no longer possible.[21] It is proof which is taken as decisive and final.

---

[12] *S v Slabbert* 1985 4 SA 248 (C) 250A. See also *S v Zaba* 1978 1 SA 646 (O) 647 and *S v Mogoregi* 1978 3 SA 13 (O) 14.

[13] 1968 4 SA 335 (A) 337.

[14] See ch 27 below.

[15] 1975 1 SA 551 (NC) 556.

[16] See ch 28 below.

[17] Van Wyk 1976 *TSAR* 255. Evidence ("getuienis") and proof ("bewys") are not synonymous: *R v V* 1958 3 SA 474 (GW).

[18] See ch 30 below.

[19] See ch 31 below.

[20] See ch 32 below.

[21] *S v Moroney* 1978 4 SA 389 (A) 406.

Prima facie proof implies that proof to the contrary is (still) possible. In the absence of proof to the contrary, *prima facie* proof will, generally speaking, become conclusive proof. *Prima facie* proof is sometimes used as a synonym for *prima facie* evidence (especially by the legislature). This approach is, strictly speaking, incorrect.[22]

2 7 ADMISSIBILITY AND WEIGHT OF EVIDENCE

The admissibility of evidence and weight of evidence should not be confused.[23] Lansdown & Campbell state that:[24]

> "If what is adduced can in law properly be put before the court, it is admissible. It is only once it has been or could be admitted that its persuasiveness, alone or in conjunction with other evidence, in satisfying the court as to the *facta probanda* has to be considered."

There are no degrees of admissibility. Evidence is either admissible or inadmissible. Evidence cannot be more or less admissible. Once admissible, however, it may carry more or less weight according to the particular circumstances of the case. The court weighs or evaluates evidence to determine whether the required standard of proof has been attained. It is only after the evidence has been admitted and at the end of the trial that the court will have to assess the final weight of the evidence. The evaluation of evidence is dealt with in chapter 30 below.

It should be borne in mind, however, that the admissibility of evidence is in principle determined with reference to its relevance. In determining relevance reference must of necessity also be made to the potential weight of the evidence.[25] This, however, is a preliminary investigation in order to determine whether such evidence, once admitted, would be of assistance when it must finally be decided whether the facts in issue have been proved.

2 8 CONDITIONAL ADMISSIBILITY[26]

Evidence may be admitted on condition that some basic defect which renders it inadmissible is cured during the course of the trial.[27] This procedure is rare and is merely one of convenience.[28] A good example of conditional admissibility is found in *S v Swanepoel*,[29] where it was held that a document can be used in

---

[22] Van Wyk in Ferreira *Strafproses in die Laer Howe* 2 ed (1979) 418–23.

[23] In *S v Fourie* 1973 1 SA 100 (D) 102H–103A it was said that it "is one thing to say that evidence is relevant and an entirely different thing to say that it is cogent or persuasive". See also the quotation from *R v C* 1949 2 SA 438 (SR) 439 in § 5 3 6 n 44 below.

[24] At 720.

[25] See § 5 3 2 below.

[26] See generally *Van Tonder v Kilian* 1992 1 SA 67 (A) and cf *S v Ntuli* 1993 2 SACR 599 (W).

[27] Tapper *Cross and Tapper on Evidence* 8 ed (1995) 65.

[28] See also s 3(1) *(b)* and 3(3) of the Law of Evidence Amendment Act 45 of 1988 as discussed by De Vos & Van der Merwe 1993 *Stell LR* 7 20. See further § 13 8 below.

[29] 1980 1 SA 144 (NC).

cross-examination in spite of its authenticity being denied by the opposing party: it is only after the state (in a criminal case) and the plaintiff (in a civil case) have closed their cases that the accused and the defendant have the opportunity to place their cases before the court and tender their evidence on the authenticity of documents. If authenticity is not proved later, the evidence initially elicited in cross-examination with regard to the content of the document in question will be inadmissible despite the fact that it was received at an earlier stage, because the rule remains that cross-examination on an inadmissible document is not allowed.[30]

2 9   CIRCUMSTANTIAL AND DIRECT EVIDENCE [31]

Circumstantial evidence often forms an important component of the information furnished to the court. In these instances the court is required to draw inferences, because the witnesses have made no direct assertions with regard to the fact in issue. These inferences must comply with certain rules of logic.[32]

Circumstantial evidence furnishes *indirect* proof.[33] In a murder trial, for example, evidence may be given that A had a motive to kill B and was seen running from B's home with a bloodstained knife. Evidence, however, is *direct* when a fact in issue is proved directly by such evidence; for example, where witness C testifies that he saw A stabbing B in the latter's home.

The distinction between direct and circumstantial evidence is of special importance in those instances where an accused decides not to testify in his own defence.[34]

2 10   PRIMARY AND SECONDARY EVIDENCE

The distinction between primary and secondary evidence is of importance with regard to documentary evidence.[35] In the fifth edition of *Cross on Evidence* it was said:[36]

> "Primary evidence is that which does not, by its very nature, suggest that better evidence may be available: 'Secondary evidence' is that which, by its very nature, does suggest that better evidence may be available. The original of a document is primary evidence, a copy secondary evidence, of its contents. The distinction is now mainly of importance in connection with documents, because their contents must, as a general rule, be proved by production of the original, but it used to be of much greater significance on account of the 'best evidence' rule which occupied a prominent place in books on the law of evidence in the eighteenth and early nineteenth centuries."

---

[30] See *R v Black* 1923 AD 388 and § 18 6 5 3 below.
[31] See generally *S v Mtsweni* 1985 1 SA 590 (A) 593D–594A.
[32] Se ch 30 below.
[33] Schmidt 4.
[34] *S v Mthetwa* 1972 3 SA 766 (A) 769. See further ch 30 below.
[35] See generally Hoffmann & Zeffertt 390. See further §§ 20 3–20 5 below.
[36] Cross *Cross on Evidence* 5 ed (1979) 15.

2 11   HEARSAY [37]

In terms of s 3(4) of the Law of Evidence Amendment Act 45 of 1988 hearsay evidence "means evidence, whether oral or in writing, the probative value of which depends upon the credibility of any person other than the person giving such evidence".

2 12   RELEVANCE

Four possible definitions of relevance are quoted in § 5 3 below.

---

[37] See ch 13 below.

SOURCES OF THE SOUTH AFRICAN LAW OF EVIDENCE AND THE IMPACT OF CONSTITUTIONAL PROVISIONS

S E van der Merwe

3 1 INTRODUCTION

The following fundamental principles and broad guidelines are important in identifying the sources of the South African law of evidence:

(a) Our law of evidence is not based on Roman-Dutch authority.

(b) Our rules of evidence are found in local statutes and, where these are silent on a specific topic or issue, the English law of evidence which was in force in South Africa on 30 May 1961 serves as our common law.[1] The CPA[2] and CPEA[3] contain provisions to this effect.

(c) South Africa has a considerable body of local case law on evidence. These cases — if decided in accordance with the applicable English common-law rules and principles as at 30 May 1961 — are binding in terms of our law of precedent. The practical result is that a South African court need not in each and every instance try to find applicable English cases. In most instances local precedents will suffice on the basis that they accurately reflect the common-law position.

(d) If a total *lacuna* is encountered, a South African court may for comparative purposes look for guidance in English cases decided after 30 May 1961. Such

---

[1] See § 3 5 below.
[2] See § 3 3 below.
[3] See § 3 4 below.

cases would normally have considerable persuasive value, but can never be binding.[4] In the event of a *lacuna*, support for a decision can also be gleaned from the law of evidence of other Anglo-American jurisdictions, for example, Australia, Canada and the United States. In § 1 4 above it was pointed out that the South African law of evidence belongs to the Anglo-American "family". We share a common heritage, that is, the English common-law system, which is based upon rules essentially and originally designed for trial by jury.

(e) The South African interim Constitution is the supreme law: *all* rules of evidence must comply with our constitutional provisions. This matter is dealt with more fully in § 3 9 below. At this stage it is sufficient to note that the interim Constitution not only governs the validity of rules of evidence but is also an important source of the law of evidence.

3 2   ORIGINAL INCORPORATION OF ENGLISH LAW: THE PRE-UNION PERIOD

In the period before South Africa became a Union (that is, before 1910) the English law of evidence was directly and indirectly incorporated into the different colonies which later became the Union.[5] Legislation which set out English common-law rules and principles was passed. This process can be referred to as *direct* incorporation. However, *indirect* incorporation also took place: it was also provided that the English law of evidence had to be followed in respect of issues or topics for which no express local statutory provision had been made.

There were several colonial statutes which had directly and indirectly incorporated English law (for example, Ordinance 72 of 1830 (Cape); Law 17 of 1859 (Natal); Ordinance 11 of 1902 (Orange Free State) and Proclamation 16 of 1902 (Transvaal)). At the original dates of incorporation *both* English statutory and common law were adopted.[6] It was generally accepted that local courts were required to follow the English statutes as these had stood on the original date of incorporation,[7] and that local courts were therefore not bound by subsequent English legislation.[8] Law 17 of 1859 (Natal), for example, provided expressly that only those English statutes in force in England in 1859 were to be applied in Natal. But amendments of the English common law brought about by English judicial precedents (or of course subsequent local legislation) had to be applied.

In some of these early statutes the English law was indirectly incorporated by referring to the law "in the Supreme Court of Judicature in England" (see, for example, s 45 of Proclamation 16 of 1902 (Transvaal)). Residuary sections (see § 3 5 below) were also employed, for example, in the Transvaal Proclamation of 1902 and the Orange Free State Ordinance of 1902. The latter proclamation

---

[4] See § 3 6 below.
[5] See Schmidt 12–14; Hoffmann & Zeffertt 6–9.
[6] Hoffmann & Zeffertt 11.
[7] O'Dowd *The Law of Evidence in South Africa* (1963) 3.
[8] Hoffmann & Zeffertt 11.

incorporated the law of the Cape of Good Hope, which, in turn, had incorporated English law.

3 3 CRIMINAL PROCEEDINGS: THE POST-UNION PERIOD

In criminal proceedings the early colonial legislation was superseded by and consolidated in the Criminal Procedure and Evidence Act 31 of 1917. But this Act was later replaced by the Criminal Procedure Act 56 of 1955. In terms of the latter Act, English law was excluded where any matter or topic relating to evidence was expressly dealt with in South African legislation. But English law had to be followed where a matter was specifically covered by a reference to the law as applied "in the Supreme Court of Judicature in England". There were also residuary clauses which invoked the English law with regard to issues not expressly covered by South African legislation.

When the Union became a Republic it was thought that further direct references to another country's laws were inappropriate.[9] The Criminal Procedure Amendment Act 92 of 1963 removed all references to "the Supreme Court of Judicature in England" from the then Criminal Procedure Act 56 of 1955: these references were replaced by references to the law as it stood on the "thirtieth May 1961" (the day before South Africa became a Republic). However, these 30 May 1961 provisions were and are nothing else but a cumbersome way of telling a South African court and lawyer to go back in time, look at the law as it stood on 30 May 1961, and then discover(!) that the law in force on that day was the law which was in force in the supreme court of judicature in England[10] (unless, of course, superseded by local legislation).

In 1977 the Criminal Procedure Act 56 of 1955 was (except for ss 319(3) and 384) superseded by the CPA. The CPA generally retained the references to the law as it stood on 30 May 1961.

The following are examples of specific topics — or aspects of specific topics — which, in our law of evidence in criminal proceedings, are still covered by references to the law as it stood on 30 May 1961: the impeachment or support of the credibility of a witness — s 190(1) of the CPA;[11] legal professional privilege — s 201 of the CPA;[12] state privilege — s 202 of the CPA;[13] the privilege against self-incrimination — s 203 of the CPA;[14] the character of an accused — s 227(1) of the CPA;[15] the character of any female or male against or in connection with whom any offence of an indecent nature is alleged to have been committed — s 227(1) as read with s 227(4) of the CPA;[16] evidence and sufficiency of evidence

---

[9] Hoffmann & Zeffertt 11.
[10] See generally Harcourt (ed) *Swift's Law of Criminal Procedure* 2 ed (1969) 536.
[11] See §§ 25 2 and 25 2 2 below.
[12] See § 10 3 1 n 98 below.
[13] See § 11 1 below.
[14] See § 10 2 below.
[15] See § 6 1 below.
[16] See § 6 2 6 1 below.

of appointment to public office — s 230 of the CPA.[17] Aspects relating to hearsay also used to be covered by references to the law as it stood on 30 May 1961. But these provisions — which were contained in s 26 and s 223 of the CPA — have been repealed by s 9 of the Law of Evidence Amendment Act 45 of 1988.[18] The latter Act regulates hearsay without any reference to the law as it stood on 30 May 1961.[19]

Sections 206 and 252 of the CPA contain *wide* residuary sections and are referred to in § 3 5 below.

3 4   CIVIL PROCEEDINGS: THE POST-UNION PERIOD

In civil proceedings the various colonial provisions which had introduced the English law of evidence were "consolidated" only when the CPEA came into operation in 1965. Section 42 of the CPEA provides that the law of evidence, including the law relating to the competency, compellability, examination and cross-examination of witnesses, which was in force in respect of civil proceedings on 30 May 1961, shall apply in any case not provided for in the CPEA or any other South African legislation. This is only an indirect way of referring the reader to the English law of evidence: on 30 May 1961 the various provisions applicable to civil proceedings in the provinces of the Union contained residuary provisions incorporating the English law for matters not specifically covered by South African statutes.

3 5   INTERPRETATION OF THE 30 MAY 1961 PROVISION

In *Rusmarc SA (Pty) Ltd v Hemdon Enterprises (Pty) Ltd* Coetzee J posed the following question:[20] "Is the result then that the South African law of evidence is English law, petrified as at 30 May 1961, with no room for judicial development by South African judges?" It is generally accepted that the South African law of evidence "remains to a certain extent frozen"[21] as at 30 May 1961. The common law that must be followed consists of English legislation that existed *on the various dates of original indirect incorporation*, as well as English case law prior to 30 May 1961.[22]

---

[17] See also Van Wyk 1981 *SACC* 277–9.

[18] See also De Vos & Van der Merwe 1993 *Stell LR* 7n2.

[19] See ch 13 below.

[20] 1975 4 SA 626 (W).

[21] Hoffmann & Zeffertt 15; *Ex parte Minister van Justisie: In re S v Wagner* 1965 4 SA 507 (A) 513G. But cf §§ 3 5 1 and 3 5 2 below.

[22] See generally *Gentiruco AG v Firestone SA (Pty) Ltd* 1972 1 SA 589 (A) 617; *Naidoo v Marine and Trade Insurance Co Ltd* 1978 3 SA 666 (A); *Smit v Van Niekerk* 1976 4 SA 293 (A); *A Sweidan and King (Pty) Ltd v Zim Israel Navigation Co Ltd* 1986 1 SA 515 (D). In the latter case counsel for the applicants submitted that where the matter had never arisen before 30 May 1961 in the House of Lords, but was after this date decided by it, this post 30 May 1961 decision was indeed binding upon South African courts because the House of Lords would in so deciding have determined what the law has always been. For purpose of his judgment Booysen J did not have to decide on the merits of this argument. But in 1986 *ASSAL* 485 Zeffertt responded as follows to the aforementioned argument. "It is submitted that the argument advanced on behalf of the applicants has, at best, a seductive and meretricious charm. It manipulates a fiction and, by so doing, achieves a result that could never have been the intention of the legislature — it is unlikely that our staunchly republican Parliament wished to leave our law of evidence in perpetual colonial servitude.

The two accepted instances where our courts have moved away from the binding effect of the "30 May 1961" provision are discussed in §§ 3 5 1 and 3 5 2 below and the value of Privy Council decisions are referred to in § 3 7 below.

A good example of a residuary provision is also found in s 206 of the CPA.[23] This section provides as follows: "The law as to the competency, compellability or privilege of witnesses which was in force in criminal proceedings on the thirtieth day of May, 1961, shall apply in this Act or any other law." In *S v Taylor* Selikowitz J pointed out that the effect of this section is that "we rely heavily on the law of England as applied at that date".[24] The practical effect of a 30 May 1961 provision is that " . . . the Legislature has . . . in its wisdom referred us to another system of law", that is, the English law.[25] Section 252 of the CPA also determines that the law as to the admissibility of evidence which was in force in respect of criminal proceedings "on the thirtieth day of May 1961" shall apply in any case not expressly provided for by the CPA[26] or any other law.

Section 42 of the CPEA is the residuary section for civil matters.[27]

3 5 1 English decisions considered to be incorrect The implication of *Van der Linde v Calitz*[28] is that our Appellate Division, as successor to the Privy Council, may deviate from an English decision if it concludes that the English decision does not correctly apply the English law.[29] In this case — which was decided in 1967 — the Appellate Division preferred an older Privy Council decision to a more recent decision of the House of Lords. A further reason for this decision, namely that the Privy Council was at the time of its decision (that is, 1931) the highest court of appeal in the South African hierarchy, has been criticized.[30] It should be borne in mind that South African appeals to the Privy Council were abolished in 1950.[31]

The whole tenor of *Van der Linde v Calitz* is against such an intention. The language of s 42 of the Civil Proceedings Evidence Act 1965 points to an intention to 'freeze' the law as it was on 30 May 1961. To maintain that that intention is defeated by an artificial jurisprudential nicety, by a mere legal fiction, is specious when it most persuades, and spurious in its intended result . . . In my submission, the primary question is: Were there relevant English decisions prior to 30 May 1961? If there were, they are binding to the extent to which the Appellate Division (or the Privy Council before appeals to it were abolished) considers them to be correct reflections of the English law (*Van der Linde v Calitz*). Since we do not have to apply the English law of procedure in its entirety, but only that part which is evidentiary, a South African 'practice' which is 'procedural' rather than exclusively 'evidentiary' would also have to be followed."

[23] See further § 22 2 below.

[24] 1991 2 SACR 69 (C) 70*h*.

[25] See *Ex parte Minister of Justice: In re R v Demingo* 1951 1 SA 36 (A). In this case the AD interpreted one of the forerunners of s 206 of the CPA.

[26] See s 240(1) of the CPA for an example where express provision is made for the admissibility of certain evidence.

[27] See § 3 4 above.

[28] 1967 2 SA 239 (A). See § 11 3 n 12 below for a discussion of this case.

[29] Hoffmann & Zeffertt 12 and 15.

[30] Davids 1967 *SALJ* 245; Kahn 1967 *SALJ* 327; Kerr 1965 *SALJ* 169.

[31] See § 3 7 below.

3 5 2 South African rules of practice incompatible with English law[32] Where an English evidentiary principle is obviously incompatible with South African law or a rule of practice (*usus fori*), such principle may be rejected.[33] In *S v Lwane*[34] the Appellate Division also created a binding rule of practice which has no counterpart in English law or practice.

3 6 VALUE OF ENGLISH DECISIONS

English decisions after 30 May 1961 are not binding upon South African courts, but do have considerable persuasive force.[35] English decision also have strong *persuasive* force in the interpretation of those South African statutory provisions which make no reference to English law but which do in effect enact rules similar to those which apply in English law.[36]

3 7 VALUE OF PRIVY COUNCIL DECISIONS[37]

The Privy Council Appeals Act 16 of 1950 abolished appeals from the Appellate Division to the judicial committee of the Privy Council. Post-1950 decisions of the Privy Council therefore merely have persuasive force. Paizes concludes as follows:[38] "Lower courts in South Africa are bound by the decision of the Appellate Division, followed by pre-1950 decisions of the Privy Council, followed by pre-30 May 1961 decisions of the English appeal courts and House of Lords." The Appellate Division may disregard a pre-1950 Privy Council decision if convinced that it was wrongly decided.[39]

3 8 FURTHER SOURCES

Obviously the CPA, CPEA and the Law of Evidence Amendment Act 45 of 1988 cannot be regarded as comprehensive codes governing the law of evidence. But they certainly are the main sources. Some examples of other statutes can be found in chapters 15 and 20 below.

3 9 THE INTERIM CONSTITUTION

The South African legal system was constitutionalized on 27 April 1994, when the South African Constitution Act 200 of 1993 (in this work called the "interim Constitution") came into operation. Parliamentary sovereignty was replaced by

---

[32] See Schmidt 19.

[33] *Ex parte Minister of Justice: In re R v Pillay* 1945 AD 653.

[34] 1966 2 SA 433 (A). See also *Magmoed v Janse van Rensburg & others* 1993 1 SACR 67 (A) 105*j*–105*h*. See further §§ 10 2 2 and 12 3 3 below.

[35] *Papenfus v Transvaal Board for the Development of Peri-Urban Areas* 1969 2 SA 66 (T) 69.

[36] *R v Hendrickz* 1933 TPD 451.

[37] See generally Hahlo & Kahn *The South African Legal System and Its Background* (1968) 259–60.

[38] Paizes in Du Toit et al *Commentary* 23-55.

[39] According to Schmidt 17–18, this is the implication of *Van der Linde v Calitz* supra.

a Constitution which is the supreme law. There is a justiciable Bill of Rights. Any statutory or common-law rule which conflicts with the rights and freedoms contained in the Bill of Rights must be declared unconstitutional unless it can in terms of s 33(1) of the interim Constitution be saved as a constitutionally permissible limitation of a constitutionally guaranteed fundamental right or freedom.[40]

Some common-law (and also some statutory) procedural and evidentiary rights of an accused have hardened into constitutional rights. These include the following: the right to be informed of certain rights;[41] the right to exercise a "passive defence right"[42], which incorporates the right to remain silent upon arrest,[43] to be presumed innocent,[44] to remain silent during plea or trial proceedings and not to testify during trial,[45] and to be a non-compellable witness against oneself.[46] The "active defence right"[47] of an accused has also been elevated to a constitutional guarantee: there is a right to adduce and challenge evidence.[48] There is, furthermore, a right to a fair trial[49] — which includes the rights as set out in s 25(3)(a)–(j) of the interim Constitution. This right to a fair trial ("due process") inevitably also has an important impact on the application of rules of evidence.[50]

The right to be informed not only of the right to legal representation[51] but also the right to silence[52] affects the admissibility of confessions and admissions (including so-called "pointings out"). There is also a constitutional right "not to be compelled to make a confession or admission which could be used in evidence against" the declarant.[53] The impact of constitutional provisions on the admissibility of admissions and confessions is discussed in chapters 16 and 17 below.

The constitutional presumption of innocence[54] has been invoked to declare

---

[40] However, see also s 35(2) of the interim Constitution. This section permits a so-called "reading down" in certain circumstances.

[41] Section 25(3)(e) as read with ss 256(2)(a) and 25(1)(c) of the interim Constitution.

[42] On the use of the term "passive defence right", see Van der Merwe 1994 *Obiter* 22 23 and Van Rooyen 1973 *De Rebus Procuratoriis* 207. See also *S v Brown en 'n ander* 1996 2 SACR 49 (NC) 56g–h.

[43] Section 25(2)(a) of the interim Constitution. This right can affect the admissibility of admissions and confessions. See generally ch 17 below.

[44] Section 25(3)(d) of the interim Constitution. This right confirms the rule that the prosecution has the burden of proof. See further § 31 1 below.

[45] Section 25(3)(d) of the interim Constitution. See further § 30 9 below, as well as the discussion of *Griffin v California* 380 US 609 (1965) by Van der Merwe in 1994 *Obiter* 1. See further *S v Brown en 'n ander* 1996 2 SACR 49 (NC).

[46] Section 25(3)(d) of the interim Constitution. See further ch 22 below.

[47] See generally Van der Merwe 1994 *Stell LR* 243 257.

[48] Section 25(3)(d) of the interim Constitution. The right to challenge evidence includes the right to cross-examine, which is discussed in §§ 18 6–18 6 5 5 below. The constitutional right to challenge evidence also affects hearsay. See ch 13 below as well as De Vos & Van der Merwe 1993 *Stell LR* 7 34–9.

[49] Section 25(3) of interim Constitution.

[50] See the discussion of *Chambers v Mississippi* 410 US 284 (1973) in § 25 3 4 below. See also § 11 4 4 below as regards the application of the so-called "informer's privilege". See further *Shabalala v Attorney-General of Transvaal & another* 1995 2 SACR 761 (CC), which is discussed in § 11 5 below. In *S v Zuma* 1995 2 SA 642 (CC) the Constitutional Court held that the right to a fair trial is not limited to those rights specified in s 25(3).

[51] Section 25(1)(c) of the interim Constitution.

[52] Section 25(2)(a) of the interim Constitution.

[53] Section 25(3)(c) of the interim Constitution.

[54] Section 25(3)(c) of the interim Constitution.

certain statutory presumptions and reverse onus clauses unconstitutional.[55] The constitutionality of presumptions is discussed in chapter 29 below.

In terms of s 23 of the interim Constitution every person has the right of access to all information held by the state or any of its organs in so far as such information is required for the exercise or protection of any of his or her rights. This provision has an impact on state privilege.[56]

However, the most far-reaching effect of the interim Constitution on our law of evidence concerns the admissibility of unconstitutionally obtained evidence. The interim Constitution does not make any specific provision for the exclusion of evidence obtained in breach of constitutional rights. But a rule of exclusion — even if it is a discretionary one — is necessary in order to ensure that constitutional rights (such as, for example, the right to privacy) are not reduced to pious pronouncements.[57] Some courts have invoked the so-called "exclusionary rule", that is, a rule in terms of which evidence obtained in violation of constitutional rights may be — and generally should be — excluded despite its high probative value and reliability. *S v Melani & others*[58] and *S v Motloutsi*[59] provide two good examples of the application of the exclusionary rule.

The proposed final Constitution contains a qualified exclusionary rule. Section 35(5) of this Constitution provides that evidence "obtained in a manner that violates any right in the Bill of Rights must be excluded if the admission of that evidence would render the trial unfair or otherwise be detrimental to the administration of justice". The exclusion of unconstitutionally obtained evidence is discussed in chapter 12 below.

In the final analysis it can be said that there is "an inseparability between rules of evidence and constitutional entitlements".[60] Our law of evidence must constantly be scrutinized in the light of constitutional provisions. Canadian and American cases can be useful in interpreting the impact of our interim Constitution on the law of evidence, because both these countries have also had constitutional provisions superimposed on their English common-law rules of evidence. In Canada it happened less than a decade and a half ago; and in the United States it happened more than two centuries ago. We can be guided by these decisions, especially since s 35(1) of our interim Constitution provides that "a court . . . may have regard to comparable foreign case law". On the other hand, our courts should be careful not to rely on foreign case law too easily: a court "must evaluate [foreign decisions] in the light of the conditions and circumstances existing in its own jurisdiction from time to time, and the facts of the case before it".[61]

---

[55] See e g *S v Bhulwana; S v Gwadiso* 1995 2 SACR 748 (CC).

[56] See generally ch 11 below.

[57] See generally Van der Merwe 1992 *Stell LR* 173.

[58] 1996 1 SACR 335 (E). Cf *S v Melani & others* 1995 2 SACR 141 (E). See further § 12 5 1 below. See also generally *Mendes & another v Kitching NO & another* 1995 2 SACR 634 (E).

[59] 1996 1 SACR 78 (C). See further § 12 5 1 below.

[60] Paizes 1989 *SALJ* 472 478.

[61] *S v Minnies* 1991 1 SACR 335 (Nm) 370*g–h*.

CHAPTER 4

THE LAW OF EVIDENCE AND SUBSTANTIVE LAW

E van der Berg

4 1 INTRODUCTION

Substantive law is usually distinguished from adjective law (of which the law of evidence forms a part)[1] on the basis that substantive law provides for rights and duties, whereas adjective law provides the procedural mechanisms whereby those rights and duties are enforced.[2]

The distinction is not as clear as it seems.[3] It is not only substantive law that creates rights and duties. Adjective law also provides for rights and duties. One merely has to think of the right of a party in a trial to call and cross-examine witnesses,[4] and the numerous rights and duties provided for by the rules of court in civil matters, for example the rules relating to the discovery of documents,[5] and the calling of expert witnesses.[6] The question arises whether the distinction between substantive and adjective law has any practical relevance, or whether it is merely of academic interest. The answer is that important consequences hinge upon this distinction.

---

[1] See § 1 1 above.

[2] Howard et al *Phipson on Evidence* 14 ed (1990) 1.

[3] Hoffmann & Zeffertt 6; Pistorius *Pollak on Jurisdiction* 2 ed (1993) 29–30; Schmidt 5–7; Zeffertt 1990 *SALJ* 579; *Universal City Studios Inc v Network Video (Pty) Ltd* 1986 2 SA 734 (A).

[4] Schmidt 6.

[5] Rule 35 of the Supreme Court; rule 23 of the magistrates' courts.

[6] Rule 36(9) of the Supreme Court; rule 24(9) of the magistrates' courts; see also § 8 7 below.

4 2   THE SIGNIFICANCE OF THE DISTINCTION

In our law the distinction between substantive and adjective law is a necessary one.[7] The historical development of our law resulted in our having Roman-Dutch law as our common law, except, however, in the law of evidence,[8] wherein we follow English law.[9] The results of following either Roman-Dutch law or following English law may be diametrically opposed. No better illustration exists than that found in *Tregea v Godart*.[10] This case concerned the burden of proof and is discussed in §§ 4 3 and 32 1 below.

Rabie points out another practical consequence of the characterization of a principle or rule as being either substantive or evidential.[11] In this instance characterization has a curious effect on the application of estoppel.[12] If estoppel is a rule of substantive law,[13] viewed as a measure of preventing prejudice, and not an instrument of gain, the relief afforded by estoppel should not extend beyond the actual damage suffered by the party entitled to assert estoppel. If, however, the rule is one of evidence,[14] then, notwithstanding the fact that the actual prejudice suffered by the representee does not extend to the full amount in question, the representor, precluded from relying on the true facts, would be unable to recover anything at all.

The dividing line between substantive law and the law of evidence is blurred by the evidential effect of some rules of substantive law which result in the exclusion of evidence by the court, thus causing the rule to appear to be one of evidence (the mistaken reasoning being that since it results in the exclusion of evidence, the rule must be one of evidence). In this context the so-called irrebuttable presumptions of law as well as estoppel and parol evidence will be discussed briefly in this chapter.

4 3   THE BURDEN OF PROOF [15]

Views on the classification of the burden of proof vary from one extreme to the other. Some hold that it is purely adjectival. Others maintain that it is substantive law. Even the view that it falls in a grey area somewhere between substantive and adjective law has found support.

As far as case law is concerned, *Tregea v Godart*[16] remains the leading but

---

[7] In *Botes v Van Deventer* 1966 3 SA 182 (A) it was held, e g, that the law of evidence determines that a vicarious admission is admissible if an identity of interest (see § 16 5 3 below) exists between a declarant and a party, but that the issue whether such identity exists is determined by substantive law (i e Roman-Dutch law). See generally Schmidt 6–7.

[8] This is not to say that it is the only exception.

[9] See chs 1 and 2 above.

[10] 1939 AD 16.

[11] Rabie *The Law of Estoppel in South Africa* (1992) 7, 68–71.

[12] See § 4 5 below.

[13] What Rabie *Estoppel* 69 refers to as the American approach.

[14] The English approach; Rabie *Estoppel* 70.

[15] The rules and principles which govern the incidence of the burden of proof are discussed in chs 31 and 32 below.

[16] 1939 AD 16. See also §§ 28 4 and 32 1 below.

doubtful authority. In this case the Appellate Division held that substantive law lays down *what* has to be proved and *by whom*, and the rules of evidence relate to the *manner* of its proof. It was also held that the burden of proof and rebuttable presumptions of law are matters of substantive law.

The issue in this case was the validity of a will. The plaintiffs sought the rejection of the will on the grounds that the testator did not have the mental capacity to execute a will. Much depended upon who carried the burden of proof. If this question was regarded as one of substantive law, Roman-Dutch law would apply, and the defendants would benefit by a presumption that a will, regular on the face of it, is valid. If, on the other hand, the matter was regulated by the law of evidence, and English law applied, the plaintiffs would have been assisted by a rule that cast the burden of proof on the defendants to prove testamentary capacity on the part of the testator. The question was held to be one of substantive law, and Roman-Dutch law was followed. The burden of proof accordingly was on the plaintiffs.

Schmidt[17] is of the opinion that *Tregea v Godart* was incorrectly decided. He points out that substantive law defines the rights and duties of persons and thus determines the *facta probanda*. The burden of proof and the rebuttable presumptions do nothing of the kind; they relate to the manner in which facts are proved and therefore belong to the law of evidence.

Certainly the various elements that constitute a cause of action, or a crime, or a defence, and thus the *facta probanda*, are requirements of substantive law; certainly, also, it is very difficult to mention the burden of proof without reference to what has to be proved. That, however, simply means that the burden pertains to the particular *probanda*. But it is for this very reason that the law of evidence is called *adjectival*. It would be more accurate to say that the incidence of the burden of proof is *dependent upon, or varies according to*, substantive law, rather than that it is *determined by* substantive law. The existence of the burden of proof, and its various consequences and qualifications,[18] must, however, be ascribed to the law of evidence.

4 4 IRREBUTTABLE PRESUMPTIONS [19]

Irrebuttable presumptions are not really presumptions in the true sense of the word, nor are they rules of evidence. Irrebuttable presumptions are rules of substantive law, directing a court to accept a situation as conclusively proved once certain (other) basic facts have been proved. There is, for example, a presumption that a girl below the age of 12 is irrebuttably presumed to be incapable of consenting to sexual intercourse.[20] This is just another way of saying that sexual intercourse with a girl below the age of 12 amounts to rape, even if the girl had consented.[21]

---

[17] At 10.
[18] See chs 31 and 32 below.
[19] The traditional classification of presumptions is discussed in §§ 28 3–28 3 3 below.
[20] *Socout Ally v R* 1907 TS 336 339.
[21] See generally *R v M* 1950 4 SA 101 (T) 102.

Once intercourse with a girl below the age of 12 is proved (and these are the basic facts which the prosecution must prove) the court is obliged to conclude that there was no consent.[22]

There is also a so-called irrebuttable presumption of law that an *infans* (a child who has not yet completed his seventh year) is criminally and delictually non-responsible (*doli* and *culpae incapax*).[23] The truth of the matter is that it is a rule of substantive law that an *infans* can never be held liable in crime or delict.[24] Evidence to the contrary will not be received because the court is required to accept — irrefutably — that an *infans* does not possess sufficient mental ability to render him legally accountable. There are no exceptions to the rule. If an *infans* is charged with fraud, the prosecution will not be permitted to lead evidence that he or she is a genius and therefore had the necessary mental ability to distinguish between right and wrong.

The above rules are rules of substantive law[25] and stem from Roman-Dutch (and not English) law. These rules — even though they clearly have some fictive content — are based on policy and clearly aimed at protecting very young persons. But such protection can go too far. The irrebuttable presumption of Roman-Dutch law that a male *impubes*[26] is presumed to be incapable of sexual intercourse[27] was abolished in South Africa by s 1 of the Law of Evidence and the Criminal Procedure Act Amendment Act 103 of 1987.[28]

The above statutory intervention does not affect the *rebuttable* presumption that male and female *impuberes* are rebuttably presumed to be *doli* and *culpae incapax*.[29] The prosecution is still required, for example, to rebut this presumption of criminal incapacity.[30] Proof beyond reasonable doubt is required.[31] It is generally accepted that it is difficult to rebut this presumption where the *impubes* has barely progressed beyond the age of the *infans*.[32] Rebuttal is easier where the *impubes* was nearly 14 at the time of the incident.[33] Rebuttal may take place by way of direct or circumstantial evidence.[34]

---

[22] This rule operates only if the girl's actual age is below 12 (*Mostert v S* 1973 2 PH H67 (C)). The rule cannot be applied, e g, where the girl's real age is 16 but her mental age is 8 (*R v S* 1951 3 SA 209 (C)). In such an instance the state's case is not aided by the rule and the state will have to prove absence of consent, e g that the girl could not, as a result of her mental defect, have given proper consent.

[23] *Q v Lourie* (1892) 9 SC 432.

[24] *Attorney-General, Tvl v Additional Magistrate for Johannesburg* 1924 AD 421.

[25] Formulated as rules of substantive law, the absurdity of terminology and contents is removed: an *infans* lacks criminal and delictual capacity; the consent of the girl below the age of 12 does not constitute lawful consent for the purposes of a defence to a charge of rape. Hoffmann & Zeffertt 531 and Schmidt 133. See further § 28 31 below.

[26] An *impubes* is a child who is no longer an *infans* but who has not attained the age of 14.

[27] See generally *S v A* 1962 4 SA 679 (E) as discussed by Schmidt 1963 *THRHR* 139 for the absurd results caused by this presumption.

[28] This section is quoted in § 28 3 1 below.

[29] See generally Snyman *Criminal Law* 3 ed (1995) 165.

[30] See generally *S v M* 1979 4 SA 564 (B).

[31] *R v K* 1956 3 SA 353 (A) 359E.

[32] *R v Nhamo* 1956 1 PH H28 (SR).

[33] *R v K* supra 358D–E.

[34] *R v Ndenxa* 1919 EDL 199 200.

4 5   ESTOPPEL

Estoppel is a term of English law, derived from the same origin as the word "stop".[35] It denotes that a party is precluded (or estopped) from denying or asserting a particular fact.[36] The doctrine of estoppel was introduced into South African law from English law on the basis that it was analogous to, or accorded with, principles of Roman and Roman-Dutch law.[37]

One comes across various expressions coupled with the term "estoppel". Amongst there are estoppel by record, by deed, by conduct, issue estoppel, estoppel *in pais*, equitable estoppel, estoppel by silence, and estoppel by negligence.[38] Only the two forms of estoppel most common in South African law, namely estoppel by representation (which covers most of the various aforementioned forms of estoppel[39]) and estoppel by judgment[40] will be considered below.

The term "estoppel" is generally used in South Africa to denote estoppel by representation.[41] The doctrine applies where a person makes a representation to another, who, believing in the truth thereof, acts thereon to his prejudice. The representor is then precluded or estopped from denying the truth of the representation.[42]

Estoppel by judgment is more commonly known in South Africa as estoppel *per rem judicatam, exceptio rei judicatae* or a plea of *res judicata*.[43] The expression signifies that a matter has been finally adjudicated on by a competent court. It may then not be raised again, if the action is between the same parties, for the same relief, upon the same cause, and provided further that the judgment was a final one on the merits of the matter.[44]

The equivalent of the aforegoing in a criminal case would be a plea of *autrefois convict* or *acquit* — that the accused has already been convicted or acquitted of the offence with which he is now charged.[45] Again the charge must relate to the same or a substantially identical offence and the verdict must have been pronounced by a competent court on (in the case of *autrefois acquit*) the merits of the matter and not merely on an irregularity in the procedure.

Some authorities in both England and South Africa have described estoppel as a rule of the law of evidence.[46] It is possible to express estoppel in the form of a rule that excludes evidence: the representor may not adduce evidence at variance with his representation;[47] evidence may not be led in contradiction of a

---

[35] Hoffmann & Zeffertt 332.

[36] Hoffmann & Zeffertt 332.

[37] Hoffmann & Zeffertt 333; Rabie *Estoppel* 21 et seq.

[38] See generally Hoffmann & Zeffertt 332 et seq; Rabie *Estoppel* 16 et seq.

[39] See Rabie *Estoppel* 16.

[40] Also called estoppel by record — see Hoffmann & Zeffertt 332; Rabie *Estoppel* 16.

[41] Rabie *Estoppel* 16.

[42] Hoffmann & Zeffertt 354–5; Rabie *Estoppel* 1.

[43] Hoffmann & Zeffertt 335; Rabie *Estoppel* 16; Schmidt 8.

[44] See generally Hoffmann & Zeffertt 335 et seq.

[45] Section 106(1) *(c)* and *(d)* of the CPA; see generally Van der Merwe in Du Toit et al *Commentary* 15-4 et seq. See also s 25(3) *(g)* of the interim Constitution.

[46] Rabie *Estoppel* 5–6.

[47] Rabie *Estoppel* 2.

judgment.[48] Estoppel has been expressed in the form of an irrebuttable presumption: a judgment is presumed to be correct.[49]

Nowadays it is fairly generally accepted, at least in South Africa, that estoppel is more correctly viewed as a rule of substantive law.[50] Proper analysis shows that estoppel by representation is a doctrine which involves the making of a representation, action on the faith thereof, resultant prejudice, and possibly fault; furthermore, it operates as a defence which has to be pleaded. Such a doctrine cannot be looked upon as a rule of the law of evidence.[51] Similarly the correct formulation of estoppel by judgment is by way of a rule that the judgment of a court is final. Even if it is expressed as an irrebuttable presumption as above, it must be borne in mind that such presumptions are merely rules of substantive law couched in the form of presumptions.[52]

These rules of substantive law cause the particular evidence in contradiction of the representation or judgment to become irrelevant and therefore, according to the law of evidence, inadmissible. The evidence is not inadmissible because estoppel as a rule of evidence prohibits such evidence; it is inadmissible because estoppel as a rule of substantive law causes the evidence to be irrelevant.[53]

4 6   PAROL EVIDENCE

4 6 1 The integration rule The parol[54] evidence rule provides that "where a jural act is incorporated in a document, it is not generally permissible to adduce extrinsic evidence of its terms".[55] "Extrinsic" refers to evidence other than, or extraneous of, the document itself.[56] The rule is accordingly also called the extrinsic evidence rule.[57] In an oft-quoted[58] passage Wigmore[59] describes the rule as follows: "[The] process of embodying the terms of a jural act in a single memorial may be termed the integration of the act, i e its formation from scattered parts into an integral documentary unity. The practical consequence of this is that its scattered parts, in their former and inchoate shape, do not have any jural effect; they are replaced by a single embodiment of the act. In other words: when a jural act is embodied in a single memorial, all other utterances of

---

[48] Schmidt 8.

[49] Schmidt 8. It seems to have been the fashion in earlier days to turn to fictions and presumptions for lack of a more scientific construction.

[50] Hoffmann & Zeffertt 335; Rabie *Estoppel* 7; Schmidt 8.

[51] Hoffmann & Zeffertt 335; Rabie *Estoppel* 7.

[52] See § 4 4 above; Schmidt 8.

[53] "Relevance" is discussed in ch 5 below. See especially § 5 3 below.

[54] Cf "*parol* . . . given orally; (of a document) not given under seal; oral declaration"; cf "*parole* . . . the release of a prisoner . . . on the promise of good behaviour; a word of honour": *The Concise Oxford Dictionary* 9 ed (1995).

[55] *LAWSA* para 538; *Purchase v De Huizemark Alberton (Pty) Ltd t/a Bob Percival Estates* 1994 1 SA 281 (W) 283I–J.

[56] Howard et al *Phipson on Evidence* 1020.

[57] *LAWSA* para 538.

[58] *National Board (Pretoria) (Pty) Ltd v Estate Swanepoel* 1975 3 SA 16 (A) 26C; *Standard Bank of SA Ltd v Cohen (1)* 1993 3 SA 846 (SE) 849E.

[59] Wigmore para 2425.

the parties on that topic are legally immaterial for the purposes of determining what are the terms of their act." From this derives a further name by which the rule is known: the integration rule.[60]

It has been pointed out that extrinsic evidence can be applied to a document for two different purposes: first, to show terms different to those contained in the document — in other words, the inquiry is aimed at determining what the terms of a particular transaction are; secondly, to show the meaning of the terms contained in the document — in issue is not the content of the document, but the meaning thereof, as it stands. Accordingly, the extrinsic evidence rule is said to comprise two distinct rules: the integration rule, which applies to the former situation, and the interpretation rule, which applies to the latter.[61]

The parol evidence rule[62] is often couched in evidential terms, disguising it as a rule of evidence:[63] "[W]hen a contract has been reduced to writing, the writing is, in general, regarded as the exclusive memorial of the transaction and in a suit between the parties no evidence to prove its terms may be given save the document or secondary evidence of its contents, nor may the contents of such document be contradicted, altered, added to or varied by parol evidence." The rule has accordingly been viewed as one of evidence[64] and was received into South African law on the assumption that it forms part of the English law of evidence, so that English precedents are followed.[65]

On proper analysis it becomes clear that the rule is one of substantive law. The rule relates to the nature and scope of a jural act, and not merely the admissibility of evidence. Certainly the distinction is a fine one and not as apparent as for instance in the case of estoppel. This is so especially since even the leading authors who hold the view that the parol evidence rule is one of substantive law explain that view with reference to the source from which the terms of the act are determined.[66] Considering the document merely as a source of information concerning the terms of a contract makes it very difficult not to regard that document as being merely the only admissible evidence, all other evidence being inadmissible (and the whole matter thus being a matter of evidence and admissibility).

If one were rather to think in terms of the document *constituting* the jural act,[67] then it would follow that whatever other actions[68] of the parties may have accompanied the jural act, as a matter of substantive law, simply form no part

---

[60] See also *Johnston v Leal* 1980 3 SA 927 (A); *Venter v Birchholtz* 1972 1 SA 276 (A); *Standard Bank of SA Ltd v Cohen (1)* 1993 3 SA 846 (SE) 849B–C; *De Klerk v Old Mutual Insurance Co Ltd* 1990 3 SA 34 (E).

[61] *Johnston v Leal* 1980 3 SA 927 (A); see generally Lubbe & Murray *Farlam & Hathaway: Contract: Cases, Materials and Commentary* 3 ed (1988) 215; Schmidt *Bewysreg* 2 ed (1982) 592, 607; Van der Merwe et al *Contract: General Principles* (1993) 125. We shall return to the matter of interpretation below.

[62] The name of the rule does not make things any easier either — calling it the integration rule has the merit of placing the emphasis where it should be, on the substantive aspect of the matter.

[63] *Union Government v Vianini Ferro-Concrete Pipes (Pty) Ltd* 1941 AD 43 47; *Purchase v De Huizemark Alberton (Pty) Ltd t/a Bob Percival Estates* 1994 1 SA 281 (W) 283I–J.

[64] See for instance *Avis v Verseput* 1943 AD 331; *Cassiem v Standard Bank of SA Ltd* 1930 AD 336.

[65] See for instance *Cassiem v Standard Bank of SA Ltd* 1930 AD 366; Lubbe & Murray *Farlam & Hathaway* 215; Schmidt *Bewysreg* 2 ed (1982) 592; Van der Merwe et al *Contract* 125.

[66] See Hoffmann & Zeffertt 291: "[T]he document is conclusive as to the terms of the transaction . . .."

[67] Whether because it is so required by the law, or because the parties have so agreed or intended it.

[68] Whether it be oral or documentary communications, or other conduct.

thereof. That being so, any such actions are irrelevant to the act, and consequently inadmissible as a matter of evidence. This approach is reflected in *De Klerk v Old Mutual Insurance Co Ltd*:[69]

> "[W]here a contract has been reduced to writing, the written document is regarded as the sole memorial of the transaction and *deprives all previous inconsistent statements of their legal effect.* The document becomes conclusive of the terms of the transaction which it was intended to record. The result is that *previous statements by the parties on the subject can have no legal consequences and are accordingly irrelevant and evidence to prove them is inadmissible.*"

The view that the matter is one of substantive law has found some acceptance in South African case law.[70] As a matter of practicality, however, it must be accepted that English precedent has become so entrenched in South African law that it must now be regarded as an ineradicable part thereof. A return to Roman-Dutch sources is unlikely.[71]

Although contracts are generally the kind of written instrument which most frequently form the subject of debate concerning parol evidence, the rule is applicable also to other written jural acts such as wills,[72] negotiable instruments,[73] and court orders.[74]

4 6 2 Some exceptions   There are several qualifications and exceptions to the general rule excluding parol evidence.[75] Some of these are not truly exceptions, but rather instances which fall outside the scope of the rule.

Where, for instance, a written contract is not intended to cover the terms of the transaction all-inclusively, evidence of further oral terms is not precluded.[76] The rule does not apply to a document which contains a mere narration of an event, and which does not constitute a jural act;[77] nor does the rule exclude evidence which throws light on the true nature of a transaction referred to in a written document.[78]

Extrinsic evidence is admissible to determine the validity of a transaction: it may be shown by oral evidence that a contract is void for fraud, mistake, illegality, impossibility or lack of consensus.[79] However, where writing is required by law, evidence cannot be produced of oral terms not included in the written document in order to invalidate the transaction through non-compliance with the require-

---

[69] 1990 3 SA 34 (E) 39D–E (my emphasis).
[70] See for instance *Slabbert, Verster & Malherbe (Bloemfontein) Bpk v De Wet* 1963 1 SA 835 (O); *Schroeder v Vakansieburo (Edms) Bpk* 1970 3 SA 240 (T); *Venter v Birchholtz* 1972 1 SA 276 (A).
[71] Hoffmann & Zeffertt 293.
[72] *Moskowitz v The Master* 1976 1 SA 22 (C).
[73] *Cassiem v Standard Bank of SA Ltd* 1930 AD 366.
[74] *Postmasburg Motors (Edms) Bpk v Peens* 1970 2 SA 35 (NC).
[75] See generally Hoffmann & Zeffertt 294 et seq; Schmidt *Bewysreg* 2 ed (1982) 592 et seq.
[76] *Johnston v Leal* 1980 3 SA 927 (A).
[77] *Purchase v De Huizemark Alberton (Pty) Ltd t/a Bob Percival Estates* 1994 1 SA 281 (W).
[78] *Purchase v De Huizemark Alberton (Pty) Ltd t/a Bob Percival Estates* 1994 1 SA 281 (W); *Moodley v Moodley* 1991 1 SA 358 (D).
[79] *Kok v Osborne* 1993 4 SA 788 (SE).

ment of writing; the correct avenue is to apply for rectification of the written agreement.[80]

The parol evidence rule applies to transactions reduced to writing, whether it be done at the instance of the parties, or because the law requires it.[81] The distinction may, however, have an effect on the admissibility of parol evidence. Parol evidence may, for instance, be admissible of a collateral agreement and additional terms[82] and subsequent oral variations,[83] but not where writing is a requirement of law, and such evidence seeks to contradict the written instrument.[84] A similar result arises where the contract contains a clause to the effect that no variation or rescission of the contract shall be valid unless it is reduced to writing.[85] But that, of course, is not due to the operation of the parol evidence rule. Curiously, even contracts that are required by law to be in writing can be cancelled orally.[86]

Suspensive conditions (or conditions precedent) which suspend the operation of a contract may be proved by parol evidence, but not if the condition forms an integral part of the agreement.[87]

4 6 3 Rectification The parol evidence rule notwithstanding, and in order to effect the rectification of the written document, extrinsic evidence is admissible to show that the document does not correctly reflect the consensus between the parties.[88] The document is made to conform with the jural act that underlies it: "[A]ll the Court does is to allow to be put in writing what both parties intended to put in writing and erroneously thought they had."[89] It is only logical that the law should not hold parties to a document which purports to reflect an agreement, when the document does not in fact do so.[90]

In *Standard Bank of SA Ltd v Cohen (1)*[91] the plaintiff sued the defendant on two written suretyship agreements. In terms of these agreements the defendant bound himself as surety and co-principal debtor for the indebtedness of a certain company. The defendant wished to adduce evidence of two terms orally agreed upon prior to the execution of the written agreements. The oral terms provided that the plaintiff would not extend credit to the company beyond a certain limit

---

[80] *Standard Bank of SA Ltd v Cohen (1)* 1993 3 SA 846 (SE); *Standard Bank of SA Ltd v Cohen (2)* 1993 3 SA 854 (SE). See, however, *Philmatt (Pty) Ltd v Mosselbank Developments CC* 1996 2 SA 15 (A), as discussed in § 4 6 3 below.

[81] As for instance in the case of the Alienation of Land Act 68 of 1981.

[82] *Avis v Verseput* 1943 AD 331; *Veenstra v Collins* 1938 TPD 458; *Du Plessis v Nel* 1952 1 SA 513 (A).

[83] *Venter v Birchholtz* 1972 1 SA 276 (A); *Johnston v Leal* 1980 3 SA 927 (A); *De Klerk v Old Mutual Insurance Co Ltd* 1990 3 SA 34 (E).

[84] *Du Plessis v Nel* 1952 1 SA 513 (A); *Venter v Birchholtz* 1972 1 SA 276 (A); *Johnston v Leal* 1980 3 SA 927 (A).

[85] *Pelser v Smith* 1979 3 SA 687 (T).

[86] *Le Grange v Pretorius* 1943 TPD 223.

[87] *Stiglingh v Theron* 1907 TS 998; *Thiart v Kraukamp* 1967 3 SA 219 (T); see, however, Hoffmann & Zeffertt 309–12 for an analysis of the difficulties in respect of such conditions.

[88] *Weinerlein v Goch Buildings Ltd* 1925 AD 282.

[89] *Weinerlein v Goch Buildings Ltd* 1925 AD 282.

[90] "[R]ectification corrects the document and not the contract itself . . .": Van der Merwe et al *Contract* 132; "All that is to be done is, upon proper proof, to correct the mistake, so as to reproduce in writing the real agreement between the parties": *Weinerlein v Goch Buildings Ltd* 1925 AD 282 290.

[91] 1993 3 SA 846 (SE).

and that no money would be advanced until the defendant had arranged a cession of the book debts of the company to himself. The object hereof was to protect the defendant. The deeds of suretyship were by law required to be in writing.[92] The agreements further contained a clause which provided that the deeds set out the entire agreement between the parties and that the plaintiff would not be bound by any term not recorded therein.

The court held that the defendant could not rely on the oral terms, since evidence thereof would be contrary to the parol evidence rule; in any event, they were not in writing as required by the statute. Nor could evidence thereof be adduced as a basis for the argument that the deeds were invalid for failure to include material clauses therein. The two written documents contained all the essential terms to constitute valid suretyships. *Ex facie* the documents they complied with the statutory requirements for validity. Evidence of the oral terms was thus irrelevant and inadmissible, unless it were presented for the purposes of rectification.

In a second judgment,[93] upon a plea of rectification by the defendant, the court found on the evidence that the two oral terms alleged by the defendant had in fact been agreed upon. The clause recording that the written deed set out the whole agreement between the parties did not constitute a bar to rectification — that right could only be excluded in explicit terms. The plea of rectification therefore succeeded, and the matter had to be adjudicated on the basis of the written agreements as they stood to be corrected.

In *Philmatt (Pty) Ltd v Mosselbank Developments CC*[94] an oral suspensive condition was the subject of dispute. Rectification was not possible as the appellant was an innocent third party. The court did not find it necessary to decide whether evidence of the condition was admissible by way of exception to the parol evidence rule. Instead, it held that evidence thereof was admissible to establish the existence of a material term not incorporated in the deed of sale in order to show that the deed of sale did not constitute a valid deed in terms of s 2(1) of the Alienation of Land Act 68 of 1981.

4 6 4 The interpretation rule If the first aspect of parol evidence, the integration rule, does not truly form part of the law of evidence, then the second aspect, the interpretation rule, does even less so.[95]

---

[92] Section 6 of the General Law Amendment Act 50 of 1956.
[93] *Standard Bank of SA Ltd v Cohen (2)* 1993 3 SA 854 (SE).
[94] 1996 2 SA 15 (A).
[95] Hoffmann & Zeffertt 32: "The construction of documents is a subject so remote from the law of evidence . . . .." See further Van der Merwe et al *Contract* 218–24 for a discussion of the interpretation rule.

CHAPTER 5

RELEVANCE, ADMISSIBILITY AND JUDICIAL DISCRETION TO EXCLUDE RELEVANT EVIDENCE

A St Q Skeen and S E van der Merwe

5 1　INTRODUCTION

Section 210 of the CPA provides that no evidence as to any fact, matter or thing shall be admissible if irrelevant or immaterial and if it cannot conduce to prove or disprove any point of fact at issue in criminal proceedings. Section 2 of the CPEA contains a substantially similar provision. These sections serve as statutory confirmation of our common law and state the rule in its negative form: irrelevant evidence is inadmissible. Courts, however, are inclined to state the rule in its positive form: "[A]ll facts relevant to the issue in legal proceedings may be proved."[1]

The present chapter serves as an introduction to chapters 6–9, which respectively deal with character evidence, similar fact evidence, opinion evidence, and evidence of previous consistent statements. These four chapters are all directly concerned with the application of the rule that irrelevant evidence is inadmissible (or, to put it differently, that relevant evidence is admissible). However, not all relevant evidence is necessarily admissible: "The . . . rule . . . is that any

---

[1] *R v Trupedo* 1920 AD 58 62; *S v Gokool* 1965 3 SA 461 (N) 475G: "The law of evidence is foundationally based on the principle that evidence is admissible if it is relevant to an issue in the case."

evidence which is relevant is admissible unless there is some other rule of evidence which excludes it."[2] Evidence — even if highly relevant and even if it happens to be the only available evidence — must be excluded where, for example, it is privileged.[3] Relevant evidence obtained in breach of constitutional rights may also be excluded.[4] Relevance is therefore not the sole test for admissibility. Certain rules of exclusion — which are largely discussed in chapters 10–17 — also come into play. The law of evidence does not allow untrammelled access to all relevant evidence.[5]

5 2 RATIONALE FOR THE EXCLUSION OF IRRELEVANT EVIDENCE

Murphy states:[6]

"The purpose of evidence being to demonstrate to the court the truth or probability of the facts upon which the success of a party's case depends in law, it follows that evidence must be confined to the proof of facts which are required for that purpose. The proof of supernumerary or unrelated facts will not assist the court, and may in certain cases prejudice the court against a party, while having no probative value on the issues actually before it."

To this can be added considerations of time, costs and inconvenience; the limitations of the human mind;[7] the undesirability of a court being called upon to adjudicate matters which are not related to the litigation at hand; the risk that the real issues might become clouded; and, further, the obvious consideration that a party against whom irrelevant evidence is adduced may find himself in a position where it could be difficult to defend himself. This last consideration is of special importance to the criminally accused, who enjoy a constitutionally guaranteed right to a fair trial.[8]

5 3 THE MEANING OF RELEVANCE AND THE DETERMINATION OF RELEVANCE

Relevance is a matter of degree[9] and is certainly easier to identify in practice than to describe in the abstract. But the following may be useful:

---

[2] *R v Schaube-Kuffler* 1969 2 SA 40 (RA) 50B.

[3] But see also § 5 5 below.

[4] See ch 12 below.

[5] Van Niekerk, Van der Merwe & Van Wyk *Privilegies in die Bewysreg* (1984) 4.

[6] Murphy *A Practical Approach to Evidence* 4 ed (1992) 8.

[7] Zuckerman *The Principles of Criminal Evidence* (1989, reprinted 1992) 49.

[8] See s 25(3) of the interim Constitution. But Choo "The Notion of Relevance and Defence Evidence" 1993 *Crim LR* 114 argues (at 125) that "the defence should generally have more liberal rights than the prosecution to adduce evidence which may not be of especially high probative value". This argument is of even greater significance in a constitutionalized system, such as ours, where an accused has the constitutional right to adduce evidence. See also generally Kuplicki "Fifth, Sixth and Fourteenth Amendments — A Constitutional Pardigm for Determining the Admissibility of Hypnotically Refreshed Testimony" (1987) 78 *Supreme Court Review* 853. See also *Chambers v Mississippi* 410 US 284 (1973). In a constitutionalized system the legislator also cannot in an arbitrary manner restrict the defence in its presentation of exculpatory evidence. See *R v Seaboyer* 1992 6 CRR 2d 35 (*R v Seaboyer; R v Gayme* 83 DLR (4th) 193) and the discussion of s 227 of the CPA in § 6 2 6 1 below.

[9] Hoffmann 1974 *SALJ* 237 238.

(a) Stephen provides the following classical formulation:[10]

"The word 'relevant' means that any two facts to which it is applied are so related to each other that according to the common course of events one either taken by itself or in connection with other facts proves or renders probable the past, present, or future existence or non-existence of the other."

(b) Rule 401 of the Federal Rules of Evidence of the United States of America defines relevant evidence as follows:

"Evidence having any tendency to make the existence of any fact that is of consequence to the determination of the action more probable or less probable than it would be without the evidence."

(c) Van Wyk has put forward the following:[11]

"[G]etuienis [is] relevant . . . wanneer dit oor die vermoë beskik, hetsy alleenstaande of tesame met ander bewysmateriaal, om die bestaan van 'n feit in geskil, direk of indirek, meer of minder waarskynlik te maak."

(d) In *DPP v Kilbourne* Lord Simon said:[12]

"Evidence is relevant if it is logically probative or disprobative of some matter which requires proof. I do not propose to analyse what is involved in 'logical probativeness' except to note that the term does not of itself express the element of experience which is so significant of its operation in law, and possibly elsewhere. It is sufficient to say . . . that relevant evidence, i e logically probative or disprobative evidence, is evidence which makes the matter which requires proof more or less probable."

It would be wrong to accept or assume that evidence is admissible simply because of its logical relevance. "Logical relevance", states McEwan (correctly, it is submitted), "is a *sine qua non* of admissibility; but it cannot guarantee that the evidence will be admitted; in fact, on its own it is far from sufficient."[13] What, then, are the precise factors and considerations which place a check on the admissibility of all evidence which is logically probative or disprobative?

5 3 1 The issues (as the essential point of departure) Relevance (and therefore admissibility) cannot be decided in a vacuum. The nature and extent of the factual and legal dispute must be considered. In *Lloyd v Powell Duffryn Steam Coal Co Ltd* it was said that the very first question that must be asked in deciding admissibility is: "What are the issues?"[14] The term "relevance" finds concrete application not only in the light of the primary *facta probanda* but also the secondary *facta probanda* (the *facta probantia* which are in dispute).[15] In *S v Mayo* Jones J held as follows:[16]

"It is not in the interests of justice that relevant material should be excluded from the Court, whether it is relevant to the issue or to issues which are themselves relevant to the issue but strictly speaking not in issue themselves, and this includes the credibility of

---

[10] Stephen *Digest of the Law of Evidence* 12 ed (1914) art 1.

[11] Van Wyk 1978 *THRHR* 1975.

[12] *DPP v Kilbourne* 1973 AC 729 756.

[13] McEwan *Evidence and the Adversarial Process: The Modern Law* (1992) 31.

[14] 1914 AC 733 738.

[15] See § 2 2 above.

[16] 1990 1 SACR 659 (E) 661*f*–662*e*.

witnesses, provided that the question of their credibility is in some way related to the issues or matter relevant to the issues . . . There remains the question of relevance. I am not satisfied on the information which is presently before me that the pocket book in question is relevant to any of the issues in this case. It is certainly not relevant to the main issues. Their contents do not appear to me to be relevant to issues which are relevant to those issues and they are not presently at any rate even relevant to credibility because it has not anywhere been suggested that the witness has said anything which will be contradicted by accused No 1, in so far as the content of his pocket book is concerned. It is not in the interest of justice that irrelevant information should be made available to the defence and used for the purposes of cross-examination, because justice requires that there be an end to cross-examination and that only relevant matter should in fact be canvassed. It seems to me therefore, that, in so far as the issue of relevance is concerned, the application should fail and I should rule against the applicant at this stage."

In *R v Solomons*[17] it was held that, subject to considerations of prejudice, a ruling on the admissibility of evidence could at a later stage be reversed in the light of new factual issues which might come to light during the course of the trial. Decisions on the admissibility of evidence are interlocutory and may therefore be re-assessed in the light of new facts.

5 3 2 Reasonable or proper inference: assessing the potential weight of the evidence "[F]acts", it was said in *R v Mpanza*,[18] "are . . . relevant if from their existence inferences may properly be drawn as to the existence of a fact in dispute." In *R v Trupedo*[19] it was held that no proper inference could be drawn from the behaviour of a police dog in its identification of a suspect. The evidence was rightly excluded as being irrelevant.[20]

Almost seven decades after the decision in *Trupedo* the Appellate Division again came to a similar conclusion in *S v Shabalala*,[21] where Nestadt JA also pointed out that if the weight of the evidence "is so inconsequential and the relevance accordingly so problematical, there can be little point in receiving the evidence . . ."[22] of identification by a police dog trained for purposes of identifying suspects by scenting.[23]

---

[17] 1959 2 SA 352 (A) 362E–F.

[18] 1915 AD 348 352 (and cited with approval in *S v Mavuso* 1987 3 SA 499 (A) 505B).

[19] 1920 AD 58.

[20] In *Trupedo* supra evidence concerning the behaviour of a trained police dog towards an accused was admitted in the court *a quo* to prove that he had committed the crime. On appeal it was submitted that evidence of this kind was inadmissible because no inferences could properly be drawn from the behaviour of police dogs towards an accused. At 62 Innes CJ remarked as follows (our emphasis): "The general rule is that all facts relevant to the issue in legal proceedings may be proved. Much of the law of evidence is concerned with exceptions to the operation of this general principle, as for example the exclusion of testimony on grounds of hearsay and remoteness. But where its operation is not so excluded it must remain as the fundamental test of admissibility. *And a fact is relevant when inferences can be properly drawn from it as to the existence of a fact in issue.*" Innes CJ also pointed out that the admission of evidence relating to the behaviour of the dog towards the accused would amount to entering " . . . a region of conjecture and uncertainty". At 64 it was concluded that there was too great and element of uncertainty to justify the court in drawing inferences from this kind of evidence in the course of legal proceedings. The evidence of the behaviour of the police dog was therefore found to be inadmissible because of its irrelevance.

[21] 1986 4 SA 734 (A).

[22] At 743F.

[23] *Shabalala* supra is discussed by Van Oosten 1987 *SALJ* 531. It must be noted that circumstances might be such that in appropriate cases reasonable inferences can be drawn from the behaviour of police dogs.

In order to determine whether a reasonable or proper inference might eventually be possible the court must make a provisional or tentative assessment of the *potential* weight of the evidence sought to be adduced. There must at least be some advance indication that the evidence, if received, would be of reasonable assistance to the court in the exercise of its ultimate fact-finding duty. Zuckerman explains that where the relevance or irrelevance of evidence is the issue and *potential* probative weight must be assessed,[24]

> "[t]he judge is not concerned to estimate the final weight of any piece of evidence. At the admissibility stage he is only concerned to make a rough and ready estimate of the potential contribution that the evidence in question might make and whether it is substantial enough to justify admission. The admissibility test is therefore a composite test made of a mesh of considerations of logical probabilities and of practical utility . . . On some occasions the potential contribution of the evidence adduced will be immediately apparent; for example, the testimony of an eyewitness to the disputed event. At other times its potential will only emerge from a juxtaposition of the evidence in question and other pieces of known facts. If upon the presentation of an individual piece of evidence the judge is in doubt about its relevance, he will ask the party offering it how it relates to the rest of the evidence he plans to adduce. If a publican claims that the brewer supplied him with bad beer, then the fact that the same brewer supplied another pub with bad beer might not be of sufficient weight to be admissible. But it would become sufficiently weighty if it is also shown that it is one of five incidents of supply of bad beer by the same brewer in the same neighbourhood within the space of a day."

5 3 3 Avoiding a proliferation or multiplicity of collateral issues[25] There is a "desire to avoid waste of time in probative exertions more or less off the bull's eye of litigation."[26]

In determining the relevance of evidence the court should of necessity also consider the following question: would the admission of the evidence lead to a protracted investigation into many collateral or side-issues which — once determined — would be of little probative value as regards the true issues? A proliferation of side-issues can, for example, arise where a court decides to admit evidence of the results of a polygraph test (a lie-detector test).[27] Was the polygraphist competent? Was he an expert in this fairly novel "technique" of determining credibility? Were appropriate questions asked during the session? Did the machine function properly? How reliable is the final result? Once all these subsidiary issues — and a host of other related but collateral issues — have been determined the court may merely end up with the following fairly useless result: the opinion of

---

See generally *S v Moya* 1968 1 PH H148 (GW); Barrie 1967 (2) *Codicillus* 44 and Hoffmann 1974 *SALJ* 237. In *Trupedo* supra it was also specifically pointed out that evidence of an animal's instinctive behaviour — as opposed to acquired behaviour — may be admissible. See also *Poswa v Christie* 1934 NPD 178.

[24] Zuckerman *The Principles of Criminal Evidence* 51.

[25] See generally Tapper *Cross and Tapper on Evidence* 8 ed (1995) 61–2.

[26] Maguire *Evidence: Common Sense and Common Law* (1947) 205. See also *Land Securities plc v Westminster City Council* 1993 4 All ER 124 128*h*, where Hoffmann J concluded that the evidence in dispute had "in itself insufficient weight to justify the exploration of otherwise irrelevant issues which its admissibility would require".

[27] See generally Van der Merwe 1981 *De Rebus* 576. On problems which may arise as regards the admissibility of hypnotically induced testimony, see Van der Merwe 1995 *Obiter* 1; 1995 *Obiter* 179; 1996 *Obiter* 1.

someone else that the witness concerned is truthful or untruthful according to a test which has as yet not received universal or broad acceptance in the scientific world. There is a real risk that the drawn-out and time-consuming investigation of collateral issues would not justify the final result. The game is not worth the candle. At any rate, it is the duty of the court to make findings of credibility wherever necessary.

In *S v Nel*[28] Marais J agreed with the trial court's refusal to allow an accused to lead psychiatric evidence. The purpose of this proposed evidence was to show that a defence witness who in her testimony had contradicted aspects of the accused's testimony was "mildly to moderately retarded" and therefore likely to "clamp up" under the strain of testifying in court. Marais J — following *R v Turner*[29] and distinguishing *S v Thurston*,[30] *Lowery v The Queen*[31] and *Toohey v Metropolitan Police Commander*[32] — remarked as follows:[33]

> "Differences in intelligence, ability to recall, ability to articulate, and the like are common-place and courts are well aware that they exist. The *ad hoc* assessments of such matters which courts make as part of the daily round of hearing witnesses testify are an integral and prominent part of the judicial function. Deficiencies in any of these abilities are not likely to remain hidden or obscured if the questioning of the witness is thorough, as it should be. Once the door is opened to evidence of this kind when is it to be shut? If a witness happens to have undergone an intelligence test and it shows the witness to be of high or low intelligence, is it to be received? Are school teachers or university dons to be called to say whether or not a witness was stupid or clever when at school or university? Or that he had a particularly good or poor memory. Is a distinction to be drawn between such witnesses and a professional psychiatrist or psychologist because of the latter's expertise in matters of the mind? The questions are rhetorical but they show, I think, that this is an evidential Pandora's box which we are being invited to open . . . All of this has of course nothing to do with the entirely different question of whether psychiatric evidence may be led to show that a witness is insane and therefore incompetent to testify. Different considerations apply there. I do not think there is any real analogy between cases of physical affliction which adversely affect the capacity of a witness to testify accurately and reliably and intellectual and psychological disabilities of a relatively normal kind. A court cannot tell merely by looking at and listening to a witness that he is so shortsighted that he could not possibly have identified correctly a person who was 100 metres away at the time. Evidence to establish that he is shortsighted should obviously be admissible. But intellectual and psychological disabilities affecting personality, powers of exposition and articulation, ability to recall, and the like are capable of being assessed reasonably adequately while the witness is engaged in giving evidence. No doubt it will be said by some that a more accurate and reliable assessment is likely to be made if evidence, and particularly expert evidence, specifically directed towards such matters is heard? Perhaps so. But then, as against that, one must weigh the cost of this additional and inessential assistance in terms of the prolongation of trials, its availability in relatively few centres and not in others, and its lack of affordability for many in both criminal and civil trials. The cost is likely to exceed by far the marginal benefit which would be gained in the administration of justice by the admission of such evidence."

---

[28] 1990 2 SACR 136 (C).
[29] 1975 1 All ER 70.
[30] 1968 3 SA 284 (A).
[31] 1973 3 All ER 662.
[32] 1965 1 All ER 506. See also generally Pattendon "Conflicting Approaches to Psychiatric Evidence in Criminal Trials: England, Canada and Australia" 1986 *Crim LR* 92.
[33] *Nel* supra 142*j*–143*f*.

5 3 4 The risk of manufactured evidence[34]   The previous consistent statements of a witness are as a rule excluded.[35] One of the reasons for the exclusion of such evidence is that the admission thereof "would make it a very straightforward matter for the unscrupulous to manufacture evidence".[36]

5 3 5 Prejudicial effect[37]   Evidence which is logically probative or disprobative can be excluded because of its prejudicial effect on the party concerned. "Prejudice" in this context does not mean that the evidence must be excluded simply because the party against whom the evidence stands to be adduced will be incriminated or implicated. It means that incrimination or implication will take place in circumstances where the party concerned may be procedurally disadvantaged or otherwise exposed to a lengthy trial involving issues which, though logically relevant, are legally too remote to assist the court in its ultimate decision on the merits. Evidence is relevant if its probative value outweighs its prejudical effect. Proof of motive provides a good example.

Evidence of an accused's motive to commit a particular crime is generally relevant for purposes of proving intention or identity.[38] In *R v Kumalo & Nkosi* Innes CJ gave the following example:[39]

> "The ordinary man does not perpetrate a grave criminal offence without a motive; and although it is not essential, nor always possible, to ascertain what it was, the matter is often of considerable importance. A crime for which no motive likely to affect the person charged can be assigned is difficult to bring home. So that the presence of such a motive is an element in favour of the [prosecution], and its absence an element in favour of the accused. Now it is seldom that direct evidence on the point, such as would be afforded by the accused's own statement, can be produced. In the majority of cases the probable existence or non-existence of motive must be deduced from external circumstances. And such circumstances may as a general rule be proved if they are relevant — that is to say if they are circumstances from which the presence or absence of the particular motive may be reasonably inferred. Thus, if a husband were charged with the murder of his wife, evidence that he had formed an adulterous connection with another woman would be admissible as showing a possible motive for the crime. On the other hand proof might be properly given of affectionate marital relations in order to negative motive."

The presence or absence of motive would be worth pursuing even if it results in further issues such as: was there an adulterous affair? was the marriage a happy one? These issues are not really collateral issues but issues which, once determined, can assist the court in making a finding as regards the *facta probanda*.[40] And the prejudicial effect of the evidence is outweighed by its potential probative value.

---

[34] Tapper *Cross and Tapper on Evidence* 62.

[35] See § 9 1 below.

[36] Cowsill & Clegg *Evidence: Law and Practice* 3 ed (1990) 207–8.

[37] In *S v Papiyana* 1986 2 PH H115 (A) the appellant at his trial appeared in prison clothes and with his feet shackled in leg-irons. The court (at 206) compared this "information" with "evidence which . . . [should be] . . . excluded on the ground that its relevance is too tenuous to compensate for its prejudicial nature".

[38] *S v Sithole* 1980 4 SA 148 (D) 150.

[39] 1918 AD 500 504.

[40] See § 5 3 3 above.

The above is an example of the relevance of a *personal* motive. However, in *R v Kumalo & Nkosi*[41] the Appellate Division actually went a great deal further and held that evidence of a motive for a crime is admissible against an individual even though its tendency is to show that all members of a certain category, or even persons of a certain tribe generally, would have had an inducement to commit the crime in question. Two accused had been charged with and convicted of the murder of a child. The body was found in the veld. The child's throat was cut and the front part of the body was also cut open from the throat to the fork of the legs. According to medical opinion the cutting open of the body had been done by a skilled hand. The heart had been taken out and the left ventricle containing the fatty portion had been removed. In order to furnish proof of a motive for the crime the prosecution called an expert witness, one Hoffman, who testified that it was (at that stage) the practice amongst Zulu tribes and especially on the part of Zulu witch-doctors to kill and mutilate young persons and use portions of the body — and particularly fat — as a charm against ill-luck. It was found that Kumalo and his accomplice were not witch-doctors but "native doctors". The evidence concerning the practice of witch-doctors could therefore not be admitted against the two accused. However, Innes CJ held that the expert evidence on the custom of Zulu people *generally* was relevant and admissible against Kumalo:[42]

> "[I]n deciding whether inferences as to motive could reasonably be drawn from Hoffman's evidence, we must have regard to those portions which dealt with the custom of Zulu tribes generally. And according to his statements the members of those tribes believed firmly in the potency of human fat not only as a charm against misfortune already sustained, but as ensuring good luck in the future, and for love philters. They generally followed the advice of a witch-doctor, but they also used the charm themselves. And in my opinion the existence of a motive for a crime like the present might be reasonably deduced from the general custom or belief described if the accused were members of the tribe or tribe referred to. Human fat taken from certain internal organs would possess a definite value for them, and would be used for important purposes, and that fact might be fairly considered as pointing to the existence of a motive for acquiring a substance which to other persons would be both useless and repulsive. Generally the circumstance relied upon as showing motive stands in direct connection with the person charged, and is clearly within his personal knowledge. Here it is merely a tribal custom. But the customs of native tribes upon vital matters are universal and binding in a very high degree. And I see nothing unreasonable or unfair in inferring from a well-established tribal custom such as has been deposed to, the existence of motive for a crime, the leading feature of which was the removal of the very substance to which the custom related. This conclusion, however, as already pointed out, is based upon the assumption that the accused are members of the tribe in question. Hoffman spoke about the customs among the Zulu tribes, and he stated that the first accused (Kumalo) was a Bacwa, a tribe which was a Zulu off-shoot. But he could not say to what tribe the second accused belonged. The evidence before us does not show him to have been a Zulu, and no inference could in his case be reasonably drawn from Hoffman's statement. That statement was therefore relevant as against the first accused only. But being relevant against him it was rightly admitted . . .."

---

[41] 1918 AD 500.
[42] *Kumalo & Nkosi* supra 505–6.

Solomon JA and C G Maasdorp JA came to a similar conclusion in their separate judgments, albeit for slightly different reasons. It is submitted that the evidence which was held admissible in *R v Kumalo & Nkosi* supra was far too tenuous to have warranted admission. There was no link between Kumalo and the practice referred to by the expert witness, except that Kumalo was a Zulu. There was no evidence that Kumalo had experienced ill-luck or was expecting imminent ill-luck. There was no personal motive. Solomon JA sought to circumvent this argument:[43]

"For Hoffman's evidence would, in my opinion, supply a motive for the commission of the crime in the case not only of Zulus falling under the class of witch-doctors, but also of members of that tribe in general. For if it is a common belief amongst them that portions of the insides of young children have a special value as medicine to be taken in case of ill-luck, it would follow that the possession of such objects of value would be considered highly desirable by anyone sharing in that belief. There would be a motive, therefore, on the part of every such person to kill a young child for the purpose of procuring those portions of its inside which have a special value. It is impossible to conceive of any ordinary civilized person killing a child simply for the purpose of extracting portions of its inside, for he would have no possible object in doing so; but in the case of a Zulu such conduct is quite intelligible, for he would have the motive of acquiring objects which in his opinion are of special value. The inducement in such a case would be on the same footing as that of a man who commits murder for the purpose of rifling the body of his victim of money or other valuables . . . It was argued indeed that evidence of motive is admissible only when it is directed to something peculiar to the individual who is charged with the commission of the offence, but not when it applies to a whole class or to persons in general. But I can see no reason for insisting upon any such limitation. One man who commits a murder may be actuated by a motive peculiar to himself, such as ill-will towards the deceased; another by a motive which is common to people in general, such as the love of gain. And evidence of motive is in my opinion admissible, even though its tendency is to show that all members of a class or even persons generally would have an inducement to commit the crime in question. It is true that in the present case the motive would naturally be a much stronger one if it had been proved that the prisoners were witch-doctors, but we are not concerned with the adequacy of the motive, which was a matter entirely for the jury."

It is submitted that this kind of reasoning is unacceptable because it is gravely prejudicial to the individual concerned. The evidence admitted by the Appellate Division was not really evidence of motive (at any rate, not *personal* motive) but simply circumstantial evidence which, we submit, was irrelevant on account of its extremely limited potential probative value and its likely prejudice to the accused. There was no evidence that the gruesome practices referred to by the expert witness did not also exist in other tribes.

5 3 6 The doctrine of precedent Judicial precedent can determine the relevance (admissibility) — but not the final weight[44] — of certain types of evidence.

---

[43] *Kumalo & Nkosi* supra 508–9.

[44] In *R v C* 1949 (2) SA 438 (SR) the accused was charged with sodomy. The prosecution sought to adduce evidence that six days after the alleged commission of the offence the accused had attempted to commit suicide. This evidence was held admissible. At 439 Tredgold J held as follows (our emphasis): "In this matter the Crown tenders in evidence certain documents relating to the fact that the accused, subsequent to the charge being laid against him, attempted to commit suicide. The main principle involved is the question as to whether attempted suicide is admissible evidence, the letters being purely subsidiary to that

In *S v Shabalala*[45] Nestadt JA came to the conclusion that the judgment of Innes CJ in *R v Trupedo*[46] did not rest solely on a factual finding concerning the reliability or otherwise of the particular dog whose activities and abilities were in issue, but was essentially rooted in the principle that evidence of the conduct of dogs in identifying an accused by scenting is inadmissible.[47] However, Nestadt JA did point out that if the untrustworthiness of such evidence could be sufficiently reduced — even though not totally removed — then "actions of the dog would become relevant and evidence thereof admissible".[48] It would seem that a cautious approach is necessary before boldly invoking judicial precedent to decide on admissibility where relevance is the issue. Facts differ from case to case and precedent can therefore at most provide useful guidelines.

5 3 7 The principle of completeness A court should not exclude harmless irrelevant evidence. A witness should as a rule and within limits be permitted to tell a coherent story, and in so doing provide the court with the general background to the disputed event.

5 4   THE COMMON-LAW DISCRETION TO EXCLUDE IMPROPERLY OBTAINED EVIDENCE[49]

The discretion to exclude relevant but unconstitutionally obtained evidence is discussed in chapter 12 below. The rest of the present paragraph deals with the common-law position. Is there a common-law discretion to exclude improperly (including illegally) obtained evidence? Such a discretion exists in civil cases.[50] The position in criminal cases is not entirely clear.

In *Kuruma v R*[51] Lord Goddard considered that "no doubt in a criminal case

---

attempt, but necessary to explain it, not only from the Crown's point of view, but from the accused's point of view. No, I must remember at this juncture that I am not concerned with the weight which may be attached to this evidence. *I am simply concerned with its admissibility, and I have no doubt whatsoever that it is legally admissible and that there is nothing improper in the Crown's leading this evidence. It is quite clear on the authorities which have been quoted that the behaviour of the of the accused subsequent to the allegations being made against him is relevant and is admissible in evidence. The weight to be attached to that behaviour must vary greatly according to the particular circumstances of each case.* But that is a matter to be decided by the jury, and not by myself. Amongst the matters which are expressly mentioned as being relevant is flight to avoid facing the charge laid against him, by the accused. Now, it seems to me that that covers in principle the case in which an accused person attempts to avoid facing the charge by committing suicide. The exact weight to be attached to any such attempts need not be dealt with now, and I think it is best reserved for the summing-up. *But I may say in conclusion that, although I am unable to recollect any specific case, I am quite satisfied that evidence of such attempts has been led before this Court on more than one occasion, and that the evidence is admissible,* and that it is for the jury to decide in all the circumstances of this particular case how far they should regard it as favourable or unfavourable to the accused."

[45] 1986 4 SA 734 (A).

[46] 1920 AD 58.

[47] *Shabalala* supra 741G–H.

[48] *Shabalala* supra 741J–742A.

[49] See generally Skeen 1988 *SACJ* 389.

[50] *Shell SA (Edms) Bpk v Voorsitter, Dorperaad van die OVS* 1992 1 SA 906 (O); *Motor Industry Fund Administrators (Pty) Ltd v Janit & another* 1994 3 SA 56 (W); *Motor Industry Fund Administrators (Pty) Ltd v Janit* 1995 4 SA 293 (A) 307B; *Lenco Holdings Ltd v Eckstein* 1996 2 SA 693 (N).

[51] 1955 AC 197 203.

the judge always has a discretion to disallow evidence if the strict rules of admissibility would operate unfairly against the accused". In South Africa there is some authority for the existence of the discretion to exclude admissible evidence. In *S v Forbes*[52] Theron J felt satisfied that the discretion to exclude evidence which was strictly admissible did exist in practice and that its exercise in rare cases could serve a useful purpose. In an *obiter dictum* in *S v Mushimba*[53] Rumpff CJ quoted with approval Lord Goddard's statement in *Kuruma v R* supra as to the discretion to exclude evidence which would operate unfairly against the accused.

In the Canadian case of *R v Wray*[54] it was said by Mortland J that the *dictum* of Lord Goddard appears to have been based on *R v Noor Mohamed*[55] and had been unduly extended in some of the subsequent cases as it appeared that Lord Goddard had indicated that the discretion should only be relied upon where the admissibility was tenuous but the evidence gravely prejudicial. *Noor Mohamed* supra was a similar fact evidence case in which it was held that a judge possesses a discretion to exclude similar fact evidence where its probative value is outweighed by its possible prejudicial effect. Lord Diplock in *R v Sang*[56] said that the Privy Council in *Kuruma* supra did not intend to extend the discretion beyond the situation where the prejudicial effect of the evidence exceeded its probative value.

Recent cases appear to recognize the existence of a discretion to exclude evidence where the prejudicial effect of the evidence outweighs its probative value.[57]

In *S v Nel*[58] Van der Walt J held that evidence obtained in an illegal manner can be excluded on two grounds: *(a)* the accused cannot be compelled to provide evidence against himself; and *(b)* evidence which is obtained by duress from the accused cannot be used against him. Paizes has indicated that this formulation should be qualified in respect of "autoptic" evidence and the exclusion of evidence where the prejudicial effect would outweigh probative value (i e, where it is irrelevant).[59]

In *S v Hammer & others*[60] Farlam J held that there is a general discretion to exclude improperly obtained evidence on the grounds of unfairness and public policy, and that the following factors may be considered in deciding whether to exercise the discretion: *(a)* society's right to insist that those who enforce the law themselves respect it, so that a citizen's precious right to immunity from arbitrary

---

[52] 1979 2 SA 594 (C) 600.

[53] 1977 2 SA 829 (A) 840.

[54] (1970) 11 DLR (3d) 673.

[55] 1949 AC 182.

[56] 1980 AC 402 434.

[57] *S v Mbatha* 1985 2 SA 26 (D); *S v Ramgobin* 1986 4 SA 117 (W). However, most of the cases refer to a discretion to exclude statements made by an accused. See also generally *S v Boesman & others* 1990 2 SACR 389 (E).

[58] 1987 4 SA 950 (W).

[59] Paizes 1988 *SACJ* 168–70.

[60] 1994 2 SACR 496 (C). Farlam J approved of the views expressed by Skeen 1988 *SACJ* 389 404 and Zuckerman 1991 *Crim LR* 492.

and unlawful intrusion into the daily affairs of private life may remain un-impaired; *(b)* whether the unlawful act was a mistaken act and whether in the case of mistake, the cogency of evidence is affected; *(c)* the ease with which the law might have been complied with in procuring the evidence in question (a deliberate "cutting of corners" tends towards the inadmissibility of the evidence illegally obtained); *(d)* the nature of the offence charged and the policy decision behind the enactment of the offence are also considerations; *(e)* unfairness to the accused should not be the only basis for the exercise of the discretion; *(f)* whether the administration of justice would be brought into disrepute if the evidence was admitted; *(g)* there should be no presumption in favour of or against the reception of the evidence and the question of an onus should not be introduced; *(h)* it should not be a direct intention to discipline the law enforcement officials; *(i)* an untrammelled search for the truth should be balanced by discretionary measures.

In *Hammer* supra the accused was 18 years old and, whilst in custody, wrote a letter to his mother. The paper was provided by the police and a policeman undertook to deliver the letter to the accused's mother. Instead the policeman read the letter and then handed it over to the office of the attorney-general. The issue at the trial was whether the prosecutor could cross-examine the accused on the contents of the letter. Farlam J, in applying the principles above, ruled against such a course. He concluded that the conduct of the policeman was morally reprehensible and amounted to an *injuria*.

5 5   DISCRETION TO ADMIT RELEVANT BUT PRIVILEGED EVIDENCE

In *S v Safatsa*[61] the issue whether a court has the power to overrule a claim of privilege validly made was discussed by Botha JA in *obiter dicta*. A consideration was whether a claim of privilege could be overruled when it might bear on the issue of the innocence of an accused.[62]

Botha JA, in discussing the question as to whether a court has the power to relax legal professional privilege relating to statements made by a prosecution witness to a lawyer, said that any claim to a relaxation of the privilege must be approached with the greatest circumspection. Botha JA concluded that it was not necessary to decide the issue in the case before him. But he did point out that such relaxation could arise only in the context of the exercise of a discretion by a trial court, and only on a consideration of all the information relevant to the question.

---

[61] 1988 1 SA 868 (A) 886–7. See further § 10 3 1 below.
[62] Such a course has been allowed in England in *R v Ataou* 1988 2 WLR 1147 (CA). See also generally Unterhalter 1988 *SALJ* 291.

5 6   DISCRETION TO EXCLUDE ADMISSIONS AND CONFESSIONS[63]

In *S v Mphalele*[64] the issue as to whether a court has the power to exclude a confession in circumstances where it was technically admissible, but where its prejudicial effects outweighed its evidential value, was considered. Miller JA expressed the view that it is not clear whether s 217(1) *(b)* of the CPA negates the existence of a discretion to exclude evidence where its prejudicial effect outweighs its probative value. Miller JA did say, however, that such discretionary power has previously been recognised by the courts.[65]

In *S v Mbatha*[66] Findlay AJ found himself "not persuaded that the general discretion . . . to exclude a statement by an accused which does not amount to a confession, if there are appropriate circumstances, is no longer part of our law".

In *S v Shabalala & another*[67] the accused had made confessions whilst in unlawful detention. The Appellate Division held that it was not clear whether it had a discretion to exclude an otherwise admissible confession on this ground. It was held that the confessions were admissible as the illegality of the arrest of the accused in no way influenced them to confess. Confessions are discussed in chapter 17 below.

---

[63] See and cf generally *S v Mpetha (2)* 1983 1 SA 576 (C); *S v Januarie* 1991 2 SACR 682 (SE); *S v Mafuya* 1992 2 SACR 370 (W); *S v Mbambeli* 1993 2 SACR 388 (E); *S v M* 1993 2 *SACR* 487 (A); *S v Yawa & another* 1994 2 SACR 709 (SE) and *S v Khumalo & andere* 1992 1 SACR 28 (W).

[64] 1982 4 SA 505 (A); cf *S v Mkanzi* 1979 2 SA 757 (T).

[65] See generally *R v Kleinbooi* 1917 TPD 86; *R v Lubela* 1923 TPD 229; *R v Lizzie* 1926 WLD 225; *R v Logan* 1935 CPD 4; *S v Forbes* 1970 2 SA 594 (C).

[66] 1985 2 SA 26 (D) 31. See also *S v Ramgobin* 1986 4 SA 117 (N).

[67] 1996 1 SACR 627 (A).

CHAPTER 6

CHARACTER EVIDENCE

PJ Schwikkard

6 1 INTRODUCTION

This chapter and chapter 7 deal with the subject of what evidence, pertaining to character and disposition, may be adduced. Whilst chapter 7 deals specifically with similar fact evidence, this chapter deals with the admissibility of evidence relating to the character of witnesses or the accused, as the case may be.

In terms of the common law character means general reputation[1] and must be distinguished from a person's disposition to think or act in a particular way.[2] In theory, at least, it is only evidence of general reputation which is relevant for the purposes of the law of evidence. However, in practice it is extremely difficult to maintain a clear distinction between disposition and reputation.[3] This difficulty is well illustrated by the following passage from Hoffmann & Zeffertt:[4]

> "The accused is always entitled to adduce evidence of his own good character either by calling witnesses to testify to it or by testifying to it himself. A witness who testifies to the accused's good character may, in theory, speak only of his reputation; but when an accused testifies, he cannot give evidence about what others say about his reputation: he may only say that his conduct has been good in certain respects."

---

[1] *R v Rowton* 1865 Le & CA 520, 169 All ER 1497. General reputation refers to a person's reputation in the community in which he lives.
[2] See generally Hoffmann & Zeffertt 28.
[3] See generally Schmidt 412–14.
[4] At 29.

The rules pertaining to character evidence applicable in criminal and civil cases are dealt with separately below.

6 2 CHARACTER IN CRIMINAL CASES

6 2 1 The character of the accused In terms of s 227(1) of the CPA the admissibility of character evidence of the accused is determined by the rules in force on 30 May 1961, these being the rules of English law. The common-law rules need to be read together with the relevant statutory provisions.

The general rule is that the accused may adduce evidence of his own good character,[5] but the prosecution is prohibited from adducing evidence of his bad character, subject to specified exceptions.

The reason for permitting evidence of the accused's good character is to be found in the *dictum* of Willes J in *R v Rowton*,[6] in which the court held that "such evidence is admissible because it renders it less probable that what the prosecution has averred is true. It is strictly relevant to the issue."[7] Evidence of the accused's bad character is excluded in English law because it might "have a disproportionately prejudicial effect upon the jury" and because it is generally considered to be irrelevant.[8] The latter reason presumably forms the basis for the rule in South African law.

There are a number of ways in which an accused may try and establish his good character: by the accused giving evidence herself, by calling witnesses to testify on her behalf,[9] or by cross-examining prosecution witnesses.[10] However, once the accused herself, or through calling witnesses, adduces evidence as to her good character the prosecution can respond by introducing evidence of bad character.[11] The accused may also render herself liable to cross-examination as to bad character in terms of s 197 of the CPA.

6 2 2 Evidence of the accused's bad character Once the accused has adduced evidence as to her own good character the prosecution may respond in three different ways: (i) adducing evidence of bad reputation; (ii) cross-examining character witnesses; and (iii) cross-examining the accused.[12]

If the accused attacks the character of prosecution witnesses but does not adduce evidence as to her own good character, the prosecution may not adduce

---

[5] *R v Gimingham* 1946 EDL 156; *R v Bellis* 1966 ALL ER 552 (CCA).

[6] 1865 Le & CA 520 540, 169 ER 1497 1506.

[7] Cf *R v Bellis* 1966 1 All ER 552 (CCA) 552, where the court described the accused's good character as "primarily a matter that goes to credibility".

[8] May *Criminal Evidence* 3 ed (1995) 118. At 121 May lists five reasons for limiting evidence as to character: *(a)* it is easy to fabricate; *(b)* it is often irrelevant; *(c)* it may lead to an investigation of collateral issues; *(d)* it frequently is nothing more than opinion evidence; *(e)* it may usurp the function of the jury.

[9] If a witness is called to testify as to the accused's character, she may be cross-examined so as to test the accuracy of her testimony. Hoffmann & Zeffertt 31 express the view that such witness may be asked whether she is aware of the accused's previous convictions. However, this view is yet to be tested by the South African courts and remains an open question.

[10] See generally Hoffmann & Zeffertt 29; May *Criminal Evidence* 3 ed (1995) 119.

[11] *R v Rowton* supra.

[12] See generally Hoffmann & Zeffertt 30–2.

evidence of the accused's bad character.[13] In these circumstances the prosecution will be limited to cross-examining the accused as to character in terms of s 197*(a)* of the CPA. In *R v Butterwasser*[14] the court of criminal appeal held that the defence's cross-examination of the prosecution witnesses as to their previous convictions did not permit the prosecution to call a police officer to testify as to the accused's previous convictions. The reason given by the court was that the attack on the prosecution witnesses was directed at putting their character in issue and not the character of the accused.[15]

Where the prosecution does call witnesses to testify as to the accused's bad character they may only state what they know about the accused's general reputation.[16] The prosecution is also restricted by the similar fact rule, which prohibits evidence of past misconduct on the part of the accused where the sole relevance of the evidence is the accused's disposition. Similar fact evidence is discussed in chapter 7.

6 2 3 Section 197 of the CPA   Section 197 of the CPA reads as follows:

> "An accused who gives evidence at criminal proceedings shall not be asked or required to answer any question tending to show that he has committed or has been convicted of or has been charged with any offence other than the offence with which he is charged, or that he is of bad character, unless —
>
> *(a)* he or his legal representative asks any question of any witness with a view to establishing his own good character or he himself gives evidence of his own good character, or the nature or conduct of the defence is such as to involve imputation of the character of the complainant or any other witness for the prosecution;
>
> *(b)* he gives evidence against any other person charged with the same offence or an offence in respect of the same facts;
>
> *(c)* the proceedings against him are such as are described in section 240 or 241 and the notice under those sections has been given to him; or
>
> *(d)* the proof that he has committed or has been convicted of such other offence is admissible evidence to show that he is guilty of the offence with which he is charged."

It is important to note that s 197 does not permit evidence of bad character to be *adduced* by the prosecution. It simply makes provision for cross-examination of the accused.

6 2 3 1 *Section 197*(a)   Section 197 protects the accused against cross-examination that is directed at showing bad character or his previous criminal record.[17] However, the accused will lose this protection (or 'shield') by: adducing evidence as to his own good character;[18] attacking the character of a prosecution witness;[19]

---

[13] *R v Paluszak* 1938 TPD 427; *R v Butterwasser* 1948 1 KB 4, 1947 2 All ER 415.

[14] Supra.

[15] At 7.

[16] *R v Rowton* supra. See § 6 1 above.

[17] See Hoffmann & Zeffertt generally 40; May *Criminal Evidence* 3 ed (1995) 134 et seq; Heydon *Evidence: Cases & Materials* 3 ed (1991) 285.

[18] Section 197*(a)*.

[19] Section 197*(a)*.

or by testifying "against any other person charged with the same offence or an offence in respect of the same facts".[20]

Section 197*(a)*, in so far as it permits cross-examination of the accused as to character if the accused introduces evidence as to his own good character, complements the common-law rule which permits the prosecution to adduce evidence of bad character in such circumstances. However, for the purposes of s 197*(a)* the meaning of good character is not restricted to general reputation and "includes evidence of individual witness's opinion and the accused's past misconduct".[21]

An accused gives evidence of his own good character when[22]

" . . . he asserts, or elicits, that he is of good character independently of his giving an account of what had happened: he must endeavour (by means of questions or his evidence) to refer to his good character in order to have it taken into account as something in his favour: a mere canvassing of the relevant facts is insufficient to penalize the accused if the facts may incidentally show his character in a good light".

Once an accused has put his character in issue his whole character will be subject to cross-examination. In *Stirland v DPP* the court held that[23]

"[a]n accused who 'puts his character in issue' must be regarded as putting the whole of his past record in issue. He cannot assert his good conduct in certain respects without exposing himself to inquiry about the rest of his record so far as this tends to disprove a claim of good character."

In terms of s 197*(a)* the accused will also expose himself to cross-examination as to character if "the nature or conduct of the defence is such as to involve imputation of the character of the complainant or any other witness for the prosecution". There are two ways in which the nature and conduct of the defence may be revealed: (1) by the accused's testimony; and (2) through cross-examination of the prosecution witnesses by the accused's legal representative or, in the case of the unrepresented accused, by himself.[24] However, if the accused is led by the prosecution into making assertions as to his good character, this will not put the accused's character into issue.[25]

The wording of s 197*(a)* is similar to that found in s 1*(f)*(ii) of the English Criminal Evidence Act 1898. In a post-30 May 1961 decision the House of Lords held that s 1*(f)*(ii) should be interpreted literally.[26] Consequently, in English law cross-examination as to character will be allowed even where imputations as to the character of prosecution witnesses is a necessary part of the accused's

---

[20] Section 197*(b)*.

[21] Hoffmann & Zeffertt 42.

[22] *LAWSA* para 491. See May *Criminal Evidence* 3 ed (1995) 134, where it is noted that "[i]t is a question of judgment and ultimately of discretion for the judge to say what evidence amounts to the establishment of good character". See also *R v Malindi* 1966 4 SA 123 (PC).

[23] 1944 AC 315 326–7.

[24] See May *Criminal Evidence* 3 ed (1995) 139. Where an accused is unrepresented the presiding officer should warn the accused of the dangers of exposing himself to cross-examination as to character.

[25] *R v Beecham* 1921 3 KB 464; May *Criminal Evidence* 3 ed (1995) 135; *LAWSA* para 491. See also *Schoultz v Voorsitter, Personeel-Advieskommittee van die Munisipale Raad van George* 1983 4 SA 689 (C).

[26] *Selvey v DPP* 1970 AC 304.

defence.[27] "The fact that an imputation is not made to discredit the witness but for another purpose is immaterial."[28] The South African courts have been reluctant to take such a literal interpretation and there is authority for the view that where the evidence sought to be elicited forms an essential portion of the accused's defence s 197*(a)* should not be invoked, even if that evidence involves an imputation as to the character of a prosecution witness.[29]

6 2 3 2 *Section 197*(b)   Section 197*(b)* makes the accused liable to cross-examination as to character if she gives evidence "against any other person charged with the same offence or an offence in respect of the same facts". In *Murdoch v Taylor*[30] the House of Lords held that "evidence against" a co-accused means evidence which supports the prosecution case in a material respect, or which undermines the defence of the co-accused.[31] The accused's intention in giving such evidence, whether in examination in chief or cross-examination, is not relevant.[32] However, "if one accused merely denies that he took part in a joint venture, that does not constitute giving evidence against a co-accused unless it implies that his co-accused did participate in it".[33] In *S v Mazibuko*[34] the court in an *obiter dictum* found that the wording of s 197*(b)* conferred no discretion and that when cross-examination is allowed in terms of s 197*(b)* the court has no general or residual discretion to restrict such cross-examination on grounds of irrelevancy. Paizes argues that "even where the shield is lifted in terms of paragraph *(a)* or *(b)*, the 'accused still has the ordinary witness's immunity against being asked question which are not relevant either to his credibility or to the issue' ".[35]

6 2 3 3 *Section 197*(c)   Section 197*(c)* provides that if the charge is one of receiving stolen property, the accused may be questioned in respect of her previous convictions and bad character. Hoffmann & Zeffertt note that although the drafter's intention was presumably "to allow the prosecution in a receiving charge to cross-examine on matters which they would be entitled to prove under ss 240 and 241"[36] of the CPA, this is not supported by a literal interpretation of s 197*(c)*.

---

[27] This rule is subject to an exception in the case of rape.
[28] May *Criminal Evidence* 3 ed (1995) 139. See also Hoffmann & Zeffertt 43.
[29] See *R v Hendrickz* 1933 TPD 451; *Spencer v R* 1946 NPD 696; *R v Persutam* 1934 TPD 253; *S v V* 1962 3 SA 365 (E). Section 197 replicates the provisions of s 1*(f)* of the English Criminal Evidence Act 1898. The incorporation of these provisions in a South African statute allows the South African courts to depart from English interpretation. See Paizes in Du Toit et al *Commentary* 23-31. See also Hoffmann & Zeffertt 45, who argue that the approach of the South African courts is to be favoured.
[30] 1965 AC 574.
[31] At 592.
[32] *Murdoch v Taylor* supra 591.
[33] Hoffmann & Zeffertt 46.
[34] 1988 3 SA 190 (A) 97.
[35] In Du Toit et al *Commentary* at 23-32A, where it is asserted that both the court's and Hoffmann & Zeffertt's reliance on *R v Bagas* 1952 1 SA 437 (A) is misplaced. Cf Hoffmann & Zeffertt 46.
[36] At 46. See also Paizes in Du Toit et al *Commentary* 23-32.

6 2 3 4 *Section 197*(d)   Section 197*(d)* provides that the accused may be cross-examined as to previous offences if the purpose of such evidence is to "show that he is guilty of the offence with which he is charged". The courts have held that s 197 does not prohibit the accused being asked questions relevant to an issue before the court even if such questions tend to show bad character or to reveal the accused's previous convictions.[37] Thus it can be said that s 197*(d)* merely confirms the similar fact rule.[38]

6 2 4 Section 211 of the CPA   Section 211 of the CPA provides:

"Except where otherwise expressly provided by this Act or except where the fact of a previous conviction is an element of any offence with which an accused is charged, evidence shall not be admissible at criminal proceedings in respect of any offence to prove that an accused at such proceedings had previously been convicted of any offence, whether in the Republic or elsewhere, and no accused, if called as a witness shall be asked whether he has been so convicted."

As a consequence of the words "[e]xcept where otherwise expressly provided for by this Act" s 211 is subject to the similar fact rule[39] by virtue of s 252 of the CPA, which applies the law that was in force on the 30 May 1961.[40]

Section 211 does not prevent an accused from testifying as to her own previous convictions. This might be done, for example, to support a defence based on an alibi.[41] When an accused chooses this course she runs the risk of having her character attacked by the prosecution in cross-examination.[42] However, in *S v Methembu*[43] the Appellate Division held that if such cross-examination is permitted, it must be limited to the extent that any further details sought are relevant to an issue in the trial.[44]

It should be noted that evidence of previous convictions are admitted during the course of bail proceedings as they are not considered criminal proceedings.[45] They are also admissible after conviction in order to assist the court in determining an appropriate sentence.[46]

6 2 5 Witnesses other than the accused   Except where a witness's credit has been impeached by evidence that she has a bad reputation, the party calling that

---

[37] *S v Mokoena* 1967 1 SA 440 (A); *S v Mavuso* 1987 3 SA 499 (A).

[38] See ch 7, where this rule is discussed fully. See also Hoffmann & Zeffertt 39; Paizes in Du Toit et al *Commentary* 23-31. See also *S v Mavuso* 1987 3 SA 499 (A) discussed in § 7 7 below; *S v January* 1995 1 SACR 202 (C).

[39] See ch 7 below.

[40] Section 211 is not only subject to s 252 but must also be read together with ss 197, 240, 241, and 271–273 of the CPA.

[41] See *R v Bosch* 1949 1 SA 548 (A); *S v Malinga* 1962 3 SA 174 (D).

[42] *S v Malinga* supra.

[43] 1988 1 SA 145 (A).

[44] At 150G.

[45] *S v Hlongwa* 1979 4 SA 112 (D). See further s 60(5)*(d)*, *(e)* and *(g)* of the CPA. It may be argued that the admission of previous convictions at bail proceedings infringes the constitutionally entrenched right to be presumed innocent. However, it is submitted that admission is likely to survive a constitutional challenge by virtue of the application of the limitations clause.

[46] Section 271 of the CPA.

witness is prohibited from adducing evidence as to the witness's good character.[47] Where a witness disputes an allegation that she has a reputation for untruthfulness the opposition may call a witness to testify from her knowledge of the impugned witness's reputation that she would not believe the latter on her oath.[48] In *S v Damalis*[49] the court held that another court's assessment of a witness's credibility may be put to a witness in cross-examination. In chapter 25 impeachment of the credit of a witness is fully discussed.

6 2 6 Character of the complainant   In all criminal cases where the complainant testifies he or she may be cross-examined, and the cross-examiner may ask questions that are pertinent to exposing the witness's credibility or lack thereof.[50] However, the point of departure is that the character or disposition of the complainant is not relevant to credibility. Consequently, evidence which is *solely* directed at establishing that the complainant has a bad character is prohibited, as is evidence of good character.[51] Nevertheless, in a few exceptional categories of cases the complainant's character is viewed as relevant. These are discussed in §§ 6 2 6 1 and 6 2 6 2 below.

6 2 6 1   *Rape or indecent assault*   In a case involving a charge of rape or indecent assault the defendant may adduce evidence as to the complainant's bad reputation for lack of chastity.[52] Prior to 1989[53] s 227 of the CPA provided that, in sexual offence cases, the admissibility of evidence as to "the character of any female" would be determined by the application of the common law. In terms of the common law the defence may question the complainant as to her previous sexual relations with the accused.[54] The accused is prohibited from leading evidence of the complainant's sexual relations with other men.[55] However, the complainant may be questioned on this aspect of her private life in cross-examination as it is considered relevant to credibility. Evidence to contradict any denials may be led only if such evidence is relevant to consent.[56]

The South African Law Commission in 1985[57] noted that in practice the application of s 227 resulted in little (if any) restrictions being placed on the admissibility of sexual history evidence.[58] In accordance with the recommenda-

---

[47] *R v Moore* 1948 2 SA 227 (C).

[48] See May *Criminal Evidence* 3 ed (1995) 155.

[49] 1984 2 SA 105 (T). See also Skeen 1984 *SALJ* 432.

[50] Hoffmann & Zeffertt 47.

[51] *R v Wood* 1951 2 All ER 112.

[52] See generally Hoffmann & Zeffertt 47.

[53] The Criminal Law and the Criminal Procedure Act Amendment Act 39 of 1989 introduced significant amendments to s 227. See also Skeen 1990 *SACJ* 77.

[54] *R v Riley* 1887 18 QBD 481. As this type of evidence was always considered relevant to the issue, evidence could be adduced to contradict a denial.

[55] *R v Adamstein* 1937 CPD 331.

[56] *R v Cockcroft* 1870 11 Cox CC 410; *R v Cargill* 1913 2 KB 271.

[57] Project 45 *Report on Women and Sexual Offences* (1985).

[58] At 48.

tion of the Law Commission, s 227 was amended.[59] The original provisions were retained and three new subsections added. In terms of these additions evidence of previous sexual history will be allowed only where leave of the court to lead such evidence is sought.[60] The court will only grant leave to lead such evidence if relevance is established.[61] In terms of s 227(3) an application to lead such evidence must be made *in camera*. However, the complainant's prior sexual history with the accused remains relevant and no application needs to be made to lead this evidence.[62] Section 227(4) makes these provisions applicable to complainants irrespective of gender.

Prior to the enactment of these provisions the common-law provisions had been criticized on a number of grounds: *(a)* whilst cross-examination concerning prior sexual history traumatizes and humiliates the victim, the evidence it elicits is irrelevant[63] and at most establishes a general propensity to have sexual intercourse; *(b)* evidence of this nature is held to be inadmissible in other cases and there are no grounds for admitting it where the case is of a sexual nature;[64] *(c)* the possibility of such cross-examination deters victims from reporting the offence.[65]

The reforms introduced by s 227, whilst addressing some of these problems, have not escaped criticism. The objections to these amendments are to the effect that the very purpose for which they were enacted is undermined by the very wide discretion conferred on judicial officers.[66] The same judicial officers who in the past failed to exercise their discretion to exclude irrelevant previous sexual history evidence are now being asked to exercise the very same discretion, albeit preceded by an application held *in camera*.[67] One way of addressing this problem would be to specify criteria for relevance.[68]

---

[59] By s 2 of the Criminal Law and Criminal Procedure Amendment Act 39 of 1989.

[60] Section 227(2).

[61] Section 227(2).

[62] Section 227(2).

[63] South African Law Commission *Report on Women and Sexual Offences* 42. See Temkin *Rape and the Legal Process* (1987) 120; Heilbron Committee (1975) para 89.

[64] South African Law Commission *Report on Women and Sexual Offences* 43. It was noted by the Heilbron Committee para 131 that "[i]n contemporary society sexual relationships outside marriage, both steady and of a more casual character, are fairly widespread, and it seems now to be agreed that a woman's sexual experiences with partners of her own choice are neither indicative of untruthfulness nor of a general willingness to consent".

[65] South African Law Commission *Report on Women and Sexual Offences* 49. Temkin *Rape and the Legal Process* 120.

[66] See generally Schwikkard 'A Critical Overview of the Rules of Evidence Relevant to Rape Trials in South African Law' in Jagwanth et al (eds) *Women and the Law* (1994) 198. Cf Skeen 1990 *SACJ* 77.

[67] Temkin 'Sexual History Evidence' 1993 *Crim LR* 3 identifies one of the major problems underlying the relevance test, namely that relevance is an insufficiently objective criterion. She refers to the following apt description by L'Heureux-Dube J in *R v Seaboyer; R v Gayme* 83 DLR (4th) 193: "Regardless of the definition used, the content of any relevancy decision will be filled by the particular judge's experience, common sense and/or logic . . . There are certain areas of enquiry where experience, common sense and logic are informed by stereotype and myth . . . This area of the law [sexual history evidence] has been particularly prone to the utilization of stereotypes in determinations of relevance."

[68] For a discussion of these criteria, see Schwikkard *Women and the Law* 205; Temkin *Rape and the Legal Process* 132.

6 2 6 2 Crimen iniuria In order to obtain a conviction on a charge of *crimen iniuria* the prosecution must prove insult to the complainant's dignity.[69] Evidence that goes to establishing that the complainant was not the type of person who would have been insulted in the circumstances will be regarded as relevant.[70]

6 3   CHARACTER IN CIVIL CASES

In civil cases the characters of the parties are generally considered irrelevant.[71] However, in certain specific cases evidence pertaining to the character of a party will be regarded as relevant either in respect of an issue or in quantifying damages.[72] For example, an essential element in an action of seduction is the plaintiff's virginity and evidence which shows that the plaintiff has a permissive disposition will be regarded as relevant.[73] In a defamation action a party who fails in her defence may adduce evidence of the plaintiff's general bad reputation in mitigation of damages.[74] However, the defendant may not refer to specific acts of misconduct and is restricted to leading evidence of general reputation.[75]

Clearly parties as witnesses may be cross-examined as to credit and in certain circumstances character evidence may be considered relevant to credibility.[76] Evidence of character may also be admitted in terms of the similar fact rule.[77]

---

[69] Hunt & Milton *South African Criminal Law and Procedure* vol II (1982) 538. The exceptions which apply are not relevant for present purposes.

[70] See *R v Van Tonder* 1932 TPD 90.

[71] Schmidt 418; *LAWSA* para 495.

[72] See generally Hoffmann & Zeffertt 49.

[73] See, e g, *Gleeson v Durheim* 1869 Buch 244; *Van Staden v Rudy* 1908 EDC 7.

[74] See *Sengke v Bredenkamp* 1948 1 SA 1145 (O); *Thole v Minister of Justice* 1967 3 SA 531 (D).

[75] *Black v Joseph* 1931 AD 132.

[76] See ch 25 below for a fuller discussion.

[77] See ch 7 below.

CHAPTER 7

SIMILAR FACT EVIDENCE

PJ Schwikkard

7 1 INTRODUCTION

Similar facts are facts that are directed at showing that a party to the proceedings (usually the accused) has behaved on other occasions in the same way as he is alleged to have behaved in the circumstances presently being considered by the court.[1] For example, George is charged with dealing in dagga; the prosecution wants to introduce evidence showing that he has dealt in dagga on previous occasions. Jennifer, in trying to dispute the admissibility of a confession made while she was in detention, tenders evidence that the police have on other occasions used improper means of interrogation.[2]

Similar fact evidence is generally inadmissible because it is irrelevant.[3] It will be admissible only when it is both logically and legally relevant.[4] When it is found

---

[1] Cf Carter *Cases and Statutes on Evidence* (1990) 440; Tapper *Cross and Tapper on Evidence* 8 ed (1995) 339.

[2] It is necessary to study this chapter in conjunction with chapter 6, which deals with the admissibility of character evidence, as similar facts are often invoked in tendering evidence as to character.

[3] Hoffmann & Zeffertt 52.

[4] *R v Pharenque* 1927 AD 57; *R v Zawels* 1937 AD 342; *Delew v Town Council of Springs* 1945 TPD 128; *Laubscher v National Food Ltd* 1986 1 SA 553 (ZS). The latter case is summarized in § 7 7 below.

to be sufficiently relevant it may be admitted in both civil[5] and criminal proceedings. It is most frequently used by the state against the accused; however, there is nothing prohibiting the accused from seeking to have similar fact evidence admitted in her defence.[6]

7 2   The Rationale for the Exclusion of Similar Fact Evidence

Similar fact evidence is generally irrelevant because its prejudicial effect outweighs its probative value. The types of prejudice emanating from similar fact evidence are numerous and varied.[7] They may pertain to prejudice to the accused. For example, a jury who is made aware of the accused's past bad conduct may decide that he deserves to be punished irrespective of whether he is guilty of the offence charged. Even worse, the jury may decide that the accused is of such a bad character that he has probably committed many other crimes without having been detected. A consequence of this type of reasoning is that the jury may convict even though a reasonable doubt as to the accused's guilt exists. It can thus be seen that the introduction of similar fact evidence has the potential to undermine the presumption of innocence.

The accused may also be prejudiced in that he not only has to defend himself in respect of the offence charged but he also has to defend past charges of misconduct.

In *S v M*[8] the court noted that in criminal trials one of the main reasons for not allowing the admission of similar fact evidence was its potential for prejudicing the accused. However, the court held that

> "where . . . the similar fact evidence does not go to show guilt on the part of an accused, prejudice is a far less sensitive issue. Indeed, the Court should be wary of putting obstacles in the way of an accused who wishes to adduce evidence in support of his or her legitimate defence."

Similar fact evidence may also result in procedural inconvenience. The accused is frequently taken by surprise when this type of evidence is introduced.[9] The investigation into collateral issues that arises out of the introduction of similar fact evidence inevitably extends the length of the trial, making the trial more costly and placing additional demands on judicial resources.[10]

If similar fact evidence is admitted too readily, it also has the potential to

---

[5] The same principles of admissibility are applied in both civil and criminal cases. "The courts, however, are less wary of receiving similar fact evidence in the civil context than they are in the criminal context": *LAWSA* para 501. See also *Mood Music Publishing Co Ltd v De Wolfe Ltd* 1976 1 All ER 763 (CA).

[6] *S v Letsoko* 1964 4 SA 768 (A); *S v Yengeni (2)* 1991 1 SACR 329 (C); *S v M* 1995 1 SACR 667 (BA). In all these cases it was alleged that the police habitually induced involuntary confessions.

[7] For a full discussion of these prejudicial factors, see Paizes in Visser (ed) *Essays in Honour of Ellison Kahn* (1989) 238. See also Tapper "Proof and Prejudice" in Campbell & Waller (eds) *Well and Truly Tried: Essay in Honour of Sir Richard Eggleston* (1982) 177; Hoffmann 1975 *Law Quarterly Review* 193.

[8] Supra at 692*d–e*.

[9] In *S v Fani* 1994 1 SACR 635 (E) 639–40 Jones J remarked, in an *obiter dictum*, that for there to be a fair trial as envisaged by the interim Constitution the state should disclose (amongst many other things) the full particulars of any similar fact or character evidence which it intends to lead.

[10] *Delew v Town Council of Springs* supra; *S v M* supra.

undermine the proper administration of justice. An overworked police force, knowing that a person's past record will be considered by the court, may be tempted to focus on past offenders. This could result in sloppy investigation techniques. It may also discourage persons who are genuinely trying to rehabilitate themselves. In addition it would make it easier for the police to bring undue pressure to bear on past offenders and in this way induce involuntary confessions and admissions.

Trial by jury has clearly influenced the formulation of the similar fact rule. In South Africa the jury system has been abolished. This has led to the questioning of the applicability of the existing formulation of the similar fact rule.[11]

7 3   FORMULATING THE RULE FOR DETERMINING THE ADMISSIBILITY OF
       SIMILAR FACT EVIDENCE

The many prejudicial factors associated with similar fact evidence have made the formulation of a workable general rule for determining the admissibility of similar fact evidence extremely difficult.

7 3 1   The formulation in *Makin v Attorney-General for New South Wales*   Probably the most influential formulation is to be found in Lord Herschell's *dictum* in *Makin v Attorney-General for New South Wales*:[12]

> "It is undoubtedly not competent for the prosecution to adduce evidence tending to show that the accused has been guilty of criminal acts other than those covered by the indictment, for the purpose of leading to the conclusion that the accused is a person likely from his criminal conduct or character to have committed the offence for which he is being tried. On the other hand, the mere fact that the evidence adduced tends to show the commission of other crimes does not render it inadmissible if it be relevant to an issue before the jury, and it may be so relevant if it bears upon the question whether the acts alleged to constitute the crime charged in the indictment were designed or accidental, or to rebut a defence which would otherwise be open to the accused."

In this case a husband and wife were charged with the murder of a young child. They had "fostered" this child in return for a sum of money that was insufficient for its maintenance. The child's body had been found buried in the garden of the house occupied by them. These facts were consistent both with the allegation that the child was murdered for the purpose of gaining the maintenance money and the defence that the child had died from natural causes accompanied by an irregular burial. However, the prosecution also adduced evidence that skeletal remains of other babies had been found in the gardens of homes previously occupied by the accused, and that four other women had given their babies over to the accused, having paid them an inadequate amount for maintenance, and that these babies had also vanished. The Privy Council found that this evidence had been correctly admitted to negative the possibility that the child's death resulted from accident or natural causes. It was not admitted to show that the

---

[11] See, e g, Paizes *Essays in Honour of Ellison Kahn*, who argues that where the trial is by judge alone the similar fact rule should be applied as no more than a cautionary rule. See § 7 8 below.
[12] 1894 AC 57 (PC) 65.

accused had a propensity to kill babies and that they were therefore guilty of the crime charged.

In explanation of Lord Herschell's *dictum* it has been held that the admissibility of similar fact evidence can be determined in accordance with which one of two chains of reasoning is employed. The evidence will be excluded if the court is asked to conclude that the accused is guilty because he has a propensity to act in a particular way. It will be admitted "if there is some relevant, probative purpose for it other than for the prohibited form of reasoning . . . but when it is received, the trier of fact must eschew the forbidden reasoning".[13] In terms of this formulation similar fact evidence may not be admitted if it is used only to establish propensity.

7 3 2 The inadequacies of the *Makin* formulation   The *Makin* formulation is inadequate in that it fails to explain several cases.[14] It is apparent that in a significant number of cases "propensity itself is so highly relevant to the issue in a particular case, that evidence of propensity itself is admitted".[15] An example of this is to be found in the case of *R v Straffen*.[16] The accused was charged with murdering a young girl (L). The prosecution tendered evidence relating to two other young girls. All three girls had been strangled, without having been sexually interfered with. In all three cases there was no apparent motive for the crime and no evidence of a struggle. Furthermore, there was no attempt to hide the bodies, although concealment was relatively easy. Straffen had at an earlier date been charged with the murder of the other two girls, but was found unfit to plead on the ground of insanity and committed to an institution. He escaped from the institution and he was seen near the place where L's body was found. During the very brief period of his escape L was murdered. There was further evidence that he had admitted to killing the two other girls. The evidence was admitted on the ground that it was relevant to identity. However, it is difficult to argue that the probative value of the evidence was not based on propensity, "since it established that the accused possessed a propensity of the most unusual kind: he was a strangler of small girls, in peculiar circumstances, and for no apparent motive".[17] It was this propensity which was highly relevant to an issue, namely the identity of the killer, which made the evidence admissible.

7 3 3 Hoffmann & Zeffertt's formulation   It is because of the difficulties outlined above that Hoffmann & Zeffertt argue that the *Makin* formulation can only be used as a basis for explaining the case law if the following proviso is added to it: "in some cases, evidence which proves only disposition will be admissible if, on the facts of the case, it is a disposition which is highly relevant to an issue

---

[13] *LAWSA* para 496.
[14] See *R v Ball* 1911 AC 47 (HL); *Thompson v R* 1918 AC 221 (HL); *R v Straffen* 1952 2 QB 911. Paizes *Essays in Honour of Ellison Kahn* 241.
[15] Hoffmann & Zeffertt 59.
[16] Supra.
[17] Williams (1979) 5 *Dalhousie LJ* 281; see also Hoffmann & Zeffertt 60.

in it".[18] They contend that, as a consequence of the inadequacies of the *Makin* formulation, the courts have tended to prefer to cite the proposition of Lawrence J in *R v Bond*:[19]

"In proximity of time, in method or in circumstances there must be a *nexus* between the two sets of facts, otherwise no inference can be safely induced therefrom."

7 3 3 1 *The* nexus *requirement* In terms of the "*nexus* requirement" there must be a link between the fact in issue (the *probandum*) and the similar fact (the *probans*). This is explained by Stephen as follows:

"You are not to draw inferences from one transaction to another which is not specifically connected with it merely because the two resemble each other. They must be linked together by the chain of cause and effect in some assignable way before you can draw your inference."[20]

Van der Merwe et al[21] submit that the "*nexus* requirement" is merely another way of stating that the evidence must be relevant. In this context the requirement of relevance demands that the evidence "must have probative value in the sense that it can give rise to reasonable inferences in deciding the facts in issue".[22]

7 3 4 The dangers of categorization An unfortunate consequence of the *Makin* formulation is that it has been interpreted by many lawyers as establishing rigid categories in which similar fact evidence will be regarded as relevant. An example of this approach is to be seen in the following passage in *Green*:[23]

"The usual ambit of the admission of 'similar fact' evidence is to prove identity, intent, guilty knowledge, or, as often in sexual cases, to rebut a defence of innocent association and the like."

Hoffmann & Zeffertt highlight the dangers of such an approach:[24]

"The danger of illustrating the application of the principle by the categorization of instances is that it may lead to an erroneous approach in which categories of admissibility are regarded as exceptions. Such an approach . . . leads to casuistry, to insoluble metaphysical problems as to the confines of the categories, and to the error of thinking that, because evidence slots into a category, it will be admissible."

The "categorization approach" was rejected in *Harris v DPP*.[25]

---

[18] At 60.

[19] 1906 2 KB 389 at 424. See *S v Green* 1962 3 SA 886 (A) 894; *S v Letsoko* 1964 4 SA 768 (A) 775; *Jones v S* 1970 2 PH H129 (A); Hoffmann & Zeffertt 60.

[20] *Digest of the Law of Evidence* (1914) note VI: articles 10, 11 & 12.

[21] *Evidence* (1983) 71.

[22] Van der Merwe et al *Evidence* 71. See *S v Green* supra; *S v Letsoko* supra; *S v M* supra.

[23] Supra 894.

[24] At 65.

[25] 1952 AC 694. Cf *R v Katz* 1946 AD 71; *S v M* supra. Although condemning the "categorization approach", most evidence texts use them to group and analyse the plethora of similar facts cases. See, e g, Hoffmann & Zeffertt 65–82; Van der Merwe *Evidence* 77–81. The following list of categories is most frequently enumerated: acts part of the transaction or *res gestae*, presence at a place, possession of a weapon etc, previous course of dealing, motive, sexual passion, acts of preparation, knowledge, intent, design or system, accident or mistake, identity, innocent association, innocent possession, proving the *actus reus*. See also Schmidt 390–406.

7 3 5 The formulation in *DPP v Boardman* In *DPP v Boardman*[26] the court stressed that it was the application of principle that was of prime importance,[27] the principle being that similar fact evidence is admissible only where its probative value exceeds it prejudicial effect.[28] This formulation was accepted by the Appellate Division in *S v D*.[29] The *Makin* rule was not rejected in *Boardman* — rather it was applauded.[30] Therefore *Boardman* must simply be read as revealing the underlying principle in *Makin*.[31]

7 4   THE REQUIREMENT OF SIMILARITY

The probative value of similar fact evidence will to a large extent be determined by the degree of similarity between a person's conduct on other occasions and on the occasion which is the subject of the court's inquiry.[32]

Lord Wilberforce[33] expressed the requirement of similarity in the following terms:[34]

"The basic principle must be that the admission of similar fact evidence (of the kind now in question) is exceptional and requires a strong degree of probative force. This probative force is derived, if at all, from the circumstances that the facts testified to by the several witnesses bear to each other such a striking similarity that they must, when judged by experience and common sense, either all be true, or have arisen from a cause common to the witnesses or from pure coincidence. The jury may therefore properly be asked to judge whether the right conclusion is that all are true, so that each story is supported by the other(s)."

Hoffmann & Zeffertt assert that "[t]he relevance of similar fact evidence depends upon the argument that the same conditions are likely to produce the same results".[35] In *Laubscher v National Food Ltd*[36] Reynolds J held that "before similar fact evidence [can] be admitted, the similarity of conditions applicable in each case . . . has to be satisfactorily established". However, the requirement of similarity should not be unduly emphasized.

7 4 1 The test of coincidence McEwan maintains that a mistake commonly made since *Boardman* is to assume that evidence of previous misconduct by the

---

[26] 1975 AC 421.
[27] At 439.
[28] At 442, 451 and 456–7. Hoffmann & Zeffertt 61 assert that *Boardman* clearly demonstrates that in similar fact cases it is the degree of relevance that is important, not the kind of relevance. Cf Paizes *Essays in Honour of Ellison Kahn* 244. In *S v M* supra the court held that "the reception of similar fact evidence has to be justified by it having so strong a probative value that it should be received in the interests in justice".
[29] 1991 2 SACR 543 (A) 543, where the court held that "the admission of similar fact evidence is exceptional and requires a strong degree of probative force".
[30] At 438, 450, 461.
[31] Paizes *Essays in Honour of Ellison Kahn* 244 queries whether the *Boardman* approach embodies a legal rule or the exercise of judicial discretion. See Hoffmann & Zeffertt 62–3 for a critique of the application of judicial discretion and similar fact evidence.
[32] *S v D* supra 546; *S v M* supra.
[33] *Boardman* supra 444 (AC Reports).
[34] See also *R v Kalkiwich and Kruger* 1942 AD 79 at 86–7; *S v M* 1985 1 SA 1 (A) 4.
[35] At 52.
[36] Supra 554.

accused will have the requisite probative value only when the other incidents are "uniquely strikingly similar".[37] She says it is preferable to see the test in terms of "whether the evidence can be explained away as coincidence".[38]

Several examples from case law support this argument. In *R v Bond*[39] the accused, a medical practitioner, was convicted of unlawfully using instruments upon a woman (J) with the intent to procure an abortion. The trial judge admitted the evidence of another woman (T) to the effect that the accused had performed a similar operation on her with similar intent some nine months previously. In the course of her examination in chief, T further testified that the accused had subsequently told her that he had "put dozens of girls right". Both women had at the material times been living at the accused's house and were pregnant by him. The defence was that instruments had been used on J in the course of a lawful medical examination, that the abortion was accidental, and there had been no intent. Why was this evidence admissible? There was no striking similarity between the other unlawful abortions performed by the accused. However, the evidence was significant in that it made the defence of accident implausible when raised by a man with apparent expertise in abortion.

In *Boardman* the appellant, the headmaster of a boarding school for boys, was charged with, inter alia, committing certain homosexual offences on S, a pupil aged 16, and with inciting H, a pupil aged 17, to commit such offences. There was no application for a separation of trials. The jury therefore heard the evidence of both S and H, who each testified only to incidents in which they themselves were concerned. The judge ruled and directed the jury that the evidence of S on the count concerning him was admissible as corroborative evidence and vice versa. In doing so, the judge drew attention to certain common features in the evidence of the two boys which justified cross-admissibility under the *Makin* rule. In particular, both boys said that Boardman had tried to instigate sexual acts in which Boardman would play the passive role. The judge apparently took judicial notice (see generally § 27 1 below) of the fact that this was a very unusual form of homosexual behaviour.

Despite the questionable judicial notice of what constituted unusual homosexual behaviour, there was no striking similarity between the two incidents. But the fact that both boys alleged that D wished to take the passive role, and the unlikelihood of them both constructing exactly the same lie, was sufficient to suggest that the resemblance between the two incidents went beyond coincidence.[40]

7 4 2 Coincidence and a *nexus* Another way of approaching the coincidence test is to say that the *nexus* referred to in *Bond* can be found in the extreme

---

[37] McEwan *Evidence and the Adversarial Process* (1992) 48.
[38] McEwan *Adversarial Process* 48. See *R v Mansfield* 1978 1 All ER 134; Schwikkard 1995 *SACJ* 389, where the approach taken by the court in *S v M* 1 SACR 667 (BA) is criticized.
[39] 1906 2 KB 389.
[40] See McEwan *Adversarial Process* 48. See also *S v R* 1990 1 SACR 413 (ZS).

unlikelihood of coincidence.[41] Take, for example, the case of *R v Smith*.[42] In this case the appellant was charged with the murder of a woman with whom he had recently gone through a bigamous marriage ceremony. She had been found dead in her bath. The accused, who stood to benefit financially from her death, had sought to show that it resulted from an epileptic fit. At the trial evidence was given that two other women had died on subsequent dates, that the appellant had gone through a form of marriage with each of these women, and that both had died in their baths in circumstances very similar to those surrounding the death of the victim in the instance case. In each case the accused again stood to benefit financially by the woman's death. On appeal the court held that the evidence had been correctly admitted in that it was sufficiently relevant to rebut the accused's defence. The court found that the occurrence of so many accidents which benefited the accused could not reasonable be explained on the basis of coincidence.

Van der Merwe et al[43] summarize the similar fact argument in *Smith* as follows: "[E]ither all three deaths were accidental, or else the accused was responsible for each of them. The improbability of coincidence may therefore often establish the required link."

7 4 3 The degree of similarity If we apply the coincidence test, it is necessary to consider disputed evidence in its context. McEwan contends that "this opens the way for unusual propensities and/or evidence which is not, *prima facie*, strikingly similar".[44] The circumstances of each case will determine the necessary degree of similarity. This can be illustrated by comparing *Makin*[45] and *Boardman*.[46] In *Makin* the similar fact evidence was required to fulfil a large part of the prosecution's task. In its absence it was difficult to sustain the contention that the accused were responsible for the death of their victims. In such cases a high degree of similarity will be required between the incidents before a sufficient link can be established. On the other hand, in cases such as *Boardman*, where there is other evidence supporting the prosecution case, the degree of similarity required is much lower.[47]

7 5 THE FACTS IN ISSUE

The relevance of similar fact evidence must be assessed in the light of the issues to be decided and the other evidence available to the court.[48] It follows that the

---

[41] See generally *R v Roets* 1954 3 SA 512 (A) 521; *R v Sims* 1946 1 All ER 697; *R v Pharenque* 1927 AD 57; *R v Smith* (1915) 11 Cr Pap Rep 229; *S v M* 1995 1 SACR 667 (BA).

[42] Supra.

[43] *Evidence* (1983) 72.

[44] *Adversarial Process* 53.

[45] Supra.

[46] Supra.

[47] McEwan *Adversarial Process* 53.

[48] McEwan *Adversarial Process* 47; Tapper *Cross and Tapper on Evidence* 8 ed (1995) 380. This approach was given approval by O'Connor J in *R v Horwood* 1970 1 QB 133.

admissibility of similar fact evidence also depends on what the issues before the court are.[49] This in turn makes it necessary to identify the issues. This is not difficult in civil proceedings, where the issues are established in the pleadings. In criminal matters the issues are far more difficult to ascertain in that the accused is entitled to deny every element of the charge or raise whatever defence that is open to him.[50] This does not mean, however, that the prosecution is given a licence to introduce similar fact evidence merely on the basis that it might conceivably be relevant.[51] In *Thompson v R*[52] Lord Sumner held that the issue "must have been raised in substance if not in so many words". In many instances the issues are relevant from the nature of the case and the prosecution need not wait until the issue is specifically raised by the accused. Hoffmann & Zeffertt give the following example:[53]

> "[I]f the charge against the accused is that he fraudulently obtained goods on credit without intending to pay for them, it would not be sufficient for the prosecution merely to prove that he bought goods and did not pay. If this is all that the evidence disclosed, the accused would be discharged at the end of the prosecution case without having to raise a defence at all. The prosecution have to adduce positive evidence that the accused intended to defraud, and to do this they would be entitled to lead evidence that the accused had made a practice of buying goods in similar circumstances and not paying for them."

The following example illustrates how the relevance of similar fact evidence can be negated by an admission made by the accused:

> "[I]f someone is charged with committing a crime in Cape Town, the prosecution could prove that he was there and had an opportunity to commit the offence by showing that on the same day he robbed a bank there, but if he admitted his presence in Cape Town, this evidence could have no purpose but prejudice."[54]

7 6   OTHER EVIDENCE

> "The question must always be whether the similar fact evidence taken together with the other evidence would do no more than raise or strengthen a suspicion that the accused committed the offence with which he is charged or would point so strongly to his guilt that only an ultra-cautious jury would acquit in the face of it."[55]

The relevance of similar fact evidence will also be determined by the strength of the other available evidence.[56] This is well illustrated by the case of *R v Ball*.[57] The accused, a brother and sister, were convicted of incest committed during certain periods in 1910. The main prosecution evidence was that the accused, who held themselves out as married, were seen together at night in a house which had only one furnished bedroom, containing a double bed showing signs of

---

[49] Hoffmann & Zeffertt 63–5; *R v Solomons* 1959 2 SA 352 (A); cf *R v Zawels* 1937 AD 342.
[50] Hoffmann & Zeffertt 63.
[51] Hoffmann & Zeffertt 63.
[52] 1918 All ER 521 at 526.
[53] *Law of Evidence* 64.
[54] Hoffmann & Zeffertt 63–4.
[55] *Boardman* supra 457.
[56] Hoffmann & Zeffertt 61.
[57] 1911 AC 47 HL.

occupation by two persons. The brother had been seen coming from the bedroom in a half-dressed state while the woman was in a nightdress. The similar fact evidence admitted by Scrutton J was that three years earlier, before incest was made criminal, the accused had lived together as man and wife sharing a bed, and that a baby had been born, the accused being registered as its parents. This similar fact evidence was highly probative, given the circumstances in which they were presently cohabiting. If the evidence had been that they lived in the same house but occupied separate bedrooms, the probative value of the evidence would have been greatly diminished.[58]

In *S v D*[59] the accused had been convicted in a local division of a multiplicity of crimes, including six counts of rape and one of robbery. He appealed, inter alia, against one of the rape convictions and the robbery conviction. These alleged offences had been committed in respect of the same complainant (X). The complainant had not been able to identify the accused and the trial court had to rely on circumstantial evidence in reaching its decision to convict. In a confession the accused had admitted to committing the other crimes with which he was charged, but not the two forming the subject-matter of the appeal. Evidence was led that the person who raped X told her to "sleep down". These were the same words used by the accused in respect of one of the other rape charges for which he had been convicted. The trial court held that these words were so distinctive that their probative value was sufficient to justify their admission in order to establish the accused's identity. However, the appeal court held that these words on their own did not have sufficient weight to confirm identity, but if they were taken together with the other striking similarities, they did indeed have the required probative value. The other rapes were all committed in a particular area within a period of four months. The robbery and rape of X occurred in the same area and in the middle of the series of the other crimes. The conduct of the perpetrator was very similar to that of the accused in respect of the other crimes for which he had been convicted, namely, all the crimes were committed during the morning or early afternoon, and the accused would enter the house surreptitiously and confront the victim. He would first demand money and then rape the victim. In almost every incident he removed or asked for the victim's watch. When the similarity of this conduct was viewed together with the evidence that the accused had been found in possession of X's keys, it was held that the accused had been correctly convicted. The appeal court upheld the trial court's rejection of the accused's contention that he had coincidentally picked the keys up in the street:[60]

"If, in truth, and without hearing any evidence to that effect, the accused had picked up those keys, then we are asked to believe that one man who is a rapist has picked up a bunch of keys abandoned by another rapist. Apart from the fact that the area is the same area where the accused lives, it is remarkable that, if the keys recovered by the police were not stolen from the complainants's house by the accused, but by a man who had raped there,

---

[58] The *Ball* case is frequently cited as an example of a case where the accused's propensity was highly relevant.
[59] 1991 2 SACR 543 (A).
[60] At 547.

they should come into the possession of another man who is a proved rapist. We think such a proposition would be stretching the bounds of coincidence beyond any possible limits.''

Despite the appeal's courts use of the words ''striking similarity'', the conduct of the accused was not of a particular or unique nature. However, the fact that the accused had committed other crimes in the same area, during the same time period, and, more importantly, that he was found in possession of the complainant's keys imbued the similar fact evidence with high probative value and made the likelihood of coincidence most improbable.

7 7 EXAMPLES OF THE EXCLUSION OF SIMILAR FACT EVIDENCE

Laubscher v National Food Ltd:[61] In this case the plaintiff was a pig farmer who claimed that his pigs had died as a result of eating contaminated foodstuff that he had bought from the defendant. He wished to adduce evidence that other pig farmers had similarly lost pigs after they had eaten the defendant's foodstuff. The court held this evidence irrelevant in that it lacked sufficient similarity. The evidence did not establish that the foodstuff had been bought during the same time period that the plaintiff purchased it. Nor did it indicate that the pigs had become ill within the same time of eating it, or that the conditions on the farms were similar, or that the animal husbandry practices were similar.

S v Mavuso:[62] The appellant was convicted in a magistrate's court of dealing in dagga. He appealed on the basis that the magistrate had incorrectly allowed the prosecution to question him as to a previous conviction on the same charge. The questioning as to the previous conviction arose in the following circumstances: the accused's defence was that he did not know that it was dagga in the bags which he was carrying in a motor vehicle, and under cross-examination he said that he had never before had anything to do with dagga. The Appellate Division held that the evidence did not pass the relevance test because the facts giving rise to the previous conviction were unknown and therefore it could not be inferred that he knew what dagga smelt like (i e there was insufficient similarity). Furthermore, the previous conviction was a long time ago and as the definition of dealing in dagga is so wide, it was not necessary that the accused had handled the dagga himself. Consequently, the evidence of the previous conviction was held to be inadmissible. It therefore could not be established whether or not the accused knew that the dagga was in the car. The conviction was set aside.[63]

Attorney-General, Northern Cape v Brühns:[64] The accused had been convicted in the magistrate's court on two counts: (1) contravention of the Road Traffic Ordinance[65] in that he failed to stop after a traffic officer had signalled him to do so;

---

[61] Supra.
[62] 1987 3 SA 499 (A).
[63] See also *S v January* 1995 1 SACR 202 (O).
[64] 1985 3 SA 686 (A), overruling *S v Khanyapa* 1979 1 SA 824 (A).
[65] Act 21 of 1966.

and (2) contravention of the regulations promulgated under the Petroleum Products Act[66] in that he drove his motor vehicle in excess of the maximum permissible speed laid down in the regulations. In respect of both offences there was no direct evidence that he was the driver of the motor vehicle in question. However, in respect of count (1) the prosecution was assisted by a statutory presumption in terms of which the registered owner of a vehicle is presumed to be the driver. The magistrate held that the two offences were so closely associated with one another in point of time and place that they were for practical purposes inseverable and, as the appellant had been found guilty on the first charge, he could also be presumed to be the person who drove the vehicle in respect of the second charge. The Appellate Division held that the finding on the first count was irrelevant and inadmissible on the second count, as it was based on a presumption that was not applicable on the second count.

This Appellate Division decision makes it clear that the similar fact rule cannot be used to import a presumption against an accused when the presumption does not apply in law.[67]

7 8   AN ALTERNATIVE APPROACH

Paizes[68] argues that the similar fact rule was formulated in accordance with the characteristics of the jury trial, and that since juries have long been abolished in South Africa, a consideration of the necessity and desirability of the similar fact rule is long overdue.

He argues that exclusion is an inappropriate way of dealing with the dangers inherent in the admission of similar fact evidence. It is absurd to require a judge to exclude evidence "whenever he envisages that its reception might induce him wrongly to convict the accused: if he is able to perceive this risk, he will be able, too, to guard against it". Paizes acknowledges that there is always a possibility that judges may make mistakes, but that such errors are best guarded against by invoking a cautionary rule.[69]

> "Such an approach would compel a judge to (i) recognize the dangers of receiving and relying on similar fact evidence, (ii) acknowledge that he has guarded against these dangers and (iii) specify precisely what part the similar fact evidence has played in his line of reasoning and in what way it has contributed to his findings on both the intermediate and the ultimate issues."

Paizes asserts that the doctrine of *stare decisis* is not an insurmountable obstacle to the adoption of such an approach. He argues there are two grounds on which a departure from *Makin* can be justified. First, as it is a pre-1952 decision of the Privy Council,[70]

---

[66] Act 120 of 1977.
[67] Hoffmann & Zeffertt 67. Cf, however, s 130 of the Road Traffic Act 29 of 1989.
[68] *Essays in Honour of Ellison Kahn* 254.
[69] At 265.
[70] At 269.

"it is to be regarded as if it were a decision of the Appellate Division itself and, may, accordingly be rejected by that court as being clearly wrong. Secondly, it may be viewed as creating a rule pertaining to the English system of jury trials that is so inappropriate to modern South African non-jury trial system that it is wrong slavishly to apply it."

Whatever the merits of Paizes' arguments, the South African courts have not to date been called upon to consider this alternate approach and we remain bound by the *Makin* formulation.[71]

---

[71] As elucidated by *Boardman* supra, the approach in *Boardman* having been adopted by the Appellate Division in *S v D* supra.

CHAPTER 8

OPINION EVIDENCE

E van der Berg and S E van der Merwe

8 1 INTRODUCTION

This chapter deals with the following question: is the opinion (inference, impression, belief)[1] of a witness — whether expert[2] or lay person[3] — admissible evidence? Should an opinion be admitted for purposes of persuading the court to rely on it in deciding the issue at hand?

The answer is that relevance remains the fundamental test for admissibility.[4] The essential and very first question must therefore be: what are the issues?[5] Broadly speaking, it may be said that if the issue is of such a nature that the opinion of an expert or lay person can assist the court in deciding the issue, the opinion evidence is relevant and admissible[6] — unless some other rule, such as hearsay, calls for exclusion. By the same token, it may be said that if the opinion relates to an issue which the court can decide without the aid of opinion evidence of an expert or lay person, the opinion is irrelevant and therefore inadmissible.[7]

---

[1] See § 8 2 below.

[2] See §§ 8 4 and 8 6–8 6 4 below.

[3] See §§ 8 4 and 8 5–8 5 3 below.

[4] See *Association of Amusement and Novelty Machine Operators & another v Minister of Justice & another* 1980 2 SA 636 (A) 660E; *R v David* 1962 3 SA 305 (SR).

[5] See § 5 3 1 above.

[6] See § 8 3 below.

[7] See *S v Nel* 1990 2 SACR 136 (C) as discussed in §§ 5 3 3 above and 25 3 1 below.

The reasons for this rule, and some refinements thereof, are discussed in § 8 3 below.

Colgate Palmolive (Pty) Ltd v Elida-Gibbs (Pty) Ltd[8] provides a good example of the difficulties that can arise, not only in applying the above rule but also in distinguishing between fact and opinion.[9] In this case the plaintiff contended that the advertisements of the defendant's product were calculated to mislead consumers into believing that the defendant's toothpaste possessed certain qualities concerning the removal and reduction of plaque and tartar on teeth, which it did not. The plaintiff sought to lead the evidence of an assistant manager of an insurance company (and thus a layman with no expert knowledge of the matter) as to how he understood the advertisement. Counsel for the defendant objected on the ground that this testimony was nothing more than the opinion of a lay person on a question that the court had to decide. It was argued that the witness was no better qualified than the court to form an opinion, and that the admission of the evidence would have the effect of usurping the court's function. However, counsel for the plaintiff submitted that the evidence was relevant and admissible because the purpose of the evidence was not to persuade the court to adopt the opinion of the witness. It was argued that the purpose of the evidence was to prove the deception — and if, during the course of his testimony in support of the personal deception experienced by the witness, an opinion had of necessity to be expressed as to the meaning, for the witness, of the advertisement, it should not be excluded on that basis alone. Van Schalkwyk J agreed with the plaintiff's counsel and overruled the objection. His reason was that the fact that an opinion was contained in the evidence of the lay witness concerned could not "preclude the evidence if its purpose is to show that as a result of his interpretation of the advertisement he was misled".[10] It may be said — at the risk of oversimplification — that the evidence of the witness was a *factum probans* which could not be proved without also permitting the witness to state his own personal conclusion. Van Schalkwyk J also made it perfectly clear that a court should "refuse to hear evidence only in circumstances where a witness, unqualified as an expert, seeks to give evidence which in its essence does no more than that which the Court is itself called upon to do . . . [T]he witness may not interpret but he may give evidence of a factual nature to act as an aid to interpretation."[11]

In *Stewarts & Lloyds of SA Ltd v Croydon Engineering & Mining Supplies (Pty) Ltd & others*[12] an issue of a different nature arose. In this case the trial court was requested by counsel for two of the defendants to examine certain handwriting under a high-power microscope, and in so doing to be guided by an expert in the field of handwriting, a certain Mr Gilchrist. Counsel claimed that this procedure would have enabled the court to make observations which would have

---

[8] 1989 3 SA 759 (W).
[9] See further § 8 2 below.
[10] *Colgate Palmolive (Pty) Ltd v Elida-Gibbs (Pty) Ltd* supra 764E.
[11] At 763H–I.
[12] 1979 1 SA 1018 (W).

assisted the court in determining the order in which two witnesses had affixed their handwriting on a document — which was an issue which could have reflected on the credibility of these two witnesses. Le Grange J held that counsel[13]

> "seeks through the witness Gilchrist to educate my eye, because he first wishes Mr Gilchrist to explain to me what he saw when he looked through the microscope. I gather this will be done, and it is necessary for Mr Gilchrist to do this, in order that I should know what to look for. Well, the Court declines the opportunity of qualifying itself in this branch of science. It appears to me that it is undesirable from every point of view that the Court should look through certain sophisticated instruments and rely upon its own observations when, from its limited knowledge of the subject, it does not know whether its observations are reliable or not and whether an inference can reliably be drawn from them or not. The Court therefore declines the invitation to look at the document through the microscope."

Of course, the *Stewarts & Lloyds* case stands on an entirely different footing from the *Colgate* case — and is also clearly discernible from cases where the court can make its own observations and form its own opinion on the basis of ordinary knowledge or skill common to the average person. In *R v Makeip*[14] the trial judge had examined plaster casts of footprints with an ordinary magnifying glass. He had also measured several distances between various marks. The Appellate Division had no quarrel with this procedure as it involved no more than ordinary everyday knowledge or skill. In fact, in the case of *S v Mkhabela* Corbett JA (as he then was) also came to the conclusion that "it will always be more satisfactory if the Court is able, by means of a photograph or a plaster cast or some other visual medium . . . to make the necessary comparisons and to assess the cogency of the footprint evidence".[15]

Makeip and *Mkhabela* supra merely illustrate that a court need not be guided by opinion evidence in respect of matters which can be assessed on the basis of ordinary knowledge or skill. But it is irregular for a court to attempt to qualify itself as an expert for purposes of the trial or to rely on its own peculiar specialist knowledge.[16]

8 2   FACT AND OPINION: SOME COMMENT[17]

It is sometimes stated that in terms of the opinion rule a witness must give evidence of facts and may not express an opinion unless he is an expert or, if not an expert, his opinion can be received as an exception to the general rule which excludes opinion evidence.[18] Apart from the fact that this formulation amounts to a gross distortion of the true rule,[19] it also fails to accommodate the practical reality that for purposes of the law of evidence it is not always possible to distinguish clearly between fact and opinion: "In a sense all testimony to

---

[13] At 1019F–H.
[14] 1948 1 SA 947 (A).
[15] 1984 1 SA 556 (A) 563D.
[16] See generally *S v Steenberg* 1979 3 SA 513 (B) 515 as discussed in § 27 5 1 below.
[17] See also Hoffmann & Zeffertt 84; Zuckermann *The Principles of Criminal Evidence* (1992) 59–60.
[18] See generally May *Criminal Evidence* 2 ed (1990) 132–3.
[19] See § 8 3 below.

matter of fact is opinion evidence; i e, it is a conclusion formed from phenomena and mental impressions".[20] Even a matter such as identification really constitutes evidence of an inference, drawn from comparison with prior experience.[21] Where the complainant testifies that it was the accused who had raped her, her evidence is in truth no more than an opinion that it is the man in the dock who committed the offence. If the rapist were someone of close acquaintance, it may seem absurd to say that she is expressing an opinion. But if the perpetrator were a stranger, never seen before, and the opportunity for observation not great, the identification can clearly be seen to constitute no more than an inference, drawn from a resemblance between the offender and the man in the dock. Identity, as such, of course cannot be perceived. All that is observed by the witness are certain physical characteristics which can be compared and which can form the basis of a conclusion in the mind of the witness. That is no more and no less than an inference. This reasoning can be extended to various forms of observation. In truth, then, the distinction between fact and opinion is a fallacious one, not borne out by scientific analysis. Support for this statement can be found in *S v Pretorius*,[22] where the identities of the accused were in issue. When defence counsel in cross-examination challenged a prosecution witness to describe one of the accused, the trial court interrupted as follows:

"Well, it is extremely difficult to describe a person . . . I have seen [the accused] yesterday, and if you were to ask me to describe No 2 or No 4, I will be completely at a loss. I have looked at them properly."

On appeal, the court agreed that[23]

"[n]atuurlik is dit baie moeilik om 'n persoon te beskryf en die onvermoë van 'n getuie om 'n persoon te kan beskryf, is nie noodwendig fataal by die vraag of die persoon deur die getuie behoorlik geïdentifiseer is nie."

It is submitted that the following analysis of the meaning of opinion is accurate and useful:[24]

"The word 'opinion' can be used in various senses. When one says, to take one meaning, 'That is a matter of opinion', one is saying that the point is open to question: it is a matter on which doubt can reasonably exist. When one prefaces an assertion with, 'In my opinion', one is indicating that it is a personal belief. Used in this sense, opinion is contrasted with fact — facts simply are, opinions are variable in that differing opinions on the same matter may without absurdity be held by different people. *Quot homines tot sententiae.* Opinion, in this sense, is inadmissible in evidence, not because of any exclusionary rule, but because it is irrelevant. Legal proceedings are concerned with facts, not with the beliefs of witnesses as to the existence of facts . . . In the opinion rule, 'opinion' carries another, special meaning. A fact in issue may be proved by the direct evidence of a witness with personal knowledge, or it may be proved by way of inference from other facts which tend logically to prove the fact in issue. *As used in the law of evidence, 'opinion' has the meaning of an inference or conclusion of fact drawn from other facts.*"

---

[20] Thayer *A Preliminary Treatise on Evidence at the Common Law* (1898) 524.
[21] Murphy *A Practical Approach to Evidence* 4 ed (1992) 324.
[22] 1991 2 SACR 601 (A).
[23] At 607*i*.
[24] Nicholas "Some Aspects of Opinion Evidence" in Kahn (ed) *Fiat Justitia: Essays in Memory of Oliver Deneys Schreiner* (1983) 225 (our emphasis).

The so-called "compendious mode" of testifying, as discussed in § 8 5 1 below, is also based on the fact that in the law of evidence opinion carries a special meaning.

Once it is accepted that it is not always possible — and certainly not always desirable — to attempt to distinguish between fact and opinion it becomes meaningless to formulate the opinion rule in terms which require, or purport to require, a strict distinction between fact and opinion.[25]

8 3   THE BASIS OF THE OPINION RULE

Any opinion, whether expert or non-expert, which is expressed on an issue which the court can decide without receiving such opinion is in principle inadmissible because of its irrelevance.[26] Such evidence is unnecessary — and can be referred to as "superfluous" or "supererogatory evidence".[27] In this instance the opinion of the witness is excluded not because of a need to preserve or protect the fact-finding duty of the court, but because such evidence makes no probative contribution, creates the risk of confusion of the main issues, can lead to prolongation of trials, and can open an "evidential Pandora's box".[28]

If the issue is of such a nature that the witness is in a better position than the court to form an opinion, the opinion will be admissible on the basis of its relevance.[29] Such an opinion has probative force. The opinion is no longer superfluous because it can assist the court in determining the issue. This explains why the opinions of lay persons[30] and experts[31] are at times received.

---

[25] There is much merit in the forceful approach adopted by the Appellate Division in *Reckitt & Colman SA (Pty) Ltd v S C Johnson & Son SA (Pty) Ltd* 1993 2 SA 307 (A). This was a passing-off case: the appellant's "Brasso" versus the respondent's "Brillo". Regarding the question whether the "Brillo" get-up was calculated to deceive, the court found that the evidence of the psychologists and linguistic experts was singularly unhelpful, if not inadmissible, because it tended to disguise opinion as a statement of scientific principle — and in so doing subtly sought to displace the court's value judgment with that of the witness.

[26] See generally *S v H* 1981 2 SA 586 (SWA).

[27] Wigmore para 1918 used this term and explained that the rule "simply endeavours to save time and avoid confusing testimony by telling the witness: 'The tribunal is on this subject in possession of the same materials of information as yourself; thus, as you can add nothing to the materials for judgment, your further testimony is unnecessary, and merely cumbers the proceedings.' " See further the discussion of *Ruto Flour Mills Ltd v Adelson (1)* 1958 4 SA 235 (T) in § 8 6 below. In this case the court relied heavily on Wigmore's views.

[28] See *S v Nel* 1990 2 SACR 136 (C) as discussed in § 5 3 3 above.

[29] Zeffertt 1976 *SALJ* 275.

[30] In *R v Vilbro* 1957 3 SA 223 (A), a unanimous decision of the Appellate Division sitting with five judges, the question concerned the descent of the appellants. It was argued on behalf of the appellants that witnesses could not be called to offer their opinions on the point: such evidence would be inadmissible, as it was merely evidence of opinion, usurping the function of the court on an issue which the court, not any witness, had to decide. Fagan CJ, delivering the judgment of the court, referred to Wigmore's concept of supererogatory evidence and his rejection of the usurpation theory. The court concluded that whereas nothing could be gained by calling witnesses at random to express an opinion on the question, there would, however, be people who could be of great assistance to the court, such as a government inspector who claimed to have experience of such affairs, as well as other persons who were familiar with the appellants. Their opinions, the court held, would be admissible. It is important to note that the suggestion here is that it is the opinion of *laymen* that could be received, on the basis that their opinion could, due to their familiarity with the appellants, assist the court, who was not as familiar with the appellants. See Hoffmann & Zeffertt 85–7 for a careful and critical analysis of *R v Vilbro*.

[31] See § 8 6 below.

The rule that opinion evidence is excluded where superfluous (because it is irrelevant) and admitted where it can assist the court (because it is relevant) has to compete with some other theories, principles and formulations governing the opinion rule. Paizes refers to these as "empty catch-phrases and misconceptions which have blurred the parameters of the rule and shifted the focus of attention away from its chief function, viz the exclusion of supererogatory evidence".[32] It is, for example, sometimes said that the exclusion of opinion is intended to preserve or protect the function of the tribunal of fact,[33] and that a witness should not be permitted to usurp this function.[34] Wigmore rejected this theory on the basis that the tribunal of fact is not and cannot be obliged to substitute the opinion of the witness for his own.[35] Support for Wigmore's reasons for rejecting this theory can be found in *S v Nieuwoudt*.[36] In this case various experts (including an electrical engineer and members of university departments of speech and drama) were called to testify as regards certain tape recordings. Hefer JA remarked as follows:[37]

> "Daarenteen is ek nie bereid om 'n submissie wat mnr *De Villiers* op een stadium gemaak het (klaarblyklik sonder dat hy self veel geloof daarin gehad het) te aanvaar nie, nl dat daar slegs gelet moet word op wat *die deskundige getuies* se waarnemings was. Om te hoor watter woorde in hierdie soort opname voorkom, verg geen deskundigheid nie en 'n geregshof kan in elk geval nie sy funksie aan die getuies delegeer nie. Natuurlik moet ag geslaan word op die getuienis; maar uiteindelik is dit die Hof se taak om te bepaal wat die woorde is en deur wie hulle gebruik is."

The theory that the opinion rule preserves or protects the fact-finding function of the court is sometimes also expressed in terms of the so-called "ultimate issue" doctrine, namely that a witness may not express an opinion on an ultimate issue which the court must decide: "The risk of usurpation by the witness of the function of the trier of fact", says Carter, "is often greatest if the witness expresses an opinion on the very question, or 'ultimate issue' which the trier of fact finally has to decide."[38] However, the ultimate issue doctrine fails to explain why courts at times permit not only experts but also lay persons to express an opinion on the very issue the court has to decide. In drunken driving cases the prosecution must prove that the accused was under the influence of intoxicating liquor at the time when he was driving. Courts receive both expert and lay opinion in this regard,[39] despite the fact that this is the very issue that the court

---

[32] Paizes in Du Toit et al *Commentary* 24-16.

[33] Cowsill & Clegg *Evidence: Law and Practice* (1990) 149.

[34] See generally *R v Louw* 1930 CPD 368 and *R v Van Tonder* 1929 TPD 365.

[35] Wigmore para 1920. See also Cowen & Carter *Essays on the Law of Evidence* (1956) 169.

[36] 1990 4 SA 217 (A).

[37] At 238C–E.

[38] Carter *Cases and Statutes on Evidence* (1981) 503.

[39] In *S v Edley* 1970 2 SA 223 (N) 226D Miller J noted: "It seems to me that the more gross and manifest the physical manifestations of intoxication noted by credible and reliable laymen are, the more readily may medical evidence be dispensed with and that the more equivocal the physical manifestations or indications of intoxication may be, the greater would be the need for the State to lead medical evidence of the accused's condition at the relevant time." *S v Skeal* 1990 1 SACR 162 (Z) is an example of a case where intoxication was found proved on the basis of the evidence of two policemen. Both lay person and expert should, however, advance reasons for their opinion. See *S v Mhetoa* 1968 2 SA 773 (O) and *R v*

must decide. The court is not bound by such an opinion, but will place much reliance on it if it is satisfied that the reasons which the witness can advance for having formed the opinion are convincing and do in fact support the opinion expressed by the witness.

The ultimate issue doctrine is often ignored in practice. In *DPP v A & BC Chewing Gum Co Ltd* Lord Parker said:[40]

" . . . I cannot help feeling that with the advance of science more and more inroads have been made into the old common-law principles. Those who practise in the criminal courts see every day cases of experts being called on the question of diminished responsibility and although technically the final question 'Do you think he was suffering from diminished responsibility?' is strictly inadmissible, it is allowed time and time again without any objection."

This case concerned the admissibility of expert opinion evidence on the issue whether certain publications tended to corrupt or deprave children. It was concluded that expert evidence would have been inadmissible if the issue had related to adults, but that it was admissible where the issue related to children. In the latter instance the tribunal would need all the help it could get.

It is significant that in 1972 the English legislator abolished the "ultimate issue" doctrine for purposes of civil proceedings. Section 3(1) of the Civil Evidence Act 1972[41] provides that where a person is called as a witness in any civil proceedings his opinion on any relevant matter on which he is qualified to give expert evidence shall be admissible in evidence. Section 3(2) determines that where a person is called as a witness in any civil proceedings a statement or opinion by him on any relevant matter on which he is not qualified to give expert evidence, *if made as a way of conveying relevant facts personally perceived by him,*[42] is admissible evidence of what he perceived. Section 3(3) determines that for the purposes of s 3 "relevant matter" includes an issue in the proceedings in question. It is important, though, to note that the statute also provides for a discretion to exclude evidence falling under s 3.

Another approach is to say that a witness should not be permitted to express an opinion which entails a conclusion of law,[43] or which requires the application of a standard of law to the facts,[44] or which relates to the meaning of words

---

Theunissen 1948 4 SA 43 (C). The opinion becomes worthless in the absence of reasons: *S v Adams* 1983 2 SA 577 (A). On a charge of drunken driving the prosecution must also prove that the skill and judgment normally required to drive a vehicle were impaired or detrimentally affected. In England a lay witness is not permitted to say whether the accused was fit or unfit to drive (*R v Davies* 1962 1 WLR 1111). But the Irish courts receive such an opinion (*G (Rudely) v Kenny* 1960 94 ILT 185 as cited by Heydon *Evidence: Cases and Materials* 3 ed (1991) 386). Expert opinion is required in South Africa, but the courts have accepted the opinion of experienced policemen. See *R v Seaward* 1950 2 SA 704 (N). It is submitted that an experienced policeman's opinion can be received on the basis that it can assist the court.

[40] 1968 AC 159 164.

[41] See Huxley & O'Connell *Blackstone's Statutes on Evidence* (1991) 142–3.

[42] See also § 8 5 1 below.

[43] See the argument advanced by counsel for the appellant in *S v Haasbroek* 1969 2 SA 624 (A).

[44] *R v Van Tonder* 1929 TPD 365 can be explained as a case based on this approach.

appearing in a statute.[45] This is just a variation of the "ultimate issue" doctrine.[46] Although this doctrine should not be discarded entirely,[47] the answer in all three aforementioned instances should be that the exclusion of supererogatory evidence remains the governing test. *Association of Amusement and Novelty Machine Operators & another v Minister of Justice & another*[48] involved the meaning of certain words in a statute. The opinion of a language expert was held irrelevant and inadmissible: the words in dispute were often encountered in common parlance, and the witness was therefore in no better position than the court to form an opinion.

In *International Business Machines SA (Pty) Ltd v Commissioner for Customs and Excise* it was said: "Under our system, questions of interpretation of . . . documents are matters of law, and belong exclusively to the Court. On such questions the opinions of witnesses, however eminent or highly qualified, are (except in regard to words which have a special or technical meaning) inadmissible."[49] The words in brackets are important, and indicate that this case is not a vindication of the "ultimate issue" doctrine; it really confirms the approach that supererogatory evidence is inadmissible.

8 4   LAY PERSONS AND EXPERTS

It is customary to approach the admission of opinion evidence on the basis that one has to distinguish between lay opinion and expert opinion. Once it is realized that admissibility does not depend on this distinction, but on the question whether the opinion of the particular witness in the particular circumstances of the case can assist the court in determining the issues, it becomes clear that the distinction between lay person and expert does not govern admissibility. The separate discussion of lay persons and experts in the next few paragraphs is for the sake of convenience, and not an attempt to identify two separate categories for purposes of admissibility. For *procedural* purposes, however, a distinction is necessary:[50] in civil cases parties should give notice of their intention to rely on expert opinion evidence; in criminal cases the prosecution is required on

---

[45] See generally *Metro Transport (Pty) Ltd v National Transport Commission* 1981 3 SA 114 (W) 120A, where it was held that "vertolking van 'n statutêre bepaling deur middel van verduidelikende getuienis nie toelaatbaar is nie".

[46] According to May *Criminal Evidence* 134, this doctrine developed because of jury trials: "It was feared that if witnesses could be asked for their opinion on the issue the jury had to decide (the 'ultimate issue'), the jury would be unduly influenced."

[47] Schmidt *Bewysreg* 3 ed (1989) 435 makes the valid point that there is a link between the "ultimate issue" doctrine and the important administrative law principle in terms of which the tribunal of fact must apply his mind to the issue (emphasis in the original): " 'n Owerheidsorgaan wat met 'n bevoegdheid beklee is, moet . . . aandag gee aan die saak waaroor hy moet beslis, en self die bevoegdheid uitoefen; hy kan hom nie aan 'n ander ondergeskik stel nie. Dieselfde beginsel geld vir geregtelike optrede. Dit is waar dat 'n getuie nie 'n hof se bevoegdhede effektief *kan* usurpeer nie, maar dit is nie waarom dit gaan nie. Die punt is dat die hof met behulp van die getuienis uiteindelik die kernvraag wat aan hom as regsprekende orgaan opgedra is, self moet beslis."

[48] 1980 2 SA 636 (A). See also § 27 5 below.

[49] 1985 4 SA 852 (A) 874A–B.

[50] Hoffmann & Zeffertt 99. See further § 8 7 below.

constitutional grounds to disclose expert opinion evidence to the accused prior to the commencement of the trial.[51]

8 5   THE OPINION OF A LAY PERSON

Application of the rule that opinion evidence must be excluded where it cannot assist the court, but admitted where it can, yields the following results: a lay witness may express an opinion on the approximate age of a person, the state of sobriety of a person, the general condition of a thing, and the approximate speed at which a vehicle was travelling. This is not an exhaustive list.

An inability to provide reasons for the opinion should in principle affect the weight and not the admissibility of the opinion.[52]

8 5 1   The compendious mode   There are instances where a witness — and more particularly a lay witness — will not be able to testify meaningfully if the law of evidence were to persist in drawing a distinction between fact and opinion for the purposes of admitting the fact and excluding the opinion. It is "never possible for a witness to eliminate altogether the results of inference from the evidence he gives".[53] In *Herbst v R* it was said:[54]

> "When an ordinary witness says 'I see a Chinaman', he generally means that from his knowledge, obtained by experience or study, he is aware of the salient external characteristics of a citizen sprung from the Celestial Empire; that the person in question appears to possess those characteristics, and that consequently he infers, deduces or opines that the man whom he sees is a Chinaman. His short statement is therefore a *compendious mode* of expressing facts and opinions. Similarly, in the identification of an accused person, the witness compares in his own mind the person he has previously seen with the person produced at the trial, forms an opinion as to the resemblance or otherwise, and states that opinion which is then received as evidence for what it is worth. A similar process takes place when a witness gives evidence as to mental and physical conditions, age, speed, value, character and handwriting. Whether, therefore, an ordinary witness simply states 'The flag was yellow', or more comprehensively says 'The writing is Smith's', there is a ratiocination in different degrees, and consequently an expression of opinion. But such evidence is clearly admissible; if it were not, the machine for trying disputed facts would come to a standstill. It is accordingly not always possible to wholly separate statement of opinion from statement of fact, and consequently, on the grounds of necessity, because this separation is not always possible, and because more direct and positive evidence is often unobtainable, experience has evolved the subsidiary rule that the opinions and beliefs of witnesses who are not experts are in certain cases admissible."

The term "compendious mode" as used in *Herbst* supra is of English law origin.[55] It is a convenient term to use in those instances where the witness offers an opinion as a brief summary of factual data perceived by him. This explains why a witness is permitted to say that the complainant was "angry", that the victim

---

[51] *Shabalala & others v Attorney-General of Transvaal & another* 1995 2 SACR 761 (CC) para [72]. See further § 11 5 below.

[52] See § 8 5 4 below.

[53] Cowen & Carter *Essays on the Law of Evidence* 166.

[54] 1925 SWA 77 80.

[55] *Wright v Tatham* 1885 Cl & Fin 670 721 as cited by Hodgkinson *Expert Evidence: Law and Practice* (1990) 18.

tried to "protect" himself or that the defendant "looked surprised". The compendious mode is permitted not only because of its practical convenience but also because the witness is better placed than the court.[56] The witness may in examination in chief, cross-examination and re-examination be questioned on the reasons for his conclusion. Admission or exclusion of the evidence tendered in compendious mode will be in the court's discretion. Much depends on the circumstances and issues, as well as the question whether for purposes of the case any meaningful attempt can be made to separate conclusion from fact.

8 5 2 Handwriting[57] Section 4 of the CPEA provides that comparison of a disputed writing with any writing proved to be genuine may be made by witnesses, and such writings and the evidence of any witness with respect thereto may be submitted as evidence of the genuineness or otherwise of the writing in dispute. Section 228 of the CPA contains a similar provision. On the basis of these provisions as well as common-law principles, a lay witness is permitted to identify handwriting. An expert may also express an opinion on handwriting.[58] The fact that an accused who has furnished samples of his handwriting to the police could have made some intentional distortions affects the weight and not the admissibility of the opinion.[59]

8 5 3 Probative value of lay opinion It is generally accepted that the admissible opinion of a lay person provides *prima facie* evidence and — if not challenged[60] — may, not must, be accepted. Much will depend on the issues and the reasons that the witness can advance in support of his conclusion.[61] If challenged,[62] the issue might be of such a nature that only expert opinion can resolve it.[63] In *S v Faltein* — where the issue was whether the substance in question was dagga — Erasmus J noted that "dagga, although unfortunately in wide use, is not so well known that just anybody can identify it as such. In order to do so special

---

[56] Cowsill & Clegg *Evidence: Law and Practice* 150.

[57] See also § 19 7 below.

[58] An "expert" on handwriting is not necessarily confined to people who are handwriting experts by profession: *R v Silverlock* 1894 2 QB 766.

[59] *S v Smith* 1978 3 SA 749 (A).

[60] *S v Gentle* 1983 3 SA 45 (N) 46F–G Booysen J said: "The evidence as to the identity of the substance can hardly be said to be challenged by challenging the evidence of possession thereof. It is one thing to say 'that exhibit is not dagga' and quite another to say 'I deny having possessed it'. In these circumstances the magistrate was quite entitled to accept that it was dagga."

[61] *S v Januarie* 1980 2 SA 598 (C) 600B–C: "[A]s to the value of an opinion expressed by a witness, there should be some sufficient enquiry not only into the reasons for the opinion, but also into the ability of the witness to express an informed and sound opinion."

[62] A challenge can be explicit or by implication in the course of cross-examination: *S v Sinam* 1990 2 SACR 308 (E) 315*a–b*.

[63] *AA Onderlinge Assuransie-Assosiasie Bpk v De Beer* 1982 2 SA 603 (A) 614.

knowledge or expertise is required."[64] The value of a policeman's opinion that a substance is dagga was dealt with comprehensively by James JP in *S v Ndaba*.[65]

8 6   THE EXPERT WITNESS[66]

There are issues which simply cannot be decided without expert guidance. Expert opinion evidence is therefore readily received on issues relating to, for example, ballistics, engineering, chemistry, medicine, accounting and psychiatry. This is not an exhaustive list. And there are cases where expert evidence — though not *absolutely* necessary — would nevertheless still be of use. Intoxication[67] and handwriting[68] are two examples.

The matter was crisply stated in *Gentiruco AG v Firestone SA (Pty) Ltd*: "[T]he true and practical test of the admissibility of the opinion of a skilled witness is whether or not the Court can receive 'appreciable help' from that witness on the particular issue."[69] In *S v Melrose* the court found it necessary to point out that the *viva voce* evidence of medical practitioners in cases involving, for example, homicide, rape and serious assaults "is very relevant indeed".[70]

Ruto Flour Mills Ltd v Adelson (1)[71] provides a good example not only of the

---

[64] 1990 2 PH H105 (E) 291.

[65] 1981 3 SA 782 (N) 784B–785A: "It has been accepted in a long series of cases that the evidence of policemen regarding the identity of dagga may be given in court and that in the absence of any challenge it may be accepted by the presiding officer. A magistrate should satisfy himself that the policeman is sufficiently familiar with dagga to be able to make a reliable identification but in the absence of any challenge a policeman's statement that he knows dagga and that what he found was in fact dagga has in the past been accepted by the Courts as sufficient identification unless the policeman's grounds for making this statement are challenged and his experience with and knowledge of dagga is put in issue. See *R v Radebe* 1960 (4) SA 131 (T) at 133; *R v S* 1956 (4) SA 118 (N) at 125D. This is in conformity with the practice in cases concerned with concoctions under the liquor laws where it has been held that the unchallenged evidence of a policeman that the liquor in question was a particular type of concoction may be accepted as *prima facie* proof that it is such a concoction. See *R v Modesa* 1948 (1) SA 1157 (T) at 1159; *R v De Souza* 1955 (1) SA 32 (T). Challenges in regard to the identity of a substance which the police aver is dagga are usually made on one of two grounds, the first being that the substance found is not dagga but something else. In such a case the policeman's evidence should not be accepted unless the policeman's claim to be able to identify a substance such as dagga has been thoroughly tested and the court feels able to accept it as so reliable that the accused's claim that the substance is something else must be rejected as false. See *S v Ngwanya* 1962 (3) SA 690 (T) and *R v Kolisi* 1960 (2) SA 374 (E). Secondly, when an accused person claims that he has no knowledge of what the substance in question is, and challenges the correctness of the identification in cross-examination, sufficient evidence must be adduced regarding the witness' experience in or knowledge of the substance in question to satisfy the court that his conclusion that the substance is undoubtedly what he claims it to be is reliable. See *S v Bertrand* 1975 (4) SA 142 (C) at 149B (a case dealing with the drug known as LSD) and the case of *S v Malefane* 1974 (4) SA 613 (O) in which the accused denied on oath that the substance was dagga and in which the cross-examination of the State witnesses clearly challenged their claim that the substance found in her possession was dagga. See also *S v Seboko* 1975 (3) SA 343 (O). Once the accused challenges the reliability of the identification on the grounds that the witness does not have the experience to give reliable evidence on the subject of dagga the State is entitled to examine the witness further on his experience and if thought advisable, call further evidence to identify the substance as dagga." See also *S v Letimela* 1979 2 SA 332 (B).

[66] See generally *S v Gouws* 1967 4 SA 527 (E) 528.

[67] See n 39 above.

[68] See § 8 5 2 above.

[69] 1972 1 SA 589 (A) 616H.

[70] 1985 1 SA 720 (Z) 724I.

[71] 1958 4 SA 235 (T).

guidance or assistance that a court can receive from an expert but also the reasons for the exclusion or admission of expert opinion evidence — a matter already dealt with in general terms in § 8 3 above. In this case an accountant was called to give evidence of the financial affairs of the bakery concerned. The accountant had experience in the financial management of bakeries and had inspected and analysed the books of the bakery. He testified that the business was conducted erratically. The court overruled an objection to this opinion, and made the following points:

(a) Supererogatory evidence is excluded simply because it is not needed: the court is as able as the witness to draw the conclusion. The evidence is not excluded because there is something objectionable regarding the reliability of the evidence.

(b) The opinion of an expert is received because and whenever his skill is greater than that of the court.

(c) The true criterion is whether the court can receive appreciable help from the opinion of the witness.

(d) When the issue is one of science or skill the expert can be asked the very question which the court has to decide.

8 6 1 The expert witness: the need to lay a foundation[72] The party seeking to adduce the opinion of a witness as an expert opinion must satisfy the court that the opinion is not supererogatory — that is, not irrelevant. For this purpose the court must be satisfied:

(a) that the witness not only has specialist knowledge, training, skill or experience but can furthermore, on account of these attributes or qualities, assist the court in deciding the issues;[73]

(b) that the witness is indeed an expert for the purpose for which he is called upon to express an opinion;[74] and

(c) that the witness does not or will not express an opinion on hypothetical facts, that is, facts which have no bearing on the case or which cannot be reconciled with all the other evidence in the case.[75]

---

[72] *S v Nangutuuala* 1974 2 SA 165 (SWA) 167C–E: "[T]ensy die grondslag van 'n getuie se kundigheid gelê word — en gewoonweg word dit gedoen deur gepaste vrae aan die getuie self — [mag] hy nie as deskundige . . . getuig nie. In die onderhawige saak was geen grondslag gelê nie . . . Geen enkele vraag in verband òf met sy akademiese kwalifikasies òf met sy praktiese ervaring is aan [die getuie] gestel nie."

[73] *Ruto Flour Mills Ltd v Adelson (1)* supra.

[74] *Goliath v Fedgen Insurance Company Ltd* 1994 2 PH F31 (E) 83: "I am, however, not satisfied that it has been established that Victor has the necessary qualifications or expertise to give expert evidence regarding the behaviour of a motor vehicle in cases where a driver is faced with the sudden deflation of a tyre and the steps which should be taken by the driver to keep the vehicle under control in such circumstances. Victor is a physicist and a motor sport enthusiast. The fact that he is a motor sport enthusiast, without more, does not qualify him to give expert evidence of the nature to which I have referred. There is no evidence before me to suggest that Victor has been involved in any research, or has conducted tests on which he is able to base the views expressed by him . . . An expert must himself have knowledge or experience in the special field on which he testifies otherwise the danger exists of a court being blinded by theory untested by knowledge or practical experience." A physician who is not expert in ballistics cannot be asked about the shape and size of bullets which caused a wound: *Barrie v R* 1959 1 PH H22 (O).

[75] *S v Mkohle* 1990 1 SACR 95 (A) 100d.

In *Menday v Protea Assurance Co Ltd* Addleson J said:[76]

"In essence the function of an expert is to assist the Court to reach a conclusion on matters
on which the Court itself does not have the necessary knowledge to decide. It is not the
mere opinion of the witness which is decisive but his ability to satisfy the Court that, because
of his special skill, training or experience, the reasons for the opinion which he expresses
are acceptable . . . However eminent an expert may be in a general field, he does not
constitute an expert in a particular sphere unless by special study or experience he is
qualified to express an opinion on that topic. The dangers of holding otherwise — of being
overawed by a recital of degrees and diplomas — are obvious; the Court has then no way
of being satisfied that it is not being blinded by pure 'theory' untested by knowledge or
practice. The expert must either himself have knowledge or experience in the special field
on which he testifies (whatever general knowledge he may also have in pure theory) or he
must rely on the knowledge or experience of others who themselves are shown to be
acceptable experts in that field."

In *Mohamed v Shaik*[77] it was said that it is the function of the court to decide
whether an "expert" has the necessary qualifications and experience to enable
him to express reliable opinions. In this case it was held that a general medical
practitioner — even though he held the degrees MB ChB and had four years'
experience — was not qualified to speak authoritatively on the significance of
findings in a pathologist's report concerning the fertility of semen.

Formal qualifications are not always essential; and in many instances the
practical experience of the witness may be decisive. An experienced stock farmer
may, for example, give expert evidence as to the value of cattle.[78] The fundamental test still is whether the evidence can assist the court — and the result is that
in certain circumstances formal qualifications without practical experience may
not be enough to qualify the witness as an expert.[79]

8 6 2 Reasons for opinion and probative value of the opinion Expert witnesses
are in principle required to support their opinions with valid reasons. But no
hard-and-fast rule can be laid down. Much will depend on the nature of the issue
and the presence or absence of an attack on the opinion of the expert.[80]

If proper reasons are advanced in support of an opinion, the probative value
of such opinion will of necessity be strengthened.[81] In *Coopers (South Africa) (Pty)
Ltd v Deutsche Gesellschaft für Schädlingsbekämpfung Mbh* it was said:[82]

"[A]n expert's opinion represents his reasoned conclusion based on certain facts or data,
which are either common cause, or established by his own evidence or that of some other
competent witness. Except possibly where it is not controverted, an expert's bald statement
of his opinion is not of any real assistance. Proper evaluation of the opinion can only be
undertaken if the process of reasoning which led to the conclusion, including the premises
from which the reasoning proceeds, are disclosed by the expert."

[76] 1976 1 SA 565 (E) 569.
[77] 1978 4 SA 523 (N).
[78] *Van Graan v Naudé* 1966 1 PH J12 (O).
[79] *Van Heerden v SA Pulp and Paper Industries Ltd* 1945 2 PH J14 (W) 31–2.
[80] *S v Ramgobin* 1986 4 SA 117 (N) 146; *S v Mthimkulu* 1975 4 SA 759 (A); *S v Claassen* 1976 2 SA 281 (O).
[81] *S v Kotze* 1994 1 SACR 214 (O).
[82] 1976 3 SA 352 (A) 371F–H.

There are extreme cases where expert evidence can be so technical that the court may not be in a position to follow the exact reasoning of the expert or observe the specific points of identification. In such an instance great emphasis will be placed upon the general repute of the witness's profession and the absence or presence of possible bias. In *R v Nksatlala* it was said:[83]

"[A] Court should not blindly accept and act upon the evidence of an expert witness, even of a finger-print expert, but must decide for itself whether it can safely accept the expert's opinion. But once it is satisfied that it can so accept it, the Court gives effect to that conclusion even if its own observation does not positively confirm it."

In *S v Blom*[84] the accused was charged with, amongst other crimes, murder. Two police fingerprint experts testified for the prosecution. At first they had not prepared comparative charts in respect of the fingerprints found at the scene of the crime, as their department had a policy not to do so unless there were at least eight points of identification in comparing the fingerprints of the accused with those found at the scene of the crime. In this case they could find only seven. Both the witnesses were satisfied that seven points of identification were more than sufficient to identify a fingerprint beyond any doubt, and that the fingerprint in question was that of the accused. It transpired that the prosecutor had told the defence counsel that only five points of identification had been found. This corresponded with the evidence of the investigating officer. When the two fingerprint experts were asked to indicate the points of identification in court their evidence was unsatisfactory in a number of respects. The court accordingly held that there was a reasonable doubt as to whether the fingerprint was that of the accused, despite the fact that the two fingerprint experts had no doubt in their minds.

In a number of cases[85] the courts have accepted the results of chemical blood-alcohol concentration tests despite opinions by medical doctors that the clinical observations of the accused did not correspond with the blood-alcohol level determined in the tests.

S v Van As[86] contains important observations and findings as regards expert opinion evidence. In this case Kirk-Cohen J — apart from emphasizing that in appropriate cases expert evidence is adduced to place the court in a better position to decide the issues — also distinguished between two situations: the first is where the expert's opinion is based on that of recognized writers or authority in the science concerned; the second is where the expert has personally conducted experiments and then in court bases his opinion on the results of his experiments. It was said that in the latter instance it is easier for the court to

---

[83] 1960 3 SA 543 (A) 546D.

[84] 1992 1 SACR 649 (E). In *Maritime & General Insurance Co v Sky Unit Engineering (Pty) Ltd* 1989 1 SA 867 (T) 877 the court rejected an argument to the effect that a court may not — in regard to scientific issues — draw its own conclusions based on criteria identified by experts.

[85] See, e g, *S v Boyce* 1990 1 SACR 13 (T); *S v De Leeuw* 1990 2 SACR 165 (NC); *S v Abel* 1990 2 SACR 367 (C).

[86] 1991 2 SACR 74 (W).

Principles of Evidence

follow the evidence, to accept it and to rely on it in deciding the issue. The expert's presentation can obviously also enhance the value of his testimony.[87]

In *S v M* [88] Kriegler J was most emphatic that a court should not lightly discard an expert's opinion where no factual premise of his or her evidence is unsound and where his or her opinion — and the reasons therefor — have been furnished in a satisfactory manner. But experts can make mistakes! In *S v Venter* Nestadt JA approved the trial court's rejection of expert testimony:[89]

"[T]he State pathologist who performed the post-mortem examination on the body of the child supported the appellant's denial. His opinion was that the child's head was not submerged in the water. The trial Court, however, refused to accept that this was so. This was a bold approach. One does not lightly depart from the uncontroverted views of an impartial, well-qualified and experienced expert. But I am persuaded that in the present matter it was warranted. The reasons given by Southwood J for rejecting the doctor's evidence are weighty. Consider the following. The photographs clearly show that the child sustained burn injuries to his head and face; the condition of the inner lining of the windpipe was consistent with the swallowing of hot water; the lungs contained fluid; and there is the singular, undisputed feature that despite the injuries having been immediately painful (intensely so, I would have thought), the child did not cry out or scream. The cumulative effect of what has been referred to supports the trial court's finding that the appellant 'plunged [the child] into the water and that his head was immersed for a number of seconds' and that there was therefore no chance for the child to cry out . . . Confirmation that the child's head was submerged in the water comes from the appellant himself."

Collateral support for the above approach can be found in *Motor Vehicle Assurance Fund v Kenny*,[90] where Eksteen J observed that direct credible evidence of what happened in a collision must generally be accorded greater weight than the opinion of an expert who attempts to reconstruct the actual events on the basis of his experience and scientific training. After all, there can in principle be

---

[87] See Bartlett "The Preparation of Experts' Reports" 1994 60 *Journal of the Chartered Institute of Arbitrators* 94 for a useful discussion of the various considerations that must be taken into account when the report of an expert is prepared.

[88] 1991 1 SACR 91 (T). In this case a specialist psychiatrist had testified in mitigation of an accused who was addicted to pethidine. The psychiatrist strongly advised against sending the accused to prison. In the opinion of the psychiatrist the accused needed extensive psychotherapy (including chemotherapy) under controlled conditions and combined with a gradual process of reintegration into society. The trial court refused to rely on this opinion. On appeal Kriegler J remarked as follows (at 99*j*–100*c*, emphasis in the original): "A court's approach to expert evidence has been dealt with on many occasions. The court is not bound by expert evidence. It is the presiding officer's function ultimately to make up his own mind. *He* has to evaluate the expertise of the witness. *He* has to weigh the cogency of the witness's evidence in the contextual matrix of the case with which he is seized. *He* has to gauge the quality of the expert *qua* witness. However, the wise judicial officer does not lightly reject expert evidence on matters falling within the purview of the expert witness's field. The judicial process is difficult enough. And the determination of an appropriate sentence is always vexed. It is all the more so in a case such as the one with which we are now dealing. A wise judicial officer will gather unto himself such aids as he can find. One does not spurn proffered aid lightly. Here a highly qualified and obviously well informed expert proffered not only expert evidence but volunteered valuable assistance in the future handling of the prisoner before the court. That witness dealt with questions beyond the field of ken of laymen. One does not reject such evidence readily where the expert has furnished his opinions — and the foundational reasons therefor — in a satisfactory manner. Here the diagnosis, prognosis and prescribed treatment were clearly articulated and carefully, if not painstakingly, explained." At 100*g* it was said that the psychiatrist's evidence "was uncontroverted by any factual or opinion evidence. It was thoroughly tested and was in all respects persuasive and weighty. It should have been accepted, not rejected."

[89] 1996 1 SACR 664 (A) 666*f–j*.

[90] 1984 4 SA 432 (E).

no obstacle to accepting direct credible evidence even though such evidence is in conflict with probabilities which arise from expert opinion evidence.[91]

The opinion of an expert must be ignored — and should strictly speaking be considered inadmissible — if it is based on some hypothetical situation which has no relation to the facts in issue or which is entirely inconsistent with the facts found proved.[92] This is a frequent problem where a psychiatrist relies solely on an accused's version of the events in assessing his or her mental condition for purposes of determining criminal responsibility.[93] In *S v Harris* Ogilvie Thompson JA said:[94]

> "[I]n the ultimate analysis, the crucial issue of appellant's criminal responsibility for his actions at the relevant time is a matter to be determined, not by the psychiatrists, but by the Court itself. In determining that issue the Court — initially, the trial Court; and, on appeal, this Court — must of necessity have regard not only to the expert medical evidence but also to all the other facts of the case, *including the reliability of appellant as a witness and the nature of his proved actions throughout the relevant period.*"

It is important that an expert witness should remain objective despite the fact that he is — in terms of our adversarial system — called by a party to testify in support of the latter's case:[95] "If he is to be helpful he must be neutral. The [opinion of an expert] is of little value where he . . . is partisan and consistently asserts the cause of the party who calls him." In *S v Kotzé*[96] Lombard J relied heavily on the opinions of experts — not only because they had advanced reasons in support of their conclusions but also because their opinions had the "stempel van objektiewe professionalisme".

No reliance can be placed on an expert's opinion if counsel puts his own interpretation to the expert witness.[97] In this way "the expert does not put his evidence across in his own words *viva voce*, but hides behind the words of counsel".[98]

When it comes to assessing the testimony of an expert, an appeal court is in as good a position as the trial court to test the reasoning of the expert.[99]

8 6 3 Hearsay and expert opinion Hearsay evidence is defined in chapter 13 below. An expert witness may not as a rule base his opinions on statements made by a person not called as a witness (but see § 8 6 4 below). In *Southern Transvaal Buildings (Pty) Ltd v Johannesburg City Council*[100] it was held, for example, that

---

[91] *Mapota v Santamversekeringsmaatskappy Bpk* 1977 4 SA 515 (A). See also § 30 2 2 below.

[92] See generally *S v Mkohle* 1990 1 SACR 95 (A) 100*c–d*; *S v Mngomezulu* 1972 1 SA 797 (A); *S v Boyce* 1990 1 SACR 13 (T) 19.

[93] See generally *S v Loubscher* 1979 3 SA 47 (A) 57F–G and 60B–C.

[94] 1965 2 SA 340 (A) 365B–C (emphasis added).

[95] *Stock v Stock* 1981 3 SA 1280 (A) 1296E.

[96] 1994 2 SACR 214 (O) 225*i*.

[97] *S v Zwane (3)* 1989 3 SA 253 (W) 278H. Zeffertt 1989 *ASSAL* 421 points out, however, that "reliance could be placed on it if it were an interpretation that were to be accepted by either the court or the witness (or both)".

[98] *S v Baleka (3)* 1986 4 SA 1005 (T) 1021D.

[99] *Stock v Stock* 1981 3 SA 1280 (A) 1296F.

[100] 1979 1 SA 949 (W) 959.

expert witnesses expressing opinions on the value of ground may not utilize or rely upon conclusions arrived at by other valuers not called as witnesses.

An expert witness may be allowed to rely on information which would technically be hearsay, but which is admitted if the conditions set out in § 8 6 4 below are satisfied. The realities of practice demand that impossible standards should not be set. In *S v Kimimbi*[101] it was said:

> "No one professional man can know from personal observations more than a minute fraction of the data which he must every day treat as working truths. Hence a reliance on the reported data of fellow scientists learned by perusing their reports in books and journals. The law must and does accept this kind of knowledge from scientific men . . . [T]o reject a profession physician or mathematician because the fact or some of the facts to which he testifies are known to him only upon the authority of others, would be to ignore the accepted methods of professional work and to insist on impossible standards."

8 6 4 The expert referring to textbooks   The expert who relies on information contained in a textbook written by someone who is not called as a witness, does in fact make use of hearsay. But he is allowed to do so if the following conditions as set out in *Menday v Protea Assurance Co Ltd* are satisfied:[102]

> "Where . . . an expert relies on passages in a text-book, it must be shown, firstly, that he can, by reason of his own training, affirm (at least in principle) the correctness of the statements in that book; and, secondly, that the work to which he refers is reliable in the sense that it has been written by a person of established repute or proved experience in that field. In other words, an expert with purely theoretical knowledge cannot in my view support his opinion in a special field (of which he has no personal experience or knowledge) by referring to passages in a work which has itself not been shown to be authoritative . . . [T]he dangers of holding the contrary are obvious."

It is irregular for the court to rely upon publications (or portions thereof) not referred to and adopted by an expert witness.[103]

8 7   PROCEDURAL ASPECTS

Rule 24(9) of the rules of the magistrates' courts and rule 36(9) of the rules of the Supreme Court provide as follows:

> "(9) No person shall, save with the leave of the court or the consent of all parties to the suit, be entitled to call as a witness any person to give evidence as an expert upon any matter upon which the evidence of expert witnesses may be received, unless he shall —
> *(a)* not less than fifteen days before the hearing, have delivered notice of his intention so to do; and
> *(b)* not less than ten days before the trial, have delivered a summary of such expert's opinion and his reasons therefor."

The above rules are confined to civil cases.[104] In criminal cases prior disclosure may be demanded — and should generally be granted — on constitutional grounds.[105]

---

[101] 1963 3 SA 250 (C) 251H–252A.
[102] 1976 1 SA 565 (E) 569H.
[103] *S v Collop* 1981 1 SA 150 (A); *S v Harris* 1965 2 SA 340 (A) 344C–D.
[104] On the purpose and application of these rules, see *Doyle v Sentraboer Co-operative (Ltd)* 1993 3 SA 176 (SE) 180–1.
[105] *Shabalala & others v Attorney-General of Transvaal & another* 1995 2 SACR 761 (CC) para [72]. See § 11 5 below.

In both civil and criminal cases there are certain statutory provisions which permit expert evidence by way of affidavit or certificate. These provisions — which are discussed in chapter 15 — do not, however, preclude the calling of the witness in person.[106]

There is a series of conflicting and confusing South African cases not only on the procedure to be adopted where an expert testifies from his written report but also on the question to what extent the written report — as opposed to the *viva voce* evidence — is received as evidence.[107] It is submitted that the following principles govern the situation:[108]

(a) "Not infrequently", said Milne JP in *S v Ramgobin*,[109] "experts are permitted to refresh their memories from reports and notes, and the reports and notes are, not infrequently, put in as exhibits. They are not, however, the evidence. The evidence is the oral evidence given by the expert, and the notes are merely an *aide-memoire*."[110] It is submitted that this principle applies only to situations which can be described as "present recollection revived" — a concept which is explained in § 24 2 below. In this instance the expert's report and notes have no independent probative value.

(b) Where the expert witness — after consultation of his report and notes — has no independent recollection of the case and can merely vouch for the accuracy of his recorded observations the contents of the report must be received as the evidence.[111] This situation can be referred to as "past recollection recorded" — a concept which is explained in § 24 2 below.

(c) In both *(a)* and *(b)* above the expert should — as a matter of convenience — be permitted to read out his report.[112] This is a necessary exception[113] to the general rule that witnesses are not permitted to read from statements prepared for purposes of the trial.[114] The expert witness should in principle confirm the correctness of his report and state his adherence to it — and he *must* do so in the case of "past recollection recorded".

8 8   THE RULE IN *HOLLINGTON*

In civil proceedings the earlier criminal convictions of a party are inadmissible to prove the *facts* upon which such convictions were based. In *Hollington v*

---

[106] See generally s 212 of the CPA and s 22 of the CPEA.

[107] See and compare generally *R v Van Schalkwyk* 1948 2 SA 1000 (O); *R v K* 1951 3 SA 180 (SWA); *R v Birch-Monchrieff* 1960 4 SA 425 (T); *S v Joubert* 1971 3 SA 924 (E).

[108] See also generally Van der Merwe *Die Geheueverfrissingsprosedure* (unpublished LLD thesis, UCT 1988) 269–80.

[109] 1986 4 SA 117 (N).

[110] 1986 4 SA 117 (N) 146F–G.

[111] See generally *S v Bergh* 1976 4 SA 857 (A) 865C–D.

[112] Wigmore para 787 (emphasis in the original): "Sometimes a prepared statement has advantages. In many cases, especially where an *expert witness* upon a subject of scientific knowledge has made an investigation or analysis and is called to testify, it makes for his own lucidity and accuracy, and for better comprehension and valuation of his testimony, if he first reads his written report stating in precise terms his observations and inferences. This practice should be freely permitted."

[113] *S v Heller (1)* 1964 1 SA 520 (W) 522B–523D.

[114] See § 24 1 below.

F Hewthorn & Co Ltd it was held, inter alia, that the opinion of the previous tribunal was irrelevant.[115] Sections 11, 12 and 13 of the English Civil Evidence Act 1968 have made previous judgments admissible in certain specified instances. In South Africa we are still bound by the English common-law rule as embodied in *Hollington*.

In *S v Khanyapa*[116] Rumpff CJ gave an indication that the rule in *Hollington* may in future be overruled by the Appellate Division. It is submitted that in order to do so some extraordinary judicial footwork would be necessary to circumvent our residuary clause as found in s 42 of the CPEA.[117] But is the rule in *Hollington* archaic and irrational? In *Land Securities plc v Westminster City Council*[118] Hoffmann J applied the rule in *Hollington* to proceedings which fell outside the ambit of the Civil Evidence Act 1968: an arbitrator's previous finding was held inadmissible in respect of the facts in dispute because such previous finding was considered an irrelevant opinion.

In *S v Mavuso*[119] Hefer J raised, but did not decide, the following question: does the rule in *Hollington* prohibit proof of an accused's previous convictions in a trial in which the prosecution seeks to prove such convictions for purposes of the merits of the case, and assuming such previous convictions are indeed relevant? Zeffertt responded as follows:[120]

> "[This] question has been asked of me, by students, at least once a year for the last twenty years. My reply has always been that the strange rule in *Hollington v Hewthorne* (which is to the effect that the fact of a conviction by a criminal court is not evidence — not even *prima facie* evidence — in a subsequent civil case, that the accused had committed the act for which he was convicted since it is the irrelevant opinion of another court) is generally regarded as wrong. Although it has been held to bind us in civil cases by virtue of the Civil Proceedings Evidence Act 25 of 1965 (see *Yusuf v Bailey* 1964 (4) SA 117 (W)), it has not been applied in proceedings that are not civil proceedings within the meaning of that Act (for instance, in proceedings to strike an attorney off the roll: *Hassim (also known as Essack) v Incorporated Law Society of Natal* 1977 (2) SA 757 (A)). It should not be extended to criminal proceedings either — a submission that is supported by the fact that s 211 of the Criminal Procedure Act 1977 envisages the proof of a previous conviction and, as we have seen, s 197(*d*) allows an accused's previous conviction to be put to him if relevant . . . The fact that my students have always seemed totally unconvinced by this reply in no way derogates from my conviction that it is the true answer."

We are as unpersuaded as Professor Zeffertt's students, but can find no quarrel with his argument! At any rate, how must one explain proof of admissible similar fact evidence[121] by way of previous convictions?

---

[115] 1943 2 All ER 35. See Cowen & Carter *Essays on the Law of Evidence* 172–204 for a detailed discussion of this rule.
[116] 1979 1 SA 824 (A) 840.
[117] See ch 3 above.
[118] 1993 4 All ER 124 128*h*.
[119] *S v Mavuso* 1987 3 SA 499 (A) 505F.
[120] 1987 *ASSAL* 433. See also Van der Berg 1987 *Obiter* 128.
[121] See ch 7 above.

CHAPTER 9

PREVIOUS CONSISTENT STATEMENTS

S E van der Merwe

9 1 INTRODUCTION

A previous consistent statement is a written or oral statement made by a witness on some occasion prior to testifying and which corresponds with or is substantially similar to his or her testimony in court. The general rule is that a witness is not allowed to testify that on a previous occasion he made an oral or written statement consistent with his evidence in court.[1] A witness may therefore not be asked in evidence in chief or re-examination whether he had made a previous statement consistent with his evidence in court.[2] A previous consistent statement of a witness may also not be proved by calling another witness.[3] This kind of statement is excluded because of its irrelevance. It lacks probative value.[4] In exceptional circumstances these statements may be sufficiently relevant to be admissible.[5]

---

[1] *S v Moolman* 1996 1 SACR 267 (A) 300*c* ; *S v Mkohle* 1990 1 SACR 95 (A) 99*c–d*; *R v Rose* 1937 AD 467; *S v Bergh* 1974 4 SA 857 (A) 865G.

[2] Hoffmann & Zeffertt 117. The cross-examiner may venture into this area should he or she deem it necessary. In *R v M* 1959 1 SA 434 (A) 438H it was accepted that a trial court could "do so *mero motu . . .* in the interests of justice (in some cases *in favorem innocentiae*) . . .".

[3] *Corke v Corke and Cook* 1958 2 WLR 110.

[4] *S v Mkohle* supra 99*d*.

[5] These instances are discussed in §§ 9 4–9 12 below.

The general rule against the admissibility of previous consistent statements is sometimes loosely described as the "rule against narrative" or the "rule against self-serving statements".[6]

Proof of previous *inconsistent* statements is as a rule admissible, because inconsistent statements are relevant to credibility.[7] Previous *consistent* statements are, however, generally excluded.

9 2   RATIONALE FOR THE EXCLUSION OF PREVIOUS CONSISTENT STATEMENTS

A previous consistent statement is generally insufficiently relevant. Its insufficient relevance can be attributed to the cumulative effect of several factors:

(a) A previous consistent statement generally has insufficient probative force.[8] A lie can be repeated as often as the truth.[9]

(b) There is also the danger of easy fabrication.[10] There is a risk of "self-made" evidence.[11] This is a factor which indirectly affects relevance and admissibility.[12]

(c) Evidence of previous consistent statements would in most cases be completely superfluous as it may be accepted that in the ordinary course of events a witness's evidence would be consistent with what he on other occasions had said about the same topic or incident.[13]

(d) Proof of previous consistent statements in each and every case would be extremely time-consuming and may pave the way for numerous collateral enquiries. A previous consistent statement, once proved, would merely duplicate the evidence already given by the witness. There is no probative contribution.

(e) The rule against self-corroboration[14] limits the probative value of a previous consistent statement to such an extent that proof of such statement is generally excluded: it has insufficient probative force (as stated in *(a)* above).

9 3   AN EXAMPLE FROM CASE LAW

In *R v Roberts*[15] the accused was charged with murder. He testified that the killing

---

[6] See generally Tapper *Cross and Tapper on Evidence* 8 ed (1995) 204.

[7] See ch 25 below.

[8] *S v Mkohle* 1990 1 SACR 95 (A) 99*d*: "[T]he general rule is that a witness' previous consistent statement has no probative value."

[9] *R v Rose* 1937 AD 467 473.

[10] See § 5 3 4 above.

[11] Cowsill & Clegg *Evidence: Law and Practice* 3 ed (1990, reprinted 1991) 207.

[12] Van Wyk in Ferreira *Strafproses in die Laer Howe* 2 ed (1979) 442 states: "Die vorige ooreenstemmende verklaring is irrelevant omdat dit baie geringe bewyskrag het en tweedens omdat die toelating daarvan daartoe kan lei dat 'n getuie of beskuldigde sy verhaal aan verskeie mense kan herhaal, met die oog daarop dat die aanhoorders dan as getuies geroep kan word om dit te bevestig. Dit is egter 'n erkende feit dat 'n leuen net so dikwels, indien nie meer nie, as die waarheid herhaal kan word. Die roep van 'n aantal getuies om dieselfde verhaal te kom vertel, soos hulle dit aangehoor het, druis in teen die relevantheidsgrondreël en neem onnodig die tyd van die hof in beslag. Voorts kan dit tot verwarring lei terwyl dit geen of weinig bewyswaarde het nie."

[13] Tapper *Cross and Tapper on Evidence* 295.

[14] See ch 30 below.

[15] 1942 28 Cr App R 102.

of his girlfriend was an accident. He was, however, not permitted to testify that two days after the killing he had told his father that the killing was an accident. The narration to his father was excluded because of its irrelevance. The court remarked:[16]

> "The law upon the matter is well-settled. The rule relating to this is sometimes put in this way, that a party is not permitted to make evidence for himself. That law applies to civil cases as well as to criminal cases. For instance, if A and B enter into an oral contract, and some time afterwards there is a difference of opinion as to what were the actual terms agreed upon and there is litigation about it, one of those persons would not be permitted to call his partner to say: 'My partner a day or two after told me what his view of the contract was and that he had agreed to do' so and so. So, in a criminal case, an accused person is not permitted to call evidence to show that, after he was charged with a criminal offence, he told a number of persons what his defence was going to be, and the reason for the rule appears to us to be that such testimony has no evidential value. *It is because it does not assist in the elucidation of the matters in dispute that the evidence is said to be inadmissible on the ground that it is irrelevant.* It would not help the jury in this case in the least to be told that the appellant said to a number of persons, whom he saw while he was awaiting his trial, or on bail if he was on bail, that his defence was this, that or the other. The evidence asked to be admitted was that the father had been told by his son that it was an accident. We think the evidence was properly refused."

9 4 EXCEPTIONS TO THE GENERAL RULE

At this stage of the development of our law of evidence it seems as if it must be accepted that the exceptions to the rule form a *numerus clausus*. These exceptions are discussed in §§ 9 5–9 12 below.

9 5 TO REBUT A SUGGESTION OF RECENT FABRICATION[17]

If it is suggested to a witness that he has fabricated his evidence within some ascertainable period of time, he may rebut this specific suggestion of fabrication by showing that prior to the time as alleged he had made a written or oral statement consistent with his evidence in court.[18] In *Menday v Protea Assurance Co Ltd* Addleson J remarked as follows:[19]

> "The word 'recent' in the term 'recent fabrication' appears to be inappropriate since in those cases in which such evidence has been admitted, it appears that the comparative 'recentness' of the fabrication has not been the deciding issue but rather the question whether between the event under investigation and the trial of the matter, the witness invented a false version of what occurred; and the statement has been admitted to show that, far from fabricating his evidence, the witness is saying what he has always said. Much depends upon the form of the challenge of the disputed evidence and much must depend on the ultimate cogency of the evidence of the previous consistent statement."

---

[16] At 105 (my emphasis).

[17] See generally *R v Oyesikuz* 1972 56 Cr App R 240; *R v Vlok* 1951 1 SA 26 (C) 27A–G; *Pincus v Solomon* 1942 WLD 237 241–2; *S v Bergh* 1976 4 SA 857 (A); *R v Dart (2)* 1951 1 SA 483 (W).

[18] The party calling the witness may prove the previous consistent statement made by the witness at a time when the latter had no motive or opportunity to fabricate a false version. See generally *R v Kizi* 1950 4 SA 532 (A) 535G–H.

[19] 1976 1 SA 565 (E) 566F–H.

This exception also applies where the allegation of recent fabrication is made by implication.[20]

General cross-examination aimed at showing that a witness is unreliable or untruthful will not open the door for the admissibility of a previous consistent statement.[21] The specific allegation or line of cross-examination must be analysed.[22]

The previous consistent statement is admissible not only where a direct or implied accusation of a recent deliberate false fabrication is made but also where it is alleged that the witness recently imagined[23] or reconstructed the event even though not with conscious dishonesty.[24]

The previous consistent statement is admitted because of its relevance. It has the potential to rebut the attack upon the credibility of the witness. The contents of the statement may not, however, be used as evidence of the truth of what the witness had said. Nor can it serve as corroboration of the witness's evidence.[25] The general rule against self-corroboration prohibits such an approach.[26] The true evidential value of the statement is to show that the story of the witness was not concocted at a later date.

9 6   COMPLAINTS IN SEXUAL CASES WHERE THERE IS A VICTIM[27]

In sexual cases evidence may be given of a voluntary complaint made by the victim within a reasonable time after the commission of the alleged sexual offence. This rule has had a peculiar historical development.[28] In the Middle Ages it was considered essential for a rape victim to have "raised the hue and cry"[29] if a charge of rape were to succeed. This rule, however, merely serves as a remote historical link with the present rule. The present rule, for example, applies to female as well as male victims[30] and is no longer confined to sexual crimes where absence of consent is an essential element.[31] There are, however, several rational requirements as regards the admissibility of such a complaint. These requirements are discussed in §§ 9 6 1–9 6 5 below.

---

[20] *Bergh* supra 868D; *S v Nieuwoudt* 1986 1 PH H3 (C) 5–6; *S v Moolman* 1996 1 SACR 267 (A).

[21] *Nieuwoudt* supra 5.

[22] *Pincus v Solomon* supra 241–2; *Moolman* supra 295*i*.

[23] In *Bergh* supra 868D Rumpff CJ said (emphasis added): "Die begrip 'onlangse versinsel' is nie 'n omlynde begrip nie en dit is die plig van die hof, by 'n probleem van hierdie aard, om vas te stel of die aanval op die getuie se getuienis wesenlik neerkom op 'n suggestie, uitdruklik of implisiet, dat vir doeleindes van die saak hy iets as 'n feit beweer wat tydens die aflê van sy getuienis 'n versinsel is of in sy *verbeelding* bestaan."

[24] See generally the decision of the High Court of Australia in *Nominal Defendant v Clement* 1961 104 CLR 476.

[25] *Bergh* supra; *Pincus v Solomon* supra 242. The sole purpose is to prove inconsistency and, in so doing, rebut the allegation of recent fabrication or reconstruction.

[26] See also § 30 3 2 below.

[27] See generally Van der Merwe 1980 *Obiter* 86; Labuschagne 1978 *De Jure* 18 and 242. See also Schwikkard in Jagwanth, Schwikkard & Grant *Women and the Law* 198–202, who argues that this exception has no rational basis and is potentially prejudicial to both the complainant and accused.

[28] See generally Nokes *An Introduction to Evidence* 4 ed (1967) 104; Harms 1965 *THRHR* 257 268–9; *R v Ellis* 1936 SWA 10; *R v Guttenberg* 1907 TS 207 211.

[29] Tapper *Cross and Tapper on Evidence* 296.

[30] *R v Camelleri* 1922 2 KB 122; *R v Burgess* 1927 TPD 14.

[31] *R v Osborne* 1905 1 KB 551.

9 6 1 Voluntary complaint[32] The complaint must have been made voluntarily. In *S v T*[33] the victim's mother had threatened to hit her if she refused to disclose what the accused had done to her. The complaint obtained in this way was held inadmissible. This case can be criticized on the basis that the court paid inadequate attention to all the surrounding circumstances.[34]

Leading or intimidating questions should not have been asked.[35] Questions such as "why are you upset?" or "what happened to your clothes?" will not render the complaint inadmissible. But a question such as "did X touch your private parts?" will affect admissibility even if the answer was given voluntarily. In *R v Osborne* it was said:[36]

> "[T]he mere fact that the statement is made in answer to a question in such cases is not of itself sufficient to make it inadmissible as a complaint. Questions of a suggestive or leading character will, indeed, have that effect . . . [B]ut a question such as this, put by the mother or other person, 'What is the matter?' or 'Why are you crying?' will not do so. These are natural questions which a person in charge will be likely to put. On the other hand, if she were asked, 'Did so-and-so . . . assault you?' 'Did he do this and that to you?' then the result would be different . . . In each case the decision on the character of the question put, as well as other circumstances, such as the relationship of the questioner to the complainant, must be left to the discretion of the presiding judge. If the circumstances indicate that but for the questioning there probably would have been no voluntary complaint, the answer is inadmissible. If the question merely anticipates a statement which the complainant was about to make, it is not rendered inadmissible by the fact that the questioner happens to speak first . . .."

9 6 2 The victim must testify It is a condition of admissibility that the victim should testify.[37] Consistency cannot be proved without the victim's version. Neither the fact that the victim complained nor the contents of the complaint may be received if the victim fails to or cannot testify.[38]

In *S v R*[39] it was alleged that the victim (a chronic alcoholic) was raped in an ambulance whilst on her way to a nursing home for treatment. The accused, who had accompanied her on the journey during which intercourse took place, alleged that she had consented. Upon their arrival at the nursing home the victim repeatedly averred that the accused had raped her. These statements were

---

[32] In *R v C* 1955 4 SA 40 (N) it was said: "To qualify for admission, the 'complaint' must have been made voluntarily, not as a result of leading or suggestive questions, nor of intimidation . . .."

[33] 1963 1 SA 484 (A).

[34] In *S v T* supra the victim also testified that the accused had threatened to kill her and the rest of her family if she were to report the incident. This allegation should have been considered and — if accepted — could have played a role in assessing the voluntariness of the complaint. There was also medical evidence of sexual interference.

[35] *R v Norcott* 1917 1 KB 347.

[36] 1905 1 KB 551 556.

[37] *R v Kgaladi* 1943 AD 255. In *Smith v Malete* 1907 TH 235 236 Bristowe J said: "If a child of three years cannot give evidence in court, how can she give evidence through her mother? The particulars of the complaint must be excluded." If the complainant does not testify, the prosecution may seek to persuade the court to receive the evidence of the complaint (as hearsay) in terms of s 3(1)(c) of Act 45 of 1988, on the grounds that such admission would be in the interest of justice. It is extremely doubtful whether such an attempt would succeed — especially where the complainant happens to be an incompetent witness. Hearsay is discussed in ch 13 below.

[38] *R v Wallwork* 1958 42 Cr App Rep 153.

[39] 1965 2 SA 463 (W).

overheard by a nurse. At the trial — and as a result of the fact that the victim's acute alcoholic condition had given rise to amnesia — she was unable to recall anything from the time she entered the ambulance. But in her evidence she denied that she could have consented to intercourse. The complaint was held admissible despite the fact that the victim was unable to repeat it in her testimony. It was also held that the complaint was admissible to prove state of mind.

9 6 3 First reasonable opportunity The complaint should as a rule have been made at the first reasonable opportunity.[40] Complaints by young children have been admitted after periods of five days,[41] seven days,[42] ten days[43] and even six weeks.[44] According to Schmidt,[45] the determination of what exactly would amount to a "first reasonable opportunity" does to a large extent depend upon *(a)* the presence or absence of a person to whom it can reasonably be expected that the victim might have complained and *(b)* the question whether the victim realized the immoral nature of the act.[46] In *S v V*[47] it was also pointed out that an important question is whether the complainant — because of the lapse of time — could possibly have made a false complaint.

In *S v S*[48] the accused was charged with the rape of an 11-year-old girl. Ebrahim JA adopted a most sensible approach:[49]

> "There is one aspect of the complainant's evidence which on first reading is puzzling and can only be clarified when it is considered from the viewpoint of a young person. This is the reason she gave for not reporting the incident to her mother in detail. She told the court she did not report it at school because she wanted to tell her mother first. This I regard as a natural reaction of one who has been through a traumatic experience such as that deposed to. But then when she arrived home she merely told her mother that her teacher had 'touched' her private parts. Out of context, this erratic behaviour might well present the prosecution with an insuperable problem, for it is a generally accepted evidential requirement that the complainant should report the offence at the earliest

---

[40] In *R v C* 1955 4 SA 40 (N) Caney J said: "To qualify for admission, the 'complaint' . . . must have been made . . . at the earliest opportunity which, under all the circumstances, could reasonably be expected, to the first person to whom the complainant could reasonably be expected to make it." See also *R v S* 1948 4 SA 419 (G) 423. In *R v Kautumundu* 1936 2 PH F154 (SWA) two complaints (relating to the same incident) were made on the same day. Both were received as having been made at the "first" reasonable opportunity. This seems to be acceptable, provided that the court must bear in mind that the complaint(s) can merely prove consistency. A witness, it was said in *R v Whitehead* 1929 1 KB 99 102, cannot corroborate himself, otherwise it would only be necessary for him to repeat his story some twenty-five times in order to get twenty-five corroborations of it. Schwikkard in Jagwanth, Schwikkard & Grant *Women and the Law* (1994) 201 states that the requirement of "first reasonable opportunity" and its application by the courts fails to take into account the many psychological and social factors which may inhibit a rape survivor from making a complaint.

[41] *R v C* 1955 4 SA 40 (N).

[42] *R v Hedges* 1909 3 Cr App Rep 262.

[43] *R v Gannon* 1906 TS 114.

[44] *R v T* 1937 TPD 398.

[45] At 383.

[46] *Gannon* supra 117: "I think . . . the complaint was made at the earliest opportunity which could reasonably have been expected. If the girl had been older, if it had been the case of a grown woman, or even a child more precocious, who knew something about the nature of the offence, the decision might be different". In *Gannon* supra the complainant was 8 years old.

[47] 1961 4 SA 201 (O).

[48] 1995 1 SACR 50 (ZS).

[49] At 56*d–h*. However, see also Schwikkard 1995 *SACJ* 100 for some criticism of this rule.

opportunity. I should emphasize that this requirement is not a rule of law and admits of exceptions in appropriate cases. The explanation proffered by the complainant for her erratic behaviour is not one I would accept from an adult, or even from an older juvenile, but it emerged so naturally from this 11-year-old, and in context to the mind of an innocent child must appear so logical that I am prepared to accept it was given without intention to deceive. The little girl said that at the time she formed the intention to tell her mother about her ordeal she was bleeding from her vagina and sore, but by the time she arrived at home the bleeding had stopped. In answer to previous questions she had deposed that she was unaware that what the appellant had done was unlawful. So, when she arrived home without visible injury, she decided not to trouble her mother with a detailed report of what, one gathers, she (the complainant) regarded as a form of punishment. I am fortified in my acceptance of this aspect of the complainant's evidence by the evidence of her mother, from which it emerges that the complainant was not infrequently detained at school for punishment. It is unlikely in these circumstances that she would wish to draw attention to a further detention by going into details about her 'punishment'."

9 6 4 Victim of sexual offence The offence must be of a sexual nature; there must be a *victim* and violence (*or* some physical element) must have been present[50] (for example, as in rape or indecent assault).

The concept "victim" includes people who voluntarily participate in a sexual offence, but who cannot in law give proper consent,[51] for example, children below certain ages and imbeciles.

The specific offence charged is not the decisive factor. The complaint may be admissible on a charge of common assault if the evidence discloses that an indecent act was also committed.[52]

9 6 5 Limited evidential value The complaint only serves to prove consistency on the part of the victim.[53] It cannot corroborate the victim. Ashworth states as follows:[54]

"A witness certainly cannot corroborate himself by pointing out that he told the same story before. The fact that the witness telling a particular story at the trial told exactly the same story to the police soon after the alleged offence cannot supply corroboration, although it may well strengthen the evidence and rebut any suggestion of subsequent fabrication. Repetition of a story does not corroborate it: and this is a corollary of the general proposition that the confirmatory evidence must come from an independent source. But this general proposition does not apply in one carefully circumscribed set of circumstances, where self-corroboration is possible — by means of the victim's distressed condition after the alleged incident."

9 7 IDENTIFICATION

Identification in court (a so-called "dock identification") is of very little probative

---

[50] See generally *S v Thys* 1974 2 PH H82 (C); *R v Gloose* 1936 2 PH F155 (SWA); *R v Westermeyer* 1911 32 NLR 197; *R v Komsame* 1928 EDL 423.
[51] See generally Hoffmann & Zeffertt 119.
[52] *R v Dray* 1925 AD 553.
[53] *R v M* 1959 1 SA 352 (A). Cf, however, *S v M* 1980 1 SA 586 (B) as discussed by Labuschagne 1980 *THRHR* 322 and Van der Merwe 1980 *Obiter* 86.
[54] Ashworth "Corroboration and Self-corroboration" 1978 *Justice of the Peace* 266 267.

value.[55] Prior identification obviously carries more weight. In *R v Rassool* it was said:[56]

> "Therefore it seems to me that the evidence of previous identification should be regarded as *relevant* for the purpose of showing from the very start that the person who is giving evidence in court identifying the prisoner in the dock is not identifying the prisoner for the first time but has identified him on some previous occasion in circumstances such as to give real weight to his identification."

The evidence of identification must go no further than mere identification. But identifying words accompanying any physical identification may be received.[57]

9 8   PART VI OF THE CPEA[58]

In terms of Part VI of the CPEA it is in certain circumstances permissible to hand in signed statements which witnesses, who are also giving oral evidence, made after the incident under investigation. Part VI of the CPEA also applies in criminal proceedings.[59] The previous written statement cannot serve as corroboration of evidence given by the person who made the statement.[60]

9 9   *RES GESTAE*

A previous consistent statement may also be received if it forms part of the *res gestae*.[61] This was confirmed by the Appellate Division in *S v Moolman*.[62] But here, too, the previous consistent statement cannot corroborate the witness.

9 10   REFRESHING MEMORY [63]

A witness's earlier statement may in certain circumstances be used to refresh his memory whilst he is in the witness-box. The evidential value of a statement used to refresh memory depends on one of two possible situations. In the case of "present recollection revived" the earlier statement has no independent probative value. However, in the case of "past recollection recorded" the contents of the statement are received. In such an instance there is no independent oral testimony (the memory of the witness is not refreshed) and the issue concerning the admissibility of a previous consistent statement does not arise.

---

[55] *S v Maradu* 1994 2 SACR 410 (W); *R v Velekaze* 1947 1 SA 162 (W).
[56] 1932 NPD 112 118 (emphasis added).
[57] Hoffmann & Zeffertt 122.
[58] Part VI of the CPEA is discussed in more detail in §§ 15 5 and 15 9 below.
[59] Section 222 of the CPA.
[60] Section 35(2) of the CPEA.
[61] Tapper *Cross and Tapper on Evidence* 303 states as follows: "The term '*res gestae*' is a blanket phrase when applied to the admissibility of statements, and may roughly be said to denote relevance through contemporaneity — part of the story."
[62] 1996 1 SACR 267 (A). In this case entries in a policeman's pocket book were held admissible as being part of the *res gestae*.
[63] Refreshing of memory and the distinction between present recollection revived and past recollection recorded are discussed in ch 24 below. See especially § 24 2 below.

9 11 STATEMENTS MADE AT ARREST OR ON DISCOVERY OF INCRIMINATING ARTICLES

These statements may be used to prove consistency.[64]

9 12 SECTION 213 OF THE CPA

In terms of this section a witness's statement may in certain circumstances be proved by consent, that is, without calling the witness. It is possible, however, that the witness may also be called upon to testify *viva voce* after his statement has been proved by consent.[65] It is submitted that in such an instance the previous written statement will merely serve to show consistency. It cannot corroborate the witness.

---

[64] See generally Gooderson "Previous Consistent Statements" 1968 26 *Cambridge LJ* 64 66–74.
[65] Section 213(4) of the CPA.

THE EXCLUSION OF RELEVANT EVIDENCE

CHAPTER 10

PRIVATE PRIVILEGE

PJ Schwikkard

10 1   INTRODUCTION

Privilege exists when a witness is not obliged to answer a question or supply information which is relevant to an issue before the court.[1] A claim of privilege must be distinguished from the non-competence or non-compellability of a witness. An incompetent witness does not have the capacity to testify; a non-compellable witness has the right to refuse to testify at all, whilst a witness who wishes to claim privilege is still required to enter the witness-box and then raise the privilege as the reason for not answering the questions put. A claim of

---

[1] Generally speaking, no adverse inference may be drawn from the fact that a person claims privilege; see *International Tobacco Co (SA) Ltd v United Tobacco Co (South) Ltd (1)* 1955 2 SA 10 (W).

privilege may be waived. However, if persons are unaware of their right to claim the privilege, the courts will be reluctant to uphold a claim of waiver.[2]

A distinction must also be drawn between private privilege and state privilege. Where evidence is excluded because to disclose or admit it would be detrimental to state interests, state privilege is claimed. Private privilege is directed at protecting the interests of individuals. When private privilege is claimed secondary or circumstantial evidence may be admitted to prove the matters protected by that privilege.[3] This may not be done when state privilege is invoked. The differences between private and state privilege are also discussed in § 11 1 below.

The effect of private privilege is to deprive the court of relevant evidence; consequently there is a tendency to restrict the instances in which privilege can be claimed.[4] For example, the courts will not recognize a privilege between journalists and their informers or doctors and their patients. This matter is dealt with in § 10 4 below.

In this chapter the following heads of privilege will be discussed: the privilege against self-incrimination; professional privilege; marital privilege; parent–child privilege.[5]

10 2 THE PRIVILEGE AGAINST SELF-INCRIMINATION

The privilege against self-incrimination prohibits a person being compelled to give evidence that incriminates him- or herself.[6] This rule is part of our common law; it is also reflected in certain statutory provisions[7] and enjoys constitutional protection.[8]

10 2 1 The rationale The privilege against self-incrimination is a natural consequence of the presumption of innocence, which plays an important role in the adversarial (accusatorial) trial.[9] It is generally accepted that historically the rule originated "in the unpopularity of the procedure in the Star Chamber under

---

[2] See *Van Lill v S* 1969 2 PH H219 (T); *S v Evans* 1981 4 SA 52 (C). A presiding officer has a duty to advise the unrepresented accused of any claim to privilege; see *S v Lwane* 1966 2 SA 433 (A).

[3] Van der Merwe et al *Evidence* (1983) 133.

[4] Public policy plays an important role in determining in respect of what interests private privilege can be invoked. See generally Tapper *Cross and Tapper on Evidence* 8 ed (1995) 453.

[5] Although not discussed in this chapter, it should be noted that a litigant may refuse to disclose a document in discovery proceedings if he would be able to claim privilege for its contents on any ground. See generally Hoffmann & Zeffertt 267. See further Van Niekerk, Van der Merwe & Van Wyk *Privilegies in die Bewysreg* (1984) 221 for the grounds on which witness statement privilege exists in civil cases: See § 11 5 below as far as "docket privilege" of the state is concerned.

[6] *R v Camane* 1925 AD 570 575.

[7] See s 14 of the CPEA and ss 203, 217 and 219A of the CPA.

[8] Section 25(2)*(a)* and *(c)*, 25(3)*(c)* and *(d)* of the interim Constitution.

[9] Van der Merwe et al *Evidence* 136. See also generally Van der Merwe 1991 *Stell LR* 102.

which those who were charged with an offence were interrogated on oath"[10] and the use of torture as an accepted legal procedure.[11]

In modern law the rationale for retaining the privilege against self-incrimination probably remains founded in public revulsion to the idea that a person should be compelled to give evidence that will expose her to the risk of criminal punishment.[12] A further justification for the privilege is that it is necessary to encourage people to testify freely;[13] people may decline to testify if they are fearful that they might be forced to incriminate themselves.[14]

In *Miranda v Arizona* Warren CJ held:[15]

"The constitutional foundation underlying the privilege is the respect a government . . . must accord to the dignity and integrity of its citizens . . . [T]o respect the inviolability of the human personality, our accusatory system of criminal justice demands that the government seeking to punish an individual produce the evidence against him by its own independent labors, rather than by the cruel simple expedient of compelling it from his own mouth."

There are distinctions in the application of the privilege to the accused, witnesses in criminal proceedings, and witnesses in civil proceedings; these will be considered below.

10 2 2 The witness in criminal proceedings In terms of s 203 of the CPA a witness may refuse to answer a question if it would expose her to a criminal charge;[16] however, the refusal will not be justified if it is based on a fear that it may give rise to a civil claim.[17] Presiding officers are required to warn witnesses in criminal proceedings of their rights under s 203. A failure to do so will ordinarily render "the incriminating evidence inadmissible in a prosecution against the witness".[18] In *S v Lwane*[19] the appellant had been a complainant at an earlier hearing at which he gave evidence against a fellow thief and murderer who had shot him. In the course of his testimony he confessed to having participated in a murder himself. He was subsequently charged and convicted of the murder. On appeal it was held that his testimony at the earlier hearing was inadmissible in that the

---

[10] Tapper *Evidence* 453. See also Hoffmann & Zeffertt 238; Wigmore paras 2250–1. It has also been suggested that the privilege originated in Jewish law; see Mazabow 1987 *SALJ* 710, where this claim is refuted.

[11] Wigmore op cit describes the history of the rule in the following words " . . .[a] long story . . . woven across a tangled warp composed in part of the inventions of the early canonists, of the momentous contest between the courts of the common law and of the church, and of the political and religious issues of the convulsive period in English history, the days of the dictatorial Stuarts."

[12] Tapper *Evidence* 454 cites *Pyneboard Pty Ltd v Trade Practices Commission* 1983 152 CLR 328 346, where the privilege was referred to as "part of the common law of human rights".

[13] See *S v Lwane* supra 438.

[14] The privilege against self-incrimination has been criticized in that it obstructs the course of justice and militates against the discovery of crimes. See Tapper *Evidence* 456; Kurzon 1992 *TRW* 1.

[15] 384 US 436 (1966).

[16] The privilege is that of the witness and generally must be claimed by her.

[17] Section 200 of the CPA.

[18] *S v Lwane* supra. The presence of a legal representative will not necessarily excuse a presiding officer from this duty. See *S v Botha* 1995 2 SACR 605 (W).

[19] Supra. See also § 12 3 3 below for a discussion of *S v Lwane* supra.

appellant had been ignorant of his right to decline to incriminate himself and had not been warned of the existence of this right.[20]

Before the privilege against self-incrimination will be upheld the court must be satisfied from the circumstances of the case and the nature of the evidence that there are reasonable grounds to believe that the witness will incriminate herself.[21] However, the witness is "given considerable latitude in deciding what is likely to prove an incriminating reply".[22]

The privilege against self-incrimination can also be claimed by a witness at inquest proceedings.[23] From the decision in *Masokanye v Additional Magistrate, Stellenbosch*[24] it would appear that the privilege is restricted at such proceedings.[25] The court held that a presiding officer at an inquest, in exercising his discretion to uphold the privilege against self-incrimination, must ensure that the salutary protection afforded by the rule against self-incrimination was not converted into a means of abuse. In exercising such a discretion it is necessary to balance the scales between the interests of the witness who demands the protection and the interests of the public, which demands full disclosure. Despite adopting this approach, the court held that a policeman at inquest proceedings is entitled to claim the privilege against self-incrimination concerning questions relating to his own activities as well as the actions of his colleagues, as inferences could be drawn from his colleagues' actions which could incriminate him. The conclusion of the court has the potential of compromising the principle of open government.[26] "The propriety of police conduct is a matter of public concern, and public policy requires that such conduct should, as far as possible, be open to scrutiny by the courts."[27] A constitutional right may be limited if such limitation is reasonable and justifiable in a democratic society and if the limitation does not negate the essential content of that right. Therefore it is possible that the

---

[20] In *Magmoed v Janse van Rensburg* 1993 1 SA 777 (A) the court found that the underlying rationale in *S v Lwane* was that the warning was required to protect persons who were ignorant of their rights and to encourage witnesses to come forward and testify. The court held that the fact that a police official had not been warned prior to giving evidence at inquest proceedings did not make his evidence inadmissible in subsequent proceedings as he must have been aware of his rights and as a police official it was his duty to give evidence concerning matters arising from the execution of his police duties (at 827). The *Magmoed* approach does not accord with the constitutional rationale for insisting that persons be informed of their right not to incriminate themselves (see § 10 2 3 1 below).

[21] *Magmoed v Janse van Rensburg* supra 819.

[22] *Magmoed v Janse van Rensburg* supra 820. In *S v Heyman* 1966 4 SA 598 (A) 608 Steyn CJ stated: "The avoidance of incriminating replies may not be a simple matter by any means. As observed in *Q v Boyes* 1861 LJR 301 (referred to in *S v Carneson* 1962 3 SA 437 (T) at 439) a question which might at first sight appear a very innocent one, might, by affording a link in a chain of evidence, become the means of bringing home an offence to the party answering." If a claim of privilege is wrongly denied, an incriminating reply may not be admitted in subsequent criminal proceedings. See *Magmoed's* case supra 821.

[23] *Magmoed v Janse van Rensburg* supra; *S v Ramaligela* 1983 2 SA 424 (V).

[24] 1994 1 SACR 21 (C).

[25] See also *S v Van Schoor* 1993 1 SACR 202 (E). The accused prior to his criminal trial had made a written statement to the police for the purposes of inquest proceedings. He was not warned before making the statement. The court found the written statement to be admissible into evidence and held that, although a witness in judicial proceedings was required to be warned, the requirement applied only to *viva voce* evidence before a judicial tribunal. In reaching this conclusion Melunsky J did not refer to any authority and no mention was made of the Judges' Rules.

[26] See Constitutional Principle IX.

[27] *Magmoed v Janse van Rensburg* supra 827.

limitations clause[28] may be successfully invoked to prevent errant police officials taking refuge behind the shield of self-incrimination.

The extent of the privilege set out in s 203 is modified by s 204 of the CPA, which is designed to encourage accomplices to testify against their co-offenders by providing an avenue for indemnity.[29] This section provides that whenever the prosecutor informs the court that a witness will be required to answer self-incriminating questions with regard to the offence specified, the court, provided the witness is competent, shall inform the witness that she is obliged to give evidence and answer incriminating questions (in respect of the offence charged).[30] If a witness answers the questions put to her frankly and honestly, she will be discharged from prosecution.[31] If such a discharge is given at preparatory examination proceedings and a witness does not testify frankly and honestly at the ensuing trial, the discharge shall be of no legal force or effect.[32] If discharge is refused, the witness still enjoys a measure of protection in that her evidence will be inadmissible at any trial in respect of the specified offence. However, the evidence will not be excluded where the charge is one of perjury or statutory perjury.[33]

The privilege against self-incrimination may also be claimed when an inquiry is held in terms of s 205 of the CPA.[34] However, the privilege falls away if the s 204 procedures are invoked during such an inquiry.[35]

10 2 2 1 *The scope of the privilege* A claim of privilege will succeed only if the court is satisfied that the witness's apprehension of being exposed to a criminal charge, if she is compelled to answer, is based on reasonable grounds.[36] Clearly if a witness has been indemnified from prosecution she will not be able to claim the privilege.

The privilege extends beyond answers that would directly incriminate the witness to those "which tend to disclose facts which are innocent in themselves but might form 'links in the chain of proof' in a possible charge against the witness".[37]

10 2 3 The accused

10 2 3 1 *Prior to trial proceedings* The accused's right to remain silent from the time of arrest has been given constitutional recognition.[38] Section 25(2)(a) of the interim Constitution provides that an arrested person shall have the right "promptly to be

---

[28] Section 33(1) of the interim Constitution.
[29] See Paizes in Du Toit et al *Commentary* 23-50, who warns that this procedure should be used cautiously.
[30] Section 204(1).
[31] Section 204(2).
[32] Section 204(3).
[33] Section 204(4).
[34] Section 205(1) is used for the purpose of obtaining statements from witnesses who refuse to make statements to the police in the course of the latter's investigation of a crime.
[35] See generally Paizes in Du Toit et al *Commentary* 23-51. Section 205 is not unconstitutional: *Nel v Le Roux NO & others* 1996 1 SACR 572 (CC).
[36] Hoffmann & Zeffertt 241.
[37] Hoffmann & Zeffertt 241; see also *Wigmore* para 2260; Tapper *Cross and Tapper on Evidence* 457–8; *S v Heyman* supra 608; Van Niekerk, Van der Merwe & Van Wyk *Privilegies in die Bewysreg* 143.
[38] Section 25(2)(a) and (c), 25(3)(c) and (d) of Act 200 of 1993.

informed, in language which he or she understands, that he or she has the right to remain silent and to be warned of the consequences of making any statement". In terms of s 25(2)(c) an arrested person may not be compelled to make an admission or confession.[39] Persons who are detained or arrested also have the right "to consult with a legal practitioner of his or her choice, to be informed of this right promptly and, where a substantial injustice would otherwise result, to be provided with the services of a legal practitioner by the state".[40]

The provisions pertaining to the warning of the right to remain silent to a large extent reflect the common-law position. At common law it is well recognized that a person should not be compelled to incriminate him- or herself.[41] In addition the Judges' Rules[42] also require the police to caution persons suspected of committing a crime before questioning them. Unfortunately, these rules have been accorded little weight by the judges themselves, who have frequently dismissed them on the ground that they are merely administrative directives.[43] In the past the courts have held that a failure to advise an arrested person of her right to remain silent and her right to legal representation does not necessarily render any incriminating statements inadmissible, the absence of a warning merely being a factor to be taken into consideration in deciding whether the state has discharged its onus of proving that the requirements of admissibility have been met. For example, in *R v Barlin*[44] the accused made an incriminating statement to a police officer. At the time this statement was made the police officer suspected but had not yet arrested the accused and did not caution him. The court held that as the accused's statement had been made freely and voluntarily, the fact that the police officer had not warned the accused of his right to remain silent did not render the statement inadmissible.

In the United States the Fifth Amendment, which gives constitutional protection to the privilege against self-incrimination, was interpreted in *Miranda v Arizona*[45] as extending to incriminating statements made by persons in police custody.[46] In the *Miranda* judgment the court, referring with approval to an earlier case *Escobedo v Illinois*,[47] found that the right to counsel was essential in

---

[39] This provision is dealt with in chs 16 and 17 below.

[40] Section 25(1)(c) read together with s 25(2).

[41] *S v Sheehama* 1991 2 SA 860 (A).

[42] At the South African Judges Conference held at Cape Town in 1931 the Judges' Rules were formulated. These rules are virtually identical to the Judges' Rules drawn by the English judges in 1913. The purpose of these rules is to protect an accused from unfair practices by the police.

[43] Hiemstra 1968 *SALJ* 187. Cf *S v Mpetha (2)* 1983 1 SA 576 (C); *S v Sampson* 1989 3 SA 239 (A); *S v Colt* 1992 2 SACR 120 (E).

[44] 1926 AD 459. See also *R v Holtzhausen* 1947 1 SA 567 (A); *R v Kuzwayo* 1949 3 SA 761 (A). In *S v Mpetha* supra 598 Williamson J noted: "Once the person being interviewed is cautioned and then indicates that he does not want to say anything it is in my opinion improper to direct further questions to him. If he answers these further question the irresistible inference is that his earlier expressed decision to say nothing has been made to crumble by the pressures of the situation in which he then finds himself." See also *S v Sabisa* 1993 2 SACR 525 (Tk). See chs 16 and 17 below for a discussion of the requirements that have to be met before an admission or confession may be admitted into evidence.

[45] Supra.

[46] See further Ghent (annotation) 31 ALR 3d 565; Smith 1974 *South Carolina LR* 699–735. *Harris v New York* 401 US 222 (1970); *Rhode Island v Innis* 446 US 291 (1980); *New York v Quarles* 1984 104 SCt 2626.

[47] 378 US 478.

order to protect the right against self-incrimination. The holding of the court in *Miranda* can be summarized as follows: statements obtained during custodial interrogation of the accused may not be admitted into evidence unless the prosecution can show that appropriate procedural safeguards were used to secure the privilege against self-incrimination. The appropriate procedural safeguards are that a person must be warned that she has the right to remain silent, that any statement she makes may be used in evidence against her, and that she has a right to the presence of an attorney. The fact that an accused may know of her rights without been warned will not effect the inadmissibility of the evidence.

The *Miranda* rule applies to all custodial interrogation, whereas s 25(2)*(a)*, which stipulates that persons must be warned of their right to remain silent and the consequences of not doing so, applies only to arrested persons and not detained persons. The Judges' Rules provide broader protection in that they stipulate that not only must arrested persons be duly warned but also persons under suspicion.[48] Furthermore, rule 4 of the Judges' Rules provides that questions should not be put to a person in custody. It would therefore seem that a person who is not arrested and not warned, but is questioned because she is suspected of having committed a crime, may not challenge the admissibility of consequent incriminating evidence on the basis that it was obtained unconstitutionally. This anomaly could be resolved if the concept of a fair trial,[49] which includes the protection of the privilege against self-incrimination, is not restricted to court procedures but begins the instant the criminal process is invoked.[50] This is not a concept foreign to South African law. The courts have frequently stressed "the undesirability of requiring a high standard of fairness in the courts while at the same time tolerating a low standard of fairness in the judicial process prior to an accused reaching court".[51] In *R v Kuzwayo*[52] Van den Heever JA, referring to the Judges' Rules noted:[53]

> "Non-compliance not infrequently results in the police embarking upon an informal and irregular 'trial' of the accused, designed to establish his guilt or innocence. When this happens, the courts of this country sit in judgment, not upon the guilt or innocence of the accused (although, of course, in theory this is what they are doing), but upon the merit or demerits of a 'trial' conducted by the police in the course of which the 'guilt' of the accused has already been determined. This development, if it were to get out of hand, would undermine our system of justice. It need hardly be stressed that a farcical situation arises if the courts, while insisting upon the maintenance of the highest standards in their procedure, accept and endorse the result of 'trials' conducted in an informal and irregular way by members of the police force. If a stage has been reached when it has become desirable in the interests of justice to subject persons suspected of crimes to interrogation

---

[48] See *S v Mafuya* 1992 2 SACR 370 (W); *S v Mpetha (2)* supra.

[49] The right to a fair trial is guaranteed in s 25(3) of the interim Constitution.

[50] In *S v Zuma* 1995 2 SACR 568 (CC) the Constitutional Court held that the right to a fair trial conferred by s 25(3) of the interim Constitution is broader than the list of specific rights set out in the section, and that it embraces a concept of substantive fairness.

[51] *Mpetha* supra 593. See also *S v Lwane* supra; *R v Kuzwayo* supra; *S v Dlamini* 1973 1 SA 144 (A); *S v Melani* 1996 1 SACR 335 (E). See also Paizes 1981 *SACC* 122 133.

[52] 1949 3 SA 761 (A).

[53] At 400. See also *S v Colt* 1992 2 SACR 120 (E) 128.

designed to establish their guilt, it is desirable that this power should be exercised in open court, and it is undesirable that the power should be exercised by the police in private."

If it is accepted that the requirements for a fair trial can only be met if the privilege against self-incrimination is upheld from the moment the criminal process is invoked, then the standards set by the Judges' Rules[54] provide an extremely useful measure for ascertaining whether the requirements of a fair trial have been met.

The duty to advise persons of their right to consult with a legal practitioner applies to both detained and arrested persons; however, legal representation will only be sponsored by the state "where substantial justice would otherwise

---

[54] The following is the text of the Judges' Rules:

"1. Questions may be put by policemen to a person whom they do not suspect of being concerned in the commission of the crime under investigation, without any caution being first administered.

2. Questions may be put to a person whom the police have decided to arrest or who is under suspicion where it is possible that the person by his answers may afford information which may tend to establish his innocence, as, for instance, where he has been found in the possession of property suspected to have been stolen, or of an instrument suspected to have been used in the commission of the crime, or where he was seen in the vicinity about the time when a crime was committed. In such a case a caution should first be administered. Questions, the sole purpose of which is that the answers may afford evidence against the person suspected, should not be put.

3. The caution to be administered in terms of rule 2 should be to the following effect:
'I am a police officer. I am making inquiries (into so and so) and I want to know anything you can tell me about it. It is a serious matter and I must warn you to be careful what you say.'
Where there is any special matter as to which an explanation is desired, the officer should add words such as: 'You have been found in possession of . . . unless you can explain this I may have to arrest you . . .'.

4. Questions should not be put to a person in custody with the exception of questions put in terms of rule 6.

5. Where a person in custody wishes to volunteer a statement, he should be allowed to make it, but he should be first cautioned.

6. A statement made by a prisoner before there is time to caution is not rendered inadmissible in evidence, merely by reason of no caution having been given prior to the commencement of his statement, but in such a case he should be cautioned as soon as possible.

7. A prisoner making a voluntary statement must not be cross-examined, but questions may be put to him solely for the purpose of removing elementary or obvious ambiguities in voluntary statements. For instance, if he has mentioned an hour without saying whether it was morning or evening or has given a day of the week and day of the month which do not agree, or has not made clear to what individual or what place he intended to refer in some part of his statement, he may be questioned sufficiently to clear up the point.

8. The caution to be administered to a person in custody should be to the following effect:
(a) where he is formally charged:
'Do you wish to say anything in answer to the charge? You are not obliged to do so, but whatever you say will be taken down in writing and may be given in evidence.'
(b) Where a prisoner volunteers a statement otherwise than on a formal charge:
'Before you say anything (or, if he has already commenced his statement, 'anything further'), I must tell you that you are not obliged to do so, but whatever you say will be taken down in writing and may be given in evidence.'

9. Any statement made in accordance with the above rules should, whenever possible be taken down in writing and in the language in which it was made. It should be read over to the person making it and he should be given full opportunity for making any corrections therein that he may wish to, and he should then be invited to sign it.

10. When two or more persons are charged with the same offence, and a voluntary statement is made by any one of them, the police, if they consider it desirable, may furnish the other person with a copy of such statement, but nothing should be said or done by the police to invite a reply. The police should not read such statement to a person furnished, unless such person is unable to read it and desires that it be read over to him. If a person so furnished wishes to make a voluntary statement in reply, the usual caution should be administered."

result".[55] In terms of the reasoning in *Miranda* the right to legal representation is essential if the privilege against self-incrimination is to be upheld.[56]

> "The circumstances surrounding in-custody interrogation can operate very quickly to overcome the will of one merely made aware of his privilege by interrogators. Therefore, the right to have counsel present at the interrogation is indispensable to the protection of the Fifth Amendment privilege under the system we delineate today. Our aim is to assure that the individual's right to choose between silence and speech remains unfettered throughout the interrogation process. A once-stated warning, delivered by those who will conduct the interrogation, cannot itself suffice to that end among those who most require knowledge of their rights. A mere warning given by the interrogators is not alone sufficient to accomplish that end. Prosecutors themselves claim that the admonishment of the right to remain silent without more 'will benefit only the recidivist and the professional' . . . Thus the need for counsel to protect the Fifth Amendment privilege comprehends not merely a right to consult with counsel prior to questioning, but also to have counsel present during any questioning if the defendant so desires."[57]

If the *Miranda* approach is to be followed, it is clearly untenable that the degree of constitutional protection afforded to accused persons is dependent upon their income.[58] It would therefore appear that if the privilege against self-incrimination and the right to equality are to be upheld, if the state finds itself unable to provide legal representation to an accused, the police must refrain from interrogating persons who desire legal representation but who are not in a position to obtain it.

The South African interim Constitution contains no explicit provisions in respect of the admissibility of evidence obtained in breach of a person's constitutional rights. However, there are several Supreme Court judgments that support the view that at the very least the court has a discretion to exclude evidence obtained unconsitutionally.[59] In the past a breach of the Judges' Rules was simply a factor taken into account in determining whether the requirements of the admissibility of confessions and admissions had been met.[60] If the traditional approach is followed, the constitutional provisions upholding the privilege against self-incrimination may in many instances be as ineffective as the Judges' Rules were in the past. Consequently, it has been argued that the privilege against self-incrimination will become a useful tool in ensuring the right to a fair trial only if evidence obtained in breach of the privilege is excluded.[61] A full discussion of unconstitutionally obtained evidence is contained in chapter 12 below.

10 2 3 1 1 *Ascertainment of bodily features*   Section 37(1) of the CPA authorizes police officials to take the fingerprints, palm-prints or footprints of any person who has been arrested or charged. The police are also authorized to take such steps as are necessary to ascertain whether the body of any arrested person has any mark, characteristic or distinguishing feature or shows any condition or

---

[55] Section 25(1) *(c)*, 25(2) and 25(3) *(e)* of the interim Constitution.
[56] See also *Escobedo* supra.
[57] *Miranda v Arizona* supra. See also Cachalia et al *Fundamental Rights in the New Constitution* (1994) 80–3.
[58] See also *Gideon v Wainwright* 372 US 335 (1963); *Douglas v California* 372 US 353 (1963).
[59] See ch 12 below.
[60] *S v Mpetha (2)* supra; *S v Sampson* supra; *S v Colt* supra.
[61] See Cachalia et al *Fundamental Rights* (1994) 82.

appearance.[62] Although police officials are prohibited from taking blood samples, this may be done by any medical officer of any prison or a district surgeon. And if requested to by the police, a registered medical practitioner or nurse can take steps, including taking a blood sample, to ascertain whether the body of an arrested person has any mark, characteristic or distinguishing feature or shows any condition or appearance.[63] Section 225(2) of the same Act allows such evidence to be admitted into evidence even if it was obtained improperly or against the will of the accused.

Obviously evidence obtained as a consequence of any of the above steps may incriminate the accused. The question then arises whether s 37 is in conflict with s 25(2) *(c)*, which provides that no one shall be compelled to make an admission which can be used in evidence against them. Prior to legislative authorization[64] there was some uncertainty as to whether the ascertainment of bodily features, without the consent of an accused, infringed the common-law privilege against self-incrimination. In *Goorpurshad v R*[65] the court set aside a conviction where the accused had been compelled during the course of a trial by the presiding officer to have his fingerprints taken. The Transvaal Provincial Division adopted a similar approach in *R v Maleke*,[66] in which the court refused to admit evidence of a footprint compelled by force. Krause J expressed his objection to the admission of such evidence as follows:[67]

> "[I]t compels an accused person to convict himself out of his own mouth; that it might open the door to oppression and persecution of the worst kind; that it is a negation of the liberty of the subject and offends against our sense of natural justice and fair play . . . ."

However, the judicial debate as to whether such evidence should be excluded because it infringed the principle against self-incrimination was brought to a close by the Appellate Division in *Ex parte Minister of Justice: In re R v Matemba*,[68] in which the court considered the admissibility of a palm-print taken by compulsion. The court found that the privilege against self-incrimination applied only to testimonial utterances. Watermeyer JA held:[69]

> "Now, where a palm-print is being taken from an accused person, he is, as pointed out by Innes CJ in *R v Camane* (1925 AD 570 at 575), entirely passive. He is not being compelled to give evidence or to confess, any more than he is being compelled to give evidence or confess when his photograph is being taken or when he is put upon an identification parade or when is made to show a scar in court. In my judgment, therefore, neither the maxim

---

[62] Section 37(1)*(c)*. See *S v Mbambeli* 1993 2 SACR 388 (E), where the court held that evidence emanating from a medical examination, authorized in terms of s 37, could also be used to refute an allegation of assault.

[63] Section 37(1)*(c)* and 37(2)*(a)*.

[64] Sections 2 and 3 of the Criminal and Magistrates' Courts Procedure (Amendment) Act 39 of 1926, replaced by ss 289 and 291 of the Criminal Procedure Act 56 of 1955, in turn replaced by s 37 and s 225 of the Criminal Procedure Act 51 of 1977.

[65] 1914 35 NLR 87.

[66] 1925 TPD 491.

[67] At 534. See also *R v B* 1933 OPD 139.

[68] 1941 AD 75.

[69] At 82–3. See also *Nkosi v Barlow* 1984 3 SA 148 (T); *S v Duna* 1984 2 SA 591 (C). See generally Labuschagne 1980 *TSAR* 58; *Wigmore* para 2265.

nemo tenetur se ipsum prodere nor the confession rule make inadmissible palm-prints compulsorily taken."

This reasoning was also invoked to justify the admission of a thing or place pointed out by the accused, even in circumstances where the pointing out was coerced. In *S v Sheehama*[70] the Appellate Division found this reasoning to be untenable and held that "a pointing out is essentially a communication by conduct and, as such, is a statement by the person pointing out". Consequently, a pointing out, like any other extra-judicial admission, has to be made voluntarily before it will be admitted into evidence.[71] However, although a pointing out, like the ascertainment of bodily features, usually results in the production of "real" evidence, it can be distinguished from the latter in that it involves some degree of active or communicative conduct.[72]

In *S v Huma (2)*[73] the accused objected on two grounds to his fingerprints being taken during the course of the trial: (1) it would infringe his constitutional right to dignity protected in ss 10 and 11 of the interim Constitution; and (2) it would infringe the privilege against self-incrimination as contained in s 25(3)*(c)* of the interim Constitution. The court held that the accused's right to dignity had not been infringed as the taking of fingerprints could not be said to be inhuman or degrading treatment.[74] With regard to the argument that fingerprinting infringed the privilege against self-incrimination, the court found it unnecessary to invoke the limitations clause. Claasen J held that the taking of fingerprints did not constitute testimonial evidence by the accused and was therefore not in conflict with the privilege against self-incrimination.[75] The court clearly found the majority decision in *Schmerber v California*[76] very persuasive. In this case the majority of the US Supreme Court held that the Fifth Amendment privilege against self-incrimination relates only to the testimonial or communicative acts of the accused and does not apply to non-communicative acts such as submission to a blood test.[77]

However, some of the American states have legislated against the admission of such evidence. For example, a South Dakota statute permits a person suspected of driving while intoxicated to refuse to submit to a blood-alcohol test, but authorizes revocation of the driver's licence of a person who refuses to submit

---

[70] 1991 2 SA 860 (A).

[71] See further ch 17 below.

[72] See *S v Binta* 1993 2 SACR 553 (C).

[73] 1995 2 SACR 411 (W). See also *S v Maphumulo* 1996 2 SACR 84 (N).

[74] At 416. The court held, at 316*j*–317*a*, that even if it was incorrect in reaching this conclusion, such infringement was a reasonable and necessary limitation in terms of ss 33(1) of the interim Constitution.

[75] At 419*g*.

[76] 384 US 757 (1966). This case was cited with approval in *Seetal v Pravitha* 1983 3 SA 827 (D). See also *S v Maphumulo* supra 88*f*–89*b*.

[77] Black J and Douglas J dissented on the ground that the compulsory blood test, against the wishes of the defendant, was a violation of the defendant's constitutional right against self-incrimination. In Canada, in terms of the common law a person may refuse to provide a sample of bodily substances; however, this has been modified by statute and in terms of s 223 of the Criminal Code a person may be required to take a "breath test". Refusal to take such a test will constitute an offence. However, this has been held not to violate s 11*(c)* of the Canadian Charter, which confers the right not to be compelled "to be a witness against oneself" as it is a privilege against testimonial compulsion, not against compulsion generally. See Hogg *Constitutional Law of Canada* 3 ed (1992) 48 4*(d)*.

to the test and allows evidence of the refusal to be admitted into evidence. In *South Dakota v Neville*[78] it was argued that the admission into evidence of such a refusal infringed the privilege against self-incrimination. The court, in rejecting this argument, held that a refusal to take such a test after a police officer has lawfully requested it is not an act coerced by the officer and is therefore not protected by the privilege against self-incrimination.

Can a clear distinction be made between the ascertainment of bodily features and testimonial or communicative statements? Black J and Douglas J, dissenting in *Schmerber*,[79] thought not:

"[T]he compulsory extraction of a petitioner's blood for analysis so that the person who analyzed it could give evidence to convict him had both a 'testimonial' and a 'communicative nature'. The sole purpose of this project which to be successful was to obtain 'testimony' from some person to prove that petitioner had alcohol in his blood at the time he was arrested. And the purpose of the project was certainly 'communicative' in that the analysis of the blood was to supply information to enable a witness to communicate to the court and jury that the petitioner was more or less drunk."[80]

In his dissenting judgment Justice Black criticized the majority's heavy reliance on the words "testimonial" and "communicative", which he found to have little clarity, and the court's narrow and technical interpretation of the bill of rights safeguard against compulsory self-incrimination.

It is submitted that even if in the future the South African courts take the more broad and liberal construction advocated by Black J, the compulsory ascertainment of bodily features authorized by s 37 of the CPA may still survive a constitutional challenge on the following basis: although the ascertainment of bodily features against the will of the accused limits the privilege against self-incrimination, such limitation may well meet the requirements of s 33(1) of the interim Constitution.[81] However, the provisions of s 225(2) have a more uncertain future as the effect of this section is to make admissible evidence that is obtained illegally or improperly. In terms of s 225(2) evidence that is obtained not in accordance with s 37, or without the necessary precautions been taken to protect the accused from hazard or trauma, will still be admissible. See, for example, *S v Britz*,[82] where the court held that the fact that the nurse taking the blood sample had not taken the appropriate sanitary precautions in drawing the blood specimen was irrelevant to admissibility.

10 2 3 1 2 *Bail proceedings* Where an accused gives evidence in a bail application he retains the privilege against self-incrimination.[83] This means that even where the accused elects to testify he can decline to answer incriminating questions.

---

[78] 459 US 553 (1983).
[79] Supra.
[80] Black J at 921.
[81] See Van der Merwe in Du Toit et al *Commentary* 3-1, where it is noted that "the ascertainment of the bodily features and 'prints' of an accused often forms an essential component of the investigation of crime and is in many respects a prerequisite for the effective administration of any criminal justice system, including the proper adjudication of a criminal trial".
[82] 1994 2 SACR 687 (W).
[83] *S v Botha* 1995 2 SACR 605 (W).

However, if the accused chooses not to testify or refuses to answer incriminating questions, he runs the risk of bail being refused. The court in *S v Botha*[84] concluded that the only way to avoid this invidious situation was to treat evidence given at bail proceedings in the same way as evidence given at a trial-within-trial.[85] This would prohibit the prosecution leading evidence of the testimony given at a bail application at the main trial.

10 2 3 2 *Trial and plea proceedings* Section 25(3) *(c)–(d)* of the interim Constitution protects the privilege against self-incrimination during trial proceedings. Section 25(3) *(c)* provides that every accused person shall have the right "to be presumed innocent and to remain silent during plea proceedings or trial and not to testify during trial". Section 25(3) *(d)* gives an accused person the right to adduce and challenge evidence and "not to be a compellable witness against himself or herself".

This once again mirrors the existing common-law right to remain silent.[86] The constitutional protection of the right to remain silent reinforces the notion that a person should not be penalized for exercising her right to remain silent at trial. Consequently, a court may not draw an adverse inference from an accused's decision not to testify at trial. Geldenhuys & Joubert give the following reasons for not drawing an adverse inference:[87]

> "[F]irst, no such inference *can* be drawn, for there may be a multitude of reasons why he does not wish to testify (he may think that State case is so weak that it does not merit an answer; he may not trust the court or legal system, or be afraid or ignorant as to strategy; or he may simply want to exercise the right to silence about which he has been informed); secondly, no such inference can logically be drawn to fill gaps in the State case: if an element of a crime (e g identity in the case of robbery) has not been covered by prima facie proof, the nothingness of the accused's silence cannot logically fill the gap in the State's case; thirdly, it would be unethical and contrary to the principle of legality to punish an accused for the exercise of a right which he has been told he may exercise."

In *S v Brown & andere*[88] it was held that no adverse inference can be drawn against an accused merely by virtue of the fact that she has exercised her constitutional right to refuse to testify. This does not mean, however, that silence cannot negatively influence an accused's defence. In § 30 9 below it is pointed out that where the state has established a *prima facie* case against the accused and the accused has failed to testify, the court is required to base its decision on the uncontradicted evidence of the state. In such a situation it may be almost inevitable that the *prima facie* case will become sufficient evidence to sustain a conviction:[89]

---

[84] Supra.

[85] See § 17 6 below for a discussion of the nature of a trial-within-trial.

[86] At common law presiding officers are required to advised unrepresented accused persons appearing before them of their right to remain silent. This requirement must also be met in bail proceedings: see *S v Mqubasi* 1993 1 SACR 196 (SE).

[87] Geldenhuys & Joubert (eds) *Criminal Procedure Handbook* (1994) 6–7. Cf 2 ed (1996) 8 of the same work.

[88] 1996 2 SACR 49 (NC) 60*f–d.* Cf *S v Scholtz* 1996 2 SACR 40 (NC).

[89] Geldenhuys & Joubert (eds) *Criminal Procedure Handbook* 2 ed (1996) 8. Hoffmann & Zeffertt 179 state: "An inference against the accused can be drawn from his silence in certain circumstances but he must first be given an opportunity to explain why he elected to remain silent. So it is permissible for a court to take into account the fact that a defence such as an *alibi* may be considerably weakened if it was disclosed

"[T]his happens simply because the defence did not 'disturb' the State case; the silence of the defence did not add anything positively to the State's case. The inference is not really an inference in the strict sense of the word, but simply an observation or conclusion that the accused could not or would not disturb the State's prima facie case, with the result that the latter stands uncontroverted and becomes proof beyond reasonable doubt."

Much will depend on the circumstances of the case and the nature of the defence raised by the accused.

It is arguable that existing legislative provisions encroach on the right to remain silent during plea proceedings. In terms of s 112 of the CPA the accused may be questioned by the presiding officer after entering a plea of guilty. This can be justified in numerous ways. The accused, by entering a plea of guilty, is clearly abdicating her right to be presumed innocent — there is no longer a contest between the state and the accused. Furthermore, questioning in terms of s 112 is aimed at protecting the accused; the accused cannot compromise herself further as she has already admitted guilt. A presiding officer may, through questioning the accused, discover that she does have a valid defence. For example, it may become apparent on a charge of culpable homicide that the accused acted in self-defence. Nevertheless, it has been held that a court should, prior to questioning, inform an accused of her right to silence.[90]

More contentious is questioning in terms of s 115 after the accused has entered a plea of not guilty. In terms of s 115(1), where an accused pleads not guilty the magistrate may ask her whether she wishes to make a statement indicating the basis of her defence. Section 115(2)(*a*) provides that where the accused does not make a statement indicating the basis of her defence, or does so and it is not clear from the statement to what extent she denies or admits the issues raised by the plea, the court may question the accused in order to establish which allegations in the charge are in dispute.

In terms of s 115(2)(*b*) the court may question the accused in order to clarify any matter with regard to the statement indicating the basis of the accused's defence, or her replies to questions directed at ascertaining which allegations are in dispute.

It is clear that an accused is not obliged to answer any questions put to her under s 115, and she must be advised of this right.[91] An unrepresented accused may find it extremely difficult to exercise this right in an alien and intimidating court environment.[92] Consequently, it is possible that s 115 may yet be challenged as effectively contravening the constitutionally protected right to remain silent.

Section 20 of the Criminal Law Second Amendment Act 126 of 1992 provides

---

too late to give the police an opportunity for checking it. The difference between saying that the failure to disclose an alibi weakens the defence and saying that it tends to show guilt may appear artificial, but it can be important in those cases in which the law requires corroboration since the accused's silence is not treated as an independent item of evidence against him." These remarks must obviously be read in the context of pre-trial silence.

[90] *S v Maseko* 1996 2 SACR 91 (W). But at 97*b–c* the court accepted that s 112(1)(*b*) of the CPA is not in conflict with the interim Constitution.

[91] See generally Geldenhuys & Joubert *Handbook* 188; *S v Evans* 1981 4 SA 52 (C); *S v Daniels* 1983 3 SA 275 (A); *S v Mabaso* 1990 3 SA 185 (A); *S v Hill* 1981 2 PH H152 (C).

[92] See generally Steytler *The Undefended Accused* (1988) 128.

a more clear-cut example of legislation that falls foul of the constitutional right to remain silent.[93] Section 20(4)(b)(i) provides that where an accused stands trial on a special offence,[94] pleads not guilty and declines to indicate what the basis of his defence is, "the court may at will, in respect of his credibility or conduct, draw an unfavourable inference regarding such failure if it is of the opinion that such an inference is justified in the light of all the evidence that was adduced at the trial". Chapter V of Act 126 of 1992 is presently not in operation.[95]

10 2 4 Other investigative inquiries   There are several statutory enactments that provide for interrogation procedures outside of the criminal process.[96] Many of these authorize designated officials to compel persons to appear before them and to answer questions, whether incriminating or not. Section 25(2)(a) and 25(3)(c) of the interim Constitution limits the right to remain silent and not to answer incriminating questions to arrested and accused persons during plea proceedings and trial.[97] Therefore, it would appear that investigative inquiries that do not form part of the criminal process will escape constitutional scrutiny provided that evidence obtained at such an inquiry is not used in subsequent criminal proceedings.[98] The admission of statements made under statutory compulsion are fully discussed in § 17 4 4 2 below.

10 2 5 The witness in civil proceedings   Section 14 of the CPEA provides:

"A witness may not refuse to answer a question relevant to the issue, the answering of which has no tendency to incriminate himself, or to expose him to penalty or forfeiture of any nature whatsoever, by reason only or on the sole ground that the answering of such question may establish or tend to establish that he owes a debt or is otherwise subject to a civil suit."

Section 14 must be read together with s 42, which provides:

"The law of evidence including the law relating to the competence, compellability and examination and cross-examination of witnesses which was in force in respect of civil proceedings on the thirtieth day of May 1961, shall apply in any case not provided for by this Act or any other law."

The effect of these two provisions is to give a wider ambit to the privilege against self-incrimination in civil cases than in criminal cases. In criminal cases the privilege applies only to answers which would expose the witness to a criminal

---

[93] See Van der Merwe 1994 *Obiter* 22. See also generally Grant & Jagwanth 1993 *SACJ* 329.

[94] The definition of a special offence is to be found in s 18(1), which provides: "If the attorney-general is of the opinion that an offence with which any person is charged or is to be charged, is an offence in which murder, robbery with aggravating circumstances, violence or intimidation is involved, that attorney-general may, irrespective of what the actual charge is, at any time before such person pleads to the charge issue a certificate to the effect that such an offence is a special offence."

[95] In terms of s 24(1) of Act 126 of 1992, ch V of the Act may be extended by the State President, with the concurrence of Parliament, for a period of one year at a time.

[96] For example, s 65 of the Insolvency Act 24 of 1936, ss 415 and 417 of the Companies Act 61 of 1973; s 66(1) of the Close Corporations Act 69 of 1984; ss 3, 4, 6, 8 and 9 of the Inspection of Financial Institutions Act 38 of 1984; ss 7, 9 and 17 of the Maintenance and Promotion of Competition Act 96 of 1979; ss 5, 7 and 14 of the Harmful Business Practices Act 71 of 1988; s 6 of the Banks Act 94 of 1990.

[97] *Park-Ross v Director, OSEO* 1995 1 SACR 530 (C). See also generally *Nel v Le Roux NO & others* 1996 1 SACR 572 (CC).

[98] See *Park-Ross v Director, OSEO* supra.

charge, whilst in civil cases it also applies where it would expose the witness to penalties or forfeiture.

10 3 LEGAL PROFESSIONAL PRIVILEGE

10 3 1 The rationale   In civil and criminal proceedings communications made between a lawyer and her client may not be disclosed without the client's consent.[99] Heydon sets out the rationale for the rule as follows:

> "The privilege is usually said to exist for the following reasons. Human affairs and the legal rules governing them are complex. Men are unequal in wealth, power, intelligence and capacity to handle their problems. To remove this inequality and to permit disputes to be resolved in accordance with the strength of the parties' cases, lawyers are necessary, and privilege is required to encourage resort to them, and to ensure that *all* the relevant facts will be put before them, not merely those the client thinks favour him. If lawyers are only told some of the facts, clients will be advised that their cases are better than they actually are, and will litigate instead of compromising and settling. Lawyer–client relations would be full of 'reserve and dissimulation, uneasiness, and suspicion and fear' without the privilege; the confidant might at any time have to betray confidences."[100]

In *S v Safatsa*[101] Botha JA expressed his agreement with the views of Dawson J in *Baker v Campbell*:[102]

> "The conflict between the principle that all relevant evidence should be disclosed and the principle that communications between lawyer and clients should be confidential has been resolved in favour of the confidentiality of those communications. It has been determined that in this way the public interest is better served because the operation of the adversary system, upon which we depend for the attainment of justice in our society, would otherwise be impaired . . . The privilege extends beyond communications made for the purpose of litigation to all communications made for the purpose of giving or receiving advice and this extension of the principle makes it inappropriate to regard the doctrine as a mere rule of evidence. It is a doctrine which is based upon the view that confidentiality is necessary for the proper functioning of the legal system and not merely the proper conduct of particular litigation . . .."

In *Safatsa* the Appellate Division for the first time recognized that legal

---

[99] This common-law rule is reflected in s 201 of the CPA. Although there is no express provision in the CPEA, by virtue of s 42 the common law applies as it was on 30 May 1961. It should be noted that a restriction is placed on the privilege by s 201, in terms of which a legal adviser is required to reveal any communications from his client made "before he was professionally employed or consulted with reference to the defence" of his client.

[100] Heydon *Evidence: Cases & Materials* 3 ed (1991) 414–15. See also Tapper *Cross and Tapper on Evidence* 8 ed (1995) 470. The basis and justification for attorney–client privilege has been the subject of much debate. See Paizes 1989 *SALJ* 109. At 120 Paizes comments favourably on the non-utilitarian foundation for professional privilege put forward by Fried, who argues that the identity between lawyer and client provides the moral foundation for an absolute privilege: "It is not only the client's lack of legal knowledge that compels him to make confidential communications to his lawyer. If we regard them as constituting one conceptual unit then, ex hypothesi, no 'communication', as such, has been made. To compel either the lawyer or the client to disclose what has passed between them would be tantamount to involuntary self-incrimination . . .." See generally Unterhalter 1988 *SALJ* 291; Haysom 1987 *De Rebus* 697; Kriegler 1991 *SALJ* 613.

[101] 1988 1 SA 868 (A) 886.

[102] 1983 49 ALR 385 at 442–5.

professional privilege is a fundamental right derived from the requirements of procedural justice, and not merely an evidentiary rule.[103]

10 3 2 The requirements for the existence of the privilege Before legal professional privilege can be claimed the communication in question must have been made to a legal adviser acting in a professional capacity, in confidence, for the purpose of pending litigation or for the purpose of obtaining professional advice. The privilege must be claimed by the client. And the lawyer can claim the privilege on behalf of his client once the latter has made an informed decision.

10 3 2 1 *Acting in a professional capacity* Whether an adviser is acting in her professional capacity will be a question of fact in each case. Although a strong inference can be drawn that this requirement has been fulfilled where a fee has been paid, the absence of such payment does not necessarily mean that an adviser was not acting in her professional capacity.[104] Hoffmann & Zeffertt[105] submit that the weight of legal opinion in England supports the view that salaried legal advisers (that is, those employed by corporations and statutory bodies) must also be considered as acting in a professional capacity for the purposes of legal professional privilege. Whether the South African courts will follow this approach remains an open question.

10 3 2 2 *The communication must be made in confidence* Whether a communication was made in confidence will always be a question of fact.[106] Confidentiality will usually be inferred where it is proved that a legal adviser was consulted in a professional capacity for the purpose of obtaining legal advice.[107] The inference of confidentiality will always be rebuttable, for example, where it is clear from the nature of the communication that it was intended to be communicated to the other party. In *Giovagnoli v Di Meo*[108] the court held that an instruction to an attorney to negotiate and effect a settlement was not privileged as it was clearly not confidential in that it was intended to be communicated to the other party.

10 3 2 3 *For the purpose of obtaining legal advice* If a communication is made in confidence, but not for the purpose of obtaining legal advice, it will not be privileged. For example, in *S v Kearney*[109] the director of a company was charged with numerous counts of theft. The admissibility of a statement that he had made

---

[103] See also *Sasol III (Edms) Bpk v Minister van Wet en Order* 1991 3 SA 766 (T); *Waymark NO v Commercial Union Assurance Co Ltd* 1992 3 SA 779 (Tk). See also generally Allan "Legal Privilege and the Principle of Fairness in the Criminal Trial" 1987 *Crim LR* 449.

[104] See *R v Fouche* 1953 1 SA 440 (W). The requirement of "professional capacity" is fully discussed by Van Niekerk, Van der Merwe & Van Wyk *Privilegies in die Bewysreg* 53–60.

[105] At 250–1.

[106] *Danzfuss v Additional Magistrate, Bloemfontein* 1981 1 SA 115 (O).

[107] *R v Fouche* 1953 1 SA 440 (W).

[108] 1960 3 SA 393 (D). See also *Resisto Dairy (Pty) Ltd v Auto Protection Insurance Co Ltd* 1962 2 SA 408 (C); *Euroshipping Corporation of Monrovia v Minister of Agricultural Economics and Marketing* 1979 1 SA 637 (C); *Kelly v Pickering (1)* 1980 2 SA 753 (R).

[109] 1964 2 SA 494 (A).

to an attorney acting on behalf of somebody else in a separate matter was disputed. The court found that this statement was a witness statement and had not been made for the purpose of seeking legal advice. As the client on whose behalf the attorney was acting had waived attorney–client privilege, the privilege could not be claimed by the accused.

Communications made between a legal adviser and her client, provided they are made for the purpose of obtaining legal advice, need not be connected to actual or pending litigation for privilege to attach to them. However, before statements taken from agents or independent third parties will be treated as privileged they must have been made in connection with contemplated litigation.[110]

Legal professional privilege will not be upheld if legal advice is sought so as to further a criminal purpose.[111]

10 3 2 4 *The client must claim the privilege* The privilege attaches to the client and it must be claimed by the client. The court will not uphold the privilege in the absence of a claim of privilege. Hoffmann & Zeffertt state:[112]

> "An attorney, when asked to disclose a privileged communication, is entitled, and in fact under a duty to claim privilege on his client's behalf, but he does this as agent for the client in the litigation and not as maker of the statement. If the client is present and indicates that he will not claim the privilege, the attorney cannot refuse to answer."

10 3 3 The scope of the rule Where a client gives evidence in respect of facts that have not been put to the opposing witnesses she may be asked whether she told her legal advisers about those facts, but she may not be asked what she told them.[113]

In *S v Mushimba*[114] the court held that legal professional privilege extended to interpreters, articled clerks, secretaries and other employees in a law firm. The privilege also applies to intermediaries who are used to convey communications by the client or adviser.[115]

However, where communications are made between the adviser/client and a third party privilege can only be claimed if: (i) the communication was made for the purpose of being submitted to a legal adviser and (ii) the communication was made after litigation was contemplated.[116] In *General Accident, Fire and Life Assurance Corporation Ltd v Goldberg*[117] an insured made a claim upon a policy of fire insurance and an assessor was appointed by the insurance company to investigate and advise whether the claimant should be paid out. The company, in claiming privilege in respect of the assessor's report, alleged that it was

---

[110] *General Accident, Fire and Life Assurance Corporation v Goldberg* 1912 TPD 494.
[111] *R v Smith* 1914–1915 All ER 262.
[112] At 254.
[113] See, e g, *S v Nkata* 1990 4 SA 250 (A).
[114] 1977 2 SA 829 (A).
[115] See Hoffmann & Zeffertt 249.
[116] *General Accident, Fire and Life Assurance Corporation Ltd* supra. See also *Potter v South British Insurance Co Ltd* 1963 3 SA 5 (W); *Bagwandeen v City of Pietermaritzburg* 1977 3 SA 727 (N); *Tshikomba v Mutual & Federal Insurance Co Ltd* 1995 2 SA 124 (T).
[117] Supra.

required for the purpose of submitting it "if necessary" to the company's attorneys. The court refused to uphold the privilege on the basis that neither of the abovementioned requirements had been fulfilled. Mason J stated the following with reference to the requirement that litigation must be contemplated:[118]

> "With reference to the first point, whether the report was made in contemplation of litigation, I do not think that the circumstances in this case, as alleged by the affidavit on behalf of the company, show that litigation was contemplated. It is not a question whether a man is very nervous or suspicious that there may be litigation, and that if he is so nervous and suspicious he is to be protected in respect of a document, whereas if he is not nervous and suspicious he is not to be protected. There must be really some contemplated litigation, some fact to indicate that litigation is likely or probable. It must not be a mere possibility which there is nothing to lead one to believe would be converted into reality according to the facts of the case."

A distinction is made between statements from agents and from independent third parties in that an agent can be prevented from disclosing the contents of a statement whilst an independent third party wishing to disclose what he said cannot be prevented from doing so.[119]

Where another person gains knowledge of a privileged communication, or possession of a privileged document, its disclosure cannot be prevented. However, if such knowledge or possession came about as a result of some unlawful act, it is possible that a court may refuse admission of such evidence on the basis of its discretion to exclude unfairly obtained evidence.[120]

In the past some South African courts have held that legal professional privilege does not prevent documents falling under this privilege from being seized by the police under a valid search warrant.[121] However, the correctness of these past decisions has fallen to be contested in view of the Appellate Division's recognition in *S v Safatsa* supra that legal professional privilege is a fundamental right that is essential for the proper functioning of the legal system. In *Bogoshi v Van Vuuren NO; Bogoshi v Director, OSEO*[122] the Appellate Division, accepting that legal professional privilege is a fundamental right, held that ordinarily the privilege can be claimed to prevent seizure by warrant of a privileged document.[123] Whether the breach of an accused's legal professional privilege constitutes an unjustifiable infringement of the constitutional right to a fair trial will depend on the nature of the breach and the circumstances in which it occurred.[124]

---

[118] At 504.

[119] See *S v Mnyaka* 1990 4 SA 299 (E).

[120] See Hoffmann & Zeffertt 257–8. Hoffmann & Zeffertt's submission that it is doubtful that such a discretion would exist in a civil cases must be reviewed in the light of *Shell SA (Edms) Bpk v Voorsitter, Dorperaad van die Oranje-Vrystaat* 1992 1 SA 906 (O), in which the court held that the judicial discretion to exclude improperly obtained evidence in a criminal case also exists in civil proceedings. See also *S v Hammer* 1994 2 SA 496 (C) and in § 5 4 n 50 above.

[121] *Andresen v Minister of Justice* 1954 2 SA 473 (W); *Mandela v Minister of Prisons* 1983 1 SA 938 (A). See also generally Haysom 1981 *SACC* 176; Cameron & Van Zyl Smit 1983 *ASSAL* 521; Unterhalter 1986 *SAJHR* 312 328.

[122] 1996 1 SA 785 (A). See also *Sasol III (Edms) Bpk v Minister van Wet en Orde & 'n ander* 1991 3 SA 766 (T).

[123] However, the claim of privilege failed as it had not been claimed in the interests of the client but in the appellants' (who were attorneys) own interest.

[124] *Klein v Attorney-General* 1995 2 SACR 210 (W). See also *S v Nkata* 1990 4 SA 250 (A); *S v Mushimba* 1977 2 SA 829 (A).

Section 23 of the interim Constitution provides that "[e]very person shall have the right of access to all information held by the state . . . in so far as such information is required for exercise or protection of his or her rights". In *Jeeva v Receiver of Revenue, Port Elizabeth*[125] an application was brought in terms of s 23 for an order that the receiver of revenue give the applicant access to certain information in its possession. The court ordered that all the requested information be disclosed except that information which was covered by legal professional privilege. The court held that legal professional privilege was a reasonable and justifiable limitation[126] on the applicant's right of access to information in terms of s 23.[127]

10 3 4 Waiver Legal professional privilege may be waived by a client. This may be done expressly or impliedly. For example, waiver may be implied when a client discloses privileged information. In *Ex parte Minister of Justice: In re S v Wagner*[128] Rumpff CJ held that an implied waiver involves

> "an element of publication of the document or part of it which can serve as a ground for the inference that the litigant or prosecutor no longer wishes to keep the contents of the document a secret".

In determining whether privilege has been impliedly waived the courts will have regard to the requirements of fairness and consistency.[129]

10 3 5 Refreshing memory in the witness-box In both civil and criminal trials the privilege attaching to a witness's statements is treated as separate from legal professional privilege. The rationale is that the distinction is necessary to protect the person who is unrepresented. However, as these two privileges overlap and are in many aspects very similar, they are for reasons of convenience dealt with under legal professional privilege.

The privilege pertaining to a witness's statement falls away when a witness uses a document to refresh her memory in the witness box. The privilege is not disturbed if witnesses refresh their memory whilst out of the witness-box;[130] and the privilege will not be lost where witnesses refresh their memory during an adjournment.[131] However, if the court is of the view that the witness has no independent recollection and has merely memorized the contents of the document, then the document must be produced.[132]

One basis for distinguishing between refreshing memory in and out of the

---

[125] 1995 2 SA 433 (SE).

[126] In terms of s 33(1) of the interim Constitution.

[127] At 453C–457B.

[128] 1965 4 SA 507 (A) 514. See also generally *S v Fourie* 1972 1 SA 341 (T); *Msimang v Durban City Council* 1972 4 SA 333 (D) 338F.

[129] *S v Boesman* 1990 2 SACR 389 (E); *Peacock v SA Eagle Insurance Co Ltd* 1991 1 SA 589 (C). See also *S v Nhlapo* 1988 3 SA 481 (T), in which, following the defence's express waiver in respect of one page of a statement, the court held that there had been an implied waiver of the document. See Unterhalter 1988 *ASSAL* 449 for a criticism of this decision.

[130] See *Ex parte Minister of Justice: In re S v Wagner* supra.

[131] *Van den Berg v Streeklanddros, Vanderbijlpark* 1985 3 SA 960 (T); *S v Tshomi* 1983 1 SA 1159 (C).

[132] *Van den Berg v Streeklanddros, Vanderbijlpark* supra. See further § 24 3 below.

witness-box is that waiver of privilege cannot be implied unless there is some element of publication. This occurs when the document is used whilst the witness is testifying in court, but not when it is used out of court.[133] The consequences of refreshing of memory from a privileged document are dealt with in ch 24 below.

10 4 OTHER PROFESSIONAL PRIVILEGES?

Professional privilege pertains only to the lawyer–client relationship and is not enjoyed by other professional relationships,[134] although bankers do have a limited privilege in that they need not produce their books unless ordered to do so by the court.[135] Privilege is not accorded to the doctor–patient relationship;[136] however, where an accused has been referred for mental observation, any statement made by her at such an inquiry will be inadmissible in criminal proceedings, "except to the extent to which it may be relevant to the determination" of her "mental condition".[137]

Priests,[138] insurers[139] and accountants[140] do not enjoy this privilege. Journalist can be compelled to disclose the sources of their information.[141] However, it would appear that some relief is available to these professionals if they can establish that they have a "just excuse" for not testifying.[142]

It is also arguable that certain professional communications may be protected from disclosure by the constitutional right to privacy. Section 13 of the interim Constitution provides:

"Every person shall have the right to his or her personal privacy, which shall include the right not to be subject to searches of his or her person, home or property, the seizure of private possessions or the violation of private communications."

For example, a communication between doctor and patient may well be regarded as a personal and private communication, and where the state seeks to compel disclosure of such a communication, privilege may be claimed on the basis of s 13. However, that privilege may be denied if the state is able to establish that the requirements of the limitations clause have been met.[143]

10 5 MARITAL PRIVILEGE

Spouses are entitled to refuse to disclose communications from the other spouse

---

[133] See *S v Tshomi* supra; *S v Toka* 1990 2 SA 225 (T).

[134] See, for example, *Trust Sentrum (Kaapstad) (Edms) Bpk v Zevenburg* 1989 1 SA 145 (C).

[135] Section 236(4) of the CPA, s 31 of the CPEA.

[136] *Botha v Botha* 1972 2 SA 559 (N); *Davis v Additional Magistrate, Johannesburg* 1989 4 SA 299 (W).

[137] See ss 77, 78 and 79 of the CPA, and especially s 79(7).

[138] *Smit v Van Niekerk* 1976 4 SA 293 (A); *S v B* 1980 2 SA 946 (A).

[139] *Howe v Mabuya* 1961 2 SA 635 (D).

[140] *Chantrey Martin v Martin* 1953 2 All ER 691.

[141] *S v Pogrund* 1961 3 SA 868 (T); *S v Cornelissen; Cornelissen v Zeelie NO* 1994 2 SACR 41 (W), in which the court, whilst holding that there was no legally recognized privilege giving journalists immunity from testifying, held that in the circumstances of the case the journalist had a just excuse for not testifying.

[142] See *Cornelissen* supra.

[143] Section 33 of Act 200 of 1993.

made during the marriage.[144] This privilege is founded on the notion that public opinion would find it unacceptable if spouses could be forced to disclose communications received from each other.[145]

There appear to be two requirements for the existence of the privilege: (1) the communication must have been made whilst the spouses were married, the privilege persisting after divorce with regard to communications made whilst the couple were still married;[146] (2) the persons must not be married in terms of customary law.[147] There can be little doubt that the second requirement will not survive a constitutional challenge under the equality clause.[148]

In terms of s 199 of the CPA each spouse may refuse to answer a question which the other spouse could not have been compelled to answer.[149] However, should the spouse who received the communication wish to disclose it, there is nothing the other spouse can do to prevent such disclosure, since marital privilege can only be claimed by the spouse to whom the communication is made. The traditionally accepted view is that a third person who hears or intercepts the communication cannot be prevented from disclosing it.[150] This common-law approach may well be challenged on the basis that it infringes the constitutional right to privacy.[151]

10 6   PARENT–CHILD PRIVILEGE

Section 192 of the CPA[152] makes it clear that parents/guardians can be compelled to testify against their children/wards and vice versa. Our courts do not recognize a privilege pertaining to communications between parent and child. The absence of privilege prevails even where the parent attends criminal proceedings in order to provide assistance to a child in terms of s 73(3) of the CPA.

There can be no doubt that an argument can be made that where parents attend criminal proceedings in order to assist their children, public policy militates against those very same parents being compelled to testify against their children. In *S v M*[153] the Appellate Division held that s 73(1) and 73(2) of the CPA, read together, conferred a right upon a child to be assisted by a parent or guardian as from the time of the child's arrest, in the same way as an adult would be entitled to the assistance of a legal adviser. From this equation of parental

---

[144] See s 198 of the CPA and s 10 of the CPEA.
[145] Hoffmann & Zeffertt 244.
[146] See s 198(2) of the CPA and s 10(2) of the CPEA. However, the privilege cannot be claimed by widows or widowers.
[147] See s 195(2) of the CPA. In *S v Johardien* 1990 1 SA 1026 (C) the court held that a woman who was married by Muslim rites was not entitled to invoke marital privilege.
[148] Section 8 of the interim Constitution.
[149] Hoffmann & Zeffertt 245 state: "It has been suggested that the privilege not to answer questions which tend to incriminate the other spouse must be regarded as excluded by implication in those cases in which one spouse is a compellable witness in a prosecution against the other."
[150] See *Rumping v DPP* 1962 3 All ER 256.
[151] Section 13 of the interim Constitution. See generally *S v Hammer* 1994 2 SACR 496 (C) as discussed in n 155 below.
[152] Read together with s 206 of the CPA.
[153] 1993 2 SACR 487 (A).

assistance with the assistance of a legal adviser follows the logical inference that parent–child communications in this context should be afforded the same privilege as communications made between legal adviser and client.

However, even where a parent does not appear to assist the child there may well be constitutional grounds for holding that communications between parent and child are privileged. In the United States the courts have recognized that confidential communications between children and their parents, guardians or other caretakers are privileged from disclosure on the basis of the constitutional right to privacy.[154] It is submitted that s 13 of the interim Constitution, which guarantees the right to privacy, is susceptible to a similar interpretation.[155]

[154] *In re A & M* 61 AD 2d 426, 403 NYS 2d 375 (1978); *People v Fitzgerald* 101 Misc 2d 712, 422 NYS 2d 309.
[155] See Van Dokkum 1994 *SACJ* 213. Article 2(21) of the African National Congress' draft Bill of Rights gave recognition to parent–child privilege. See also *S v Hammer* 1994 2 SA 496 (C), in which an 18-year-old accused, whilst in police custody, after receiving permission to write a letter to his mother, asked a member of the South African Police Services to deliver the letter to his mother. The policeman, instead of delivering the letter, read it and handed it over to the prosecution. Although the court did not base its decision on the constitutional right to privacy, it found the evidence to be inadmissible in that it had been improperly obtained. The court found that the policeman had in all probability committed an *injuria* against the accused, that he had acted unlawfully and immorally in reading and handing the letter over to the Attorney-General, and that this was a serious and deliberate breach of the accused's common-law right to privacy. The court concluded that the evidence was to be excluded as it had been unfairly obtained and to admit it would bring the administration of justice into disrepute.

CHAPTER 11

STATE PRIVILEGE*

S E van der Merwe

11 1 INTRODUCTION

This chapter largely concerns the exclusion of evidence which, if admitted, would prejudicially affect the security of the state, the public interest, or the efficient detection of crime.[1] The evidence is excluded despite its relevance and irrespective of the extreme probative value it may have. Relevance is not the test. The rationale for excluding such evidence is that its reception would be contrary to public policy.[2] There are categories of evidence which may be excluded on grounds of public policy.[3]

The governing provision concerning the exclusion of such evidence in criminal proceedings is s 202 of the CPA. The effect of this section is that, except where otherwise provided by the CPA or any other law, no witness may be compelled or permitted to give evidence as to any fact, matter or thing, or as to any communication made to him, if he would not have been compelled or permitted to do so on 30 May 1961 on the ground of public policy or with regard to the public interest. There is a proviso, however, to the effect that any person may in criminal proceedings adduce evidence of any communication alleging the commission of an offence if the making of that communication *prima facie* constitutes

---

* §§ 11 1–11 4 2 of this chapter were originally written by Prof A P Paizes, School of Law, University of the Witwatersrand, and published as ch 12 in Van der Merwe (ed) *Evidence* (1983) 147–156 and later in Du Toit et al *Commentary on the Criminal Procedure Act* (1987, as revised). Prof Paizes' kind permission to retain his original text for purposes of the present book is appreciated. Of course, the present author carries responsibility for amendments, updating, style, and ultimate accuracy of the contents.

[1] See generally Van Niekerk, Van der Merwe & Van Wyk *Privilegies in die Bewysreg* (1984) 240–74.

[2] *Minister van Justisie v Alexander* 1975 4 SA 530 (A) 544–5.

[3] Hoffmann & Zeffertt 268. It is against public policy that discussions and deliberations between a presiding officer and his assessors be disclosed. See *S v Baleka & others (4)* 1988 4 SA 688 (T).

an offence,[4] that is, if such communication amounted to criminal *iniuria*, criminal defamation, treason, statutory treason, or perjury. It is for the presiding judge or judicial officer to decide whether such communication *prima facie* constitutes an offence.

The effect of s 202 is to apply the English law on this topic as it was on 30 May 1961. The same effect has been achieved in civil proceedings by s 42 of the CPEA.[5] As regards evidence which affects the security of the state, however, the law has been modified by s 66 of the Internal Security Act 74 of 1982.[6]

It is important, at the outset, to note some differences between private and state privilege.[7] Whereas secondary or circumstantial evidence is admissible to prove a matter which is protected in terms of private privilege, such evidence is generally inadmissible in respect of state privilege.[8] Further, whereas the court may in appropriate circumstances enforce state privilege *mero motu*,[9] private privilege must be claimed. And finally, whereas private privilege can be waived, it seems that state privilege may be waived only on the clear authority of the ministerial head of a department.[10]

11 2   STATE SECURITY

Section 66(1) of the Internal Security Act 74 of 1982, which repeals but substantially reincorporates the provisions of s 25(1) of the General Law Amendment Act 102 of 1972, reads as follows:

> "Notwithstanding anything to the contrary in any law or the common law contained, no person shall be compelled and no person shall be permitted or ordered to give evidence or to furnish any information in any proceedings in any court of law or before any body or institution established by or under any law or before any commission as contemplated in the Commissions Act, 1947 (Act No 8 of 1947), as to any fact, matter or thing or as to any communication made to or by such person, and no book or document shall be produced in any such proceedings, if an affidavit purporting to have been signed by the Minister responsible in respect of such fact, matter, thing, communication, book or document, or, in the case of a provincial administration, the Administrator concerned, is produced to the court of law, body, institution or commission concerned, to the effect that the said Minister or Administrator, as the case may be, has personally considered the said fact, matter, thing, communication, book or document, that, in his opinion, it affects the security of the State and that disclosure thereof will, in his opinion, prejudicially affect the security of the State."

---

[4] See generally *S v Gcali* 1992 1 SACR 372 (Tk) 378*b–c*.

[5] See § 3 4 above.

[6] See §§ 11 2 and 11 3 below. See also generally s 12(6)*(b)* of the Drugs and Drug Trafficking Act 140 of 1992 and s 23(5) of the Criminal Law Second Amendment Act 126 of 1992. State privilege clearly raises constitutional issues. In terms of s 23 of the interim Constitution every person shall have the right of access to all information held by the state or any of its organs at any level of government in so far as such information is required for the exercise or protection of his or her rights. See also n 11 below as regards the constitutionality of the procedure contained in s 66(1) of the Internal Security Act 74 of 1982. See also generally *Jeeva v Receiver of Revenue, Port Elizabeth* 1995 2 SA 433 (SE).

[7] See Schmidt 537.

[8] *Redelinghuys v Geidel* 1963 2 SA 274 (W); *Ministry of Community Development v Saloojee* 1963 4 SA 65 (T).

[9] See *Conway v Rimmer* 1968 1 All ER 874; *Van der Linde v Calitz* 1967 2 SA 239 (A).

[10] *Nyangeni v Minister of Bantu Administration and Development* 1961 1 SA 547 (E).

This section removes any uncertainty there might have been at common law by making it clear that the minister's affidavit is final and may not be questioned by the court. It must be noted, however, that s 66(1) deals *only* with matters concerning the security of the state; the other grounds of public interest are dealt with in s 66(2).

Only the political head is competent to avail himself of s 66(1). No authorized person may act on his behalf; and if the affidavit satisfies the statutory requirements, then the court has no right to examine the evidence itself, and the matter must be decided without the help of such evidence. Ousting the court's jurisdiction is, however, unconstitutional.[11]

11 3   PUBLIC INTEREST

Section 66(2) of the Internal Security Act 74 of 1982 provides as follows:

> "The provisions of subsection (1) shall not derogate from the provisions of any law or of the common law which do not compel or permit any person to give evidence or to furnish any information in any proceedings in any court of law or before any body or institution established by or under any law or before any commission as contemplated in the Commissions Act, 1947, as to any fact, matter or thing or as to any communication made to or by such person, or to produce any book or document, in connection with any matter other than a matter affecting the security of the State."

The effect of this subsection, read with s 202 of the CPA and s 42 of the CPEA, is that the common law, or the English law as it applied on 30 May 1961, governs those areas of the subject not covered by statute. This includes objection to the disclosure of evidence on grounds of public policy that do not concern the security of the state.[12]

---

[11] Van Wyk et al (eds) *Rights and Constitutionalism: The New South African Legal Order* (1994) 431 point out that the effective ousting of the court's jurisdiction (in terms of s 66(1) of the Internal Security Act 74 of 1982) is unconstitutional "and once it is established that the information is necessary to enable a person to exercise or protect her rights [in terms of s 23 of the interim Constitution] the minister will have a very onerous task establishing that the privilege claimed is reasonable and necessary". The right to have justiciable disputes settled by a court of law is contained in s 22 of the interim Constitution.

[12] According to the common law, a court may of its own accord exclude evidence prejudicial to the public interest (see *Van der Linde v Calitz* supra). In addition, it is open to the executive to object to the reception of such evidence, in which case the responsible political head must make his objection in proper form (see *Van der Linde v Calitz* supra 260). In order to make such objection the political head must either attend court in person or submit an affidavit, from which it must appear that he has himself read and considered each item of evidence in question and is of the opinion that the disclosure of this evidence would be contrary to the public interest (see *Van der Linde v Calitz* supra 260). He should also give reasons for his opinion as fully as is possible without defeating the purpose of the privilege (see *Van der Linde v Calitz* supra 260). The political head may object to the reception of oral evidence as well as documents, but he would probably have to state clearly in his affidavit what matters are considered contrary to public policy, and his representative at the trial would have to object to specific questions related to these matters. The *effect* of such an objection has been settled, after some uncertainty (see *Duncan v Cammell Laird and Co Ltd* 1942 1 All ER 587), by the decisions in *Van der Linde v Calitz* supra and *Conway v Rimmer* 1968 1 All ER 874. In the last two cases it was held that at common law the courts have a residual power to overrule a properly tendered objection where they are satisfied that the objection is unjustifiable or cannot be sustained on any reasonable grounds, and that the court itself is in a position to examine the relevant evidence and reach a decision (see *Van der Linde v Calitz* supra 260). In *Van der Linde v Calitz* supra 259 Steyn CJ warned, however, that this residual power must be exercised with strict circumspection, and pointed out the gravity of overruling an objection where the court is not normally aware of all the considerations on which the political head's opinion is founded. If the court feels that the reasons for the opinion are not sufficiently

11 4 THE DETECTION OF CRIME

In order to promote the efficient detection of crime a privilege has arisen to protect communications which would tend to reveal the identity of an informer or which would otherwise expose the channels of communication of a crime, such as communications between officials in the course of an investigation. This privilege, being an aspect of state privilege, is governed by s 202 of the CPA, and accordingly rests for its authority on English law.[13] The rationale underlying this principle is reflected by the following remarks of Solomon J:[14] "The whole business of crime is conducted in secret and devious ways against the interests of the state, and the work of defeating the operations of criminals must also be conducted, obviously, by similar methods."

11 4 1 Communications tending to expose the methods used to investigate crimes[15]
In *R v Abelson*[16] the accused was charged with contravening a Liquor Act. He called as a witness the divisional criminal investigation officer for the Witwatersrand, who, when asked to produce certain reports made to him by two detectives concerning the charges, refused on the ground that such reports were confidential. The court upheld the claim of privilege, holding that the disclosure of the evidence would be contrary to public policy as it would lay bare to the public the methods used by the police to control the liquor traffic. And in *S v Peake*,[17] where the police had used a tape recorder to record a conversation, the court disallowed cross-examination relating to the manner in which the recording had been obtained, even though the recording itself was admissible evidence. Of course, in our present constitutionalized system courts will have to be careful to ensure that any claim to privilege concerning methods of investigation is not merely an attempt to cover up the fact that evidence was unconstitutionally obtained. Evidence of conversations which were unlawfully recorded (and thus in breach of the right to privacy) should be excluded.[18]

---

convincing, it may call upon him to elaborate on or clarify such reasons by way of either oral evidence or a further affidavit (*Van der Linde v Calitz* supra 262). The common-law procedure, however, is confined to spheres of public interest other than the security of the state because s 66(1) of the Internal Security Act 74 of 1982 provides expressly that the political head's properly raised objection, where the security of the state is concerned, is final in the sense that the court cannot overrule it. But see n 11 above as regards the constitutionality of s 66(1).

[13] One of the most important English decisions in this regard is *Marks v Beyfus* 1890 25 QBD 494.

[14] *R v Abelson* 1933 TPD 227 231.

[15] See also generally Van Niekerk, Van der Merwe & Van Wyk *Privilegies in die Bewysreg* 270–4. At 271 the authors point out that the purpose of the privilege which arises in this regard is not to protect the police, but to ensure that their sources of information concerning crime and their methods of investigation are protected: "Die reg moet enersyds sorg dra dat die polisie nie hul funksies en aktiwiteite verrig op 'n heimlike wyse wat nadelig kan wees vir die breër belange van die regspleging nie, maar andersyds dat hulle in die uitvoering van hul pligte nie só gekortwiek word dat die breër belange van die regspleging benadeel word nie."

[16] 1933 TPD 227.

[17] 1962 4 SA 288 (C).

[18] See generally ch 12 below.

11 4 2 Communications tending to reveal the identity of an informer[19]   There are at least three reasons for the so-called "informer's privilege": *(a)* to protect the informer and his family from those against whom he informs; *(b)* to ensure that the informer can be used in future; and *(c)* to encourage the public to come forward with information about crimes. The rule, accordingly, is that no question may be asked and no document may be received in evidence that would tend to reveal the identity of an informer or the content of the information supplied by him, and there is a *duty* on the court to ensure that this privilege is upheld regardless of whether or not the parties to the litigation claim it.[20]

After a period in our law when, owing to different procedures regarding prosecutions in South Africa and England, our courts adopted a more stringent practice of exclusion, it was settled in *Ex parte Minister of Justice: Re R v Pillay* that the privilege should only operate[21]

" . . . when public policy requires the name of the informer or his information to be kept secret, because of some confidential relationship between the state and the informer, or because the state desires its sources of information to be kept secret for the reason that the informer's information relates to matters in respect of which he might not inform if he were not protected, or for the reason that the candour and completeness of his communications might be prejudiced if he were not protected, or for some other good reason. To give a comprehensive definition which will include all such cases would be impossible."

The learned Chief Justice then gave examples of instances where the rule could appropriately be relaxed: *(a)* when it is material to the ends of justice; *(b)* if it is necessary or right to do so to show the accused's innocence; and *(c)* when the reason for secrecy no longer exists, for example, when the identity of the informer is known.[22]

It seems to have been a subject of controversy in our law whether this privilege

---

[19] Who is an "informer" for purposes of this privilege? In *R v Van Schalkwyk* 1939 AD 543 548 Stratford CJ observed that while no definition has been authoritatively laid down in the English cases, these cases "seem to lay down that any person who gives information to the authorities of the commission of a crime, or information which leads to the detection of a crime, is one who, in the public interest, ought to be protected. In other words, anyone who gives useful information about the commission of a crime and needs protection against those who may suffer from his disclosures, should get that protection so as to encourage these disclosures." Accordingly, not every person who makes a statement to the police in connection with a prosecution may claim this privilege, but only informers properly so called, whose identity must be kept secret in the public interest (*Scheepers v S* 1971 2 PH H101 (NC)). A person who has laid a charge is normally regarded as an informer (*R v Olifant* 1937 2 PH H191 (T)), except where he is the complainant in a charge relating to the person or property of an individual, in which case he would not need encouragement to lodge his complaint (*Naylor v Wheeler* 1947 2 SA 681 (D)). For the same reason, a person interrogated by the police when the accused has already been arrested is not an informer (*Attorney-General v Van Wyk* 1932 TPD 359 361). A policeman is not ordinarily an informer, as he requires no encouragement to disclose information (*Suliman v Hansa* supra); this may not be true, however, of a policeman who operates secretly or in disguise in order to procure information.

[20] *Tranter v Attorney-General* 1907 TS 415; Van Wyk in Ferreira *Strafproses in die Laer Howe* 2 ed (1979) 493.

[21] 1945 AD 653 658.

[22] See also *R v Van Schalkwyk* 1938 AD 543. The scope of the privilege was considered further in *Suliman v Hansa* 1971 4 SA 69 (D). Fannin J approved and applied the views of Wigmore para 2285 that the following four fundamental conditions must be satisfied to establish the privilege: "(1) The communications must originate in a *confidence* that they will not be disclosed; (2) This element of *confidentiality must be essential* to the full and satisfactory maintenance of the relation between the parties; (3) The *relation* must be one which in the opinion of the community ought to be sedulously *fostered*; and (4) The *injury* that would inure to the relation by the disclosure of the communications must be *greater than the benefit* thereby gained for the correct disposal of litigation."

may be waived, and, if it can, in what circumstances. It has been held that the protection afforded an informer is a matter of public policy and cannot be waived.[23] This view was also taken by the court in *Natal Fertilizers Ltd v Van Dam*,[24] where Dove-Wilson JP held that the privilege would be upheld even if the informer were willing to divulge his identity in the witness-box; he would "be protected in spite of himself". And again, in *Robinson v Benson and Simpson*[25] the court emphasized that as the privilege did not pertain to the witness who was called, but rested on public policy, the court was "absolutely prohibited" from allowing such information to be disclosed. These views were, however, rejected by the Appellate Division in *R v Van Schalkwyk*,[26] where Stratford CJ approved the following approach laid down by Tatham J in *R v Harris*:[27]

> "The rule protecting an informer is based upon the theory that public policy requires his protection, because otherwise persons would be discouraged from giving information, but it is difficult to see how public policy is served by prohibiting him from himself disclosing the fact, indeed public interests would be ill-served in many cases if there were any such rule."

An important qualification to this principle was added, however, by Tatham J and endorsed in *R v Van Schalkwyk*:[28] if the dictates of public policy would require that the identity of the informer be kept secret, then, provided this is shown by the state, such evidence should be excluded notwithstanding the informer's willingness to disclose his identity.[29]

The informer's privilege should as a rule also apply for purposes of any civil action[30] which might stem from the police investigation.

11 4 3 Extension of the informer's privilege   In the English case *Blake and Austin v Director of Public Prosecutions*[31] the accused were convicted of indecent behaviour in a church yard in contravention of s 2 of Ecclesiastical Courts Jurisdiction Act of 1860. Two police officers had observed the activities of the accused from an observation post in neighbouring domestic premises. The court held that there was no reason why the precise location from which the observation had been made had to be disclosed: there is no essential difference between informers and the providers of observations posts, who both in different ways provide the police with indispensable assistance in the prevention of crime. There does not seem to be any South African decision on this very point. There is, however, ample

---

[23] *R v Olifant* 1937 2 PH H191 (T). Cf generally *S v Rossouw* 1973 4 SA 608 (SWA).
[24] 1922 NPD 157 162.
[25] 1918 WLD 1 4–5.
[26] 1938 AD 543 553–5.
[27] 1927 NPD 330 345.
[28] Supra 554–5.
[29] Hoffmann & Zeffertt 276–7.
[30] *Marais v Lombard* 1958 4 SA 224 (E) 231A. See also Van Niekerk, Van der Merwe & Van Wyk *Privilegies in die Bewysreg* 266–7.
[31] 1993 *Crim LR* 283.

English authority to support the decision in *Blake and Austin v Director of Public Prosecutions*.[32] It is submitted that these decisions should be followed in South Africa. After all, it is nothing else but the practical combination of the informer's privilege and the privilege which relates to police methods of investigation.

11 4 4   The constitutionality of the informer's privilege   In *McCray v Illinois*[33] an informer gave three police officers information that someone (M) was dealing in drugs. The informer accompanied the police in their vehicle to a street where M was talking to people. The informer pointed out M and then left on foot. When M spotted the police vehicle he hurriedly disappeared between two buildings. Two of the officers promptly arrested M on the basis that they had probable cause for an arrest and search without a warrant — the informer concerned was known to them as someone who had always furnished them with accurate information on drug dealers. Heroin was found on M. At a preliminary hearing defence counsel asked each of the officers to disclose the identity of the informer. In both instances the prosecution objected successfully. M eventually took the matter to the Supreme Court of the United States, claiming that his constitutional right to due process had been violated and that he was given no opportunity to confront and cross-examine the informer. The Supreme Court rejected M's argument and pointed out that there was no due process violation if the police had made the arrest and search in reliance upon facts furnished by an informer whom they had reason to trust: nothing in due process requires that a court must assume that the police were committing perjury. The informer was not a material witness. The Supreme Court distinguished M's case from *Roviaro v United States*,[34] which was decided a decade earlier. In the latter case the Supreme Court had confirmed that there could be no fixed rule as regards disclosure of the identity of an informer. A balance must be struck between the public interest and the right of the individual to prepare and present his defence. In *Roviario v United States* supra Burton J held that where the disclosure of the informer's identity — or disclosure of the contents of his communications — is relevant and helpful to the accused, the privilege must be lifted. On the facts in *Roviaro v United States* supra it was held that the trial court had erred in refusing disclosure of the identity of the informer concerned. The informer was with the accused when the alleged crime

---

[32] See generally *R v Rankine* 1986 *Crim LR* 464; *R v Brown & Daley* 1988 *Crim LR* 426; *R v Johnson* 1988 *Crim LR* 831, where certain guidelines were provided to police in obtaining observation posts; *R v Hewitt & Davis* 1992 *Crim LR* 650. In a commentary on the latter case DJB 1992 *Crim LR* 651 remarked as follows: "Two grounds are given for the rule about informers: first, the need to secure the informer's own safety, and secondly the desire to ensure that the supply of information does not dry up (see e g *Hennessey* (1978) 68 Cr App R 419). Both apply equally to the supplier of an observation post: in fact it could be argued that the need for protection on both grounds is greater, as *(a)* the supplier of an observation post may be an easier target for retaliation, particularly if it is the supplier's own home which has been used, and *(b)* where the need is to police a particular locality where crime is rife, the loss of an observation post may be an irreparable blow."

[33] 386 US 300 (1967).

[34] 353 US 53 (1957).

was committed and *could have been a material witness* on the issue whether the accused had knowingly transported the drugs as charged.[35]

The above two cases make it clear that the informer's privilege *per se* is not unconstitutional,[36] but that the constitutional right to a fair trial must be considered in deciding whether the privilege must give way. It is submitted that this approach merely confirms the common-law principles which govern the relaxation of the informer's privilege and which were set out in § 11 4 2 above.

11 5   THE POLICE DOCKET AND CONSTITUTIONAL PROVISIONS[37]

Prior to constitutionalization it was generally accepted that the state had some kind of "blanket docket privilege" in terms of which statements obtained for purposes of a criminal trial were as a rule privileged from disclosure[38] — in much the same way as parties in a civil dispute can claim privilege in respect of statements obtained from their respective witnesses.[39]

The prosecution's so-called docket privilege — which, as will be shown, has now shrunk drastically on account of constitutional provisions — was and is not really part of "state privilege" in the true sense of the word. In this work, however, it is dealt with in the context of state privilege because matters which fall under state privilege (the informer's privilege, state secrets, police methods of investigation) are now for all practical purposes the main (but most certainly not sole) grounds upon which the state can seek to withhold statements in the police docket. In the past all statements — other than a statement obtained from the accused[40] and certain documents such as an identification parade form[41] — could have been withheld simply because these statements were obtained for purposes of the criminal trial.[42] The "blanket docket privilege" — sometimes also referred to as "witness statement privilege" — did not survive Chapter 3 of the interim Constitution: it conflicted with the provisions of ss 23[43] and 25(3)[44] of the interim Constitution. After a spate of conflicting Supreme Court decisions

---

[35] See further Van Niekerk, Van der Merwe & Van Wyk *Privileges in die Bewysreg* 268–9 for a brief summary of the informer's privilege in the USA.

[36] This is also the clear implication of *Shabalala v Attorney-General of Transvaal & another* 1995 2 SACR 761 (CC) para [72] (subpara 5). See § 11 5 below.

[37] The pre-constitutional era as well as the post-constitutional era are discussed by Paizes in Du Toit et al *Commentary* 23-39 to 23-42N.

[38] *R v Steyn* 1954 1 SA 324 (A); Van Niekerk, Van der Merwe & Van Wyk *Privileges in die Bewysreg* 219–36.

[39] See generally *S v Yengeni & others* 1991 1 SACR 639 (C) and *International Tobacco Co (SA) Ltd v United Tobacco Co (South) Ltd (2)* 1953 3 SA 879 (W).

[40] See s 335 of the CPA. See also *S v Mpetha (1)* 1982 2 SA 253 (C) 259F.

[41] *S v Jija & others* 1991 2 SA 52 (E).

[42] *S v B* 1980 2 SA 964 (A).

[43] Section 23 of the interim Constitution provides as follows: "Every person shall have the right of access to all information held by the state or any of its organs at any level of government in so far as such information is required for the exercise or protection of any of his or her rights." This section was relied on in several Supreme Court decisions in which it was held that statements of state witnesses had to be handed over to the defence. These cases appear in n 52 of the Constitutional Court judgment in *Shabalala v Attorney-General of Transvaal & others* 1995 2 SACR 761 (CC) 775.

[44] This section provides for the right to a fair trial.

and several academic opinions,[45] the Constitutional Court finally resolved the matter in *Shabalala v Attorney-General of Transvaal & another* and made an order declaring that:[46]

> "1. The 'blanket docket privilege' expressed by the rule in *R v Steyn* 1954 (1) SA 324 (A) is inconsistent with the Constitution to the extent to which it protects from disclosure all the documents in a police docket, in all circumstances, regardless as to whether or not such disclosure is justified for the purposes of enabling the accused properly to exercise his or her right to a fair trial in terms of s 25(3).
>
> 2. The claim of the accused for access to documents in the police docket cannot be defeated merely on the grounds that such contents are protected by a blanket privilege in terms of the decision in *Steyn's* case.
>
> 3. Ordinarily an accused person should be entitled to have access to documents in the police docket which are exculpatory (or which are *prima facie* likely to be helpful to the defence) unless, in very rare cases, the State is able to justify the refusal of such access on the grounds that it is not justified for the purposes of a fair trial.
>
> 4. Ordinarily the right to a fair trial would include access to the statements of witnesses (whether or not the State intends to call such witnesses) and such of the contents of a police docket as are relevant in order to enable an accused person properly to exercise that right, but the prosecution may, in a particular case, be able to justify the denial of such access on the grounds that it is not justified for the purposes of a fair trial. This would depend on the circumstances of each case.
>
> 5. The State is entitled to resist a claim by the accused for access to any particular document in the police docket on the grounds that such access is not justified for the purposes of enabling the accused properly to exercise his or her right to a fair trial or on the ground that it has reason to believe that there is a reasonable risk that access to the relevant document would lead to the disclosure of the identity of an informer or State secrets or on the grounds that there was a reasonable risk that such disclosure might lead to the intimidation of witnesses or otherwise prejudice the proper ends of justice.
>
> 6. Even where the State has satisfied the Court that the denial of access to the relevant documents is justified on the grounds set out in paragraph 5 hereof, it does not follow that access to such statements, either then or subsequently, must necessarily be denied to the accused. The Court still retains a discretion. It should balance the degree of risk involved in attracting the potential prejudicial consequences for the proper ends of justice referred to in paragraph 5 (if such access is permitted) against the degree of the risk that a fair trial may not enure for the accused (if such access is denied). A ruling by the Court pursuant to this paragraph shall be an interlocutory ruling subject to further amendment, review or recall in the light of circumstances disclosed by the further course of the trial."

An important point to note in respect of the above Constitutional Court order is that it also fully accommodates s 22 of the interim Constitution, that is, the fundamental right to have justiciable disputes settled by a court of law. The court can now in all cases decide on the issue of disclosure — and it must exercise this discretion in the context of the constitutional right of the accused to a fair trial and such legitimate claims that the state may have, for example, state privilege and protection of witnesses from possible intimidation.

Closely linked to — and almost a natural or inevitable extension of — the

---

[45] See, e g, Schwikkard 1994 *SACJ* 323; Du Plessis 1994 *SACJ* 295; Meintjies-Van der Walt 1995 *SACJ* 127.
[46] Supra para [72] 790*c*–791*b*. The Constitutional Court did not rely on s 23, but on the right to a fair trial contained in s 25(3). See para [34] of the judgment.

former "blanket docket privilege" was the ethical rule of practice that the defence could not without the consent of the prosecution have had interviews with (potential) state witnesses.[47] In *Shabalala v Attorney-General of Transvaal & another* supra the Constitutional Court also addressed this matter by making the following order:[48]

> "1. Insofar and to the extent that the rule of practice pertaining to the right of an accused or his legal representative to consult with witnesses for the State prohibits such consultation without the permission of the prosecuting authority, in all cases and regardless of the circumstances, it is not consistent with the Constitution.
>
> 2. An accused person has a right to consult a State witness without prior permission of the prosecuting authority in circumstances where his or her right to a fair trial would be impaired, if, on the special facts of a particular case, the accused cannot properly obtain a fair trial without such consultation.
>
> 3. The accused or his or her legal representative should in such circumstances approach the Attorney-General or an official authorised by the Attorney-General for consent to hold such consultation. If such consent is granted the Attorney-General or such official shall be entitled to be present at such consultation and to record what transpires during the consultation. If the consent of the Attorney-General is refused the accused shall be entitled to approach the Court for such permission to consult the relevant witness.
>
> 4. The right referred to in paragraph 2 does not entitle an accused person to compel such consultation with a State witness:
>   (a) if such State witness declines to be so consulted; or
>   (b) if it is established on behalf of the State that it has reasonable grounds to believe such consultation might lead to the intimidation of the witness or a tampering with his or her evidence or that it might lead to the disclosure of State secrets or the identity of informers or that it might otherwise prejudice the proper ends of justice.
>
> 5. Even in the circumstances referred to in paragraph 4(b), the Court may, in the circumstances of a particular case, exercise a discretion to permit such consultation in the interest of justice subject to suitable safeguards."

Once again, it should be noted that the ultimate power to regulate the matter is in the hands of the court. The right to a fair trial governs the issue; and the constitutional right to have access to information held by the state was not the basis of the decision.

---

[47] See generally *S v Hassim & others* 1972 1 SA 200 (N).
[48] Supra para [72] 791*c–h*.

CHAPTER 12

UNCONSTITUTIONALLY OBTAINED EVIDENCE

P J Schwikkard and S E van der Merwe

12 1   INTRODUCTION

This chapter deals with the ambit of a court's discretion to exclude evidence obtained in breach of constitutionally guaranteed rights. However, before examining the relevant provisions of the interim and 1996 Constitutions, as well as the applicable case law, the interests that compete in defining the parameters of such a discretion must be considered.[1] In *Lawrie v Muir*[2] Lord Cooper described these competing interests in the following terms:

> "The law must strive to reconcile two highly important interests which are liable to come into conflict — *(a)* the interest of the citizen to be protected from illegal or irregular invasion of his liberties by the authorities, and *(b)* the interest of the state to secure that evidence bearing upon the commission of crime and necessary to enable justice to be done shall not be withheld from courts of law on any mere formal or technical grounds."

Depending on what weight is accorded to these respective interests the courts may choose between favouring an inclusionary or exclusionary approach. In terms of the inclusionary rule all relevant evidence should be admitted no matter

---

[1] See Van der Merwe 1992 *Stell LR* 175 for extensive references to both local and international materials. §§ 12 1–12 5 of this chapter are based on his article.
[2] 1959 Scots LT 37 39–40.

how it was obtained. The exclusionary rule demands that unconstitutionally obtained evidence be excluded despite its relevance.

The present chapter is confined to the criminal justice system. The exclusion of unlawfully obtained evidence in civil cases was dealt with in § 5 4 above.

12 2   THE RATIONALE OF THE INCLUSIONARY RULE

The argument in favour of the inclusionary rule is essentially pragmatic and expedient. It runs along the following lines:

— The end justifies the means.[3]
— Two wrongs do not make a right.[4]
— The probative value of evidence is not impaired by unlawful methods employed in acquiring such evidence,[5] and the relevance of such evidence cannot be affected by the mere fact that it was unlawfully procured.
— The exclusionary rule necessarily requires an investigation and adjudication of collateral issues, shifting the focus of the trial from an enquiry into the guilt or innocence of the accused to an enquiry into the conduct of the police. The true issues get blurred.[6]
— There are sufficient (other) remedies available to an accused whose constitutional or common-law rights have been violated.[7]
— Policing is a social service aimed at protecting society and, for purposes of effective law enforcement, society must of necessity tolerate illegal police conduct.
— The deterrent effect of an exclusionary rule is minimal.[8]
— It is not the function (purpose) of the law of evidence to deter illegal police conduct and the rules of evidence were never meant to promote "an indirect form of punishment".[9]

---

[3] The following dissenting judgment of Brandeis J in *Olmstead v United States* 277 US 438 485 (1928) provides clear grounds for rejecting this argument: "Decency, security, and liberty alike demand that government officials shall be subjected to the same rules of conduct that are commands to the citizen. In a government of laws the existence of the government will be imperiled if it fails to observe the law scrupulously. Our government is the potent, the omnipresent, teacher. For good or for ill, it teaches the whole people by its example. Crime is contagious. If the government becomes a lawbreaker, it breeds contempt for the law; it invites every man to become a law unto himself; it invites anarchy. To declare that in the administration of the criminal law the end justifies the means — to declare that the government may commit crimes to secure the conviction of a private criminal — would bring terrible retribution. Against that pernicious doctrine this court should resolutely set its face."

[4] Wigmore paras 2183 and 2184.

[5] Schlesinger *Exclusionary Injustice: The Problem of Illegally Obtained Evidence* (1977) 62.

[6] See generally Peiris "The Admissibility of Evidence Obtained Illegally: A Comparative Analysis" (1981) 13 Ottawa LR 309 343.

[7] See *People v Defore* 150 NE 585 (1926); *Wolf v Colorado* 338 US 25 (1949); Shanks "Comparative Analysis of the Exclusionary Rule and it's Alternatives" 1983 57 *Tulane LR* 648. But see §§ 12 3 2 and 12 3 4 below for a counter-argument. See also *Brinegar v United States* 338 US 160 173 (1949); *Mapp v Ohio* 367 US 643 (1961); Traynor "*Mapp v Ohio* at Large in the 50 States" 1962 *Duke LJ* 319.

[8] Schlesinger *Exclusionary Injustice* 61; Peterson "Restrictions in the Law of Search and Seizure" 1958 52 *Northwestern Univ LR* 46 55.

[9] Wigmore para 2183.

— The exclusionary rule "protects" only the guilty from conviction.[10]
— Criminals do not impose restrictions upon themselves in their choice of weapons; why should the police?[11]
— The exclusionary rule frustrates or hampers effective policing in an age of rising crime rates.[12]
— An exclusionary rule puts it in the power of any police official to frustrate the judicial process: he can, through his unlawful conduct, control the volume of evidence available to the prosecution at the trial; and he can in this way also determine, almost in advance, what evidence a court may or may not receive.[13]
— Public policy considerations do not militate against the admission of unlawfully obtained evidence.[14]
— A court that excludes unlawfully obtained evidence might in effect be condoning the unlawful acts of the accused.[15] If this is not the actual effect of the exclusionary rule, then it is at least the citizen's perception of the rule.[16] And it is undesirable that a criminal justice system should be held in disrespect by the public at large.
— An exclusionary rule may, according to Schlesinger, have the "perverse and unintended" result of limiting the ambit of fundamental rights: judges who are required to apply an exclusionary rule might give an extensive interpretation to probable cause "in order to admit crucial evidence".[17]
— A (rigid) exclusionary rule allows no room for "proportionality", that is, an approach in terms of which a court should at least have a discretion to determine the question of evidential admissibility by comparing the gravity

---

[10] This criticism of the exclusionary rule can be rejected on the basis that it views the rule solely from the angle of the "guilty". Dworkin "Fact Style Adjudication and the Fourth Amendment: The Limits of Lawyering" 1973 48 *Indiana LJ* 329 330–1 has pointed out that the exclusionary rule protects "the rest of us from unlawful invasions of our security and [maintains] the integrity of our institutions . . . The innocent and society are the principal beneficiaries of the exclusionary rule."

[11] Kamisar " 'Comparative Reprehensibility' and the Fourth Amendment Exclusionary Rule" 1987 86 *Michigan LR* 1 43 dismisses this argument (emphasis in the original text): "I wince when I hear a law enforcement official protest: 'We . . . are forced fight to by Marquis of Queensberry rules while criminals are permitted to gouge and bite'. If criminals didn't gouge and bite they wouldn't be criminals. And if police officers *did* gouge and bite they wouldn't (or at least shouldn't) be police officers."

[12] Stewart "The Road to *Mapp v Ohio* and Beyond: The Origins, Development and Future of the Exclusionary Rule in Search and Seizure Cases" 1983 83 *Columbia LR* 1365 1394 notes that "there is absolutely no evidence that the exclusionary rule is in any way responsible for the horrible increase in the crime rate in the United States . . .". See also LaFave *Search and Seizure: A Treatise on the Fourth Amendment* 2 ed (1987); Kamisar 1987 86 *Michigan LR* 1 131.

[13] Cardozo J in *People v Defore* supra. But there is a fundamental flaw in this line of reasoning. If you are going to deal with a corrupt or ignorant policeman, there will always be loss of reliable evidence irrespective of the fact whether an exclusionary or inclusionary rule is adopted. See also Heydon *Evidence: Cases and Materials* 3 ed (1991) 260–4.

[14] *R v Mabuya* 1927 CPD 181 182.

[15] Barrett "The Exclusion of Evidence Obtained by Illegal Searches — A Comment on *People v Cahan*" 1955 43 *California LR* 565 582.

[16] Waite "Judges and the Crime Burden" 1955 54 *Michigan LR* 169 192.

[17] *Exclusionary Injustice* 63.

and nature of the offence with the gravity and nature of the unconstitutional conduct of the police.[18]

— A prosecutor who is apprehensive that the exclusionary rule might result in the acquittal of an accused might accept a plea of guilty to a lesser charge in circumstances where such acceptance cannot be justified.[19]

Many of the above arguments merit little consideration and several of the counter-arguments are dealt with in the corresponding footnotes. However, the danger of creating a situation where society perceives the relevant criminal justice system as one which "frees" persons who commit serious crimes on account of a constable's blunder must be taken seriously.[20]

12 3   THE EXCLUSIONARY RULE : ITS THEORETICAL AND PRACTICAL JUSTIFICATION

In contradistinction to those pragmatic considerations which underlie the inclusionary rule the arguments in favour of an exclusionary rule are less concrete and more subtle.

12 3 1   The "preventive effect" argument   In *Elkins v United States*[21] the court held that the purpose of the exclusionary rule is " . . . to deter — to compel respect for the constitutional guaranty in the only effective way by removing the incentive to disregard it".[22] This deterrent purpose or basis of the exclusionary rule has been subjected to severe criticism.[23] In response it has been argued that "deterrence" must not be viewed in a narrow traditional sense and that its "educative" role and ultimate preventive[24] effect are more important than immediate deterrence. Kamisar notes:[25]

"Deterrence suggests that the exclusionary rule is supposed to influence the police the way the criminal law is supposed to affect the general public. But the rule does not, and cannot be expected to, deter the police the way the criminal law is supposed to work. The rule does not inflict a punishment on police who violate the Fourth Amendment: exclusion

---

[18] It is interesting to compare the German approach as set out by Morissette "The Exclusion of Evidence under the Canadian Charter of Rights and Freedoms: What to do and not to do" 1984 29 *McGill LJ* 521 530: "The *Rechtsstaatsprinzip* (or Rule of Law) requires the exclusion of evidence, regardless of its weight or value, in cases of police brutality or other aggravated illegality. The *Verhältnismässigkeit* (or principle of proportionality) calls for the exclusion of probative evidence where the means by which it was obtained are excessively intrusive in view of the triviality of the offence investigated and the particular sphere of privacy thus invaded. According to one fitting metaphor, the principle of proportionality means that one should not shoot sparrows with a cannon." Stewart 1983 83 *Columbia LR* 1365 1396 concludes as follows: "[D]isproportionality is significant only if one conceives the purpose of the rule as compensation for the victim. Because I view the exclusionary rule as necessary to preserve Fourth Amendment guarantees, I do not find this criticism persuasive."

[19] Schlesinger *Exclusionary Injustice* 63.

[20] See generally Shanks "Comparative Analysis of the Exclusionary Rules and its Alternatives" 1983 57 *Tulane LR* 648.

[21] 364 US 206 217 (1960).

[22] See also LaFave *Search and Seizure* 17.

[23] Oaks "Studying the Exclusionary Rule in Search and Seizure" 1970 37 *University of Chicago LR* 665.

[24] See *Stone v Powell* 428 US 465 492 (1976).

[25] Kamisar 1987 86 *Michigan LR* 1 34n147.

of the evidence does not leave the police in a worse position than if they had never violated the Constitution in the first place. Because the police are members of a structural governmental entity, however, the rule influences them, or is supposed to influence them, by systemic deterrence i e through a department's institutional compliance with Fourth Amendment standards.''

However, it would appear that there are much stronger arguments that justify an exclusionary rule. These are dealt with in §§ 12 3 2–12 3 6 below.

12 3 2 Due process in the context of a bill of rights The exclusionary rule is founded in the concept of due process, in terms of which the idea that there must be ascertainment of the truth at any cost is rejected. Relevant improperly obtained evidence should be excluded because its admission compromises other more important values.[26] It is argued that the primary function or goal of a criminal justice system is not merely to secure the conviction of an accused but to ensure that a conviction takes place in terms of a procedure which duly and properly acknowledges the rights of an accused at every critical stage during pre-trial, trial and post-trial proceedings. This due process argument gathers momentum when presented in the light of a bill of rights which demands and guarantees due process, and places important constitutional limitations upon official power. For if evidence is obtained in breach of these constitutional rights and allowed into evidence, the status of these constitutional guarantees will inevitably be undermined.[27]

The exclusionary rule is concerned with legality in the criminal process. This legality ranges from search, seizure, and arrest through to trial proceedings and final appeal or review. The police and prosecution are required to operate within a system in which civil liberties and due process are constitutionally guaranteed. Therefore it is inappropriate to justify or condemn the exclusionary rule on the basis of whether it provides an incentive for the police to comply with constitutional guarantees. If the exclusionary rule provides an incentive for compliance, this must merely be considered an additional advantage. Similarly, the fact that incentives to comply with the law might also be gained from departmental enquiries or civil actions is also irrelevant.

Where due process is constitutionally guaranteed the prosecution's attempt to introduce unconstitutionally obtained evidence may be viewed as a request that the court act contrary to the spirit and perhaps express provisions of the Constitution. Evidence, however relevant and persuasive it might be, should in principle be excluded where the admission of such evidence would undermine the value system created and guaranteed by a bill of rights. In terms of this argument the exclusionary rule is not merely an evidential barrier to factfinding; it is a constitutional barrier.[28] It can be argued that real meaning and effect are given to constitutional provisions through the medium of the law of evidence.[29]

---

[26] Packer *The Limits of the Criminal Sanction* (1968) 149–72. See also generally Herrmann 1978 *SACC* 3.
[27] See *Weeks v United States* 232 US 383 393 (1914); Oaks 1970 37 *University of Chicago LR* 665.
[28] See *Mapp v Ohio* 367 US 643 662 (1961).
[29] See Paizes 1989 *SALJ* 472 478.

The reason for excluding unconstitutionally obtained evidence is not to provide the aggrieved accused with some form of personal remedy[30] or some distorted form of "compensation", but to ensure that a court of law can in accordance with its constitutional duty make a valuable contribution to the upholding of constitutional principles which govern the criminal justice system as a whole.[31]

Although the exclusionary rule may sometimes result in the factually guilty being acquitted, this undesirable result is justified on the basis that the purpose of the exclusionary rule is not to provide a remedy to that particular accused — but to ensure that in the long run other citizens are not deprived of their constitutional rights. In this context the interests of social justice prevail over those of individual justice.[32]

12 3 3 The doctrine of legal guilt The role that the exclusionary rule plays in ensuring that the notion of legality is retained in the criminal justice system is supported by the due process doctrine of legal guilt. In terms of this doctrine of legal guilt[33]

> " . . . a person is not to be held guilty of a crime merely on a showing that in all probability, based upon reliable evidence, he did factually what he is said to have done. Instead, he is to be held guilty if and only if these factual determinations are made in procedurally regular fashion and by authorities acting within competences duly allocated to them."

This doctrine can also be detected in the South African criminal justice system.[34] For example, in *S v Lwane*[35] the prosecution had tendered, and the trial court had received, evidence which had been obtained from the accused at an earlier preparatory examination where he had testified and inculpated himself in his capacity as a witness. At the preparatory examination the accused (witness) had not been warned that he was not obliged to give evidence exposing himself to a criminal charge. The trial court convicted the accused on the basis of his self-incriminating evidence which he had, as a witness, given at the preparatory examination. On appeal Holmes JA held:[36]

> "The . . . question is whether such evidence given in the absence of judicial warning is admissible on the prosecution of the witness. As to that, the pragmatists may say that the guilty should be punished and that if the accused has previously confessed as a witness it is in the interests of society that he be convicted. The answer is that between the individual and the day of judicial reckoning there are interposed certain checks and balances in the interests of a fair trial and the due administration of justice. The rule of practice to which I have referred is one of them, and it is important that it be not eroded. According to the high judicial tradition of this country it is not in the interests of society that an accused should be convicted unless he has had a fair trial in accordance with accepted tenants of adjudication."

---

[30] See Clearly (ed) *McCormick on Evidence* 3 ed (1984) 463.

[31] See Gard (ed) *Jones on Evidence: Civil and Criminal* 13.

[32] See generally Kamisar 1987 86 *Michigan LR* 130; Diamond "The State and the Accused: Balance of Advantage in Criminal Procedure" 1960 69 *Yale LJ* 1149.

[33] Packer *The Limits of the Criminal Sanction* 166. See also Van Rooyen 1975 *Acta Juridica* 70 78.

[34] See, e g, *S v Mushimba* 1977 2 SA 829 (A); *S v Zulu* 1990 1 SA 655 (T); *S v Ebrahim* 1991 2 SA 553 (A).

[35] 1966 2 SA 433 (A).

[36] At 444C–E.

12 3 4 Judicial integrity The Supreme Court of the United States has identified "the imperative of judicial integrity" as an important rationale of the exclusionary rule.[37] It would appear that there are at least four interrelated facets to this rationale, namely, that by admitting unconstitutionally obtained evidence *(a)* courts themselves will violate the Constitution;[38] *(b)* courts will act contrary to their oath to uphold the Constitution;[39] *(c)* courts will indirectly encourage violations of the Constitution;[40] and *(d)* courts will somehow create the impression that they sanction or condone unconstitutional conduct by government officials.[41]

12 3 5 The principle of self-correction An effective due process system must have the inherent ability to correct abuses within the system;[42] and it must be able to do so at the first moment that it is established that there has been an abuse. To argue that a separate criminal charge (or a civil action for damage to property, for assault, or for an illegal arrest, etc) against the perpetrator is the appropriate remedy amounts to a tacit admission that the relevant criminal justice system:

— is not truly a due process one, because, for purposes of adjudication, it tolerates infringements of rights which are otherwise considered essential for due process;

— is for the maintenance or perpetuation of its status as a fair and just system dependent upon (or in need of being propped up by) whatever civil action the accused may or may not institute against the perpetrator, or whatever criminal charges the authorities (or the accused) may follow up;

— cannot operate unless abuses are accommodated on an internal level.

Acceptance of the principle of self-correction leads to a further valid argument. The exclusionary rule is not primarily aimed at discouraging unconstitutional official conduct: *its true purpose is to serve as an effective internal tool for maintaining and protecting the value system as a whole.* But if officials are as a result of the exclusionary rule deterred from infringing fundamental rights, then so much the better.

12 3 6 Primary rules and the secondary rule (the exclusionary rule) It can also be argued that the exclusionary rule merely reinforces existing rules regulating police powers. Van Rooyen makes this point as follows:[43]

"It is usually said against the exclusionary rule that exclusion of illegally obtained evidence

---

[37] *Elkins v United States* supra. See also generally Osakwe "The Bill of Rights for the Criminal Defendant in American Law: A Case Study of Judicial Lawmaking in the United States" in Andrews (ed) *Human Rights in Criminal Procedure: A Comparative Study* (1982) 259 280.

[38] *Janis v United States* 428 US 433 458 (1966).

[39] *Elkins v United States* supra 223.

[40] *Janis v United States* supra.

[41] See *Olmstead v United States* 277 US 438 485 (1928). Cf Kaplan "The Limits of the Exclusionary Rule" 1974 26 *Stanford LR* 1027.

[42] See Packer *The Limits of the Criminal Sanction* 167–8; Damaska "Evidentiary Barriers to Conviction and Two Models of Criminal Procedure" 1973 121 *University of Pennsylvania LR* 506 583.

[43] 1975 *Acta Juridica* 70 79.

infringes the principle that all relevant and credible evidence should be admitted at an accused's trial. However, upon close analysis it is clear that the policy decision that certain relevant and credible evidence may not be obtained unless certain prerequisites are met — i e that relevant and credible evidence should not be gathered at all costs — has already been taken by the rules regulating pre-trial police powers (which I shall call 'primary rules') and is not newly imposed by the exclusionary rule (the 'secondary rule'). The secondary rule merely 'enforces' the primary rules: if, for example, the police in a given case voluntarily obey the primary rules, the result may well be that certain evidence is lost and will accordingly not be used at the trial — a calculated risk that we must run if we are to have legal limits on police powers to infringe individual interests; if, on the other hand, the police flout the primary rules, the secondary rule simply achieves the same result."

12 4 CRITICISM OF THE EXCLUSIONARY RULE

Despite the many cogent theoretical arguments in support of the exclusionary rule, the question remains: to what extent is society prepared to accept the "release" of criminals as a consequence of the exclusion of incriminating evidence of strong probative value, excluded as a result of a policeman's trivial, technical and inadvertent infringement of a primary rule? The American experience has shown that the strict application of a rigid exclusionary rule can bring the criminal justice system into disfavour.[44] As a result the United States Supreme Court has relaxed the rigidity of the exclusionary rule in cases of good faith, for example, where a law enforcement officer had reasonably relied and acted upon a statute which was only at a later stage held to be in violation of the Fourth Amendment.[45]

12 5 THE CANADIAN APPROACH

If a Canadian court is satisfied that evidence was obtained in a manner which infringed or denied any rights or freedoms guaranteed by the Canadian Charter of Rights and Freedoms, the evidence shall be excluded if it is established that, having regard to all the circumstances, the admission of such evidence would bring the administration of justice into disrepute. This provision is contained in s 24(2) of the Canadian Charter. In *R v Collins*[46] the court considered the method of ascertaining the meaning of "disrepute". Seaton JA held as follows:[47]

"Disrepute in whose eyes? That which would bring the administration of justice into disrepute in the eyes of a policeman might be the precise action that would be highly regarded in the eyes of a law teacher. I do not think that we are to look at this matter through the eyes of a policeman or a law teacher, or a judge for that matter. *I think that it is the community at large, including the policeman and the law teacher and the judge, through whose eyes we are to see this question.* It follows, and I do not think this is a disadvantage to the suggestion, that there will be a gradual shifting. *I expect that there will be a trend away from admission of improperly obtained evidence . . .* I do not suggest that the court should respond

[44] Schlesinger *Exclusionary Injustice* 3–5.
[45] *Illinois v Krull* 1987 107 SCt 1160. See also generally *United States v Leon* 468 US 897 (1984); *Massachusetts v Sheppard* 468 US 981 (1984); LaFave *Search and Seizure: A Treatise on the Fourth Amendment* 47.
[46] 1983 5 CCC (3d) 141 (BCCA).
[47] At 150–1 (emphasis added). See also Morisette 1984 29 *McGill LJ* 521 538.

to public clamour or opinion polls.[48] *I do suggest that the views of the community at large, developed by concerned and thinking citizens, ought to guide the courts when they are questioning whether or not the admission of evidence would bring the administration of justice into disrepute.*"

There have been several Canadian decisions interpreting s 24(2) of the Charter.[49] The Canadian courts have attempted to identify three categories of factors which must be assessed and balanced in the application of s 24(2).[50] The first category covers the fairness of the trial process. The second one refers to the seriousness of the violation[51] of the Charter. The third relates to the consequences of admitting the evidence, namely the question whether the reputation of the system will be better served by admitting or excluding the evidence.[52]

The ultimate result is a compromise:[53]

"The core idea is simple. An effective and stable legal system must enjoy the support of the public. To admit unconstitutionally obtained evidence where that would bring the system into disrepute in the eyes of the public would be to compromise the public's support for the legal system. Conversely, to exclude evidence under circumstances where this would bring the administration of justice into disrepute would again undermine public support of the legal system. Hence the 'compromise' reflected in s 24(2)."

12 6   THE CONSTITUTION OF THE REPUBLIC OF SOUTH AFRICA

Prior to South Africa's new constitutional dispensation there were no express legislative provisions applicable to the admissibility of unlawfully obtained evidence. South African courts were required to refer to the English common law in force on 30 May 1961.[54] In terms of the English common-law approach there is *in principle* no bar to the admissibility of relevant evidence obtained in an unlawful manner.[55] The common-law discretion to exclude improperly obtained evidence is discussed in §§ 5 4–5 6 above.

12 6 1   The interim Constitution   The interim Constitution does not contain any express provision dealing with the admissibility of evidence obtained in breach of its provisions. However, s 7(4) of the interim Constitution provides that when

---

[48] See generally Gibson "Determining Disrepute: Opinion Polls and the Canadian Charter of Rights and Freedoms" 1983 61 *The Canadian Bar Review* 337.

[49] See generally Marin *Admissibility of Statements* 7 ed (1989) 171–205. See also *R v Richardson* 1991 49 CRR 304 and cf this case with the decision by Van Deventer J in *S v Mhlakaza & others* 1996 2 All SA 130 (C). See further Labuschagne 1994 *SACJ* 353 for a discussion of *R v Dersch* 1994 85 CCC (3d) 1.

[50] See *R v Cohen* 1983 5 CCC (3d) 156 (BCCA).

[51] See *R v Therens* 1985 18 CCC (3d) 481.

[52] See generally *R v Collins* supra; *R v Debot* 1989 73 CR (3d) 129 (SCC); *R v Leclair & Ross* 1989 67 CR (3d) 209 (SCC); *R v Genest* 1989 45 CCC (3d) 385 (SCC) 403–10.

[53] Bryant et al "Public Attitudes Foward the Exclusion of Evidence: Section 24(2) of the Canadian Charter of Rights and Freedoms" 1990 69 *Canadian Bar Review* 1 5. See also generally Charles, Cromwell & Jobson *Evidence and the Canadian Charter of Rights and Freedoms* (1989) 199–343; Gibson & Gibson "Enforcement of the Canadian Charter of Rights and Freedoms (Section 24)" in Beaudoin & Ratushny *The Canadian Charter of Rights and Freedoms* 2 ed (1989) 825–38.

[54] Section 252 of the CPA. See also § 3 5 above.

[55] See generally Keane *The Modern Law of Evidence* 2 ed (1989) 37–8; Howard et al *Phipson on Evidence* 14 ed (1990) para 28-08; Murphy *A Practical Approach to Evidence* 27–32. See also *S v Nel* 1987 4 SA 950 (W) and Paizes 1988 *SACJ* 389.

it is alleged that any right entrenched in the bill of rights has been threatened or infringed, a person may apply to a competent court for appropriate relief. In a number of Supreme court decisions it has been held that the exclusion of unconstitutionally obtained evidence may constitute appropriate relief.[56]

In *S v Melani*[57] the court, in ascertaining what constituted appropriate relief, rejected both the rigid exclusionary and rigid inclusionary approaches. Froneman J found that a strict exclusionary approach failed to take into account the interests of the community as a whole. He held that a rigid inclusionary approach was inappropriate in a legal system which recognized the supremacy of the Constitution and that it denied the court the opportunity of granting effective "appropriate relief". In favouring and applying a discretionary approach, which allowed the court to admit evidence if its exclusion would bring the administration of justice into discredit and dishonour,[58] the court noted that the seeds for such an approach could be detected in the case law prior to the enactment of the interim Constitution.[59] In addition the court held that this discretionary approach provided the best mechanism for balancing the legitimate interests of the accused and those of the community at large.[60] In a later judgment bearing the same name[61] Froneman J held that s 25 of the interim Constitution provided a further reason for the exclusion of unconstitutionally obtained evidence, "namely the need to ensure the fairness and integrity of the criminal process at least from arrest up to and including the trial".[62]

The court in *S v Motloutsi*[63] found the test of whether the admission of unconstitutionally obtained evidence would bring the administration of justice into disrepute unsatisfactory. The court favoured the approach taken by the Irish courts in *The People (Attorney-General) v O'Brien*.[64] Farlam J held that "the presiding Judge has a discretion to exclude evidence of facts ascertained by illegal means where it appears to him that public policy, based on a balancing of public interest, requires such exclusion".[65] However, the court found that a stricter approach was needed where the evidence was obtained as a consequence of a deliberate breach of the accused's constitutional rights.[66] In such cases the evidence should only be admitted if "extraordinary excusing circumstances exist, such as the imminent destruction of vital evidence or the need to rescue a victim in peril"

---

[56] See *S v Botha (1)* 1995 2 SACR 598 (W); *S v Melani* 1995 2 SACR 141 (E); *S v Melani* 1996 1 SACR 335 (E). See also generally Meintjies-Van der Walt 1996 *SACJ* 83.

[57] 1995 2 SACR 141 (E).

[58] *S v Motloutsi* 1996 1 SACR 78 (C).

[59] See, e g, *S v Forbes* 1970 2 SA 594 (C); *S v Ebrahim* 1991 2 SA 553 (A); *S v Hammer* 1994 2 SACR 496 (C). For a discussion of the common-law position, see §§ 5 4 and 5 6 above. See also § 17 8 3 below.

[60] At 153*b–e*.

[61] *S v Melani* 1996 1 SACR 335 (E) at 351*b*. See also *S v Zuma* 1995 2 SA 642 (CC); cf *S v Rudman; S v Mthwana* 1992 1 SA 343 (A).

[62] At 351*b*. See also *S v Botha (1)* 1995 2 SACR 598 (W). In *S v Mhlakaza & others* 1996 2 All SA 130 (C) Van Deventer J held that a failure to allow legal representation at an identification parade constituted a violation of an accused's right to a fair trial.

[63] 1996 1 SACR 78 (C).

[64] 1965 IR 142.

[65] At 84*i–j*. He also relied on *S v Forbes & another* 1970 2 SA 594 (C).

[66] At 85*b*.

or when the evidence is obtained by "a search incidental to and contemporaneous with a lawful arrest although made without a valid search warrant".[67] The
court stressed that a claim of ignorance of law would not assist police officials in
contradicting an allegation that there had been a deliberate and conscious
breach of the accused's rights.[68]

12 6 2 The 1996 Constitution Section 35(5) of the 1996 Constitution provides:

> "[E]vidence obtained in manner that violates any right in the Bill of Rights must be
> excluded if the admission of that evidence would render the trial unfair or otherwise be
> detrimental to the administration of justice."

Section 35(3) lists certain basic requirements for the existence of a fair trial.[69]
If s 35(5) is read together with s 35(3), it is certainly open to the interpretation
that if any of the rights falling under the umbrella of s 35(3) are violated, the
evidence must be excluded, that is, the courts do not have a discretion to include
it. However, it must be borne in mind that the limitations clause[70] must be applied
before the constitutional exclusionary rule comes into play. Consequently, a
person arguing for the exclusion of evidence, on the basis that it was obtained
in contravention of the accused's right to a fair trial, would not succeed if the
prosecution persuaded the court that the violation was reasonable and justifiable
in terms of the limitations clause.

It is also clear that once it is established that the admission of evidence would
"be detrimental to the administration of justice" the courts do not have a
discretion to admit it. What remains to be determined is the test to be applied
in establishing when the admission of evidence will be detrimental to the
administration of justice. Clearly, if it would undermine public support of
the legal system, it would be detrimental to the administration of justice.[71]
Froneman J in *S v Melani*[72] noted that "a public opinion poll would probably
show that the majority of our population would at this stage in the history of our
country be quite content if the courts allow evidence at a criminal trial, even if
it was unconstitutionally obtained". However, in *S v Makwanyane*[73] — which

---

[67] At 85–6, quoting from *The People (Attorney General) v O'Brien* supra.

[68] At 87*f–j*.

[69] In *S v Zuma* supra the Constitutional Court in interpreting the corresponding provision in the interim
Constitution (s 25(3)) held that the right to a fair trial is not limited to those rights specified in the section.

[70] Section 36 of the 1996 Constitution provides:

> "(1) The rights in the Bill of Rights may be limited only in terms of law of general application to the
> extent that the limitation is reasonable and justifiable in an open and democratic society based on
> human dignity, equality and freedom, taking into account all relevant factors including —
> *(a)* the nature of the right;
> *(b)* the importance of the purpose of the limitation;
> *(c)* the nature and extent of the limitation;
> *(d)* the relation between the limitation and its purpose; and
> *(e)* less restrictive means to achieve the purpose."

[71] See generally Skeen 1988 *SACJ* 389 for a discussion of the factors a court may take into account in
exercising its discretion to exclude improperly obtained evidence. See also Bradley "The Emerging
International Consensus as to Criminal Procedure Rules" 1993 14 *Michigan Journal of International Law*
172.

[72] 1996 1 SACR 335 (E) 352.

[73] 1995 3 SA 391 (CC) para [88].

concerned the death penalty — the Constitutional Court noted that, whilst public opinion did have some relevance, "it is no substitute for the duty vested in the Courts to interpret the Constitution and to uphold its provisions without fear or favour". Clearly, the interests of the criminal justice system should also accord with the "longer-term purpose of the Constitution, to establish a democratic order based on, amongst other, the recognition of basic human rights".[74] The reasonable person test as applied by the Canadian court in *R v Collins*[75] in determining disrepute provides a useful mechanism for incorporating public opinion whilst avoiding compromising judicial integrity. In terms of this test the court is required to take into account the views of the reasonable person, who is usually the average person in the community, "but only when the community's current mood is reasonable".[76] However, the court in exercising its discretion must consider "long-term community values" and "not render a decision that would be unacceptable to the community when that community is not being wrought with passion or otherwise under passing stress due to current events".[77] If the Constitution is viewed as reflecting "long-term community values", this adds weight to the argument that the maintenance of judicial integrity requires the courts to exclude evidence obtained unconstitutionally in the absence of extraordinary excusing circumstances.[78]

---

[74] *S v Melani* 1996 1 SACR 335 (E) 353.
[75] Supra. This test was approved in *S v Melani* 1996 1 SACR 335 (E). See also § 12 6 above.
[76] At 136.
[77] At 136.
[78] *The People (Attorney-General) v O'Brien* supra.

SECTION D
HEARSAY

CHAPTER 13

THE RULE AGAINST HEARSAY

A St Q Skeen

13 1 INTRODUCTION AND HISTORY

Prior to October 1988 hearsay evidence in civil and criminal cases was admissible or inadmissible as the case might have been on 30 May 1961.[1] The effect was to rely on the English common-law hearsay rule as applied and understood in this country at the given date.[2] Certain statutory exceptions to the hearsay rule were created and are still in force.[3] On 3 October 1988 new provisions relating to hearsay were brought into effect in terms of s 3 of the Law of Evidence Amendment Act.[4]

---

[1] See generally ch 3 above as regards the interpretation of the 30 May 1961 provisions.

[2] See generally ch 14 below for a brief discussion of the common-law position.

[3] See ch 15 below for a discussion of some of these statutes.

[4] Act 45 of 1988; s 216 of the CPA was repealed by Act 45 of 1988. See also Schutte 1991 *THRHR* 495; De Vos & Van der Merwe 1993 *Stell LR* 7.

13 2   THE MEANING OF HEARSAY

At common law hearsay encompasses oral or written statements made by persons who are not parties and who are not called as witnesses and which are tendered for the purpose of proving the truth of such statements.[5]

The mere fact that a statement was made by a non-witness did not make it hearsay — it only became hearsay if the reported statement was used to prove the truth of its contents.[6] The common-law approach to hearsay is assertion-oriented.

In terms of s 3 of Act 45 of 1988 hearsay is now defined as written or oral evidence, the probative value of which depends on the credibility of any person other than the person giving such evidence. This approach may be described as declarant-oriented.

13 3   REASONS FOR THE EXCLUSION OF HEARSAY AND THE NEED FOR REFORM

Various reasons have been given for the exclusion of hearsay. All these reasons basically stress the inherent possibility of unreliability. There is a real danger of inaccuracy through repetition — especially as regards oral statements.

13 3 1 Best evidence rule   At one stage it was thought that hearsay evidence should not be admitted as it was not original evidence and thus not the best evidence. This view has now been rejected.

13 3 2 Not on oath   It has been said that hearsay should be excluded because the original statement was not made under oath. This reason for exclusion was often given in earlier cases.

13 3 3 Unreliable as no opportunity for cross-examination   The purpose of cross-examination is to show that the witness is untruthful or mistaken; it also attempts to elicit points that are favourable to the cross-examiner's case. None of these tests or purposes can be applied to hearsay statements, thus, sometimes, making them suspect. It can confidently be submitted that this reason is the best explanation for the exclusion of hearsay.

13 3 4 The need for reform   The rigidity of the old rule meant that hearsay evidence could not be received unless it fell within the bounds of a common-law exception or a statutory provision. The fact that the evidence was both highly relevant and trustworthy could not assist as the Appellate Division decided in *Vulcan Rubber Works (Pty) Ltd v SAR & H*[7] that it could not create new exceptions.

---

[5] *S v Holshausen* 1984 4 SA 852 (A).

[6] *International Tobacco Co (SA) Ltd v United Tobacco Co (South) Ltd* 1953 3 SA 343 (W).

[7] 1958 3 SA 285 (A).

The new declarant-oriented approach considers all hearsay evidence as potentially unreliable, but allows for its admission under certain circumstances, which are considered below. The most important innovation is the introduction of a discretion, which is explained in § 13 7 below. It is to be preferred to the rigidity of the common law.

13 4   SECTION 3 OF THE LAW OF EVIDENCE AMENDMENT ACT 45 OF 1988

This section allows for the admission of hearsay as defined in s 3(4). But the requirements of the section must be met.

The common-law exceptions are abolished both in criminal and civil proceedings. The court is now given a discretion to admit hearsay evidence.

Section 3 is set out below and is then analysed in subsequent paragraphs:

"3. (1) Subject to the provisions of any other law, hearsay evidence shall not be admitted as evidence at criminal or civil proceedings, unless —

(a) each party against whom the evidence is to be adduced agrees to the admission thereof as evidence at such proceedings;

(b) the person upon whose credibility the probative value of such evidence depends himself testifies at such proceedings; or

(c) the court having regard to —
  (i) the nature of proceedings;
  (ii) the nature of evidence;
  (iii) the purpose for which the evidence is tendered;
  (iv) the probative value of the evidence;
  (v) the reason why the evidence is not given by the person upon whose credibility the probative value of such evidence depends;
  (vi) any prejudice to a party which the admission of such evidence might entail; and
  (vii) any other factor which should in the opinion of the court be taken into account,
is of the opinion that such evidence should be admitted in the interests of justice.

(2) The provisions of subsection (1) shall not render admissible any evidence which is inadmissible on any ground other that that such evidence is hearsay evidence.

(3) Hearsay evidence may be provisionally admitted in terms of subsection (1) (b) if the court is informed that the person upon whose credibility the probative value of such evidence depends, will himself testify is such proceedings; Provided that if such person does not later testify in such proceedings, the hearsay evidence shall be left out of account unless the hearsay evidence is admitted in terms of paragraph (a) of subsection (1) or is admitted by the court in terms of paragraph (c) of that subsection.

(4) For the purposes of this section —
'**hearsay evidence**' means evidence, whether oral or in writing, the probative value of which depends upon the credibility of any person other that the person giving such evidence;
'**party**' means the accused or party against whom hearsay evidence is to be adduced, including the prosecution."

13 5   STATUTORY DEFINITION OF HEARSAY IN TERMS OF ACT 45 OF 1988

Section 3(4) of Act 45 of 1988 defines hearsay as "evidence, whether oral or in writing, the probative value of which depends upon the credibility of any person other than the person giving such evidence".

The words "depends upon" are important in the application of this definition.

According to Paizes,[8] all evidence depends to some extent on the credibility of a person other than the witness as evidence is a blend of individual perception, accumulated information, and visual and audial communication. The words "depends upon" obviously cannot be this widely applied, otherwise the section would be unworkable.

On the other hand, the words "depends upon" cannot mean "solely depends upon", as in every case the witness who gives the evidence must have his or her credibility considered, i e the relating of what has been told to the witness must depend to some degree on the credibility of the witness.

In *Hewan v Kourie NO*[9] it was indicated that the words "depends upon" cannot mean "to rest entirely upon". It has been suggested that the most useful way to look at the matter is to consider all evidence as hearsay if it depends sufficiently for its probative value on the credibility of some person other than the witness.[10]

13 6   ADMISSION BY CONSENT

Apart from the factors to be considered under s 3(1)(c) (see §§ 13 7–13 7 6 below), hearsay evidence may be admitted in both criminal and civil cases if consent is given by the party against whom the evidence is to be led. Such consent must be an informed consent, which should include knowledge of the prejudice which may result from the admission of the evidence. In *S v Ngwani*[11] it was held that, prior to the admission of hearsay by consent, the relevant law must be explained to an unrepresented accused person. The accused must also be heard on the issue as to whether the hearsay evidence should be admitted in terms of the discretion.

13 7   DISCRETION IN TERMS OF ACT 45 OF 1988

The discretion to admit hearsay evidence must be exercised in a judicial manner. Section 3(1)(c) enjoins the court to consider six specific factors, and any other factor which it is of the opinion should be taken into account, before forming an opinion that the hearsay evidence should be admitted in the interests of justice. It involves a guided discretion.[12]

13 7 1   The nature of the proceedings: s 3(1)(c)(i)   The distinction between civil and criminal cases is important. Courts more readily admit hearsay in civil cases. In criminal cases the presumption of innocence and the court's intuitive reluctance to permit untested evidence to be used against an accused are of importance. The section should therefore rarely be used in criminal cases. This

---

[8] In Du Toit et al *Commentary on the Criminal Procedure Act* (1987, as revised) 24-5.

[9] 1993 3 SA 233 (T).

[10] Paizes in Du Toit et al *Commentary on the Criminal Procedure Act* 24-46.

[11] 1990 1 SACR 449 (N).

[12] On the exercise of the discretion, see generally *Metadad v National Employers' General Insurance Co Ltd* 1992 1 SA 494 (W).

was the view of Van Schalkwyk J in *Metadad v National Employers' General Insurance Co Ltd.*[13]

In application proceedings, it is submitted, the court would more readily accept hearsay evidence.[14]

13 7 2 The nature of the evidence: s 3(1)(c)(ii) The issue as to whether the hearsay evidence is reliable or not is central to the exercise of the discretion on the above ground. Relevant factors to consider are: Was the statement against the interest of the original declarant? Was there a motive to misrepresent? What is the relationship between the parties? Was the statement spontaneous? Is the statement first- or secondhand hearsay?

In *S v Cekiso & another*[15] hearsay evidence was tendered on the question of identity and as to whether the faces of the accused had been covered in order to conceal identity. There had been conflicting non-hearsay evidence on this point. The court held that the hearsay could not be tested in the normal manner, and thus it would not be in the interests of justice to admit it.

In *S v Mpofu*[16] the appellant had been convicted of culpable homicide arising out of a hit-and-run motor-vehicle accident. The deceased's husband had been given a piece of paper with a number written on it by a passer-by. This person did not give evidence. It was alleged that the number of the vehicle involved had been written down on the piece of paper. On appeal it was held that the evidence ought to have been excluded by the trial court. Spontaneity was not proved. It was held that the probative value was so open to conjecture that admission of the recorded number would amount to unjustified prejudice to the accused. In rejecting the evidence the court also indicated that there was "no objective way of testing" the opportunity that the passer-by had for observation.[17] The reliability of what was recorded could therefore not be tested. The passer-by was for all practical purposes an absent witness.

The dangers in the reiteration of oral statements are noted in *Mnyama v Gxalaba.*[18] But the reliability of the oral hearsay evidence, although important, is not an overriding requirement for admissibility.[19]

13 7 3 The purpose for which the evidence is tendered: s 3(1)(c)(iii) In some cases it has been suggested that a factor against admissibility is that the hearsay was tendered to prove a fundamental issue rather than a side or subsidiary issue.[20] However, in *S v Mpofu*[21] it was said that if the evidence is relevant, its degree of

---

[13] 1992 1 SA 494 (W); see also *Hewan v Kourie NO* 1993 3 SA 233 (T).

[14] *S v Cekiso* 1990 4 SA 320 (E). See also *Syfrets Mortgage Nominees Ltd v Cape St Francis Hotels (Pty) Ltd* 1991 3 SA 276 (SE). See further De Vos & Van der Merwe 1993 *Stell LR* 7 26.

[15] 1990 4 SA 320 (E).

[16] 1993 2 SACR 109 (N).

[17] At 117*e*.

[18] 1990 (1) SA 650 (C) 654. See also § 13 7 6 below.

[19] *Hewan v Kourie NO* supra.

[20] *Hlogwane v Rector, St Francis College* 1989 3 SA 318 (D); *Hewan v Kourie NO* supra.

[21] *R v Mpofu* supra.

importance should not be decisive. If the evidence carries the hallmark of truthfulness and reliability, then its reception is justified.

Evidence tendered for a legitimate purpose would be more readily accepted than that tendered for a doubtful purpose.[22]

13 7 4 The probative value of the evidence: s 3(1)(c)(iv) Relevance has two variables which must be considered and weighed before deciding to admit the evidence in question. These are *(a)* the probative value of the evidence; and *(b)* the prejudicial factors which may militate against its acceptance. These are factors to be considered in deciding whether to admit hearsay evidence.

13 7 5 The reason why the evidence is not given by the person upon whose credibility the probative value depends: s 3(1)(c)(v) Trustworthiness and necessity were the basis for the admission of hearsay at common law.[23] These factors would still be relevant under s 3 and such factors as the nature of the evidence (see § 13 7 2 above) will be considered in deciding on the trustworthiness of the evidence. Necessity would depend on such factors as the death of the declarant, illness (mental or physical), absence from the country, and the fact that the witness cannot be traced after all reasonable efforts have been made to locate him or her.[24]

Further factors such as intimidation of or apprehension of harm to the witnesses may be considered. In *Hlongwane v Rector, St Frances College*[25] the applicants had been suspended from a college because of allegations that they were ringleaders in certain agitations. The rector acted on hearsay statements because he feared that, should the identity of his informants be disclosed, the applicants might take violent reprisals against the informants. It was decided that it was in the interests of justice to admit the hearsay.

13 7 6 Prejudice to opponents: s 3(1)(c)(vi) By its very nature hearsay cannot be tested by conventional procedural safeguards such as direct confrontation and cross-examination. Section 25(2)(d) of the interim Constitution gives an accused person the right to adduce and challenge evidence. Hearsay cannot be challenged by cross-examination.

However, in the United States the principle of direct confrontation has been dispensed with where the utility of the hearsay evidence is low or the hearsay evidence is both reliable and necessary.[26] The same approach, it is submitted, should apply in this country if the issue of hearsay and its constitutionality should arise.[27] Hearsay and its constitutionality should also be assessed in terms of the limitations clause as contained in s 33 of the interim Constitution.

---

[22] *Metadad v National Employers' General Insurance Co Ltd* supra.
[23] Wigmore paras 1420–3.
[24] These are also factors considered under s 34(1)(b) of the Civil Proceedings Evidence Act 25 of 1965; see generally ch 15 below.
[25] 1989 3 SA 318 (D).
[26] *Ohio v Roberts* 448 US 56 (1960).
[27] See generally De Vos & Van der Merwe 1993 *Stell LR* 7 34–9 for the impact of a Bill of Rights on hearsay.

13 7 7 Any other factor which in the opinion of the court should be taken into account: s 3(1)(c)(vii) In *Mnyama v Gxalaba*[28] it was said that one of the factors which a court is entitled to take into account in exercising the discretion to admit hearsay is that it would have been admissible under the common law. In *S v Mpofu*[29] it was held that logically the court could not ignore considering factors which allowed for admissibility at common law.

In *Hewan v Kourie*[30] the court warned against seeking the safety of the common-law rules. But the court also said that the common-law exceptions and the rationale behind them provide collective wisdom which can be utilized under the new rule.

13 8 PROVISIONAL ADMISSION OF HEARSAY[31]

In terms of s 3(3) of the Law of Evidence Amendment Act[32] hearsay evidence may be provisionally admitted if the court is advised that the person upon whose credibility the probative value of the evidence depends will also testify. But there is a proviso that if such person does not later testify, the hearsay evidence shall be left out of account unless admitted by consent[33] or in terms of the discretion.[34]

This provision allows a party to lead evidence in a particular order without having to call the maker of a statement as an earlier witness.[35]

---

[28] 1990 1 SA 650 (C).

[29] 1993 2 SACR 109 (N).

[30] 1993 2 SA 233 (T).

[31] See generally De Vos & Van der Merwe 1993 *Stell LR* 7 20. See also *S v Ramavhale* 1996 1 SACR 639 (A), where prejudice was caused by admitting hearsay at judgment stage.

[32] Act 45 of 1988.

[33] Section 3(1)(a) of Act 45 of 1988. See § 13 6 above.

[34] Section 3(1)(c) of Act 45 of 1988. See §§ 13 7–13 7 7 above.

[35] See also § 2 8 above.

CHAPTER 14

A SELECTION OF COMMON-LAW EXCEPTIONS TO THE HEARSAY RULE: A BRIEF PERSPECTIVE

A St Q Skeen

14 1   INTRODUCTION

In § 13 7 7 above it was pointed out that cases such as *Mnyama v Gxalaba*,[1] *S v Mpofu*[2] and *Hewan v Kourie NO*[3] have indicated that common-law exceptions to hearsay — although abolished — may be taken into account by a court in the exercise of its discretion in terms of s 3(1)(c) of the Law of Evidence Amendment Act 45 of 1988.[4]

The purpose of the present chapter is not to "revive" the common-law exceptions, but to provide some examples of factual situations which — in terms of the common law and prior to the commencement of the Law of Evidence Act 45 of 1988 — would have qualified as exceptions to the hearsay rule as applied and understood at that stage. What follows is not an overview of all common-law exceptions but a selection of those exceptions which might be of assistance to the court in exercising its discretion created by s 3(1)(c) of Act 45 of 1988.

---

[1] 1990 1 SA 650 (C).

[2] 1993 2 SACR 109 (N).

[3] 1993 2 SA 233 (T).

[4] Section 3(1)(c)(vii) of Act 45 of 1988 permits the approach suggested in *Mnyama v Gxalaba* supra, *S v Mpofu* supra and *Hewan v Kourie NO* supra. Section 3(1)(c)(vii) refers to "any other factor which should in the opinion of the court be taken into account . . .".

14 2   VARIOUS STATEMENTS BY DECEASED PERSONS AS EXCEPTIONS

Six classes of statements made by *deceased* persons are included in the exceptions to the hearsay rule. These are statements against interest, statements in the course of duty, statements in the case of murder or culpable homicide, statements concerning pedigree, statements as to public and general rights, and statements as to the contents of wills by testators.

14 2 1 Statements against interest An oral or written statement made by a deceased person was admissible in evidence if it was, to his knowledge, against his pecuniary or proprietary interest at the time it was made. The rationale of this exception is that a man is unlikely to make a false statement when it is against his interest. Certain requirements had to be met.[5]

14 2 2 Statements in the course of duty Oral or written statements made by a deceased person are admissible to prove the truth of the contents if made as a result of a duty to record or report contemporaneously and if made with no motive to misrepresent. An example is *Price v Earl of Torrington*,[6] where entries, made by a deceased delivery man in certain records, were held admissible to prove a beer delivery which was the subject of the action. In the case of *Nolan v Barnard*[7] entries made by a deceased farm manager in a diary in the course of duty were admissible to prove that strange cattle had made their appearance on the farm. Certain requirements had to be satisfied.[8]

---

[5] The conditions of admissibility were as follows: *(a) The declarant must have died. (b) The statement must have been against the pecuniary or proprietary interest of the declarant at the time of making.* It appears that *Sussex Peerage* 1844 11 Cl and Fin 85 decided that a declaration which only exposed the maker to criminal liability was inadmissible. The most common type of statement against pecuniary interest is an admission that the maker owes money or, conversely, that he is not owned money. Statements by a person who knows he is dying may be admissible against his estate. A statement by a possessor of a movable that he is not the owner would amount to a declaration against proprietary interest. The statement must have been against interest at the time it was made. In *Smith v Blakey* 1867 LR 2 QB 326 a clerk in charge of an office wrote to his employers to advise them of three crates of shoes which had been received from the defendant and the terms on which they had been accepted. It was held that the letter was inadmissible to prove the terms of the contract as the possibility of the clerk becoming liable if the cases were lost was too remote. The statement need only be *prima facie* against interest. *(c) The declarant must have known that the statement was against his interest.* In *Tucker v Oldbury Urban Council* 1912 2 KB 317 a claim by dependants for workmen's compensation was brought as a result of a workman dying from blood-poisoning consequent upon an injury to his thumb. It was held that a statement by the deceased that the injury was due to a whitlow was inadmissible as he was unaware that he could make a claim, i e the statement was not knowingly against interest when made. *(d) There is uncertainty as to whether the declarant must have had personal knowledge of the fact he stated.* The better view is that he should have had personal knowledge, otherwise hearsay upon hearsay would be received. In the event of the declaration being admissible it may be used to prove collateral facts. See *Relief Brothers v Du Plessis* 1928 CPD 387.

[6] 1703 1 Salk 285.

[7] 1908 TS 142.

[8] The conditions for admissibility were as follows: *(a) The declarant must have died.* In *Naik v Pillay* 1923 AD 471 it was held that entries by a sick bookkeeper were, in terms of this exception, admissible *ex necessitate rei.* This decision must be considered wrong because the bookkeeper was not dead but only unavailable. The subsequent case of *Vulcan Rubber Works (Pty) Ltd v SAR & H* 1958 3 SA 285 (A) expressly set its face against the creation of new exceptions to the hearsay rule *ex necessitate. (b) There must have been a duty to record or report.* The duty must have been owed to another person and it must have related to acts by the declarant. See *Vianini Ferro-Concrete (Pty) Ltd v Union Government* 1941 TPD 252. *(c) The recording or reporting of the act must be contemporaneous with the act itself.* The precise time lapse permissible was not laid down in

14 2 3 Dying declarations in cases of murder or culpable homicide[9] This exception did not apply to civil cases. Section 223 of the CPA, repealed in 1988 in South Africa, provided that a declaration made by a deceased person upon the apprehension of impending death shall be admissible or inadmissible in evidence if such a declaration would have been admissible or inadmissible on 30 May 1961. The law as it stood on that date was, in general, English law.[10] The general rules for admissibility are that the oral or written declarations of a deceased person are admissible to show what occasioned his death, provided the declaration refers to his death and that he was under a settled hopeless expectation of death and, further, that he would have been a competent witness at the time of the declaration.

The rationale behind this exception is that no person would wish to be untruthful just prior to his death. This reason is questionable, to say the least.

The leading South African case on the subject is *R v Heine*.[11] The accused was charged with murdering Dora van Breda by performing an illegal abortion on her. The deceased died on 19 May 1910. Two days before her death a magistrate was called to the hospital and recorded a declaration from the deceased. It commenced with the words, "I, Dora van Breda, with the fear of death before me and without hope of recovery, make the following statement . . .", and concluded, "I am going to die, Mrs Hine is the cause of it all. I want her to go to the Breakwater." The statement was received in evidence because the declarant knew that she was dying. There were five requirements that had to be satisfied.[12]

---

the cases. In *The Henry Coxon* 1878 3 PD 156 entries made in a ship's log by a mate two days after a collision were not admissible because of the time lapse. In *Re Djambi (Sumatra) Rubber Estates Ltd* 1912 107 LT 631 a report made one month after a survey was rejected. See also *Murray v Opperman* 1904 TS 965. *(d) There must have been no motive to misrepresent.* In *The Henry Coxon* supra one of the grounds of rejection of the log entries was that the mate had a motive to misrepresent. This should really have been a matter affecting weight and not admissibility.

[9] See generally Hoffmann & Zeffertt 643–6.

[10] See ch 3 above.

[11] 1910 CPD 371.

[12] The requirements for admissibility were as follows: *(a) The declarant must have died.* This is self-explanatory. *(b) Declarations are accepted only in cases of murder or culpable homicide.* The statement can only be used to prove the way in which the deceased met his or her death. The statement may be used in favour of the accused. In *R v Scaife* 1836 2 Lew CC 150 a statement by the deceased that he would not have been struck if he had not provoked the accused was held to be admissible. *(c) The declarant must have had a settled hopeless expectation of death.* The deceased must have given up all hope of recovery, but need not have died immediately after having made the declaration. It is not fatal to admissibility if the deceased later entertained hopes of recovery. The belief he held when making the statement is decisive. In *R v Moseley* 1825 1 Mood CC 97 the deceased did not die until eleven days after the statement was recorded. The statement was admitted. In *R v Nzobi* 1932 WLD 98 a statement was excluded where the declarant said that he was very weak and did not think he would recover. His statement was to some extent equivocal and did not exhibit a hopeless expectation of death. Much depends upon the circumstances of each case. *(d) The declarant must have been a competent witness.* A lunatic and very young children would thus be excluded from this category. *(e) The statement must be complete.* If the statement is incomplete because of supervening death or unconsciousness, it will be inadmissible as it is impossible to speculate as to what the deceased left unsaid. See *R v Waugh* 1950 AC 203. There was no requirement that the exact words used by the deceased had to be tendered, as long as the statement accurately reflected what was said by the deceased. See *R v Baloi* 1949 1 SA 491 (T). Questions might have been asked of the deceased during the making of the declaration, but suggestions should not have been made. See *R v Abdul* 1905 TS 119. In this case it was also decided that where the deceased expressed his expectation of death in the middle of the statement both the earlier and subsequent parts may be admitted.

14 2 4 Statements concerning pedigree[13] Declarations as to pedigree may be admitted in evidence in both civil and criminal cases. The statement may be oral or written and must relate to matters actually in issue. The declarant must be a blood relation (or spouse of a blood relation) to the person whose pedigree is in issue. Section 38*(b)* of the CPEA provides that any documentary evidence of declarations relating to pedigree shall not be rendered admissible if it would not have been admissible at common law. Consequently the common-law rules must be applied.

The most common written pedigree declarations are to be found in family Bibles, which may set out the family's genealogy. Inscriptions on tombstones also serve as common examples of written pedigree declarations.

In *Ex parte Lottering*[14] an application was made to the Registrar of Births to issue a birth certificate and register the birth. The applicant's case depended on an entry relating to his birth in his mother's Bible. The court refused to accept the entry as the date of birth was not relevant to a pedigree question. The applicant merely wanted a birth certificate for convenience.

14 2 5 Statements as to public and general rights[15] An oral or written declaration made by a deceased person concerning matters of public or general rights is admissible if it was made before a dispute arose and if the declarant was competent to make the declaration. A general right is a right that affects a class of persons, for example, grazing rights gained by immemorial use.[16]

14 2 6 Statements by testators as to the contents of their wills Oral or written statements by a deceased testator were admissible to prove the contents of the will if made after its execution. This exception was created by *Sugden v Lord St Leonards*.[17] The declaration was inadmissible to prove the execution of the will, its alteration or destruction *animo revocandi*.[18]

---

[13] The requirements for admissibility were as follows. *(a) The declarant must have died. (b) The declarant must have been a blood relation (or spouse of a blood relation) of the person whose lineage is in dispute and the relationship must also have been a legitimate one.* This is illustrated by the case of *R v Ndabazonke* 1915 EDL 132. The accused was charged with committing incest with his granddaughter. The prosecution led evidence of hearsay statements concerning the parentage of the girl. As the girl was illegitimate, the statements were held to be inadmissible. The declaration will be admissible where other evidence *prima facie* establishes a legitimate relationship. *(c) The declaration must have been made before a family dispute arose.*

[14] 1936 TPD 29.

[15] The requirements for admissibility were as follows: *(a) The declarant must be dead.* It would seem that the case of *Fuchs & Downing v Port Elizabeth Municipality* 1944 EDL 254 was wrongly decided as there was no evidence that the declarant was dead. *(b) The declaration should deal with the reputed existence of a public or general right.* In *Du Toit v Lydenburg Municipality* 1909 TS 527 the boundaries of the town lands were proved by evidence that an old resident, who had known the beacons for forty years, had pointed them out to his son. *(c) The declaration must have been made before the dispute arose.* It was held in *Berkeley Peerage* 1811 4 Camp 401 that the admissibility of the statement would not be affected if it was made to cover future contingencies. *(d) The declarant must have been qualified to speak.* Each member of the public is presumed capable to speak of public rights; but with general rights it would seem as if only a person who has an interest in the right is competent.

[16] *Municipality of Swellendam v Surveyor-General* 1848 3 Menz 578.

[17] 1876 1 PD 154.

[18] *Dukada v Dukada* 1937 EDL 372.

14 3   SPONTANEOUS EXCLAMATIONS

The so-called spontaneous exclamation constituted an exception to the hearsay rule.

In *R v Ratten*[19] it was said that if a sudden event had assumed such intensity and pressure that the utterance can safely be regarded as a true reflection of what was actually happening, then it ought to be received.[20]

A party who wishes to introduce a statement under cover of this exception to the hearsay rule assumes the burden of laying the foundation for its reception.[21]

It was formerly thought that the declarant must be shown to be unavailable as a witness. But in *Titus v Shield Insurance Co Ltd* it was said (*obiter*) that the unavailability of the declarant is not an essential requirement for the admission of a spontaneous statement. This approach is sound. The extra-curial statement made spontaneously at the time of or immediately after the event will ordinarily be of more value than a statement made in court by the same person in his capacity as a witness and after weeks or months have passed.[22] The spontaneous exclamation has a strong guarantee that a story was not contrived. The declarant had no time to reflect or reconstruct. There was no chance for the declarant "to trim his sails".

A statement in writing may also be admitted as a spontaneous exclamation.[23]

There are basically four conditions for the admissibility of spontaneous statements. These conditions overlap to a great extent.

14 3 1   Startling occurrence   There must have been an occurrence startling enough to produce a stress of nervous excitement. Typical examples are assaults,[24] collisions,[25] explosions, or even a robbery.[26] It would be impossible to state a *numerus clausus* of events startling enough to produce a stress of nervous excitement in a declarant.

14 3 2   Spontaneity   It is required that the statement should have been made while the stress was still so operative upon the speaker that his reflective powers may be assumed to have been in abeyance.[27] This is a crucial condition and can be illustrated with reference to *S v Qolo*.[28] In this case A saw a man covered in blood and immediately went to his assistance. A saw that the man was seriously injured and asked him what the matter was. The man then pointed his finger at a tree approximately ten metres away and said "lo tsotsi". Through the foliage

---

[19] 1971 3 All ER 803 807.
[20] See also *R v Taylor* 1961 3 SA 616 (N).
[21] *Titus v Shield Insurance Co Ltd* 1980 3 SA 119 (A).
[22] Van der Merwe 1981 *THRHR* 94 96.
[23] *S v Tuge* 1966 4 SA 565.
[24] *R v Taylor* supra.
[25] *Titus v Shield Insurance Co Ltd* supra; *Vermaak v Parity Insurances Co Ltd* 1966 2 SA 312 (W).
[26] *S v Tuge* supra.
[27] *S v Tuge* supra. Cf *S v Mpofu* 1993 2 SACR 109 (N), which was decided after the Law of Evidence Amendment Act 45 of 1988 had come into operation.
[28] 1965 1 SA 174 (A).

A saw the accused, who was thereafter caught and brought to the injured man, who then slapped the accused in the face. The injured man subsequently died from one of three stab wounds. There was no evidence as to when the stabbing actually took place. It was held that the deceased's utterance was not admissible as a dying declaration. It was also held that it had not been shown that the utterance to A was so contemporaneous with the assault that it formed part of the *res gestae*. It was further held, however, that the physical act of slapping the face of the appellant was admissible. But the court held that the evidence of identification (that is, the pointing out of the accused) could not be admitted as a spontaneous exclamation because there was no evidence as to when the stabbing actually took place. Spontaneity was not proved. The deceased could have reconstructed the events or contrived a story. The test of contemporaneousness and spontaneity was not satisfied. But in *Titus v Shield Insurance Co Ltd* supra it was said that the emphasis should rather be on the probable spontaneity of the utterance than on strict contemporaneousness, even though the lapse of time may be one of the factors determining probable spontaneity. Spontaneity is a secondary *factum probandum*, whilst contemporaneousness may serve as a *factum probans*. But the real test is whether the statement was made at a time when the effect, upon the declarant, of the shocking occurrence to which the statement related was still operative, thus rendering it unlikely, according to common human experience, that the declarant would at the time of making the statement have concocted it, or attempted to reconstruct the occurrence in his mind.[29]

14 3 3 No reconstruction of past events In *S v Tuge* it was also said that the statement must not amount to a reconstruction of a past event.[30]

14 3 4 Narrative parts excluded Purely narrative matter will be excluded from a spontaneous exclamation.[31] The rationale of this rule is also fairly obvious: any narration is a strong indication that reflective powers were not in abeyance; that the declarant had sufficient time to think or reason and that the statement was therefore not made spontaneously.[32]

---

[29] *Titus v Shield Insurance Co Ltd* supra 128.
[30] Supra 573.
[31] *Joubert v SAR & H* 1930 TPD 164.
[32] Lansdown & Campbell 826.

CHAPTER 15

STATUTORY EXCEPTIONS TO THE HEARSAY RULE

A St Q Skeen

15 1   INTRODUCTION

The restrictive nature of the hearsay rule as developed by the common law was mitigated by considerable statutory inroads in the form of additional exceptions. These exceptions provide for the admissibility of certain documents which contain hearsay. These exceptions are vital to the proper functioning of the law of evidence in a complex and modern industrial society (see, for example, §§ 15 4, 15 10, and 15 11 below.)

These exceptions antedate s 3 of the Law of Evidence Amendment Act 45 of 1988, which has revolutionized the law relating to hearsay. It may be possible to introduce documentary hearsay which does not comply with the requirements of s 3 of Act 45 of 1988.

15 2   PROOF OF CERTAIN FACTS BY AFFIDAVIT

Both the CPA and the CPEA permit the proof of certain facts by affidavits. The salient feature of these exceptions is that they apply in the main to affidavits made by persons employed by the state, provincial administrations and banks.

15 2 1 Proof of certain facts by affidavit or certificate in criminal proceedings (ss 212 and 212A of the CPA)   Section 212(1) provides that the question as to whether any fact or transaction or occurrence did or did not take place in any state department or provincial administration, in any court of law or in any bank, may, subject to certain formalities, be proved by an affidavit. The affidavit is admissible on its mere production as *prima facie* evidence of the matters stated in it.

Section 212(2) provides that the question of whether a person bearing a particular name did or did not provide information or documents to a state or provincial administration official shall be *prima facie* proved by means of an affidavit from the official concerned.

Section 212(3) relates to the question as to whether anything has been registered under any law or whether any fact or transaction has been recorded under a particular law. It provides that any affidavit by the person whose duty it is to perform the act shall be admissible (on its mere production) and shall be *prima facie* proof of its contents.

Section 212(4) provides that where any fact is established by an examination or process involving skill in biology, chemistry, physics, astronomy, geography, anatomy, human behavioural sciences, pathology, toxicology or the identification of fingerprints or palmprints, an affidavit from a person in the state or provincial service, or attached to the South African Institute for Medical Research, or in the service of any university in the country or any other body duly gazetted, shall on its mere production be *prima facie* proof of such fact. In cases where the deponent has skill in chemistry, anatomy or pathology a certificate may be furnished instead of an affidavit. In *S v Ratsane*[1] it was held that an affidavit which identified an exhibit as fine cord in terms of a certain Act and which contained no allegation as to what skill was required to identify it was inadmissible. In *S v Nkhahale*[2] it was decided that a certificate handed in in terms of s 212(4)*(a)* must be regarded as *prima facie* evidence of the facts contained in it unless the judicial officer is convinced that he cannot rely on it.[3] *Prima facie* proof will become conclusive proof in the absence of other credible evidence.[4] The section may be used by both the state and defence and applies to a plea of guilty and not guilty.[5]

Where the state relies on a certificate in terms of s 212(4) and (8) regarding

---

[1] 1979 4 SA 864 (O). See also *S v Easter* 1995 2 SACR 350 (W) and see generally *S v Britz* 1994 2 SACR 687 (W); cf *S v Farenden* 1994 1 SACR 229 (T).

[2] 1981 1 SA 320 (O).

[3] See also *S v Van der Merwe* 1982 1 SA 313 (O); *S v Greeff* 1995 2 SACR 687 (A). However, a further consideration arises in respect of an undefended accused. In *S v Nkhumeleni* 1986 3 SA 102 (V) it was held improper to make use of s 212(4) of the CPA to submit evidence of a medico-legal report in the case of an undefended accused. It was suggested that the court should employ s 220 of the CPA by asking the accused whether he admits or denies the contents. See generally Zeffertt 1986 *ASSAL* 477 for a critical discussion of this procedure.

[4] *S v Veldthuizen* 1982 3 SA 413 (A).

[5] *S v Naidoo* 1985 2 SA 32 (N).

the analysis of a sample and receipt of such a sample where there is no indication that there was a significant lapse of time between receipt and analysis, it is not necessary, in order to constitute *prima facie* proof, that the analyst should allege that the sample remained in his custody from the time he received it until he analysed it.[6]

The person who signs a certificate in terms of s 212(4) *(a)* must say that he or she determined the relevant fact.[7]

Section 212(5) deals with proof of the existence, nature, mass or value of precious stones or metals by means of an affidavit from an appraiser in the service of the state. This affidavit is admissible on its mere production and is *prima facie* proof of its contents.

Section 212(6) concerns the finding, lifting of and dealing with fingerprints and palmprints. An affidavit is *prima facie* proof of the matters stated in it.

Section 212(7) deals with the identity and physical condition of any deceased person or body. An affidavit (which is *prima facie* proof of its contents) made by a person in the employ of a hospital, nursing home, ambulance or mortuary is admissible to show the physical characteristics or condition of the deceased person or body and that, whilst under the deponent's care, the body received no further wounds or injuries. This subsection is often used to provide the chain of evidence to show that no *novus actus interveniens* occurred in cases of murder or culpable homicide.

Section 212(8) concerns the receipt, custody, packing, marking or delivery of any fingerprint or palmprint, article of clothing, specimen, tissue or any other object of whatever nature and which is relevant to the issue. A person of the status referred to in the subsection may make an affidavit dealing with the receipt, delivery and despatch of such items and such affidavit shall be admissible on its mere production as *prima facie* proof of its contents.[8]

Section 212(9) concerns consignment of goods by rail. An affidavit as to the consignment and delivery of goods may be made by a person in the service of the railways administration and shall be *prima facie* proof of its contents on mere production.

Section 212(10) allows the Minister to prescribe in respect of any measuring instrument and by notice in the *Gazette* the conditions and requirements which must be complied with before any reading by such measuring instruments may be accepted in criminal proceedings. Once the gazetted conditions are complied with, the measuring instrument shall be accepted as proving the fact recorded by it unless the contrary is proved.[9] An affidavit which declares that the requirements have been complied with shall, on its mere production, be admissible. This subsection is used, inter alia, to prescribe the formalities for various speed

---

[6] *S v Jantjies* 1993 2 SACR 475 (A).
[7] *S v Paulsen* 1995 1 SACR 518 (C).
[8] See, e g, *S v Mirirai* 1995 2 SACR 134 (T).
[9] See *S v Easter* 1995 2 SACR 350 (W).

trapping devices.[10] The affidavit which is used must comply with the terms of the Justices of the Peace and Commissioners of Oaths Act.[11]

Section 212(11) provides that the Minister may make regulations in the *Gazette* concerning any syringe intended for drawing blood and any receptacle intended for the storing of blood. Requirements may also be prescribed concerning the cleanliness and sealing of these items. An affidavit from a person who has satisfied himself before using the items that the regulations have been complied with shall be admissible on mere production and shall be *prima facie* proof of its contents. This section is often used in cases of drunken driving and driving with an excess blood-alcohol level.[12]

Section 212(12) allows the court, at its discretion, to cause any deponent to an affidavit made under s 212 to give evidence or answer interrogatories.[13]

Section 212(13) provides that the section is additional to and not in substitution of the law concerning the admissibility of documentary evidence.

Section 212A allows for the proof of any act, transaction or occurrence in a foreign official department, court or bank by an affidavit, which must be duly authenticated.

15 2 2 Proof of certain facts by affidavit in civil proceedings Section 22 of the CPEA provides that an affidavit shall be admissible on its mere production to prove any fact ascertained requiring skill in bacteriology, biology, chemistry, physics, astronomy, anatomy or pathology. The deponent must be a person in the state or provincial administration service, or attached to the South African Institute for Medical Research, or any university in the Republic or any other institution that may be gazetted. It is provided that no affidavit shall be admissible unless a copy has been delivered to the opposing party at least seven days before its production. The court may, on application, order the deponent to give evidence or answer interrogatories.

15 3 ADMISSIBILITY OF WRITTEN STATEMENTS BY CONSENT (SECTION 213 OF THE CPA)

Section 213 of the CPA provides that a written statement by any person, other than an accused in the proceedings, shall, subject to certain conditions, be admissible as evidence to the same effect as oral evidence by such person. The main conditions are that the statement should be signed and should contain a

---

[10] See GN R389 in *Reg Gaz* 2607 of 3 March 1978 as amended by GN 2051 in *Reg Gaz* 2675 of 13 October 1978; see also *S v Baum; S v Booysen; S v Murison* 1979 2 SA 671 (E). In *S v Van der Merwe* 1979 2 SA 760 (T) it was held that the mere fact that a manufacturer states that a machine is identical to one the Minister has approved in the *Gazette* does not mean that the Minister has approved that particular machine. In *S v Mwanusi* 1978 4 SA 806 (O) the accused was charged with speeding. A traffic officer had used a gazetted radar device and stated, in an affidavit, that he had set up the machine in terms of s 212(10) *(a)* and that all the stated requirements were satisfied. The court held that evidence was required to show what had been done to satisfy the requirements.

[11] Act 16 of 1963; *S v Stevens* 1983 3 SA 649 (A).

[12] See generally Strauss 1979 *SACC* 179.

[13] See *S v Veldthuizen* 1982 3 SA 413 (A).

declaration of the maker's knowledge that it was made subject to penalties (in the event of it being used in evidence where the maker knew it was false or where he did not believe it to be true). A copy should be served on the opposite party. Any objection should be received from the opposite party at least two days before the proceedings. It is possible for the parties to agree to production of the statement even if it had not been served on the opposing party.[14] There is provision for either party to require the maker to give evidence.

Section 213 is based on s 9 of the English Criminal Justice Act of 1967. Such a provision is probably more suited to a country where legal aid and representation are more widespread than in this country. The idea behind the section is that statements which were in the nature of agreed facts could be admitted to obviate the calling of the witness in question. The main danger is that an accused who is ignorant of the consequences may, by default, allow the admission of a statement which is adverse to his case without fully realizing this. It is true to say that he could later require the court to call the maker of the statement, but ignorance may prevent him from following this course.[15] The only statements which may not be produced under s 213 are admissions and confessions made by the accused (see generally chapters 16 and 17 below). The section is designed to save time and expense. A more appropriate way would be by means of formal admissions in court after the presiding officer had advised the accused of the consequences of making admissions (see § 28 4 4 below).

15 4   ADMISSIBILITY OF TRADE OR BUSINESS RECORDS IN CRIMINAL CASES

Section 221 of the CPA closely follows the wording of s 1 of the English Criminal Evidence Act of 1965. The English Act was passed as a result of the case of *Myers v DPP*.[16] The question in issue was whether the identity of stolen motor vehicles could be proved by the production of the manufacturer's records made by unidentified workmen. The House of Lords held that the records were hearsay as they were used to prove the identity of the vehicles.

The material part of s 221 of the CPA reads as follows:

"In criminal proceedings in which direct oral evidence of a fact would be admissible, any statement contained in a document and tending to establish that fact shall, upon production of the document, be admissible as evidence of that fact if —

(a) the document is or forms part of a record relating to any trade or business and has been compiled in the course of that trade or business, from information supplied directly or indirectly, by persons who have or may reasonably be supposed to have personal knowledge of the matters dealt with in the information they supply; and

(b) the person who supplies the information recorded in the statement in question is dead or outside the Republic or is unfit by reason of his physical or mental condition to attend as a witness or cannot with reasonable diligence be identified or found or cannot reasonably be expected, having regard to the time which has elapsed since he supplied

---

[14] This agreement must be reached before the statement is tendered; *S v Serapelo* 1979 4 SA 567 (B).
[15] See generally Van Wyk 1977 *SACC* 213.
[16] 1965 AC 1001, 1964 2 All ER 881.

the information as well as all the circumstances, to have recollection of the matters dealt within the information he supplied."

Section 221(2) states that in determining the admissibility of the document the court may draw an inference from the form or contents of the document. It may also have reference to a medical certificate in deciding whether or not the person is fit to attend as a witness. Section 221(3) deals with the matters to be considered in determining the weight to be given to a statement which is admissible under the section; namely the accuracy or otherwise of the statement, whether the information was supplied contemporaneously, and whether anyone concerned with the making of the statement had any incentive to conceal or misrepresent the facts.

"Business", in terms of s 221(5), includes any public transport, public utility or similar undertaking carried on by a local authority, and the activities of the post office and the railways administration. "Document" includes any device by means of which information is recorded or stored; and "statements" include any representation of fact, whether made in words or otherwise. This definition is sufficient to include tape recordings, computer printouts[17] and microfilm.[18]

The section contains no definition of the word "record". The English courts have held that a single document relating to one transaction (such as a bill of lading) is admissible as a record.[19] There are no reported cases in South Africa, but it is submitted that our courts should arrive at a similar conclusion. English courts have also doubted whether a file, containing correspondence, which was added to from time to time as letters were received, could constitute a record. However, it could be argued that a file containing correspondence may amount to a record in terms of the Act if it constitutes a complete history surrounding a fact in issue. The record need not be continuous as is required by s 34(1)(a)(ii) of the CPEA.

Once the conditions set out in s 221(1) of the CPA have been met the document is admissible and the court will have no discretion to exclude it. It does, however, have a discretion as to how much weight to afford to the document.

15 5 PART VI OF THE CPEA AS APPLIED TO CRIMINAL CASES (SECTION 222 OF THE CPA)

Section 222 of the CPA provides that the provisions of ss 33–38 (inclusive) of the CPEA shall, *mutatis mutandis*, apply with reference to criminal proceedings. The provisions of these sections were first introduced, for civil proceedings, in 1962 and were substantially identical to the English Evidence Act of 1938. A number of the cases cited below are English cases. South African courts are not bound

---

[17] See *S v Harper* 1981 1 SA 88 (D).
[18] See § 21 4 below for a discussion of the admissibility of computer printouts.
[19] *R v Jones; R v Sullivan* 1978 2 All ER 718.

by these decisions, but they serve as useful guides as to how the English courts have interpreted identical provisions.

Section 33 defines a document as including any book, map, plan, drawing or photograph.[20] "Statement" includes any representation of fact, whether made in words or otherwise. The definition of a statement is taken, when referring to statements of fact, to include a statement of opinion if the opinion would have been admissible in oral evidence. This is illustrated by the English case of *Dass (an infant) v Masih*.[21] Evidence was required from an expert on Punjabi writing. Such an expert was not available in England and a written report was obtained from India. The court of appeal held that this report was admissible.

Section 34(1) sets out the main requirements for the admissibility of documentary evidence and reads as follows:

"In any civil proceedings where direct oral evidence of a fact would be admissible, any statement made by a person in a document and tending to establish that fact shall on production of the original document be admissible as evidence of that fact provided —
(a) the person who made that statement —
    (i)   had personal knowledge of the matters dealt with in the statement; or
    (ii) where the document in question is or forms part of a record purporting to be a continuous record, made the statement (in so far as the matters dealt with therein are not within his personal knowledge) in the performance of a duty to record information supplied to him by a person who had or might reasonably have been supposed to have personal knowledge of those matters; and
(b) the person who made the statement is called as a witness in the proceedings unless he is dead or unfit by reason of his bodily or mental condition to attend as a witness or is outside the Republic, and it is not reasonably practicable to secure his attendance or all reasonable efforts to find him have been made without success."[22]

It is to be observed that the original document must be produced, but the presiding officer may, in terms of s 34(2)(b), allow the production of a copy or of the material part proved to be a true copy. He can only do so to avoid undue delay or expense. In *Bowskill v Dawson*[23] it was held that the provisions appear to indicate that the original must be in existence because no amount of inconvenience or delay would enable its production.[24]

Section 34(4) provides that a statement in a document shall not, for the purposes of the section, be deemed to have been made by a person unless the document or the material part was written, made or produced by him with his own hand, or was signed or initialled by him or otherwise recognized by him in

---

[20] An affidavit has been held to be a document in this context; *Schimper v Monastery Diamond Mining Corporation (Pty) Ltd* 1982 1 SA 612 (O).

[21] 1968 2 All ER 226.

[22] In *Magwanyana v Standard General Insurance Co Ltd* 1996 1 SA 254 (D) the court held that s 34(1) required proof that the statement in the document in question was made by the person in question. The court found that the statement in issue was essentially a statement by an interpreter of what the deponent had told him and, as the interpreter had not been called to testify, the document could not be admitted under s 34.

[23] 1954 1 QB 288.

[24] If this is so, microfilm would in most cases, where the original has been destroyed, be inadmissible; Paizes 1984 *BML* 91. A copy must be proved a true copy: *Rawoot v Marine & Trade Insurance Co Ltd* 1980 1 SA 260 (C).

writing as one for the accuracy of which he is responsible. In *Da Mata v Otto*[25] handwritten and signed carbon copies satisfied the requirements of the section. In *Putter v Provincial Assurance Co Ltd*[26] a thumbprint of a deceased person was regarded as a signature. A document which had been dictated to a typist and corrected in his own hand by the person who dictated it has been held admissible on the ground that he had acknowledged in writing the accuracy of the document.[27]

The phrase "continuous record" has given rise to certain judicial interpretations. In *Thrasyvoulos Ioannou v Papa Christoforas Demetriou*[28] Lord Tucker said:

> ". . . [W]ithout attempting to give a definition of continuous record it is sufficient to say that the mere existence of a file containing one or more documents of a similar nature dealing with the same or a kindred subject-matter does not necessarily make the contents of the file a continuous record within the meaning of the section."

In this case the court refused to receive in evidence a report (of an official inquiry into water rights) which was filed together with other documents of a similar nature. The refusal was based on the fact that there was no evidence that it formed part of a continuous record. In *Simpson v Lever*[29] a policeman's notebook recording details of a motor-vehicle accident was held to be a continuous record.

Section 34(2) provides that the court may, if it is satisfied that undue delay or expense would otherwise occur, admit a statement admissible under s 34(1) notwithstanding that the person who made the statement is available but is not called as a witness. This provision gives the court a fairly wide discretion once it is satisfied that undue delay or expense would occur. In criminal cases it would appear that this can be done at the request of either the prosecution or defence. In *Hladhla v President Insurance Co Ltd*[30] it was held that a plan plus its accompanying key were admissible without the maker, a policeman, giving evidence.

Section 34(3) provides that nothing in the Act shall render admissible as evidence any statement made by a person interested at the time when proceedings were pending or anticipated involving a dispute as to any fact which the statement might tend to establish. It is a moot point whether it is sufficient that the person who recorded the statement under a duty was not interested or whether such a statement would be inadmissible if the informant was interested. In *Barkway v South Wales Transport Co Ltd*[31] it was held that the statement should be excluded if either the maker or the informant was an interested person. This approach tends to ensure that only reliable hearsay is admissible. There are

---

[25] 1972 3 SA 859 (A).
[26] 1963 3 SA 145 (W).
[27] *Re Powe* 1955 3 All ER 448.
[28] 1952 AC 84.
[29] 1962 3 All ER 870. Cf generally *S v Moolman* 1996 1 SACR 267 (A).
[30] 1965 1 SA 614 (A).
[31] 1949 1 KB 54.

numerous decisions as to what constitutes interest.[32] In *Boshoff v Nel*[33] the court held that the term "interest" should not be construed to allow a mere indirect interest to render a statement inadmissible, as the concept "person interested" has a more limited context, implying a more tangible interest. On the other hand, it should not be interpreted so restrictively that it can only be an interest which entitles a person to join or be joined in proceedings. A personal interest, whether financial or otherwise, may be included provided it is not too remote.

Interest is not confined interest,[34] but the witness must have a personal interest in the outcome.[35] It was held in *Laubscher v Commercial Union Assurance Co of SA Ltd*[36] that a person who was an accused in criminal proceedings would be an interested person in subsequent civil proceedings. It is submitted that anyone who may be liable to prosecution for an offence would be termed interested. The same approach should apply to complainants, except in the so-called victimless crimes.

In the case of *Jarman v Lambert and Cooke (Contractors) Ltd*[37] the word "anticipate" was taken to mean that proceedings were regarded as likely or reasonably probable. It was further held that the subjective anticipation of the maker is important and not what the reasonable man would have anticipated. In *Da Mata v Otto*[38] "anticipated" was said to mean "expect". It has been held, in a civil case, that the fact that only a criminal charge was anticipated was sufficient to exclude a statement. There is no reason why this should not apply in the reverse situation.[39]

Section 34(5) provides that in deciding whether a document is admissible the court may draw any reasonable inference from the document. It may also have regard to a medical certificate in deciding whether a person is fit to attend court as a witness.

Section 35 provides that in determining the weight, if any, to be attached to a statement regard should be had as to whether the person who made the statement had any incentive to conceal or misrepresent facts.

Section 36 states that in any civil proceedings an instrument, the validity of which requires attestation, may, instead of being proved by an attesting witness, be proved in the manner which it might be proved if no attesting witness were alive, provided that this will not apply to wills or other testamentary writings. This means that the document in question can be proved by evidence identifying the writing of the author.

---

[32] *Bearmans Ltd v Metropolitan Police District Receiver* 1961 1 All ER 384; *Barkway v South Wales Transport Co Ltd* 1948 2 All ER 40.

[33] 1983 2 SA 41 (NC).

[34] *Boshoff v Nel* supra.

[35] *Holton v Holton* 1946 2 All ER 534.

[36] 1976 1 SA 908 (E); see also *Colgate-Palmolive (Pty) Ltd v Elida-Gibbs (Pty) Ltd* 1990 2 SA 516 (W). In *United Tobacco Co Ltd v Goncalves* 1996 1 SA 209 (W) it was held that a person is "interested" if the statement in question was made when criminal proceedings were anticipated against its maker.

[37] 1951 2 KB 937.

[38] 1972 3 SA 858 (A).

[39] *W & W Wood (Haulage) Ltd v Redpath* 1967 2 QB 520.

Section 37 provides that documents which are more than twenty years old and come from proper custody are presumed to have been duly executed if there is nothing to suggest the contrary.

The next matter to consider is whether computer output would be admissible under s 34. Various difficulties arise: *(a)* the definition of document is more restrictive than the definition in s 221 of the CPA; *(b)* a computer is not a person;[40] *(c)* it is unlikely, to say the least, that the computer operator would acknowledge in writing that he is responsible for its accuracy.[41]

15 6   PROOF OF ENTRIES IN BANKERS BOOKS IN CRIMINAL CASES (SECTIONS 236 AND 236A OF THE CPA)

The entries in the accounting records of a bank and any document which is in the possession of the bank relating to the entries or to any transaction of the bank shall on their production be *prima facie* proof of the matters recorded if accompanied by an affidavit by a person who works for the bank in question, that the accounting records or documents were or are the ordinary books of the bank, that the entries were made in the normal course of business, and that the records or documents are in the custody or under the control of the bank. "Document" is defined to include a recording or transcribed computer print-out produced by any mechanical or electronic device by means of which information is stored or recorded.

Provisions are made for copies to be produced subject to the presence of an accompanying affidavit. The opposing party may, on the order of a court, inspect the original entries in question. No bank is compelled to produce its books unless the court so orders. Strict compliance regarding the formalities and contents of the affidavits is necessary.[42]

Section 236A provides for proof of entries in accounting records and documentation of banks in countries outside the Republic.

15 7   PRESUMPTIONS RELATING TO CERTAIN DOCUMENTS IN CRIMINAL CASES (SECTION 246 OF THE CPA)

Section 246 of the CPA provides that any document (which includes any book, pamphlet, letter, circular letter, list, record, placard or poster) which was at any time on premises occupied by any association, incorporated or unincorporated, or in the possession or under the control of any office bearer, officer or member of such association shall be *prima facie* proof that an accused was an office bearer or member of the association if his name appears on the document as an office bearer or member. If the accused appears to be the author of the document and the name of a person which corresponds with the accused's name appears on the document, the document, on its mere production, shall serve as *prima facie*

---

[40] *Narlis v South African Bank of Athens* 1976 2 SA 573 (A).
[41] Skeen 1984 *SALJ* 675. See § 21 4 below, where computer-generated evidence is discussed.
[42] *R v Bhoola* 1960 4 SA 895 (T); *S v Smit* 1966 1 SA 638 (O).

proof that the accused was the author. In the same section provision is also made for minutes, or copies thereof, of an association or committee thereof, which on mere production shall be *prima facie* proof thereof. Any document which discloses the objects of the association shall also be *prima facie* proof of the objects.

In *S v Matsiepe*[43] a document which contained the constitution of an organization was held to be proof, without any additional evidence, of the aims of the organisation. A "corresponding" name must show some similarity.[44]

The section, which was first introduced in 1958, was intended to facilitate the control of subversive organizations.

15 8   PRESUMPTIONS RELATING TO ABSENCE FROM THE REPUBLIC

Section 247 of the CPA provides that any document (including any newspaper, periodical, book, pamphlet, letter, circular letter, list record, placard, or poster) on the face of which it appears that a person of a name corresponding to that of an accused has, at a particular time, been outside the Republic or made a statement whilst outside the Republic, shall be *prima facie* proof that the accused was outside the Republic or made the statement.

The document, which is admissible on its mere production, must be accompanied by a certificate from the Director-General of Foreign Affairs that he is satisfied that the document is of foreign origin. This section is intended to be used in cases where persons are charged with undergoing military training abroad and allied "political offences". There is no need for the document to emanate from the country in which the accused allegedly was; it is merely necessary that it is certified to be a foreign document.

15 9   PART VI OF THE CPEA RELATING TO DOCUMENTS IN CIVIL CASES

The application of Part VI to criminal cases was considered in § 15 5 above. Part VI applies equally to civil and criminal cases with an identity of principles.

15 10   ENTRIES IN BANKERS BOOKS IN CIVIL PROCEEDINGS (SECTIONS 28–32 OF THE CPEA)

Section 28 of the CPEA provides that the ledgers, day-books, cash books and other account books of any bank shall be *prima facie* evidence of the matters concerned therein if an affidavit is furnished by a bank official stating that the books have been or are the ordinary books of the bank and have come from the control or custody of the bank.

If these requirements are satisfied, then books shall be received in evidence as *prima facie* proof of their contents. Section 29 allows for the admissibility of copies of documents subject to the presence of an accompanying affidavit.

---

[43] 1962 4 SA 708 (A); see also *S v Alexander* 1965 2 SA 818 (C).
[44] *S v Sethlodi* 1962 1 PH H35 (T); *S v Mothopeng* 1965 4 SA 484 (T).

Section 30 requires that at least ten days' notice of the intention to produce must be given to the opposing party. The opposing party, on at least three days' notice to the bank, shall be allowed to inspect and make copies of the documents. Section 31 provides that no bank shall be compelled to produce documents without a court order. Section 32 expressly provides that the provisions of ss 28–31 shall not apply when the bank is a party to a case. The time limits and requirements for the affidavit must be strictly complied with.[45]

The essential difference between these sections and s 236 of the CPA is that no notice of production need be given in criminal cases.

15 11 COMPANIES ACT 61 OF 1973

Section 94 of this Act provides that a certificate signed by two directors of a company or by one director and one officer duly authorized by the directors, specifying any shares or stock of the company, shall be *prima facie* evidence of the title of the member to such shares or stock.[46] Section 109 of this Act provides that the register of members shall be *prima facie* evidence of any matters directed or authorized to be entered therein by the Act. Section 204 provides that the minutes of meetings of the company, which purport to be signed by the chairman of that or the succeeding meeting, shall be evidence of the proceedings.

15 12 MISCELLANEOUS

Various statutes provide that certain documents shall be admissible on their mere production and shall be *prima facie* proof of the matters contained in the document.

15 12 1 Birth and death certificates Section 28(2) of the Births and Deaths Registration Act 51 of 1992 provides that a birth or death certificate shall serve as *prima facie* evidence of the particulars which it contains. A foreign certificate would normally be considered a public document.

15 12 2 Further exceptions in terms of the CPA Section 237 of the CPA provides for a presumption of lawful marriage entered into by an accused charged with bigamy. Section 238(2) of the CPA provides that whenever the fact that any lawful and binding marriage was contracted is relevant to the issue at criminal proceedings at which an accused is charged with incest, such fact may be proved *prima facie* in the manner provided in s 237 for the proof of the existence of a lawful and binding marriage of a person charged with bigamy.

Sections 214, 215 and 235 deal with the admissibility of evidence in former proceedings.

---

[45] *Grubb v Mouton* 1958 1 SA 463 (T); *Van der Westhuizen v Kleynhans* 1969 3 SA 174 (O).

[46] See *Marine and Trade Insurance Co Ltd v Van der Schyff* 1972 1 SA 26 (A) for the meaning of *prima facie* evidence in this respect.

THE ADMISSIBILITY AND PROOF OF THE CONTENTS OF RELEVANT DETRIMENTAL STATEMENTS

CHAPTER 16

INFORMAL ADMISSIONS

PJ Schwikkard

16 1 INTRODUCTION

An admission is a statement made by a party, in civil or criminal proceedings, which is adverse to that party's case. Informal admissions, which are usually made out of court, must be distinguished from formal admissions made in the pleadings or in court. Formal admissions are binding on the maker, and are generally made in order to reduce the number of issues before the court,[1] whereas informal admissions merely constitute an item of evidence which can be contradicted or explained away.

---

[1] See ch 26 for a fuller discussion of formal admissions.

Informal admissions may be admitted to prove the truth of their contents. The rationale for admitting such evidence would appear to be that a person is unlikely to make an admission adverse to his interests if the contents of that admission are not true. However, since a statement may constitute an admission even though a party is unaware that what he is saying is contrary to his interests,[2]

> "[i]t is probably better to say that admissions or confessions do not have some of the drawbacks inherent in hearsay because a party can hardly complain that when he made the statement he was not on oath or did not have an opportunity to cross-examine himself".[3]

Van der Merwe et al describe informal admissions as constituting an exception to the rule against hearsay.[4] This observation was made prior to the Appellate Division decision in *S v Holshausen*[5] (in which it was held that a statement by a party cannot be hearsay) and prior to the redefinition of hearsay in s 3 of the Law of Evidence Amendment Act.[6] Section 3(4) defines hearsay evidence as "evidence, whether oral or in writing, the probative value of which depends upon the credibility of any person other than the person giving such evidence".

Hoffmann & Zeffertt argue that the words "depend upon" must be interpreted as meaning "to rest primarily upon or to be governed by".[7] Consequently,[8]

> "[i]f a witness testified that X had admitted something to him, the probative value of his testimony would depend to some extent on the credibility of X, but it would usually rest primarily upon the credibility of the witness, or be governed by it. In other words its probative value would not 'depend upon' a person other than the person who is giving the evidence and, therefore, would not be hit by s 3."

On the other hand, Paizes takes the view that s 3(4) brings confessions and admissions within the hearsay rule and that the probative value of a statement depends on the credibility of its maker.[9] However, he concludes that s 3 does not require any significant departure from the traditional approach to the admission of confessions and admissions, because[10]

> "the more contentious aspects of the problem of the admissibility of confessions or admissions are not the concern of s 3. And, since it is difficult to imagine how the interest of justice could be served by the exclusion of a relevant, voluntarily made admission or confession which satisfies the other statutory requirements, it is submitted that subjecting such evidence to the scrutiny required in s 3 will be a harmless but usually futile exercise. The hearsay objection will be met, in any event, should the accused himself testify at his trial . . .."

Once part of a statement has been allowed into evidence as an admission the maker is entitled to have the whole statement put before the court, even where

---

[2] The test employed in determining whether a statement or conduct constitutes an admission is objective. See *R v Barlin* 1926 AD 459 at 465; *S v Grove-Mitchell* 1975 3 SA 417 (A) 420.

[3] Hoffmann & Zeffertt (1988) 4 ed 172.

[4] Van der Merwe (ed) *Evidence* (1983) 216.

[5] 1984 4 SA 852 (A).

[6] Act 45 of 1988. See further ch 13 below.

[7] At 175.

[8] Hoffmann & Zeffertt 175.

[9] Paizes in Du Toit et al *Commentary* 24-50E. See also Paizes 1985 *SALJ* 258, where the decision in *Holshausen* is criticized.

[10] Paizes in Du Toit et al *Commentary* 24-50E.

it includes self-serving statements,[11] provided the two components form part of a single statement.[12]

An informal admission which is made extra-judicially must also be distinguished from a statement made against a party's interest during the course of a trial. The latter is treated as ordinary evidence.

16 2 REQUIREMENTS FOR ADMISSIBILITY

In civil matters there is only one general requirement for admissibility, and that is relevance.[13] An additional requirement must be met where statements are made in the course of negotiations for the settlement of a dispute, in that such statements cannot be disclosed without the consent of both parties.[14] In criminal matters an admission must be proved to have been made voluntarily before it can be admitted into evidence.[15]

16 3 ADMISSIONS BY CONDUCT

Admissions may be contained in a verbal or written statement and they may also be inferred from conduct. For example, in *S v Sheppard*[16] it was held that a party's payment of an invoice was an admission that the services specified in that invoice had been performed.[17] However, conduct does not need to be positive to constitute an admission, and an admission may be inferred from silence.

16 3 1 Admissions by silence Silence in the face of an accusation may amount to an admission when it forms the basis of a commonsense inference against a party.[18] For example, in *Jacobs v Henning*[19] the plaintiff, in bringing an action for damages for seduction, led evidence that the defendant, when confronted and accused by the plaintiff's father of having caused his daughter's pregnancy,

---

[11] *R v Valachia* 1945 AD 826; *S v Cloete* 1994 1 SACR 420 (A). See §§ 16 7 2 and 30 12 below.
[12] *R v Vather* 1961 1 SA 350 (A). See also *S v Yelani* 1989 2 SA 43 (A); *S v Mkhize* 1992 2 SACR 347 (A). See also § 30 12 below.
[13] In respect of informal admissions the effect of s 42 of the CPEA is to apply the English law as it was on 30 May 1961.
[14] See § 16 6 below.
[15] See § 16 7 below.
[16] 1966 4 SA 530 (W).
[17] See Hoffmann & Zeffertt 176, where the following distinction in respect of inferences is also noted: "There is an important distinction between conduct by a party from which an inference can be drawn as to the existence, or non-existence of a fact in issue, and conduct from which an inference can be drawn that he is admitting a fact in issue. For instance, one must be careful to distinguish between conduct that warrants an inference that the accused had knowledge of a relevant fact, from conduct from which an inference can be drawn that an accused admits a relevant fact. This is well illustrated by *S v Shezi* [1985 3 SA 900 (A)]: the appellant had given a demonstration at a police station that indicated that he had intimate knowledge of how to dismantle and assemble demolition, limpet and anti-personnel mines; this demonstration did not constitute an admission of an averment against him, but was evidence of an act done by him from which an inference could be drawn that he had knowledge of the working of mines, and, as such, was admissible without proof that the demonstration had been freely and voluntarily given."
[18] See Van der Merwe *Evidence* 219. See also Elliot (ed) *Elliott & Phipson Manual of The Law of Evidence* 12 ed (1987) 181 for a discussion of the dangers arising from drawing "commonsense inferences".
[19] 1927 TPD 324.

remained silent and simply lowered his head. The court found that this conduct was sufficient corroboration of the plaintiff's version. In *R v Barlin*[20] a detective, whilst searching the accused's shop, found a number of shirts from which the name tabs had been removed. The accused, on been asked for an explanation, remained silent. The court held that this tended to show a consciousness of guilt.

Obviously, the nature of the inference that can be drawn from silence will always depend on the surrounding circumstances:[21]

> "[O]nly if a person's reaction can fairly be taken as an adoption of the statement made in his presence, and if such adoption can fairly be taken as evidence of guilt, is the statement evidence against him. This means that if the circumstances are such that no reply could reasonably be expected, or that although a reply could be expected, there is some other probable explanation of his silence, the statement made in his presence is not evidence against him. Indeed, strictly, that statement is never evidence of what it asserts, it is his reaction which is the evidence . . .."

The interpretation of silence will also depend on whether it occurs in the context of a civil or criminal matter. One reason for drawing a distinction between civil and criminal cases is that in civil cases the parties are likely to be on a more equal footing. In a criminal case the accuser will most often be a person in authority and the accused may well feel that it is futile to raise an argument in the circumstances.[22]

More importantly, in criminal trials, both at common law and in terms of s 25 of the interim Constitution, the accused has a right to remain silent from the time of arrest. In the past the courts have held that once an accused has been informed of his right to remain silent no inference as to guilt can be drawn from his silence.[23] However, whether this was also the position when the accused had not been cautioned was viewed as an open question. As the right to be cautioned and the right to remain silent are now constitutional rights, it is submitted that it would be absurd to draw a negative inference from silence where the accused was not advised of his constitutional right to remain silent.[24]

16 3 2 Failure to answer letters In certain circumstances an admission may be inferred from the failure to answer a letter. However, as responding to a letter requires a greater degree of positive conduct than an oral denial, the courts are more reluctant to draw such an inference. For example, in *R v West*,[25] where the accused had failed to respond to a letter from the complainant alleging that he was the cause of her pregnancy, the court held that an acknowledgement of paternity could not be inferred from his silence.

In each case, before an admission can be inferred, it must be established in the light of the surrounding circumstances that it would be reasonable to draw

---

[20] 1926 AD 459.

[21] Elliot *Elliot & Phipson* 182.

[22] See Hoffmann & Zeffertt 177.

[23] *R v Patel* 1947 AD 903. See also *S v Maritz* 1974 1 SA 266 (NC).

[24] See also § 10 2 3 2 above for a discussion of the privilege against self-incrimination and the right to remain silent during plea proceedings.

[25] 1939 CPD 393.

the inference that the party did not respond because he acknowledged that the contents of the letter were true. Thus in *Mc Williams v First Consolidated Holdings*[26] Miller JA held:

> "I accept that 'quiesence is not necessarily acquiescence' (see *Collen v Rietfontein Engineering Works* 1948 (1) SA 413 (A) at 422) and that a party's failure to reply to a letter asserting the existence of an obligation owed by such party to the writer does not always justify an inference that the assertion was accepted as the truth. But in general, when according to ordinary commercial practice and human expectation firm repudiation of such an assertion would be the norm if it was not accepted as correct, such party's silence and inaction, unless satisfactorily explained, may be taken to constitute an admission by him of the truth of the assertion, or at least will be an important factor telling against him in the assessment of the probabilities and in the final determination of the dispute. And an adverse inference will the more readily be drawn when the unchallenged assertion had been preceded by correspondence or negotiations between the parties relative to the subject-matter of the assertion."

16 3 3 Statements in the presence of a party A statement made in the presence of a party may be put before the court in order that the court may assess whether the party's response to hearing the statement amounted to an acceptance of its truth. It is not necessary for the party to assent to the statement for an inference to be drawn, as agreement as to the truth of the statement may be inferred from silence. An inference may even be drawn from a denial if, for example, the court finds that the party's demeanour contradicts the denial. However, if the statement is not accepted and is devoid of any other relevance, it must be disregarded.[27]

In *Rex v Jackson*[28] the accused was charged with contravening the Transvaal Liquor Ordinance. A witness, when found in possession of the illegally supplied liquor and asked by a detective where she got the liquor, pointed to the accused, but the accused did not assent to the truth of this "statement". It was argued by the defence that this evidence should not be admitted unless the accused assented to the statement at the time that it was made. The court held that the evidence "was admissible in reference to the demeanour of the accused at the time", but not as proof of the correctness of the fact stated.[29] The court noted:[30]

> "There may well be cases in which statements of the kind made in the presence of an accused would be calculated to prejudice him, unless carefully guarded. As whether the witness making the statement was not called . . . or where a question of disputed identity arises."

Where one co-accused makes a statement in the presence of another, or where the accused is presented with what a co-accused has said by the police, the statement can be used against the accused in whose presence it was made, provided that he has accepted it as true. As this occurs even though an accused is not a competent witness for the prosecution against his co-accused, the practice is discouraged by rule 10 of the Judges' Rules, which provides:

---

[26] 1982 2 SA 1 (A) 10.

[27] See Hoffmann & Zeffertt 182; *R v A* 1959 3 SA 498 (FC) 502.

[28] 1917 AD 556.

[29] At 558.

[30] At 558. See also *R v Christie* 1914 AC 545; cf *R v Norton* 1910 KB 496.

"When two or more persons are charged with the same offence, and a voluntary statement is made by one of them, the police, if they consider it desirable, may furnish each of the persons with a copy of such statement, but nothing should be said or done by the police to invite a reply. The police should not read such a statement furnished to a person unless such a person is unable to read it and desires that it be read over to him. If a person so furnished desires to make a voluntary statement in reply, the usual caution should be administered."

The Judges' Rules (see § 10 2 3 1 n 54 above for the full text of these rules) were formulated at a South African judges conference held in Cape Town in 1931. They are administrative directives to the police designed to protect accused persons from unfair practices by the police. Although they have no legal force, a contravention of the rules may still impact on admissibility. In *S v Sampson*[31] the court held that a contravention of rule 10 would be a factor taken into consideration by the court in determining whether a confession has been improperly obtained. To date the Judges' Rules have had a limited influence on judicial decisions whether to admit confessions into evidence,[32] but a contravention of these rules has not been used to exclude admissions. This is probably attributable to the more stringent requirements of admissibility applicable to confessions.[33] It is argued below[34] that this distinction between the requirements of admissibility is unconstitutional, and the view is expressed that compliance with the Judges' Rules should be seen as a prerequisite for a fair trial.[35] From these arguments it follows that a breach of the Judges' Rules must be as relevant to the admissibility of admissions as it would be to confessions.

16 4   VICARIOUS ADMISSIONS

As a general rule an admission is not admissible against anyone except its maker.[36] A statement made out of court, by a person who is not a party to the suit, is excluded because it is hearsay in nature.[37] It follows that an extra-curial statement will be admissible only if it can qualify as an exception to the hearsay rule.[38] However, it has been argued that there are other reasons for excluding vicarious admissions and therefore such statements should not be admitted merely because they fall to be admitted as an exception to the hearsay rule.

Prior to *Mdani v Allianz Insurance Ltd*[39] it was widely accepted that certain exceptions existed in terms of which an admission of a third person (X) could be proved against a party (Y) to litigation.[40] These exceptions are referred to as

---

[31] 1989 3 SA 239 (A) 244. See also *S v Colt* 1992 2 SACR 120 (E); *S v Mafuya* 1992 2 SACR 370 (W).

[32] See §§ 10 2 3 1 above and 17 4 4 1 below for further discussion of the Judges' Rules.

[33] See §§ 16 7 and 17 4 below.

[34] In § 16 7 1 1 below.

[35] See also § 10 2 3 1 above.

[36] This rule does not apply to admission or confessions made in the witness box. See *R v Zawels* 1937 AD 342.

[37] See *Union and South West Africa Insurance Co Ltd v Quntana NO* 1977 4 SA 410 (A); *Mdani v Allianz Insurance Ltd* 1991 1 SA 184 (A).

[38] See ch 13 above for a full discussion of hearsay.

[39] Supra.

[40] See Hoffmann & Zeffertt 184.

vicarious admissions. There are two main categories of vicarious admissions. First, where X has implied or express authority to make a statement on behalf of Y the admission may be proved against Y. Secondly, the statement may be admitted where X and Y share a privity or identity of interest. For example, in *Botes v Van Deventer*[41] the plaintiff claimed damages for loss incurred as a result of a lorry colliding with his race horse. One of the issues to be decided by the court was whether an admission made by the driver of the defendant's lorry (the driver being the defendant's employee) was admissible against the defendant. The driver had made a statement to a police constable in which he admitted that his negligence was the cause of the accident. However, the driver was not available to give evidence at the trial. The court held the statement to be admissible, its reasoning can be summarized as follows: an employer is vicariously liable for a delict committed by his employee acting in the course and scope of his employment. The liability of the employer is identical to the liability of the employee. Consequently, an employee's statement pertaining to the subject-matter of the liability is admissible against the employer.

However, the relevance of these exceptional categories in terms of which vicarious admissions are admissible needs to be reassessed following the Appellate Division's decision in *Mdani*.[42] In this case the evidence in issue consisted of extra-curial statements made by an insured driver, who was not party to the suit, which was tendered against a third-party insurer. The court *a quo* found the evidence to be inadmissible in accordance with its interpretation of *Union and South West Africa Insurance Co Ltd v Quntana NO*,[43] that not only are such statements inadmissible because they are hearsay in nature but also because of their vicarious nature. Therefore, by application of s 3(2) of the Law of Evidence Amendment Act,[44] the fact that s 3(1) of the Act permits hearsay to be admitted in certain circumstances does not enable the court to override the rule that vicarious extra-curial admissions and statements are generally inadmissible. On appeal the court held that it was quite clear from the judgment in *Quntana's* case "that the statement in question was held to be inadmissible on a single ground, viz that it was hearsay".[45]

It would therefore appear that the admissibility of extra-curial admissions made by a person who is not a party to the suit will depend solely on whether the statement is exceptionally admissible as hearsay in terms of s 3(1) of the Law of Evidence Amendment Act.[46]

Zeffertt, although acknowledging the above implications of *Mdani*, criticizes the decision on the following basis:[47]

---

[41] 1966 3 SA 182 (A).

[42] Supra.

[43] Supra.

[44] Act 45 of 1988. Section 3(2) provides that "[t]he provisions of subsection (1) shall not render admissible any evidence which is inadmissible on any ground other than that such evidence is hearsay evidence".

[45] At 188.

[46] Act 45 of 1988. See Zeffertt 1991 *ASSAL* 537; Schwikkard 1991 *SALJ* 410.

[47] 1991 *ASSAL* 538.

"Inadmissible admissions are categorized as an inadmissible species of hearsay. When a vicarious admission is rejected for failing to meet the requirements of admissibility (for instance, that there must either be authorization or privity of interest or obligation if a vicarious admission is to be admissible) it is excluded as hearsay but there are other reasons that warrant the exclusion . . . It does not follow, therefore, that because evidence in *Quntana* was excluded as hearsay, that the theoretically true basis of its exclusion was not, in reality, the vicarious-admission rule."

Paizes shows a similar disquiet and submits that the vicarious admission rule still has a role to play in the law of evidence. He argues that vicarious admissions are also excluded because they are irrelevant and even though such an admission may pass the hearsay test, it should still be excluded if it is not sufficiently relevant:[48]

"Vicarious admissions constitute, technically, an exception to the rule against hearsay. Since it is an exception that has not been accorded any specific statutory recognition, it may be thought that the rules governing their admissibility have been abolished — along with the other 'common-law exceptions' — by the repeal of s 216 and the enactment of s 3 of the Law of Evidence Amendment Act 45 of 1988. This may not be entirely true, however, since these rules are not the product of the hearsay problem alone. An admission made by A is, for instance, normally irrelevant when tendered against B, and the categories of admissible vicarious admissions are exceptional instances when such admissions are relevant. It could be argued, too, that the principle that an admission should only be admissible against its maker is a salutary policy which warrants independent recognition apart from any considerations regarding hearsay. It may be, therefore, that the rules governing the admissibility of vicarious admission have, to some extent, survived the enactment of s 3 and the repeal of the old s 216 by virtue of the provisions of s 210 and s 235. It may be simpler, however, to put aside labels which have outlived their usefulness and to view the admissibility of such admissions purely in the light of the general principles relating to relevance and hearsay . . .."

16 5   EXAMPLES OF EXCEPTIONS TO THE VICARIOUS ADMISSIONS RULE

It is submitted that should *Mdani* be interpreted in the future as abolishing the exceptions to the vicarious admissions rule, the categories of exception will still be relevant in that they will be a factor taken into consideration in the exercise of the court's discretion to admit hearsay evidence.

16 5 1   Express or implied authority

16 5 1 1   *Agents and servants*   Statements made by an agent within the scope of his authority may be admitted against his principal. Admissions by servants are similarly admissible. However, where the admission relates to a matter on which servant and master have incurred joint liability the statement will be admitted on the basis that servant and master have an identity of interest.[49] Agents are rarely specifically authorized to make admissions, but authorization will be established if it is shown that the statement was one of a type or class which the agent was expressly or impliedly authorized to make.

---

[48] Paizes in Du Toit et al *Commentary* 24-70A. See also ch 13 above.

[49] See *Botes v Van Deventer* supra.

For example, in *Kirkstall Brewery Co v Furness Railway Co Ltd*,[50] in which the plaintiff claimed damages for the loss of a parcel, the court held that a statement made by the station master to a policeman that the goods had been stolen by a porter was admissible in evidence against the railway company as the station master had the requisite authority to make such a communication to the police.

At common law directors and servants of companies are in the same position as any other agent. However, the position has been altered by statute with regard to criminal proceedings instituted against a corporate body. Section 332(3) of the CPA provides:

> "In criminal proceedings against a corporate body, any record which was made or kept by a director, servant or agent of the corporate body within the scope of his activities as such director, servant or agent, or any document which was at any time in the custody or under the control of any such director, servant or agent within the scope of his activities as such director, servant or agent, shall be admissible in evidence against the accused."[51]

16 5 1 2 *Partners* An admission made by a partner concerning partnership affairs is admissible against his partners. Partners are subject to the same principles applicable to agents. However, as a consequence of the contractual liability of partners, admissions made after the dissolution of the partnership may be admitted against ex-partners if they pertain to a transaction which occurred before the dissolution of the partnership.[52]

16 5 1 3 *Legal representatives* An admission made at trial by a legal representative is admissible against the client.[53] However, it must first be established that the legal representative was properly instructed. That a legal representative has general authority to act on behalf of his client will often be inferred from the surrounding circumstances.[54] It is only admissions of fact that are vicariously admissible and not expressions of opinion on the evidence adduced.[55]

16 5 1 4 *Spouses* An admission by one spouse is generally inadmissible against the other spouse unless it relates to the joint interest of the spouses in the community estate,[56] or in a deferred sharing of profits under the accrual system

---

[50] 1874 LR 9 QB.

[51] See *S v Harper* 1981 1 SA 88 (D).

[52] For example, in *R v Jaspan* 1940 AD 9 the court held that the lodging of a statement of affairs of partnership by one partner under s 16 of the Insolvency Act 1936 was an act of the partnership and, in the absence of a repudiation of the contents of such statement by another partner, such statement was evidence against both partners of the correctness of the figures in such statement.

[53] *S v Gouws* 1968 4 SA 354 (GW). See also *SOS Kinderdorf International v Effie Lentin Architects* 1993 2 SA 481 (NmH), where the court held that a litigant is bound by counsel's conduct of the case (within the limits of counsel's brief) and by admissions which a legal representative makes in the pleadings or in the drafting of an affidavit, unless satisfactory reasons are given to show that counsel had no right to make such admissions. In the absence of a satisfactory explanation a litigant will not be permitted to lead evidence to withdraw an admission made in an affidavit. See also *Brummund v Brummund's Estate* 1993 2 SA 494 (NmH) and *S v Gope & others* 1993 2 SACR 92 (Ck).

[54] *Dhlamini v Minister of Law and Order* 1986 4 SA 342 (D).

[55] *S v Gouws* supra.

[56] See *Oelofse v Grundling* 1952 1 SA 338 (C).

introduced by the Matrimonial Property Act.[57] However, the court may find on the facts that an express or implied agency has been created and apply the principles pertaining to agents.

16 5 1 5 *Referees* Statements made by someone to whom a party has referred others for information may be proved against him as an admission concerning the subject-matter of the reference. For example, in *Van Rooyen v Humphrey*,[58] an action for damages resulting from a fire, a dispute arose as to whether the fire had taken place on the appellant's instructions. Evidence that the appellant had instructed the respondent to ask two of the appellant's employees how the fire occurred, and their answers, were held to be admissible against him.[59]

16 5 2 Acts and declarations in furtherance of a common purpose If A, B and C are engaged in a common purpose, and A makes a statement in furtherance of that common purpose, it will be admissible against B and C.[60]

Hoffmann & Zeffertt state:[61]

> "There is some uncertainty as to whether this topic should be treated as an exception to the rule that admissions are not vicariously admissible. Some say that it should, but the better view, it is submitted, is that the reception of the declarations of persons engaged in a common purpose stands on the same footing as acts done; in other words, they are received when they are relevant acts. They are relevant . . . when they are 'executive' statements; they are inadmissible when they are 'narrative', that it to say, when they are not made in furtherance of a common purpose but an account or admission of past events. An admission contained in narrative is inadmissible precisely because admissions are not, in general, vicariously admissible but they may, of course be received against the persons making them."

R v Blake and Tye [62] provides an example of the distinction drawn between executive and narrative statements. The accused were charged with a conspiracy to pass goods through customs without paying duty. Tye had made entries incriminating both himself and Blake in two books. The entry in one book was a necessary part of the fraud, whereas the entry in the other book was solely a record for his own private purposes. It was held that the first entry was admissible against Blake as something done in the furtherance of the common purpose (an executive statement), but the second entry merely constituted evidence against Tye because it did not advance the common purpose (a narrative statement).

Before executive statements can be admitted into evidence the conspiracy and the accused's participation in it must be proved.[63] In deciding these preliminary issues the court is permitted to look at the statements of the alleged

---

[57] Act 88 of 1984. In such instances it can be said that an identity of interest or obligation exists.

[58] 1953 3 SA 392 (A).

[59] See also *Kroon v JL Clark Cotton Co (Pty) Ltd* 1983 2 SA 197 (E).

[60] *R v Levy* 1929 AD 312; *R v Cilliers* 1937 AD 278; *R v Mayet* 1957 1 SA 492 (A); *S v ffrench-Beytagh* 1972 3 SA 430 (A).

[61] At 190.

[62] 1844 6 QB 126.

[63] See *S v Sibanda* 1993 1 SA 691 (ZS), where the court held that the exception applied only to statements made whilst the conspiracy was still operating.

conspirators.[64] The Appellate Division in *S v ffrench-Beytagh*[65] held that "it is immaterial whether the existence of the conspiracy or the participation of the defendants be proved first, although either element is nugatory without the other". There must be some evidence aliunde establishing the existence of the common purpose before the relevant statements can be considered at the end of the case.[66]

Hoffmann & Zeffertt comment that there is no reason why this exception should be confined to criminal cases — "an executive act or declaration does not depend on the kind of proceedings for its relevance".[67]

16 5 3 Privity or identity of interest or obligation   Where two people share a privity or identity of interest or obligation, statements by one of them will be admissible against the other.[68] Hoffmann & Zeffertt make the following distinction between privity and identity:[69]

> "Generally speaking privity exists between persons who have successive interests in the same property, and in the case of an owner and predecessor in title. Identity exists between persons who have concurrent joint interests or liabilities. This rule originates in the law or correality of obligation, the theory being that there is only a single right or obligation enforceable by or against all or any of the parties jointly interested and which may therefore be affected by the acts or statements of any one of them."

Schmidt, acknowledging the difficulties of establishing whether privity or identity exists, suggests that the case law is the best guide in determining the existence of privity or identity.[70]

16 5 3 1 *Predecessors in title*   The statement of a predecessor in title of a party to litigation is admissible against that party, provided that it relates to the title and was made during the existence of the predecessor's interest.[71] For example, in *Head v Du Toit*[72] the plaintiff sought a declaration to the effect that he was entitled to free and undisturbed use of a road across the defendant's property on the basis that such right had been acquired by prescription. The court held that evidence of the defendant's predecessor in title, to the effect that he recognized the existence of such a right in favour of a predecessor of the plaintiff, was admissible,

16 5 3 2 *Master and servant*   In terms of substantive law a master is vicariously liable for a delict committed by his servant in the course of his employment. It

---

[64] *R v Mayet* supra 494.
[65] Supra 455.
[66] *S v ffrench-Beytagh* supra.
[67] *Law of Evidence* 191.
[68] *Botes v Van Deventer* supra 199.
[69] *Law of Evidence* 192. See also *Knouwds v Administrateur* 1981 1 SA 544 (C) 522, where the court held that the concept of privity was not rigidly defined.
[70] At 483.
[71] See Tapper *Cross and Tapper on Evidence* 8 ed (1995) 649.
[72] 1932 CPD 287.

follows from this rule of substantive law that a servant's statement will be admissible against the master.[73]

16 5 3 3 *Nominal and real parties* When litigation is conducted by a nominal party an admission by the 'real' party may be proved against the nominal party. For example, where a guardian litigates on behalf of a child an admission made by that child may be proved against the guardian.[74]

16 6   STATEMENTS MADE WITHOUT PREJUDICE

The general rule in civil matters is that an admission will be accepted into evidence provided that it is relevant. However, admissions included in a statement by a person involved in a dispute which are genuinely aimed at achieving a compromise are protected from disclosure. Such admissions may only be accepted into evidence with the consent of both parties.

The rationale of the rule is based on public policy which encourages the private settlement of disputes by the parties themselves.[75] Clearly, parties would be reluctant to be frank if what they said might be held against them in the event of negotiations failing.

It is the habit of legal representatives to preface such statements with the words "without prejudice", meaning that the statement is made without prejudice to the rights of the person making the offer in the event of the offer being refused.[76] However, the words "without prejudice" do not by themselves protect the statement from disclosure. If the communication constitutes a *bona fide* attempt to settle the dispute, it will be "privileged"[77] even though it has not been prefaced with the words "without prejudice".[78] Conversely, even if the words are invoked, the statement may still be disclosed if it was not made during the course of genuine negotiations.[79] Before the "privilege" will prevail there must be some connection with or relevance to the settlement negotiations.[80]

A "without prejudice" offer will only be protected from disclosure if it is made

---

[73] *Botes v Van Deventer* supra.

[74] Phipson *Evidence* 14 ed (1990) 633–6; Hoffmann & Zeffertt 193.

[75] See *Naidoo v Marine and Trade Insurance Co Ltd* 1978 3 SA 666 (A) 677. The various theories concerning the exclusion of statements made without prejudice are discussed by Van Niekerk, Van der Merwe & Van Wyk *Privileges in die Bewysreg* (1984) 202–4.

[76] A without prejudice offer will not be taken into account by the court when determining an order for costs. See *Tshabalala v President Versekeringsmaatskappy Ltd* 1987 4 SA 73 (T) 76A.

[77] In *Naidoo v Marine and Trade Insurance Co Ltd* supra 667 Trollip JA noted that to describe "without prejudice" statements as privileged was inaccurate but convenient. The label is inaccurate in that they are not governed by the same rules that are applicable to privileged communications, the most important distinction being that secondary evidence can be given of privileged communications, whereas it cannot be given in respect of "without prejudice" statements.

[78] *Millard v Glaser* 1950 3 SA 547 (W) 554; *Gcabashe v Nene* 1975 3 SA 912 (D) 914; *Jili v South African Eagle Insurance Co Ltd* 1995 3 SA 269 (N).

[79] *Brauer v Markow* 1946 TPD 344 at 350.

[80] *Naidoo v Marine and Trade Insurance Co Ltd* supra 678–9. Hoffmann & Zeffertt 197 favour the approach taken in *Patlansky v Patlansky (2)* 1917 WLD 10, in terms of which the statement will be protected from disclosure provided it is not wholly unconnected, albeit irrelevant, to the negotiations in issue. The Appellate Division is yet to decide the issue.

in good faith. If the statement contains statements which are criminal or fraudulent, it will not automatically be presumed to be made in bad faith, and the criminal or fraudulent content will only be relevant to admissibility if it tends to show bad faith.[81] On the other hand, even if a statement is made in good faith, it will be admissible if the attempt at settlement constitutes an act of insolvency or an offence or an incitement to commit an offence, provided that the statement is tendered to prove the commission of the act.

If the statement is accompanied by a threat of litigation should the offer not be accepted, it will remain privileged since such a threat is implicit in every offer of compromise.[82] However, where an offer contains a threat which is relevant to establishing that the offer was not *bona fide*, evidence of both the offer and threat will be heard by the court. For example, in *Davenport v Davenport*[83] the defendant, in a letter marked "without prejudice", warned the plaintiff (his wife) that unless she withdrew a divorce application he would ensure that criminal proceedings would be instituted against her. The court held that the letter was admissible.

Once a settlement is reached the "privilege" ceases to exist, the rationale for its existence having fallen away.[84] However, if the same or some connected issue is later disputed, the earlier "without prejudice" statement will remain protected from disclosure.[85]

16 7   ADMISSIONS BY THE ACCUSED

16 7 1 The requirements for admissibility   At common law an extra-judicial statement made by an accused may not be admitted into evidence unless it is proved to have been made freely and voluntarily.[86] In this context the words "freely and voluntarily" have a technical and restricted meaning and an admission will be found to be involuntary only if it has been induced by a promise or threat *proceeding from a person in authority.*[87]

Section 219A of the CPA provides:

> "(1) Evidence of any admission made extra-judicially by any person in relation to the commission of an offence, shall, if such admission does not constitute a confession to that offence and is proved to have been voluntarily made by the person, be admissible in evidence against him at criminal proceedings relating to that offence."

In *S v Yolelo*[88] the Appellate Division held that s 219A merely codified the

---

[81] See *Brauer v Markow* supra; *Coetzee v Union Government* 1941 TPD 1.
[82] *Hoffend v Elgeti* 1949 3 SA 91 (A).
[83] 1930 WLD 202.
[84] *Gcabashe v Nene* supra.
[85] *Patlansky v Patlansky* supra.
[86] *S v Cele* 1965 1 SA 82 (A).
[87] *R v Barlin* supra 462.
[88] 1981 3 SA 1002 (A).

common law as regards the meaning of voluntariness in relation to admissions.[89] As the voluntariness of an admission will be compromised only if it has been induced by a promise or threat emanating from a person in authority, it is necessary to look more closely at the meaning of these terms.

A threat or a promise will be found to have been made if a person, by means of words or conduct, indicates to the accused that they will be treated more favourably if they speak, or less favourably if they don't. Whether such a threat or promise was made will be a question of fact in each case.[90] Proof of such threat or promise does not necessarily establish the absence of voluntariness. The test of whether the threat or promise actually affected the accused's freedom of volition is subjective.[91] It follows from the subjective nature of the test that the threat or promise must be operative on the mind of the accused at the time that the admission is made.[92] This subjective test makes it impossible to specify precisely what will constitute a threat or a promise. Clearly, an admission induced by violence or a threat of violence will not be admissible, nor will an admission made in response to a promise of lenient treatment be admitted. However, an admission made under police interrogation will not necessarily be inadmissible. It will be excluded only if on the facts it appears that it was induced by a threat or promise.[93] Similarly, whether or not an exhortation or invitation to speak amounts to a threat or a promise negating volition will depend on the surrounding circumstances.[94]

A threat or promise will not be relevant unless it emanates from a person in authority. A person in authority is "anyone whom the prisoner might reasonably suppose to be capable of influencing the course of the prosecution".[95] Rose Innes J, in *S v Robertson*,[96] commented that the requirement that duress must flow from a person in authority is a concept to be found in English law and is not referred to in the CPA. He held that for the purposes of the South African law a person in authority is

> "enigiemand, of hy 'n amptelike posisie beklee aldan nie, wat mate van outoriteit, bv die van 'n vader teenoor 'n seun, of 'n oom teenoor 'n neef of 'n werkgewer teenoor 'n werknemer".[97]

Having thus broadened the definition of a person in authority, the court found that the accuseds' admissions were inadmissible as they had been intimidated

---

[89] At 1009C. See also *S v Schultz* 1989 1 SA 465 (T); cf *S v Mpetha(2)* 1983 1 SA 576 (C). Paizes in Du Toit et al *Commentary* 24-76A notes that the courts have in general adopted an artificial interpretation of the voluntariness requirement. For example, in *R v Moiloa* 1956 4 SA 824 (A) the court found admissions made under a statutory obligation to give information to be admissible.

[90] *R v Magoetie* 1959 2 SA 322 (A); *R v Nhleko* 1960 4 SA 712 (A).

[91] *R v Magoetie* supra.

[92] *S v Radebe* 1968 4 SA 410 (A).

[93] See *S v Thwala* 1991 1 SACR 494 (N), where the court excluded an admission made after lengthy and traumatic interrogation.

[94] In *R v Dhlamini* 1949 3 SA 976 (N) 979 the court held that the words "You must realize that you stand at the prison doors and that you must speak the truth" did not amount to a threat or promise.

[95] Hoffmann & Zeffertt 203. The courts have held that a person in authority includes a magistrate, police officer, and a complainant, and in *R v Dhlamini* 1949 3 SA 976 (N) it was held to include a complainant's employer.

[96] 1981 1 SA 460 (C) 467.

[97] At 467A–C.

into making them by an unidentified member or members of a prison gang.[98] Whether the court was entitled to take this approach is a question for debate.

In *S v Peters*[99] Jones J rejected this extended definition on the basis that the court had not properly distinguished the requirements of admissibility for confessions from those pertaining to admissions.[100] He concluded that as the threats in question had not emanated from persons who could influence the prosecution, the admission could not be said to be involuntary.

Accepting that the court in *Peters'* case was bound by Appellate Division authority to the effect that the common-law meaning of "voluntarily" is retained for the purposes of s 219A, and is restricted to a promise or a threat emanating from a person in authority,[101] the question that remains is whether the court was correct in its restrictive interpretation of the term "person in authority".

Authority for "defining a person in authority" as a person "whom the prisoner might reasonably suppose to be capable of influencing the course of the prosecution" appears to derive from two sources, namely Cross *On Evidence*[102] and *R v Wilson; R v Marshal-Graham*.[103] However, no such proposition is to be found in the case of *R v Wilson; R v Marshall-Graham*, in which Lord Parker CJ held that there was no authority clearly defining who constituted a person in authority and declined to make any such definition.[104] Furthermore, in the sixth edition of Cross[105] it is noted that the House of Lords in *Commissioners of Customs and Excise v Harz*[106] clarified the old rule and "rejected the view that the inducement or threat need relate to the prosecution".

In the absence of Appellate Division authority to the contrary there would appear to be no reason for further restricting the concept of "person in authority" to mean only a person capable of influencing the course of the prosecution. Whether the purpose of the admission requirements is to ensure reliability and/or to discourage improper police behaviour,[107] it would make more sense to define a person in authority as someone the accused believes to be capable of carrying out what he says, rather than someone able to influence the course of the prosecution.[108]

---

[98] At 467.

[99] 1992 1 SACR (E).

[100] At 295. See Schwikkard 1992 *SACJ* 351, where it is submitted that the fact that the court in *Robertson's* case went to some length to deal with the question of what constitutes a person in authority would indicate that it was aware of the different requirements of admissibility applicable to admissions and confessions.

[101] *S v Yolelo* supra. See also *S v Mpetha (2)* supra 581, where the court held that "voluntarily" must be accorded its ordinary common law meaning as "where statute deals with a specific matter also specifically dealt with by the common law, one does not readily give the same words or concepts different meanings . . . and it seems to me that stronger indications than are to be found in the provisions of ss 217 and 219A are required in order to justify a departure from the accepted common law meaning." It should be noted that Farlam AJ in *S v Williams* 1991 1 SACR 1 (C) 7, in an obiter dictum questioned whether the common law did indeed place such a restrictive interpretation on the meaning of the word "voluntarily".

[102] 5 ed (1979) 54.

[103] 1967 2 QB 406. See Hoffmann & Zeffertt 203; *S v Schultz* supra.

[104] At 415.

[105] Cross *On Evidence* 6 ed (1985) 536.

[106] 1967 AC 760, 1967 1 All ER 177.

[107] See Hoffmann & Zeffertt 201.

[108] See Lansdown & Campbell 852. Paizes in Du Toit et al *Commentary* 24-76A submits "that since the

16 7 1 1   *Section 25(2)(c) of the interim Constitution*   Section 25(2)*(c)* of the interim Constitution may well provide the courts with the opportunity for departing from the artificial and technical common-law interpretation of the requirement of "voluntariness".

Section 25(2)*(c)* provides that an arrested person shall have the right "not to be compelled to make a confession or admission which could be used in evidence against him or her". Section 35(1) of the same Act instructs a court, when interpreting the Chapter on Fundamental Rights, to

> "promote the values which underlie an open and democratic society based on freedom and equality and shall, where applicable, have regard to public international law applicable to the protection of the rights entrenched in this Chapter, and may have regard to comparable foreign case law".

It is therefore permissible and instructive to look at the approach taken in other jurisdictions. As the South African law of evidence has been deeply influenced by the English law, it is appropriate to look at modern developments in that jurisdiction. Following the recommendations of the Criminal Law Revision Committee[109] and the Royal Commission on Criminal Procedure,[110] the Police and Criminal Evidence Act[111] came into being. This Act, which introduced substantial reforms to the law of evidence and criminal procedure, provides that with regard to the requirements of admissibility no distinction should be drawn between full confessions and admissions.[112] As a result of this equation the restrictive interpretation of "voluntary" is no longer applicable to admissions.

In a similar vein the United States Supreme Court has held that admissions should receive the same cautious treatment accorded to confessions.[113] The obvious reason for taking this approach is that all the reasons for excluding involuntary confessions apply equally to involuntary admissions.[114] Involuntary confessions and admissions are excluded not only because they are potentially unreliable but also because a conviction based on an involuntary admission or confession would be one obtained without due process of law.[115] The American courts have also held that the admission of such evidence would also be in contravention of the Fifth Amendment ban against compulsory self-incrimination.

There is nothing in s 25(2)*(c)* to suggest that admissions and confessions should be treated differently. Section 217 of the CPA[116] requires a confession to be made freely and voluntarily whilst the maker is in his sound and sober senses and without having been unduly influenced thereto. In *R v Barlin*[117] Innes CJ

---

concept of voluntariness is a subjective one, the test for excluding involuntary admissions should not be determined by such objective factors as the nature of the influence or status of the person exerting such influence".

[109] Cmnd 4991 (1972) 34–47.

[110] Cmnd 8092 (9181) ch 4.

[111] 1984.

[112] Section 82(1). For a full discussion, see Tapper *Cross and Tapper on Evidence* 8 ed (1995) 675 et seq.

[113] *Opper v United States* 348 US 84.

[114] *People v Atchley* 53 Cal 2d 160, 346 P2d 764, cert dismd 366 US 207.

[115] *Brown v Allen* 344 US 443.

[116] Confessions are considered in detail in ch 17 below.

[117] Supra 462–3.

held that the requirement of undue influence pertaining to confessions was "elastic" and went beyond the ambit of voluntariness, which was restricted to an inducement, threat or promise coming from a person in authority. It can be argued that the constitutional entrenchment of the principles of due process and the right to a fair trial in s 25 as well as the wording of s 25(2) *(c)*, which draws no distinction between admissions and confessions, favours an interpretation of voluntariness which escapes the restrictive common-law approach.

16 7 2 Plea proceedings Section 115 of the CPA provides:

"(1) Where an accused at a summary trial pleads not guilty to the offence charged, the presiding judge, regional magistrate or magistrate, as the case may be, may ask him whether he wishes to make a statement indicating the basis of his defence.

(2) *(a)* Where the accused does not make a statement under subsection (1) or does so and it is not clear from the statement to what extent he denies or admits the issues raised by the plea, the court may question the accused in order to establish which allegations in the charge are in dispute.

(b) The court may in its discretion put any question to the accused in order to clarify any matter raised under subsection (1) of this section, and shall enquire from the accused whether an allegation which is not placed in issue by the plea of not guilty, may be recorded as an admission by the accused of that allegation, and if the accused so consents, such admission shall be recorded and shall be deemed to be an admission under section 220.

(3) Where the legal adviser of an accused on behalf of the accused replies, whether in writing or orally, to any question by the court under this section, the accused shall be required by the court to declare whether he confirms such reply or not."

What is the evidentiary value of an admission made by an accused who pleads not guilty and makes certain admissions in response to questions raised by the presiding officer, but does not consent to having them recorded as formal admissions or is not asked whether he so consents?

In *S v Sesetse*[118] the Appellate Division held that in these circumstances the state is still required to prove the facts admitted in the informal statement. However, the court held that such informal admissions still constitute evidentiary material.[119] This means that it can be proved against the accused in evidence, it can be the subject of cross-examination, and its probative value will be assessed in the light of all the surrounding circumstances.[120]

However, the position was not as clear where the accused's responses to the presiding officer included *exculpatory* statements. One view is that exculpatory statements should be accorded no evidential value as they are inadmissible as prior inconsistent statements.[121] The Appellate Division, in *S v Cloete*,[122] was called upon to consider precisely this issue. The court, in considering the earlier Appellate Division decision in *Sesetse*,[123] found that the basis of the judgment in

---

[118] 1981 3 SA 353 (A).

[119] See also *S v Mjoli* 1981 3 SA 1233 (A). Hoffmann & Zeffert 233 state this "is in line with principle: there is nothing to prevent the prosecution from adducing unrecorded statements, at common law, not as formal admissions but as informal ones".

[120] Cf *S v October* 1991 SACR 455 (C).

[121] See *S v Malebo* 1979 2 SA 636 (B). See also Hoffmann & Zeffertt 234, where this view is discussed.

[122] 1994 1 SACR 420 (A).

[123] Supra.

Sesetse's case was "that statements in an explanation of plea are treated in the same way as extra-curial statements".[124] Grosskopf JA noted:[125]

"An accused is not entitled to lead evidence of exculpatory extra-curial statements made by him, except to rebut a suggestion of recent fabrication . . . Where an explanation of plea is entirely exculpatory it will be before the court, but if the analogy with extra-curial statements holds good, it will have no evidential value in favour of an accused. Statements in terms of s 115 are, however, seldom entirely exculpatory. The purpose of the statement is to define the issues raised by a plea of not guilty, and, since such a plea places all elements of the charge in issue, a definition of the issues normally involves admissions on the part of the accused. In practice most explanations therefore consist of a mixture of incrimination and exculpatory statements as in the present case."

He then concluded that if the explanation of plea were to be treated as an extra-curial statement, it would not be possible for a court in convicting an accused to rely solely on the incriminating parts of the plea whilst ignoring the exculpatory ones.

The court referred to the following extract from *R v Valachia* with approval:[126]

"[T]he rule is that when proof of an admission made by a party is admitted, such party is entitled to have the whole statement put before the Court and the judicial officer or jury must take into consideration everything contained in the statement relating to the matter in issue . . . Naturally, the fact that the statement is not made under oath, and is not subject to cross-examination, detracts very much from the weight to be given to those portions of the statement favourable to its author as compared with the weight which would be given to them if he had made them under oath, but he is entitled to have them taken into consideration, to be accepted or rejected according to the court's view of their cogency."

The court rejected[127] the holdings in *S v Mkhize*[128] and *S v Mothlaping*[129] that the exculpatory part of a s 115 statement could not be accepted as evidential material because in terms of s 196(3) of the CPA the accused is prohibited from making an unsworn statement from the dock. Grosskopf JA held:[130]

"A s 115 statement is not 'an unsworn statement . . . in lieu of evidence'. It is a statement in explanation of plea, and is expressly permitted, and indeed encouraged by the Act. The only question is what effect it has."

The court noted that in many respects s 115 was similar to s 169(5) of the Criminal Procedure Act 56 of 1955, and that in terms of s 169(5) "[a] court was required to give proper regard to an exculpatory statement".[131] Grosskopf JA concluded[132]

"that the evidential value of informal admissions in s 115 derives from the ordinary common law of evidence. That being so, there would appear to be no reason or principle why the rule enunciated in *R v Valachia (supra)* should not be applicable also to such statements. The prohibition in s 196(3) of the Act on unsworn statements in lieu of

---

[124] At 424.
[125] At 424–5.
[126] Supra 837. See also § 30 12 below.
[127] At 427.
[128] 1978 2 SA 249 (N).
[129] 1988 3 SA 757 (NC).
[130] At 247.
[131] At 427.
[132] At 428.

evidence has no bearing on the matter. And I can think of no other reason why a court should be entitled to have regard to the incriminating parts of such statements while ignoring the exculpatory ones."

Although acknowledging that an accused may try to abuse s 115, Grosskopf JA found that this could be guarded against by the court "refusing to attach any value to statements which are purely self-serving, and, generally, by determining what weight to accord to the statement as a whole and to its separate parts".[133] He concluded that this was the light in which *Sesetse* should be understood.

16 7 3 The burden of proof In accordance with the presumption of innocence, the prosecution bears the burden of proving beyond a reasonable doubt that the accused made an admission freely and voluntarily.[134] However, s 219A(1) of the CPA provides

"that where the admission is made to a magistrate and reduced to writing by him or is confirmed and reduced to writing in the presence of a magistrate, the admission shall, upon the mere production at the proceedings in question of the document in which the admission is contained —

(a) be admissible in evidence against such person if it appears from such document that the admission was made by a person whose name corresponds to that of such person and, in the case of an admission made to a magistrate through an interpreter, if a certificate by the interpreter appears on such document to the effect that he interpreted truly and correctly and to the best of his ability with regard to the contents of the admission and any question put to such person by the magistrate; and

(b) be presumed, unless the contrary is proved, to have been voluntarily made by such person if it appears from the document in which the admission is contained that the admission was made voluntarily by such person."

Ackermann J, in *S v Dhlamini*,[135] held that to meet the requirements of s 219A(1)*(a)* it was necessary to show that the name of the person who made the admission was sufficiently similar to that of the accused, so that there could be reasonable certainty that the accused was the person who made the admission. Further, it had to be shown that the person to whom the admission was made was a magistrate, and where an interpreter is used it must be proved that the person who issued the certificate was the person who interpreted the statement. It must also be clear that the certificate relates to the admission in question. These requirements will not be met by the mere production of the document containing the admission.

In *S v Yolelo*[136] the court held that the requirements set out in s 219A(1)*(a)* did not have to be met before the onus was placed on the accused as these requirements were concerned only with the facilitation of proof. The onus will shift to the accused where it appears beyond reasonable doubt from the document containing the admission that the accused made the admission voluntarily.[137]

[133] At 428. See also § 30 12 below.
[134] *S v Cele* 1965 1 SA 82 (A).
[135] 1981 3 SA 1105 (W).
[136] Supra.
[137] *S v Dhlamini* supra.

Once the onus shifts to the accused the accused must establish that the requirement of voluntariness has not been met on a balance of probabilities.[138]

It is questionable whether the presumption contained in s 219A(1)*(b)* will survive a constitutional challenge. In *S v Zuma*[139] the Constitutional Court found a similar presumption contained in s 217(1)*(b)*(ii) of the CPA, pertaining to confessions, to be unconstitutional in that by placing the burden of proving the absence of voluntariness on the accused it violated the presumption of innocence.[140]

The impact of the interim Constitution on the interpretation and application of statutory presumptions is dealt with more fully in chapter 29 below.

16 7 4 Trial within a trial The admissibility of an admission is determined at a 'trial within a trial'. At this stage of the criminal proceedings both the defence and the prosecution will lead evidence as to the circumstances in which the admission was obtained. The presiding officer (sitting with or without assessors[141]) will then make a determination with regard to admissibility. The same procedure is invoked in determining the admissibility of confessions, and is discussed in more detail in § 17 6 below.

---

[138] *S v Mpetha (2)* supra.

[139] 1995 1 SACR 568 (CC).

[140] This case is more fully discussed in §§ 17 4 5 2 and 29 3 below. See also *S v Shangase* 1994 2 SACR 659 (D).

[141] See s 145(4) of the CPA. See further § 1 6 above.

CHAPTER 17

CONFESSIONS IN CRIMINAL TRIALS

PJ Schwikkard

17 1   INTRODUCTION

Confessions are a special type of comprehensive admission. A statement will constitute a confession when the maker of the statement admits, out of court, to all the elements of the crime charged.[1] Confessions are subject to special rules

---

[1] The meaning of the term "confession" is discussed in § 17 3 below.

of admissibility which do not apply to admissions and which are invoked only in criminal proceedings.

17 1 1 The rationale for excluding involuntary admissions and confessions The dominant reason for excluding involuntary admissions and confessions at common law was the danger of unreliability.[2] However, the possibility that a forced admission or confession might be unreliable was never the only reason for exclusion.[3] Even where a confession was proved to be true by the subsequent discovery of physical evidence, such as the murder weapon or corpse, the confession was still not admitted into evidence. This would suggest that the exclusionary rule had another purpose: to uphold the privilege against self-incrimination.[4] There has also been judicial acknowledgement that involuntary confessions must be excluded in order to protect citizens from abuse. In *S v January; Prokureur-Generaal, Natal v Khumalo*[5] Van Heerden JA held that the primary reason for excluding evidence of involuntary confession and admissions was one of policy,[6]

> "because in a civilized society it is vital that person in custody or charged with offences should not be subjected to ill treatment or improper pressure in order to extract confessions".

This policy has been given recognition by s 25(2)(c) of the interim Constitution, which provides that an arrested person shall have the right "not to be compelled to make a confession or admission which could be used in evidence against him or her". Section 25(3)(d) of the interim Constitution also makes the privilege against self-incrimination an essential component of a fair trial.

17 2 THE IMPORTANCE OF DISTINGUISHING BETWEEN ADMISSIONS AND CONFESSIONS

In § 16 7 1 1 above an argument is put forward as to why it is constitutionally unsound to distinguish between admissions and confessions in respect of the requirements for admissibility. However, the matter has not as yet come before the South African courts and both the common law and existing statutory provisions make it necessary to distinguish between admissions and confessions. This is because the requirements for admissibility are far more onerous in respect of confessions than is the case with admissions. Furthermore, s 209 of the CPA provides that an accused may be convicted of an offence on the single evidence of a confession if the confession is confirmed in a material respect or if the offence is proved by evidence, other than such confession, to have been actually committed.[7]

---

[2] *R v Warickshall* 1783 1 Leach 263; *R v Samhando* 1943 AD 608. See also Wigmore III para 823.

[3] See *S v Radebe* 1968 4 SA 410 (A) 418–19.

[4] See *R v Duetsimi* 1950 3 SA 674 (A); *S v Sheehama* 1991 2 SA 860 (A). The rationale for upholding the privilege against self-incrimination is discussed in § 10 2 1 above.

[5] 1994 2 SACR 801 (A).

[6] See also *S v De Vries* 1989 1 SA 228 (A) 233, quoting from *R v Wong Kam-ming* 1980 AC 247 (PC) 261.

[7] See *S v Erasmus* 1995 2 SACR 373 (E), in which the court held that the necessary confirmation could be found in another extra-curial statement made by the accused. See further §§ 30 3 3–30 3 3 4 below.

17 3 THE MEANING OF A CONFESSION

As there is no statutory definition of a confession, it is necessary to look at the common law to ascertain what a confession is. The general tendency of the courts has been to interpret the word "confession" as strictly as possible,[8] and in *R v Becker*[9] the court held that a confession was "an unequivocal acknowledgement of guilt, the equivalent of a plea of guilty before a court of law". This definition has been enthusiastically adopted by the courts and strictly applied.[10] The result is that "[t]he accused is credited with remarkable semantic ingenuity and his words are meticulously scrutinized to see whether he still has an opportunity for equivocation".[11]

For example, in *S v Grove-Mitchell*[12] the accused, who was charged with murder, told the police that he had shot the deceased, that he had "shot her six times" and had "emptied the gun on her", and that she was "full of holes". The court held that these statements did not amount to a confession as they did not exclude the possibility of a valid defence.[13] If the accused had said, "I murdered her" or "I unlawfully killed her", then his statement would have amounted to a confession. Some relief is to be found in that the court, in determining whether a statement constitutes a confession, can have regard to the circumstances surrounding the statement.[14] However, the courts are restricted to considering those circumstances "which put the statement in its proper setting and which help to ascertain the true meaning of the words used".[15] In reaching a decision as to whether a statement amounts to a confession the court is required to look at the confession in its entirety, including the necessary implication of the words.[16]

17 3 1 Offences which place a burden of proof on the accused There are numerous statutory offences which place either the burden of proof or an evidentiary burden on the accused.[17] However, even in these circumstances the accused's statement will not amount to a confession unless it excludes the possibility of a defence. For example, in *R v Khumalo*[18] the accused was charged and convicted of the statutory offence of having an unlicensed revolver in his possession. The accused, whilst driving a motor vehicle, had been stopped by the

---

[8] See Hoffmann & Zeffertt 208 and Van der Merwe (ed) *Evidence* (1983), where it is noted that the courts' strict approach in interpretation was due to the initial unfavourable view of the strict requirements for admissibility. See, e g, the *dictum* of Wessels J in *R v Hans Veren* 1918 TPD 218 at 221, approved by the Appellate Division in *R v Becker* 1929 AD 167.

[9] Supra 171. See also *S v Grove-Mitchell* 1975 3 SA 417 (A).

[10] See, e g, *R v Viljoen* 1941 AD 366; *S v Grove-Mitchell* supra.

[11] Hoffmann & Zeffertt 209.

[12] Supra.

[13] For example, self-defence.

[14] See *S v Yende* 1987 3 SA 367 (A).

[15] *S v Motara* 1963 2 SA 579 (T). See also *Yende* supra 374.

[16] Supra 375.

[17] See ch 28 below and particularly ch 29 below for a discussion of the constitutionality of these provisions. And see ch 31 below for a discussion of the burden of proof and the evidentiary burden.

[18] 1949 1 SA 620 (A).

police, who found a revolver near the driver's seat. The accused claimed the revolver as his and admitted that he did not have a licence. The prosecution invoked a statutory presumption[19] which provided that:

"Any person who is . . . in charge of . . . any vehicle . . . in which there is . . . any arm, shall, until the contrary is proved, be deemed for the purposes of this Act to be the possessor of such . . . arm."

Nevertheless, the court found that the accused's claim of ownership coupled with the admission that he did not have a licence did not amount to a confession as he could have still led evidence to show that he was not in possession of the firearm.

Similarly in *R v Xulu*[20] the accused was charged with unlawfully possessing dagga for the purpose of sale or supply in contravention of Act 13 of 1928.[21] Section 90 of that Act placed the onus of proving that possession was lawful on the accused. The accused, when questioned by the police, admitted to possessing the dagga. The court found that his statement did not constitute a confession and held:[22]

"The point is that his statement was not an unequivocal admission of guilt on that charge. It was still open to him to try to prove that he had a permit or other right to possess dagga or . . . to allege that the dagga had been put there without his authority by someone else who had used his car. The fact that such defences would be hopeless in the light of the circumstances to which the police would testify does not provide the missing elements in the statement so as to make it a confession."

Hoffmann & Zeffertt state:[23]

"The logical conclusion from these cases is that in crimes which require *mens rea*, an account by the accused of his actions, however detailed and damning, will hardly ever amount to a confession (*unless there be something in the surrounding circumstances to indicate that what was said amounted to an unequivocal admission of guilt, and unless, taking the statements as a whole, the necessary implication is that he confessed*) because it would almost always be possible to give some further explanation which would negative the necessary mental intent."

17 3 2 Incriminating statements intended to be exculpatory Is a statement that is intended to be exculpatory, but which is actually inculpatory, a confession? Until *S v Yende*[24] there was a great deal of uncertainty as to which approach to follow in such circumstances.[25] In *Yende* the Appellate Division held that it was necessary to take an objective approach. If an objective approach is taken, it "is not whether the accused intends to admit that he is guilty but whether he intends to admit facts which make him guilty, whether he realizes it or not".[26]

---

[19] Section 32 of Act 28 of 1937.
[20] 1956 2 SA 288 (A).
[21] Which is now repealed.
[22] At 294A–B.
[23] At 211 (emphasis in the original).
[24] Supra.
[25] See Zeffertt 1987 *SALJ* 537.
[26] The words of Greenberg J in *R v Kant* 1933 WLD 128 at 129. However, it should be noted that subjective factors are not totally irrelevant in that they may be one of the surrounding circumstances taken into account in determining the objective meaning of the statement. See *S v Yende* supra 374; see also *S v Motloba* 1992 2 SACR 634 (BA) 638, in which the court approved and applied the objective test, but noted that the intention of the person making the statement may be important in certain circumstances, for example, to resolve an ambiguity.

17 3 3 Exculpatory statements incriminating as to a lesser offence Does a statement constitute a confession where the accused's statement is exculpatory in relation to the main charge, but incriminating in relation to a lesser charge?

For example, an accused is charged with raping a girl under the age of 16 and he makes a statement admitting to having had sexual intercourse with her by consent. The statement is exculpatory with regard to the charge of rape, but inculpatory in respect of the statutory offence of having sexual intercourse with a girl under the age of 16. Does the statement constitute a confession to the statutory offence? The case law does not provide clear guidance. On substantially the same facts as given in the example above two provincial divisions reached opposite conclusions. In *R v Goliath*[27] the court held that such a statement was a confession to the lesser offence, whereas in *S v F*[28] the court held that the statement could not amount to a confession either because the accused intended to exculpate himself when he made it, or, if the objective test was applied, because the statement did not exclude the defences open to him in terms of the statute.[29] Although *Yende*[30] cannot be said to be of direct application, there is no reason why the objective test laid down by the Appellate Division should not be applied in determining whether a statement amounts to a confession of a lesser offence. Following this approach, Hoffmann & Zeffertt formulate the test as follows:[31]

"[D]id the accused, when he made a statement that was exculpatory in relation to the main charge against, him intend to admit facts that make him guilty of the lesser crime for which he could be convicted on the main charge, whether he realized or not those admissions made him guilty of it?"

It does not matter whether the accused subjectively intended to exculpate himself — if objectively his statement amounts to an unequivocal admission of guilt, then it will amount to a confession to the lesser offence.

17 4   REQUIREMENTS FOR ADMISSIBILITY

17 4 1 Generally Section 217(1) of the CPA provides:

"Evidence of any confession made by any person in relation to the commission of any offence shall, if such confession is proved to have been freely and voluntarily made by such person in his sound and sober sense and without having been unduly influenced thereto, be admissible in evidence against such person at criminal proceedings relating to such offence: Provided —

(a) that a confession made to a peace officer, other than a magistrate or justice, or, in the case of a peace officer referred to in section 334, a confession made to such peace officer which relates to an offence with reference to which such peace officer is

---

[27] 1941 CPD 3.

[28] 1967 4 SA 639 (W).

[29] In Van der Merwe (ed) *Evidence* 250 it is noted that the bulk of authority favours the view taken by Lansdown & Campbell 866–7, "that where the statement is an unequivocal admission equivalent to a plea of guilty to a lesser offence of which the accused could competently be convicted on the indictment, then it ranks as a confession of that lesser offence". See *S v Gcaba* 1965 2 SA 325 (N); *R v Ahmed* 1940 AD 333; *S v Ori* 1963 2 PH H165 (D); *S v Lalamani* 1981 1 SA 999 (V) 1001.

[30] Supra.

[31] At 214.

authorized to exercise any power conferred upon him under that section, shall not be admissible in evidence, unless confirmed and reduced to writing in the presence of a magistrate or justice; and

(b) that where the confession is made to a magistrate and reduced to writing by him, or is confirmed and reduced to writing in the presence of a magistrate, the confession shall, upon the mere production thereof at the proceedings in question —

(i) be admissible in evidence against such person if it appears from the document in which the confession is contained that the confession was made by a person whose name corresponds to that of such person, and in the case of a confession made to a magistrate or confirmed in the presence of magistrate through an interpreter, if a certificate by the interpreter appears on such document to the effect that he interpreted truly and correctly and to the best of his ability with regard to the contents of the confession and any question put to such person by the magistrate; and

(ii) be presumed, unless the contrary is proved, to have been freely and voluntarily made by such person in his sound and sober senses and without having been unduly influenced thereto, if it appears from the document in which the confession is contained that the confession was made freely and voluntarily by such person in his sound and sober senses and without having been unduly influenced thereto."

Consequently, before a confession will be admitted into evidence the general rule is that the prosecution must establish that the confession was made freely and voluntarily by the accused whilst in sound and sober senses and without having been unduly influenced thereto. In § 17 4 5 2 below it is pointed out that s 217(1)*(b)* has been declared unconstitutional.

17 4 2 Freely and voluntarily The requirements that the statement be made "freely and voluntarily" and "without undue influence" are treated as separate requirements, each having a distinct meaning.[32] The requirement of freely and voluntary is assigned its common-law meaning: the statement must not be induced by a threat or promise emanating from a person in authority.[33] This requirement is also applicable to admissions and is discussed in § 16 7 1 above. The meaning of undue influence is discussed in § 17 4 4 below. The elasticity of this concept is such that "it in effect covers all cases in which external influences have operated to negative the accused's freedom of volition".[34] Consequently, in practice the inquiry as to whether the statement was made voluntarily is of little relevance, it being subsumed in the inquiry as to whether the statement was made without undue influence.[35]

17 4 3 Sound and sober senses Before a confession will be admitted into evidence it must be proved that the accused understood what he was saying. This is all that is meant by the requirement that the accused must be in his sound and sober senses. Consequently, the fact that the accused was intoxicated, or

---

[32] *S v Radebe* 1968 4 SA 410 (A); *S v Lebone* 1965 2 SA 837 (A).

[33] The fact that a confession is found to contain material untruths will give rise to doubts as to the voluntariness of the confession. See *R v Wong Kam-ming* 1980 AC 247 (PC), 1979 1 All ER 939; *S v Blom* 1992 1 SACR 649 (E).

[34] Van der Merwe (ed) *Evidence* 253; Hoffmann & Zeffertt 217.

[35] See Hoffmann & Zeffertt 217; *S v Radebe* 1968 4 SA 410 (A); *R v Kuzwayo* 1949 3 SA 761 (A).

extremely angry, or in great pain will not in itself lead to the conclusion that this requirement has not been met, unless it is established that he could not have appreciated what he was saying.[36]

17 4 4 Without being unduly influenced thereto Undue influence will be present where some external factor operates so as to extinguish the accused's freedom of will.[37] The undue influence need not emanate from a person in authority.[38] Clearly violence or a threat of assault would constitute undue influence, but the concept includes subtler forms of influence such as the promise of some benefit,[39] or an implied threat or promise.[40] The view has been expressed that any practice that is repugnant to the principles upon which the criminal law is based is an undue one.[41] Even if a statement is found to have been made voluntarily, it will be excluded if it was induced as a consequence of undue influence.[42]

17 4 4 1 *The test of undue influence* In *S v Mpetha (2)*[43] the court held that the object of an inquiry into the existence of undue influence was to determine whether the accused exercised his will freely, and that consequently the inquiry was a subjective one. Williamson J explained the relevance of objective factors as follows:[44]

> "It is his will as it actually operated and was affected by outside influences that is the concern . . . Obviously, if in a particular case there is evidence of factors which a court thinks are objectively calculated or likely to influence the will of a person, then from a purely pragmatic point of view it will not be easy for the prosecution to satisfy the court that there is no reasonable possibility of these factors in fact having had an influence subjectively on the particular accused. Conversely, if there are factors which the court thinks are not objectively calculated or likely to influence the will of an accused, then it will, practically speaking, not be easy for the defence to persuade a court that there is a reasonable possibility that these factors in fact subjectively influenced the will of the particular accused . . . An improper influence which is trivial must be ignored; so also an improper influence, which, though not trivial in itself, is shown in fact not to have had any meaningful influence on the will of the confessor."

The subjective inquiry requires the undue influence to have been operative on the accused's mind when he made the statement.[45] The subjective approach has allowed courts in the past to conclude that a confession made after lengthy interrogation, or after detention without trial, did not amount to undue influence.[46] Similarly, a breach of the Judges' Rules will not automatically render a

---

[36] *R v Blyth* 1940 AD 355; *R v Mtabela* 1958 1 SA 264 (A); *R v Ramsamy* 1954 2 SA 491 (A).

[37] See *R v Kuzwayo* 1949 3 SA 761 (A) 768.

[38] *R v Nhleko* 1960 4 SA 712 (A); *R v Masinyama* 1958 1 SA 616 (A); *S v W* 1963 3 SA 516 (A).

[39] *R v Masinyana* supra.

[40] *R v Jacobs* 1954 2 SA 320 (A).

[41] Williamson J in *S v Mpetha (2)* 1983 1 SA 576 (C). See also *S v Pietersen* 1987 4 SA 98 (C); *S v Williams* 1991 1 SACR 1 (C); *S v Colt* 1992 2 SACR 120 (E); cf *S v Mafuya (1)* 1992 2 SACR 370 (W).

[42] *S v Pietersen* supra.

[43] 1983 1 SA 576 (C) 585.

[44] At 585C–D.

[45] *S v Mkwanazi* 1966 1 SA 736 (A). See also *S v Mpetha (2)* supra 585.

[46] *S v Christie* 1982 1 SA 464 (A). Cf *S v Wanna* 1993 1 SACR 582 (Tk), in which the court held that, as a matter of general principle, a threat of detention, particularly detention in solitary confinement, would constitute undue influence.

confession inadmissible, and will merely be a factor the court will take into consideration in determining whether a confession has been made freely and voluntarily and without being unduly influenced thereto.[47]

The courts have held that the failure to advise an accused of his right to legal representation from the time of arrest[48] may be a factor taken into consideration in determining whether the requirements of s 217(1) have been met.[49] In *S v Yawa*[50] the accused had pointed out certain places and had made explanatory statements accompanying the pointing out. It was common cause that these statements constituted a confession and that the pointing out and accompanying statements were inseparable. The court therefore held that the provisions of s 217(1) had to be met before the pointing out could be admitted into evidence. The court found that the accused had not been advised of his right to legal representation at the time of his arrest or at any time before making the pointing out and that it was highly probable that if he had been advised of his right to representation, he would have exercised it. Further, if the accused had exercised this right he would

"prior to pointing anything out, have been in a position to and would have had the opportunity to consider whether or not to take part in the pointing out in the light of whatever advice his legal representative may have furnished him . . . Once it is accepted that accused No 1's decision to participate in the pointing out was affected by his lack of appreciation that he was entitled to legal representation, it follows that such lack of appreciation had an influence on the decision accused No 1 took."[51]

However, the court took care to stress that the failure to advise the accused of his right to legal representation amounted to undue influence when considered together with *all the circumstances of the case*. Therefore it cannot be concluded that there is a general principle in terms of which the failure to advise persons of their right to legal representation amounts to undue influence.[52]

In *S v M*[53] the Appellate Division, equating the right of a juvenile to be assisted by his parents with the right to legal representation, held that[54]

"the failure to afford a young person the assistance of a parent or guardian where this is reasonably possible before taking a confession from such person, could conceivably lead to the conclusion that the confession was not made freely, voluntarily, or without undue influence".

---

[47] The Judges' Rules are discussed in § 10 2 3 1 above and quoted in full in § 10 2 3 1 n 54 above. There is now clear judicial recognition that confessions are not merely excluded for potential unreliability, but because people should not be subjected to ill treatment or improper abuses. The Judges' Rules were designed especially to prevent such abuse; therefore logic dictates that a breach of the Judges' Rules should at least provide a *prima facie* case for exclusion.

[48] The courts have also suggested that the right to legal representation should be explained to the accused when he is brought before a magistrate to have his confession recorded. *S v Januarie* 1991 2 SACR (SE); *S v Mbambeli* 1993 2 SACR 388 (E).

[49] *S v Molefe* 1991 4 SA 266 (E).

[50] 1994 2 SACR 709 (SE).

[51] At 717*g–i*. See also *S v Melani* 1996 1 SACR 335 (E).

[52] *S v Khumalo* 1992 1 SACR 28 (C).

[53] 1993 2 SACR 487 (A).

[54] The Canadian Supreme Court in *R v T (E)* 109 DLR (4th) 141, referring to both the Charter of Rights and the Young Offenders Act RSC 1985, held that parental assistance is not an alternative to legal representation and found that where a young person was assisted by a parent but not advised of the right to counsel the constitutional guarantee of the right to counsel had not been upheld, and consequently the confession made by the young offender was held to be inadmissible. See also Schwikkard 1994 *SACJ* 141.

Following this approach, the court in *S v Kondile*[55] held confessions made by two juveniles to be inadmissible. Although the accused had been advised of their right to legal representation and their right to remain silent, they were not given the opportunity of being assisted by their parents or guardians. There was no suggestion of any other type of improper influence; however, the court found that it was highly probable that the absence of parental assistance influenced the accused in their decision to make the confessions and pointing outs.

Section 25(1)*(c)* and 25(2) of the interim Constitution stipulate that an accused must be advised of his or her right to consult with a legal practitioner. Therefore, the absence of such advice may not only lead to the conclusion that the accused was subject to undue influence[56] but also to the conclusion that the confession should be excluded as it was obtained unconstitutionally.[57]

A distinction needs to be drawn between a confession obtained as a result of undue influence and a confession obtained in breach of constitutional provisions. The test to be applied in determining the presence of undue influence is subjective. However, it is submitted that the test as to whether a constitutional guarantee has been violated must be objective. For example, whether the absence of legal representation amounts to undue influence will be subjectively determined, but whether or not the accused was advised of his right to legal representation in accordance with s 25 of the interim Constitution is an objective question of fact.

17 4 4 2 *Statements made under statutory compulsion* Is a statement made under statutory compulsion admissible? In *R v Carson*[58] the court was required to consider the admissibility of evidence taken in terms of s 55 of the Insolvency Act.[59] Section 55 of the now repealed Act provided for the examination, by the commissioner, of an insolvent under oath, and directed that an insolvent could not refuse to answer questions on the basis that they might incriminate him. The court held that the provisions of the statute made it clear that such evidence could be admitted in both civil and criminal proceedings. Further, the court found that the provisions of s 273 of the Criminal Procedure and Evidence Act,[60] requiring confessions to be made freely and voluntarily before being admissible into evidence, were of no relevance as regards the admissibility of a statement

---

[55] 1995 1 SACR 394 (SE).

[56] At § 10 2 3 1 above it is argued that failure to *provide* legal representation compromises the privilege against self-incrimination; clearly, if this argument is persuasive, a confession made in the absence of legal representation will be obtained in breach of the constitutionally protected privilege against self-incrimination.

[57] *S v Melani* supra. See ch 12 above for a full discussion of the admissibility of unconstitutionally obtained evidence.

[58] 1926 AD 423.

[59] Act 32 of 1916.

[60] Act 31 of 1917.

elicited in terms of s 55.[61] The court held that both provisions were "affirmatively couched", s 55 stipulating that the entire statement of an insolvent, whether or not it is included a confession, was admissible in criminal proceedings, while, on the other hand, s 272 stipulating that all confessions must be shown to have been made freely and voluntarily. It was therefore necessary to apply "a well-known principle of construction that a general affirmative provision does not repeal an earlier specific affirmative provision, unless language is used which clearly indicates an intention to repeal".[62] Consequently, the court found that "the provisions for regulating the admission of statements of insolvents in criminal proceedings against themselves dealt with a special subject, and were intended to be distinct and separate from the provisions governing the admission of confessions generally".[63] In *R v Moiloa*[64] the court held that "there would seem to be no reason to exclude an admission made in answer to a question which is required by law to be answered, for there is no threat or inducement to the party questioned to make him give an answer falsely incriminating himself".[65] Fagan JA held:

> "The effect of the statutory compulsion is merely to remove the protection embodied in the maxim *nemo tenetur se ipsum accusare*, leaving the question of admissibility in other proceedings to be decided by the principles applicable to that branch of the law; and these have been so construed as not to make the statutory compulsion a ground for ruling the statement to be inadmissible."[66]

The court found that in deciding upon the admissibility of the statement it was bound to follow the English law governing admissions and left open the question whether the conclusion would be the same in regard to confessions.

However, now that the privilege against self-incrimination and the right to remain silent have been afforded constitutional protection the approach of the courts needs to be reconsidered. In *Park-Ross v Director, OSEO*[67] an application was brought on the basis that s 5 of the Investigation of Serious Economic Offences Act[68] infringed the right to a fair trial and infringed the constitutional right to remain silent. Section 5(1)(a) of the Act provides that

> "[i]f the Director [of the Office for Serious Economic Offences] has reason to suspect that a serious economic offence has been or is being committed or that an attempt has been made or is being made to commit such an offence, he may hold an inquiry on the matter in question".

---

[61] The successor to the 1916 Act, the Insolvency Act 24 of 1936, has similar provisions. However, s 65(2A)(a) prohibits the publication of any information obtained at such interrogation and s 65(2A)(b) stipulates that incriminating questions and answers given at such an interrogation are not admissible in criminal proceedings except where the offence charged is one of perjury. In *S v Vermaas (2)* 1994 2 SACR 622 (T) the court held that these provisions did not prohibit the Master of the Supreme Court from handing over the record of the s 65 interrogation to the Attorney-General.

[62] At 424.

[63] *R v Carson* supra 424. See also *S v Hlekani* 1964 4 SA 429 (E); *S v African Bank of South Africa Ltd* 1990 2 SACR 585 (W).

[64] 1956 4 SA 824 (A).

[65] At 831C.

[66] At 834A.

[67] 1995 1 SACR 530 (C). See also *Nel v Le Roux NO & others* 1996 1 SACR 572 (CC).

[68] Act 117 of 1991.

The director may compel certain persons to attend such an inquiry in terms of s 5(8) *(a)*. A person so summoned "shall not be entitled to refuse to answer any questions upon the ground that the answer would tend to expose him to a criminal charge". Section 5(8) *(b)* provides that "[n]o evidence regarding any questions and answers contemplated in paragraph *(a)* shall be admissible in any criminal proceedings". The court held that s 25(2) *(a)* and (3) *(c)* of the interim Constitution limit the right to remain silent and not to answer incriminating questions to arrested and accused persons during plea proceedings and trial. Therefore such rights were not applicable to an inquiry under s 5, as such inquiry could not be said to be part of the criminal process. However, the court held that the use of evidence obtained at such an inquiry in subsequent criminal proceeding against the person who gave the evidence would constitute a violation of the right to remain silent.[69] However, as s 5(8) *(b)* could be "read down" so as to prohibit both direct testimony and derivative evidence from being used in criminal proceedings, s 5 could not be said to be in conflict with the interim Constitution.[70] It would therefore appear that the constitutionality of statutory provisions which operate outside of the criminal process and which override the right to remain silent will depend on the inclusion of corresponding provisions prohibiting the use of evidence obtained in breach of the privilege against self-incrimination in criminal proceedings.

In Canada similar statutory provisions have been attacked on numerous constitutional grounds and survived scrutiny.[71] In *Stelco Inc v Canada (AG)*[72] the Supreme Court of Canada held that s 17 of the Combines Investigation Act,[73] in terms of which persons who are being investigated may not refuse to answer questions, was constitutional. The court held:

"The privilege against self-incrimination, as it exists in Canada does not permit these witnesses to refuse to answer questions during the course of an investigative hearing. It clearly cannot provide them the right to refuse to attend. They are fully protected against the subsequent use of any incriminating answers by the Canada Evidence Act and s 20(2) of the Combines Investigation Act, as well as s 13 of the Charter."[74]

Section 13 of the Canadian Charter of Rights and Freedoms provides that "[a] witness who testifies in any proceedings has the right not to have any incriminating evidence so given used to incriminate the witness in any other proceedings, except in a prosecution for perjury or for the giving of contradictory evidence". The South African interim Constitution contains no similar provisions. However, it is submitted that the constitutional privilege against self-incrimination and the right to remain silent[75] are sufficient to prohibit the admission of evidence

---

[69] At 546*j*.

[70] At 548*c–f*.

[71] It is submitted that in South Africa the position would be similar and should these provisions be challenged in terms of other provisions contained in chapter 3, for example s 13 (the right to privacy), they will most probably be found to meet the requirements of the limitations clause. See *Podlas v Cohen and Bryden* 1994 4 SA 662 (T).

[72] 68 DLR (4th) 518.

[73] RSC 1970.

[74] At 522c.

[75] See s 25(3) *(c)* and *(d)* of the interim Constitution.

elicited under statutory compulsion at an investigative hearing in a later criminal hearing.

In *Davis v Tip*[76] the applicant was the subject of an inquiry instituted by his employer, the Greater Johannesburg Transitional Metropolitan Council, into allegations of, inter alia, bribery, corruption and theft. The applicant requested that the inquiry be postponed until after the conclusion of the criminal proceedings on the basis that if the inquiry proceeded, his right to remain silent at trial would be infringed. The request was denied, but the applicant was given the opportunity to seek relief from the Supreme Court. Nugent J declined the relief on the basis that the applicant was not compelled to testify at the inquiry. The court appeared to accept the contention that if the applicant chose not to testify, he would in all likelihood be found guilty of misconduct and dismissed, but held that this did not constitute compulsion. The court held that dismissal would simply be the consequence of a choice made by the applicant, "but not a penalty for doing so".[77] Compulsion would be found to be present only where "the alternative which presents itself constitutes a penalty, which serves to punish a person for choosing a particular route as an inducement to him not to do so".[78] The court appears to have overlooked the plethora of cases that identify the criteria of voluntariness as the cornerstone for determining whether the privilege against self-incrimination has been infringed.[79] It is submitted that the better approach would have been to recognize the non-applicability of s 25(2) and (3) of the interim Constitution to the inquiry, leaving the admissibility of any evidence obtained as a consequence of the violation of the privilege against self-incrimination to be determined at the relevant criminal proceedings.

17 4 5 Confessions made to peace officers   Section 217(1) provides that where a confession is made to a peace officer who is not a magistrate or justice of the peace, the confession must be confirmed or reduced to writing in the presence of a magistrate or justice of the peace.

17 4 5 1 *"Peace officer"*   Section 1(xv) defines a peace officer as including

"any magistrate, justice, police official, member of the prisons service as defined in section 1 of the Prisons Act, 1959 (Act 8 of 1959), and, in relation to any area, offence, class of offence or power referred to in a notice issued under section 334(1)[80] any person who is a peace officer under that section".

It has been held that this definition is exhaustive[81] and the onus rests on the accused to show that the person to whom he made the confession is a peace

---

[76] 1996 1 SA 1152 (W).

[77] At 1159B.

[78] At 1158I. Cf *Williams v Deputy Superintendent of Insurance* 1993 18 CRR (2d) 315.

[79] See § 16 7 1 1 above for a discussion of the requirement of voluntariness. See also *S v Botha* 1995 2 SACR 605 (W) discussed in § 10 2 3 1 2 above.

[80] Section 334(1) empowers the Minister, by notice in the *Government Gazette*, to declare certain persons to be peace officers for certain prescribed periods.

[81] *R v Debele* 1956 4 SA 570 (A).

officer.[82] The confession must be addressed to the peace officer,[83] and it will not be said to have been made to a peace officer if the confession is merely made in the presence of a peace officer or if a peace officer is used solely as an interpreter.[84]

Once a confession made to a peace officer is confirmed and reduced to writing in the presence of a magistrate or justice of the peace, it is treated as if it were a new confession.[85]

17 4 5 2 *Confessions made to peace officers who are also magistrates and justices of the peace*   Confessions made to peace officers who are also magistrates or justices of the peace need not be reduced to writing and will be admissible if they are made freely and voluntarily, in sound and sober senses, and without undue influence.[86] In terms of s 217(1) *(b)*(ii) of the CPA, if a confession is reduced to writing[87] and confirmed in the presence of magistrate, it is deemed to be admissible in evidence upon mere production and if it appears from the document that the confession was made freely and voluntarily, the confession is presumed to have been made freely and voluntarily in sound and sober senses and without undue influence.

The Consitutional Court in *S v Zuma*[88] found that the presumption in s 217(1) *(b)*(ii) placed on the accused the burden of proving that the confession was not made freely and voluntarily and required him to discharge the onus on a balance of probabilities. The court held that the common-law rule placing the burden of proof on the state to prove that a confession was made voluntarily was integral and essential to: the right to remain silent after arrest; the right not be be compelled to make a confession; and the right not to be a compellable witness against oneself. The court held that by reversing the burden of proof all these

---

[82] *R v Debele* supra; *R v Tshetaundzi* 1960 4 SA 569 (A).

[83] *R v Hans Veren* 1918 TPD 218.

[84] *R v Tshetaundzi* supra. The prosecution may invoke s 231 of the CPA in order to prove that a confession was made to, or recorded by, a magistrate (see *S v Kekane* 1986 2 SA 466 (W)). Section 231 provides that the mere production of a document that purports to bear the signature of a holder of public office, and which bears a stamp or seal purporting to be that of his department, office or institution, is *prima facie* proof that he signed it. In *S v Jika* 1991 2 SACR 489 (E) the court held that in the absence of such stamp or seal, before the documents in question could be proved by their mere production and before the onus would shift to the accused in terms of s 217*(b)*(ii), it had to be established by *viva voce* evidence that the statements had been recorded by the magistrate.

[85] *R v Jacobs* 1954 2 SA 320 (A). In *S v Mkize* 1992 2 SACR 347 (A) the accused made two admissible confessions, at different times and contained in separate statements. The statements contradicted each other in material respects and the court had to determine whether the two statements should be dealt with as part of one and the same exposition by the accused of his version of events. The court held that the logical rationale behind regarding statements as a composite whole was that, where one part of what was said qualified or altered another, both should be considered together, but where part of what was said did not so qualify, alter or explain another part, but merely contradicted it, different considerations apply, and when the parts are made at different times they cannot artificially be brought together to form one identity.

[86] In *S v Potwana* 1994 1 SACR 159 (A) the court noted that although policeman of certain rank are entitled to record confessions, it is obviously preferable for an accused to be brought before a magistrate.

[87] In *S v Mogale* 1980 1 SA 457 (T) the court held that a confession by means of a tape-recording and the transcription thereof did not meet the requirement of writing and did not fulfil the requirements of s 217(1) *(a)*. This decision has been the subject of much criticism. See Van der Merwe (ed) *Evidence* 259.

[88] 1995 1 SACR 568 (CC).

rights would be seriously compromised and undermined. The Constitutional Court found that the right to a fair trial conferred by s 25(3) of the interim Constitution was broader than the list of specific rights listed in that section. It held that the right to a fair trial embraces a concept of substantive fairness and consequently the common-law rule on the burden of proof was inherent in the rights specifically mentioned in s 25(2) and 25(3). The court concluded that s 217(1)(*b*)(ii) violated the provisions of the interim Constitution and was invalid.[89] *S v Zuma* supra is also discussed in § 29 3 below.

17 4 5 3 *Confessions confirmed and reduced to writing in the presence of a magistrate or justice of the peace and undue influence* The circumstances in which confessions are reduced and confirmed to writing by magistrates and justices of the peace have frequently provided fertile ground for allegations of undue influence.

The courts have consistently expressed the view that it is undesirable for a police officer, involved in the team investigating the accused's conduct,[90] to record the accused's confession or to be used as an interpreter for the purpose of recording the confession.[91] However, the Appellate Division in *S v Mbatha*[92] held that it was wrong to view this type of conduct as an irregularity,[93] the undesirable conduct simply being a factor taken into account in determining whether the confession was made freely and voluntarily and without undue influence.[94] In *S v Latha*[95] the court held that the failure to take heed of judicial advice to the effect that it was undesirable for a police officer attached to a particular unit which investigated the matter to take a confession meant that the state bore the onus of proving that the confessions were made freely and voluntarily.

In *S v Colt*[96] the court held that the onus would not shift unless the following requirements were fulfilled:

> "Where an accused person is brought to a magistrate for the purpose of making a confession and it appears that he has already made a statement, it is necessary that the questioning of the accused by the magistrate be such firstly, to pierce the veil adverted to in *S v Gumede and Another* 1942 AD 398 at 433, i e the 'veil between the previous interrogations by the police and the subsequent appearance of the interrogated person before the magistrate' and, secondly, to ensure that the result of such piercing is that the Court is satisfied beyond reasonable doubt that whatever possible untoward circumstances may have

---

[89] The court held that any application of s 217(1)(*b*)(ii) was invalid in any criminal trial which commenced before, on, or after 27 April 1994 and in which a verdict had not been given by 27 April 1994. See also *S v Mhlungu* 1995 2 SACR 277 (CC). For further discussion of *Zuma*, see Govender 1995 *SACJ* 205; Jagwanth 1995 *SACJ* 380.

[90] *S v Mdluli* 1972 2 SA 839 (A); *S v Mahlabane* 1990 2 SACR 558 (A).

[91] *S v Dhlamini* 1971 1 SA 807 (A).

[92] 1987 2 SA 272 (A).

[93] See also *S v Mavela* 1990 1 SACR 582 (A). Cf *S v Mbele* 1981 2 SA 738 (A); *S v Magwaza* 1985 3 SA 29 (A). In *S v Jantjie* 1992 1 SACR 24 (SE) the state failed to provide the accused with a copy of a confession allegedly made by the accused. The court held this was manifestly unjust and unfair and constituted an irregularity and that the only way the accused could have a fair and just trial would be to exclude the confession from evidence.

[94] See also *S v Khoza* 1984 1 SA 57 (A) 59–60.

[95] 1994 1 SACR 447 (A).

[96] 1992 2 SACR 120 (E) 123*h*–124*a*. See also *S v Jika* 1991 2 SACR 489 (E); *R v Gumede* 1942 AD 398.

prevailed at the time the accused made the statement to the police were no longer operative at the time when the accused appeared before the magistrate. The reason for this is that there is a danger that by reason of untoward conduct on the part of the police the accused might have been brought to a confessing state of mind which might persist at the time of his appearance before the magistrate and which might give rise to an apparent but deceptive voluntariness on his part to make a statement to the magistrate. The magistrate should, therefore, enquire of the person appearing before him 'whether he has already made a statement and, if so, the nature of such statement and especially the reasons actuating him in wishing to repeat the statement'."

Now that there is no longer a shift in onus when a confession is reduced to writing and confirmed in the presence of a magistrate the significance of the above factors may well be diminished. However, reduction to writing remains a requirement for admissibility where the confession is made to a peace officer who is not a magistrate or justice of the peace. Consequently the circumstances in which a confession was reduced to writing will remain a factor to be taken into consideration in determining whether a confession was made freely and voluntarily, in sound and sober senses and without undue influence.

17 5   THE BURDEN OF PROOF

It is now clear that the prosecution will always bear the burden of proving that a confession was made freely and voluntarily in sound and sober senses and without undue influence.

17 6   PROCEDURE: TRIAL WITHIN A TRIAL

The admissibility of a confession is determined at a trial within a trial.[97] The failure to hold a trial within a trial when the admissibility of a confession is disputed constitutes a material irregularity.[98]

At this stage of the proceedings both prosecution and defence will adduce evidence as to the circumstances in which the confession was made. The judge and assessors[99] will decide whether or not the requirements of admissibility have been met. In order to avoid potential prejudice to the accused the court will not consider the contents of a confession before determining whether it is admissible or not.[100] The purpose of the inquiry is not to establish the accused's guilt or

---

[97] Where two or more accused are being tried, and a number of them challenge the admissibility of a confession, the trials within trials may be consolidated in order to be fair and just to the accused. See *S v Letsoko* 1964 4 SA 768 (A); *S v Yengeni (2)* 1990 4 SA 429 (C).

[98] *S v Mofokeng* 1992 2 SACR 261 (O); *S v Ntuli* 1995 1 SACR 158 (T). Cf *S v Mndebele* 1995 1 SACR 278 (A): on appeal it was argued that evidence of certain pointings out had been incorrectly considered as part of the merits when they should have been considered at a trial within a trial. The Appellate Division held that there had been no irregularity in the circumstances of the case: the defence had not insisted on a trial within a trial and had expressly informed the court that the issue was not one of admissibility but rather of accuracy.

[99] The admissibility of a confession may be decided by a judge sitting alone if the judge is of the opinion that it is in the interests of the administration of justice to do so. See s 145(4) of the CPA 1977.

[100] *S v Gaba* 1985 4 SA 734 (A). In *S v Nkata* 1990 4 SACR 250 (A) the court held that an inadmissible confession may not be referred to by the prosecution at any stage of the proceedings for any purpose whatsoever.

innocence but the admissibility of the confession, and the accused may not be cross-examined on the issue of his guilt.[101] Consequently at the trial within a trial the general rule is that an accused may not be cross-examined as to whether the confession is true or not.[102] However, cross-examination of this nature may be allowed where the accused alleges that the confession is false and that the true authors were the police.[103] The purpose of the cross-examination is to test the accused's credibility and not the truth of the confession.[104] In such circumstances the prosecution may cross-examine on the contents of the confession and only those portions referred to in cross-examination may become part of the record.[105] In *S v Potwana*[106] the court, when assessing evidence pertinent to the voluntariness of the confession, warned against attaching undue significance to the fact that an accused person lied with regard to the truth of the content of the confession.

Once the court is satisfied that the requirements for admissibility set out in s 217(1) of the CPA have been met the confession will be admitted into evidence. However, if during the course of the trial evidence comes to light which causes the court to question its earlier ruling, it is entitled to overrule its own decision.[107] Conversely, a court may not provisionally admit a confession on the basis that evidence may emerge later to justify its admission.[108]

In accordance with the principle that the issue of admissibility must be kept separate from the issue of guilt the prosecution in the main trial may not lead evidence regarding the accused's testimony at the trial within a trial. Nor may a presiding officer in deciding the issue of guilt have regard to the evidence given at the trial within a trial.[109] The accused is not precluded from leading the same evidence adduced at the trial within a trial during the course of the main trial. This may be done in order to persuade the court that, owing to the circumstances in which the confession was made, little weight should be attached to it.[110]

---

[101] *R v Dunga* 1934 AD 223; *S v De Vries* 1989 1 SA 228 (A). In *S v Yengeni (3)* 1991 SACR 387 (C) the court held that the accused could be cross-examined on his guilt only where the accused himself raised the issue of guilt or innocence in support of his argument that the confession was inadmissible.

[102] See Hoffmann & Zeffertt 228.

[103] *S v Lebone* 1965 2 SA 837 (A); *S v Khuzwayo* 1990 1 SACR 365 (A); *S v Mriba* 1995 2 SACR 585 (E).

[104] See *S v Lebone* supra; *S v Talane* 1986 3 SA 196 (A); *S v Mafuya (2)* 1992 2 SACR 381 (W); *S v Gxokwe* 1992 2 SACR 355 (C), in which the rationale for this exception is clearly set out at 358.

[105] *S v Lebone* supra; *S v Potwana* 1994 1 SACR 159 (A).

[106] Supra.

[107] *R v Melozani* 1952 3 SA 639 (A); *S v W* 1963 3 SA 516 (A); *S v Mkwanazi* 1966 1 SA 736 (A).

[108] *S v Ntuli* 1993 2 SACR 599 (W).

[109] *S v De Vries* 1989 1 SA 228 (A); *S v Sithebe* 1992 1 SACR 347 (A); *S v Malinga* 1992 1 SACR 138 (A); *S v Mlomo* 1993 2 SACR 123 (A); *S v Shezi* 1994 1 SACR 575 (A). But see also generally *S v Nglengethwa* 1996 1 SACR 737 (A). In *De Vries* and *S v Sithebe* supra the court left open the question as to whether an accused who elects to testify at the main trial can be cross-examined on what he said in the trial within a trial about the merits. Cf *S v Gquama (2)* 1994 2 SACR 182 (C), where the court held that once a statement and pointing out had been ruled admissible at the trial within a trial the accused could be cross-examined in the main trial on the contents of his evidence during the trial within a trial.

[110] *S v Mkwanazi* supra.

17 7   INADMISSIBLE CONFESSIONS WHICH SUBSEQUENTLY BECOME ADMISSIBLE

A confession excluded by s 217(1) is "unconditionally . . . inadmissible",[111] and as a general rule cannot become admissible by virtue of waiver or consent on the part of the accused. Consequently the prosecution is prohibited from introducing evidence of an inadmissible confession either in evidence in chief or in the course of cross-examination of the accused or other defence witnesses. In *S v Nkata*[112] the court held that not even the preamble to an inadmissible confession could be used in cross-examination of the accused and to do so would constitute an irregularity. However, it is not entirely clear what the position is where the accused elicits evidence of the inadmissible confession whilst leading or cross-examining witnesses.

Section 217(3) of the CPA provides:

"Any confession which is under subsection (1) inadmissible in evidence against the person who made it, shall become admissible against him —

(a) if he adduces in the relevant proceedings any evidence, either directly or in cross-examining any witness, or any oral or written statement made by him either as part of or in connection with such confession; and

(b) if such evidence is, in the opinion of the judge or judicial officer presiding at such proceedings, favourable to such person."[113]

In *S v Nieuwoudt*[114] the court held that the "words 'in connection with' " indicated that the provision is not limited to cases where the accused elicits the favourable part of the confession. The Appellate Division approved the following definition of "in connection with" provided in *R v Mzimsha*:[115]

"If the defence elicits a portion of the verbal conversation or transaction which is favourable to the accused person it does so at the risk of the unfavourable portion also becoming admissible in evidence, but either the favourable statements must be a natural part of the confession tendered or the two matters, the favourable statement and the confession, must . . . be parts of substantially the same transaction. It would . . . be competent to admit the evidence if the alleged confession took place at later stage of the same conversation or transaction in which the favourable statement was made. Although then not a part of the confession there is an intimate connection in point of time in that both form part of the same transaction."

The court in *Nieuwoudt* found the approach of the court in *Mzimsha* to be acceptable, provided it was understood that everything said during the same conversation is not necessarily "in connection with" the matter in question.

Section 217(3) has not assisted the courts in reaching consensus on the admissibility of a confession elicited by the accused in cross-examination of a prosecution witness in circumstances where the requirements of s 217(3) have not been met. For example, in *R v Bosch*[116] the accused, in cross-examining a state

---

[111] *R v Perkins* 1920 AD 307.

[112] 1990 4 SA 250 (A).

[113] Paizes in Du Toit et al *Commentary* 24-66F says: "The principle contained in this section is an extension of the common-law rule of completeness." See *R v Valachia* 1945 AD 826; *S v Cele* 1985 4 SA 767 (A); *S v Nieuwoudt* 1990 4 SA 217 (A).

[114] 1990 4 SA 217 (A).

[115] 1942 WLD 82 85–6.

[116] 1949 1 SA 548 (A).

witness, asked the witness why he was sure that he had not made a mistake in identifying the accused. The witness replied "to put it bluntly, the Criminal Investigation Department told me that you admitted guilt". The court held that this response was inadmissible to show that the accused had admitted his guilt, but that it was admissible to show why the witness was sure he was not making a mistake in identifying the accused.[117] However, subsequently the courts have not been consistent in their interpretation of *Bosch.* In *S v Magagula*[118] the court interpreted *Bosch* as providing authority for the view that the confession would be inadmissible unless its reception into evidence would be to the advantage of the accused. However, the court in *S v Olifant,*[119] also applying *Bosch,* reached a different conclusion: a confession elicited in this way will be admissible provided that the witness's reply was a direct and fair answer to the question.[120] Hoffmann & Zeffertt,[121] who favour this latter approach, submit that this is suggested in *Bosch,* but that *Bosch* "does not go so far as to hold it". In contrast, Paizes[122] submits that *Bosch's* case does not furnish authority for the broad proposition that a confession that has been elicited by an accused may be used as evidence of the truth of its content to prove the accused's guilt.[123]

In *S v Jeniker*[124] the court questioned the correctness of the court *a quo's* decision in permitting a confession that was not admissible against the accused (as it had not been proved to have been made freely and voluntarily) to be admitted for the specific purpose of assisting a co-accused in his defence. The Appellate Division held that it was doubtful whether the fact that the confession could assist the accused in his defence was sufficient basis for admitting the evidence. The accused did not testify and it therefore appeared that the confession constituted inadmissible hearsay evidence. However, the court found it unnecessary to reach a conclusion on these points and presumed that the confession was admissible, but held that no weight could be attached to it as there was another statement before the court by the accused repudiating the confession and alleging that it was coerced.

---

[117] At 554.

[118] 1981 1 SA 771 (T).

[119] 1982 4 SA 52 (NC).

[120] See also *S v Mokoena* 1978 1 SA 229 (O); *S v Minnie* 1986 4 SA 30 (E); *S v Mvambo* 1995 1 SACR 180 (W), in which Marais J, whilst favouring this approach, held that where the accused is unrepresented the court must be fully satisfied that the accused is fully aware of the risk attaching to the question. He also noted that his proviso should extend to all cases and that the court should warn inexperienced counsel of the dangers of putting such questions.

[121] At 231.

[122] Paizes in Du Toit et al *Commentary* 24-66G.

[123] Ibid: "Greenberg JA was at pains to stress that the confession in *Bosch's* case could not be used for such a purpose, but since it could be used for another, non-hearsay purpose, its reception was not irregular."

[124] 1994 1 SACR 141 (A).

17 8 FACTS DISCOVERED AS A CONSEQUENCE OF AN INADMISSIBLE ADMISSION OR CONFESSION

The admissibility of facts discovered as a consequence of an inadmissible admission or confession is governed by s 218 of the CPA, which provides:

"(1) Evidence may be admitted at criminal proceedings of any fact otherwise admissible in evidence, notwithstanding that the witness who gives evidence of such fact, discovered such fact or obtained knowledge of such fact only in consequence of information given by an accused appearing at such proceedings in any confession or statement which by law is not admissible in evidence against such accused at such proceedings, and notwithstanding that the fact was discovered or came to the knowledge of such witness against the wish or will of such accused.

(2) Evidence may be admitted at criminal proceedings that anything was pointed out by an accused appearing at such proceedings or that any fact or thing was discovered in consequence of information given by such accused, notwithstanding that such pointing out or information forms part of a confession or statement which by law is not admissible in evidence against such accused at such proceedings."

17 8 1 Section 218(2) In terms of this subsection evidence that the accused pointed out anything may be admitted as well as evidence that any fact or thing was discovered in consequence of information given by the accused, even though the pointing out or information forms part of an inadmissible confession or statement.

17 8 2 Evidence discovered as a consequence of a pointing out A pointing out has been defined as "an overt act whereby the accused indicates physically to the inquisitor the presence or location of some thing or some place actually visible to the inquisitor".[125] Evidence of a pointing out will be admissible even if no concrete facts are discovered as a result of the pointing out. It is only necessary to show that the accused knew of a fact relevant to his guilt.[126] For example, in *R v Tebetha*[127] the accused was arrested and interrogated in connection with a robbery. The police, prior to arresting the accused, had already found the van and empty tins used to carry money. The court held that the fact that the accused later pointed out the place where the van and tins had been found was admissible in evidence notwithstanding that the pointing out was conducted as a consequence of an inadmissible statement.[128]

This subsection does not permit statements accompanying the pointing out to be admitted into evidence[129] and the courts have held a confession in the guise

---

[125] *S v Nkwanyana* 1978 3 SA 404 (N) 405H.

[126] See *R v Tebetha* 1959 2 SA 337 (A) 346, where Hoexter JA held that "the mere pointing out . . . is sufficient by itself to prove his knowledge of the thing pointed out or some fact connected with it". See *S v Mncube* 1991 3 SA 132 (A); *S v Francis* 1991 1 SACR 198 (A) 207*g–h* as to what inferences can be drawn from the fact of the accused's knowledge.

[127] 1959 2 SA 337 (A).

[128] See Paizes in Du Toit et al *Commentary* 24-67, where the majority decision in *Tebetha* is criticized. See also Zeffertt "Pointing Out" *Fiat Iustitia: Essays in Memory of Oliver Deneys Schreiner* (1983) 395.

[129] *R v Nhleko* 1960 4 SA 712 (A).

of a pointing out will not be admissible.[130] In *S v Magwaza*[131] it was held that where "the court has certain knowledge not only that the pointing out forms part of an inadmissible confession but also what the precise contents of the inadmissible confession are" it should exclude the evidence of the pointing out. However, the court in *S v Masilela*,[132] although distinguishing the facts of the case from those in *Magwaza*, made it clear that it disagreed with the approach taken in *Magwaza* on the basis that the provisions of s 218(2) make the fact that a pointing out forms part of an inadmissible confession irrelevant to the question of admissibility.[133] Stafford J, in *S v Mmonwa*,[134] found that the words "[e]vidence *may* be admitted" gave the courts a discretion whether or not to admit such facts. *Masilela* and *Mmonwa* are reconcilable if it is borne in mind that there are numerous considerations other than the mere inadmissibility of the confession that can influence the court in its determination regarding the admissibility of the pointing out.[135] The question then arises as to what factors will guide the court in determining the admissibility of evidence obtained as a consequence of a pointing out.

17 8 3 Factors affecting admissibility Prior to *S v Sheehama*[136] and *S v January; Prokureur-Generaal, Natal v Khumalo*[137] it was clear that central to judicial arguments for admitting a pointing out was that facts discovered in consequence of an inadmissible confession, unlike the confession itself, cannot be rejected on the basis that they are likely to be unreliable.[138] In *Samhando* the court held that evidence of a pointing out forming part of an inadmissible statement could be admitted in accordance with the theory of confirmation by subsequently discovered facts. In terms of this theory the reason for excluding an admission or confession obtained by inducement is that the evidence is potentially unreliable. However, if the contents of the admission can be proved to be true by other evidence, the problem of unreliability falls away. Clearly if the confirmation argument were carried to its logical conclusion, the whole confession could be admitted if confirmed in material respects by subsequently discovered facts. The courts have declined to go this far and have expressly held that a confession will not be admitted in the guise of a pointing out. In *Sheehama* the court noted that the reliability argument was dependent on an element of discovery and was therefore not applicable where the pointing out simply confirmed already known

---

[130] *S v Mbele* 1981 2 SA 738 (A).

[131] 1985 3 SA 29 (A) 39.

[132] 1987 4 SA 1 (A).

[133] See also *S v Mathebula* 1991 1 SACR 306 (T).

[134] 1990 1 SA 81 (T).

[135] See *S v Sheehama* 1991 2 SA 860 (A) 881. See also Schwikkard 1991 *SACJ* 318. It can be argued that the inadmissibility of the confession does remain relevant in so far as it would be absurd if the provisions of s 217 were negated by permitting the prohibited confession to be admitted through manipulation of s 218(2).

[136] Supra.

[137] 1994 2 SACR 801 (A).

[138] *R v Warickshall* 1783 1 Keach 263; *R v Samhando* 1943 AD 608; *S v Duna* 1984 2 SA 591 (Ck). Cf *R v Camane* 1925 AD 570.

facts.[139] This approach has led the courts to express disapproval of police practices that might compromise the discovery element in a pointing out. The courts have found the following practices to be undesirable: a member of the investigating unit being involved in the pointing out;[140] the involvement of any person in conducting the pointing out who has prior knowledge of the relevant places or objects;[141] using an interpreter, during the course of the pointing out, who is attached to the investigating unit.[142]

Prior to the enactment of s 245(2) of the Criminal Procedure and Evidence Amendment Act 29 of 1955 and its successor s 218(2), there were some judicial objections to the admission of evidence discovered as a consequence of a pointing out on the basis that it infringed the common-law privilege against self-incrimination.[143] However, the provisions of s 245(2) were used to strengthen the argument that a pointing out could not infringe the common-law privilege against self-incrimination, as evidence of pointing out was not admitted in evidence on the basis that it amounted to an extra-curial admission,

> "but on the basis that it shows that the accused has knowledge of the place or thing pointed out, or of some fact connected with it, from which knowledge it may be possible, depending on the facts of the case concerned, to draw an inference pointing to an accused's guilt".[144]

The courts went as far as to hold that evidence of a pointing out would be admissible notwithstanding that it was obtained as a result of the use of violence.[145] This view was expressly rejected by the Appellate Division in *Sheehama*,[146] in which the court held:

> "[A] pointing out is essentially a communication by conduct and, as such, is a statement by the person pointing out. If it is a relevant pointing out unaccompanied by any exculpatory explanation by the accused, it amounts to a statement by the accused that he has knowledge of relevant facts which *prima facie* operates to his disadvantage and it can thus in an appropriate case constitute an extra-judicial admission. As such the common law, as confirmed by the provisions of s 219A of the Criminal Procedure Act 51 of 1977, requires that it be made freely and voluntarily. It is also a basic principle of our law that an accused cannot be forced to make self-incriminating statements against his will, and it is therefore inherently improbable that the legislature, with a view to sound legal policy, could ever have had the intention in s 218(2) of Act 51 of 1977 to authorize evidence of forced pointings out."[147]

However, the court in *Sheehama* left open the question whether an involuntary pointing out may nevertheless be admitted where there is the requisite element of discovery ("the *Samhando* exception"). The answer was provided in *S v January; Prokureur-Generaal, Natal v Khumalo*,[148] where the Appellate Division held that

---

[139] Supra 877.
[140] *S v Mbele* 1981 2 SA 738 (A).
[141] *S v Nyembe* 1982 1 SA 835 (A).
[142] *S v Mahlabane* 1990 2 SACR 558 (A).
[143] See *R v Camane* supra; *R v Duetsimi* 1950 3 SA 674 (A). Cf *R v Samhando* supra.
[144] *S v Tsotsobe* 1983 1 SA 856 (A).
[145] *S v Ismail (1)* 1965 1 SA 446 (N); *R v Samhando* supra.
[146] Supra 879 and 880.
[147] Headnote.
[148] Supra.

s 219A could not be interpreted so as to preserve the common law as expounded in *Samhando*.[149] It found the provisions of s 219A(1) to be unambiguous and that in terms of this section involuntary admissions are inadmissible and that "linguistically the subsection admits of no exception".[150] The court referred with approval to *S v Khumalo*,[151] in which it was held that the reliability principle had been disapproved of in our law — consequently "the theory of confirmation by subsequently discovered facts" must by implication be rejected.

Where a pointing out cannot be separated from the confession, or where it constitutes a confession itself, a requirement for admission is that the state must prove that it was made freely and voluntarily, in sound and sober senses and without undue influence.[152] In *S v Mjikwa*[153] the court held a pointing out made approximately nine hours after the making of an involuntary confession to be inadmissible. The court found that it was probable that the accused had been asked to make the pointing out as a result of the confession and that the factors that had induced him to make the confession continued to persist at the time of making the pointing out.

The interim Constitution upholds the privilege against self-incrimination and provides that no person shall be compelled to make a confession or admission.[154] It is argued above[155] that these constitutional provisions support the argument that admissions and confessions should not be treated differently, and that the requirement of voluntariness should not be given its restrictive common-law interpretation. Obviously, this argument extends to admissions arising out of a pointing out and, if followed, would require that a pointing out be made freely and voluntarily, in sound and sober senses and without undue influence before being admitted into evidence.[156]

Evidence obtained as a consequence of a pointing out may also be excluded if obtained unconstitutionally.[157] In *S v Melani*[158] the court considered the admissibility of pointings out made by the three accused. Accused No 3 had been wounded on arrest and declined to make a statement to a magistrate two days after his arrest. But, despite this, he was a few days later taken to make a pointing out. The court found that these circumstances were sufficient to raise a reasonable doubt as to whether the accused exercised a free will at the time of making the pointing out.[159] Consequently the pointing out was excluded from evidence

---

[149] Supra. Cf *S v Jordaan* 1992 2 SACR 498 (A).

[150] At 806.

[151] 1992 2 SACR 411 (N).

[152] See, e g, *S v Zimmerie* 1989 3 SA 484 (C), in which the court held an explanation and demonstration by the accused of how they had broken open a window and entered the premises was not a pointing out but an inadmissible confession. See also *S v Yawa* supra.

[153] 1993 1 SA SACR (A).

[154] See s 25(2) *(a)* and *(c)*.

[155] In § 16 7 1 1 above.

[156] See, e g, *S v Melani* 1996 1 SACR 335 (E).

[157] In *S v Melani* 1995 2 SACR 141 (E) the court held that it had a discretion to *admit* such evidence if its exclusion would bring the administration of justice into discredit.

[158] 1996 1 SACR 335 (E).

[159] At 342*g–h*.

without reference to the Constitution. (The court appears not to have found it necessary to determine whether the pointing out constituted an admission or confession.) Accused Nos 1 and 2 had not been properly informed of their right to legal representation prior to making their pointings out. Furthermore, accused No 1 had not been warned that the evidence obtained as a result of the pointing out could be used against him. Froneman J held that non-compliance with the Judges' Rules and the failure to advise an accused of his right to legal representation was not, at common law, a ground for a ruling of inadmissibility.[160] The court then considered the defence argument that the pointings out should be excluded as they had been obtained in breach of s 25(1)*(c)* of the interim Constitution. This section provides, inter alia, that every detained person has the right to consult with a legal practitioner and to be informed of this right promptly. Froneman J held that the provisions of s 25 required the court to look beyond the reliability and voluntariness of the evidence and to consider the impact of admitting the evidence on the "fairness of the criminal justice system as a whole and not only the fairness of the actual trial itself".[161] The court concluded that the pointings out were inadmissible as their admission would bring the administration of justice into disrepute.[162] The admissibility of unconstitutionally obtained evidence is dealt with in chapter 12 above.

17 8 4 Facts discovered in consequence of information given by the accused It is not only facts discovered as a result of a pointing out that are admissible in terms of s 218(2) but also evidence of any fact or thing discovered in consequence of information given by such accused, even where that information forms part of an inadmissible statement. And in terms of s 218(1) evidence of a fact will be admissible notwithstanding that the witness discovered or obtained knowledge of the fact in consequence of an inadmissible confession. It also specifically provides that such fact will be admissible even though it came to the knowledge of the accused against the wish or will of the accused. The meaning of this latter provision was explained by Milne JP in *S v Ismail*,[163] where he held that the words "against the wish or will" of the accused apply[164]

> "to the actual discovery of the fact sought to be led in evidence, not to the confession containing information which led to the discovery. A confession may be made to a policeman that the accused had stolen a large sum of money but the accused might well decline to say where he had hidden it because he wished to lay his hands upon it after undergoing his punishment for stealing it. But if the policeman to whom he has made the confession, as a result of information contained in it, finds the sum of money, evidence that it was so found is admissible notwithstanding that the discovery was made against his wish or will . . . It seems to me that, although the words are capable of having a meaning

---

[160] At 344*b*. However, the court did acknowledge that it may be incorrect in reaching this conclusion.

[161] At 349*d*. See also § 12 6 2 above.

[162] At 351*g* In Zimbabwe and Namibia evidence of involuntary pointings out have been excluded on the basis that the admission of such evidence would be contrary to the constitutional provisions of those countries. See *S v Nkomo* 1990 1 SACR 682 (ZS); *S v Minnies* 1991 3 SA 364 (NmH).

[163] 1965 1 SA 446 (N) 450H–451B; the court in this case dealt with s 245 of Act 56 of 1955, which was the precursor to s 218 and contained substantially the same provisions.

[164] Cf *S v Duna* 1984 2 SA 591 (Ck).

sufficient to indicate that the evidence would be admissible, even though the confession was obtained against the wish or will of the accused, that is not what the words where intended to mean. The confession itself, even though made voluntarily, would be inadmissible because it was made to a policeman, unless it was reduced to writing before a magistrate.''

The view that s 218(1) applies only where the confession is found to be inadmissible on grounds other than that it was made involuntarily or subject to undue influence accords with the fundamental rule that persons should not be compelled to incriminate themselves.

In *S v Mokahtsa*[165] the court held that the requirement of voluntariness must also be met in circumstances where facts are discovered in consequence of information given by the accused where the supplying of such information amounted to an admission by conduct. However, there was an interesting twist in this judgment. The facts can be summarized as follows: the accused was arrested in connection with a bank robbery. After intensive interrogation the accused's wife was brought to him and he instructed her to hand over the money to the police. The accused's wife took the police to the place where the money was hidden. The court found that the information supplied by the accused had not been given voluntarily and consequently the accused's statements were not admissible. But it held that the fact that it was the accused's wife who was responsible for the recovery of the stolen money was admissible. The court held that evidence which connected the accused in another way with the object involved in the commission of the offence, that is in a manner independent of the admission by conduct, was not inadmissible merely because the pointing out of the object or the supplying of information leading to the discovery thereof had not been made voluntarily. The court used the following analogy: if an accused is coerced into pointing out the murder weapon, evidence that the accused pointed out the weapon will be inadmissible; however, evidence that the accused's fingerprints were found on the weapon will be admissible, even though the weapon was found only as a result of a coerced pointing out.[166]

Whether the courts have a discretion to exclude evidence of this nature on the basis that it was obtained as a consequence of a breach of the accused's constitutional right not to be compelled to make an admission or confession is discussed in chapter 12 above.

17 9   CONFESSION ADMISSIBLE ONLY AGAINST MAKER

A confession is admissible only against the person who made the confession, and may not be admitted either directly or indirectly against any other person.[167] This general rule is also applicable to admissions and to evidence arising out of a pointing out that constitutes an admission. In *S v Jili*[168] the court distinguished

---

[165] 1993 1 SACR 408 (C).

[166] This analogy can be challenged on the basis that the fingerprints would be admissible in terms of s 225(2) of the CPA and not s 218. See § 10 2 3 1 above for a discussion of the ascertainment of bodily features.

[167] *R v Baartman* 1960 3 SA 535 (A). *S v Serobe* 1968 4 SA 420 (A).

[168] 1989 4 SA 921 (N).

between two types of evidentiary material that may arise out of a pointing out. The first kind are facts that are discovered as a result of the pointing out. These facts which exist objectively, if found to be admissible, can be taken into account for all purposes against all accused. The second is the fact that the accused did the pointing out. The relevance of this evidence is to establish the extent of the accused's knowledge by virtue of his ability to do the pointing out, which amounts to an admission and consequently is admissible only against the person who did the pointing out.

17 10 AN ARGUMENT FOR LAW REFORM

In chapter 16 above it is argued that if the constitutional privilege against self-incrimination is to be upheld, a distinction should not be drawn between the requirements of admissibility for confessions and admissions, and that both admissions and confessions should be required to be made freely and voluntarily in sound and sober senses and without undue influence. In this chapter it is noted that the courts have taken an overly technical approach in distinguishing between admissions and confessions and that the reluctance to classify statements as confessions appears to have its origins in judicial disapproval of the requirement that a confession made to a peace officer be reduced to writing. This requirement, prior to *Zuma*, was coupled with a proviso that once a confession was reduced to writing in the presence of a magistrate and certain requirements were met it would be presumed to be have been made freely and voluntarily, in sound and sober senses and without undue influence. This proviso has been found to be unconstitutional and has been held to be an infringement of the presumption of innocence.[169] The requirement of writing and confirmation in the case of certain peace officers has not provided the intended protection to accused persons as it has "had the effect of dropping a veil between the treatment of the accused by his custodians and his resulting confession".[170] Therefore there would appear to be little reason to retain it. The scrapping of this requirement should also reduce resistance to the notion of making both admissions and confessions subject to the same requirements of admissibility. Once the distinction between confessions and admissions is removed the necessity of retaining the restrictive and technical common-law interpretation of voluntariness is removed, there being little sense in retaining it when it can be subsumed under the broader umbrella of undue influence.

[169] See *S v Zuma* supra; *S v Shangase* 1994 2 SACR 659 (D).
[170] Lansdown & Campbell 874.

KINDS OF EVIDENCE AND THE PRESENTATION THEREOF

ORAL EVIDENCE

A St Q Skeen

18 1 INTRODUCTION

Generally, evidence for either party must, in both criminal and civil cases, be given orally by the witnesses in the presence of the parties. There are certain exceptions such as the receiving of evidence by way of commission, interrogatories or affidavit.[1] Section 170A of the CPA allows for evidence to be given through intermediaries where it appears to the court that a witness under the age of 18 years would be exposed to undue mental stress or suffering if he or she testifies in open court. All questioning will then take place through the intermediary. Medical practitioners, family counsellors, child care workers, social workers, certain teachers, and psychologists may be appointed as intermediaries. The witness may be seated in an informal setting, out of the sight of the accused, or even in a separate room linked by closed circuit television. The idea behind these provisions is to protect a child witness, particularly in cases of sexual abuse.[2]

The rationale of this practice of orality is that parties should have an opportunity to confront the witnesses who testify against them, and should be able to challenge the evidence by questioning.

Section 161 of the CPA provides that a witness in criminal proceedings should (except where the CPA or any other law provides otherwise) give evidence *viva voce* (which in the case of a deaf-and-dumb person is deemed to include gesture-language). An accused who disrupts proceedings may be removed from the court.[3] A witness and an accused may give evidence through an interpreter.

Section 42 of the CPEA incorporates the general common-law provision that a witness should give oral evidence in civil proceedings. An example of an exception to this rule was discussed in § 15 2 2 above.

18 2 EVIDENCE MUST GENERALLY BE GIVEN ON OATH OR AFFIRMATION

Section 162 of the CPA provides that no person shall be examined as a witness unless he has taken the oath in the form set out in the section. The oath must be administered by the judge, registrar, or presiding officer.[4] Section 163 of the CPA allows a person who objects to taking the oath (either at all or in the prescribed form) to make an affirmation to speak the truth. An affirmation has the same legal effect as an oath and the maker of both an oath and affirmation may be charged with perjury or statutory perjury. The oath or affirmation may be administered through or by an interpreter instructed by the court.[5]

Section 39 of the CPEA provides that no person (other than a person referred

---

[1] See §§ 18 11–18 14 below.

[2] See further §§ 18 17–18 17 3 below.

[3] Section 159 CPA.

[4] *S v Bothma* 1971 1 SA 332 (C). In *S v Shezi* 1987·1 SA 552 (N) it was held that where the record of the proceedings show that the accused has been sworn, the record is *prima facie* proof that it was correctly recorded. The administration of the oath by a judge's clerk and in his absence by a court orderly acting temporarily as court registrar is proper or substantial compliance: *S v Orphanou* 1990 2 SACR 429 (W). The oath may not be administered by the prosecutor: *S v Bothma* supra.

[5] A failure to administer the oath to a witness or administration of the oath through an interpreter who has not been sworn results in the "evidence" being inadmissible: *S v Naidoo* 1962 2 SA 625 (A).

to in ss 40 and 41 (see § 18 2 1 below)) may give evidence except on oath. The oath is to be administered in the manner which most clearly conveys to the witness the meaning of an oath and which the witness considers to be binding on his conscience. Section 40 provides for an affirmation to be made in lieu of an oath.

A person who attends court in obedience to a *subpoena duces tecum* is not necessarily a witness and consequently need not take an oath[6] unless he is required to prove the document (that is, where he is required to go into the witness-box and identify and hand in the document).

18 2 1 Unsworn evidence exceptionally allowed Section 164 of the CPA provides that a person who, from ignorance arising from youth, defective education or other cause, does not understand the nature and import of the oath or affirmation may in criminal proceedings give evidence without taking the oath or making an affirmation. There is, however, a proviso that he should be admonished by the judge or presiding officer to speak the truth. A person who falsely and wilfully states an untruth after he has been admonished may be charged with perjury or statutory perjury. Section 41 of the CPEA has similar provisions for the reception of unsworn evidence.

18 2 2 Witness with no religious belief A witness with no religious belief shall make an affirmation at the direction of the presiding officer.[7]

18 3 EXAMINATION IN CHIEF

The purpose of examination in chief is to present evidence favourable to the version of the party calling the witness. The method most frequently adopted is the question-and-answer technique. This method is used to control the witness so that he does not speak of inadmissible or irrelevant matters. On the other hand, it is sometimes advisable to allow a witness to tell his story without interruption as, in this way, a person may tell a story more convincingly and clearly.[8] A mixture of these two approaches may be the happy medium provided the person leading the evidence has control of the witness so that he can prevent the introduction of inadmissible evidence. There is no rule as to which method should be employed; it lies within the discretion of the person leading the evidence. Strict adherence to the question-and-answer technique is normally unnecessary where the witness is experienced in court appearances (for example, a district surgeon or policeman).

18 3 1 Leading questions generally prohibited A leading question is one which either suggests the answer or assumes the existence of certain facts which might

---

[6] *Waterhouse v Shields* 1924 CPD 155.

[7] For example, see s 163(1) *(d)* of the CPA.

[8] O'Dowd *The Law of Evidence in South Africa* (1963) 154; Wigmore para 767.

be in issue.[9] The reason for the prohibition on leading questions is that the witness might be favourably disposed to the person calling him and readily adopt the suggested answer.[10] Hoffmann & Zeffertt[11] suggest that human laziness must also be considered; it is easy to say yes or no when asked something. However, not all questions which suggest a yes or no answer are leading questions. Wigmore[12] states that questions may legitimately suggest to the witness the topic of the answer required, but not the specific tenor of the answer desired. In practice this distinction will depend on the circumstances of each case.[13]

18 3 2 Situations where leading questions are permitted Leading questions are allowed with regard to introductory or uncontested matters. Most examinations commence by suggesting the witness's name ("Are you Joe Soap?"), his address ("Do you live at 14 Jan Smuts Avenue?") and his personal knowledge of a party ("Do you know the accused?"). Likewise, in a vehicle accident case the date, place and time of the accident may be led if these facts are not in dispute. It is often permissible to use leading questions with regard to such matters as identification of persons or things.[14] The general rule is that leading questions may be asked in *cross-examination*; but a question which suggests the existence of unproved facts may not be allowed in cross-examination[15] (see generally § 18 6 2 below).

18 4   IMPEACHMENT OF OWN WITNESS DURING EXAMINATION IN CHIEF

Generally speaking a person who calls a witness is considered to hold him out as a truthful person. However, it sometimes happens that the witness unexpectedly gives evidence unfavourable to the party calling him. The general rule is that a party may not discredit his own witness unless the witness has been declared by the court to be a hostile witness (see § 25 3 3 below). There is, however, nothing to prevent the party from calling other witnesses to contradict the evidence of an unfavourable witness (see § 25 3 1 below). The party may also in terms of s 190 of the CPA impeach the testimony of the witness and prove a previous inconsistent statement.[16] A similar approach is possible in civil proceedings (see § 25 3 2 below). The impeachment of the credit of a witness is dealt with in detail in chapter 25 below.

---

[9] Hoffmann & Zeffertt 444.
[10] Lansdown & Campbell 775.
[11] At 444.
[12] Paragraph 767.
[13] O'Dowd *Evidence* 154.
[14] Hoffmann & Zeffertt 445.
[15] Skeen in Du Toit et al *Commentary* 22-22.
[16] *R v Loofer* 1952 3 SA 798 (C). See further § 25 3 2 below.

18 5 EXAMINATION IN CHIEF: LIMITED USE OF WITNESS'S PREVIOUS CONSISTENT STATEMENT

A party almost invariably presents the evidence in chief of his witnesses on the basis of earlier extra-curial written statements made by the witnesses concerned. These earlier statements may generally not be proved or referred to by the party conducting examination in chief. During examination in chief (and other stages of a trial) the earlier written statement serves an extremely limited purpose: it merely assists a party to examine his witness on facts falling within the latter's knowledge. But there are some instances where a witness's previous consistent oral or written statement may — either during examination in chief or during re-examination — be put to more use on account of its relevance (see § 9 5 above). A witness's previous written statement may also be used to refresh his memory whilst he is in the witness-box, but certain strict requirements must be satisfied. These requirements are discussed in §§ 24 5–24 5 6 below.

18 6 CROSS–EXAMINATION

Cross-examination is a fundamental procedural right.[17] It is one of the essential components of the accusatorial or adversary trial and a natural and integral part of our trial system, where emphasis is placed upon orality. Cross-examination is the name given to the questioning of an opponent's witness. It succeeds examination in chief. The essence of any defence should as a rule be introduced during cross-examination.[18]

Failure to allow cross-examination constitutes a gross irregularity. The court has no right to prevent cross-examination — even if the purpose is to protect the witness.[19]

18 6 1 The purpose and general scope of cross-examination The purpose of cross-examination is to elicit facts favourable to the cross-examiner's case and to challenge the truth or accuracy of the witness's version of the disputed events.[20]

The scope of cross-examination is wider than that of examination in chief. The cross-examiner is also not restricted to matters covered by the witness in his evidence in chief.[21]

A number of methods may be used in cross-examination to test the reliability, credibility and observation of the witness. A witness may be asked the same question more than once in cross-examination in order to test the witness; but pointless repetition may be stopped by the court.[22] The court should not forbid the cross-examiner the right to ask a witness to repeat something that has already

---

[17] As far as criminal cases are concerned, see s 25(3)(d) of the interim Constitution.
[18] *S v Nkomo* 1975 3 SA 598 (N). See also § 31 4 2 below.
[19] *S v Mcolweni* 1973 3 SA 106 (E); *R v Ndawo* 1961 1 SA 16 (N).
[20] *Carroll v Carroll* 1947 4 SA 37 (N).
[21] *Distillers Korporasie (SA) Bpk v Kotze* 1956 1 SA 357 (A).
[22] *R v De Bruyn* 1957 4 SA 408 (C); *R v Amod* 1958 2 SA 658 (N).

been said in chief merely because it has already been said.[23] But the court may curtail cross-examination where the cross-examiner endeavours to wear the witness down.

18 6 2 Leading questions Leading questions may as a rule be asked in cross-examination (compare § 18 3 1 above). But there is a measure of dispute as to whether leading questions may be put to witnesses who are obviously favourably disposed to the cross-examiner.[24] A court is obviously entitled to attach less weight to answers given to leading questions put by a cross-examiner to a favourable witness.[25] A cross-examiner who wishes to put blatant leading questions to a favourable witness must therefore consider the risk.

18 6 3 Who may be cross-examined The right to cross-examine arises as soon as any witness of an opponent has been sworn or admonished or has made an affirmation. This right may be exercised even if the witness does not give evidence in chief. One accused may also be cross-examined by another accused. The cross-examination of witnesses called by the court is discussed in § 18 10 below.

A party may as a rule not cross-examine his own witness. Those exceptional cases where a party is allowed to cross-examine his own witness are discussed in detail in § 25 3 3 below.

18 6 4 The duty to cross-examine A party has a duty to cross-examine on aspects which he disputes.[26] His failure to cross-examine may in appropriate cases have serious evidential consequences in that an adverse inference may be drawn against him (see § 30 8 below). The rationale of this duty to cross-examine is that if it is intended to argue that the evidence of the witness should be rejected, he should be cross-examined so as to afford him an opportunity of answering points supposedly unfavourable to him.[27]

A failure to cross-examine does not preclude a party from disputing the truth of the evidence, but such a failure may often be decisive in deciding on the guilt of an accused. Generally the failure of the prosecutor to cross-examine an accused may be decisive.[28]

A failure to cross-examine by a simple peasant does not necessarily signify guilt.[29]

---

[23] *S v Mngogula* 1979 1 SA 525 (T).

[24] *R v Ismail* 1943 CPD 418; *Novick v Comair Holdings Ltd* 1978 3 SA 333 (W).

[25] *R v Milne and Erleigh (7)* 1951 1 SA 791 (A).

[26] *R v Malele* 1975 4 SA 128 (T); *Small v Smith* 1954 3 SA 434 (SWA).

[27] *R v M* 1946 AD 1023.

[28] *S v Gobosi* 1975 3 SA 88 (E). A failure to explain the right to cross-examine constitutes an irregularity which does not necessarily amount to a gross irregularity; *S v Wellington* 1991 1 SACR 144 (Nm); *S v Modiba* 1991 2 SA CR 286 (T); *S v Khambule* 1991 2 SACR 277 (W).

[29] *S v Mngomezulu* 1983 1 SA 1152 (N).

It is the duty of the court to tell an undefended accused to put relevant portions of his defence to a witness.[30] The court must assist illiterate persons and undefended persons.[31]

It is, for example, also an established rule that a legal representative should introduce an accused's defence during the course of cross-examination (see § 31 4 2 below).

18 6 5 The limits of cross-examination There are limits beyond which cross-examination should not go. The most important limits are discussed in §§ 18 6 5 1–18 6 5 5 below.

18 6 5 1 *Curial courtesy* Vexatious, abusive, oppressive or discourteous questions may be disallowed.[32] Much will depend, however, upon the demeanour of the witness who is being cross-examined. The court will allow a cross-examiner to cut a rude or sarcastic witness down to size, but will adopt a different approach where a witness is for no reason harassed by abusive cross-examination. The dignity of the court must, above all, be maintained. Cross-examination need not always be aggressive in order to be effective.

In *S v Omar*[33] it was held that the conduct of the prosecutor in cross-examining the accused was unseemly and unfair, being hectoring, rude and unreasonable, and that, even though the accused's counsel had not objected to such cross-examination, the presiding officer was not absolved from ensuring that he received a fair trial or from requiring those who appear before him to comport themselves properly in his court. It is the duty of the court to prevent unfair questions as often as is necessary.[34]

18 6 5 2 *Misleading statements put by cross-examiner* Misleading or vague statements should not be put to a witness. In *S v Khubeka* it was said:[35]

> "[W]hile it is perfectly permissible cross-examination to test a witness's version of events by ascertaining the details thereof and then by interrogating him about them, one ought not in cross-examination so to couch one's questions that they appear as statements of fact to which others will depose when in truth the 'facts' in question are not part of one's case and no evidence is intended to be led thereon. Questions put in this way are apt to mislead the witness."

A cross-examiner should take care before asserting that a witness has

---

[30] *S v Govazela* 1987 4 SA 297 (O).

[31] *S v Sebatana* 1983 1 SA 809 (O). See also *S v Dipholo* 1983 4 SA 757 (T). It is absurd to draw an inference against an accused for a failure to cross-examine where the defence was fully explained in the plea: *S v Kibido* 1988 1 SA 802 (C). It is also improper to tell an undefended accused that he can put his defence during cross-examination but that he is not obliged to disclose his defence to the court: *Govazela* supra; see *S v M* 1989 4 SA 421 (T).

[32] *S v Sello* 1993 1 SACR 497 (O).

[33] 1982 2 SA 357 (N). See also *S v Gidi* 1984 4 SA 537 (C).

[34] *S v Nisani* 1987 2 SA 671 (O); *S v Nkibane* 1989 2 SA 421 (NC).

[35] 1982 1 SA 534 (W) 536.

previously said something in his evidence which had in fact not been said; and the court should curb this type of questioning.[36]

18 6 5 3 *Inadmissible evidence* Inadmissible evidence may not be put to nor elicited from a witness. An accused may, for example, not be cross-examined on the basis of an inadmissible confession.[37] Cross-examination on the basis of a privileged statement is also inadmissible.[38]

In civil cases, where a person elicits inadmissible evidence which is unfavourable to him or fails to object to such type of evidence, he *may* be held to have consented to its admission.

In criminal cases, generally, where an accused elicits unfavourable evidence which is inadmissible, this evidence does not become admissible. However, there are certain qualifications.[39]

In *R v Bosch*[40] the accused elicited an inadmissible hearsay confession which presumably formed a natural part of the answer. This did not constitute an irregularity. According to Lansdown & Campbell,[41] the effect of this decision is that a statutory or common-law exclusionary rule of evidence which would prevent the state or the court from eliciting certain inadmissible evidence cannot be applied to the accused who elicits inadmissible evidence during cross-examination (provided the evidence is to the advantage of the accused and was elicited by a purposive question put by the defence). Hiemstra[42] argues that a confession elicited by an accused in cross-examination is admissible against him to prove not only state of mind but also guilt (even if such confession was made to a peace officer). It is submitted that *R v Bosch* is merely authority for the rule that if an accused elicits inadmissible evidence, he may not later on appeal or review argue that as a result of the recording of such inadmissible evidence an irregularity took place.[43] The evidence may not be used to prove the guilt of the accused.[44] The issues which arose in *R v Bosch* and the effect of s 217(3) of the CPA were discussed in greater detail in § 17 7 above. It should also be borne in mind that s 217(3) of the CPA (quoted in § 17 7 above) has to some extent modified *R v Perkins*,[45] where it was held that an accused could not by waiver or consent render admissible a statement which the legislator had expressly and unconditionally declared to be inadmissible.

18 6 5 4 *Sections 197 and 211 of the CPA* In terms of ss 197 and 211 of the CPA an accused who gives evidence may neither be asked nor be required to answer

---

[36] *S v Tswai* 1988 1 SA 851 (C).
[37] *S v Nkwanyana* 1978 3 SA 404 (N); *R v Black* 1923 AD 388.
[38] *Israelsohn v Power (1)* 1953 2 SA 499 (W).
[39] *LAWSA* para 573.
[40] 1949 1 SA 548 (A).
[41] At 790.
[42] 1981 *SACC* 22 28–9.
[43] See generally Schmidt 283–4.
[44] *R v Bosch* supra 554–5.
[45] 1920 AD 307.

any questions which tend to show that he has been convicted of or charged with any other offence apart from the one on which he is standing trial. But s 197 also makes provision for specific instances where questions of this nature are admissible. These instances were discussed in detail in §§ 6 2 3 1–6 2 3 4 above.

18 6 5 5 *Cross-examination as to credit* This aspect and the rule that answers given to questions in cross-examination relating to collateral issues are final are discussed in greater detail in chapter 25 below. A few introductory remarks are necessary at this stage.

A witness may be cross-examined as to his memory, perception and accuracy in relating his story.[46] Fairly wide bounds are permitted in cross-examination. But in *R v Sacks*[47] a cross-examiner was not allowed to ask a witness whether he had previously been in trouble for illicit diamond buying as this could not have affected his credibility. In *Gillingham v Gillingham*[48] a question as to whether a witness had committed adultery was disallowed as it had no bearing on his credibility and the answer could not in any way have assisted the court in determining the issues. In *Heystek v Alge and Paiken*[49] it was held that a witness could be asked if his testimony had been rejected in previous proceedings, but if he denies, the answer must be taken as final (see § 25 2 1 below).

An answer to a question which solely concerns the credibility of a witness must be accepted as final (see § 25 2 1 below). This is so as to prevent endless collateral issues from being investigated.[50] It is sometimes difficult to decide whether an issue is sufficiently relevant to allow contradictory evidence to be led.[51]

If an accused is charged with rape or indecent assault, the complainant may be asked about her general sexual behaviour and also about specific instances. If she denies the instances put to her, evidence may be led to show that she previously had voluntary sexual intercourse with the accused. Her denial of intercourse with other men must be accepted as final and rebutting evidence cannot be led as it involves collateral issues.[52] The procedural rules determined by s 227 of the CPA and discussed in § 6 2 6 1 above come into play.

There are, however, two situations where cross-examination as to credit may be followed up with contradicting evidence. These situations are dealt with in detail in §§ 25 2 2 and 25 2 3 below.

---

[46] Hoffmann & Zeffertt 459.

[47] 1931 TPD 188.

[48] 1904 TS 126.

[49] 1925 TPD 1. See also *S v Damalis* 1984 2 SA 105 (T). However, in *Maxwell v White* 1936 SR 59 it was decided that English law, which disallows such conduct, should be followed. See Skeen 1984 *SALJ* 431, where *S v Damalis* is criticized as not reflecting the English law as it stood on 30 May 1961. However, in *S v Zwane* 1993 1 SACR 748 (W), 1993 3 SA 393 (W) the advantages in allowing such questioning are stated. See also 1993 *ASSAL* 732.

[50] *Wood v Van Rensburg* 1921 CPD 36; *S v ffrench-beytagh (3)* 1971 4 SA 571 (T).

[51] Hoffmann & Zeffertt 459. See also § 25 2 1 below.

[52] *R v Samuels* 1930 CPD 67; *R v Riley* 1887 18 QB 481; *R v Hendricks* 1957 1 SA 138 (C); *S v Sinkankanka* 1963 2 SA 531 (A).

18 7   PROCEDURAL MATTERS PERTAINING TO CROSS–EXAMINATION

Cross-examination usually takes place immediately after examination in chief. Cross-examination may be reserved, but it is solely within the discretion of the court whether to allow this to happen.[53] In criminal cases it is customary to allow the accused to cross-examine in the order that they are listed in the charge sheet.[54] Parties in civil cases will usually cross-examine in the order that their names appear on the record.[55] Defence witnesses called by one accused may be cross-examined by a co-accused before the prosecutor cross-examines.[56]

The cross-examiner is not obliged to state in advance the relevance of questions he may wish to ask. But he should as a matter of principle avoid setting out on a "fishing expedition". There ought to be some latent relevance.[57]

It is perfectly proper for the court to draw a cross-examiner's attention to matters on which cross-examination is, in its view, desirable.[58] Such an approach is desirable where counsel is inexperienced or where the accused is undefended.

The court should explain to undefended parties — especially an accused — that they have a right to cross-examine.

18 8   RE–EXAMINATION

Re-examination follows cross-examination and is conducted by the party who initially called the witness. A party has a right to re-examine.

The purpose of re-examination is to clear up any point or misunderstanding which might have occurred during cross-examination; to correct wrong impressions or false perceptions which might have been created in the course of cross-examination; to give the witness a fair opportunity to explain answers given by him under cross-examination which, if unexplained, may create a wrong impression or be used to arrive at false deductions; to put before the court the full picture and context of facts elicited during cross-examination; or to correct patent mistakes made under cross-examination. Re-examination can be, and frequently is, a very important mechanism of presenting a full picture and thus of arriving at the truth. The *right* to re-examine is not restricted to matters raised for the first time during cross-examination.[59] But new matters may only be canvassed with leave of the court, which should then allow further cross-examination on the new evidence. Re-examination is conducted in accordance with the rules which cover examination in chief; consequently leading questions

---

[53] *Gumede and Daines v Attorney-General* 1952 2 SA 315 (T).

[54] The court may not interfere if the accused persons decide on a different order: *S v Mpetha (1)* 1983 1 SA 492 (C). However, in *S v Ngobeni* 1981 1 SA 506 (B) it was held that a departure from the numerical order should be allowed only if the court so permits and if the court is of the opinion that it is in the interests of justice. See further § 23 3 2 below.

[55] O'Dowd *The Law of Evidence in South Africa* (1963) 156.

[56] *R v Herholdt (4)* 1956 3 SA 313 (W).

[57] See generally Lansdown & Campbell 790.

[58] Lansdown & Campbell 788; *S v Solomons* 1959 2 SA 352 (A).

[59] *S v Ramalope* 1995 1 SACR 616 (A).

will not be permitted. If part of a document has been referred to in cross-examination, the whole document may be referred to in re-examination.[60]

18 9 EXAMINATION BY THE COURT

The court has the right to question a witness at any stage of the proceedings and the rule against leading questions does not apply. But it is desirable that leading questions should be avoided. Very often questioning by the court takes place after re-examination. The main purpose of such questioning should be to clear up any points which are still obscure. The court should play a limited role. In *Yuill v Yuill* Lord Greene expressed the following sentiments on the subject:[61] "The judge who himself conducts the examination . . . descends into the arena and is liable to have his vision clouded by the dust of conflict. Unconsciously he deprives himself of the advantage of calm and dispassionate observation." Similiar observations were made in *Hamman v Moolman*.[62] In *S v Rall*[63] it was said that it is difficult and undesirable to define precisely the limits within which judicial questioning should be confined. Certain broad limitations were mentioned: *(a)* the judge must conduct the trial so that his impartiality and fairness are manifest to all concerned; *(b)* a judge should refrain from questioning in such a way or to such an extent as to lose judicial impartiality and objectivity; and *(c)* a judge should desist from questioning in a way which may intimidate or disconcert a witness so as to affect his demeanour or impair his credibility.

In criminal cases a judge has more latitude, subject to the rules mentioned above, to intervene to see that justice is done and the truth ascertained. In civil proceedings his intervention should be less frequent.[64]

Section 115 of the CPA does not entitle a court to cross-examine an accused during the so-called explanation of plea procedure.[65] A similar approach applies with regard to s 112(1)*(b)* of the CPA.[66]

18 10 EXAMINATION OF WITNESSES CALLED BY THE COURT

In chapter 23 below it will be pointed out that the court may in certain circumstances also call a witness. The court should in a fair and impartial manner lead the evidence of any witness it may call. The court will usually allow cross-examination of a witness called by it, but has a right to control such

---

[60] O'Dowd *The Law of Evidence in South Africa* (1963) 158.
[61] 1945 1 All ER 183 189.
[62] 1968 4 SA 340 (A).
[63] 1982 1 SA 828 (A); Skeen 1982 *SACC* 180–2.
[64] *S v Baartman* 1960 3 SA 535 (A); *S v Roopsing* 1956 4 SA 509 (A); *Jones v National Coal Board* 1957 2 All ER 155.
[65] *S v Seleke* 1980 3 SA 745 (A); Van der Merwe, Barton & Kemp *Plea Procedures in Summary Criminal Trials* (1983) para 6 6 3.
[66] *S v Jacobs* 1978 1 SA 1176 (C) 1177; *S v Gumede* 1978 1 PH H81 (N).

cross-examination as may take place.[67] A witness who has been recalled by the court may also only be cross-examined with leave of the court.[68]

18 11 EVIDENCE ON COMMISSION IN CRIMINAL CASES

A commission involves the evidence of witnesses being taken by a commissioner appointed by the court to hear evidence. The evidence will be recorded and sent back to the court which issued the commission and it will become part of the evidential material. Section 171 of the CPA allows for the issue of a commission in criminal cases if the evidence of any witness is necessary in the interests of justice and if the evidence of the witness cannot be obtained without undue delay, expense or inconvenience. If the witness is resident in the Republic, the commissioner will be a magistrate and if the witness is resident outside the country, any competent person may be appointed.

The commissioner will record the evidence on oath and the evidence will be read back to the witness, who, if he adheres to it, will sign it. Legal representation and cross-examination are permitted. In most cases (but by no means all) the evidence taken on commission is of a formal nature. *S v Hoare* [69] sets out the circumstances in which a commission will be granted. In this case a commission was granted to hear the evidence of the crew of the aircraft and the director of aviation in the Seychelles. James AJP quoted with approval the case of *S v ffrench-Beytagh (2)*,[70] where it was said that the decision whether to issue a commission must depend on the facts of each case. It is accepted that a person who asks for a commission is at a disadvantage: less weight may be attached to such evidence as the court does not have the opportunity to observe the demeanour of the witness. However, it is also accepted that if such a person is refused a commission, his disadvantage will be even greater because the evidence cannot be put before the court at all.

In *R v Levy*[71] and *S v Hassim*[72] it was held that a wide discretion is conferred on the judge in deciding whether or not to grant a commission and that a court should only grant such applications sparingly and in unusual circumstances. There is no justification for limiting the provisions of the section only to formalistic evidence.[73]

18 12 EVIDENCE ON COMMISSION IN CIVIL CASES

Supreme Court rule 38(3) provides that a court may, where it appears convenient or necessary for the purposes of justice, make an order for the taking of evidence

---

[67] *R v Masofi* 1956 1 SA 167 (N); *R v Kumalo* 1952 3 SA 223 (T).
[68] Hoffmann & Zeffertt 474.
[69] 1982 3 SA 306 (N).
[70] 1971 4 SA 426 (T).
[71] 1929 AD 312 332.
[72] 1973 3 SA 433 (A).
[73] *S v Hoare* 1982 3 SA 306 (N); *S v Mzinyathi* 1982 4 SA 118 (T). A useful summary fo the cases and principles relating to the grant or refusal of a commission is to be found in *S v Banda* 1990 2 SACR 44 (B).

before a commissioner. Magistrates' courts may issue commissions in terms of s 53 of the Magistrates' Courts Act 32 of 1944. A review of the authorities and principles concerning the issue of commissions is to be found in the case of *Federal Insurance Co Ltd v Britz*.[74] The courts have consistently followed the sentiments expressed in *Robinson v Randfontein Estates Gold Mining Co Ltd*[75] to the effect that the court will normally grant a commission rather than lose the evidence.

It has been held that a commission may be issued in respect of both formal as well as contentious factual issues.[76] As a rule evidence taken on commission will carry less weight than evidence given before the court because the court did not have the opportunity of observing the demeanour of the witnesses (see generally § 30 4 below). Right of representation and cross-examination will be afforded at the hearing of the commission.

18 13 INTERROGATORIES

In civil cases interrogatories may be granted in terms of Supreme Court rule 38(5) and s 32 of the Supreme Court Act 59 of 1959. In magistrates' courts the appropriate section is s 52 of the Magistrates' Courts Act 32 of 1944.

The principles governing the issues of interrogatories are similar to those for the issue of commissions (see § 18 12 above). A list of proposed questions is drawn up by the parties. The court may also add questions of its own. The interrogatories are then sent to the court having jurisdiction where the witness is present. This court then summons the witness, puts the questions to him, records the answers, and returns the record to the original court. The interrogatories will be read as evidence at the trial and form part of the evidential material.

18 14 EVIDENCE BY WAY OF AFFIDAVIT

Evidence received by way of affidavit in terms of s 212 of the CPA and s 22 of the CPEA was discussed in §§ 15 2 1 and 15 2 2 above.

18 15 EVIDENCE IN FORMER PROCEEDINGS

Section 214 of the CPA allows for the reading of a witness's evidence at a preparatory examination at a subsequent trial if it is proved to the satisfaction of the court that the witness is dead or incapable of giving evidence or too ill to attend the trial or is being kept away from the trial by the means and connivance of the accused and if the evidence was recorded by a magistrate or regional court

---

[74] 1981 4 SA 74 (T); Skeen 1982 *SALJ* 338.

[75] 1918 TPD 420.

[76] *Smitham v De Luca* 1977 2 SA 582 (W). The strength or weakness of a party's case is quite irrelevant to whether a commission should be granted. What is important is the relevance of the evidence and whether the taking of the evidence is convenient or necessary for the interests of justice. *Myerson v Health Beverages (Pty) Ltd* 1989 4 SA 667 (C).

magistrate. It must also be shown that the accused (or state as the case may be) had had an opportunity to cross-examine the absent witness.[77] It is provided that if a witness, after having given evidence at a preparatory examination, cannot be found after a diligent search or cannot be compelled to attend the trial, his evidence may be read if it is apparent from the record that the opposing party had had the opportunity to cross-examine the witness. The court is given a discretion whether to allow the production of the evidence of a witness who cannot be found. In *R v Stolz*[78] it was held that the discretion should be exercised sparingly and, where the nature of the evidence would depend on the credibility of the witness, the court should be very slow to admit the evidence.[79]

18 16 PRESERVED EVIDENCE

In terms of s 23(1) of the CPEA and s 19(1)*(c)* of the Supreme Court Act 59 of 1959 a Supreme Court has the power to order evidence to be taken on commission on the application of a person who alleges that he will become entitled to an interest in some asset upon the happening of a future event, but who cannot bring an action before the event occurs.[80]

18 17 THE INTERMEDIARY[81] AND RELATED PROCEDURES[82]

In April 1989 (exactly five years prior to constitutionalization[83]) the South African Law Commission concluded[84] that the ordinary adversarial trial procedure with its strong emphasis on cross-examination was insensitive and unfair to the child witness — especially the alleged sexually abused child witness, who had to go through the traumatic experience of facing the accused in court and who had to be subjected to cross-examination which could be intimidating, aggressive, tormenting and humiliating.

In its final report on the matter in 1991 the Commission recommended[85] that *in certain circumstances* a so-called "intermediary" could be appointed. It also recommended that, in the event of such an appointment, face-to-face confrontation should be eliminated by using electronic or other devices.

Section 170A was inserted[86] into the Criminal Procedure Act 51 of 1977 on

---

[77] *R v McDonald* 1927 AD 11; *R v Matyeni* 1958 2 SA 573 (E); *R v Goliath* 1946 EDL 310; *R v Mkwanazi* 1935 TPD 129.

[78] 1925 WLD 38.

[79] *R v Andrews* 1920 AD 290.

[80] See generally Hoffmann & Zeffertt 440; *Ross v Silbermann* 1963 2 SA 296 (W).

[81] The rest of this chapter was written by S E van der Merwe and consists of extracts of an article previously published in 1995 *Obiter* 194. The intermediary is known as "tussenganger" in Afrikaans.

[82] See also Skeen in Du Toit et al *Commentary* 22-31.

[83] The interim Constitution came into operation in April 1994.

[84] See *Working Paper 28 of the SA Law Commission: The Protection of the Child Witness: Project 71* (April 1989).

[85] See *Report of the SA Law Commission on the Protection of Child Witnesses: Project 71* (February 1991), especially paras 5 48 and 5 49.

[86] See s 3 of the Criminal Law Amendment Act 135 of 1991. However, s 170A only came into operation on 30 July 1993 (Proc R64 *Government Gazette* 15025 dated 30 July 1993).

the basis of the Commission's recommendations. Section 170A(1) provides that whenever criminal proceedings are pending before any court and it appears to such court that the proceedings would expose any witness under the age of 18 years to undue mental stress of suffering if he or she testifies, the court may appoint an intermediary in order to enable such witness to give his or her evidence through that intermediary.

In terms of s 170A(2) *(a)* of the CPA no examination in chief, cross-examination or re-examination of any witness in respect of whom a court has appointed an intermediary shall take place in any manner other than through that intermediary. This means that the parties may at no stage question the witness directly. It is only the court that may question the witness without intervention by the intermediary.

A crucial provision is contained in s 170A(2) *(b)* of the CPA: "The . . . intermediary may, unless the court directs otherwise, convey the general purport of any question to the relevant witness." This means that — subject to the court's final control — any question put by the prosecutor and the defence may be "blocked" by the intermediary in the sense that the intermediary may "relay" the question to the witness in a different form. The "general purport" of the question is conveyed and the *ipsissima verba* of the original question may be ignored. The court may *mero motu* or in response to objections raised by one or more of the parties direct the intermediary to put the original question or, if necessary, to make another attempt at conveying the general purport of the original question. Or the court may take a shortcut and put the original question in the form that it thinks fit. But the nature of the court's question must be such that the court does not descend — or is not perceived to be descending — into the arena. The court may not cross-examine.

Whenever an intermediary has been appointed the witness concerned is in another room and does not hear the original questions as put by the prosecutor or defence counsel. The witness only hears — and therefore merely responds to — the prosecutor's or defence counsel's question as relayed by the intermediary to the witness, either in its original or amended form.

The intermediary is not a lawyer. In terms of s 170A(4) *(a)* the Minister of Justice may by notice in the *Gazette* determine the persons or the category or class of persons who are competent to be appointed by the court as intermediaries. At least seven categories of persons have been determined in this manner.[87] In practice, however, intermediaries are largely appointed from only two of these categories: social workers and psychologists. The intermediary is indeed a court official, and must display the necessary impartiality despite his or her close contact with the child witness and the inevitable rendering of some "emotional support" to the child during the latter's testimony.

Section 170A(3) of the CPA provides that *if a court appoints an intermediary* in terms of s 170A(1), the court may direct that the witness concerned shall give his evidence at any place

---

[87] The Minister of Justice has in GN R1374 *Government Gazette* 15024 of 30 July 1993 determined that certain categories or classes of persons are competent to be appointed as intermediaries.

"*(a)*   which is informally arranged to set that witness at ease;

(b)   which is so situated that any person whose presence may upset that witness, is outside the sight and hearing of that witness; and

(c)   which enables the court and any person whose presence is necessary at the relevant proceedings to see and hear, either directly or through the medium of any electronic or other devices, that intermediary as well as that witness during his testimony."

One obvious purpose of these provisions — which can be invoked only if an intermediary is appointed — is to ensure that during the course of the witness' testimony a full and proper opportunity is given to the prosecutor, the accused, defence counsel and the court (including assessors) of observing the demeanour of the child witness and the behaviour of the intermediary. Closed-circuit television or one-way mirrors can be employed.

18 17 1   A general assessment of the use of an intermediary in the context of an adversarial trial[88]   It must be stressed that an intermediary cannot conduct his or her own independent questioning of the witness. The intermediary's power to interfere can only be exercised in response to a question put by one of the parties. This is an important check or restriction on the functions of the intermediary. The parties are, broadly speaking, still in control of the witness. They can — through their questions — confine the witness *and* the intermediary to those aspects of the case which they wish to probe. And in this respect there has been no real deviation from the adversarial model.

The appointment of an intermediary and the use of related procedures are *not* confined to the situation where the child witness happens to be the victim of a sexual offence. Section 170A can be invoked in all criminal proceedings. The only criterion for appointing an intermediary is whether it appears to the court that a witness under the age of 18 will suffer "undue mental stress or suffering" if he or she testifies. In practice, however, s 170A has been invoked only in sexual abuse cases and then only in those cases where the child witness happened to be a witness for the prosecution.

Seen from a practical point of view, s 170A of the CPA impacts largely on the case for the defence. It may affect cross-examination by the defence of a child witness testifying on behalf of the prosecution. Admittedly, all questioning by the prosecutor must also be conducted through the intermediary. It may therefore be argued that both parties — the prosecutor as well as the defence — have similar difficulties whenever an intermediary participates in the proceedings. But this is not a valid argument. In South Africa — as in most other countries where criminal trial procedure is adversarial in nature — the examination of one's own witness is "witness friendly".

The following valid questions arise: What is the purpose of an intermediary if the court does in fact have the power ultimately to control and determine the question? Why was the court not given the power to interfere more actively and

---

[88] See § 1 5 2 above for a brief discussion of the principles of the adversarial trial.

to fulfil some inquisitorial role? These questions must be considered in the light of the following remarks made by the South African Law Commission.[89]

It was felt that the presiding officer should in principle retain the role of arbitrator or passive umpire and that the appointment of an intermediary who is controlled by the presiding judicial officer would most closely resemble or retain the theoretical structure of the adversarial trial. The court does in principle remain aloof from the proceedings and is there to ensure that the rules of procedure and evidence are observed by the prosecution and the defence. What is new, however, is that the intermediary — whilst certainly neither a witness in nor a party to the proceedings — becomes a further participant in the adversarial trial (or game, as some would have it). The intermediary participates quite independently from the prosecution and defence.

It is submitted that participation by intermediaries in the administration of the criminal justice system is in accordance with democratic theory. Their participation rests upon the same philosophical or ideological basis upon which other non-lawyers — such as lay assessors in South Africa[90] and jurors in other countries — are called upon and permitted to participate: enhancement not only of the general legitimacy of the system but also the fact-finding process. The fact that intermediaries are not adjudicators and are not really lay persons does not destabilize or destroy the essence of this argument. The use of intermediaries adds a new dimension to the ways in which the legitimacy of the system and the search for the truth can possibly be promoted or reinforced.

18 17 2 The essential content of the right to confront It has been claimed that the right to confront can be traced to the primitive ordeal of "trial by battle",[91] and that the notion that demeanour must be observed finds its early roots in the *corsnaed* or so-called "ordeal of the accursed morsel".[92] But whatever the historical origins of "confrontation" may be,[93] the fact of the matter is that the right to confront is presently a procedural right generally deemed essential for a fair trial.

More than two centuries ago the Sixth Amendment to the Constitution of the USA granted an accused the right "to be confronted with the witnesses against him". One of the original purposes of this guarantee was to prevent the improper introduction of hearsay evidence and to restrict the use of *ex parte* affidavits in criminal trials. The Supreme Court of the USA has also said that the Sixth Amendment right to confront " . . . (1) insures that the witness will give evidence under oath — thus impressing him with the seriousness of the matter and guarding against the lie by the possibility of a penalty for perjury; (2) forces the

---

[89] Paragraphs 2 8–2 11 of the *Report of the SA Law Commission on the Protection of Child Witnesses: Project 71* (February 1991).

[90] See generally s 93*ter* of the Magistrates' Courts Act 32 of 1944. See generally § 1 6 above.

[91] Re "Oral v Written Evidence: The Myth of the Impressive Witness" 1983 57 *Australian LJ* 679. See also § 1 3 1 above.

[92] Paton & Derham (eds) *A Textbook of Jurisprudence* 4 ed (1972) 597. See also § 1 3 1 above.

[93] See generally Pollitt "The Right of Confrontation: Its History and Modern Dress" 1959 8 *Journal of Public Law* 381.

witness to submit to cross-examination . . . [and] (3) permits the [court] to observe the demeanor of the witness".[94]

The decision in *Coy v Iowa*[95] in 1988 provides a good example of the extent to which the majority of the US Supreme Court will go in upholding the right of an accused to be confronted with the witnesses against him. In this case the accused was charged with the sexual assault of two 13-year-old girls. In accordance with an Iowa statute the trial court had permitted the placing of a large screen between the accused and the two complainants. The screen was used only during the testimony of the witnesses. With certain lighting adjustments the screen enabled the accused "dimly to perceive" the two complainants. But these two witnesses could not see the accused at all. The accused was convicted despite his claim that use of the screen had violated his Sixth Amendment right to confront the two witnesses.

An appeal was lodged to the Supreme Court of Iowa. This court, however, confirmed the conviction and expressed the view that there had been no violation of the constitutional right to confront. The Iowa Supreme Court pointed out, first, that direct examination and cross-examination of the two witnesses had occurred in full view of the judge and jury and, secondly, that counsel for the defence had cross-examined both witnesses fully and without limitation while they were under oath.

But a further appeal to the US Supreme Court was successful. A majority reversed the judgment of the Supreme Court of Iowa on the basis that[96]

"(1) the confrontation clause of the Sixth Amendment guarantees a criminal defendant a face-to-face meeting with witnesses appearing before the trier of fact; (2) in the case at hand, the defendant's right to such a meeting with the two child witnesses was violated, where *(a)* the screen was specifically designed to enable the witnesses to avoid viewing the defendant as they gave their testimony, *(b)* the screen was successful in its objective, and *(c)* despite the state's claim that such a procedure was necessary to protect victims of sexual abuse, the conviction could not be sustained by any conceivable exception to the right to face-to-face confrontation, for the recently passed statute, which created a generalized, legislatively imposed presumption of trauma, was not firmly rooted in the nation's jurisprudence, and there had been no individualized findings that the particular witnesses needed special protection . . .".

O'Connor J — who had agreed with the majority — also wrote a separate judgment in which she was at pains to point out that an accused's rights under the confrontation clause are not absolute. According to her, these rights may in suitable cases "give away . . . to other competing interests so as to permit the use of certain procedural devices designed to shield a child witness from the trauma of courtroom testimony".[97] O'Connor J noted that she would allow use of a particular trial procedure which entailed something other than face-to-face confrontation if such a procedure was essential to promote an important public policy. And the protection of child witnesses, said O'Connor J, " . . . is . . . just such

---

[94] *California v Green* 399 US 149 158 (1970).
[95] 487 US 1012, 101 LEd 2d 857 (1988).
[96] Quotation taken from the headnote of the case as reported in 101 LEd 2d 857–8 (1988).
[97] *Coy v Iowa* supra 868.

a policy"[98]. White J concurred in this separate judgment even though he, like O'Connor J, also agreed with the majority that *in the case at hand* Coy's constitutional rights under the confrontation clause in the Sixth Amendment had been violated by the implementation of the Iowa legislation under discussion.

Blackmun J wrote a dissenting judgment, in which he was joined by Rehnquist CJ. They concluded that the screening procedures permitted by the Iowa legislation and employed by the trial court had not violated[99]

"(1) the confrontation clause, because *(a)* the important public policy in protecting child witnesses from the fear and trauma associated with such children's testimony in front of a defendant outweighed the confrontation clause's 'preference' for face-to-face confrontation, and *(b)* the child witnesses had testified under oath and in full view of the jury, and had been subjected to unrestricted cross-examination; or (2) due process, because the procedure was not inherently prejudicial".

There are, of course, significant differences[100] between the procedure provided for in s 170A of the CPA and that provided for by the Iowa legislation which was the subject of dispute in *Coy v Iowa* supra. But the point remains that this case illustrates the impact of the constitutional right to confront on legislative measures which seek to assist child witnesses.

Hard on the heels of *Coy v Iowa* came the decision in *Maryland v Craig*.[101] The latter concerned a Maryland statute which had permitted the use of one-way closed circuit television if the judge came to the conclusion that testimony by the child in the courtroom would have resulted in "serious emotional distress such that the child cannot reasonably communicate".[102] A minority (four judges) of the US Supreme Court expressed the view that the Maryland procedure conflicted with the accused's constitutional right to a face-to-face confrontation. But a majority (five judges) held that a face-to-face confrontation was not an indispensable element of the Sixth Amendment's confrontation guarantee. Writing for the majority, O'Connor J said:[103]

"Maryland's statutory procedure, when invoked, prevents a child witness from seeing the defendant as he or she testifies against the defendant at trial. We find it significant, however, that Maryland's procedure preserves all of the other elements of the confrontation right: the child witness must be competent to testify and must testify under oath; the defendant

---

[98] *Coy v Iowa* supra 869.

[99] Quotation taken from the headnote of the case as reported in 101 LEd 2d 857 (1988).

[100] The two important differences are as follows: *(a)* Section 170A requires the court to make a case-specific finding as regards the child before the measures contained in this section can be invoked. The Iowa legislation amounted to a "legislatively imposed presumption of trauma", and did not call for an individualized finding. *(b)* In terms of s 170A the defence must at all relevant times be able to observe the child witness. Use of the screen as permitted by the Iowa legislation confined the defence to observing a mere silhouette.

[101] 497 US 836 (1990).

[102] The full text of the Maryland statute is cited in 111 LEd 2d 666 675 (1990). In the event of the court concluding that the child would suffer serious emotional distress to the extent that the child's ability to communicate reasonably is affected, the court should — apart from directing the use of closed-circuit television — also adopt the following procedure: the judge, jury and accused remain in the courtroom, whereas the child witness, the prosecutor and defence counsel should withdraw to a separate room, where the witness may then be examined and cross-examined whilst being observed by the judge, jury and accused. The witness cannot see the accused. The latter is at all times in electronic communication with his or her counsel. Objections can be made as if the child witness is in the courtroom.

[103] 111 LEd 2d 666 682 (1990).

retains full opportunity for contemporaneous cross-examination; and the judge, jury, and defendant are able to view (albeit by video monitor) the demeanor (and body) of the witness as he or she testifies. Although we are mindful of the many subtle effects face-to-face confrontation may have on an adversary criminal proceeding, the presence of these other elements of confrontation — oath, cross-examination, and observation of the witness; demeanor — adequately ensures that the testimony is both reliable and subject to rigorous adversarial testing in a manner functionally equivalent to that accorded live, in-person testimony. These safeguards of reliability and adversariness render the use of such a procedure a far cry from the undisputed prohibition of the Confrontation Clause: trial by *ex parte* affidavit or inquisition . . ..''

It is distinctly possible that Anglo-American systems over-estimate the value of oath-taking in open court. The usefulness of providing the finder(s) of fact with an opportunity to observe the demeanour of a witness who is taken through examination in chief, cross-examination and re-examination might also be overrated. Demeanour, according to the South African Appellate Division, is a ''tricky horse to ride''.[104] It is, furthermore, quite possible that cross-examination is not — as Wigmore so smugly but in obvious hyperbolical terms had claimed — '' . . . the greatest legal engine ever invented for the discovery of the truth''.[105]

18 17 3 The constitutionality of s 170A of the CPA In *K v The Regional Court Magistrate NO & others*[106] a Full Bench of the Eastern Cape Division of the Supreme Court held that the physical separation of the complainant from the courtroom did not violate the right to a public trial. According to the court, the right to a public trial is not violated merely because the complainant gives evidence in a separate room. This conclusion is supported. However, the court also concluded that, even giving a broad and liberal interpretation to the fundamental rights of the accused, the right to cross-examine has not been violated by the provisions of s 170A. Having come to this conclusion, it was not necessary for the court to have considered the second stage of the constitutional inquiry, namely, whether the infringement or denial was a constitutionally permissible limitation in terms of s 33(1) of the interim Constitution.

It is distinctly possible that other courts may conclude that s 170A does infringe the right to cross-examine. In this event the second stage will be entered: can the ''offending legislation'' — that is, s 170A of the CPA — be saved in terms of the limitation clause?

The threshold test is whether s 170A is indeed a ''law of general application''. This test seeks to ensure that there is equality before the law and equal protection of the law. Section 170A passes this threshold test. It is a law which applies to all those cases where it appears to the court that a witness under the age of 18 years might be subjected to undue mental stress or suffering. The intermediary is appointed for purposes of a certain category of cases and not for purposes of a certain type of individual who stands accused of crime. There is no unequal treatment of accused persons similarly situated. For the same reasons it can be

---

[104] *S v Kelly* 1980 3 SA 301 (A) 308B. See § 30 4 below.
[105] Wigmore para 1367.
[106] 1996 1 SACR 434 (E).

said that s 170A(3) *(b)* also passes the "threshold test". This section determines that if an intermediary is appointed, the court may direct that the witness shall give his evidence at any place which is so situated that any person whose presence might upset the witness is outside the sight and hearing of that witness.

In addition to the threshold test, the limitation shall also be permissible only to the extent that it is reasonable and, furthermore, justifiable in an open and democratic society based on freedom and equality. Section 170A seeks to protect the child witness from the trauma of courtroom testimony in the adversarial trial. It is neither capricious nor arbitrary. It is not aimed at hampering the defence or impeding the fact-finding process. In fact, s 170A might even enhance the fact-finding process.

The impact of s 170A on the right to challenge evidence is reasonable because the measures contained in s 170A not only stem from considerations which are of sufficient importance to interfere with the right to challenge evidence but are also proportional to the objective sought to be achieved. Whilst it is certainly true that s 170A does impair the right to challenge evidence, it does so only to the extent that it is necessary to protect the child. The right to challenge evidence is infringed as little as possible. Consider the following: *(a)* Face-to-face confrontation is eliminated, *but the defence can at all times observe the witness.* The opportunity to observe the demeanour of the witness remains intact. *(b)* The intermediary may convey the general purport of any question, *but the court may in its discretion (and either* mero motu *or in response to an objection raised by defence counsel or the prosecutor) direct that the original question be put.* The final decision rests with the court — and this is the kind of control that the court should or could, even in the absence of an appointed intermediary, have exercised if defence counsel's questions were unfair, confusing, insensitive or otherwise improper.

It also follows from *(a)* and *(b)* above that the essential content of the right to challenge evidence is not negated by s 170A of the CPA. Section 170A therefore complies with the provisions of s 33(1) *(b)* of the Constitution.

Are the provisions of s 170A of the CPA "justifiable in an open and democratic society based on freedom and equality", as required by s 33(1) *(a)*(ii) of the Constitution? This is a nebulous — if not murky — provision which can at best be described as an open-ended value statement. It is to a large extent based upon s 1 of the Canadian Charter of Rights and Freedoms, which provides that the Charter "guarantees the rights and freedoms set out in it subject only to such reasonable limits prescribed by law as can be demonstrably justified in a free and democratic society". According to the Canadian Supreme Court's decision in *R v Oakes*,[107] a court should, in its consideration of what is justifiable in a free and democratic society, also turn to other provisions contained in the Charter. South African courts ought to follow this decision, especially since s 35(1) of the South African Bill of Rights states that in interpreting the Bill of Rights "a court of law . . . may have regard to comparable foreign case law". *R v Oakes* supra is such a comparable foreign decision because of the similarities which exist between

---

[107] 1986 19 CRR 308.

s 1 of the Canadian Charter and s 33(1)(*a*)(ii) of the South African Bill of Rights.

Now, upon turning to other relevant provisions in the South African Bill of Rights, one finds that there is a separate section which deals specially with the rights of children. In terms of s 30(1)(*c*) "[e]very child shall have the right . . . to security . . . and social services". And in terms of s 30(1)(*d*) "[e]very child shall have the right . . . not to be subject to neglect or abuse". Section 30(3) states that for the purposes of s 30 a "child" is someone under the age of 18 years. The following important provision is also found in s 30(3): "[I]n all matters concerning such child his or her best interest shall be paramount."

It is submitted that these s 30 provisions must be given more than considerable weight in deciding whether the limited adverse impact of s 170A of the CPA on the constitutional right to challenge evidence is in terms of s 33(1)(*a*)(ii) justifiable in an open and democratic society based on freedom and equality. A democratic South Africa has decided that the basic legitimate needs of children should be elevated to rights which form part and parcel of the Bill of Rights. A democratic South Africa has decided that there must be a constitutional provision that in all matters concerning children their best interests shall be paramount. A democratic South Africa values the well-being of the child to such an extent that the very limited restrictions which s 170A of the CPA might place on the constitutional guarantee to challenge evidence should be accepted as a constitutionally permissible limitation. The measures contained in s 170A are justifiable because they stem from, and represent, precisely those values which a democratic South Africa has secured in its Bill of Rights.

Are the measures contained in s 170A necessary? The right to challenge evidence is a procedural right contained in s 25(3)(*d*) of the interim Constitution. In terms of the limitation clause contained in s 33(1)(*aa*) of the interim Constitution any limitation of a s 25 right must, in addition to being reasonable as required in terms of s 33(1)(*a*)(i), also be necessary. "Necessary" does not mean "necessary in absolute terms". And yet it must mean something more than "reasonable". It has been suggested that a South African court which considers the necessity of a limitation should invoke "a standard stricter than *sufficient* importance, for instance *absolute* or *compelling* or *overriding* importance . . . to adjudicate the limitation of the right in question".[108] It is submitted that protection of the child witness in the adversarial trial is of compelling importance for the reasons advanced not only in our local official reports,[109] literature[110] and case law[111] but also in the official reports[112] and literature[113] of foreign countries.

---

[108] Du Plessis & Corder *Understanding South Africa's Transitional Bill of Rights* (1994) 128.

[109] See nn 84 and 85 above.

[110] See, e g, Schwikkard 1991 *SACJ* 44; Sieff 1991 *SACJ* 21; Hammond & Hammond 1987 *SACC* 3; Key 1988 *De Rebus* 54.

[111] See, e g, *S v Basil Simons* (unreported, DCLD 84/88, but referred to by Zieff 1991 *SACJ* 21 35).

[112] See, e g, *Report on the Evidence of Children and Other Potentially Vulnerable Witnesses* Scottish Law Commission, Study no 125, Edinburgh (1990).

[113] See, e g, Morgan & Plotnikoff "Children as Victims of Crime: Procedure at Court" in Spencer, Nicholson, Flin & Ball (eds) *Children's Evidence in Legal Proceedings: An International Perspective* (1990) 189–92;

One is driven to agree with the following words of Blackmun J in his dissenting judgment in *Coy v Iowa*: "[A] State properly may consider the protection of child witnesses . . . an important public policy."[114] And the fact that other countries have taken legislative steps to protect the child witness[115] provides further ground for concluding that there is a compelling importance which justifies legislative measures which conflict with the right of the accused directly to challenge the evidence of a child witness by way of cross-examination in a face-to-face confrontation.

McEwan "Child Evidence: More Proposals for Reform" 1988 *Crim LR* 813; Adler "Prosecuting Child Sexual Abuse: A Challenge to the Status Quo" in Maquire & Pointing (eds) *Victims of Crime: A New Deal?* (1988) 138–46; Hardin "Guardians *ad litem* for Child Victims in Criminal Proceedings" 1986–1987 25 *Journal of Family Law* 687; Pynoos & Eth "The Child Witness to Homicide" 1984 40 *Journal of Social Issues* 87; Pynoos & Eth "Witnessing Violence: Special Intervention Programs for Child Witnesses to Violence" in Lystadt (ed) *Violence in the Home* (1986) 193–216; Spencer "Children's Evidence: How Not to Reform the Law" 1988 137 *New Law Journal* 497; Goodman "The Child Witness: Conclusions and Future Directions for Research and Legal Practice" 1984 40 *Journal of Social Issues* 157; Black & Kaplan "Father Kills Mother: Issues and Problems Encountered by a Child Psychiatric Team" 1988 153 *British Journal of Psychiatry* 624; Harmon "Examination of Children in Sexual Offences: The Israeli Law and Practice" 1988 *Crim LR* 263; Aman & Hirschman "Child Sexual and Physical Abuse: Children's Testimony" in Ceci, Ross & Toglia (eds) *Children's Eye-witness Memory* (1987) 142; Libai "The Protection of the Child Victim of a Sexual Offence in the Criminal Justice System" 1969 15 *Wayne LR* 980; Graham "Indicia of Reliability and Face to Face Confrontation: Emerging Issues in Child Sexual Abuse Prosecutions" 1985 *University of Miami LR* 19; Oates "Children as Witnesses" 1990 64 *Australian LJ* 129; Christiansen "The Testimony of Child Witnesses: Fact, Fantasy and the Influence of Pre-trial Interviews" 1987 62 *Washington LR* 709; Malamquist "Children Who Witness Parental Murder: Post Traumatic Aspects" 1986 25 *Journal of the American Academy of Child Psychiatry* 320.

[114] 487 US 1012, 101 LEd 2d 857 874 (1988).

[115] See, e g, the discussion of the position in England by Morgan & Zedner *Child Victims: Crime, Impact, and Criminal Justice* (1992) 134–5. See also the Canadian cases *R v Levogiannis* 18 CR (2d) 242 and *R v Toten* 16 CRR (2d) 49.

REAL EVIDENCE

A St Q Skeen

19 1   INTRODUCTION

"Real evidence" is the term used to cover the production of material objects for inspection by the court.[1] Real evidence may include any thing, person[2] or place which is observed by the court in order that a conclusion may be drawn as to any fact in issue. The following are some of the types of material objects used as real evidence: the weapon used in the commission of a crime, the appearance of persons, tape recordings, fingerprints, photographs, films, video recordings, handwriting, documents (when presented as a chattel rather than for their contents) and blood tests. The list is by no means exhaustive.[3]

Real evidence usually owes its efficacy to the evidence of a witness who explains how the exhibit was used. A witness normally clarifies the relevance of the production of real evidence. In the case of injuries sustained by a person evidence should generally be led to link the exhibit with the injuries. Medical evidence is useful to show whether the weapon in question could have caused the injuries and, if so, what approximate degree of force had been used. Exhibits are usually labelled and numbered on their production. Sometimes the working of a machine may be demonstrated to the court; for example, the functioning of a telephone call-box apparatus may be demonstrated to the court to show how coins can illegally be removed from the apparatus.

The court should describe the exhibit carefully so that the details may be embodied in the record. The court should not attempt to make any observations which require expert knowledge.[4] But it may measure exhibits. In *R v Makeip*[5]

---

[1] Tapper *Cross and Tapper on Evidence* 8 ed (1995) 49.
[2] See generally *Newell v Cronje* 1985 4 SA 692 (E).
[3] See generally Hoffmann & Zeffertt 405–14.
[4] O'Dowd *The Law of Evidence in South Africa* (1963) 111.
[5] 1948 1 SA 947 (A). See further § 8 1 above.

the judge examined some plaster casts of footprints (which were exhibits) with a magnifying glass and also measured the distance between the various marks. The Appellate Division held that this procedure was permissible as it did not require more than ordinary knowledge or skill. The true value of real evidence was discussed in *S v Msane*.[6]

19 2 APPEARANCE OF PERSONS

A person's physical appearance and characteristics are real evidence. The court may examine wounds sustained by a person and, if it does so, should describe its observations for the purposes of the record. Identity may be established by a person's physical characteristics. His size, strength, dexterity and other physical peculiarities may be relevant to the issue of guilt or innocence.

The resemblance of a child to its reputed mother or father may afford some evidence of parentage, although the value of such evidence is marginal.[7] The evidence may carry slightly more weight if the alleged parents are of different races and the child is in appearance of mixed blood.[8] Where a person's ethnic descent is in dispute his appearance may be real evidence.[9] The evidence of experts in racial classification may be admissible to prove a person's racial identity.[10] The physical appearance of a person may also serve as real evidence of his approximate age.[11]

19 3 TAPE RECORDINGS

Tape recordings may be admissible as real evidence. The main danger concerning this type of evidence is the possibility of editing or alteration of the tapes.[12] The court should be satisfied that it is shown prima facie that the recording is original. The recording must also be sufficiently intelligible. Sometimes a transcript of the recording will be produced in evidence subject to the court being satisfied as to the accuracy of the transcription. In *Hopes v HM Advocate*[13] a Scottish court held that a typist who prepared a transcript after playing over the recording many times could be considered an expert in respect of the particular recording. The transcript must be identified by the person who made it.[14] There must be evidence to identify the speakers.[15] This may be done in several ways, for example,

---

[6] 1977 4 SA 758 (N).

[7] *R v Jood* 1949 1 SA 298 (GW); *Russel v Russel* 1923 129 LT 151.

[8] *R v P* 1957 3 SA 444 (A); *R v D* 1958 4 SA 364 (A).

[9] *R v S* 1954 3 SA 522 (A).

[10] *R v Vilbro* 1957 3 SA 223 (A); *S v Wyngaard* 1966 2 SA 372 (C).

[11] See generally Schmidt 311–14; s 337 of the CPA; *S v Mavundla* 1976 2 SA 162 (N).

[12] See *S v Ramgobin* 1986 4 SA 117 (N) and the discussion of this case in § 19 5 below.

[13] 1960 SC (J) 106. But cf *Ramgobin* supra 163I–J.

[14] *S v Singh* 1975 1 SA 330 (N).

[15] *R v Behrman* 1957 1 SA 433 (T).

either by a person who heard the speech or conversation or by inference from what was said.[16] See § 19 5 below for a discussion of video recordings.

19 4 FINGERPRINTS

Evidence that fingerprints were found at the scene of the crime or on a particular object is often of strong probative value in linking the accused with the commission of a crime. The usual manner in which fingerprint evidence is obtained is as follows: a policeman will lift a print by means of folien from the object and then send off the folien and fingerprints taken from the suspect to a police expert stationed at a main centre; the expert will then compare the fingerprints of the suspect with those found at the scene; the expert will mount enlarged photographs of the two sets of prints side by side and mark the points of similarity. If the expert attends court, he will often re-take the accused's fingerprints and compare them with the prints found at the scene. Seven points of similarity are sufficient to prove beyond doubt that the prints were made by one and the same person.[17] The evidence of comparison may be given orally or by affidavit (s 212(4) and (6) of the CPA; see § 15 2 1 above). Once the court accepts that the witness is an expert it will as a general rule accept his evidence.[18] The procedural requirements relating to comparative charts are set out in a number of cases.[19]

Footprints do not require explanation by an expert and the court is not obliged to accept an opinion as to the identity of footprints.[20]

19 5 PHOTOGRAPHS, FILMS AND VIDEO RECORDINGS

Photographs may be produced as real evidence of such matters as injuries or accident damage. A photograph may also be used where an item is too bulky to produce in court. Section 232 of the CPA expressly allows for the production of photographs. Witnesses may also identify persons by examining photographs. A photograph is a document in terms of part VI of the CPEA (s 33) and may be admissible in both civil and criminal proceedings (s 222 of the CPA) if the photographer has acknowledged in writing that he is responsible for its accuracy. In other instances there must be evidence that the photograph is a true likeness of the items shown in it. The principles regarding the use of films as real evidence are the same as those for photographs. In *The Statue of Liberty*[21] a radar station's films and recordings of echoes of ships on the River Thames were accepted as real evidence. The cases dealing with the admissibility of film and video recordings show differing approaches.

---

[16] *S v Peake* 1962 4 SA 288 (C).

[17] *S v Kimimbi* 1963 3 SA 250 (C); *S v Nala* 1965 4 SA 360 (A).

[18] *R v Nksatlala* 1960 3 SA 543 (A); *S v Nala* supra. But see also *S v Blom* 1992 1 SACR 649 (E) as discussed in § 8 6 2 above.

[19] *S v Phetshwa* 1982 3 SA 404 (E); *S v Malindi* 1983 4 SA 99 (T); *S v Van Wyk* 1982 2 SA 148 (NC); *S v Nyathe* 1988 2 SA 211 (O) (overruling *S v Segai* 1981 4 SA 906 (O)); Skeen 1988 *SACJ* 339.

[20] *R v Makeip* 1948 1 SA 947 (A); *R v Debati* 1951 1 SA 421 (T). See also generally § 8 1 above.

[21] 1968 2 All ER 195.

In *S v Mpumlo*[22] the court held that a video film was not a document but was real evidence which, so long as it satisfied the requirement of relevance, could be produced, subject to any dispute as to authenticity or interpretation. In that case a copy was produced, but this was said only to go against the weight that may be attached to the evidence.

In *S v Ramgobin*[23] Milne JP held that there was no difference in principle between the admission of audio tapes and video recordings. Milne JP held that the state had to prove the following factors beyond a reasonable doubt: *(a)* originality; *(b)* that no interference had taken place; *(c)* that they related to the incident in question; *(d)* that the recording was faithful; *(e)* that the identity of the speakers was identified; and *(f)* that the recordings were sufficiently intelligible.

In *S v Baleka (1)*[24] it was held that sound recordings and video recordings, and a combination of the two, are real evidence to which the rules relating to documentary evidence are not applicable. In *S v Baleka (3)*[25] Van Dijkhorst J found himself unable to agree with the stringent test for admissibility laid down in *S v Ramgobin* supra because it is absurd to exclude evidence because it is potentially dangerous. Reliability need be established only later — all that need be established for admissibility is that *prima facie* the recordings had some probative value.

19 6   INSPECTIONS *IN LOCO*

It is open to the court to hold an inspection *in loco* to observe the scene of an incident or the nature of an object which cannot be produced in court. The decision to hold an inspection *in loco* is solely within the discretion of the court. A court of appeal will be slow to hold that the trial court was wrong in refusing to hold an inspection.[26] The power to hold inspections *in loco* is conferred on a court, in criminal cases, by s 169 of the CPA and in civil cases by Supreme Court rule 39(16) *(d)* and magistrates' courts rule 30(i) *(d)*.

An inspection *in loco* may achieve two purposes: *(a)* it may enable the court to follow the oral evidence more clearly or *(b)* it may enable the court to observe some real evidence which is additional to the oral evidence. It is undesirable that an inspection *in loco* should take place after the evidence and arguments have been completed, because observations made by the court should be recorded and the parties should be afforded the opportunity of making submissions and leading evidence to correct an observation which seems to them to be incorrect.[27]

---

[22] 1986 3 SA 485 (E).

[23] 1986 4 SA 117 (N).

[24] 1986 4 SA 192 (T).

[25] 1986 4 SA 1005 (T).

[26] *R v Sewpaul* 1949 4 SA 978 (N); *R v Robertson* 1958 1 SA 676 (A) 679; *East London Municipality v Van Zyl* 1959 2 SA 514 (E); *S v Solani* 1987 4 SA 203 (NC); *S v Mkohle* 1990 1 SACR 95 (A) 99*h–i*.

[27] *Goldstuck v Mappin and Webb Ltd* 1927 TPD 723; *Kruger v Ludick* 1947 3 SA 23 (A); *Bayer v Viljoen* 1990 2 SA 647 (A).

The inspection should be held in the presence of both parties, but the presiding officer may make the inspection on his own.[28] If witnesses point out items and places during the inspection, they should subsequently be called or recalled to give evidence on what was indicated at the inspection.[29] It is irregular for the inspection to be held in the presence of only one of the parties or his witnesses.[30]

19 7   HANDWRITING

Comparisons of disputed writing with any writing proved to be genuine may be made by a witness. Such writings and the evidence of the witnesses may be submitted as proof or otherwise of the writing in dispute (s 228 of the CPA and s 4 of the CPEA). The writing submitted for comparison is real evidence.[31] An expert in the comparison of handwriting is usually known as a "questioned document examiner". Such an expert will usually mount the disputed writing side by side with the genuine writing and indicate points of similarity. The court is not bound by an expert's opinion.[32] A layman may give evidence concerning the comparison of writing that he knows. It is also open to the court to form its own conclusions from its own comparisons.[33] Identification of handwriting in the context of opinion evidence is also discussed in § 8 5 2 above.

19 8   BLOOD TESTS, TISSUE TYPING AND DNA IDENTIFICATION

The results of blood tests may be used in litigation. This is usually done in cases of driving under the influence of alcohol or driving with an excess blood-alcohol level. In paternity cases red blood cell tests can at the most give a negative result. All that can be said is that the alleged father could not have been the father.[34] The HLA tissue typing test may be used to prove paternity to a much more certain degree than red blood cell tests. In *Van der Harst v Viljoen*[35] evidence showed a probability of 99,85 per cent that the defendant was the father. However, such testing is merely corroborative of the evidence of the complainant.

In paternity cases it is disputed whether a person may be forced to submit to blood or tissue tests in civil cases by order of the Supreme Court.[36]

---

[28] *R v Mouton* 1934 TPD 101; *R v Akoon* 1926 NPD 306. Schmidt 310 correctly criticizes the rule that the court may make an inspection on its own.

[29] *R v Van der Merwe* 1950 4 SA 17 (O).

[30] *R v Bereng* 1949 AC 253. *S v Douglas* 1993 1 PH F14 (C); *S v Dippenaar en 'n ander* 1990 1 SACR 208 (T).

[31] See *S v Smith* 1978 3 SA 749 (A).

[32] *Annama v Chetty* 1946 AD 146; *R v Smit* 1952 3 SA 447 (A).

[33] *R v Kruger* 1941 OPD 33. Hoffmann & Zeffertt 105 maintain that such a course should be discouraged.

[34] See Darroll 1965 *SALJ* 317.

[35] 1977 1 SA 795 (C): see Böhm & Taitz 1986 *SALJ* 662 and 1987 *SALJ* 307. The HLA test is based on the white blood cells.

[36] In *Seetal v Pravitha NO* 1983 3 SA 827 (D) it was held that the Supreme Court had the power as upper guardian to consent to a minor undergoing a blood test against parental wishes and in *M v R* 1989 1 SA 416 (O) it was held that the Supreme Court had the power to order both a minor and an adult to submit to a blood test; see Zeffertt 1989 *ASSAL* 412–13. These decisions turned on the court's power to regulate its procedure; see also *O v O* 1992 (4) SA 137 (C). However, in *Nell v Nell* 1990 (3) SA 889 (T) the court declined to order a child to undergo a tissue test on the grounds that such an order was not a purely

However, an important presumption has been created by the Children's Status Act 82 of 1987. This section is cited in § 28 5 4 below.

A far more precise method of identification is to be found in the so-called DNA 'fingerprinting'.[37] In essence, each person has a unique genetic code and the 46 chromosomes which hold the code are made up of the chemical DNA (deoxyribonucleic acid). A sequence amongst the genes in the DNA of each person repeatedly occurs along the length of the DNA molecule and all copies of these are unique to an individual, with the sole exception of identical twins.

DNA fingerprinting can be done on blood samples, semen, hair roots, shin scrapings. It can be taken from samples up to two years old. In Britain DNA fingerprinting has been used both to establish guilt and to prove innocence and relationship.

The chance of error is very remote and a properly conducted test is said to be proof of identity beyond any doubt.[38]

---

procedural matter in which the court could exercise its inherent power to regulate its procedure. See also *E v E* 1940 TPD 333 and *S v L* 1992 (3) SA 713 (E), where it was held that the court possessed no such power. The right to privacy under s 13 of the interim Constitution might alter the situation and make such tests unconstitutional unless shown to be reasonable limitations. See also *Crow v McMynn* 1991 49 CRR 290. In criminal cases s 37 of the CPA applies. See further § 10 2 3 1 1 above.

[37] See Böhm & Taitz 1986 *SALJ* 662 and 1987 *SALJ* 307; White & Greenwood 1988 *Modern LR* 145; 1987 *The Law Society's Gazette* 2161 and 3637; 1988 *Journal of the Law Society of Scotland* 124; 1991 *Crim LR* 583.

[38] Dr A J Jeffreys of Leicester University developed the test and ICI hold the patent.

CHAPTER 20

DOCUMENTARY EVIDENCE

A St Q Skeen

20 1 INTRODUCTION

Documentary evidence consists of statements made in writing which are intended to be relied on. Three main rules have to be complied with before a document will be admissible: *(a)* the statements contained in the document must be relevant and admissible; *(b)* its authenticity must be proved; and *(c)* the original document must normally be produced. There are various exceptions to the last rule. These are considered in § 20 5 below.

A document may be produced as a thing or chattel like any other real evidence[1] where no reference is to be made to its contents; for example, a stolen document which is the subject-matter of a charge of theft could be produced in the manner applicable to other exhibits without the necessity of compliance with the three rules referred to above. In such an instance the document constitutes real evidence as discussed in ch 19.

20 2 DEFINITION OF DOCUMENT

In *R v Daye*[2] it was said that a document is "any written thing capable of being evidence". It was held that it is immaterial what the writing was made on. In terms of s 33 of the CPEA a "document" is defined as including any book, map, plan,

---

[1] See § 19 1 above; see generally on documents Van der Merwe 1994 *Obiter* 64–84.
[2] 1908 2 KB 330 340.

drawing or photograph (see § 15 5 above). Section 221 of the CPA defines a "document" as including any device by means of which information is stored or recorded. This definition has been held to include computer output in certain circumstances.[3] In terms of ss 246 and 247 of the CPA the definition of document includes any book, pamphlet, letter, circular letter, list, record, placard or poster.[4] On the definition of document see generally *Seccombe v Attorney-General*,[5] *S v Tsapo*,[6] and *S v Mpumlo*.[7]

20 3 PRODUCTION OF THE ORIGINAL DOCUMENT

If a party wishes to produce a document as proof of its contents, the original document must be produced unless the non-production of the original is satisfactorily explained.[8] This requirement that primary evidence of a document's contents should be adduced may be a remnant of the best evidence rule.[9]

There may be more than one original document. If the document is executed in duplicate, both copies are originals; the same applies to carbon copies.[10] A roneoed copy of a document has been held to be an original.[11] If one copy of an agreement is signed by one party and another by the other, each copy ranks as primary evidence against the person who signed it. This type of copy is known as a counterpart.[12] In the case of a telegram (where it is intended to use the contents against the maker) the original is the form handed in at the post office.[13] Certified copies of a telegram would be admissible in terms of s 234 of the CPA[14] and s 20 of the CPEA.[15]

The holder of a licence or the terms contained in the licence can be proved only by the production of the licence or copies expressly authorized by statute.[16] Proof of ownership of immovable property can be properly proved only by the production of the title deeds or register or a duly certified copy under s 18 of the CPEA.[17]

---

[3] See *S v Harper* 1981 1 SA 88(D) 95; § 15 4 above.

[4] See §§ 15 7 and 15 8 above.

[5] 1919 TPD 270 277.

[6] 1970 2 SA 256.

[7] 1986 3 SA 485 (E) 489.

[8] O'Dowd *The Law of Evidence in South Africa* (1963) 115; *Standard Merchant Bank v Creser* 1982 4 SA 671 (W) 674.

[9] Hoffmann & Zeffertt 390. See further § 2 10 above.

[10] *Lynes v International Trade Developer Inc* 1922 NPD 301; *Forbes v Samuel* 1913 3 KB 706 722; *Da Mata v Otto* 1972 3 SA 858 (A) 880.

[11] *Herstigte Nasionale Party van Suid-Afrika v Sekretaris van Binnelandse Sake en Immigrasie* 1979 4 SA 274 (T).

[12] *Houghton v Koenig* 139 ER 1358.

[13] *R v Regan* 1887 16 Cox CC 203.

[14] See § 20 11 below.

[15] See § 20 11 below.

[16] *R v Hullet* 1948 1 SA 808 (N); *S v Van Pittius* 1973 3 SA 814 (C); *R v De Meyer* 1949 3 SA 892 (O); *R v Koro* 1950 3 SA 797 (0); *R v Sonday* 1954 3 SA 641 (C).

[17] *Gemeenskapsontwikkelingsraad v Williams (1)* 1977 2 SA 692 (W); *R v Mabinandla* 1960 4 SA 307 (E). In *Goudini Chrome (Pty) Ltd v MCC Contracts (Pty) Ltd* 1993 1 SA 77 (A) it was accepted that the best evidence of ownership of immovable property is the title deed, which is a public document. Such documents are admissible in terms of s 18 of the CPEA and a copy may be received if it is certified to be a true copy or an extract from the register.

20 4   ILLUSTRATIONS OF THE ORIGINAL DOCUMENT RULE

In *Macdonnell v Evans*[18] one of the witnesses for the plaintiff was asked in cross-examination whether a letter written by him was written as a reply to a letter (which was an exhibit) in which he was accused of forgery. The question was not allowed as the latter letter was not produced. In *R v Pelunsky*[19] the accused was alleged to have attempted to defraud a municipality by making out false entries on tickets as to the number of sheep taken into the market. The prosecution attempted to prove the entries on the tickets by producing the counterfoils which were made at the same time as the originals. This secondary evidence was held to be inadmissible as no explanation was given as to the absence of the original tickets.

The primary or best evidence rule applies only where the contents of the document are in dispute. The rule does not apply where the document helps to prove some fact which can be proved by other means. In *R v Amod and Co (Pty) Ltd*[20] the accused was charged with selling goods in excess of the maximum price. The customer (who was a police trap) had been handed an invoice and a cash slip. The documents were subsequently lost and it was held that secondary evidence was admissible because the offence could be proved without the necessity of producing the documents.

In *R v Lombard*[21] it was held that the fact that the accused was a retail butcher in a controlled area could be proved by evidence other than the contents of a registration certificate. This case also illustrates the fact that the rule does not apply *(a)* where the fact in issue is the existence of the document rather than its contents and *(b)* where what is to be proved is the existence of a relationship or status flowing from the document.

20 5   SECONDARY EVIDENCE ADMISSIBLE IN CERTAIN CIRCUMSTANCES

The general rule is that secondary evidence is inadmissible. There are, however, numerous exceptions to this rule. Before secondary evidence as to the contents of a document may be led the absence of the original must be satisfactorily explained.

The following are some of the more important instances where secondary evidence is permitted. *(a)* Evidence that the original is destroyed or cannot be located after a diligent search will pave the way for the admissibility of secondary evidence.[22] *(b)* Secondary evidence is allowed where the production of the original would be illegal: in *R v Zungu*[23] the production of an original public-service vehicle certificate was excused as it was illegal to remove the certificate

---

[18] 1852 11 CB 930.
[19] 1914 AD 360; see also *Singh v Govender Bros Construction* 1986 3 SA 613 (N); *S v Mgesi* 1986 2 SA 244 (E); *S v Tshabalala* 1980 3 SA 99 (A).
[20] 1947 3 SA 32 (A).
[21] 1957 2 SA 42 (T) 46.
[22] *Boon v Vaughan* 1919 TPD 77; *Ex parte Ntuli* 1970 2 SA 278 (W).
[23] 1953 4 SA 660 (N).

from the vehicle. *(c)* Secondary evidence is allowed where production of the original is impossible, that is, where the writing is fixed onto an immovable object.[24] *(d)* Secondary evidence is also allowed where the original is in the possession of the opposing party or a third party, who refuses to produce it or who cannot be compelled to produce it.[25] In civil litigation notice to produce must first be given in terms of Supreme Court rule 35(10) and magistrates' courts rule 23(4). Where the document is in the possession of a third party he should by means of a *subpoena duces tecum* be informed to produce it (see, for example, s 179 of the CPA).

Various other statutory exceptions will be considered in § 20 7 below. Once secondary evidence is allowed any form of secondary evidence may be produced; there are therefore no degrees of secondary evidence.

20 6 PROOF OF DOCUMENTS

The general rule is that a party wishing to produce a document must prove that it is authentic. The usual manner of proving authenticity is by leading evidence of the maker, signatory or a person who witnessed the signing or who can identify the writing or signature of the author.[26] If it is relevant that a document was in the possession of a particular person, such possession must be proved.

In terms of Supreme Court rule 35(9) a party to civil proceedings may not be required to prove authenticity if he serves a notice on his opponent calling on him to admit authenticity. If consent is unnecessarily refused, the opponent may be required to bear the costs of proof. There are conflicting decisions as to whether evidence is necessary to prove the authenticity of a document which is mentioned in a discovery affidavit.[27] O'Dowd[28] submits that discovery does not necessarily involve any admission of authenticity. If the authenticity of a document is not proved or admitted, the document is inadmissible and may not be used for the purpose of cross-examination.[29] Foreign documents may be proved as authentic in the normal manner or in terms of Supreme Court rule 63.[30]

20 7 PROOF OF AUTHENTICITY AND SECONDARY EVIDENCE ALLOWED BY STATUTE

In some cases proof of authenticity is not required by virtue of the terms of certain

---

[24] *R v Watt & Darlow* 1919 NLR 108.
[25] *Dalgleish v Israel* 1909 TH 229; *R v Goldberg* 1924 EDL 311; *R v Southhall* 1921 TPD 403; *S v Miles* 1978 3 SA 407 (N). See also generally *Singh v Govender Brothers Construction* 1986 3 SA 613 (N) 617H–J.
[26] *Policansky Bros v L and H Policansky* 1935 AD 89.
[27] *Christie v Liquidator, Beersheba Options Ltd* 1927 TPD 662; *Cloete v Union Corporation* 1929 TPD 668.
[28] *The South African Law of Evidence* (1963) 113.
[29] *Israelsohn v Power* 1953 2 SA 499 (W); *Howard and Decker v De Souza* 1971 3 SA 937 (T) 940, but see the discussion of *Swanepoel* 1980 1 SA 144 (NC).
[30] See *Kaplan v Kaplan* 1936 WLD 51; *Stift v Stift* 1952 4 SA 216 (O); *Friend v Friend* 1962 4 SA 115 (E); *Chopra v Sparks Cinemas (Pty) Ltd* 1973 2 SA 352 (D).

statutes. Some statutes also allow the use of secondary evidence. Only the most important instances will be considered.

Section 231 of the CPA provides that any document which purports to bear the signature of any person holding public office and which bears a seal or stamp of the department, office or institution to which such person is attached shall, upon the mere production of the document at criminal proceedings, be *prima facie* proof that such person signed the document. In *S v Kariola*[31] an appeal was allowed as a notice served under the Group Areas Amendment Act 57 of 1957 did not bear the seal or stamp of the department in question. Section 6 of the CPEA is to the same effect.

Section 37 of the CPEA (which in terms of s 222 of the CPA applies to criminal proceedings as well) provides that documents which are proved or purported to be not less than twenty years old, and come from proper custody, are presumed to have been duly executed if there is nothing to suggest the contrary.

In terms of s 234 of the CPA it is sufficient to prove an original official document which may or may not be a public document and which is under the control of or in the custody of any state official by virtue of his office if a copy or extract is certified as being true by the head of department concerned or any state official authorized by the head to do so. The certified document may be led in evidence. The section further provides that an original official document may not be produced (except for records of judicial proceedings) without an order from the Attorney-General.

Section 20 of the CPEA has similar provisions to those of s 234 of the CPA covering the production of copies. Section 19 of the CPEA provides that no original document in the custody of a state official shall be produced except on the order of the head of department concerned or an official authorized by him.

Section 25 of the CPEA makes provision for the admissibility of an official report at any proceedings in which an order is sought to presume a soldier is dead. The report must be accompanied by an affidavit made by the secretary of defence setting out certain matters which are contained in the section.

Section 229 of the CPA and s 26 of the CPEA provide that the times of sunrise and sunset at particular places in the Republic may be proved, on mere production, by tables drawn up by an official observatory if the tables have been approved by the Minister in the *Gazette*. This matter is also dealt with in § 27 4 3 below.

20 8   PUBLIC DOCUMENTS

Public documents are documents which are made by a public official, in the execution of a public duty and for public use and access.

Section 18 of the CPA provides that certified copies of public documents are admissible if certified as a true copy or extract by the officer to whom the custody of the original is entrusted. Section 233 of the CPA is to the same effect.

---

[31] 1966 1 SA 343 (T).

20 9 JUDICIAL RECORDS AND DOCUMENTS

Judicial records of court cases are admissible in certain circumstances.

20 9 1 Civil cases In terms of s 17 of the CPEA the conviction or acquittal of a person may be proved in a civil case by the production of a document certified (by the registrar or clerk of the court or their deputies who have custody of the record) as being a correct copy of the record or a part of it. Section 18 of the Supreme Court Act 59 of 1959 provides that certified copies of court records certified by the registrar of the particular court under its seal shall be *prima facie* evidence of the record without the need to authenticate the registrar's signature. Rule 61 of the magistrates' courts rules provides that the clerk of the court may produce in evidence any original record, entry or document of the same court in a different matter. Where it is necessary to give evidence in another court a certified copy of the original is admissible without the production of the original.

20 9 2 Criminal cases Section 235 of the CPA provides that in criminal cases it is sufficient to prove an original record of judicial proceedings if a copy of the record is certified by the clerk of the court, registrar, their deputies or any person having custody of the record. Where the record is taken down by shorthand or mechanically a certificate by the person who transcribed the record is sufficient.

20 10 STAMP DUTIES ACT 77 OF 1968

Section 12 of this Act provides that no instrument which is to be stamped under this Act shall be made available for any purpose whatsoever unless it is duly stamped, and in particular shall not be produced or given in evidence or be made available in any court of law.

This prohibition does not apply to criminal proceedings (s 251 of the CPA) or in an action brought by the state for the recovery of stamp duty (s 12*(b)* of Act 77 of 1968). It is possible for an unstamped document to be admitted in evidence if it is stamped late and penalties have been paid (proviso to s 12 of Act 77 of 1968).

It was held in *Gleneagles Farm Dairy v Schoombie*[32] that the document could be stamped even during an appeal and before the registrar of the appeal court. The document would then be validated retrospectively and a copy may be stamped as if it were an original so as to prove it as secondary evidence.[33]

20 11 LETTERS AND TELEGRAMS

The ordinary way in which a letter is proved is by the writer giving evidence and being asked whether the signature is his and whether he was the author of the letter.[34]

---

[32] 1947 4 SA 67 (E).
[33] *Steyn v Gagiano* 1982 3 SA 562 (NC).
[34] *Policansky Bros v L and H Policansky* 1935 AD 89; *R v Wilken* 1939 EDL 151.

The post mark on an envelope is *prima facie* evidence as to the date on which and place where it was posted.[35] The fact that a letter has been posted raises a rebuttable presumption of fact (gives rise to an inference) that it has been delivered.[36] In the case of telegrams the form handed in at a post office is the original document (see § 20 3 above).

20 12 DISCOVERY OF DOCUMENTS

Discovery is a procedure, provided for in terms of Supreme Court rule 35 and magistrates' courts rule 23, whereby a party in civil proceedings is able to ascertain what documents relating to the case are, or have been, in the possession of the opposing party. The party requiring discovery serves a notice on the opposing party calling on him to make discovery. Discovery should then be made by means of an affidavit in which the deponent states that the documents listed in the schedule attached to the affidavit are the only documents relevant to the matter which are in his possession or control (those documents in the possession of a party's agent or attorney are considered to be under his control). The person requesting discovery may then inspect and make copies of the disclosed documents. If a party fails to make discovery after a request, he may not use the document at the trial without the permission of the court. In the magistrates' courts all relevant documents which are to be used in the action or which tend to prove or disprove either party's case have to be discovered. A party need not disclose privileged documents.[37]

---

[35] May *South African Cases and Statutes on Evidence* (1962) para 620.
[36] May *South African Cases and Statutes on Evidence* para 620. See further § 28 5 6 1 below.
[37] See chs 10 and 11 above for a detailed discussion of privilege.

CHAPTER 21

MACHINE-GENERATED EVIDENCE AND RELATED MATTERS

A St Q Skeen

21 1 HISTORY

In 1976 the Appellate Division in *Narlis v South African Bank of Athens*[1] held that a computer print-out was not admissible in terms of s 34 of the CPEA. A computer, it was said, is not a person.

The hiatus relating to the admissiblity of computer-generated evidence, which was starkly highlighted by the decision in *Narlis,* led the Clearing Bankers' Association to be concerned about the implications of the decision. The Association asked the South African Law Commission to investigate the need for specific legislation on the subject. Mr Justice J M Didcott prepared a report and a draft bill on behalf of the Clearing Bankers' Association. After various representations had been received, a draft bill was published in the *Government Gazette* in September 1981.

The report of the South African Law Commission on the admissibility in civil proceedings of evidence generated by computers was presented to the Minister of Justice in April 1982.[2] The report contained a consideration of the need for reform to the law of evidence to accommodate the admissibility of computer records, as well as a draft bill which aimed to provide the vehicle for this reform.

The Law Commission emphasized that the ever-increasing usage of computers required the courts to be aware of contemporary business practices. Because of the restrictive nature of the common-law hearsay rule, there was inadequate provision for the admissibility of computer output in evidence. As a result of the restrictions contained in s 34 of the CPEA, the Law Commission considered that an amendment to this section would not solve all the problems relating to

---

[1] 1976 2 SA 573 (A).

[2] South African Law Commission *Report on the Admissibility in Civil Proceedings of Evidence Generated by Computers. Project 6. Review of the Law of Evidence* (1982).

computerized records. It also held the view that a basic disparity existed between human and electronic output, which could best be distinguished by a separate statute.

In 1983 the legislature passed the Computer Evidence Act,[3] which very closely resembled the draft bill proposed by the Law Commission. The Act applies only to civil cases. Arguably it may be possible to produce computer output under s 3 of the Law of Evidence Amendment Act 45 of 1988 if the requirements of the Computer Evidence Act are not met. Hearsay is discussed in ch 13 above.

21 2   COMPUTER EVIDENCE ACT 57 OF 1983 (IN CIVIL CASES)

Section 3 of the Computer Evidence Act provides that an authenticated computer print-out is admissible, on its production, as evidence of any fact recorded in it in circumstances where direct oral evidence of the fact would be admissible. It is provided that the court may give as much or as little weight to the print-out as all the circumstances of the case dictate. "Authenticated computer print-out" is defined as meaning a computer print-out accompanied by an affidavit authenticating the computer print-out.

"Processing" includes treating by calculation, compilation, arrangement, sorting, comparison, analysis, synthesis, classification, selection, summarizing or consolidation. "Computer print-out" means the documentary form in which information is produced by a computer or a copy or reproduction of it, and includes whatever information needs to be transcribed, translated or interpreted after its production by the computer in order that it may take such form and be intelligible to the court. "Information" is defined to include any information expressed in or conveyed by letters, figures, characters, symbols, marks, perforations, patterns, pictures, diagrams, sounds or any other visible, audible or perceptible signals.

Various safeguards are embodied in an attempt to ensure the reliability of the print-out. Section 2 of the Computer Evidence Act requires that a computer print-out be authenticated by an affidavit termed an "authenticting affidavit". The affidavit must *(a)* identify the print-out and confirm that it is a computer print-out as defined in the act; *(b)* identify the print-out and confirm that it is a true copy, reproduction, transcription or interpretation of the information; *(c)* describe in general terms the nature, extent and sources of the data, instructions supplied to the computer and the purpose and effect of the data processed by the computer; *(d)* certify that the computer was correctly supplied with data and functioned correctly; *(e)* certify that no reason exists to doubt or suspect the truth or reliability of any information recorded or contained in the resultant print-out. It is sufficient compliance with *(c)*, *(d)* and *(e)* for the maker of the affidavit to state that the information and certifications are given to the best of his knowledge and belief.

The deponent to the authenticating affidavit must be a person who has

---

[3] Act 57 of 1983

knowledge and experience of computers and of the particular system in question. He must also have examined all the records and facts to hand concerning the operation of the computer, the data and the instructions supplied to it. The records and facts must be verified by him if he has control of or access to them in the ordinary course of his business, employment, duties or activities. If not, then a supplementary affidavit must be made by a person who has control of or access to them. Records and facts are sufficiently verified if the deponent states that, to the best of his knowledge and belief, they comprise all the relevant records and facts. The above requirements concerning the deponent do not apply to a computer print-out of any public institution, which must be accompanied by an authenticating affidavit from an official or employee of the institution. A public institution is defined as any government department, any provincial administration or local authority or financial institution as defined in the Inspection of Financial Institutions Act or any mutual building society and the Land and Agricultural Bank.[4]

The definitions are designed to overcome several apparently insuperable obstacles to the production of computer output in evidence in terms of s 34 of the CPEA. Section 34 provides that any document containing a statement made by a person and tending to establish a fact is admissible on the production of the original document if either *(a)* the maker of the statement had personal knowledge of the matters dealt with in the statement, or *(b)* the document was part of a continuous record made under a duty by the maker to record information supplied by persons who may reasonably be supposed to have personal knowledge of the matters. Further requirements are that the maker has to be called as a witness "unless he is dead", is unfit (mentally or physically) or is outside the Republic (and it is not reasonably practicable to secure his attendance) or cannot be traced after all reasonable efforts have been made to trace him. The court may, however, if it is satisfied that undue delay or expense would otherwise be caused, admit the document without the oral testimony of the person who made the statement, despite his being available. The statement contained in a document is not to be deemed to have been made by a person unless the document or the material part of it was written, made or produced by him with his own hand or was signed or initialled by him or otherwise recognized by him in writing as one for the accuracy of which he is responsible. Section 33 of the CPEA defines "document" as including any book, map, plan, drawing or photograph.

The following are some of the difficulties which either were or could have been encountered in attempting to produce computer output in evidence under s 34 of the CPEA:

(a) Personal knowledge by the maker of the statement: it would be a rare occasion that a computer operator would have personal knowledge of items fed into the computer by him.

(b) The record must be a continuous record. This is difficult to interpret

---

[4] Act 68 of 1962.

judicially. In *Thrasyvoulos Ioannou v Papa Christoforos Demetriou* Lord Tucker said:[5]

> "Without attempting to give a definition of 'continuous record' it is sufficient to say that the mere existence of a file containing one or more documents of a similar nature dealing with the same or a kindred subject-matter does not necessarily make the contents of the file a 'continuous record' within the meaning of the section."

Consequently the court refused to find that an official report of an inquiry into water rights, which was filed with other documents of a similar nature, was part of a continuous record. In *Simpson v Lever*[6] a policeman's notebook containing details of an accident was held to be a continuous record.

(c)   There must be, at some stage or another, personal knowledge of the matters recorded either by the recorder or by the maker of the statement. In the case of a computer operator this would be an extraordinary situation.

(d)   Section 34 requires that the statement be made by a "person".

The definitions contained in the Computer Evidence Act appear largely to overcome the problems mentioned above. Personal knowledge is not required, the record need not be continuous, the operator need not acknowledge authorship, and the definition of "computer print-out" allows for reproductions or copies to be produced without any further requirements having to be satisfied. One of the most far-reaching of the innovations provides for the admissibility of processed information, which is much more flexible than the ordinary storage or recording of information.

Section 2 provides what on the face of it are adequate safeguards to allay the fears and suspicions of the wary. The Law Commission acknowledged that it was "well aware of the fact that computers are the object of deep public suspicion". The requirements to be satisfied before an authenticating affidavit and the print-out are admissible are fairly extensive. Such stringent requirements will not apply to a print-out of a public institution (as defined in s 1), as such a print-out will not be hit by subsecs (3), (4) and (5) of s 2. The Law Commission gave the following reason for this dispensation: "They could find it very inconvenient to comply with all the requirements of clause 3 of the bill. On the other hand, their nature is such that they are unlikely to attempt fraud on the public."

The court may place such weight on the print-out as the circumstances may dictate.

21 3   POSSIBLE PROBLEMS ARISING FROM THE COMPUTER EVIDENCE ACT 57
        OF 1983

Various difficulties may be encountered by the deponent to an authenticating affidavit. In terms of s 2(1)(d)(ii) he is required to certify that, to the best of his knowledge and belief, the computer was unaffected by any malfunction, interference, disturbance or interruption which might have had a bearing on such

---

[5] 1952 AC 84 (PC) 92, 1952 1 All ER 179 184.
[6] 1963 1 QB 581, 1962 3 All ER 870.

information or its reliability. The data-processing manager may often state in an affidavit that the computer was working properly. This is the expression of an opinion, and with a large and complex computer system it may be doubtful whether the manager could have enough knowledge concerning the computer system to be capable of forming such an opinion based on fact. Different aspects of the computer system must be considered, and a number of independent experts may be required, with the data-processing manager merely testifying that no faults came to his notice at the particular time.[7]

Another related problem is that errors in the output of the computer may occur in a number of ways. The hardware may develop faults because the machine is working in an unsuitable environment, such as when the air-conditioning is faulty. Changes in voltage may also have an adverse effect on the machine. There may be faults in the software (programmes) or such faults may develop when the software is interacting with other components of a particular network. Some computer systems have safety systems to stop undetectable corruption of output. These safeguards may sometimes be ineffective. The newer the type of system, the greater the possibility of unforeseen problems which have not yet been ironed out. Machines can and do malfunction, for short or long periods, without the reason being readily ascertainable.

Further problems may lie in the fact that the identification of the computer operator in question will be unknown (there is increasing mobility of skilled persons); and it may be impossible to evaluate the operator's reliability, any motives he might have had to misrepresent, and other human variables that may affect the correct and competent handling of the computer. The computer is a technological marvel, but the correctness of its output must ultimately be dependent on the absence of any foibles and failings of its human operators and programmers.

It is true that the court may attach what weight it considers fit to the print-out, but very often it will be unable to read into the affidavit matters that cannot be affirmed by the deponent. Suspicions may be swept under the carpet by a bland and reassuring affidavit made by someone who cannot possibly speak on all the surrounding circumstances. Section 3 of the Act provides that a properly authenticated affidavit is admissible on its production. The court has no discretion to exclude it; its only discretion is as to the weight it will attach to it. In order to assess this weight the court may consider matters raised in the affidavit.

21 4 COMPUTER EVIDENCE AND CRIMINAL CASES

Section 221 of the CPA would appear to allow the use of computer print-outs. Apart from minor variations to meet local needs, s 221 is identical in wording to s 1 of the English Criminal Evidence Act of 1965. The English Act was passed as

---

[7] Kelman & Sizer *The Computer in Court* (1982) 19. See generally on difficulties relating to affidavits Steele 1983 *SALJ* 505; Delport 1983 *Obiter* 140; Skeen 1984 *SALJ* 675; Ebden 1985 *SALJ* 687; Van der Merwe *Computers and the Law* (1986) 123–5; Van Der Merwe 1994 *Obiter* 64–84.

a direct result of the decision in the case of *Myers v Director of Public Prosecutions*,[8] where the House of Lords refused to create a new exception to the hearsay rule. The prosecution attempted to introduce microfilmed records, made by unidentified workmen on assembly lines, concerning numbers of stolen vehicles. These records were ruled inadmissible as being hearsay.

The material part of s 221 of the CPA reads as follows:

> "(1) In criminal proceedings in which direct oral evidence of a fact would be admissible, any statement contained in a document and tending to establish that fact shall, upon production of the document, be admissible as evidence of that fact if —
>
> (a) the document is or forms part of a record relating to any trade or business and has been compiled in the course of that trade or business, from information supplied, directly or indirectly, by persons who have or may reasonably be supposed to have personal knowledge of the matters dealt with in the information they supply; and
>
> (b) the person who supplied the information recorded in the statement in question is dead or outside the Republic or is unfit by reason of his physical or mental condition to attend as a witness or cannot with reasonable diligence be identified or found or cannot reasonably be expected, having regard to the time which has elapsed since he supplied the information as well as all the circumstances, to have any recollection of the matters dealt with in the information he supplied."

Section 221(2) states that in determining the admissibility of the documents the court may draw an inference from the form or contents of the document and it may have reference to a medical certificate in deciding whether or not the person is fit to attend as a witness. Section 221(3) deals with the factors to be considered in determining the weight to be given to a statement which is admissible under the section: namely, the accuracy or otherwise of the statement, whether the information was supplied contemporaneously and whether anyone concerned with the making of the statement had any incentive to conceal or misrepresent the facts.

"Business", in terms of s 221(5), includes any public transport, public utility or similar undertaking carried on by a local authority, and the activities of the post office and the railways administration. "Document" includes any device by means of which information is recorded or stored, and "statement" includes any representation of fact, whether made in words or otherwise.

The Act contains no definition of a record. The English courts have decided that a single document relating to one transaction, such as a bill of lading, is admissible as a record.[9] There are no reported cases in South Africa in point, but it is submitted that a similar conclusion would be reached. The definition of "document" would appear to extend to computer output. There is no requirement of direct personal knowledge on the part of the maker of the document, but the original informant must have personal knowledge. This point is clearly made in the English case of *R v Pettigrew; Newark*.[10] The accused was convicted of burglary. A significant factor in the proof of the prosecution case was that the

---

[8] 1965 AC 1001 (HL), 1964 2 All ER 881.

[9] *R v Jones; Sullivan* 1978 2 All ER 718 (CA).

[10] 1980 71 Cr App 39 (CA). See also *R v Ewing* 1983 2 All ER 645 (CA), where hearsay evidence was accepted under the English Criminal Evidence Act of 1965.

accused was found in possession of three new £5 notes which came from a bundle of notes stolen in the burglary. The prosecution tried to prove this by the production of a Bank of England computer print-out identifying the serial numbers of a bundle of notes sent to a bank, parts of which could be traced to another bank. On appeal it was held that the print-out was inadmissible, as the information was not supplied by a person who had or could have had personal knowledge of the matters dealt with. This decision turned on the mode of operation of the machine. The sequence of events was this: the operator placed bundles of newly minted notes into the machine which made the print-out. Each note bore a serial number. The computer rejected defective notes and recorded the first and last serial numbers of each bundle of one hundred notes in addition to the serial numbers of rejected notes. Serial numbers could be taken to be consecutive except where notes had been rejected. The operator noted on a card the first serial number of a batch, but did not examine the bundle any further. On these facts the Court of Appeal held that the operator could not be said to have personal knowledge of the rejected notes. A further point taken, but not decided on, was whether the issue of banknotes was an activity forming part of any trade or business.

It seems that once the conditions set in terms of s 221(1) of the CPA have been satisfied the document will become admissible and the court will have no discretion to exclude it. However, in terms of s 221(3) the judicial officer has a discretion as to what weight to afford the document.

Smith[11] and Tapper[12] suggest that in *Pettigrew* supra the evidence from the computer was not hearsay but direct evidence. As the information was recorded by mechanicl means without the intervention of the human mind, the record made by machine was admissible so long as it was accepted that the machine was reliable, such as in the cases of the temperature recorded by a thermometer, a camera picture, a tape recording and the reading of a speed-trapping device. The authors accept that the computer varies from the above instruments in that it can perform a number of functions, but these functions are done mechanically. Smith and Tapper also contend that judicial notice of the reliability of computer operation should be taken, as it has been with the examples listed above. The answer to this may lie in justifiable judicial conservatism in the consideration of the workings of new technology. Smith concedes that in many cases the information recorded by computer is derived, directly or indirectly, from a human mind and then the hearsay rule will apply, unless there is an exception under either the common law or statute.

The line of thought that machine-produced information is not hearsay relies on the reasoning to be found in the English case of *The Statue of Liberty*.[13] This case concerned the collision of two ships. One of the parties wished to produce a film of the radar echoes of the ships and a series of photographs from the film in order to show how the vessels collided. Sir Jocelyn Simon P held that the

---

[11] 1981 *Crim LR* 387; see also Van Der Merwe 1994 *Obiter* 64–84.
[12] 1982 *Oxford Journal of Legal Studies* 128.
[13] 1968 2 All ER 195. See also § 19 5 above.

film was not hearsay but real evidence which was brought into existence by purely mechanical means without any human intervention. It may be argued, on the one hand, that hearsay rules apply only where the assertion is made by a human being.[14] Conversely, it has been argued that although machine-generated evidence did not exist when the hearsay rule was developed, the hearsay rule is an exclusionary rule and, in the light of the rationale behind the rule, machine-created evidence should be covered by it.[15] Pengilley answers Smith in the following terms: "It is submitted that if the legislation that modifies the rule against documentary hearsay adverts expressly to machine information then it would be applicable to machine information even if machine information was not hearsay."[16]

In the South African case of *S v Harper & another*[17] the meaning of 'document' as defined in s 221 was considered. The question in issue was whether computer print-outs are documents. Milne J made the following finding:[18]

> "The extended definition of 'document' is clearly not wide enough to cover a computer, at any rate where the operations carried out by it are more than the mere storage or recording of information . . . The wording of the section . . . is entirely appropriate to the production of microfilm as evidence since the microfilm itself can be produced. Furthermore microfilm is a means by which information is stored, and recorded."

It was held that the computer print-outs were admissible in evidence, as they fell within the ordinary grammatical meaning of the word "document".

It appears from *Pettigrew* supra that information obtained from computer print-outs is admissible only if the function of the computer was purely passive in that it merely recorded or stored the information. Implicit in the decision is the conclusion that if the computer carried out active functions, over and above storage, then the fruits of its endeavours would be inadmissible. This conclusion would appear to be derived for two reasons, namely, the passive attributes given to a computer by the definition of "document" and because personal knowledge would be required, either directly or indirectly, by the person supplying the information. In *Narlis v South African Bank of Athens* Holmes JA summed up the status of a computer as follows:[19] "Well, a computer, perhaps fortunately, is not a person." This remark aptly expresses the underlying reasons for the decision in *Pettigrew* supra.

Section 236 of the CPA allows for the production of the accounting records of a bank and any document in the possession of the bank subject to the requisite supporting affidavits. The term "document" is defined to include a recording or transcribed computer print-out produced by any mechanical or electronic device and any device by means of which information is recorded or stored. Section 236A of the CPA has a similar definition relating to the proof of entries

---

[14] Cross 1969 *Melbourne University LR* 1.
[15] Pengilley 1982 *Melbourne University LR* 617 623.
[16] At 626.
[17] 1981 1 SA 88 (D); see also *S v De Villiers* 1993 1 SACR 574 (Nm).
[18] At 95E–H.
[19] 1976 2 SA 573 (A) 577H.

in foreign bank's accounting records. The problems encountered in *Narlis* supra will not be encountered in the production of bank records in criminal cases.

21 5   COMPUTER EVIDENCE AS REAL EVIDENCE

The next matter to consider is whether oral evidence would be admissible to prove the output of a computer in the absence of an authenticating affidavit. The answer appears to lie in s 2(1) of the Computer Evidence Act, where it is provided that a computer print-out may be authenticated for the purposes of the Act. This, in my view, allows for the proof of computer-generated evidence in ways other than by means of an authenticated computer print-out. It could apply only to real evidence in the form of evidence made by the machine without the intervention of the human mind. If the evidence were derived in part or in whole from a human statement, the party seeking to adduce the evidence would run foul of the hearsay rule unless the maker of the statement testified.

The problem of machine-generated evidence has been considered earlier. The proponents of the view that it is real evidence place great store on the decision in *The Statue of Liberty*.[20]

If machine-generated evidence may, in certain circumstances, be real evidence, an assumption which will be made, various problems of proof can arise. The person operating the computer would have to be an expert on the workings of the machine, as the courts are unlikely, at this stage in any event, to take judicial notice of them. This problem may be illustrated by reference to three cases that were decided in three different jurisdictions. In the New Zealand case of *Holt v Auckland City Council*[21] evidence was admitted in the court *a quo* from a scientist who was an expert in the analysis of blood samples by means of gas chromatography. It was held on appeal that the analyst was not qualified to give expert evidence as to the method of operation of the microprocessor which was employed to convert certain comparative results into blood-alcohol levels, for she had nothing to do with the programming, testing or maintaining of the machine. It was held that judicial notice could not be taken of the accuracy of the machine. In *Mehesz v Redman*,[22] which was decided in South Australia, blood analysis by gas chromatography was again in issue. The analyst followed instructions in a manual and carried out certain acts accordingly. He was unable to explain the process or the significance of what he was doing. Not surprisingly it was found that the analyst was not an expert. In the local case of *S v Terblanche*[23] the court was unwilling to take judical notice of the working of a gas chromatograph. It was held that evidence was necessary to explain how the machine functioned.

---

[20] 1968 2 All ER 195, 1968 1 WLR 739.
[21] 1980 2 NZLR 124.
[22] 1974 21 SASR 569.
[23] 1981 1 SA 791 (T).

21 6   SPEED-MEASURING DEVICES

Section 212(10) of the CPA allows the Minister to prescribe in respect of any measuring instrument, by notice in the *Gazette,* the conditions and requirements which must be complied with before any reading made by such instruments may be accepted in criminal proceedings. Once the conditions are complied with the measuring device shall be accepted as proving the fact recorded unless the contrary is proved.

An apparatus which takes a photograph of a speeding vehicle is not a "computer" and the photograph is not a "computer print-out" as defined in the Computer Evidence Act 57 of 1983. It therefore does not have to be authenticated.[24]

---

[24] *S v Fuhri* 1994 2 SACR 829 (A). See also generally Van Dokkum 1995 *SACJ* 322.

SECTION G
WITNESSES

CHAPTER 22

THE COMPETENCE AND COMPELLABILITY OF WITNESSES

Wouter L de Vos

22 1 INTRODUCTION

The competence and compellability of a witness should not be confused with the possible privileges which he might claim. Cowen & Carter[1] explain as follows:

"A competent witness is a person whom the law allows a party to ask, but not to compel, to give evidence. A compellable witness is a person whom the law allows a party to compel to give evidence. There are certain questions which a witness may refuse to answer if he so wishes. He is said to be privileged in respect of those questions. It should be clear, therefore, that competence without compellability (or bare competence) is not the same as privilege. Compellability is concerned with whether a witness can be forced by a party to give evidence at all. Privilege is concerned with whether a witness who is already in the box is obliged to answer a particular question. The protection of privilege is exactly the same whether the witness is barely competent and of his own free will elected to give evidence or the witness is compellable and was forced to give evidence."

It follows that a competent and compellable witness who wishes to rely on, for example, the privilege against self-incrimination may not refuse to enter the

---

[1] *Essays on the Law of Evidence* (1956) 220.

witness-box: he may only claim his privilege once the relevant question is put to him.[2]

Seen from a historical perspective, the general development has been towards competence rather than incompetence. It was, for example, formerly held that a person who had been sentenced to death was an incompetent witness because he hardly had a reason to fear prosecution for perjury. In the modern era, however, such a person is not considered an incompetent witness solely on the basis of the fact that he awaits capital punishment.[3] His evidence may be tested in cross-examination and he is indeed a competent witness.[4] Since the death penalty has recently been declared unconstitutional by the Constitutional Court this issue has now become irrelevant.[5]

Today it is also accepted that a person's religious belief — or no such belief at all — cannot make him an incompetent or non-compellable witness.[6]

22 2 THE GENERAL RULE

In both civil and criminal proceedings the general rule is that every person is presumed to be competent and compellable to give evidence.[7] The so-called residuary clauses, for example s 206 of the Criminal Procedure Act of 1977, refer us to the English law. The effect of this section was discussed in § 3 5 above, where brief reference was made to *Ex parte Minister of Justice: In re R v Demingo*.[8]

22 3 GENERAL PROCEDURAL MATTERS

Parties cannot consent to the admission of an incompetent witness's evidence.[9] The court must decide any question concerning the competence or compellability of any witness.[10] The method of examining and deciding issues relating to competence or compellability is normally that of a trial within a trial.[11] It may be necessary for the court to hear evidence, for example, on the issue whether a deaf mute can communicate properly.[12] However, the court can also decide the issue of competence on the basis of its own observations, without requiring a trial within a trial.[13] A competent and compellable witness who refuses to attend the

---

[2] See generally § 10 1 above. However, cf *S v Boesman & others* 1990 2 SACR 389 (E) 396*e–g*, where this rule was for practical considerations not followed.

[3] *R v Tom* 1914 TPD 318.

[4] Scoble *The Law of Evidence* 3 ed (1952) 256.

[5] See *S v Makwanyane* 1995 3 SA 391 (CC).

[6] Cf s 163 of the CPA.

[7] Hoffmann & Zeffertt 371; s 8 of the CPEA read with s 42; s 192 of the CPA read with s 206.

[8] 1951 1 SA 36 (A).

[9] *S v Thurston* 1968 3 SA 284 (A) 291; Hoffmann & Zeffertt 372.

[10] See, e g, s 193 of the CPA.

[11] *S v Thurston* supra 291; Hoffmann & Zeffertt 372. The so-called trial within a trial was also briefly referred to in § 16 7 4 above.

[12] See § 22 6 below.

[13] *S v Zenzile* 1992 1 SACR 444 (C) 446.

proceedings may be brought before the court by means of a warrant of arrest.[14] Such a witness, or one who does attend but refuses to testify, may also be tried and punished summarily by the court for his failure or refusal. The witness concerned can, however, avoid punishment by presenting an acceptable excuse.[15]

22 4   CHILDREN

There is no statutory provision governing a child's capacity to give evidence. At common law there is also no specific age limit. Even very young children may testify provided that they *(a)* appreciate the duty of speaking the truth;[16] *(b)* have sufficient intelligence; and *(c)* can communicate effectively. A child who is competent may be sworn in, provided that the court is of the opinion that he understands the nature and religious sanction of the oath. If the child is unable to understand that, he may give his evidence without taking the oath; but in this event the court must admonish him to speak the truth.[17]

Children are competent and compellable to testify against their parents. But in *R v Zulu*[18] it was pointed out that it is in principle undesirable that children should be compelled to do so. The decision to call them, however, rests in the discretion of the prosecutor and will normally depend upon considerations such as the availability of other witnesses and the seriousness of the offence with which the parent is charged.[19]

The evidence of children is approached with caution.[20]

22 5   MENTALLY DISORDERED AND INTOXICATED PERSONS

Section 194 of the CPA provides that no person appearing or proved to be afflicted with mental illness or to be labouring under any imbecility of mind due to intoxication or drugs or the like and who is thereby deprived of the proper use of his or her reason shall be a competent witness whilst so afflicted or disabled.[21] It follows that an intoxicated person, for example, will regain his competence and compellability when sober.[22] It is also clear that the section is directed at a certain degree of mental illness or imbecility of mind. Therefore, a

---

[14] Cf ss 170(2) and 188 of the CPA; ss 30 and 31 of the Supreme Court Act 59 of 1959; Uniform Rule 38; s 51 of the Magistrates' Courts Act 32 of 1944 and rule 26 of the rules of these courts.

[15] The terminology in civil and criminal proceedings differs and the punishment in criminal proceedings is more severe than in civil cases. But in essential respects the procedure in the respective proceedings is the same. Cf ss 22, 170, 188 and 189 of the CPA; ss 30 and 31 of the Supreme Court Act; s 51 of the Magistrates' Courts Act.

[16] Section 164(1) of the CPA.

[17] Section 164(1) of the CPA; see further Hoffmann & Zeffertt 375–7.

[18] 1947 2 PH H302 (N).

[19] Bosman (ed) *Social Welfare Law* (1982) 45.

[20] See § 30 11 3 below.

[21] See also s 9 of the CPEA.

[22] *R v Creinhold* 1926 OPD 151.

person who is affected to some extent but still endowed with the proper use of his reason will be a competent witness.[23]

22 6 DEAF-AND-DUMB PERSONS

These persons are competent and compellable if they can communicate with the court.[24] The CPA also provides that in the case of deaf-and-dumb persons oral evidence shall be deemed to include gesture-language.[25]

22 7 JUDICIAL OFFICERS

Judges and magistrates are not competent to give evidence in cases over which they preside or have presided.[26] If they have personal knowledge of a fact in dispute, they should recuse themselves.[27] They may then testify after recusal.[28] No recusal is necessary where judicial notice may take place.[29]

If a judge is competent to testify in a given case, a subpoena may nevertheless not be issued against him without leave of the Supreme Court.[30]

22 8 OFFICERS OF THE COURT

Attorneys, advocates and prosecutors are competent witnesses in cases in which they are professionally involved. But it is extremely undesirable that they testify in such cases.[31] By so doing they would compromise their independence with regard to the case and put their credibility at stake.[32]

22 9 THE ACCUSED

An accused, whether or not charged jointly with another accused, is at any appropriate stage in criminal proceedings competent to testify in his own defence.[33] He may not, however, be called as a witness except upon his own application.[34] The accused is therefore a competent but non-compellable witness. It should be borne in mind, however, that an accused who has given evidence may be recalled by the court.[35]

---

[23] Schmidt 209.
[24] *R v Ranikolo* 1954 3 SA 255 (O). They may, if necessary, communicate through an interpreter; *S v Naidoo* 1962 2 SA 625 (A).
[25] Section 161(2).
[26] See generally Hoffmann & Zeffertt 377; Schmidt 210.
[27] See generally Ferreira *Strafproses in die Laer Howe* 2 ed (1979) 47–57.
[28] Phipson *On Evidence* para 48.
[29] Judicial notice is discussed in ch 27 below.
[30] Section 25 of the Supreme Court Act 59 of 1959.
[31] *R v Nigrini* 1948 4 SA 995 (C); *Elgin Engineering v Hillview Motor Transport* 1961 4 SA 450 (N).
[32] Schmidt 211.
[33] Section 196(1) of the CPA.
[34] Section 196(1)*(a)* of the CPA. This rule also finds expression in s 25(3)*(c)* and *(d)* of the interim Constitution.
[35] See s 167 of the CPA.

22 10 THE ACCUSED AND CO-ACCUSED IN THE SAME PROCEEDINGS

An accused who testifies in his own defence may in the process give evidence favourable to a co-accused. But since every accused testifies only of his own volition, a co-accused cannot compel another accused to give evidence on his behalf. An accused may also incriminate a co-accused whilst giving evidence on his own behalf. But the state cannot call him as a witness for the prosecution since his competence is confined to being a witness for his own defence. It is only by terminating his status as an accused in the same proceedings as the co-accused that he can become a witness for the prosecution against the latter.[36]

Such a change of status can be achieved in the following ways:[37]

(a) *If the charge against the accused is withdrawn.* This does not amount to an acquittal and the former accused can be prosecuted again. But by testifying he can in certain circumstances qualify for an indemnity from prosecution.[38]

(b) *If the accused is found not guilty and discharged.* In terms of s 6(b) of the CPA a prosecution may be stopped even after an accused has pleaded, in which event he must be acquitted. In such an instance the accused may not be prosecuted again but may be called as a state witness.

(c) *If the accused pleads guilty the trials of the accused and his co-accused are separated.* Furthermore, it is desirable that the accused should be convicted and sentenced before being called as a witness.[39]

(d) *If the trials of the accused and his co-accused are separated for another valid reason.*[40] In this event it is also desirable that the accused, if convicted, should be sentenced before being called to testify for the prosecution.

Since the former accused is ordinarily an accomplice, the cautionary rule in this regard will apply.[41]

22 11 SPOUSES

The position regarding the competence and compellability of a spouse to be called as a witness for or against the other spouse depends on the nature of the proceedings.

22 11 1 Civil cases In these proceedings the spouse of a party is a competent and compellable witness for and against the party concerned.

22 11 2 Criminal cases In this context a distinction must be drawn between the case where the spouse of an accused testifies on behalf of the defence and where the spouse is called as a witness on behalf of the prosecution. For the sake of

---

[36] See Schmidt 217–19; Hoffmann & Zeffertt 382–5.

[37] See Schmidt 218–19; Hoffmann & Zeffertt 382–5.

[38] In terms of s 204 of the CPA; see § 10 2 2 above.

[39] *Ex parte Minister of Justice: In re R v Demingo* supra; *R v Zonele* 1959 3 SA 319 (A).

[40] See s 157(2) of the CPA.

[41] See § 30 11 1 below.

convenience the husband is in paras (i) and (ii) below cast in the role of the accused, whilst his wife assumes the role of the witness.

(i) *Witness for the defence.* The spouse of an accused is a competent witness for the defence, whether or not the accused is charged jointly with any other person.[42] If the spouse is called to testify on behalf of the accused, she is both competent and compellable[43] to do so. The spouse is also a competent witness for any co-accused of the accused. But in this case she cannot be compelled to testify.[44]

(ii) *Witness for the prosecution.* The spouse of an accused is a competent witness for the prosecution, but as a rule she cannot be compelled to testify in this capacity.[45] However, she is both a competent and compellable witness for the prosecution where the accused is charged with a crime falling within the following categories:[46] *(a)* any offence committed against the person of either of them or of a child of either of them; *(b)* any offence under Chapter 8 of the Child Care Act 1983 committed in respect of any child of either of them; *(c)* any contravention of any provision of s 11(1) of the Maintenance Act 1963, or of such provision as applied by any other law; *(d)* bigamy; *(e)* incest; *(f)* abduction; *(g)* any contravention of any provision of s 2, 8, 9, 10, 11, 12, 12A, 13, 17 or 20 of the Immorality Act 1957; *(h)* perjury committed in connection with or for the purpose of any judicial proceedings instituted or to be instituted or contemplated by the one of them against the other, or in connection with or for the purpose of criminal proceedings in respect of any offence included in this subsection; *(i)* the statutory offence of making a false statement in any affidavit or any affirmed, solemn or attested declaration if it is made in connection with or for the purpose of any such proceedings as are mentioned in para *(h)*.

The rule of non-compellability is based on the consideration that the marital relationship between the accused and his spouse should be protected.[47] However, in the case of the crimes listed above this consideration loses its validity since these crimes are generally directed against the person of the spouse, or one of their children, or they affect the marriage in some way. In these circumstances

---

[42] Section 196(1) of the CPA.

[43] This follows by implication from the wording of the section — cf Schmidt 212.

[44] Section 196(1)*(b)* of the CPA.

[45] Section 195(1) of the CPA; see generally Schmidt 213–16; Hoffmann & Zeffertt 385–8. It should be noted that a person married in accordance with black law or custom is, for purposes of the law of evidence in criminal proceedings, regarded as an unmarried person — s 195(2) of the CPA. However, in Kwazulu-Natal a marriage in accordance with Zulu law and customs is recognized for purposes of the law of evidence in lower courts: Kwazulu Criminal Procedure Amendment Act 11 of 1982. It should be noted that a marriage entered into for ulterior purposes is nevertheless a valid marriage, provided that the parties intend the normal legal consequences to flow from such union. See, for example, *S v Leepile* 1986 2 SA 352 (W), in which the court found that although the motive of the witness and the accused in entering into a marriage was to afford the witness a just excuse for refusing to testify, the validity of the marriage was not affected. Accordingly, the court held that the witness (spouse) had a just excuse as contemplated in s 189(1) of the CPA.

[46] Section 195(1)*(a)–(i)* of the CPA.

[47] See generally Schmidt 213.

there is, therefore, no reason why the spouse should not be treated like any other competent witness for the prosecution and thus also be compellable.

The words "offence . . . against the person" have generally been interpreted restrictively by our courts. In principle the phrase has been confined to charges of assault or charges involving assault.[48] However, it seems doubtful whether this approach accords fully with the legislative intent behind the provision. There appears to be no valid reason why crimes that infringe the personality rights of a person, such as *crimen iniuria*, should not be included under this section.[49]

In *S v Taylor*[50] the court decided that the words "wife or husband" contained in ss 195 and 196 of the Criminal Procedure Act include the former spouse of an accused if she is required to testify to events which occurred *stante matrimonio*. Accordingly, if the former spouse is called as a witness by the state or the court, she is competent to testify about these events, but not compellable.[51] The position would be the same if she is called to testify on behalf of a co-accused of her former husband.[52] The former spouse is only competent and compellable if the accused requires her evidence for his defence.[53]

In terms of the common law a former spouse was in the same position as a current spouse. Both were incompetent witnesses for the prosecution in relation to matters that occurred whilst their respective marriages to the accused existed. The legislature changed this general rule by declaring the spouse to be a competent witness for the state in the normal course of events.[54] Although the former spouse is not mentioned in this provision, she must clearly be included within its ambit. If not, the common-law principle of incompetence would still apply to the former spouse. To treat the current spouse as competent and the former spouse as incompetent would be an absurd situation that could not have been contemplated by the legislature.[55] It is therefore submitted that the above decision correctly expresses the legislative intent.

22 12   HUSBAND AND WIFE AS CO–ACCUSED

In the case where a husband and wife are charged jointly it is self-evident that neither of them can be called as a witness for the prosecution. The rules as set out in § 22 10 above apply. But if either of them testifies in his/her own defence and incriminates the other party, such evidence will be admissible, notwithstanding the fact that the former might not be a competent witness for the state against the latter.[56] Since the spouse of an accused is now generally a competent witness for the prosecution, the necessity for the above rule of admissibility might

---

[48] Compare *R v Dhlamini* 1966 4 SA 149 (N) 152.

[49] See generally Schmidt 214.

[50] 1991 2 SACR 69 (C).

[51] At 72–3.

[52] Section 196(1)*(b)* of the CPA.

[53] Section 196(1) of the CPA.

[54] Section 195(1) of the CPA as amended by s 6 of Act 45 of 1988.

[55] *S v Taylor* 1991 2 SACR 69 (C) 71*i*–72*a*.

[56] Section 196(2) of the CPA.

be questioned. However, the rule might still be justified on the basis that s 195 covers only the position of the spouse called by the state and does not sanction the situation where she testifies in her own defence and incriminates her co-accused husband.

22 13 MEMBERS OF PARLIAMENT

In terms of s 7(1) of the Powers and Privileges of Parliament Act[57] Members of Parliament cannot be required to give evidence in civil proceedings while in attendance at Parliament (but they may be required to do so if the court holds its sitting at the seat of Parliament).

22 14 HEADS OF STATE AND DIPLOMATS

The president of the Republic is clearly a competent witness, but there seems to be some uncertainty about his compellability. Although the sovereign in England is regarded as competent but not compellable, it seems doubtful whether the South African president enjoys the same privilege. The reason is that there is no statutory provision or other legal ground on which the non-compellability of the president can be based. It is therefore suggested that the president should be regarded as a competent and compellable witness.[58]

In terms of s 3 of the Diplomatic Immunities and Privileges Act[59] foreign heads of states and diplomatic agents (and various other persons in diplomatic missions or public international organizations and institutions) are immune from the civil and criminal jurisdiction of South African courts. Such immunity obviously includes non-compellability as witnesses.

---

[57] Act 91 of 1963.
[58] Cf Schmidt 219–20; Hoffmann & Zeffertt 388.
[59] Act 74 of 1989.

CHAPTER 23

THE CALLING OF WITNESSES

Wouter L de Vos and S E van der Merwe

23 1 INTRODUCTION

This chapter is largely of a procedural nature and briefly sets out the rules in terms of which witnesses are called to testify. The general rule is that all evidence should be given *viva voce*.

23 2 WITNESSES: GENERAL PROCEDURAL MATTERS

The attendance of a witness may be secured by means of a *subpoena*. A *subpoena duces tecum* is issued to a witness who is required to bring documentary evidence to court.

23 2 1 Witnesses to wait outside Witnesses are generally required to wait outside before being called upon to testify.[1] The purpose of this rule is to ensure that a witness is not influenced by what other witnesses in the same case have said.[2] The position of the accused is different and is discussed in § 23 4 2 below.

---

[1] The court may make such an order. See s 187 of the CPA.
[2] See further § 30 7 below.

Expert witnesses[3] are sometimes allowed to be present in court before being called upon to testify. This is an exception to the general rule. The purpose of this procedure is to give the expert an opportunity of assessing the issues, background, circumstances, and nature of the case. This procedure may place the expert witness in a better position to give a valued opinion when he is eventually called upon to testify. The court may grant the expert permission to be present prior to his testifying.

23 2 2 The oath, affirmation or admonition[4] Witnesses may be examined only if they are under oath or if they have made an affirmation or if they have been admonished by the presiding officer to speak the truth.

23 3 EXAMINATION OF WITNESSES

Only one witness at a time is called and examined. In both criminal and civil proceedings there are three basic stages during which a witness may be examined:[5] *(a)* examination in chief by the party who called the witness; *(b)* cross-examination by the opponent or opponents of the party who called the witness; and *(c)* re-examination by the party who initially called the witness. The court may also question a witness.[6]

23 4 CRIMINAL PROCEEDINGS

The calling of witnesses in criminal proceedings is discussed in §§ 23 4 1–23 4 4 below. The position of the accused who testifies in his own defence is examined in § 23 4 2 below, and must be read with the discussion in §§ 22 9 and 22 10 above.

23 4 1 Witnesses called by the state In criminal cases the state leads evidence first. Before any evidence is adduced the prosecutor may address the court for the purpose of explaining the charge and indicating, without comment, what evidence the state intends to adduce in support of its allegations against the accused.[7] The prosecutor then calls his first witness and examines him in terms of the rules which govern examination in chief.[8] In terms of s 150(2) *(a)* of the CPA the prosecutor may examine the witness and adduce such evidence as may be admissible to prove that the accused committed the offence referred to in the charge or any other offences which might be competent verdicts[9] on the charge. At the completion of examination in chief the accused or his legal representative

---

[3] See generally § 8 7 above.
[4] See § 18 2 above.
[5] See §§ 18 3, 18 6 and 18 8 above.
[6] See § 18 9 above.
[7] Section 150(1) of the CPA.
[8] See §§ 18 3–18 5 above.
[9] See ss 256–270 of the CPA.

has a right[10] and a duty[11] to cross-examine the witness. Cross-examination should not be conducted by the accused *and* his legal representative.[12] The prosecutor has a right to re-examine the witness upon completion of cross-examination by the defence.[13] The prosecutor may thereafter call the next witness (if any) and this witness will in turn be taken through examination in chief by the prosecutor, cross-examination by the defence, and (if necessary) re-examination by the prosecutor.

The prosecutor closes his case after all the witnesses for the state have testified. At this stage the defence may apply for the discharge of the accused in terms of s 174 of the CPA.[14] The court may also grant a discharge *mero motu*.[15]

23 4 2 Witnesses called by the defence If there is no discharge in terms of s 174 of the CPA, the accused is left with several options. He may rely on his constitutional active defence right[16] by testifying in his own defence[17] and calling one or more defence witnesses.[18] The accused may also rely on his passive defence right[19] by closing his case without testifying and without calling any defence witnesses. Or the accused can combine his active and passive defence rights:[20] as a constitutionally non-compellable witness[21] he may refuse to testify and merely call one or more defence witnesses. The accused may also elect to testify without calling any defence witnesses.

The court has a duty to explain the above options to an accused who has no legal representative.[22] In *S v Brown & 'n ander* Buys J held that the court must inform an undefended accused that *he has a constitutional right to silence and that no adverse inference can be drawn from the mere fact that he has opted for silence.*[23] Buys J, however, added the following rider: the accused must also be informed of the prejudicial consequence of exercising the constitutional right to refuse to testify, namely that the prosecution's *prima facie* case that he committed the crime will be left uncontradicted and — in the absence of an account given by the accused — the court will decide the case on the prosecution's version.[24] This rider is necessary in order to ensure that the undefended accused makes an informed

---

[10] Section 25(3)(d) of the interim Constitution and s 166(1) of the CPA.

[11] See also § 31 4 2 below.

[12] *R v Baartman* 1960 3 SA 535 (A); *S v Nkwanyama & others* 1990 4 SA 735 (A).

[13] Section 166(1) of the CPA.

[14] See further § 31 5 below.

[15] See *S v Amerika* 1990 2 SACR 480 (C).

[16] See § 3 9 above.

[17] Section 196(1) of the CPA; see also § 22 9 above.

[18] Section 25(3)(d) of the interim Constitution and s 151 of the CPA. See also s 25(3)(c) of the interim Constitution.

[19] See § 3 9 above.

[20] See generally Van der Merwe 1994 *Stell LR* 243 257.

[21] Section 25(3)(d) of the interim Constitution; s 196(1) of the CPA. See further § 22 9 above.

[22] *R v Sibia* 1947 2 SA 50 (A).

[23] 1996 2 SACR 49 (NC) 65f. See also § 30 9 below and the discussion of *Griffin v California* 380 US 609 (1965) by Van der Merwe in 1994 *Obiter* 1. Cf *S v Makhubo* 1990 2 SACR 320 (O) 322g.

[24] At 65g. See generally *S v Scholtz* 1996 2 SACR 40 (NC).

decision.[25] The effect of an accused's silence in response to the prosecution's case is dealt with in more detail in § 30 9 below.

An accused who wishes to adduce evidence on behalf of the defence may address the court for the purpose of indicating to the court, without comment, what evidence he intends adducing on behalf of the defence.[26]

Section 151(1)(b)(i) of the CPA provides that an accused who intimates that he wishes to testify shall, except where the court on good cause shown allows otherwise, be called as a witness before any other witness for the defence.[27] Section 151(1)(b)(ii) of the CPA provides that if an accused changes his mind and elects to testify after one or more defence witnesses have testified, the court may draw such inference from the accused's conduct as may be reasonable in the circumstances. The purpose of s 151(1)(b) is to create a situation where an accused who wishes to testify does so before having heard the evidence of his defence witnesses. He has a right to be present at his trial and — unlike other witnesses — cannot be asked to wait outside whilst the defence witnesses give their testimony. It has been suggested that s 151(1)(b) is unconstitutional.[28] Before the CPA came into operation in 1977 there were no statutory provisions which had attempted to prescribe the order in which an accused and his defence witness(es) were to testify.[29] However, from a tactical point of view it was — and still is — best for an accused to testify before having heard his own witness(es) in court.[30] If he testifies after having heard their testimony, he may be cross-examined on the reasons for this sequence and — depending upon his explanations — may run the risk that at the end of the trial the court may conclude that he had tailored his evidence in the light of the evidence given by the defence witnesses. The extent to which an adverse inference can be drawn as one of the "reasonable" inferences which the court may draw in terms of s 151(1)(b)(i) of the CPA is discussed in § 30 7 below.

Section 151(1)(b) does not apply where there are more than one accused.[31] In *S v Ngobeni*[32] it was also pointed out that s 151 of the CPA does not prescribe the order in which several accused should respectively put their cases to the court.

---

[25] *S v Brown & 'n ander* supra 65d.

[26] Section 151(1)(a) of the CPA.

[27] See generally *S v Nene (2)* 1979 2 SA 520 (N).

[28] Van der Merwe 1994 *Stell LR* 243. *Brooks v Tennessee* 406 US 605 (1972) is discussed in this article. In this case the majority of the Supreme Court of the USA held that Tennessee legislation, which had determined that an accused "desiring to testify shall do so before any other testimony for the defense is heard", was unconstitutional in view of procedural guarantees contained in the Fifth and Fourteenth Amendments of the Constitution of the USA. This legislation foreclosed later testimony by the accused if he had decided to call his witnesses first. It is submitted that s 151(1)(b) of the CPA does not have this effect: the accused remains a competent witness even if he deviates from the order which s 151(1)(b) seeks to secure. But it is submitted that s 151(1)(b) is nevertheless unconstitutional for the reasons advanced in 1994 *Stell LR* 243 251–9.

[29] In *S v Nkomo* 1975 3 SA 598 (N) 601H it was said that "there is no obligation whatsoever upon an accused person to testify before his witnesses are called. He is perfectly entitled to say 'I wish my witness to testify before I give evidence' or even to say 'I wish them to testify before I elect whether or not I will give evidence . . . or myself remain silent'."

[30] See further § 30 7 below as well as Tansley *SALJ* 109.

[31] *S v Swanepoel* 1980 2 SA 81 (NC) 83.

[32] *S v Ngobeni* 1981 1 SA 506 (B).

It is, however, an established practice that if there are several accused, they should put their cases in numerical order, that is, in the order in which they are listed in the charge. The court can order a departure from this rule of practice if one of the parties applies for such departure in circumstances where the court is of the opinion that none of the parties would be prejudiced and, further, that such departure would be in the interests of fairness and justice.

In *S v Mpetha (1)*[33] it was held that if counsel for all the accused are agreed that they should present the cases for the accused in an order different to that in which the accused appear in the indictment, then it is their right and duty to do so. It was also held that counsel should not be called upon to explain to the court why they want to depart from the usual practice.

It is an incorrect procedure to ask an accused to exercise his choice of giving evidence and/or calling witnesses *before* the accused preceding him in numerical order has closed his case.[34] An accused who has closed his case without having testified will be permitted to testify if he is unexpectedly incriminated by a co-accused.[35]

23 4 3 Witnesses called by the court

Section 186 of the CPA provides as follows:

"The court may at any stage of criminal proceedings subpoena or cause to be subpoenaed any person as a witness at such proceedings, and the court shall so subpoena a witness or so cause a witness to be subpoenaed if the evidence of such witness appears to the court essential for the just decision of the case."

This section introduces an inquisitorial element into our basically accusatorial trial system.[36] It is an irregularity if the court fails to call a witness whose evidence is essential for the just decision of the case.[37]

In terms of s 166(2) of the CPA the prosecutor and the accused may, with leave of the court, examine or cross-examine any witness called by the court in criminal proceedings.

Section 186 of the CPA does not empower the court to call the accused as a witness. The accused may testify only upon his own application.[38] The court may, however, recall an accused who testified in his own defence (see § 23 4 4 below).

23 4 4 Witnesses recalled by the court[39]

Section 167 of the CPA determines, inter alia, that the court may recall and re-examine any person, *including an accused*, already examined at the proceedings and *shall* recall the person concerned if his evidence appears to the court essential to the just decision of the case.

---

[33] 1983 1 SA 492 (C).
[34] *S v Ngobeni* supra.
[35] *S v Simelane* 1958 2 SA 302 (N).
[36] See generally Snyman 1975 *CILSA* 100.
[37] *S v B* 1980 2 SA 946 (A) 953.
[38] Section 196(1) *(a)* of the CPA. See also § 22 9 above.
[39] See generally *S v Shezi* 1994 1 SACR 575 (A).

23 5   Civil Proceedings

The calling of witnesses in civil proceedings is governed by the principle of party control. It is, therefore, for the parties, or rather their legal representatives, to decide which witnesses they wish to call and in what sequence the witnesses are to testify. In accordance with the position in criminal proceedings, the evidence is also presented by means of questioning conducted by the parties. Every witness called to testify also undergoes examination in chief, cross-examination and re-examination. The court, on the other hand, plays a passive and neutral role with regard to the presentation of evidence. The judge is, however, entitled to ask questions of the witnesses in order to clear up any obscure points. And he must see to it that the parties follow the correct procedure in the presentation of their evidence. But the judge must refrain from going beyond this by taking the examination of witnesses upon himself. In a common-law-orientated procedural system, like ours, this would be regarded as improper interference by the judge.[40]

23 5 1 The right or duty to begin[41] In a civil case the party who bears the onus of proof has the right (or duty) to present his case first.[42] As a rule the plaintiff carries the onus to prove all the facts in issue and therefore has the right (duty) to begin. But in some cases the onus may be on the defendant to prove certain facts, such as a special defence.[43] Hoffmann & Zeffertt explain the position as follows:

> "[T]he plaintiff has the right (or duty) to begin if the burden of proof on any issue is upon him, but he may close his case without leading any evidence on those issues on which the burden is on the defendant. It is then the defendant's turn to lead his evidence on all the issues, after which the plaintiff may do so on those issues on which he led no evidence at first."[44]

The party who bears the onus of proof is sometimes relieved of the duty to begin. This is the case where an evidentiary burden is cast upon his opponent at the outset of the trial, by reason of admissions the latter has made in the pleadings. In other words, the former has established a *prima facie* case on the pleadings, which calls for an answer from the latter at the outset.[45]

If there is a dispute as to which party bears the burden of proof, the court must give a ruling on the issue.[46]

23 5 2 Witnesses called by the parties In the normal course of events the plaintiff begins by presenting his evidence. He may testify and he may call witnesses to testify on his behalf. Thereafter he closes his case. In certain circumstances absolution from the instance may be granted against the plaintiff

---

[40] See generally *Hamman v Moolman* 1968 4 SA 340 (A) 344; Schmidt 293–4.
[41] This topic is examined in detail in §§ 32 3 and 32 4 below.
[42] Supreme Court rule 39(5) and (9); magistrates' courts rule 29(7)(*a*) and (8).
[43] Schmidt 34.
[44] At 440; cf Supreme Court rule 39(13) and magistrates' courts rule 29(9)(*a*).
[45] Schmidt 30; Hoffmann & Zeffertt 496.
[46] Supreme Court rule 39(11); magistrates' courts rule 29(9)(*a*).

at this stage.[47] If that does not happen, the defendant is required to present his case. This he does in the same manner as the plaintiff: he may testify and call witnesses to testify on his behalf.

23 5 3 Expert witnesses called by the parties A party who wishes to call an expert witness to testify on his behalf must comply with the notice requirement laid down in the rules of court.[48] The reason for this requirement is to enable the opponent to do the necessary preparation for the trial.

23 5 4 Witnesses called by the court In a civil case the court has no power to call a witness, except if the parties give their consent in this regard. If a witness has already testified, the court has a discretion to recall the witness for further examination or cross-examination.[49] This position is in accordance with the principle of party control that holds sway in our system.

23 6 REOPENING A CASE AND EVIDENCE IN REBUTTAL

A party who has formally closed his case will generally not be permitted to present further evidence by calling further witnesses. The purpose of this general rule is to promote the finality of litigation. There are, however, several exceptions to this rule.

The court may permit a party to present evidence in rebuttal in respect of new matter introduced during the course of the opponent's evidence if the party concerned could not reasonably have foreseen the presentation of the new issue. In other words, the opponent must have come up with something in the nature of a surprise.[50] The court will refuse reopening if the opponent had during the trial given an indication of the matter, for example through cross-examination.[51] This is another reason why it is essential that a defence should be put during cross-examination.[52]

Section 248(1) of the Criminal Procedure Act creates a presumption that the accused possessed a particular qualification or acted in a particular capacity if such allegation is made by the prosecution in the charge.[53] Section 248(2) provides that if such allegation is denied or evidence is led to disprove it after the prosecution has closed its case, the prosecution may adduce any evidence and submit any argument in support of the allegation as if it had not closed its case.

Reopening may also be allowed to prove a previous inconsistent statement;[54] to introduce facts to show that a witness is biased if such bias is denied under

---

[47] See § 23 7 below.

[48] Supreme Court rule 36(9); magistrates' courts rule 24(9); see § 8 7 above.

[49] Hoffmann & Zeffertt 474–5; cf magistrates' courts rule 29(12). For a somewhat different view, see Schmidt 245.

[50] *Coetzee v Union Periodicals Ltd* 1931 WLD 37; *R v Lipschitz* 1921 AD 282.

[51] *R v Lukas* 1923 CPD 508.

[52] See generally §§ 18 6 4 above and 31 4 2 below.

[53] See, on presumptions, ch 28 below.

[54] See § 25 2 4 below.

cross-examination;[55] and to call a witness to express an opinion as to the veracity of an opponent's witness.[56]

An accused who has closed his case without having testified will be allowed to testify if he is later unexpectedly incriminated by a co-accused.[57]

The exercise of the court's general discretion to allow a party to lead fresh evidence at any time up to judgment is summarized as follows by Hoffmann & Zeffertt:

> "The aim of the court is to preserve a balance between abstract justice and the need for finality in litigation . . . Factors which it will consider in the exercise of its discretion are the reasons why the evidence was not led before, the materiality of the evidence — whether it is likely to have any effect on the result of the case — and the possible prejudice to the opposing party, who may no longer have available the witnesses who could have testified in rebuttal."[58]

In the early cases the courts followed a rather strict approach, by refusing leave, unless the evidence could not by the exercise of due diligence have been led at the proper time.[59] But recent decisions have adopted a more liberal attitude by allowing a party to adduce further evidence which had been omitted through mere inadvertence or mistake. This approach is only qualified by the requirement that the opponent should not suffer any prejudice that cannot be addressed by an award of costs.[60] This trend must be welcomed since it is clearly in the interests of justice that the parties should be allowed all reasonable opportunities to present all the evidence on which they rely.

23 7   WITNESSES CALLED ON APPEAL

In exceptional circumstances a court of appeal may hear evidence on appeal or review or remit the case to the trial court for the purposes of hearing further evidence.[61]

---

[55] Hoffmann & Zeffertt 475; see also § 25 2 3 below.

[56] Hoffmann & Zeffertt 475; see also § 25 2 5 below.

[57] *S v Simelane* 1958 2 SA 302 (N); Hoffmann & Zeffertt 476.

[58] At 477.

[59] Hoffmann & Zeffertt 477, citing *May v May* 1931 NPD 223.

[60] Hoffmann & Zeffertt 477, referring to *Barclays Western Bank Ltd v Guna* 1981 3 SA 91 (D) 95D; *Hladhla v President Insurance Co Ltd* 1965 1 SA 614 (A); *Coetzee v Jansen* 1954 3 SA 173 (T).

[61] See, e g, ss 304(2)(*b*) and 316 of the CPA; s 22(*a*) of the Supreme Court Act 59 of 1959; s 87(*b*) of the Magistrates' Courts Act 32 of 1944.

CHAPTER 24

REFRESHING THE MEMORY OF A WITNESS

S E van der Merwe and H Rademeyer

24 1 INTRODUCTION[1]

The law of evidence assigns great importance to the principle of orality in the adjudication of disputes. Witnesses are as a rule required to give independent oral testimony in the sense that they are generally not permitted to rely on, or refer to, a statement, note or document whilst testifying.[2] This general rule creates the impression that preference is given to memory over writing as a means of preserving evidence. This preference can hardly be reconciled with the simple truth embodied in the saying "Ink does not loose its hold on paper, as facts do on the memory". Why is this preference for oral evidence retained? The answer lies in the common-law evidential system, where cross-examination plays a pivotal role: greater weight is attached to *viva voce* statements of witnesses than to their earlier recorded statements.

---

[1] This chapter is an abbreviated and updated version of an article by Van der Merwe in 1991 *Stell LR* 62.
[2] *S v Molefe* 1975 3 SA 495 (T). The expert witness is to some extent treated as an exception. See Schmidt 302. See also § 8 7 above.

Legislation has amended the position to a certain extent. Part VI of the CPEA (as read with s 222 of the CPA)[3] gives effect to the valid argument that the written statement of a witness may, depending upon circumstances, be more accurate than his recollection in court. In certain circumstances a prior written statement can in terms of Part VI be submitted in order to supplement — but not corroborate[4] — the evidence of a witness who cannot recall an event or some details thereof.[5]

Part VI cannot, however, be relied upon in all circumstances.[6] Where Part VI does not find application, recourse must be had to the common-law rules which provide for refreshing the memory of a witness. This procedure entails that a witness, who for some reason has forgotten a part (or all) of the events in respect of which he is to testify, may read or rely on his earlier record or statement in an attempt to refresh his memory.

Refreshing the memory of a witness with the aid of his earlier record or statement is really a necessary exception to the general rule that witnesses must testify on the basis of an independent recollection of the relevant facts. Human memory is fallible, especially in those situations where considerable time has lapsed between the actual event and the witness's narration in court. The complexity of some issues may also make it extremely difficult or impossible for a witness to testify without the aid of his earlier record.[7] In this context "record" may include an ordinary written statement, a tape recording,[8] a policeman's notebook,[9] hospital records,[10] a ship's logbook,[11] and entries in a family Bible.[12]

Refreshing the memory of a witness may take place only if certain conditions have been met. These conditions are referred to as the common-law foundation requirements and will be discussed later in this chapter. Evidence must also be led to show compliance with these conditions.[13]

---

[3] Part VI is discussed in ch 14 above.
[4] Section 35(2) of the CPEA.
[5] *Rawoot v Marine & Trade Insurance Co Ltd* 1980 (1) SA 260 (C).
[6] See generally ch 14 above.
[7] See generally the discussion of expert witnesses in § 8 7 above.
[8] *R v Mills* 1962 3 All ER 298.
[9] *Lenssen v R* 1906 TS 154.
[10] *R v Rose* 1937 AD 467.
[11] *Anderson v Whalley* 175 ER 460.
[12] *R v Sherrin* 1913 TPD 474.
[13] *R v Ndlovu* 1950 4 SA 574 (N).

24 2   "REFRESHING OF MEMORY" VERSUS THE DISTINCTION BETWEEN "PRESENT RECOLLECTION REVIVED" AND "PAST RECOLLECTION RECORDED"

The phrase "refreshing the memory of a witness" is really a misnomer.[14] Hoffmann & Zeffertt state that:[15]

> "It is not necessary that the witness, even after looking at the document, should have any independent recollection of the facts which it records. It follows that the term 'refreshing memory' is not strictly accurate, since the witness's memory may remain exhausted. He is nevertheless entitled to say 'I do not remember anything about the matter, but if that is what I wrote, then that must be what I did at the time'."

In the United States this problem is acknowledged and a distinction is drawn between "present recollection revived" and "past recollection recorded".[16] "Present recollection revived" ("herinneringsherlewing") refers to the situation which mostly closely resembles a true "refreshing of memory". Consulting the record or statement (or part thereof) merely serves as a trigger that re-establishes (or stimulates) the memory of the witness: the witness can actively recall the forgotten events and can testify without further recourse to the written source. On the other hand, "past recollection recorded" ("herinneringsherhaling") refers to the situation where the witness, after having examined the written source, still has no independent recollection and can only vouch for the accuracy and reliability of the written source. "Past recollection recorded" thus refers to a situation where there is, in effect, no memory to refresh. It refers to a "recollection which *once existed,* but now, having irrevocably vanished, depends

---

[14] Lansdown & Campbell 781. See also *Estate Parry v Murray* 1961 3 SA 487 (T) 491. Morgan "The Relation between Hearsay and Preserved Memory" 1928 40 *Harvard LR* 712 717–18. Newark & Samuels "Refreshing Memory" 1978 *Crim LR* 408 remark as follows (our emphasis): "In dealing with the problem of refreshing memory it is necessary to draw a distinction between the *different senses* in which a witness's memory may be said to be revived. *First,* the witness may be unable to recall the incident or important details of it but when referred to his notes it all comes back to him and he is able to swear to the facts from his present recollection. *Secondly,* the witness may be unable to recall the incident or important details thereof but on referring to his notes is prepared to swear to the accuracy of those notes although he has no present recollection. *Thirdly,* there are cases where the witness is unable to recall the incident or important details of it but on referring to his notes he is prepared to swear to some facts from his present memory and to vouch for the accuracy of his record of other facts."

[15] Hoffmann & Zeffertt 345.

[16] *United States v Landof* 591 F 2d 36 (9th Cir 1978); *State v Carter* 449 A 2d 1280 (1982); *State v Contreras* 253 A 2d 612 (1969); *United States v Ricardi* 174 F 2d 883 887 (3d Cir 1949); *United States v Rappy* 157 F 2d 964 (2d Cir 1946); *Johnstone v Earle* 313 F 2d 686 (9th Cir 1962); *Williams v United States* 365 F 2d 21 22 (7th Cir 1966); *Thompson v United States* 342 F 2d 137 140 (5th Cir 1965); Wigmore para 727; Lilly *An Introduction to Evidence* (1978) paras 27, 28, 66 and 67; Cleary (ed) *McCormick on Evidence* 3 ed (1984) para 9; Hutchins & Slesinger "Some Observations on the Law of Evidence — Memory" 1927 41 *Harvard LR* 860 861–3; Maquire & Quick "Testimony: Memory and Memoranda" 1957 41 *Harvard LJ* 11 14; Walker "Witness' Use of Memoranda: Present Recollection Revived and Past Recollection Recorded" 1975 6 *Cumberland LR* 472; Westman "Past Recollection Recorded: The 'Forward-looking' Federal Rules of Evidence Lean Backwards" 1975 50 *Notre Dame Lawyer* 737. The fundamental differences between present recollection revived and past recollection recorded have led the American courts to adopt a so-called liberal approach with regard to present recollection revived: *any* document (despite its nature, authenticity or origin) may serve to stimulate the memory of the witness. It is accepted that a memory stimulated to recall an event functions quite independently of the actuating cause. Of course, the court must at all times be satisfied that the witness's memory is truly refreshed. In the absence of such a finding the common-law foundation requirements concerning the nature, authenticity and origin of the document — which is then no longer considered a mere "trigger" — should be met.

on artificial preservation".[17] Psychological theory and knowledge of human memory confirm the validity of distinguishing between "present recollection revived" and "past recollection recorded".[18] The two situations are not, however, separated by a rigid and distinguishable boundary. Often situations may arise where it is difficult to distinguish between "present recollection revived" and "past recollection recorded". In *United States v Ricardi*[19] it was pointed out that the difference between the two categories will frequently be one of degree.

Although an argument can be made out that the distinction between "present recollection revived" and "past recollection recorded" should be ignored because of the difficulty in establishing which of the two is applicable in a given case, the advantages of identifying, accepting and using such distinction far outweigh the disadvantages. A proper approach should be to distinguish between "present recollection revived" and "past recollection recorded" and to accept the natural consequences of such a distinction: oral evidence is received in the case of present recollection revived (because the witness testifies from memory) and documentary evidence is received in the case of past recollection recorded (because the witness relies on the contents of documents). There are strong indications that our Appellate Division may be prepared to adopted such an approach. In *S v Bergh* it was stated:[20] "By verfrissing van geheue is die aanteke-ning wat gebruik word nie getuienis in die saak nie, alhoewel dit miskien getuienis skyn te word indien die getuie geen onafhanklike herinnering van die inhoud het nie."

24 3   REFRESHING OF MEMORY BEFORE THE WITNESS GIVES EVIDENCE

No general rule exists which precludes a witness from reading his or her statement before entering the witness-box.[21] There are several reasons why a witness should be allowed to refresh his memory before testifying. First, the common-law approach that witnesses should as a rule testify from memory[22] indirectly encourages parties and their witnesses to refresh their memories out of court. Secondly, a rule prohibiting pre-trial refreshment of memory can create serious problems for the honest witness and will have little or no effect on the dishonest witness.[23] Thirdly, it is possible to argue that pre-trial refreshment of memory is a procedural right based on the fundamental rule that a party should be given an adequate opportunity to prepare for the trial.[24] Section 35(3) (b) of the final Constitution specifically states that an accused person must be afforded adequate time and facilities to *prepare a defence*. Fourthly, testimony in the

[17] Wigmore para 725 (emphasis in the original).
[18] Van der Merwe 1989–1990 *Obiter* 49.
[19] 174 F 2d 883 889 (3d Cir 1949).
[20] 1976 4 SA 857 (A) 865C–D.
[21] *R v Richardson* 1971 2 All ER 773.
[22] *R v Molefe* 1975 3 SA 495 (T).
[23] *Lau Pak Ngam v The Queen* 1966 Crim LR 443–4.
[24] Van der Merwe 1990 *SACJ* 117 118.

witness-box will become a test of memory (rather than truthfulness) if witnesses were denied the opportunity to refresh their memories prior to trial.[25] Our courts have indeed had no hesitation in holding that a witness may refresh his memory before entering the witness-box.[26]

A document used for pre-trial refreshing of memory need not be made available to the court and the opposing party. Any privilege which might exist with regard to a document therefore remains intact. Where, however, it becomes clear during the course of a witness's testimony that he has merely memorized the contents of his statement before trial, and in fact has no independent recollection of the events, the opposing party may demand, and the court should order, that the privileged document be produced. Again it is a matter of distinguishing between present recollection revived and past recollection recorded. But the court will have to be satisfied that the *holder* of any possible privilege (for example, the client in respect of a document which falls within the ambit of legal professional privilege) has expressly or by necessary implication waived his privilege.[27] If the privileged document is withheld, the evidence should of course be excluded.[28]

24 4   REFRESHING OF MEMORY DURING AN ADJOURNMENT

There is no rule of law which prohibits a witness whose testimony has been interrupted by an adjournment from refreshing his memory during the course of such an adjournment.[29] What are the evidential consequences which flow from such conduct? Again the answer boils down to the distinction between present recollection revived and past recollection recorded. If it is clear that the witness had memorized the contents of his statement during the adjournment, then the document must be produced.[30] But if it is clear that the witness is still testifying from memory after the adjournment, the document need not be produced.[31]

May the court adjourn for the *specific* purpose of giving a witness, who is busy testifying, an opportunity of refreshing his memory from his statement which —

---

[25] *Lau Pak Ngam v The Queen* supra.

[26] *Yskor Utiliteitswinkel (Edms) Bpk v Maia* 1985 2 PH F32 (A); *Ex parte Minister van Justisie: In re S v Wagner* 1965 4 SA 507 (A).

[27] *Bowes v Friedlander* 1982 2 SA 504 (C). See also § 10 3 5 above.

[28] Van der Merwe *Die Geheueverfrissingsprosedure* (unpublished LLD thesis, UCT 1988) 311.

[29] There are, of course, certain ethical rules which attempt to limit and, in certain circumstances, prohibit interviews with witnesses after they have been sworn: see para 4 2 of the *Uniform Rules of Ethics*. It is extremely unlikely that a South African court will approve the procedure adopted in *State v Henson* 234 SW 832 (1921). In this case a prosecutor was allowed an adjournment so that he could privately refresh the memory of a witness who got stuck in the course of her testimony. See also the criticism by Anon "Evidence: Not Error for Prosecutor to Withdraw Witness and Privately Refresh his Recollection" 1922 20 *Michigan LR* 673.

[30] *Van der Berg v Streeklanddros, Vanderbijlpark* 1985 3 SA 960 (T) 963F–G: "In so 'n geval is die verklaring altyd die beste getuienis en moet dit aan die hof en verdediging voorgelê word."

[31] See generally *Bowes v Friedlander* 1982 2 SA 504 (C) and *Van den Berg v Streeklanddros, Vanderbijlpark* supra 967F: "Verder kan dit nie gesê word dat hierdie getuie nie 'n onafhanklike herinnering gehad het oor die gebeure nie. Al wat hy gedoen het, is net om sy geheue weer te stimuleer. Hy het wel getuig oor die gebeure wat hy kon onthou. Hy was nie aangewese op die dokument vir die getuienis nie en gevolglik kan die dokumente ook nie op daardie grond toegelaat word as getuienis in die hof nie."

on account of the requirement as set out in § 24 5 4 below — cannot be used for purposes of refreshing his memory while he is being questioned? In *R v Da Silva* it was held that the following procedure should be adopted to meet this situation:[32]

> "In our judgment, therefore, it should be open to the judge, in the exercise of his discretion and in the interests of justice, to permit a witness who has begun to give evidence to refresh his memory from a statement made near to the time of events in question, even though it does not come within the definition of contemporaneous, provided he is satisfied (1) that the witness indicates that he cannot now recall the details of events because of the lapse of time since they took place, (2) that he made a statement much nearer the time of the events and that the contents of the statement represented his recollection at the time he made it, (3) that he had not read the statement before coming into the witness box and (4) that he wished to have an opportunity to read the statement before he continued to give evidence . . . We do not think it matters whether the witness withdraws from the witness-box and reads his statement, as he would do if he had had the opportunity before entering the witness-box, or whether he reads it in the witness-box. What is important is that, if the former course is adopted, no communication must be had with the witness, other than to see that he can read the statement in peace. Moreover, if either course is adopted, the statement must be removed from him when he comes to give his evidence and he should not be permitted to refer to it again, unlike a contemporaneous statement which may be used to refresh memory while giving evidence."

24 5 REFRESHING OF MEMORY WHILE THE WITNESS IS IN THE WITNESS-BOX: THE COMMON-LAW FOUNDATION REQUIREMENTS

Certain requirements must be met before a witness in the witness-box may refresh his memory from an earlier record. The party who wishes to refresh the memory of the witness must prove that these requirements have been met.[33]

24 5 1 Personal knowledge of the event   The witness must have had personal knowledge of the events recorded, and a finding to this effect is necessary. The need for this requirement is of course to avoid the inadvertent admission of hearsay.[34] Proof of personal knowledge may be difficult in the case of past recollection recorded, but the law of evidence is flexible in this regard, and inferences drawn from circumstantial evidence can assist the court in determining the presence or absence of personal knowledge.[35]

24 5 2 Inability to recollect   It must be shown that the witness is unable to recollect fully a matter on which he is being examined. The court should at all

---

[32] 1990 1 All ER 29 33*c–e*.

[33] *Vumendlini v Boardman* 1946 EDL 165.

[34] *R v Mawena* 1961 3 SA 362 (SR).

[35] In *Maugham v Hubbard* 108 ER 948 951 Bayley J explained as follows (our emphasis): "Where a witness called to prove the execution of a deed sees his signature to the attestation, and says that he is, *therefore*, sure that he saw the party execute the deed, that is sufficient proof of the execution of the deed, though the witness add that he has no recollection of the fact of the execution of the deed."

times be satisfied that the witness's claim that he cannot recollect is genuine.[36] In the normal course of events the witness's mere *ipse dixit* may be sufficient,[37] whereas certain other circumstances may demand a careful enquiry.

24 5 3 Verification of the document used to refresh memory The witness must have made the recording. But it is also accepted that in at least two instances a witness may use the record of somebody else, namely, where the recording took place upon the instructions of the witness[38] (in which event the original recorder should also testify),[39] or where the witness read the record and accepted its accuracy[40] (in which event the original recorder need not testify).[41] It must be shown that the facts were fresh in the mind of the witness when he made the recording[42] or gave the instructions[43] or read and verified the recording.[44] The requirement "fresh in the memory" is discussed in § 24 5 4 below.

In *R v Kelsey*[45] the Court of Appeal ruled that it is sufficient if it can be shown that the witness verified the record by hearing it, as opposed to reading it.[46] In this case witness A saw a motor vehicle at the scene of the crime. Some twenty minutes late he gave an oral account of the registration number of this vehicle to witness B, a policeman. B recorded the number and read it back aloud to A who — without reading what B had written down — confirmed that the number was correct. The court concluded as follows:

> "The question we have to decide is . . . whether witness A can verify a note he dictates to B only by reading it himself, or whether it is sufficient if the note is read back by B to A at the time for confirmation. In most cases we would expect the note to be read by A if it is made in his presence. But what of the instant case, or cases involving the blind or illiterate? In our view there is no magic in verifying by seeing as opposed to verifying by hearing . . . What must be shown is that witness A has verified in the sense of satisfying himself whilst the matters are fresh in his mind, (1) that a record has been made, and (2) that it is accurate."[47]

It should be borne in mind that in *R v Kelsey* supra witness B testified that he had correctly recorded the number given to him by A and, further, that he had

---

[36] In *United States v Goings* 377 F 2d 753 760 (8th Cir 1967) it was pointed out that the whole adversary system will have to be revised if a party were to be allowed to offer a previous statement under "the guise of 'refreshing recollection' ".

[37] Newark & Samuels 1978 *Crim LR* 408 maintain that where it is clear that the witness will at some stage have to refer to his notes, the court will allow this at the outset to save time.

[38] *R v O'Linn* 1960 4 SA 545 (N); *S v Smuts* 1972 4 SA 358 (T); Hoffmann & Zeffertt 447.

[39] See generally *S v Van Tonder* 1971 1 SA 310 (T).

[40] *Dyer v Best* 1866 4 H and C 189, 1866 LR 1 Exch 152; *R v Mullins* 1848 12 JP 776; *Digby v Stedman* 1 Esp 328 329 (1795); *Burrough v Martin* 1809 2 Camp 112; *Anderson v Whalley* 1952 3 Car and Kir 54; *Topham v McGregor* 1844 1 Car and Kir 320; *R v McClean* 1968 Cr App R 80; *R v Varachia* 1947 4 SA 266 (T) 270. Written confirmation of the accuracy of the other person's record is not required, but can facilitate proof of verification.

[41] Van der Merwe *Die Geheueverfrissingsprosedure* 163–75.

[42] *Druker v Timmerman* 1939 SWA 42; *R v Isaacs* 1916 TPD 390; *Reference by the Attorney-General under Section 36 of the Criminal Justice Act 1972 (No 2 of 1979)* 1979 69 Cr App R 411.

[43] *R v O'Linn* 1960 4 SA 545 (N).

[44] *S v Van Tonder* 1971 1 SA 310 (T); *Harris v Mayer* 1911 AD 260; *Groves v Redbart* 1975 *Crim LR* 158.

[45] 1982 74 Cr App R 213.

[46] Succinctly stated, *R v Kelsey* supra raised the question of "verification by hearsay".

[47] At 217.

correctly read back the number to A. *R v Kelsey* supra can be distinguished from *S v Van Tonder*.[48]

24 5 4 Fresh in the memory[49]   At an early stage during the development of the English common law it was required that the writing should have been brought into existence contemporaneously or almost contemporaneously with the events.[50] It was, however, soon realized that a strict requirement of contemporaneity or substantial contemporaneity is inappropriate.[51] The test should be whether the writing came into being, or was checked and verified, at a time when the facts were still fresh in the memory of the witness.[52] The presence or absence of substantial contemporaneity is merely a factor which can assist the court in determining whether the writing came into existence at a time when the facts were still fresh in the memory of the witness. Much will depend upon the circumstances of the case.[53]

24 5 5 Use of the original document   The original document must be used where the witness has no independent recollection, that is, in the case of past

---

[48] 1971 1 SA 310 (T). In this case E, at the time of the incident, dictated the registration number of a motor vehicle to his daughter. She recorded the number on a piece of paper and E, at a time when the number was still fresh in his memory, confirmed the correctness of his daughter's recording. At a later stage a policeman took a statement from E, and E also gave his daughter's note to the police. At the trial and in the course of E's testimony it became clear that E had no independent recollection of the number. In re-examination the prosecutor "refreshed the memory" of E with the aid of the statement which the policeman had taken from E. But E never testified that the policeman had correctly copied the number from the daughter's note and the policeman was not called as a witness. The daughter testified that she had recorded a number. However, she never mentioned the exact number in her evidence and her note was never produced. The trial court allowed witness E to refresh his memory from his statement taken by the policeman. But on appeal it was concluded that without the policeman's evidence the court cannot find that the policeman correctly recorded what was said by E or what appeared on the note paper. See 313F–G of the report. Nowadays the court has a discretion to admit hearsay: see ch 13 above and cf generally *S v Mpofu* 1993 2 SACR 109 (N).

[49] See generally *Druker v Timmerman* 1939 SWA 42; *R v Isaacs* 1916 TPD 390; *Groves v Redbart* 1975 *Crim LR* 158; *R v Bryant & Dickson* 1946 31 Cr App R 1436; *R v Woodcock* 1963 *Crim LR* 273; *R v Simmons* 1967 51 Cr App R 316. In *R v Governor of Gloucester: Ex parte Miller* 1979 2 All ER 1103 1105*e–j* it was remarked that the requirement of contemporaneity ("fresh in the memory") is a mere rule of practice and not of law. Carter *Cases and Statutes on Evidence* (1981) 183 rightly describes this case as "open to doubt". It should also be appreciated that the requirement that the document should have come into existence while the events were still fresh in the memory "is by no means as stringent as the proximity demanded by, for example, the *res gestae* doctrine . . . The basis of the rule is not that the statement must have been forced from the witness by an irresistible pressure of events perceived by him but simply that he must have been able to remember the situation at the time the statement was made" (Howard 1972 *Crim LR* 351 352–3).

[50] *Doe d Church & Phillips v Perkins* 1790 3 Term Rep 749 753, 100 ER 838.

[51] See generally Wigmore para 745 and Cleary (ed) *McCormick on Evidence* 4 ed (1984) para 301.

[52] A period of twenty-two days between the event and the recording thereof has been accepted: *R v Fotheringham* 1975 *Crim LR* 710. In *R v Isaacs* 1916 TPD 390 a period of eight days was accepted. At 392 the court concluded that if the recording was made "so soon afterwards as to render it probable, in the opinion of the court, that the facts which it purports to narrate, were still fresh in the memory of the person writing them down, or reading them, as the case may be, then the witness is allowed to refresh his memory".

[53] Newark & Samuels 1978 *Crim LR* 409 remark as follows: "In the case of detailed or humdrum matters, e g a previously unknown car or telephone number, only a record made instantaneously or at least within a few minutes might be sufficient. In other cases a record made the same day may be acceptable. In some other cases where the information is either straightforward and/or unusual and striking it will fade much less quickly and a record made the following day or even some days later may be regarded as sufficiently contemporaneous."

recollection recorded.[54] This rule may, however, be departed from where the opponent fails to object[55] or where it can be shown that the original has been lost or destroyed.[56] Where the original is not used the accuracy of the copy or extract must be proved.[57] Where present recollection revived is present the approach is more flexible because memory, and not the document, is seen as the "source" of the oral evidence.[58]

24 5 6 Production[59] of the document[60] A document used to refresh memory whilst the witness is in the witness-box must[61] be made available to the court and the opponent in order to enable them to inspect it.[62] A witness is thus precluded from using a document which he refuses to produce.[63] Where the document is privileged the holder of the privilege has two options: either waive the privilege so that the document can be produced (and the witness may use it) or claim privilege so that the document cannot be produced (and the witness may not use it).[64] The opposing party may waive his right of access to a document used by a witness. Furthermore, a court has a discretion to restrict cross-examination, relating to the produced document, to those parts which were used by the witness.[65]

The effect of the Constitutional Court's decision in *Shabalala v Attorney-General & others*[66] must be noted. The prosecution no longer has a "blanket docket privilege" on statements obtained from (potential) state witnesses.[67] In most instances the defence will already be in possession of the statement of the witness.

---

[54] *S v Bergh* 1976 4 SA 857 (A) 865; *Doe d Church & Phillips v Perkins* 1790 3 Term Rep 749 753, 100 ER 838; *R v Harvey* 1869 11 Cox CC 546; *R v Alward* 1976 32 CCC 2nd 416; *R v Jonathan* 1947 1 PH K4 (C).

[55] *R v Mohafa* 1950 2 PH H103 (E). In *R v Carr* 1949 4 SA 132 (T) 134 it was said: "If defending counsel objected to the extracts and wanted the original register, they would no doubt have been produced. I cannot agree that it is legitimate for them to keep a point of this sort up their sleeve to be taken on appeal."

[56] *Burton v Plummer* (1934) 2 A & E 341, 11 ER 132.

[57] *Topham v McGregor* (1844) 1 Car & Kir 320, 174 ER 829.

[58] Tapper *Cross and Tapper on Evidence* 8 ed (1995) 288.

[59] "Production" here is "used in the sense of 'made available', not 'put in as an exhibit' ": Buzzard, May & Howard *Phipson on Evidence* 13 ed (1982) paras 33–42n60. See also *De Bruin v Rex* 1945 2 PH H255 (T). There is a rule of practice — well illustrated in *R v Smit* 1946 AD 862 867 — in terms of which a memorandum from which a witness refreshed his memory in court may, in the absence of an objection and for the sake of convenience, be utilized as a convenient record of the evidence of the witness. But this rule of practice does not elevate the memorandum to the status of evidence.

[60] See generally Ratushny "Basic Problems in Examination and Cross-Examination" 1974 *Canadian Bar Rev* 209 215.

[61] Wigmore para 753(4) seems to take the view that production is essential only if the opponent so requests. This approach might be valid in an accusatorial system, where both parties are equally familiar with the rules of trial, but is certainly invalid in respect of, e g, an undefended accused: see generally *R v Elijah* 1963 3 SA 86 (SR) 89C.

[62] *R v Elijah* supra; *MacDuff & Co (in Liquidation) v Johannesburg Consolidated Co Ltd* 1923 TPD 318 319.

[63] *Michael v Additional Magistrate of Johannesburg & Attorney-General* 1926 TPD 331 333; *R v Grieve* 1947 2 SA 264 (T); *R v Scoble* 1958 3 SA 668 (N) 669; *R v Alward* 1976 32 CCC 2d 416; *R v Smith (No 2)* 1938 71 CCC 394; *R v Bass* 1953 1 All ER 1064. Production of the document is not confined to past recollection recorded: *R v Elijah* 1963 3 SA 86 (SR).

[64] See generally *Bowers v Friedlander* 1982 2 SA 504 (C) 511F–G.

[65] *R v Bass* 1953 1 All ER 1064 1068A; *R v Scoble* 1958 3 SA 668 (N) 670D; *R v Grieve* 1947 2 SA 264 (T) 266.

[66] 1995 2 SACR 761 (CC).

[67] See § 11 5 above.

However, the statement must still be made available to the court if used to "refresh memory" — irrespective of the fact whether present recollection revived or past recollection record is at hand.

24 7 THE PROBATIVE VALUE OF A DOCUMENT USED TO REFRESH MEMORY

The probative value of a document used to refresh memory depends upon the existence of one of three possible situations: present recollection revived, past recollection recorded, and the conduct of the cross-examiner.

24 7 1 Present recollection revived   Oral evidence is received in this instance.[68] The memory is merely "triggered" and the witness testifies on his own "mental power".[69]

24 7 2 Past recollection recorded   In § 24 2 above it was pointed out that in *S v Bergh*[70] our Appellate Division seems to have acknowledged the validity of accepting the viewpoint that the document is received as evidence in the case of past recollection recorded. The unequivocal acceptance of this viewpoint would neither conflict with the hearsay rule nor amount to a subtle or disguised circumvention of the rule against previous consistent statements.[71]

24 7 3 Conduct of the cross-examiner   The course taken in cross-examination can also determine the value of the document. If the cross-examiner confines his questions to those parts of the document used by the witness to refresh his memory, the document does not become evidence.[72] But if he cross-examines on other parts of the document, he "lets in the whole, and that part referred to by the witness originally also becomes evidence".[73]

The rationale for this dual approach adopted by the common law is explained as follows by Newark & Samuels:[74]

"When a cross-examiner confines his cross-examination to the part of the document used by the witness to refresh his memory he is merely testing the genuine nature of the refreshment of the witness's memory or challenging the accuracy of the past recollection

---

[68] See § 24 2 above.

[69] Walker 1975 6 *Cumberland LR* 471 474.

[70] 1976 4 SA 857 (A) 865C–D.

[71] Schmidt 303; Van der Merwe *Die Geheueverfrissingsprosedure* 245: "Anders as in die geval van herinnerings-herlewing, kan daar nie in die geval van herinneringsherhaling beweer word dat die bewys van die inhoud van die aantekening met die gemeenregtelike reël teen vorige ooreenstemmende verklarings bots nie. Daar is geen risiko van selfstawing nie. Die skriftelike stuk is die enigste bron." See also § 9 10 above. There will also be no infringement of the hearsay rule as the "witness" is available for cross-examination. See further ch 13 above.

[72] See generally *R v Fenlon* 1980 71 Cr App Rep 307 312; *Estate Parry v Murray* 1961 3 SA 487 (T) 492; *R v Rose* 1937 AD 467 471; *R v Elijah* 1963 3 SA 86 (SR) 88H–89A; *R v Wilken* 1939 EDL 151 154; *De Bruin v Rex* 1945 2 PH H255 (T); *R v Isaacs* 1916 TPD 390 392; *Gregory v Tavernor* 1833 6 Car and P 280, 172 ER 1241.

[73] *Estate Parry v Murray* supra 292A. There is also another rule, independent of the one under discussion, which states that if a party calls for and inspects a document held by the other, he is bound to put it in evidence if required to do so: *Senat v Senat* 1965 2 All ER 505.

[74] 1978 *Crim LR* 408 411.

recorded and deposed to by the witness. But when he cross-examines on other parts of the document he is attempting to elicit testimony from the witness, or to discredit him by means of a document that is not before the jury as evidence in the case. The argument is that it would be wrong to allow the cross-examiner to make use of the document in a way quite unrelated to the testing of the refreshment of memory, and then to complain about being required to put the document in evidence."

A document which is received in evidence in the manner explained above has extremely limited evidential value.[75] It can merely show consistency or inconsistency, and cannot corroborate the witness.[76] The general rule against self-corroboration remains intact.[77]

24 8   REMARKS IN CONCLUSION

The present South African rules governing refreshing of memory are the products of a trial system which seeks to maintain orality and which views "refreshing of memory" as a method of receiving oral evidence — even in those instances where the witness has no independent recollection and relies exclusively on his recorded recollection. This fiction should be rejected.

It is true that the common-law procedure of "refreshing the memory" of a witness should be understood in the light of the principle of orality and the evolution of the accusatorial trial system with its concomitant exclusionary rules of evidence, which largely came about as a result of trial by jury, the doctrine of precedent and the desire to protect the adversary. But it is also submitted that the distinction between present recollection revived and past recollection recorded can be easily reconciled with the fundamental rules and principles of the common-law trial and evidentiary system. It is not only a matter of employing accurate terminology. It is also a matter of establishing a sound analytical framework to solve practical problems.

---

[75] *R v Wilken* 1939 EDL 151.
[76] *R v Virgo* 1978 67 Cr App R 323.
[77] See also § 9 10 above and § 30 3 1 below.

CHAPTER 25

IMPEACHING THE CREDIBILITY OF A WITNESS

S E van der Merwe and S S Terblanche

25 1 INTRODUCTION

The credibility of a witness is mainly impeached through cross-examination — a procedure that has already been discussed in §§ 18 6–18 7 above and which — in § 1 5 2 above — was identified as an essential feature of the common-law adversarial trial system. In certain circumstances it is also possible for a party to lead evidence which — though not directly relevant to the *facta probanda* — is nevertheless received on account of the impact that it may have on the credibility of an opponent's witness who has testified on matters relating to the *facta probanda*. It is, furthermore, possible that a party may experience the real need to attack the credibility of her *own* witness. May she do so through cross-examination? May she adduce evidence to contradict the evidence of a prior witness called by her?

The purpose of the present chapter is to identify and explain principles and rules which govern the situation where impeachment of the credibility of an opponent's witness as well as one's own witness is attempted through cross-examination or the leading of evidence, or cross-examination as well as the leading of evidence. It is necessary to distinguish between impeachment of the credibility of an opponent's witness and that of one's own witness: different rules come into play.

25 2 IMPEACHING THE CREDIBILITY OF AN OPPONENT'S WITNESS

Section 190(1) of the CPA provides, inter alia, that a party in criminal proceedings may impeach the credibility of any witness called against such party. In terms of this section it may done in any *manner* in which — and by any *evidence* by which — the credibility of such witness might on 30 May 1961 have been impeached by such party. Section 42 of the CPEA has a similar effect. A South African court must therefore apply the common law as it stood on 30 May 1961. The common-law methods and means of impeaching the credibility of an *opponent's* witness — as well as the applicable rules and principles — are set out in §§ 25 2 1–25 2 5 below. The rules and principles as set out in these paragraphs are really refinements of and limitations on a party's right to cross-examine and adduce evidence.

25 2 1 Cross-examination as to credit or some collateral issue: the finality of the response An answer given by a witness under cross-examination in response to a question which concerns matters which are relevant to the issue may be contradicted by other evidence. But if an answer is given to a question which is relevant solely to the credit of the witness or some other matter which is collateral, the answer must as a general rule[1] be accepted as final in the sense that the cross-examiner may not adduce evidence to contradict the answer.[2] In *S v Zwane*[3] it was held that a witness could be asked if he has been disbelieved in previous judicial proceedings. But the court also noted as follows:[4]

"If the finding by a previous court on the credibility of a witness whose credibility is sought to be impugned is purely a collateral matter — as it frequently will be — such material can nevertheless be used to cross-examine the witness; but if the witness gives a reply under cross-examination which contradicts the previous finding, or his evidence on the issues in the previous matter, then (always assuming that the previous finding and his previous evidence are not relevant to the issue before the court in the subsequent proceedings) such reply is conclusive and the cross-examiner is neither entitled to adduce evidence, nor is he permitted to put portions of the record of the previous proceedings to the witness, to contradict such reply. The furthest that the cross-examiner could go in the face of a denial . . . would be to show the relevant portion of the previous record to the witness and say: 'Look at this paper: do you still adhere to your answer?' If the witness does adhere to his answer, that is the end of the enquiry . . .."

The rule that an answer given by a witness under cross-examination on a collateral matter is final must be understood in the context of the principle that

---

[1] See §§ 25 2 2 and 25 2 3 below.

[2] *Grant v SA National Trust and Assurance Co Ltd & others* 1948 3 SA 59 (W); *S v ffrench-Beytagh (3)* 1971 4 SA 571 (T); *S v Sinkanka & another* 1963 2 SA 531 (A). The rule does not mean that the court must necessarily accept the truth of the answer given by the witness, nor is the cross-examiner obliged to concede the truth thereof. See Murphy *A Practical Approach to Evidence* 4 ed (1992) 486–7.

[3] 1993 1 SACR 748 (W). See also § 18 6 6 5 above, as well as *S v Damalis* 1984 2 SA 105 (T) and Skeen *SALJ* 431.

[4] At 750*d–e.*

in the course of litigation a proliferation or multiplicity of collateral issues must be avoided — a matter already dealt with in § 5 3 3 above.

The difficulty, of course, is to decide whether an issue is collateral or not. In *Attorney-General v Hitchcock* the following test was suggested:[5]

> "The test whether a matter is collateral or not is this: if the answer of a witness is a matter which you would be allowed on your own part to prove in evidence — if it had such a connection with the issues that you would be allowed to give it in evidence — then it is a matter on which you may contradict him."

It has often been remarked that the exact meaning of "collateral" is not entirely clear. The reason is that the meaning of "collateral" is difficult to describe in the abstract, and concrete application of the term is only possible by relying on "relevance" in the context of the specific facts of the case: "*Relevance to the issue before the court determines whether or not evidence is collateral, and what is relevant depends on the facts of each case*".[6]

In *R v Marsh*[7] a witness for the prosecution denied under cross-examination that he had threatened the accused. The trial court denied the accused an opportunity to adduce evidence to contradict the denial. The court of appeal did not agree. An integral part of the accused's defence was that he had every reason to believe that the witness had intended to attack him. The issue was therefore not a collateral one — and the accused should have been allowed to adduce evidence in an attempt to contradict the denial.[8] *Wood v Van Rensburg*,[9] on the other hand, provides an example of a case where a party was irregularly permitted by the trial court to rebut answers which the witness had given under cross-examination on collateral matters. The questions which the plaintiff had put were admissible, but "not material to the issue".[10] Their sole relevance was to assail the credit of the witness. It was held that the trial court had erred by allowing rebutting evidence (taken by means of interrogatories) in contradiction of the defendant's answers: having regard to the facts of the case,[11] such evidence could have made no real probative contribution as regards the issues. It merely involved general credibility and caused the court to get side-tracked into collateral matters. *Wood v Van Rensburg* should be understood in the light of the following remarks by Lawrence J in *Harris v Tippett*:[12]

> "I will permit questions to be put to a witness as to any improper conduct of which he may have been guilty, for the purpose of trying his credit; but when those questions are irrelevant to the issue on the record, you cannot call other witnesses to contradict the answer he gives."

---

[5] 1847 1 Exch 91 99.

[6] *S v Zwane* supra 750*g* (emphasis added).

[7] 1986 83 Cr App R 165.

[8] The evidence was also relevant to determine whether the accused or the witness was the aggressor.

[9] 1921 CPD 36.

[10] At 38.

[11] The plaintiff had sued the defendant for an amount due to him as a result of certain building work. The defendant pleaded that at the time of the summons the work had not been completed. At the trial the defendant was cross-examined on the point whether he was legally married and whether he did not have some revolvers in his possession without a permit.

[12] 1811 2 Camp 637.

25 2 2 Cross-examination as to credit and the right to contradict a denial: previous convictions On the basis of the 30 May 1961 provision as contained in s 190(1) of the CPA and s 42 of the CPEA, the credit of an opponent's witness may be impeached with reference to his previous convictions.[13] The witness may be asked whether he has any previous convictions and — in the event of a denial or refusal to admit or answer — the cross-examiner may prove such previous convictions.[14] In the application of this rule it must of course be kept in mind that an accused as a witness in his own defence is entitled to the protection granted to him in terms of local statutory provisions as well as common-law rules.[15] Counsel defending an accused who has a criminal record would normally be wise to steer clear of impeaching the credit of a prosecution witness on the basis of the latter's previous convictions. Such impeachment of the credibility of a prosecution witness would cause the accused to lose the shield of protection which he enjoys in terms of s 197 of the CPA, and the prosecution may then prove the previous convictions of the accused.

25 2 3 Cross-examination as to credit and the right to contradict a denial: bias A witness may be cross-examined on facts which tend to show that she is biased in favour of the party who called her[16] or that she is prejudiced against the case of the cross-examiner,[17] as the case may be. In the event of a denial evidence may be called to contradict her.[18] It is sometimes said that this approach is an exception to the rule that the answer given by a witness under cross-examination in relation to a collateral matter is final. However, it is possible to argue that the matter of bias or prejudice is not really a collateral matter. The presence of bias or prejudice should be brought to the attention of the court in order to enable the court to make a proper assessment of the evidence concerned — and if such prejudice or bias is denied by the witness, the matter should be clarified by adducing evidence. In *Thomas v David*[19] the plaintiff called his female house-keeper, who was one of the attesting witnesses to the defendant's signature on a promissory note. In the course of cross-examination it was alleged that she was the mistress of the plaintiff and regularly slept with him — an allegation which she denied. The defendant was permitted to call a witness to contradict this denial. Coleridge J remarked and held as follows:[20]

---

[13] Section 6 of the English Criminal Procedure Act of 1865 applies.

[14] Any previous conviction can be proved, irrespective of the fact whether it involved dishonesty or not: *Clifford v Clifford* 1961 3 All ER 231.

[15] See ch 6 above.

[16] *Thomas v David* 1836 7 C & P 350.

[17] *R v Phillips* 1936 26 Cr App R 17.

[18] *R v Mendy* 1976 64 Cr App R 17 is a case which seems to go slightly beyond "bias" or "prejudice" as an exception to the general rule. In this case the husband of the accused denied under cross-examination that, whilst waiting outside court to be called as a defence witness, he had been given information as to testimony given by a detective. The Court of Appeal confirmed that it was correct to have allowed evidence in contradiction of this denial as the court (and jury) should not have been kept in ignorance of the alleged behaviour of the husband as a witness.

[19] 1836 7 C & P 350.

[20] As cited by Carter *Cases and Statutes on Evidence* (1981) 208. Cf *Crankshaw v Galloway* 1887 5 SC 202, which is critically discussed by Hoffmann & Zeffertt 468.

"Is it not material to the issue, whether the principal witness who comes to support the plaintiff's case is his kept mistress? If the question had been whether the witness had walked the streets as a common prostitute, I think that would have been collateral to the issue, and that, had the witness denied such a charge, she could not have been contradicted; but here, the question is whether the witness had contradicted such a relation with the plaintiff as might induce her to move readily to conspire with him to support a forgery, just in the same way as if she had been asked if she was the sister or daughter of the plaintiff, and had denied that. I think the contradiction is admissible."

25 2 4 Cross-examination on and proof of a previous inconsistent statement made by an opponent's witness   A witness may be cross-examined with reference to a prior statement made by her and which is inconsistent with her testimony in court.[21] But proof of the prior inconsistent statement is permitted only if it is relevant, going beyond mere collateral matters.[22] The statement may be proved if the witness denies having made it. The rules and principles which govern the proof and evidential value of a previous inconsistent statement are set out in § 25 4 below. The rules and principles set out in § 25 4 below must, however, also be read in conjunction with s 5 of the English Criminal Procedure Act of 1865. Section 5 of this Act applies to criminal as well as civil proceedings in South Africa. It not only governs the situation where an opponent's witness is cross-examined with reference to a prior inconsistent written statement but also regulates the procedure to be followed in proving such a statement. Section 5 of the English Criminal Procedure Act of 1865 provides as follows:

"A witness may be cross-examined as to previous statements made by him in writing or reduced to writing relative to the subject-matter of the indictment or proceeding, without such writing being shown to him; but if it is intended to contradict such witness by the writing, his attention must, before such contradictory proof can be given, be called to those parts of the writing which are to be used for the purpose of so contradicting him; provided always, that it shall be competent for the judge, at any time during the trial, to require the production of the writing for his inspection, and he may thereupon make such use of it for the purposes of the trial as he may think fit."

The fact that the presiding officer "may make such use of the statement for the purpose at the trial as he may think fit" does not entitle the presiding officer to treat the contents of the statement as evidence.[23]

25 2 5 Calling a witness to testify on veracity[24]   There is an archaic rule — which has some historical link with the ancient system of calling compurgators[25] — in terms of which a witness may be called to say that he would not believe the testimony of the opponent's witness under oath. The witness is in fact called upon to express an opinion on the credibility of the opponent's witness. The purpose

---

[21] See ss 4 and 5 of the English Criminal Procedure Act of 1865. These sections apply by virtue of the provisions of s 190(1) of the CPA and s 42 of the CPEA.

[22] Both ss 4 and 5 of the English Criminal Procedure Act of 1865 require that the previous statement must be "relative to the subject-matter of the indictment or proceedings".

[23] See generally *R v Birch* 1924 18 Cr App R 172. See further § 25 4 *(e)* below.

[24] *R v Adamstein* 1937 CPD 331; *R v Richardson & Longman* 1968 2 All ER 761.

[25] See generally § 1 3 2 above.

of the evidence is to discredit all the evidence given by the opponent's witness. The opinion amounts to evidence of bad character. The witness must base his opinion on his own personal knowledge of the veracity of the impugned witness and may also refer to the latter's general reputation for veracity. But in neither instance may the witness refer to specific incidents. It can be argued that abolition of this rule would not leave the law of evidence any poorer.

25 3 IMPEACHING THE CREDIBILITY OF YOUR OWN WITNESS[26]

The general rule is that a party is not permitted to impeach the credibility of a witness called by her. There are various historical reasons for this rule.[27] The early procedure of calling up so-called "compurgators" or "oath-helpers"[28] is probably the most important historical reason. This procedure gave rise to the idea that a party vouches for or guarantees the credibility of the witness called by him.[29] The procedure of calling an oath-helper would have made very little sense if a party could be permitted to contradict the very oath-helper called by him. However, the idea that a witness called by a party should not be contradicted by such a party was carried into early English trial procedure when witnesses were called upon to testify as to the events and not merely to confirm a party's oath. In 1681 North LCJ said (rather rudely, it seems):[30]

"Look you, Mr Colledge, I will tell you something for the law and set you right. Whatsoever witness you call, you call them as witnesses to testify the truth for you; and if you ask them any questions, you must take what they have said as truth; . . . let him answer you if he will, but you must not afterwards go to disprove him."

The rule against impeachment of your own witness became part of the adversarial system: it was accepted that a party had a right to cross-examine an opponent's witness but could as a general rule not cross-examine a witness called by herself. The "modern" justification for the rule — though not beyond criticism — was set out as follows by Wessels J in *R v Wellers*:[31]

"It appears to me that the first principle as to why a party is not entitled to cross-examine his own witness as being adverse is that if this were allowed, a party may find that the witness is not giving evidence in accordance with his anticipation, and then in order to bring the witness back to what he conceives to be the true statement, or the statement he happens to have before him, he may put leading questions and so get the witness to give evidence in accordance with counsel's brief. *This the court cannot allow.* On the other hand, you may have a case where the witness in the box is giving the true statement but the counsel examining him is disappointed at the trend of his evidence, and wishes to bring him away from the true story which he is actually telling, in order, either by browbeating or confusing him, to throw doubt on his evidence. If, therefore, counsel were allowed to cross-examine his own witness the court might be led to doubt evidence which is really true."

---

[26] See Engelbrecht 1988 *De Rebus* 105 for a useful discussion of this topic.

[27] See generally Marler *The Hostile Witness in English and South African Law of Evidence* (unpublished LLM thesis, University of Stellenbosch 1990) 14–26.

[28] See generally § 1 3 2 n 23 above.

[29] See generally *Chambers v Mississippi* 410 US 284 296 (1973) and § 25 3 4 below.

[30] 1681 8 How St Tr 549 (cited by Marler *The Hostile Witness in English and South African Law of Evidence* 17).

[31] 1918 TPD 234 237 (emphasis added).

But in certain circumstances a party may attempt to contradict her own witness by calling another witness; she may also prove a previous inconsistent statement against her own witness; and — in one exceptional situation — she may even cross-examine her own witness. These circumstances and the applicable rules are set out in §§ 25 3 1–25 3 3 below and must be seen as exceptions to the general rule that a party may not impeach the credibility of her own witness. The impact of constitutional provisions on this general rule is — as far as an accused is concerned — examined in § 25 3 4 below.

25 3 1 Calling another witness A party may always call a witness to contradict the evidence given by a witness who was also called by that party.[32] However, the second witness — like the first witness and all other witnesses in every trial — may, of course, only give admissible evidence. Thus, in *S v Nel*[33] Marais J agreed with the trial court's refusal to allow defence counsel to lead psychiatric evidence: the sole purpose of the evidence — which was really expert opinion evidence which was supererogatory and therefore inadmissible[34] — was to show that a defence witness who in her testimony had contradicted aspects of the accused's testimony was "mildly to moderately retarded" and therefore likely to "clamp up" under the strain of testifying in court. It was held that intellectual and psychological disabilities of a relatively normal kind and which merely affect personality, powers of articulation and ability to recall can be assessed reasonably adequately by the court while the witness is testifying. Marais J noted the obvious admissibility of medical evidence of a *physical affliction* which adversely affects the ability of the witness to testify accurately and reliably. For example, is the previous witness so shortsighted that he could not possibly have identified a person who was 100 metres away at the time?[35] Marais J also noted that although expert evidence of *mental abnormality* could be used to impeach the credibility of the first witness, it could not be said that "the grounds upon which it was sought to lead the evidence of the psychiatrist in the case before us are fairly comparable".[36] The principles relied upon in *Nel* supra would, of course, also apply to the situation where an attempt is made to impeach the credibility of an opponent's witness.[37]

---

[32] *Ewer v Ambrose* 1825 3 B & C 746. In this case Littledale J said (as cited by Carter *Cases and Statutes on Evidence* 195): "Where a witness is called by a party to prove his case, and he disproves that case . . . the party is still at liberty to prove his case by other witnesses. It would be a great hardship if the rule were otherwise, for if a party had four witnesses upon whom he relied to prove his case, it would be very hard that, by calling first the one who happened to disprove it, he should be deprived of the testimony of the other three . . . The order in which the witnesses happen to be called ought not, therefore, to make any difference . . .." The mere fact that a witness has failed to support the case of the party who called him does not entitle the court to disregard the evidence of the witness on this ground alone. See *R v Ratner* 1910 TPD 1327 and Engelbrecht 1988 *De Rebus* 105.

[33] 1990 2 SACR 136 (C). See also § 5 3 3 above.

[34] See § 8 3 above.

[35] At 143*d–e*.

[36] At 114*c*.

[37] See *Toohey v Metropolitan Police Commissioner* 1965 1 All ER 506, where it was held that medical evidence (tendered by the defence) was wrongly excluded as such evidence related to the mental illness which could have shown that the witness (the complainant) was incapable of giving reliable evidence.

The fact that a party may call another witness to contradict her own previous witness or otherwise impeach the latter's credibility is a clear indication that the idea that a party somehow "guarantees" the credibility of his witness is based on a fiction.

25 3 2 Proving a previous inconsistent statement against your own witness At common law a party did not have an unqualified right to impeach the credibility of his own witness by proving an inconsistent statement made by the latter.[38] The position was changed by s 57 of the General Law Amendment Act 46 of 1935 and is presently governed by s 190(2) of the CPA and s 7 of the CPEA. The latter section — which is substantially similar to s 190(2) of the CPA — provides as follows:

> "Any party who has called a witness who has given evidence in any civil proceedings (whether that witness is or is not, in the opinion of the person presiding at such proceedings, adverse to the party calling him) may, after the said party or the person so presiding has asked the witness whether he has or has not previously made a statement with which his evidence in the said proceedings is inconsistent, and after sufficient particulars of the alleged previous statement to designate the occasion when it was made, have been mentioned to the witness, prove that he previously made a statement with which his said evidence is inconsistent."

The most important rules and principles which regulate proof of a previous inconsistent statement are set out in § 25 4 below. The fact that a party has proved a previous inconsistent statement against his own witness does not automatically entitle the party to embark upon cross-examination of the witness concerned: cross-examination can take place only once the party has successfully applied to the court to have her witness declared hostile — a procedure which is dealt with in § 25 3 3 below.

Neither s 190(2) of the CPA nor s 7 of the CPEA requires that the statement should be relevant "to the subject-matter of the indictment or proceeding".[39] Both these sections also make it clear that proof of a previous inconsistent statement against a party's own witness may proceed regardless of the fact whether the witness is or is not, in the opinion of the court, adverse to the party who called him.

25 3 3 Cross-examination of your own witness: the hostile witness[40] An application to have a witness declared hostile may be brought in the course of evidence in chief or re-examination. The purpose of such an application is to obtain the right to cross-examine one's own witness in the same way as if the latter had been called by an opponent. The decision to bring such an application is a tactical one, and such an application may at times be necessary despite the fact that the credibility of the witness has been destroyed by proof of a previous inconsistent

---

[38] See generally Cross & Tapper *Cross on Evidence* 8 ed (1995) 312–13 for a discussion of the early common-law position.

[39] Cf s 5 of the English Procedure Act of 1865 as cited in § 5 2 4 above and which applies in respect of proof of a previous inconsistent statement made by an opponent.

[40] The common law applies as a result of the provisions of s 190(1) of the CPA and s 42 of the CPEA.

statement.[41] The party concerned must weigh the risks: would an opportunity to cross-examine promote her case? or would it merely give the witness a further opportunity to give evidence supporting the opponent's case?

"Hostile" is not the equivalent of "adverse" or "unfavourable".[42] The party bringing the application has the burden[43] of satisfying the court that the witness is "not desirous of telling the truth at the instance of the party calling him"[44] — an antagonistic *animus* must be proved.[45] The test is a subjective one.[46] The party seeking a declaration of hostility has a difficult task: he must prove that the witness has an antagonistic *animus* so that he may cross-examine him — and yet if he could cross-examine, he would have a better chance of exposing the required *animus*.[47]

The mere fact that a party's own witness has given evidence contradicting what was expected of him does not *per se* render him hostile. Proof of a previous inconsistent statement is merely *one* of the factors to be considered.[48] In *City Panel Beaters v Bhana & Sons* Findlay AJ said that it "may well be that the nature of the statement and the inconsistency are such that the inference of hostility is very strong and that no more is required to establish this".[49] In *S v Steyn en andere* it was also said that the nature of the contradictions ("weersprekings") can create a strong probability of hostility.[50] In this case Le Roux J also referred to the "demeanour" test as being decisive: can hostility be inferred from the behaviour of the witness in the witness-box?[51] Further factors — none of which is necessarily decisive — are the relationship between the witness and parties involved in the dispute;[52] the fact that the witness is a prosecution witness who was warned in terms of s 204 of the CPA and who therefore has prospects of receiving indemnity;[53] the fact that a witness has deceived a party into calling him as a witness.[54] This is not an exhaustive list, as is evident from the following remarks by Findlay AJ:[55]

"[I]n order to be satisfied that a witness is hostile, the court will evaluate that witness's stance towards the party calling him. It is clearly undesirable to lay down any rigid formula to be applied, since what is under consideration is, by its very nature, the attitude of the witness, which obviously requires an entirely subjective assessment of that witness in the given circumstances of the case before the court. Accordingly the general guidelines derived from the authorities such as the witness being shown to have made a previous inconsistent statement, his demeanour, his position towards the party calling him, his relationship to any party and what are loosely described as 'the general circumstances of

---

[41] See generally *S v Steyn en andere* 1987 1 SA 353 (W) 355C–D.

[42] *S v Steyn en andere* supra 355F.

[43] *S v Steyn en andere* supra 358G–H.

[44] A test put forward by Stephen *Digest of the Law of Evidence* 12 ed Article 147 — as cited by Hoffmann & Zeffertt 454 and accepted and applied in *S v Steyn en andere* supra 357H.

[45] Scoble *The Law of Evidence* 3 ed (1952) 352.

[46] *S v Steyn en andere* supra 355H.

[47] Scoble *The Law of Evidence* 352.

[48] *Jabaar v South African Railways and Harbours* 1982 4 SA 552 (C).

[49] 1985 2 SA 155 (D) 160C–D.

[50] 1987 1 SA 353 (W) 357C–D.

[51] At 357A–B.

[52] *Jabaar v South African Railways and Harbours* supra 555D; *S v Steyn en andere* supra 358F.

[53] *S v Steyn en andere* supra 357F.

[54] *S v Wellers* 1918 TPD 234.

[55] *City Panel Beaters v Bhana & Sons* supra 160H–J.

the case' (which necessarily preserves a measure of flexibility in the enquiry) are no more than factors, no one of which will necessarily be decisive, which the court will take into account when deciding the question.''

25 3 4 The rule that a party may not cross-examine its own witness unless declared hostile: a constitutional perspective In terms of s 25(3)(d) of the interim Constitution an accused shall have the right to a fair trial, which shall include the right to challenge evidence. The right to challenge evidence includes the right to cross-examine.[56] The following question arises: does the constitutional right to cross-examine have any impact on the common-law rule that a party — and in this instance it is the accused — may not cross-examine his own witness unless declared hostile?

In *Chambers v Mississippi*[57] the accused had called one McDonald to introduce the latter's written confession to the crime with which the accused was charged. This was duly done. But under cross-examination by the state, McDonald repudiated the confession and asserted an alibi. The accused thereupon sought permission to cross-examine McDonald with regard to the circumstances of his repudiation of the written confession and the alibi as asserted, as well as three other oral confessions allegedly made by McDonald. The trial court refused to give such permission. The refusal was based on a Mississippi rule prohibiting a party from impeaching his own witness unless found "adverse". The accused was convicted. On appeal, the Mississippi Supreme Court confirmed the conviction and noted, inter alia, that the testimony of McDonald was not adverse to the accused as McDonald had at no stage "pointed a finger" (incriminated) the accused. But the Supreme Court of the USA did not agree. It held that — having regard to the circumstances of the case — the accused had been denied his constitutional due process right to a fair trial, including the right to confront and cross-examine. The following remarks and findings are significant:[58]

"In this case, petitioner's request to cross-examine McDonald was denied on the basis of a Mississippi common-law rule that a party may not impeach his own witness. The rule rests on the presumption — without regard to the circumstances of the particular case — that a party who calls a witness 'vouches for his credibility . . .' Although the historical origins of the 'voucher' rule are uncertain, it appears to be a remnant of primitive English trial practice in which 'oath-takers' or 'compurgators' were called to stand behind a particular party's position in any controversy. Their assertions were strictly partisan and, quite unlike witnesses in criminal trials today, their role bore little relation to the impartial ascertainment of the facts . . . Whatever validity the 'voucher' rule may have once enjoyed, and apart from whatever usefulness it retains today in the civil trial process, it bears little present relationship to the realities of the criminal process. It might have been logical for the early common law to require a party to vouch for the credibility of witnesses he brought before the jury to affirm his veracity. Having selected them especially for that purpose, the party might reasonably be expected to stand firmly behind their testimony. But in modern criminal trials, defendants are rarely able to select their witnesses: they must take them where they find them. Moreover, as applied in this case, the 'voucher' rule's impact was doubly harmful to Chambers' efforts to develop his defense. Not only was he precluded

---

[56] See generally Van der Merwe 1995 *Obiter* 194 196.
[57] 410 US 284 (1973).
[58] At 296–8 (emphasis in the original).

from cross-examining McDonald, but, as the State conceded at oral argument, he was also restricted in the scope of his direct examination by the rule's corollary requirement that the party calling the witness is bound by anything he might say. He was, therefore, effectively prevented from exploring the circumstances of McDonald's three prior oral confessions and from challenging the renunciation of the written confession . . . In this Court, Mississippi has not sought to defend the rule or explain its underlying rationale. Nor has it contended that its rule should override the accused's right of confrontation. Instead, it argues that there is no incompatibility between the rule and Chambers' rights because no right of confrontation exists unless the testifying witness is 'adverse' to the accused. The State's brief asserts that the 'right of confrontation applies to witnesses *'against'* an accused'. Relying on the trial court's determination that McDonald was not adverse, and on the State Supreme Court's holding that McDonald did not 'point the finger at Chambers', that State contends that Chambers' constitutional right was not involved . . . The argument that McDonald's testimony was not 'adverse' to, or 'against', Chambers is not convincing. The State's proof at trial excluded the theory that more than one person participated in the shooting of Liberty. To the extent that McDonald's sworn confession tended to incriminate him, it tended also to exculpate Chambers. And, in the circumstances of this case, McDonald's retraction inculpated Chambers to the same extent that it exculpated McDonald. It can hardly be disputed that McDonald's testimony was in fact seriously adverse to Chambers. The availability of the right to confront and to cross-examine those who give damaging testimony against the accused has never been held to depend on whether the witness was initially put on the stand by the accused or by the State. We reject the notion that a right of such substance in the criminal process may be governed by that technicality or by any narrow and unrealistic definition of the word 'against'. The 'voucher' rule, as applied in this case, plainly interfered with Chambers' right to defend against the State's charges."

The Supreme Court of the USA did not declare the Mississippi rule unconstitutional, but held that, as applied to the facts of the case, it had violated the constitutional rights of the accused.

It is submitted that in our law the rule that an accused may not cross-examine his defence witness unless declared hostile may have to be reconsidered in the light of the accused's constitutional right to cross-examine. The constitutional right to a fair trial should be the ultimate test and not the question of whether the accused has proved the defence witness "hostile" in the technical sense of the word.

25 4   RULES AND PRINCIPLES WHICH GOVERN THE PROOF AND PROBATIVE VALUE OF A PREVIOUS INCONSISTENT STATEMENT

The following rules and principles govern the proof or probative value of previous inconsistent statements — irrespective of whether one is dealing with an opponent's witness or one's own witness:

(a) The witness must — at some stage prior to the attempt to prove her previous inconsistent statement — be asked whether she has made a prior statement inconsistent with her testimony in court.

(b) Proof of a previous inconsistent statement may also take place only once the witness has been given sufficient particulars of the alleged previous inconsistent statement to designate the occasion on which it was made.[59]

---

[59] *Oosthuizen v Stanley* 1938 AD 322 332–3.

(c) The witness must be given an opportunity of explaining the inconsistency if she admits having made the statement.

(d) If the witness denies having made the statement, the statement — whether oral or in writing — must be proved in a proper manner, for example, through witnesses who heard or recorded it.[60] It is not properly proved if read from the bar.[61]

(e) Proof of a previous inconsistent statement merely has an impact on credibility. It proves inconsistency. The contents of the statement can never[62] be elevated to the status of "evidence"[63] despite the fact that the statement is received and marked as an exhibit.

(f) The degree to which proof of a previous inconsistent statement affects the credibility of the witness depends upon the facts.[64] What is the nature of the inconsistency? And what is the extent thereof?

(g) A witness who is confronted with a previous inconsistent statement should not be urged to adhere to her previous statement: she should be called upon to speak the truth.[65]

---

[60] *R v Kupeka & others* 1957 1 SA 399 (A).

[61] *R v Tladi* 1924 CPD 545.

[62] Unless it can be received in terms of Part VI of the CPEA as read with s 222 of the CPA.

[63] *R v Beukman* 1950 4 SA 261 (O).

[64] *International Tobacco Co (SA) Ltd v United Tobacco Co (South) Ltd (1)* 1955 2 SA 1 (W) 8.

[65] *S v N* 1979 4 SA 632 (O). At any rate, if it is an own witness who has not been declared hostile, any form of cross-examination is prohibited.

SECTION H

PROOF WITHOUT EVIDENCE

CHAPTER 26

FORMAL ADMISSIONS

PJ Schwikkard and S E van der Merwe

26 1   INTRODUCTION

The general rule is that all relevant facts must be proved on the basis of evidence presented by the parties. However, there are several exceptions to this rule. Evidence need not be adduced to prove a fact where a formal admission is made by one of the parties or where the court takes judicial notice of a fact.[1] The application of a presumption of law may also have the effect of dispensing with the necessity to adduce evidence pertaining to a particular fact.[2]

26 2   THE NATURE AND RATIONALE OF FORMAL ADMISSIONS

For the purposes of trial a party may formally admit one or more facts. These facts then no longer need to be proved by her adversary.[3] Time and costs are saved.

A formal admission can only be made in respect of an adversary's claim. A formal admission by X implies that X places beyond dispute a fact alleged by Y. The formal admission is detrimental to X and to the advantage of Y, as Y no longer has to prove the fact admitted by X. In other words, X's admission supports Y's case. The court in *S v Dingoos*[4] pointed out that a formal admission is

---

[1] See ch 27 below.
[2] See chs 28 and 29 below.
[3] See *S v Daniels* 1983 3 SA 275 (A).
[4] 1980 1 SA 595 (O). See also generally *S v Martin* 1996 1 SACR 172 (W) 174.

concerned with the acceptance of a fact which has been alleged by the state and not by the accused herself. In *S v Kuzwayo*[5] the court held that a party cannot employ a formal admission as a means of getting on record something which the opponent does not propose to make part of his case.

26 2 1 The distinction between formal and informal admissions   It is necessary to distinguish between formal and informal admissions.[6] An informal admission is usually made out of court and merely constitutes an item of evidence which can be contradicted or explained away. The weight accorded by the court to an informal admission will vary according to the surrounding circumstances.[7] In contrast a formal admission is generally made in the pleadings or in court and is considered to be "conclusive proof" of the fact admitted. Formal admissions are binding on their makers and cannot be withdrawn or contradicted unless certain legal requirements have been satisfied.[8] But the maker of an informal admission is always free to lead evidence to contradict such an admission or explain it away.

Whilst formal admissions serve to narrow down the issues, informal admissions frequently give rise to additional issues, for example, the question whether it was made freely and voluntarily.[9]

A party must intend to make a formal admission and the existence of the requisite intention will be determined by means of a subjective test. In contrast the maker of an informal admission need not even be aware that she is making an admission.[10]

26 3   THE INTENTION OF THE MAKER

Clearly a formal admission has important and serious evidential implications for its maker. Consequently, in both civil and criminal proceedings the courts require that before an admission is treated as a formal admission the maker must intend the admission to be an admission of a fact which she does not wish to dispute. In *AA Mutual Insurance Association Ltd v Biddulph*[11] Trollip JA held that "it must clearly and unequivocally appear from the pleadings that the alleged admission has been made expressly, or by necessary implication, or according to rule 22(3) by omitting to deny or deal with the relevant allegation of fact in the plaintiffs claim".[12]

---

[5] 1964 3 SA 55 (N).
[6] See also § 16 1 above.
[7] See Murphy *A Practical Approach to Evidence* 4 ed (1992) 218.
[8] See § 26 4 1 below.
[9] See § 16 2 above.
[10] See *Naik v Pillay's Trustee* 1923 AD 471; Wigmore para 1049.
[11] 1976 1 SA 725 (A) at 375.
[12] See also *Gordon v Tarnow* 1947 3 SA 525 (A); *Rance v Union Mercantile Co Ltd* 1922 AD 312. A similarly cautious approach is adopted in criminal cases. See, e g, *R v Van der Merwe* 1952 1 SA 143 (SWA); *S v Mavundla* 1976 4 SA 731 (W).

26 4 CIVIL PROCEEDINGS

In civil proceedings a formal admission can be made in the pleadings or at the trial. Section 15 of the CPEA provides that "[i]t shall not be necessary for any party in any civil proceedings to prove, nor shall it be competent for any such party to disprove any fact admitted on the record of such proceedings". Supreme Court rule 22(2) requires the defendant in his plea "either [to] admit or deny or confess and avoid all material facts alleged" by his adversary. This rule must be read together with rule 22(3), which provides that "[e]very allegation of fact in the combined summons or declaration which is not stated in the plea to be denied or to be admitted, shall be deemed to be admitted".

26 4 1 Amendment of pleadings and withdrawal of a formal admission In *Whittaker v Roos*[13] Wessels J held that the court was reluctant to deny a party the opportunity to amend its pleadings. The aim and function of the court was to do justice between the parties. It should therefore not base its decision on admitted facts which it knew to be wrong.[14] The Appellate Division in *S v Daniels*[15] held that in both civil and criminal cases the court has a discretion to relieve a party from the consequences of a formal admission made in error.[16] Before a civil litigant will be granted leave to amend its pleadings it must establish (1) that a *bona fide* mistake was made; and (2) that the amendment will not cause prejudice to the other side which cannot be cured by an appropriate order as to costs. In *President Versekeringsmaatskappy v Moodley*[17] Hiemstra J held that amendments involving a withdrawal of an admission should be treated on the same basis as all other amendments. However, he noted that[18]

> "the withdrawal of an admission is usually more difficult to achieve because (i) it involves a change of front which requires full explanation to convince the court of the *bona fides* thereof, and (ii) it is more likely to prejudice the other party, who had by the admission been led to believe that he need not prove the relevant fact and might, for that reason, have omitted to gather the necessary evidence".

A *bona fide* mistake would, for example, be an error of judgment such as a failure to appreciate the crucial nature of the fact formally admitted.[19] The mere fact that withdrawal may defeat the opponent's claim or defence is not a matter amounting to prejudice in the legal sense.[20]

In *SOS Kinderdorf International v Effie Lentin Architects*[21] the court held that a

---

[13] 1911 TPD 1092 at 1102–3.

[14] See *Frosso Shipping Corporation v Richmond Maritime Corporation* 1985 2 SA 476 (C) 485D, where the court referred with approval to the following passage from *Canaric NO v Shevil's Garage* 1932 TPD 196 at 199: "[The court may] disregard an admission made in the pleadings where it is clear after a full investigation that this admission is contrary to the facts and where injustice will result from an adherence to the admission."

[15] 1983 3 SA 275 (A) at 298H.

[16] See also *Gordon v Tarnow* 1947 3 SA 525 (A).

[17] 1964 4 SA 109 (T).

[18] At 110–11.

[19] See, e g, *Fleet Motors (Pty) Ltd v Epsom Motors (Pty) Ltd* 1960 3 SA 401 (N); *S v Seleke* 1980 3 SA 745 (A).

[20] *Zarug v Parvathie NO* 1962 3 SA 872 (N).

[21] 1993 2 SA 481 (Nm).

party is bound by admissions made by its legal representative (within the limits of counsel's brief) in pleadings or in the drafting of affidavits unless a satisfactory explanation is given to show that the legal representative had no right to make such admissions. However, the court still retains a discretion to grant relief to a party where the pleadings were drafted ineptly or with insufficient precision. See, for example, *Absa Bank Ltd v Blumberg and Wilkinson*,[22] where the court held that Supreme Court rule 22(3), which provides that every allegation of fact "which is not stated in the plea to be denied or to be admitted, shall deemed to be admitted", could not be applied "so as to deprive a party of a defence which is plainly, though perhaps imprecisely, raised on the pleadings".[23]

Once a formal admission has been withdrawn it is no longer binding on the maker. However, it may still be taken into account as an item of evidence.[24] This merely means that the initial making of the formal admission and the circumstances which led to its withdrawal may be considered for whatever probative value they might have.[25]

26 4 2 Procedure for withdrawal A party who wishes to withdraw a formal admission should normally present oral evidence or evidence by way of affidavit in order to satisfy the requirements set out in the previous paragraph.[26] In *Brummund v Brummund's Estate*[27] the withdrawal of a formal admission made in an affidavit during application proceedings was in issue. The court held that "the applicant was obliged to give a full and satisfactory explanation *on affidavit* as to how the admissions came to be made and, if they were made in error, to apply formally for their withdrawal. It was insufficient to instruct counsel to state from the Bar that a mistake had been made and that the admissions would be ignored."[28] Whether an explanation from the Bar might be considered sufficient in certain circumstances remains an open question.[29]

26 5   CRIMINAL PROCEEDINGS: THE COMMON LAW AND SECTION 220 OF THE CPA

At common law the defence was unable to make any formal admissions.[30] However, the present position is regulated by statute. Section 220 of the CPA provides that an accused or her legal adviser may in criminal proceedings admit any fact placed in issue at such proceedings and any such admission shall be "sufficient proof of such fact".[31] Section 220 contains no reference to the state

---

[22] 1995 4 SA 403 (W) at 408I, 409D–E.
[23] See also *Robinson v Randfontein Estates GM Co Ltd* 1925 AD 173 198.
[24] Hoffmann & Zeffertt 429; *S v Mbothoma* 1978 2 SA 530 (O).
[25] Schmidt 196.
[26] *Slion v Couzyn* 1927 TPD 438; Schmidt 196.
[27] 1993 2 SA 494 (Nm).
[28] At 498E (emphasis in the original). See also *Sliom v Couzyn* 1927 TPD 438.
[29] See, e g, *Watersmeet (Pty) Ltd v De Kock* 1960 4 SA 734 (E) 736B.
[30] *R v Thornhill* 1838 8 C & P 575 (173 ER 624).
[31] See further generally Paizes in Du Toit et al *Commentary* 24-79.

because the state can in terms of our common law make a formal admission.[32] This explains why it is in practice accepted that the state can bind itself by way of an admission.[33]

26 5 1 The effect and withdrawal of a formal admission in criminal proceedings
In *S v Seleke*[34] it was held that an admission made in terms of s 220 of the CPA has the effect that the accused cannot later allege that what she admitted must still be proved by the state. The court found that the words "sufficient proof" in s 220 absolved the state from the burden of proving in any other manner the particular fact which has been admitted, unless the state, for special reasons, wished to adduce before the trial court any further evidence concerning the admitted fact. In this decision it was also said that "sufficient proof" does not amount to "conclusive proof" and can later be rebutted by the accused, for example, on the grounds of duress or mistake or by other legally acceptable facts. In *S v Sesetse*[35] it was also held that if the formal admission is still standing at the end of the trial, it becomes "conclusive proof" in respect of the fact to which the admission has reference. A different approach was adopted in *S v Malebo*.[36] In this case Hiemstra CJ expressed the view that in s 220 the legislator meant to refer to conclusive proof because no further proof is required from the state.

Which is the correct approach? This depends on the interpretation given to the words "conclusive proof". If these words are understood as meaning decisive proof of the relevant fact which excludes all other evidence which may disprove it,[37] then the approach taken in *Sesetse* must be favoured, because until the conclusion of the trial the accused may still attempt to rebut the admission.[38]

As in civil cases, once a formal admission has been withdrawn the fact that it was made in the first place will be an item of evidence for consideration by the court. The weight that will attach to such an item of evidence will depend on the accused's explanation as to why it was made.[39]

A formal admission is binding on the maker only in respect of the proceedings at which it is made. However, at other proceedings it may be proved against the maker in the same way as any other informal admission.[40] A formal admission made in terms of s 220 is not binding on a co-accused.[41]

---

[32] Richings 1975 *SALJ* 246 247; Schmidt 197.
[33] *S v Davidson* 1964 1 SA 192 (T) 194. See generally Hoffmann & Zeffertt 430.
[34] 1980 3 SA 745 (A).
[35] 1981 3 SA 353 (A).
[36] 1979 2 SA 636 (B).
[37] See *S v Mjoli* 1981 3 SA 1233 (A) 1247C, where Viljoen JA, referring to s 220, stated: "I do not think that the legislature, when it formulated the provision, had in mind the distinction or meant to distinguish between *prima facie* and conclusive proof." See also *S v Moroney* 1978 4 SA 389 (A).
[38] See *S v Shabalala* 1986 4 SA 734 (A) at 746. Cf Van der Merwe et al *Evidence* (1983) 366, where it is argued that a formal admission made in terms of s 220 constitutes conclusive proof the moment it is made. See generally Kotze 1980 *De Jure* 416 419; Van der Merwe 1980 *TSAR* 284 286; Schmidt 203.
[39] See generally Hoffmann & Zeffertt 434.
[40] See Hoffmann & Zeffertt 433–4.
[41] See *S v Long* 1988 1 SA 216 (NC); Paizes in Du Toit et al *Commentary* 24-81.

26 5 2 The plea of guilty: s 112(1)(b) and s 113 CPA   A plea of guilty requires that an accused admit all the allegations against her and therefore places nothing in dispute. Paizes notes that case law supports the view that s 220 does not apply once a plea of guilty has been entered because "a plea of guilty constitutes an admission of every material fact alleged in the charge [and therefore] a formal admission would be tautologous".[42] However, s 112(1)(b) of the CPA provides, inter alia, that upon a plea of guilty the presiding officer should, in certain circumstances, question the accused with reference to the alleged facts of the case in order to ascertain whether he admits the allegations in the charge to which he has pleaded guilty.[43] Section 113 of the CPA stipulates that if the court, at any stage of the proceedings under s 112 and before sentence is passed, is in doubt whether the accused is in law guilty of the offence to which he has pleaded guilty or is satisfied that the accused does not admit an allegation in the charge or that the accused has incorrectly admitted any such allegation or that the accused has a valid defence to the charge, the court should record a plea of not guilty and require the prosecutor to proceed with the prosecution. A proviso to s 113 is to the effect that any allegation — other than an allegation referred to above — admitted by the accused up to the stage at which the court records a plea of not guilty shall in any court stand as proof of such allegation.[44] Formal admissions are therefore established in this manner.

26 5 3 The explanation of plea: s 115 of the CPA   Section 115(1) of the CPA provides that where an accused pleads not guilty the court may ask him whether he wishes to make a statement indicating the basis of his defence. If the accused makes no statement or if his statement is not clear as to what extent he admits or denies the issues raised by the plea, the court may question him to establish which allegations are in dispute.[45] Section 115(2)(b) provides, inter alia, that the court shall enquire whether an allegation which is not placed in issue may be recorded as an admission and, if the accused consents, the admission can be recorded as a formal admission in terms of s 220 of the CPA.[46] Facts admitted in this manner are then placed beyond dispute.[47] Where the accused does not consent to an admission being recorded the admission will be treated as an informal admission.[48]

26 5 4 The rules of practice and s 220   In *S v Mdladla*[49] it was said that it is

---

[42] Paizes in Du Toit et al *Commentary* 24-79. See *R v Fouche* 1958 3 SA 767 (T); *R v Philip* 1960 2 SA 267 (N); *S v Phongoma* 1976 1 SA 367 (O); cf *R v Mazibuko* 1947 4 SA 821 (N); *R v McWilliam* 1958 2 SA 243 (E).

[43] See generally Van der Merwe, Barton & Kemp *Plea Procedures in Summary Criminal Trials* (1983) para 2 3.

[44] See generally *S v Fikizolo* 1978 2 SA 676 (NC).

[45] Section 115(2)(a) of the CPA.

[46] See generally Skeen 1982 *SACC* 158 159.

[47] Schmidt 199 maintains that s 115(2)(b) can only be employed with regard to primary *facta probanda* and that s 220 should be used with regard to secondary *facta probanda*. See generally § 2 2 above for the distinction between primary and secondary *facta probanda*.

[48] This type of informal admission is discussed in § 16 7 2 above.

[49] 1972 3 SA 53 (N).

absolutely necessary that formal admissions be meticulously and unequivocally made to obviate any doubt or misunderstanding as to which matters thereafter remain in dispute. Where a formal admission by an accused is equivocal or ambiguous and permits of more than one interpretation that construction which is more favourable to the accused must be adopted.[50]

An accused need not assist the state in discharging its burden of proof. It follows that an unrepresented accused should be warned by the court that she is under no obligation to make a formal admission.[51] It is necessary that a similar warning be given with regard to admissions made in terms of s 115(2)(b) of the CPA and that a full record of how the accused's rights were explained should appear from the record.[52]

26 5 5 Formal admissions of facts outside the maker's personal knowledge The maker of a formal admission need not necessarily have personal knowledge of the facts which he is prepared to admit.[53] However, the courts take a particularly cautious approach where the accused has no legal representation. In *S v Adams*[54] it was held that a court may not simply accept an accused's admission of an unknown fact. Before a court can be satisfied of the accused's guilt in such circumstances there must be additional grounds on which the court can rely to establish that the admitted fact is true. In *S v Mavundla*[55] it was said that where an accused who lacks legal representation makes a formal admission of a fact which is beyond the range of his personal knowledge the presiding officer, before accepting the formal admission, should satisfy himself that the accused's decision to make it has been taken with full understanding of its meaning and effect. The court noted in *S v Ndlela*[56] that "[a]lthough there is no legal rule that an accused cannot admit something which is beyond his personal knowledge, the weight of such an admission will no doubt depend upon the facts and circumstances of a particular case . . .".

Informal admissions of facts outside a party's knowledge are admissible in civil as well as criminal proceedings.[57] However, the weight to be attached to such admissions will necessarily depend upon the particular circumstances of each case.

26 6 FORMAL ADMISSIONS BY CROSS-EXAMINER

Questions put in cross-examination may be of such a nature as to involve an explicit assertion of fact by the cross-examiner. For example, the legal repre-

---

[50] *S v Maweke* 1971 2 SA 327 (A).
[51] *S v M* 1967 1 SA 70 (N).
[52] See *S v Mahlangu* 1985 4 SA 447 (W); *S v Evans* 1981 4 SA 52 (C) 59. In *S v Ndlovu* 1987 3 SA 827 (N) the court held that the prosecution was entitled to lead *viva voce* evidence to prove that an accused's rights had been explained to him prior to his making a statement containing admissions in terms of s 115.
[53] Van der Merwe et al *Plea Procedures in Summary Criminal Trials* (1983) para 6 6 5.
[54] 1986 3 SA 733 (C).
[55] 1976 4 SA 731 (N).
[56] 1984 4 SA 131 (N) 134H.
[57] Richings 1975 *SALJ* 246.

sentative of an accused might put to a state witness that the accused will say that
she (the accused) was the driver of the motor vehicle at the alleged place and
time, but that she was not involved in any accident. In *S v Magubane*[58] it was said
that such assertions, for example, the driving of the vehicle and the presence of
the accused at the scene, are to be accepted as unequivocal admissions of the
facts so asserted. A statement that the accused was not involved in the accident
cannot be an admission as it is not a fact unfavourable to the accused.[59]

In *S v W*[60] it was held that assertions which amount to admissions and which
are deliberately and specifically made by the cross-examiner during the course
of her cross-examination require no formal proof before they may be used
against the party concerned. It would seem as if this type of admission should for
all practical purposes be treated as a formal admission.[61]

[58] 1975 3 SA 288 (N).
[59] See § 16 1 above.
[60] 1963 3 SA 516 (A), followed in *S v Gope* 1993 2 SACR 92 (Ck).
[61] See generally Schmidt 201; Paizes in Du Toit et al *Commentary* 24-79. Cf *S v Mjoli* 1981 3 SA 1233 (A) 1248A.

CHAPTER 27

JUDICIAL NOTICE

PJ Schwikkard and S E van der Merwe

27 1 THE NATURE OF AND RATIONALE FOR JUDICIAL NOTICE

It is in the nature of the accusatorial process that judicial officers should play a passive role and be aloof from the proceedings.[1] This serves to enhance the perception of impartiality. A judicial officer must withdraw from a case (recuse himself) if he happens to have private information concerning the facts of the case before him.[2] However, the law of evidence does to a limited extent allow a judicial officer to accept the truth of certain facts which are known to him even though no evidence was led to prove these facts. This process is known as judicial notice and must be distinguished from the procedure of receiving evidence.[3] For example, a judicial officer may, without hearing evidence, accept the fact that Pretoria is in South Africa and that there are twelve months in a year. These facts

---

[1] See § 1 5 2 above.
[2] Lansdown & Campbell 725.
[3] See § 27 2 below; Tapper *Cross and Tapper on Evidence* 8 ed (1995) 74.

are so well known[4] or can so easily be ascertained[5] that evidence to prove them would be completely unnecessary and even absurd.

In *Cross and Tapper on Evidence* the following reasons for the existence of the doctrine of judicial notice are identified:[6]

"In the first place it expedites the hearing of many cases. Much time would be wasted if every fact which was not admitted had to be the subject of evidence which would, in many instances, be costly and difficult to obtain. Second, the doctrine tends to produce uniformity of decision on matters of fact where a diversity of findings might sometimes be distinctly embarrassing."

The process of judicial notice deprives the parties of an opportunity to cross-examine and consequently the courts apply the doctrine with caution.[7]

27 2   Judicial Notice and the Reception of Evidence

Some facts are judicially noticed without any inquiry, that is, without consulting a specific source, whereas other facts may be judicially noticed only with reference to a source of indisputable authority. This distinction is important because in the former instance evidence may generally not be led to refute facts which have been properly noticed, whilst in the second instance evidence may generally be led concerning the disputability or indisputability of the source in question.[8]

How do we distinguish between receiving evidence and the taking of judicial notice? The distinction is easy to make when judicial notice is taken without any inquiry. In such a case the court is relying on its own knowledge,[9] which is something entirely different from the reception of evidence. However, the distinction is more difficult to make when the taking of judicial notice is preceded by either referring to texts or the hearing of evidence. "If learned treatises are consulted, it is not easy to say whether evidence is being received under an exception to the rule against hearsay or whether the judge is equipping himself to take judicial notice."[10] In *McQuaker v Goddard*[11] the court, before taking judicial notice of the fact that camels are domesticated animals, consulted books about camels and heard evidence from witnesses regarding the nature of camels. The Court of Appeal in affirming the decision noted that the trial judge, when hearing the witness's testimony as to the nature of camels, had not been taking evidence in the ordinary sense — the witnesses were merely assisting him in "forming his view as to what the ordinary course of nature in this regard in fact is, a matter of which he is supposed to have complete knowledge".[12]

---

[4] See § 27 4 1 below.

[5] See § 27 4 3 below.

[6] Tapper *Cross and Tapper on Evidence* 78.

[7] See *R v Tager* 1944 AD 339, *S v Imene* 1979 2 SA 710 (A). However, see Redgment 1984 *SALJ* 459 and Van der Berg 1986 *SALJ* 103, whose articles indicate that the caution is more apparent than real.

[8] See Lansdown & Campbell 726.

[9] However, a presiding officer may not act on her personal knowledge of a fact. See § 27 4 below.

[10] Tapper *Cross and Tapper on Evidence* 74.

[11] 1940 1 KB 687, 1940 All ER 471.

[12] At 700.

In these circumstances the distinction between taking judicial notice and the reception of evidence lies in the effect of the inquiry.[13] When judicial notice is taken a precedent is established and in England a judge may withdraw a fact that has been judicially noticed from the jury.[14] Furthermore, evidence is not admissible in rebuttal of a judicially noticed fact.[15] In Lansdown & Campbell the following observation is made:[16]

"Evidence is inadmissible to controvert facts properly noticed; they have more than merely *prima facie* validity, being irrefutable. This does not of course disregard the fact that whether something is indisputable may itself be a matter of dispute."

It should be noted that Schmidt[17] holds a different view and asserts that "[g]eregtelike kennisname toon heelwat ooreenkoms met die weerlegbare vermoede wanneer die in werking gestel is". This, Zeffertt argues, is true only if one takes the view that a fact judicially noticed can be rebutted, a view which is contrary to the English law by which we are bound.[18]

27 3 PROCEDURE

The question whether a fact should be judicially noticed is one of law and should be decided by the court, which should, where possible, inform the parties in advance (that is during the trial and before verdict) of its intention to take judicial notice of a certain fact which is of such a nature that it might give rise to conflicting views. In *R v Tager*[19] the court held that in these circumstances the parties may lead evidence to dispel any erroneous impression under which the court may labour.[20] Some circumstances may allow no evidence but only argument.[21]

27 4 THE LIMITS OF JUDICIAL NOTICE: BASIC PRINCIPLES

Facts which are judicially noticed are either well known to all reasonable persons or to a reasonable court in a specific locality.[22] It is not sufficient for a presiding officer to act on his personal knowledge of facts.[23] In *S v Mantini*[24] the court held that a magistrate had erred in making use of his personal knowledge to take judicial notice of the fact that the climate of a mountain range was suitable for the cultivation of dagga.

---

[13] See Hoffmann & Zeffertt 416.

[14] Tapper *Cross and Tapper on Evidence* 75.

[15] See Tapper *Cross and Tapper on Evidence* 75; Hoffmann & Zeffertt 416–17.

[16] At 726.

[17] At 174.

[18] Zeffertt 1987 *ASSAL* 429. Cf *S v Lund* 1987 4 SA 548 (N). For a contrary view see Schmidt 175–6.

[19] Supra.

[20] See also Redgment 1984 *SALJ* 459.

[21] See § 2 3 above for the distinction between evidence and argument.

[22] Hoffmann & Zeffertt 417; Schmidt 176. Schmidt expresses the view that the question is not the knowledge of the reasonable person that is in issue but whether the fact would be known to any court having jurisdiction in the matter.

[23] *R v Tager* 1944 AD 339 343–4. Tapper *Cross and Tapper on Evidence* 75.

[24] 1990 2 SACR 236 (E).

Generally, presiding officers must take judicial notice of certain laws[25] and matters which have been noticed by well-established practices or precedents of the courts.[26] However, the courts *may* also take judicial notice of facts which they are not *required* to notice.[27] In terms of our common law judicial notice should be taken of notorious facts and facts which are readily ascertainable. Special common-law and statutory rules apply where rules of law are concerned.[28]

27 4 1 Notorious facts (general knowledge) According to Hoffmann & Zeffertt,[29] notorious facts can be divided into two categories: facts of general knowledge, and specific facts which are notorious within the locality of the court. Facts of general knowledge would include, for example, the fact that there is a national road network in South African and that these roads are public roads;[30] the fact that chess, billiards and table-tennis are games of skill;[31] and the fact that there are seven days in a week. In *R v African Canning Co SWA Ltd*[32] it was said that notorious facts include elemental experience in human nature, commercial affairs and everyday life. It was held in *S v Mirirai*[33] that it is so well known that the Limpopo River forms the boundary between South Africa and Botswana between Martinsdrif and Groblersbrug that the court can summarily take judicial notice thereof.

27 4 2 Facts of local notoriety Facts may be judicially noticed even if they are not of general knowledge. However, the proviso is that these facts should be notorious among all reasonably well-informed people in the area where the court sits.[34] In *R v Levitt*[35] a local court took judicial notice of the fact that Franschhoek is not a small place and it contains a number of streets. Judicial notice has also been taken of the distance between well-known local places and that a specific local road is a public road within the local town or city in the jurisdiction of the court.

27 4 3 Facts easily ascertainable Facts which are not generally known but which are readily and easily ascertainable should also be judicially noticed.[36] However, they should be easily ascertainable from sources of indisputable authority, for example, maps and surveys issued under governmental or other reliable authority.[37] Sections 229 of the CPA and 26 of the CPEA contain provisions to

---

[25] See § 27 6 below.
[26] *Phipson on Evidence* 14 ed (1990) para 2-07.
[27] Ibid. See *R v Refanis* 1929 OPD 195 202.
[28] See § 27 6 below.
[29] At 417.
[30] *R v Bikitsha* 1960 4 SA 181 (E).
[31] *Ex parte Minister van Justisie: In re S v Conclaves* 1976 3 SA 629 (A).
[32] 1954 1 SA 197 (SWA) 199F; see also *Rowe v Assistant Magistrate, Pretoria* 1925 TPD 361 368.
[33] 1995 2 SACR 134 (T).
[34] Hoffmann & Zeffert 421; *S v Mosala* 1968 3 SA 523 (T).
[35] 1933 CPD 411 412.
[36] See generally Hoffmann & Zeffertt 423; Schmidt 183.
[37] *R v Pretoria Timber Co (Pty) Ltd* 1950 3 SA 163 (A) 172.

the effect that certain official tables, approved in the *Gazette*, may on the mere production thereof serve as proof of the exact times of sunrise and sunset at specific places in South Africa. In *S v Sibuyi*[38] the court held that, although a court might take judicial notice of the accuracy of almanacs, diaries or calendars as regards days and months, they could not be regarded as indisputably accurate as regards the phases of the moon, setting and rising of the sun, or the state of the tides. The basis of the court's reasoning was that such evidence was hearsay and did not merit being admitted as an exception to the hearsay rule.[39] The court also noted that such information could not even be regarded as being *prima facie* correct.[40]

27 5   ASSORTED EXAMPLES

27 5 1 Animals The instinctive behaviour of domesticated animals should be judicially noticed.[41] However, in *S v Soko*[42] it was held that judicial notice may not be taken of the fact that ordinary fowls do not wander off like other stock.

In *S v Steenberg*[43] one of the issues was whether certain duikers were blue duikers and as such protected game. The trial court took notice of this fact, which was really a matter that should have been ascertained with the aid of expert testimony. On appeal it was held that, even if the trial court had had the required special knowledge, judicial notice was still irregular: the matter was neither immediately and accurately ascertainable nor of general knowledge. It has also been held that judicial notice is irregular in respect of the following: the local market value of animals;[44] the manner of estimating the age of animals;[45] and that a particular skin (which was admitted as real evidence) was that of a particular species of buck.[46]

The following facts have been judicially noticed: scab is a well-known sheep disease;[47] dangerous wild animals remain potentially dangerous even after docile behaviour has come about as a result of semi-domesticity;[48] brand marks on cattle do not fade completely;[49] and rhinoceros are rarer than elephants.[50] All these facts were apparently considered to be of such general knowledge that judicial knowledge was justified.[51]

---

[38] 1988 4 SA 879 (T), in which the court found the decision in *S v Mpharu* 1981 2 SA 464 (NC) to have been wrong.

[39] At 881F–G.

[40] At 880I.

[41] *Parker v Reed* 1904 SC 496.

[42] 1963 2 SA 248 (T). In *S v Olyn* 1990 1 PH H107 (B) it was held that a court could not take judicial notice that goats always return to their own kraals.

[43] 1979 3 SA 513 (B) 515.

[44] *R v Pretorius* 1934 TPD 76.

[45] *R v Sombana* 1939 EDL 71.

[46] *R v Butelezi* 1959 1 SA 191 (N).

[47] *R v Bunana* 1958 1 SA 573 (E).

[48] *Bristow v Lycett* 1971 4 SA 223 (O).

[49] *R v Maduna* 1946 EDL 334.

[50] *S v Mazweinzini* 1964 4 SA 201 (SR).

[51] For a more sceptical approach, see Redgment 1984 *SALJ* 459.

27 5 2 Racial characteristics The doctrine of judicial notice has not escaped the effects of the historically inherent injustice of the South African social structure. Although overturned on appeal, trial courts have taken judicial notice of the "fact" that "natives" are able to see in the dark;[52] that "Bantu" women submit to rape without protest;[53] that "bantu" women are unlikely to support the evidence of their husbands against a lover;[54] that "native" witnesses who give evidence in support of an alibi may be judicially assumed to be liars.[55] Rumpff CJ in *S v Augustine*[56] made the startling assertion that "coloured" and "black" men sometimes stab others without reason. Clearly, such racially based generalizations are not matters which should be the subject of judicial notice.[57]

27 5 3 Political and constitutional matters The sovereignty of foreign states and the existence of a state of war may normally be judicially noticed.[58] In *Nasopie (Edms) Bpk v Minister van Justisie*[59] it was held that the court was entitled to take judicial notice of the constitutional development which led to the promulgation of an Act under which independence was granted to Bophuthatswana. It was also held that the court was compelled to take judicial notice of the creation of the self-governing area of Bophuthatswana and its later independence.

An appropriate certificate may be obtained from the executive if the court does not have sufficient information to take judicial notice of certain political and state matters, for example whether a war has been declared. According to *Cross and Tapper on Evidence*[60] this certificate is, for reasons of public policy, treated as one of indisputable accuracy: it is undesirable that the judicial and executive branches of government should hold conflicting views with regard to relationships with other states. In cases concerning extradition agreements a certificate from the Minister of Justice is an appropriate method of informing the court of the attitude of the government.[61] In *Inter-Science Research v Republica de Mocambique*[62] it was held that, in proceedings against a foreign government, recognition of such government as the government of the foreign state concerned may be a matter of judicial notice. However, if there is any doubt on the matter, the court should receive a certificate from the Minister of the appropriate state department

---

[52] *R v Tusini* 1953 4 SA 406 (A).
[53] *R v A* 1952 3 SA 212 (A); *S v M* 1965 4 SA 577 (N).
[54] *S v Sihlani* 1966 3 SA 148 (E).
[55] *Mcunu v R* 1938 NPD 229.
[56] 1980 1 SA 503 (A).
[57] For a fuller criticism of these cases, see Van der Berg 1986 *SALJ* 550. For a bizarre defence of the assertion that "coloureds and blacks stab each other without reason", see Marais 1987 *SALJ* 204.
[58] See generally Hoffmann & Zeffertt 423.
[59] 1979 3 SA 1228 (NC). See also generally *S v Wellem* 1993 2 SACR 18 (E) 20g–i.
[60] Tapper *Cross and Tapper on Evidence* 65.
[61] *S v Devoy* 1971 3 SA 899 (A).
[62] 1980 2 SA 111 (T).

of South Africa.[63] Certificates are usually required where inter-state relationships are in issue.[64]

Certain political circumstances (for example, the existence of a specific political system) in a specific area or country may be judicially noticed if sufficiently notorious.[65]

27 5 4 Matters of science and scientific instruments According to Lansdown & Campbell,[66] matters of science may not be judicially noticed unless "they have permeated into the background knowledge of non-specialists". Such matters can be said to be noticed on the basis of general notoriety. Judicial notice has been taken of the fact that no two fingerprints are exactly the same,[67] but not of the age at which a girl reaches puberty.[68] The normal period of human gestation has been judicially noticed, but not the possible limits within which the period may be abnormal except in the most extreme cases.[69]

When evidence includes measurement by a mechanical or scientific instrument it is ordinarily required to be accompanied by testimony as to the trustworthiness of the method or process used to make the measurement as well as the accuracy of the instrument used.[70] However, in certain circumstances the courts will take judicial notice of the reliability of the measuring device and expert evidence will not be necessary.[71] "The acceptance of the evidence of recordings of scientific instruments . . . depends on whether they are sufficiently well known for their trustworthiness to enable a court to take judicial notice of their reliability."[72] A court may, for example, take judicial notice of the process of weighing on an assized scale.[73] In *S v Fuhri*[74] the court held that the relevant science pertaining to the taking of photographs and the recording of speed by a device known as a speed camera had advanced to such a level of general acceptance that judicial notice could be taken that the photograph in question reflected a true image of what had appeared in front of the camera lens at that specific moment.[75]

---

[63] For example, the Department of Foreign Affairs.

[64] *Hassim v Naik* 1952 3 SA 331 (A). But see also *S v Mataboge* 1991 1 SACR 539 (B) 548*i–j*, where the court without any certificate not only took judicial notice of the fact that (the former) Bophuthatswana did not enjoy extradition facilities with Botswana but also that the latter did not recognize (the former) Bopthuthatswana as an independent state. The court also took judicial notice that no border formalities were required to pass from one country to the other and that border control was lax. This was done for the purposes of a bail application where the ordinary rules of evidence are relaxed.

[65] *Grgin v Grgin* 1961 2 SA 84 (W).

[66] At 727–8.

[67] *R v Morela* 1947 3 SA 147 (N).

[68] *S v M* 1969 1 SA 70 (N).

[69] *S v Segwoolam* 1961 3 SA 79 (N); *Mitchell v Mitchell* 1963 2 SA 505 (D); Hoffmann & Zeffertt 419.

[70] *S v Mthimkulu* 1975 4 SA 759 (A) 764.

[71] Ibid.

[72] *R v Harvey* 1969 2 SA 193 (RA) 200D.

[73] *S v Mtkimkulu* supra.

[74] 1994 2 SACR 829 (A).

[75] See also Wigmore para 190. Cf *S v Hengst* 1975 2 SA 91 (SWA).

27 5 5 Financial matters and commercial practices Judicial notice has been taken of the fact that the value of money has declined over the years;[76] that most public companies are incorporated for the purpose of making a profit from income;[77] the practice of furnishing bank guarantees in sales of land;[78] and the practice of making payment by cheque.[79] In *Van Huyssteen v Minister of Environmental Affairs and Tourism*[80] the court held that it was permissible to take judicial notice of the fact that "sites for holiday homes will be more valuable if they are in close proximity to beautiful and unspoilt natural areas and that they will be much less valuable if such areas are polluted or otherwise detrimentally affected".[81] However, the courts have held that judicial notice cannot be taken of the rate of exchange between South African rands and a foreign currency and that proof of the rate of exchange must be provided.[82]

27 5 6 Functioning of traffic lights If we take the view that a fact judicially noticed cannot be rebutted by adducing evidence to the contrary,[83] then those cases in which the courts have taken judicial notice of the functioning of traffic lights must be subject to some scrutiny. In *Gomes v Visser*[84] the court held that in civil cases a court can "take judicial notice of the fact that when the lights facing in one direction at a right-angled intersection are green those facing at right angles to them should be, and probably are red". However, in *S v De Lange*[85] the court found that in a criminal case it was not competent for the court to take judicial notice of the fact that if one light is green, the one at right angles to it must, beyond reasonable doubt, be red. The Natal Provincial Division in *S v Lund* reached a different conclusion and held:[86]

> "If the court is entitled to take judicial notice of a fact in a civil case, it is entitled to take notice of it in a criminal case. Once it has taken judicial notice of it, it is still a question of fact whether or not that fact establishes what the state has to prove in the case in question, and establishes it sufficiently clearly for it to be said to be established beyond reasonable doubt."

Although the court was undoubtedly correct in that no distinction should be made between the taking of judicial notice in civil and criminal trials, it failed "*to recognize that the common law lays down that when, as a result of inquiry judicial notice is taken of a fact, there is no longer an issue about the fact*".[87] Zeffertt argues that

---

[76] *Bryant v Foot* 1868 LR 3 QB 497.
[77] *R v African Canning Co (SWA) Ltd* 1954 1 SA 197 (SWA).
[78] *Trichardt v Muller* 1915 TPD 175.
[79] *Schneider and London v Chapman* 1971 TPD 497.
[80] 1996 1 SA 283 (C) 302D.
[81] In *S v Van den Berg* 1996 1 SACR 19 (Nm) the court took judicial notice of the fact that a specific company was mining rough and uncut diamonds at Oranjemund and that the security arrangements related to rough and uncut diamonds. These the court held were notorious facts.
[82] *Barclays Bank of Swaziland v Mnyeketi* 1992 3 SA 425 (W).
[83] See § 27 2 above.
[84] 1971 1 SA 276 (T).
[85] 1972 1 SA 139 (C).
[86] 1987 4 SA 548 (N) 553A–B.
[87] Hoffmann & Zeffertt 416 (emphasis in the original); see also 417, where authorities supporting the opposite view are cited.

although there is presumption of fact[88] "that traffic lights are *probably* in a working condition . . . it would be wrong to infer that they are *beyond a reasonable doubt* in a working order".[89] It is submitted that the basis for the confusion arising out of these cases is the incorrect labelling of a presumption fact as judicial notice.

27 5 7 Historical facts, words and phrases There is no general rule that facts which are reliably (as opposed to easily *and* reliably) ascertainable can be judicially noticed.[90] However, our courts have used history books to establish historical facts.[91] In *S v Mkhwanazi*[92] a magistrate had taken judicial notice of two facts: (i) statistics submitted by the agricultural union of Ermelo which contained inter alia data regarding the number of reports of theft of sheep and (ii) that organized agriculture in Ermelo had donated a substantial amount of money to the South African Police for use as rewards to informers in stock-theft cases. On review the court held that the magistrate had misdirected himself in taking judicial notice of the first fact as it did not fall within the local community's knowledge. With regard to the second fact, the court found that the magistrate had erred on the basis that although a court can take judicial notice of a historical fact mentioned in history books, it cannot take notice of a specific occurrence or incident. Zeffertt argues that "[a] specific instance may be of such general notoriety as to warrant it being noticed despite its being too recent to appear in a history book". The example he gives is the release of Nelson Mandela.[93]

The courts have also made use of dictionaries to establish the meaning of words. In *Association of Amusement and Novelty Operations v Minister of Justice*[94] it was held that the opinions of language experts and other witnesses as to the meaning and status of words as used in a statute are generally inadmissible and that recourse could be had to any authoritative dictionary of the language employed by the legislature.

27 6 LAW

Judicial notice must be taken of South African law. This is a rule of convenience. It would be very tedious and absurd if in each and every case expert witnesses were necessary in order to prove the relevant legal rules. Parties may not lead evidence in order to clarify the nature or ambit of a South African legal rule. They may, however, do so by way of argument, and indeed should be given an opportunity of doing so. This is particularly necessary where the court on its own initiative has consulted case law, legislation or authoritative textbooks in order to seek clarification of a legal rule.[95]

---

[88] For discussion of presumptions of facts, see § 28 3 3 below.
[89] 1987 *ASSAL* 429.
[90] *LAWSA* para 621.
[91] *Consolidated Diamond Mines of South West Africa v Administrator of South West Africa* 1958 4 SA 572 (A).
[92] 1989 2 SA 802 (T).
[93] 1989 *ASSAL* 418.
[94] 1980 2 SA 636 (A). See also § 8 3 above: expert testimony is unnecessary.
[95] For a distinction between evidence and argument, see § 2 3 above.

27 6 1 Statute and common law Judicial notice is taken of Acts of Parliament and of the provincial legislatures. Colonial statutes and provincial ordinances are judicially noticed in terms of our common law, whilst subordinate legislation (for example, proclamations, regulations and by-laws) and private Acts of Parliament are judicially noticed in terms of statutory law.[96] The common law also provides for judicial notice to be taken of proclamations, which have the force of original legislation.[97] Judicial notice should also be taken of any law which purports to be published under the superintendence or authority of the Government Printer.[98]

The rules of our common law are judicially noticed. There are no exceptions to this rule. The mere fact that a particular rule is vague will not entitle a party to adduce expert evidence, for example, by calling a professor of law who has specialized in the rule concerned.

27 6 2 Public international law Public international law (also known as the law of nations, or *ius gentium*) consists of the body of rules governing the relations between states in times of peace and war.[99] Public international law that has acquired the status of custom[100] "is applied directly as part of the common law, but conflicting statutory rules and acts of state are to prevail over international law and treaties are not be applied without legislative incorporation".[101] As customary international law is seen as forming part of the common law the courts should take judicial notice of it.[102] Section 231(4) of the interim Constitution provides that "[t]he rules of customary international law binding on the Republic, shall, unless inconsistent with this Constitution or an Act of Parliament, form part of the law of the Republic". [103]

27 6 3 Indigenous custom and foreign law Prior to the Law of Evidence Amendment Act 1988[104] the courts of chiefs and headmen could take judicial notice of indigenous laws and customs. But this was not the position in the ordinary courts, where such indigenous law and custom were treated as foreign law.[105] Until 1988 foreign law had to be proved by calling an expert witness and

---

[96] Section 224(*a*) of the CPA and s 5(1) of the CPEA.

[97] *R v Foster* 1922 EDL 166.

[98] Section 224(*b*) of the CPA and s 5(2) of the CPEA.

[99] Hahlo & Kahn *The South African Legal System and Its Background* (1973) 111–12.

[100] A rule of international law will be accorded customary status when it has general or widespread acceptance. Although in *Nduli v Minister of Justice* 1978 1 SA 893 (A) at 906D the court indicated that universal acceptance was required, the correctness of this view has been questioned in subsequent decisions and it would appear that general acceptance is sufficient. See *Inter-Science Research v Republica de Mocambique* 1980 2 SA 111 (T) 124–5; *S v Petane* 1988 3 SA 51 (C) 56–7; Dugard *International Law: A South African Perspective* (1994) 27.

[101] Dugard *International Law* 37; *Nduli v Minister of Justice* supra 906B; *Inter-Science Research and Development Services (Pty) Ltd v Republica Popular de Mocambique* supra 124H.

[102] See, e g, *South Atlantic Islands Development Corporation Ltd v Buchan* 1971 1 SA 234 (C), in which the court refused to admit an affidavit from an expert on international law on the ground that international law is not foreign law and therefore cannot be proved by affidavit.

[103] For a general discussion of the role of international law in interpreting the Bill of Rights, see Dugard 1994 *SALJ* 208.

[104] Act 45 of 1988.

[105] *Rowe v Assistant Magistrate, Pretoria* 1925 TPD 361.

could not be judicially noticed.[106] Judicial notice may now be taken in respect of both indigenous[107] and foreign law[108] in terms of s 1 of the Law of Evidence Amendment Act, which provides:

"1 (1) Any court may take judicial notice of the law of a foreign state and of indigenous law in so far as such law can be ascertained readily and with sufficient certainty: Provided that indigenous law shall not be opposed to the principles of public policy or natural justice: Provided further that it shall not be lawful for any court to declare that the custom of lobola or bogadi or other similar custom is repugnant to such principles.

(2) The provisions of subsection (1) shall not preclude any party from adducing evidence of the substance of a legal rule contemplated in that subsection which is in issue at the proceedings concerned.

(3) In any suit or proceedings between Blacks who do not belong to the same tribe the court shall not in the absence of any agreement between them with regard to the particular system of indigenous law to be applied in such suit or proceedings, apply any system of indigenous law other than that which is in operation at the place where the defendant or respondent resides or carries on business or is employed, or if two or more different systems are in operation at that place (not being within a tribal area), the court shall not apply such system unless it is the law of the tribe (if any) to which the defendant or respondent belongs.

(4) For the purposes of this section 'indigenous law' means the Black law or customs as applied by the Black tribes in the Republic or in territories which formerly formed part of the Republic."

The application of this section in respect of foreign law was considered in *Harnischfeger Corporation v Appleton*.[109] The court held that even though the words "readily" and "sufficient certainty" defied definition, they could not be ignored.[110] Fleming DJP, finding that accessible library holdings on the relevant topic of American law were inadequate, came to the conclusion that the American law in point was neither readily accessible nor ascertainable and consequently the common law had to be applied. At common law "each aspect of foreign law is a factual question and any evidence on that aspect must emanate from someone with the necessary expertise".[111] It will be presumed that there is no distinction between foreign and South African law and the onus rests on the person asserting a distinction to produce evidence.[112] In *Harnischfeger* the court held that this presumption applied to both common and statutory law.[113]

The status of indigenous law is reaffirmed in Constitutional Principle XIII,[114]

---

[106] *S v Masilela* 1968 2 SA 558 (A).

[107] See, e g, *Thibela v Minister van Wet en Order* 1995 3 SA 147 (T).

[108] See, e g, *Holz v Harken* 1995 3 SA 521 (C). Note that s 35(1) of the interim Constitution provides, inter alia, that in interpreting the provisions of chapter 3 the courts "shall, where applicable have regard to public international law . . . and may have regard to comparable foreign law". See further *Shabalala v Attorney-General, Transvaal; Gumede v Attorney-General, Transvaal* 1995 1 SACR 88 (T) 125*d–g; S v Makwanyane* 1995 2 SACR 1 (CC).

[109] 1993 4 SA 479 (W).

[110] At 485D–E.

[111] At 485H. See *Schlesinger v Commissioner for Inland Revenue* 1964 3 SA 389 (A); *S v Masilela* 1968 2 SA 558 (A). See also Kahn 1970 *SALJ* 145–9.

[112] *Bank of Lisbon v Optichem Kunsmis (Edms) Bpk* 1970 1 SA 447 (W). Cf Kahn 1970 *SALJ* 145.

[113] At 486–7. In *S v Kruger* 1987 4 SA 326 (T) it was held that the presumption did not apply in criminal proceedings.

[114] Schedule 4 of the interim Constitution.

which provides that "[i]ndigenous law, like common law, shall be recognized and applied by the courts subject to the fundamental rights contained in the Constitution and to legislation dealing specifically therewith".

27 7   RULE 34 OF THE CONSTITUTIONAL COURT RULES

Rule 34(1) of the Constitutional Court rules provides that any party to any proceedings before the court, and an *amicus curiae* properly admitted by the court,[115] shall be entitled, in documents lodged in terms of the rules of the Constitutional Court, to canvass factual material which is relevant to the determination of the issues and which does not specifically appear on the record. The proviso, however, is that such facts must be *either* common cause or otherwise incontrovertible[116] *or* of an official scientific, technical or statistical nature, capable of easy verification.[117] In terms of rule 34(2) all other parties are entitled to admit, deny, controvert or elaborate upon such facts to the extent necessary and appropriate for a proper decision by the Constitutional Court.

The above rule should be understood in the context of the distinction between so-called "adjudicative facts" and "legislative facts".[118] This distinction was first drawn by Davis in 1942[119] and later again explained by him in 1955:[120]

"When a court or an agency finds facts concerning the immediate parties — who did what, where, when, how, and with what motive or intent — the court or agency is performing an adjudicative function, and the facts so determined are conveniently called adjudicative facts. When a court or an agency develops law or policy, it is acting legislatively; the courts have created the common law through judicial legislation, and the facts which inform the tribunal's legislative judgment are called legislative facts . . . Stated in other terms, the adjudicative facts are those to which the law is applied in the process of adjudication. They are the facts that normally go to the jury in a jury case. They relate to the parties, their activities, their properties, their businesses. Legislative facts are those which help the tribunal to determine the content of law and policy and to exercise its judgment or discretion in determining what course of action to take. Legislative facts are ordinarily general and do not concern the immediate parties. In the great mass of cases decided by courts and by agencies, the legislative element is either absent, unimportant, or interstitial, because in most cases the applicable law and policy have been previously established. But whenever a tribunal is engaged in the creation of law or of policy, it may need to resort to legislative facts, whether or not those facts have been developed on the record . . . The exceedingly practical difference between legislative and adjudicative facts is that, apart from facts properly noticed, the tribunal's finding of adjudicative facts must be supported

---

[115] An *amicus curiae* is strictly, speaking, not a party to the case, but someone who has a special interest in the outcome of the case. The admission of and submissions by an *amicus curiae* are largely governed by rule 9 of the Constitutional Court rules. See also generally *Ferreira v Levin NO; Vryenhoek v Powell* 1996 1 SA 984 (CC) para 4.

[116] Rule 34(1) *(a)* of the Constitutional Court rules.

[117] Rule 34(1) *(b)* of the Constitutional Court rules.

[118] See generally Charles et al *Evidence and the Canadian Charter of Rights and Freedoms* (1989) 112; Wormuth "The Impact of Economic Legislation upon the Supreme Court" 1957 6 *Journal of Public Law* 296 308; Delisle *Evidence: Principles and Problems* 2 ed (1989) 183–91.

[119] Davis "An Approach to Problems of Evidence in the Administrative Process" 1942 55 *Harvard LR* 364 402.

[120] Davis "Judicial Notice" 1955 55 *Columbia LR* 945 952. See also Davis *Administrative Law Treatise* vol 3 2 ed (1980) para 15 2.

by evidence, but finding or assumptions of legislative facts need not, frequently are not, and sometimes cannot be supported by evidence."

Rule 34 cannot be relied upon by the parties in respect of facts which are essentially "adjudicative". In respect of these facts the parties are bound by the evidence on record and the normal common-law and statutory rules which govern judicial notice. But for purposes of "legislative facts", they may go beyond the record of the case by relying on rule 34. Judicial notice of legislative facts might be necessary when the court must decide upon the constitutional validity of a statute or common-law rule "upon grounds of policy, and the policy is thought to hinge upon social, economic, political or scientific facts".[121] Rule 34 seeks to ensure that the Constitutional Court is well informed about the general background of a specific rule before upholding it, striking it down, expanding or limiting it.[122]

Rule 34 can be described as our own local version of the so-called "Brandeis brief", which originated in the United States of America.[123] In 1908 the United States Supreme Court[124] had to decide on the constitutional validity of an Oregon state law of 1903, which had determined that "no female [shall] be employed in any mechanical establishment, or factory, or laundry in this state for more than ten hours during one day". Brandeis was briefed by the state. Apart from traditional legal argument, Brandeis also submitted extracts from over ninety reports of committees, bureaus of statistics, commissioners of hygiene, inspectors of factories, "to the effect that long hours of work are dangerous for women primarily because of their special physical organization". The court not only upheld the Oregon statute but also accepted extracts on the basis that it took "judicial cognizance of all matters of general knowledge".[125] The truth of the matter is that the court accepted the extracts for the sake of convenience and in order to familiarize itself with the policy considerations which had given rise to the Oregon statute's limitation on female working hours in certain industries. The evidentiary short-cut taken by the Supreme Court in *Muller v Oregon* had the result that the term "Brandeis brief" came to be used "to refer to briefs filled with factual, as well as legal arguments".[126] Brandeis later also became a judge of the United States Supreme Court and in several of his own judgments went outside the record, relying on official reports and similar sources in respect of legislative facts.[127] Hogg claims that there are justifications for the "Brandeis brief":[128]

---

[121] Clearly (ed) *McCormick on Evidence* 2 ed (1984) para 328.
[122] See generally the cases referred to in n 129 below.
[123] See generally Alfange "The Relevance of Legislative Facts in Constitutional Law" 1966 114 *University of Pennsylvania LR* 637 667; Hogg "Proof of Facts in Constitutional Cases" 1976 26 *University of Toronto LJ* 386 395.
[124] *Muller v Oregon* 208 US 412 (1908).
[125] At 421.
[126] De Witt (ed) *The Supreme Court and its Work* (1981) 32.
[127] See generally Davis 1955 44 *Columbia LR* 945 953.
[128] Hogg 1976 26 *University of Toronto LJ* 387 396.

"There are two justifications for the Brandeis brief. The first is the pragmatic one that the Brandeis brief may be the only practicable way to inform the court of the full range of professional opinion on a particular point of social science. It is true that expert opinion evidence could be adduced, but on many topics no one expert or group of experts could easily canvass the entire range of professional opinion within the limits of the law of evidence, and especially the hearsay rule. Moreover, any attempt to do so by conventional sworn testimony, subject to cross-examination, would be extremely time-consuming and expensive . . . The second justification for the Brandeis brief is more principled and more conclusive. The nature of judicial review is such that it is not necessary to prove legislative facts as strictly as adjudicative facts which are relevant to the disposition of litigation, the court need not be so definite in respect of legislative facts in constitutional cases. The most that the court can ask in respect of legislative facts is whether there is a rational basis for the legislative judgment that the facts exist."

The South African Constitutional Court has on several occasions[129] referred to and relied upon so-called discussion documents submitted by the parties. After all, it is better to seek information and be informed than to guess or rely on personal perceptions or beliefs.

---

[129] See generally *S v Ntuli* 1996 1 BCLR 141 (CC) para 27 (statistics); *Ferreira v Levin NO; Vryehoek v Powell* supra para 4 (memoranda submitted by professional bodies); *S v Makwanyane* 1995 2 SACR 1 (CC) para 24 (statistics); *Shabalala v Attorney-General of the Transvaal* 1995 2 SA 761 (CC) para 18 (annual reports of the Department of Justice).

CHAPTER 28

REBUTTABLE PRESUMPTIONS OF LAW

PJ Schwikkard

28 1 WHAT ARE PRESUMPTIONS?

A precise and readily identifiable definition of the term "presumption" is probably impossible to formulate because the nature and effect of presumptions are so varied. Elliot defines a presumption "as a conclusion which may or must be drawn in the absence of contrary evidence".[1] Heydon asserts that in terms of this definition presumptions merely state the effect of the rules as to the burden of proof.[2] For example, the presumption of innocence requires the prosecution to prove the accused's guilt; ". . . it is not in itself an item of evidence".[3] There is another kind of presumption: "[A] conclusion (the 'presumed fact') which may or must be drawn if another fact (the 'basic fact') is first proved."[4] For example, once it is shown that two people went through what appeared to be a marriage ceremony their marriage will be presumed to be valid. In *R v Bakes*[5] Dickson CJC noted:

---

[1] Elliot *Elliot and Phipson Manual of the Law of Evidence* 12 ed (1987) 77.
[2] Heydon *Evidence: Cases & Materials* 3 ed (1991) 46.
[3] Heydon *Evidence* 46.
[4] Heydon *Evidence* 46.
[5] 1986 26 DLR (4th) 200.

"Presumptions can be classified in two general categories: Presumptions *without* basic facts and presumptions *with* basic facts. A presumption without a basic fact is simply a conclusion which is to be drawn until the contrary is proved. A presumption with a basic fact entails a conclusion to be drawn upon proof of the basic fact . . .."

28 2   SOME REASONS FOR PRESUMPTIONS

Presumptions form part of our legal system for a number of reasons.[6] They are a convenient way in which to express conclusions which would be reached by applying common sense; "or at least, the conclusion is so likely to be true that it ought to be reached in favour of one party unless the other disproves it".[7] For example, it is presumed that the child of a married woman was fathered by her husband. In this sense presumptions also save time by not requiring a party to prove something that is most probably true. However, this is certainly not a basis for explaining all presumptions. The presumption of innocence is not applied because common sense tells us that most accused persons are likely to be innocent, but is applied for reasons of policy.[8] Many presumptions exist as an expression of public policy. In *R v Downey*[9] the court held that the objective of the statutory presumption that a person who lives with or is habitually in the company of prostitutes is living on the earnings of prostitution was "to deal with the cruel and pervasive evil associated with pimping" and that the presumption was necessary because of the reluctance of prostitutes to testify against their pimps.

28 3   THE CLASSIFICATION OF PRESUMPTIONS

Presumptions are traditionally classified in terms of three categories: irrebuttable presumptions of law, rebuttable presumptions of law, and presumptions of fact.[10]

28 3 1 Irrebuttable presumptions of law Irrebuttable presumptions of law furnish conclusive proof of the fact presumed and cannot be rebutted by evidence to the contrary. The term "presumptions" in this context is misleading because irrebuttable presumptions of law are really rules of substantive law. As many of these presumptions exist for reasons of public policy and not because they necessarily reflect reality, it has been argued that they should not be disguised as presumptions.[11] For example, because a child under the age of 7 is presumed to be incapable of discerning between good and evil she cannot be held to be criminally or delictually liable.[12] Obviously some children under the age of 7 may be capable of distinguishing between good and evil, and for this reason Hoffmann & Zeffertt submit that the rule would be better phrased as

---

[6] For a general discussion, see Heydon *Evidence* 46–8.
[7] Heydon *Evidence* 48.
[8] See further § 31 4 1 below.
[9] 1992 90 DLR (4th) 449. See § 29 2 below for a discussion of this case.
[10] See generally Hoffmann & Zeffertt 530; Schmidt 132.
[11] See § 4.4 above and Hoffmann & Zeffertt 530.
[12] *Q v Lourie* 1892 9 SC 432.

follows: "No child under 7 may be convicted of a criminal offence."[13] The same criticism can be levelled at the presumption that a girl under the age of 12 is incapable of consenting to sexual intercourse. One such presumption that gave rise to certain anomalies is the presumption that a boy under the age of 14 is incapable of sexual intercourse. In *S v A*[14] a mother was charged with incest and the prosecution proved that she had had sexual intercourse with her 9-year-old son. The court, applying the presumption that boys under the age of 14 are incapable of sexual intercourse, held that she could only be convicted of attempted incest and not incest itself. If the rule had been stated as a rule of substantive law ("A boy under the age of 14 cannot be convicted of an offence of which sexual intercourse is an element"), the court could have avoided reaching such an artificial conclusion.[15] Fortunately, this anomaly has been removed by s 1 of the Law of Evidence and the Criminal Procedure Act Amendment Act,[16] which provides:

> "Notwithstanding the provisions of any law or the common law, but subject to any rule of law relating to the accountability of any person under the age of 14 years, evidence may be adduced in legal proceedings where the question in issue is whether a boy under the age of 14 years has had sexual intercourse with any female, that such sexual intercourse has taken place, and no presumption or rule of law to the effect that such a boy is incapable of sexual intercourse shall come into operation."

28 3 2 Rebuttable presumptions of law Rebuttable presumptions of law "are rules of law (within the law of evidence) compelling the provisional assumption of a fact. They are provisional in the sense that the assumption will stand unless it is destroyed by countervailing evidence."[17] For example, in terms of s 21(3) of the Sexual Offences Act,[18] once a person is proved to reside in a brothel or to live with or to be habitually in the company of a prostitute and to have no visible means of subsistence the court is required to assume that she or he is living off the earnings of prostitution. This assumption will stand until the accused satisfies the court to the contrary.

It is not necessary that the presumed fact constitutes a logical inference from the evidence which gives rise to the presumption.[19] In *R v Fourie*[20] Stratford ACJ said that

> " the judge's mind does not — and ought not to — advert to the reason for the presumption, and the presumption must be accepted as proof of the fact presumed until rebutted".

28 3 3 Presumptions of fact Elliot describes presumptions of fact as "merely frequently recurring examples of circumstantial evidence".[21] Similarly Hoffmann

---

[13] At 531. See also § 4 4 above.
[14] 1962 4 SA 679 (E).
[15] Schmidt 1963 *THRHR* 139.
[16] Act 103 of 1987.
[17] *LAWSA* para 607.
[18] Act 23 of 1957.
[19] Hoffmann & Zeffertt 534.
[20] 1937 AD 31 44.
[21] *Elliot & Phipson* 89. See also § 30 5 4 below.

& Zeffertt state that a presumption of fact "is a mere inference of probability which the court may draw if on all the evidence it appears to be appropriate".[22] A court is not obliged to draw the inference dictated by a presumption of fact if such an inference would not accord with common sense.[23] For example, it can be presumed that a person found in possession of recently stolen goods stole them or received them knowing that they were stolen. In *S v Skweyiya*,[24] when the accused was stopped at a road block, he lied to the police in telling them that he did not have a key to the boot. When the boot was eventually opened it was found to contain stolen property (hi-fi equipment and bedspreads). The accused lied again and told the police that he had not known that the goods were in his boot. The court, finding that the goods were of the type that could be quickly sold, held that the facts did not justify invoking the presumption that the accused himself actually stole them. Consequently, he was found guilty of receiving stolen property but not guilty of theft.

As these inferences reflect no more than ordinary reasoning and common sense, it has been suggested that it is misleading to call them presumptions. Ogilvie Thompson JA in *Arthur v Bezuidenhout and Mieny* referred with approval to the following remarks made by Wigmore:[25]

> "[T]he distinction between presumptions 'of law' and presumptions 'of fact' is in truth the difference between things that are in reality presumptions and things that are not presumptions at all . . . There is in truth but one kind of presumption; and the term 'presumption of fact' should be discarded as useless and confusing."

28 4   The Effect of Presumptions on the Burden of Proof

In § 28 1 above it was said that presumptions which operate without the requirement of proof of any basic facts can be viewed as merely stating the rules as to the burden of proof. The effect of these presumptions on the burden of proof is generally easily ascertainable: for example, the presumption of innocence requires the state to prove the guilt of the accused beyond a reasonable doubt, whilst the presumption of sanity requires a person alleging insanity to provide proof on a balance of probabilities.[26] However, the effect on the burden of proof by presumptions that require proof of a basic fact is not always as clear. In *R v Downey*[27] the court classified presumptions in terms of their effect on the burden of proof as follows:

> "*(a)* Permissive Inferences: Where the trier of fact is entitled to infer a presumed fact from the proof of a basic fact, but is not obliged to do so. This results in a tactical burden whereby the accused may wish to call evidence in rebuttal, but is not required to do so . . .
> *(b)* Evidential Burdens: Where the trier of fact is required to draw a conclusion from proof

---

[22] At 531.

[23] See Elliot *Elliot & Phipson* 89; Hoffmann & Zeffertt 531.

[24] 1984 4 SA 712 (A).

[25] 1962 2 SA 566 (A) 574. The quotation is from Wigmore para 2491.

[26] The constitutionality of this presumption may also be challenged on the same basis as those statutory presumptions which have the effect of placing the burden of proof on the accused. See § 31 4 1 below.

[27] Supra 456. The burden of proof is discussed in chs 31 (criminal cases) and 32 (civil cases) below.

of the basic fact in the absence of evidence to the contrary. This mandatory conclusion results in an evidential burden whereby the accused will need to call evidence, unless there is already evidence to the contrary in the Crown's case . . . *(c)* Legal Burdens: Similar to the burden in *(b)* except that the presumed fact must be disproved on a balance of probabilities instead of by the mere raising of evidence to the contrary. These are also referred to as 'reverse onus clauses'."

The above analysis of presumptions was found to be useful by the Constitutional Court in *S v Zuma*.[28] The constitutionality of presumptions that have the effect of placing a burden of proof on the accused is discussed in chapter 29 below.

Presumptions of fact, in terms of the *Downey* analysis, must be regarded as permissive inferences and clearly have no effect on the incidence of the burden of proof, merely casting a tactical burden on the accused to adduce evidence. Hoffmann & Zeffertt assert that whether a rebuttable presumption of law casts an evidential burden or legal burden on the person against whom the presumption operates can be ascertained by looking at the language in which the presumption is cast.[29] When a provision states that "X has happened unless the contrary has been proved (or other words to that effect)"[30] then a legal burden rests on the party who has the task of rebutting the presumption. In *Zuma*[31] the court held that the words "unless the contrary is proved", contained in s 217(1)*(b)*(ii) of the CPA, cast a legal burden on the accused to prove that his confession did not meet the requirements of admissibility.[32]

However, where it is stated "that evidence of one fact constitutes '*prima facie* proof of', or '*prima facie* evidence of' " only an evidential burden is created. The words "in the absence of evidence to the contrary" have the same effect.[33]

Presumptions which create a legal or evidential burden must, in so far as they affect the incidence of the burden of proof, be regarded as forming part of the substantive law, and consequently the incidence will be governed by English law.[34] On the other hand, the existence of a presumption as a rule of law will be determined by reference to Roman-Dutch law.[35]

28 5   SOME EXAMPLES OF PRESUMPTIONS

There are so many presumptions both at common law and in terms of statute that any detailed discussion of them would be "an unprofitable and monstrous task".[36] A few examples have been selected for discussion in order better to illustrate the effect of presumptions.

---

[28] 1995 1 SACR 568 (CC); *S v Bhulwana; S v Gwadiso* 1995 2 SACR 748 (CC). See §§ 29 4 and 29 5 for further discussion.
[29] At 534.
[30] At 534.
[31] Supra.
[32] See §§ 17 5 above and 29 4 below.
[33] Hoffmann & Zeffertt 534.
[34] *Tregea v Godart* 1939 AD 16. See § 4 3 above for a discussion of this case.
[35] See Hoffmann & Zeffertt 535. See also § 4 3 above.
[36] Heydon *Evidence* 49, quoting Thayer *A Preliminary Treatise on Evidence at the Common Law* (1989) 313.

28 5 1 Marriage   There is no presumption of marriage.[37] However, the validity
of a marriage will be presumed once evidence is adduced showing that a marriage
ceremony was performed.[38] The onus is on the person who challenges the validity
of such a marriage to show that it is invalid.[39] This rebuttable presumption of law
creates a legal burden in that the validity of the marriage must be disproved on
a balance of probabilities. The presumption as stated in Halsbury's *Laws of
England*[40] also requires proof that the parties subsequently lived together as
husband and wife. However, Hoffmann & Zeffertt state that although in most of
the decided cases there was proof of cohabitation, evidence of cohabitation does
not appear to be essential to raise a presumption of validity.[41]

In Halsbury[42] it is also stated that "[m]ere cohabitation as man and wife if the
parties were esteemed and reputed as such by those who knew them may be
sufficient to raise the presumption" (that is the presumption of marriage).
Although in *Aronegary v Vaigalie*[43] the presumption was held to persist "unless the
contrary be clearly proved", it is argued that an analysis of the majority of cases
would indicate that this is a presumption of fact.[44] For example, in *Fitzgerald v
Green*[45] one of the issues that the plaintiffs had to prove was that they were the
legitimate children of their parents (F and H). The defendant alleged that F and
H had not been legally married. In support of his contention the defendant
established that there was no record of the marriage in the relevant registers.
However, it was also clear from the evidence that the registers had not been
properly kept and were incomplete. The court, although noting that the ordinary
way of proving a marriage was to produce the register or a certified extract from
it, held that it could be proved in other ways, for example, by evidence of witnesses
who were present at the marriage ceremony or by satisfactory evidence of
cohabitation and repute.[46] The plaintiffs produced evidence of a court order
granting a decree of divorce, which they argued was proof that their parents had
been married. The court held that in the circumstances of the case the parties
had not been strangers to one another and the decree of divorce was evidence
of the marriage of F and H.[47] However, the court held that apart from the decree
of divorce the plaintiffs had established a lawful marriage between their parents
by the production of evidence of cohabitation and repute. A witness testified that
he had known F and H before they were married, and after hearing that they
were to be married he saw them go to a church. He also saw them leaving the
church and thereafter heard them being congratulated as bridegroom and bride.

---

[37] *Acar v Pierce* 1986 2 SA 827 (W) 832.
[38] *Fitzgerald v Green* 1911 EDL 432; *Ex parte L* 1947 3 SA 50 (C).
[39] *Ochberg v Ochberg's Estate* 1941 CPD 15 33.
[40] Hailsham (ed) vol 13, s 702 at 634.
[41] Hoffmann & Zeffertt 538.
[42] *Laws of England* 634.
[43] 1881 6 App Cas 364 371.
[44] Hoffmann & Zeffertt 538.
[45] 1911 EDL 432.
[46] At 449.
[47] At 452.

Several other witnesses testified that F and H lived together as husband and wife and were generally considered to be married. Evidence was also led that the plaintiffs had been baptized in the Roman Catholic Church and that this Church did not baptize children "of parents living in sin together".[48] The court held that all this evidence considered together established a very strong *prima facie* case that F and H were legally married.[49] Common sense tells us that the court did not have to invoke a presumption of law to reach this conclusion as the facts alone were sufficient to establish a *prima facie* case. Consequently, it would appear that a presumption of fact and not a presumption of law was applied in this case. The court held that the finding in *Aronegary v Vaigalie*,[50] that where a man and woman are proved to have lived together as man and wife, the law will presume, *unless the contrary be clearly* proved, that they were living together in consequence of a valid marriage and not in a state of concubinage, also reflected the correct position in South African law.[51] This is the language of a rebuttable presumption of law and it is submitted that this is the correct classification of the presumption.

Every marriage is presumed to be in community of property until the contrary is proved.[52] In *Brummund v Brummund's Estate*[53] the parties' marriage certificate did not reflect whether they were married with or without an antenuptial contract, the relevant space on the certificate having been left empty. The court held that the presumption that they were married in community of property could be defeated by satisfactory evidence to the contrary. Although in *Acar v Pierce*[54] the court appears to have regarded the presumption as one of fact, *Brummund's* case would appear to indicate that it is a rebuttable presumption of law.[55]

28 5 2 Bigamy Section 237 of the CPA reads as follows:

"(1) At criminal proceedings at which an accused is charged with bigamy, it shall, as soon as it is proved that a marriage ceremony, other than the ceremony relating to the alleged bigamous marriage, took place within the Republic between the accused and another person, be presumed, unless the contrary is proved, that the marriage was on the date of the solemnization thereof lawful and binding.

(2) At criminal proceedings at which an accused is charged with bigamy, it shall be presumed, unless the contrary is proved, that at the time of the solemnization of the alleged bigamous marriage there subsisted between the accused and another person a lawful and binding marriage —

(a) if there is produced at such proceedings, in any case in which the marriage is alleged to have been solemnized within the Republic, an extract from the marriage register which purports —

   (i) to be a duplicate original or a copy of the marriage register relating to such marriage; and

---

[48] At 454.

[49] At 459.

[50] Supra.

[51] At 457. See also *Nyokana v Nyokana* 1925 NPD 227.

[52] *Edelstein v Edelstein NO* 1952 3 SA 1 (A).

[53] 1993 2 SA 494 (Nm).

[54] 1986 2 SA 827 (W).

[55] See also Hoffmann & Zeffertt 539, where they state that it is not clear into which category this presumption falls.

> (ii) to be certified as such a duplicate original or such copy by the person having the custody of such marriage register or by a registrar of marriages;
> (b) if there is produced at such proceedings, in any case in which the marriage is alleged to have been solemnized outside the Republic, a document which purports —
>   (i) to be an extract from a marriage register kept according to law in the country where the marriage is alleged to have been solemnized; and
>   (ii) to be certified as such an extract by the person having the custody of such register, if the signature of such persons on the certificate is authenticated in accordance with any law of the Republic governing the authentication of documents executed outside the Republic.
> (3) At criminal proceedings at which an accused is charged with bigamy, evidence —
> (a) that shortly before the alleged bigamous marriage the accused had been cohabiting with the person to whom he is alleged to be lawfully married;
> (b) that the accused had been treating and recognizing such persons as a spouse; and
> (c) of the performance of a marriage ceremony between the accused and such person,
> shall, as soon as the alleged bigamous marriage, wherever solemnized, has been proved, be *prima facie* proof that there was a lawful and binding marriage subsisting between the accused and such person a the time of the solemnization of the alleged bigamous marriage."

The words "unless the contrary is proved" contained in subsecs (1) and (2) place a legal burden on the accused, whilst the words "*prima facie* proof" in subsec (3) place an evidential burden on the accused.[56]

28 5 3 Legitimacy   Once a party alleging legitimacy has proved that the child in question was conceived by a woman whilst she was married the child will be presumed to be legitimate, and the party contesting legitimacy must prove on a balance of probabilities that the child was not conceived as a result of intercourse between the spouses. It is clear that a legal burden is created by this presumption. This presumption can be rebutted by leading evidence of a blood test showing that the spouse was not the father, or by establishing that the husband was sterile at the relevant time. It has been held that proof that contraceptives were used at the material time will carry little weight.[57] In terms of s 226 of the CPA either spouse may give evidence that the parties did not have sexual intercourse during the period when the child was conceived. A similar provision is found in s 3 of the CPEA.[58]

28 5 4 Paternity of illegitimate children   Section 1 of the Children's Status Act[59] provides:

> "If in any legal proceedings at which it has been placed in issue whether any particular person is the father of an extra-marital child, it is proved by way of a judicial admission or otherwise that he had sexual intercourse with the mother of the child at any time when that child could have been conceived, it shall in the absence of evidence to the contrary, be presumed that he is the father of the child."

---

[56] See also Hoffmann & Zeffertt 540.
[57] *R v Van der Merwe* 1952 1 SA 647 (O).
[58] Prior to 1935 such evidence was prohibited in terms of the common law. See *Russel v Russel and Mayer* 1924 AC 687.
[59] Act 82 of 1987.

A similar presumption exists at common law.[60] In terms of the common law the person against whom the presumption operated had to prove that he could not possibly be the father, not merely that he probably was not the father.[61] On this basis, Hoffmann & Zeffertt state the *exceptio plurium concubentium,* or defence based on evidence that the woman slept with other men, is not part of modern law.[62] Applying Hoffmann & Zeffertt's analysis of the wording of statutory presumptions,[63] the words "in the absence of evidence to the contrary" indicate that the statutory presumption merely places an evidential burden on the putative father in contrast to the common-law presumption, which creates a legal burden, that is, a burden of proof.

Section 2 of the Children's Status Act provides:

> "If in any legal proceedings at which the paternity of any child has been placed in issue it is adduced in evidence or otherwise that any party to those proceedings, after he has been requested thereto by the other party to those proceedings, refuses to submit himself or, if he has parental authority over that child, to cause that child to be submitted to the taking of a blood sample in order to carry out scientific tests relating to the paternity of that child, it shall be presumed, until the contrary is proved, that any such refusal is aimed at concealing the truth concerning the paternity of that child."

This presumption would appear to give rise to a legal burden.[64]

28 5 5 Death In terms of both the Inquests Act[65] and the common law, in certain circumstances, a person can be presumed to have died. Section 16(1) of the Inquests Act provides:

> "If in the case of an inquest where the body of the person concerned is alleged to have been destroyed or where no body has been found or recovered, the evidence proves beyond a reasonable doubt that a death has occurred, the judicial officer holding such inquest shall record a finding accordingly . . .."

Once such a finding has been made the magistrate is required to submit the record of the inquest to a provincial or local division of the Supreme Court for review.[66] Once the finding is confirmed by the Supreme Court it is no longer necessary to make an application to court for an order presuming death.[67]

It would appear that at common law death is not required to be proved beyond reasonable doubt and the applicant is required to persuade the court that death can be "inferred on a preponderance of probability from the evidence".[68] A

---

[60] There is uncertainty whether the common-law presumption can be invoked only by an admission of intercourse, or whether it also comes into operation when intercourse is proved by some other means. See *S v Swart* 1965 3 SA 454 (A).

[61] *Mahomed v Shaik* 1978 4 SA 523 (N).

[62] At 542–3. The matter was left open by the Appellate Division in *S v Swart* supra.

[63] See § 28 2 above.

[64] There is conflicting authority as to whether or not the Supreme Court as upper guardian can consent to a minor undergoing a blood test or tissue test against the wishes of a custodian parent, or order an adult to undergo a blood test. See *E v E* 1940 TPD 333; *Seetal v Pravitha NO* 1983 3 SA 827 (D); *M v R* 1989 1 SA 416 (O); *Nell v Nell* 1990 3 SA 889 (T); *S v L* 1992 3 SA 713 (E). See further § 19 8 n 36 above.

[65] Act 58 of 1959.

[66] Section 18(1) of Act 58 of 59.

[67] Section 18(2) and (2A).

[68] *Ex parte Govender* 1993 3 SA 721 (D) 722.

judicial declaration of death is a presumption in that it is based on circumstantial evidence and can be invalidated if the person is subsequently proved to be alive.[69]

Unlike the English law, which requires a person to have been unheard of for seven years before a persuasive presumption of death will be found to exist,[70] the South African law does not require any specific facts to be proved before death will be presumed. The court will not presume death merely because a person has been missing for a number of years.[71] For example, in *Ex parte Govender*[72] the applicant's husband had been missing for eight years. Ten days after the day on which he disappeared a suicide note was found in his jacket pocket. In the note he gave financial difficulties as the reason for taking his life. The suicide note was dated some five months before his disappearance. The court, noting that it was extremely rare for the body of a suicide victim not to be found and that the suicide victim had not left the note in a place where it could easily be discovered, held that it was also possible that the applicant's husband had disappeared in order to avoid his creditors. The court held that, although there was an inherent possibility of suicide, there were insufficient facts from which to infer that on a preponderance of probabilities death had occurred.[73]

However, in some circumstances the mere passage of time will make it unlikely that the person is still alive. In *Ex parte Engelbrecht*[74] death was presumed when the man had been missing for thirty-five years, and would have been 93 years old at the date of the application. In *Ex parte Rungsamy*[75] a presumption of death was made when the woman who was the subject of the application had been missing for only four years. However, she was 83 or 84 years of age, known to be in frail health, and had not collected her pension during the years when she was missing.

Most often when an application is made for a presumption of death the court will issue a rule *nisi* calling upon all persons to show cause why an order presuming death should not be made. The rule *nisi* will be issued once the applicant has established a *prima facie* case.[76] The court will only decide on the return day whether there is sufficient evidence to support a presumption of death. Hoffmann & Zeffertt suggest that if there is no response to the rule *nisi*, a presumption of death will be made.[77] However, in *Ex parte Dieters*,[78] despite the absence of a response to the rule *nisi*, the court declined to presume death. This can perhaps be explained on the basis that a *prima facie* case does not mean that a court must find in favour of the applicant, but simply that it may find in favour of the applicant. The disadvantages suffered by an applicant who goes to the expense of publishing the rule *nisi*, but fails in her application despite the

---

[69] Hoffmann & Zeffertt 87.
[70] Heydon *Evidence* 49.
[71] *Re Beaglehole* 1908 TS 49.
[72] 1993 3 SA 721 (D).
[73] At 723I.
[74] 1956 1 SA 408 (E).
[75] 1958 4 SA 688 (D).
[76] *Ex parte Alexander* 1956 2 SA 608 (A) 611.
[77] At 557.
[78] 1993 3 SA 379 (D).

absence of a response, is ameliorated in that the court may find that there is sufficient evidence to enable the court to appoint a *curator bonis* to manage the missing person's affairs.[79] The court may even order that the estate be distributed to the heirs, usually with the proviso that security be given.[80] For example, in *Ex parte Dieters*[81] the court, having issued a rule *nisi*, found that there was not sufficient evidence to order a presumption of death. However, the court authorized the distribution of the money held in the guardian's fund to the missing man's children without the necessity of the children providing security.[82]

28 5 5 1 *Presumption of death and dissolution of marriage* Section 2 of the Dissolution of Marriages on Presumption of Death Act[83] provides that when a married person has been presumed dead in terms of the Inquest Act "the marriage in question shall for all purposes be deemed to have been dissolved by death". The surviving spouse need not make application for an order dissolving the marriage.

Section 1 of the Act provides that when an application for an order presuming the death of a married person is made the Supreme Court granting the order may at the same time make an order that the marriage is deemed to be dissolved. If the orders are not made simultaneously, the surviving spouse may at any later stage make an application for an order dissolving the marriage.

28 5 5 2 *The date of death* The court will presume death to have occurred on or before a particular date only if the evidence supports such a finding.[84] In *Nepgen NO v Van Dyk NO*[85] Lansdown JP held that there was no presumption in our law such as the English law presumption that if the order of death is uncertain the younger is deemed to have survived the elder. Consequently, the party alleging a particular order of death bears the onus of proof. Where people have died in a common disaster the court has frequently held that they died simultaneously. Examples of orders presuming simultaneous death include cases where ships had been torpedoed during wartime;[86] the death of a mother and sister during the German occupation of Poland;[87] the death of passengers in an air crash.[88] This presumption is one of fact and will generally only be invoked where on the facts it appears most probable that the deaths were simultaneous. However, it would also appear that factors such as the absence of prejudice and the intention of the

---

[79] *Ex parte Thomson* 1919 CPD 277.

[80] *Ex parte Heppinstall* 1923 OPD 134.

[81] Supra.

[82] Section 73(1) of the Administration of Estates Act 66 of 1965 provides that the Master may appoint a curator of the property of a person whose whereabouts are unknown but who has not been presumed dead.

[83] Act 23 of 1979.

[84] See *Ex parte Graham* 1963 4 SA 145 (D), in which the court held that the presumptions referred to in Voet 34 5 3 and 36 1 16 were not part of our law; *Kakuva v Minister van Polisie* 1983 2 SA 684 (SWA).

[85] 1940 EDL 123.

[86] *Ex parte Bagshaw* 1943 2 SA PH F77 (C); *Ex parte Martienssen* 1944 CPD 139.

[87] *Ex parte Chodos* 1948 4 SA 221 (N).

[88] *Ex parte Graham* supra.

testator also affect the willingness of the court to presume simultaneous death. For example, in *Ex parte Chodos*[89] there was little, if any, evidence to show that the parties had died simultaneously; however, the court made an order declaring that the two people had died simultaneously, noting that the order would not prejudice anybody's rights. The court in *Ex parte Graham*[90] held that there was evidence to show that the testators, in using the word 'simultaneously' in their will, had foreseen their deaths happening on one occasion as a result of a single disaster, whether or not there was a difference in time between the technical moments of death. It was therefore found that the parties had died simultaneously.[91]

28 5 6 Regularity   The presumption of regularity is based on the maxim *omnia praesumuntur rite esse acta.* Hoffmann & Zeffertt, noting that the presumption is ill-defined, describe it in the following terms:[92]

> "In some cases it appears to be no more than an ordinary inference, based upon the assumption that what regularly happens is likely to have happened again. In other cases it is treated as a presumption of law, sometimes placing an onus upon the opposing party and sometimes creating only a duty to adduce contrary evidence. It has been applied in a wide variety of cases which are impossible to catalogue exhaustively."

28 5 6 1   *Letters*   Circumstantial evidence can be adduced to prove that a letter was posted. The party alleging posting may lead evidence establishing the existence of a routine used for posting letters and showing that the letter in question was dealt with in this routine manner. This is more easily done in the case of public officials as the court will take judicial notice of the existence of an office routine.[93] Wessel CJ in *Cape Coast Exploration Ltd v Scholtz* held:[94]

> "We must presume that an official will carry out the ordinary routine work of his office, for in our experience this is what usually occurs. Hence we must presume that if an official letter is written and a copy filed, that the former is dispatched in the ordinary course of business to the person concerned and that he has received it."

However, in the case of persons working in the private sector the court generally requires evidence of an office routine from which posting can be inferred.[95] This is a presumption of fact; therefore the burden of proof is not affected.

An unregistered letter that is presumed to be posted will not be presumed to have been received. For example, in *Goldfield Confectionery and Bakery (Pty) Ltd v Norman Adman (Pty) Ltd*[96] the court assumed in the defendant's favour that an envelope containing a cheque had been posted and that if it had been placed in the plaintiff's post-office box by postal officials, this would constitute delivery.[97]

---

[89] Supra.
[90] Supra.
[91] See 1978 *ASSAL* 364–6.
[92] At 545.
[93] *Cape Coast Exploration Ltd v Scholtz* 1933 AD 56.
[94] 1933 AD 56 76.
[95] *Barclays National Bank Ltd v Wall* 1983 1 SA 149 (A).
[96] 1950 2 SA 763 (T).
[97] At 768.

Counsel for the defendant argued that there was a presumption that a letter which has been posted had reached the addressee. Ramsbottom J rejected this contention and held that the word "presumption" in this context

> "means no more than that the fact that a letter was posted is evidence from which an inference that it reached the addressee may be drawn. But all the circumstances must be considered in order to decide whether on a balance of probabilities the inference ought to be drawn."

The court concluded that in the present case there was no evidence that the envelope was addressed to the plaintiff's post box and consequently delivery could not be inferred.[98]

However, the position in respect of registered letters is different both at common law and in terms of statute. In *S v Buys*[99] the court held that evidence that a letter had been posted and that a post-office slip had been received constituted *prima facie* proof that the request had been received and that the appellant's failure to testify elevated the *prima facie* proof to proof beyond reasonable doubt. It would therefore appear that proof that a letter was sent by registered post will give rise to a presumption that it was received. The presumption casts an evidentiary burden on persons alleging that they did not receive the letter.

Section 7 of the Interpretation Act[100] provides:[101]

> "Where any law authorizes or requires any document to be served by post, whether the expression 'serve', or 'give', or 'send' or any other expression is used, then unless the contrary intention appears, the service shall be deemed to be effected by properly addressing, prepaying, and posting a registered letter containing the document, and unless the contrary is proved, to have been effected at the time at which the letter would be delivered in the ordinary course of post."

Hoffmann & Zeffertt comment on the strangeness of this presumption, in that by allowing the addressee to rebut the presumption that he received it at particular time, it will "always be open to the addressee to prove that the service was in fact ineffective because the document did not reach him".[102] It would appear that this presumption casts a legal burden on the person disputing the time of delivery.

28 5 6 2 *Validity of official acts* Public officials are rebuttably presumed to have been properly appointed. This presumption places a legal burden on the party alleging the contrary.[103] It is also presumed that an official has acted in compliance

---

[98] See Hoffmann & Zeffertt 547, where it is noted that "cases in which receipt of a letter is inferred from posting must be distinguished from those in which, as a matter of substantive law, posting is all that needs to be proved".

[99] 1988 2 SA 201 (O).

[100] Act 33 of 1957.

[101] For examples of the application of this provision, see *Maron v Mulbarton Gardens (Pty) Ltd* 1975 4 SA 123 (W); *Allen v Casey NO* 1991 3 SA 480 (D).

[102] At 548.

[103] *Naidoo v R* 1909 TS 43.

with prescribed formalities.[104] Wigmore[105] sets out the following conditions for the operation of the presumption:[106]

> "The general experience that a rule of official duty, or the requirement of legal conditions, is fulfilled by those upon whom it is incumbent, has given rise occasionally to a presumption of due performance. This presumption is more often mentioned than enforced; and its scope as a real presumption is indefinite and hardly capable of reduction to rules . . . It may be said that most of the instances of its application are found attended by several conditions; first, that the matter is more or less in the past, and incapable of easily procured evidence; secondly, that it involves a mere formality or detail of required procedure, in the routine of litigation or of a public officer's action; next, that it involves to some extent the security of apparently vested rights, so that the presumption will serve to prevent an unwholesome uncertainty, and, finally that the circumstances of the particular case add some element of probability."

The effect of the presumption on the burden of proof varies:[107]

> "In some criminal cases it has been said to place an onus upon the accused, but in others the judges have used language which indicated that the presumption could be rebutted by some evidence upon which the court could find that the requisite formalities were not complied with . . . In civil cases, however, the presumption has often been treated as placing an onus upon the opposing party, and in cases where proof of non-compliance with a formality would involve the disturbance of old and vested rights, the onus of rebuttal has been very heavy indeed."

The presumption should not be interpreted as meaning that it will be presumed that all official acts are lawful. For example, in *R v Jenkins*[108] the court held that it could not be presumed that an arrest was lawful.

It would appear that the presumption applies in a very diluted form to private acts, and is merely an ordinary inference of probability.[109]

28 5 7   *Res ipsa loquitur*   The maxim *res ipsa loquitur* means "the matter speaks for itself". It is almost exclusively applied where the cause of an accident is unknown.[110] If it is the type of accident that does not ordinarily occur in the absence of negligence, an inference of negligence may be drawn from the accident itself.[111] For example, in *Authur v Bezuidenhout and Mieny*[112] the appellant's vehicle had suddenly swerved to its right onto the incorrect side of the road and collided head-on with the respondent's vehicle. Both drivers had been killed and there was no clear explanation as to the cause of the accident. The court

---

[104] *R v Naran Samy* 1945 AD 618; *Byers v Chinn* 1928 AD 322; *Tshivhase Royal Council v Tshivhase* 1990 3 SA 828 (V).

[105] Wigmore para 2534.

[106] This passage was approved by the Appellate Division in *Beyers v Chinn* 1928 AD 322 at 332; *Natal Estates v Secretary for Inland Revenue* 1975 4 SA 177 (A).

[107] Hoffmann & Zeffertt 549–50.

[108] 1945 3 SA 560 (C).

[109] O'Dowd *The Law of Evidence in South Africa* (1963) 108. Hoffmann & Zeffertt 550. See *Knocker v Standard Bank of SA Ltd* 1933 AD 128 133, where the court, although not deciding, suggests that it is inappropriate to apply the presumption to private acts.

[110] *Madyosi v SA Eagle Insurance Co Ltd* 1990 3 SA 442 (A).

[111] In *Groenewald v Conradie; Groenewald v Auto Protection Insurance Co Ltd* 1965 1 SA 184 (A) the court held that in the decision whether a particular matter is one where *res ipsa loquitur* applies, the court must look solely at the occurence itself. See also *Stacey v Kent* 1995 3 SA 344 (E).

[112] 1962 2 SA 566 (A).

found the maxim *res ipsa loquitur* applied and negligence was inferred. In *Madyosi v SA Eagle Insurance Co Ltd*[113] the court found that the maxim did not apply. A bus had left the road and overturned after the left front tyre burst. The court found that the only known facts relating to the negligence did not only consist of the occurrence itself. It was known that the bus left the road and overturned because of the burst tyre. It was held that the burst tyre was not a neutral fact as regards the alleged negligence. It explained why the bus left the road. Although the burst tyre was not inconsistent with a negligent failure to maintain the tyres, no such negligence had been pleaded. The court concluded that the fact of the burst tyre precluded the inference being drawn from the mere fact of the occurrence.[114]

As this presumption is not based on a rule of law but on commonsense reasoning, it should not strictly be classified as a presumption but rather as a permissible inference which may be drawn if it is sustained by the proven facts.[115]

The maxim does not effect the incidence of the burden of proof. In *Sardi v Standard and General Insurance Co Ltd*[116] the court held:

> "The person against whom the inference of negligence is sought to be drawn, may give or adduce evidence seeking to explain that the occurrence was unrelated to any negligence on his part. The court will test the explanation by considerations such as probability and credibility . . . At the end of the case, the court has to decide whether, on all the evidence and the probabilities and the inferences, the plaintiff has discharged the onus of proof on the pleadings on a preponderance of probability, just as the court would do in any other case concerning negligence. In this final analysis the court does not adopt the piecemeal approach of *(a)* first drawing the inference of negligence from the occurrence itself, and regarding this as a *prima facie* case; and then *(b)* deciding whether this has been rebutted by the defendants explanation."

Where an inference of negligence is drawn an evidential burden is cast on the defendant; however, this does not mean that he must prove that he was not negligent. He must merely show that the facts are as consistent with an inference not involving negligence, or he must adduce evidence so as to raise a reasonable doubt.[117]

The maxim *res ipsa loquitur* is also discussed in § 30 5 4 below.

---

[113] Supra.

[114] At 445.

[115] See, e g, *Steenberg v De Kaap Timber (Pty) Ltd* 1992 2 SA 169 (A); *Stacey v Kent* supra. See also § 30 5 4 below.

[116] 1977 3 SA 776 (A) 780. See also *Arthur v Bezuidenhout and Mieny* supra 574; *Madyosi v SA Eagle Insurance Co Ltd* supra; *Osborne Panama SA v Shell & BP South African Petroleum Refineries (Pty) Ltd* 1982 4 SA 890 (A).

[117] *Authur v Bezuidenhout and Mieny* supra. See Hoffmann & Zeffertt 554.

CHAPTER 29

A CONSTITUTIONAL PERSPECTIVE ON STATUTORY PRESUMPTIONS

A St Q Skeen

29 1   INTRODUCTION

Section 25 of the interim Constitution provides that every accused person shall have the right to a fair trial, which includes the right[1] to be presumed innocent and to remain silent during plea proceedings or trial and not to testify during the trial. Certain presumptions in favour of the state are to be found in various statutes and may run foul of the constitutional presumption of innocence.[2] This is particularly so in the case of so-called reverse onus provisions which are found in some statutes,[3] where the prosecution may be relieved of bearing the burden of proving all of the elements of a criminal charge. This may result in a conviction occurring despite the existence of a reasonable doubt. A reverse onus requires an accused to prove a certain fact on a balance of probabilities. The presumption of innocence has long been a fundamental component of our system of criminal law and procedure[4] and the entrenchment of the presumption of innocence in terms of s 25(3)*(c)* must be interpreted in this context.[5] Under the previous constitutional system the legislature was empowered to limit the principle and impose on an accused the burden of proving the absence of an element of an offence.[6] Under the present constitutional system such a limitation would have to be justified under s 33 of the interim Constitution.[7]

---

[1] Section 25(3)*(c)* of Act 200 of 1993.

[2] The Constitutional Court has already invalidated such presumptions: see §§ 29 3 and 29 4 below as well as *S v Julies* 1996 2 SACR 108 (CC) and *S v Mbatha; S v Prinsloo* 1996 1 SACR 371 (CC). See also generally *S v Chogugudza* 1996 1 SACR 477 (ZS); *S v Pineiro* 1993 2 SACR 412 (Nm); *S v Van der Berg* 1996 1 SACR 19 (Nm).

[3] See §§ 29 3 and 29 4 below.

[4] *Woolmington v DPP* 1935 AC 462 (HL); *R v Ndhlovu* 1945 AD 369.

[5] *S v Bhulwana; S v Gwadiso* 1995 12 BCLR 1579 (CC) 1585B.

[6] *R v Ndhlovu* supra; *Woolmington v DPP* supra; *R v Britz* 1949 3 SA 293 (A).

[7] See § 29 5 below.

29 2   CANADIAN JURISPRUDENCE ON STATUTORY PRESUMPTIONS

In *S v Zuma*[8] Kentridge AJ indicated that Canadian cases on reverse onus provisions under the Canadian Charter of Rights and Freedoms were particularly helpful to South African law because of their persuasive reasoning and because s 1 of the Charter is analogous to the South African limitation clause in s 33 of the interim Constitution.

It is proposed to look at three leading Canadian cases on the subject, the first of which is *R v Oakes*.[9] This case considered a challenge of s 8 of the Narcotic Control Act.[10] This section provided that on a charge of possessing a narcotic drug for the purpose of trafficking, the trial must be conducted in two parts. The prosecution must first prove possession of the narcotic beyond a reasonable doubt. Thereafter the accused must establish on a balance of probabilities that he did not possess the narcotic for the purpose of trafficking.

The issue for decision was whether s 89 of the Narcotic Control Act violated the presumption of innocence embodied in s 11(d) of the Charter. Dickson CJC[11] considered the general nature of presumptions, which can be placed in two general categories: presumptions without basic facts, and presumptions with basic facts. A presumption without a basic fact is simply a conclusion which must be drawn until the contrary is proved, whereas a presumption with a basic fact entails a conclusion to be drawn on proof of the basic fact. Basic fact presumptions, Dickson CJC indicated, can be further categorized into permissive and mandatory presumptions. A permissive presumption leaves it optional as to whether to draw the inference or not, whilst a mandatory presumption requires the inference to be made. Rebuttable presumptions may be rebutted either (a) by the accused raising a reasonable doubt as to the existence of the presumed fact; (b) by the accused bearing an evidentiary burden to lead sufficient evidence to bring into question the truth of the presumed fact; or (c) the accused may have a legal or persuasive burden to prove on a balance of probabilities the non-existence of the presumed fact. Dickson CJC concluded that s 8 of the Narcotic Control Act was a basic fact presumption which was mandatory in its effect. The presumption was rebuttable by the accused, upon whom the legal burden of proof was placed to prove on a balance of probabilities that he was not in possession of the narcotic for the purpose of trafficking.[12] This type of provision is often referred to as a "reverse onus clause".

In considering whether s 8 of the Narcotic Control Act offended against the presumption of innocence as guaranteed by s 11(d) of the Charter Dickson CJC described the importance of the presumption of innocence as follows:[13]

---

[8] 1995 2 SA 642 (CC) 654, 1995 1 SACR 568 (CC), 1995 4 BCLR 401 (SA). See also Govender 1995 *SACJ* 205.
[9] 1986 26 DLR (4th) 481.
[10] RSC 1970 (now RSC 1985).
[11] At 209–10.
[12] At 212.
[13] At 212–13.

"The presumption of innocence protects the fundamental liberty and human dignity of any and every person accused by the State of criminal conduct. An individual charged with a criminal offence faces grave social and personal consequences, including potential loss of physical liberty, subjection to social stigma and ostracism from the community, as well as other social, psychological and economic harms. In light of the gravity of these consequences, the presumption of innocence is crucial. It ensures that until the State proves an accused's guilt beyond all reasonable doubt, he or she is innocent. This is essential in a society committed to fairness and social justice. The presumption of innocence confirms our faith in humankind; it reflects our belief that individuals are decent and law-abiding members of the community until proven otherwise."

After an examination of the common-law position, previous Canadian decisions, and the Universal Declaration of Human Rights of 1948 Dickson CJC decided[14] that the presumption of innocence requires that s 11(d) of the Charter should have at the minimum three basic components: (i) an accused must be proved guilty beyond a reasonable doubt; (ii) the state bears the onus of proof; and (iii) prosecutions must be carried out in accordance with lawful procedures and fairness.

Dickson CJC then considered United States of America cases on reverse onus provisions and the presumption of innocence. In *Tot v United States*[15] Roberts J outlined the following test:

"[A] statutory presumption cannot be sustained if there be no rational connection between the fact proved and the ultimate fact presumed, if the inference of the one from the proof of the other is arbitrary because of lack of connection between the two in common experience."

In *Leary v United States*[16] Harlam J had indicated a more stringent test for invalidity:

"[A] criminal statutory presumption must be regarded as 'irrational or arbitrary', and hence unconstitutional, unless it can at least be said with substantial assurance that the presumed fact is more likely than not to flow from the proved fact on which it is made to depend."

In the case of *County Court of Ulster County, New York v Allen*[17] it was held that where a mandatory criminal presumption was imposed by statute the state may not rest its case entirely on a presumption unless the fact proved is sufficient to support the inference of guilt beyond a reasonable doubt. Dickson CJC concluded:[18]

"In general one must, I think, conclude that a provision which requires an accused to disprove on a balance of probabilities the existence of a presumed fact, which is an important element of the offence in question, violates the presumption of innocence in s 11(d). If an accused bears the burden of disproving on a balance of probabilities an essential element of an offence, it would be possible for a conviction to occur despite the existence of a reasonable doubt. This would arise if the accused adduced sufficient evidence to raise a reasonable doubt as to his or her innocence but did not convince the jury on a balance of probabilities that the presumed fact was untrue."

Section 8 of the Narcotic Control Act was found to violate s 11(d) of the Charter as an accused is compelled to prove that he is not guilty of the offence of

---

[14] At 214.
[15] 319 US 463 (1943) 467.
[16] 395 US 6 (1969) 36.
[17] 442 US 140 (1979) 167.
[18] *R v Oakes* supra 222.

trafficking narcotics. He is thus denied, said Dickson CJC, his right to be proved guilty — which is radically and fundamentally inconsistent with the societal values of human dignity and liberty.

Consideration was then given to the question as to whether s 8 of the Narcotic Control Act could be upheld as a reasonable and demonstrably justifiable limitation under s 1 of the Charter. Dickson CJC indicated that the rights and freedoms guaranteed by the Charter are not absolute and it may become necessary to limit rights and freedoms in circumstances where their exercise would be inimical to the realization of collective goals of fundamental importance. It was held that the onus of proving that a limit on a right or freedom guaranteed by the Charter is reasonable and demonstrably justified in a free and democratic society rests on the party who wishes to apply a limitation. The standard of proof required is the civil standard, namely proof on a balance of probabilities. A court would also need to know what alternative measures were available to the legislature for implementing the objective.

Dickson CJC said two criteria had to be satisfied:

(1) The objective must be of sufficient importance to warrant overriding a constitutionally protected right or freedom.
(2) The party invoking s 1 must show that the means chosen are reasonable and demonstrably justified. This involves a proportionality test which has three component parts:
  (a) the measures adopted must be carefully designed to achieve the object that is rationally connected;
  (b) the means should impair as little as possible the right or freedom in question; and
  (c) there must be proportionality between the effects of the measures and the objective.

Applying these to s 8 of the Narcotic Control Act, Dickson CJC indicated that the degree of seriousness of drug trafficking was a sufficiently important objective to warrant overriding a Charter right in certain cases. However, s 8 did not survive the rational connection test as the provision of a small quantity of narcotics does not support the inference of trafficking. It was thus found that s 8 was inconsistent with s 11*(d)* of the Canadian Charter and thus of no force and effect.

In *R v Whyte*[19] the issue was whether s 237(1) *(a)* of the Canadian Criminal Code offends the presumption of innocence by providing that on a charge of care or control of a motor vehicle whilst the accused's ability to drive was impaired the accused shall be deemed to have had care or control of the vehicle if he occupied the seat ordinarily occupied by the driver unless he establishes he did not enter or mount the vehicle for the purpose of setting it in motion.

It was held that this presumption violated s 11*(d)* of the Charter, but that it constituted a reasonable limit in terms of s 1 as the provision was designed to serve an objective which was sufficiently important to permit overriding the

---

[19] 1988 51 DLR (4th) 481.

presumption of innocence. The section was a response to a major social problem and there was a rational connection to the objective.

In *R v Downey*[20] the issue was whether s 212(3) of the Criminal Code infringed the right to be presumed to be innocent as set out in s 11(d) of the Canadian Charter of Rights and Freedoms. Section 212(3) provides: "Evidence that a person lives with or is habitually in the company of prostitutes . . . is in the absence of evidence to the contrary, proof that the person lives on the avails of prostitution." It was held that this presumption infringed s 11(d) of the Charter because it could result in the conviction of an accused despite the existence of a reasonable doubt. The fact that someone lives with a prostitute does not lead inexorably to the conclusion that the person is living on avails.

However, the majority of the court held that s 212(3) was valid as a reasonable limit in terms of s 1 of the Charter. The objective of dealing with the pervasive social evil associated with pimping is of sufficient importance to override the protection afforded by s 11(d) of the Charter.

The presumption was necessary, said Cory J, speaking for the majority, because of the documented reluctance of prostitutes to testify against their pimps. It was held that the provision met the proportionality test and the rational connection test as it was a reasonable inference that persons maintaining close ties with prostitutes are living on the avails of prostitution.

Cory J said that as regards minimal impairment Parliament is not required to choose the absolutely least intrusive alternative. Rather the consideration is whether Parliament could reasonably have chosen alternative means which could have achieved the objective as effectively. The test requires a balancing of societal and individual interests. The section was aimed not only at remedying a social problem but also at providing some measure of protection for prostitutes by eliminating the need of testimony from them.

The minority of the court were of the opinion that s 212(3) did not meet the proportionality test. There had to be a very high degree of internal rationality in that there must be a logical connection between the basic fact and the presumed fact. It would not be enough that the evidence of the presumed fact would be a rational inference in some cases.

29 3   *S V Zuma* AND PRESUMPTIONS

In *S v Zuma*[21] s 217(1)(b)(ii) of the CPA was challenged on the grounds that it was in conflict with s 25 of the Constitution.

The provision reads as follows:

"Provided —

. . .

(b) that where the confession is made to a magistrate and reduced to writing in the presence of a magistrate, the confession shall, upon the mere production thereof at the proceedings in question —

---

[20] 1992 90 DLR (4th) 448.
[21] 1995 2 SA 642 (CC), 1995 1 SACR 568 (CC), 1995 4 BCLR 401 (CC).

(i) be admissible in evidence against such person if it appears from the document in which the confession is contained that the confession was made by a person whose name corresponds to that of such person and, in the case of a confession made to a magistrate or confirmed in the presence of a magistrate through an interpreter, if a certificate by the interpreter appears on such document to the effect that he interpreted truly and correctly and to the best of his ability with regard to the contents of the confession and any question put to such person by the magistrate; and

(ii) be presumed, unless the contrary is proved, to have been freely and voluntarily made by such person in his sound and sober senses and without having been unduly influenced thereto, if it appears from the document in which the confession is contained that the confession was made freely and voluntarily by such person in his sound and sober senses and without having been unduly influenced thereto."

Subparagraph (ii) was under attack as the words "unless the contrary is proved" place an onus on the accused which must be discharged on a balance of probabilities. If at the end of the trial within a trial the probabilities are evenly balanced, the presumption prevails.[22] This constitutes a reverse onus. Kentridge AJ, in delivering the judgment of the Constitutional Court, referred with approval to the approach adopted in the Canadian cases discussed in § 29 2 above. Kentridge AJ examined the common-law rule that a confession must be made freely and voluntarily, which has a history of over three hundred years. The rule developed in reaction to the oppressive manner in which confessions were extracted by the court of the Star Chamber in the seventeenth century. At the same time the privilege against self-incrimination and the right to silence developed. Kentridge AJ concluded that the common-law rule in regard to the burden of proving that a confession was voluntarily made rested on the state and that it was an integral and essential part of the right to remain silent after arrest, the right not to be compelled to make a confession, and the right not to be a compellable witness against oneself.

Kentridge AJ said[23] that these rights are in turn the necessary reinforcement of the "golden thread" running throughout our criminal law that the prosecution must prove the guilt of the accused beyond a reasonable doubt.[24] Reverse the burden, Kentridge AJ emphasized, and all these rights are seriously compromised. Kentridge AJ concluded that the common-law rule on the burden of proof is inherent in the rights mentioned in s 25 of the interim Constitution (the right not to make a confession, the presumption of innocence, and the right not to be compelled to be a witness against oneself) and forms part of the right to a fair trial. It was decided that s 217(1) *(b)*(ii) of the CPA violated the provisions of the interim Constitution and was invalid. It was also held that s 217(1) *(b)*(ii) was not a reasonable limitation under s 33 of the Constitution.[25]

---

[22] *S v Mphahlele* 1982 4 SA 505 (A) 512.
[23] At 659H.
[24] *Per* Lord Sankey in *Woolmington v DPP* supra.
[25] See § 29 5 below.

29 4   DRUGS AND DRUG TRAFFICKING ACT 140 OF 1992 AND PRESUMPTIONS OF DEALING

Section 21(1)(a)(i) of the Drugs and Drug Trafficking Act[26] provided that if it was proved that an accused was found in possession of more than 115 grams of dagga, it shall be presumed, until the contrary is proved, that the accused dealt in dagga. This provision was attacked in the Constitutional Court in *S v Bhulwana; S v Gwadiso*[27] on the grounds that it imposed a reverse onus on an accused contrary to the presumption of innocence in terms of s 25(3)(c) of the interim Constitution. O'Regan J delivered the judgment of the court and traced the origin of the provision back to 1954, when the presumption was inserted into previous legislation. She concluded that the words "until the contrary is proved" constitute a reverse onus provision rather than an evidential burden. O'Regan J indicated that the effect of the provision is that once the state has proved that the accused was found in possession of an amount of dagga in excess of 115 grams the accused will have to show on a balance of probabilities that he was not dealing in dagga. Even if the accused were to raise a reasonable doubt, but failed to show on a balance of probabilities that he was not dealing, he must nevertheless be convicted of dealing. Thus the provision gives rise to a breach of s 25(3)(c) of the interim Constitution. In reaching this conclusion O'Regan J referred to *S v Zuma* and the North American cases cited therein.[28] The provision was held not to be a reasonable limitation in terms of s 33 of the Constitution[29] and was declared invalid.

29 5   LIMITATIONS UNDER SECTION 33 OF THE INTERIM CONSTITUTION

Section 33(1) of the Constitution provides:

"The rights entrenched in this Chapter may be limited by law of general application, provided that such limitation —
(a) shall be permissible only to the extent that it is —
(i)   reasonable; and
(ii)   justifiable in an open and democratic society based on freedom and equality; and
(b) shall not negate the essential content of the right in question,
and provided further that any limitation to —
(aa)   a right entrenched in section . . . 25
. . .
shall, in addition to being reasonable as required in paragraph (a)(i), also be necessary."

Thus where a competent court decides that statutory provision is contrary to a provision of s 25 of the Constitution it must then consider whether the provision is a reasonable, necessary and justifiable limitation. If it is held to be so, then the court must consider whether the limitation negates the essential content of the right. This involves a balancing test which includes the nature of the right, its

---

[26] Act 140 of 1992.
[27] 1995 12 BCLR 1579 (CC). See also further *S v Julies* 1996 2 SACR 108 (CC).
[28] See n 8 above.
[29] See § 29 5 below.

importance to an open and democratic society, the purpose for which the right is limited, the importance of that purpose to society, the extent of the limitation, its efficacy, and whether the desired results could be achieved by other means less damaging.[30] The more substantial the inroad into fundamental rights, the more persuasive the grounds of justification must be.[31]

In *S v Bhulwana; S v Gwadiso*[32] it was held that, although the need to suppress the illegal drug trade is an urgent and pressing one, it was not clear how, if at all, the presumption furthers such an objective. There was no logical connection between the fact proved (possession of 115 grams of dagga) and the presumed fact (dealing). It was held that it was not logical to presume that a person found in possession of 115 grams of dagga is more likely than not to have been dealing in dagga. The court was advised that 115 grams would make between 50 and 100 cigarettes, which it would not be unreasonable for a regular user to possess.

In *S v Zuma*[33] the court found that the presumption was designed to prevent accused from attempting dishonestly to retract confessions which they made before a magistrate; and to prevent unduly long trials within trials. There was nothing before the court to show that the common-law rule caused substantial harm to the administration of justice and it was debatable whether the reverse onus provision shortened trials within trials. It was concluded that the provision was not a reasonable and necessary limitation.

An example of a reverse onus provision that was found to be reasonable was in the Canadian case of *R v Downey*, which is discussed in § 29 2 above.

---

[30] As articulated by Chaskalson P in *S v Makwanyane* 1995 3 SA 391 (CC), 1995 6 BCLR 665 (CC).
[31] *S v Bhulwana; S v Gwadiso* supra 1586*c*.
[32] Supra.
[33] See § 29 3 above.

WEIGHT OF EVIDENCE AND STANDARDS AND BURDENS OF PROOF

CHAPTER 30

The Evaluation of Evidence

S E van der Merwe and S S Terblanche

30 1 Introduction

In § 1 1 above it was pointed out that a court should first determine the factual basis of the case before pronouncing on the rights, duties and liabilities of the parties engaged in the dispute. The factual basis is determined by evaluating all the probative material admitted during the course of the trial. The difficult task of finally analysing and assessing the weight or cogency of probative material arises after all the parties have closed their respective cases and delivered their arguments (see § 3 3 above for a discussion of the difference between evidence and argument). The presiding judge or magistrate — and assessors where they have been used[1] — must then assess the weight of the probative material in order to determine whether the party carrying the burden of proof has proved its allegations in accordance with the applicable standard of proof.[2]

Maguire once said that the rules of exclusion have kept Anglo-American lawyers so fully occupied that they have not yet satisfactorily explored the importance of evidential cogency; they have been too busy deciding what should be kept out to make — much less teach — a systematic appraisal of what they finally let in.[3] This allegation is probably partly true. However, it is also true that the court's duty to evaluate probative material is in many respects similar to the function of any prudent non-judicial finder of fact: credibility is determined, inferences are drawn, and probabilities and improbabilities are considered. In the evaluation of evidence there are a few legal rules — largely stemming from case law — which can assist the court and which can act as a check (see §§ 30 2 1–30 12 below). But the difficult mental task of sifting truth from falsehood, of determining credibility, of relying on probabilities, and of inferring unknown facts from the known is by and large a matter of common sense, logic and experience. Inferences which are drawn should, for example, be in accordance with the rules of logic (see § 30 5 below) and circuitous reasoning is obviously not permissible.[4] The absence of extensive legal rules governing the evaluation of probative material must also be understood in the light of the following statement by Van den Heever J: In the process of adjudication two factors are constant, namely what must be proved and to what degree of persuasion; but the third factor, namely the quantum and quality of the probative material required so to persuade the court, is subject to great variety.[5]

The purpose of the present chapter is to identify some of the main principles and rules which govern the determination of the quantum and quality of probative material.[6]

---

[1] See § 1 6 above for a brief discussion of assessors and their function. For a useful article on fact-finding, see Bingham "The Judge as Juror: The Judicial Determination of Factual Issues" 1985 38 *Current Legal Problems* 1.

[2] See chs 31 (criminal cases) and 32 (civil cases) below for a discussion of the burden and standard of proof.

[3] Maguire *Evidence: Common Sense and Common Law* (1947) 10.

[4] *S v Abrahams* 1979 1 SA 203 (A).

[5] *S v Van Wyk* 1977 1 SA 412 (NC) 414E–F.

[6] In the rest of this chapter the term "evidence" is used in its widest possible sense and as a synonym for "probative material". This is necessary as most courts do not distinguish between "evidence" ("getuienis") in its wide sense and "evidence" in a narrow sense. See further § 2 4 above as regards the distinction between evidence and probative material. Cf also generally the use of the word "oortuigingsmateriaal" as used by Fleming J in *S v Cronje* 1983 3 SA 739 (W) 744A–B and *S v Mosendu* 1981 1 SA 323 (O) 325B.

30 2   Basic Principles

Two basic principles should be kept in mind whenever evidence is evaluated: First, evidence must be weighed in its totality (see § 30 2 1 below); secondly, probabilities and inferences must be distinguished from conjecture or speculation (see § 30 2 2 below).

30 2 1 Avoidance of piecemeal processes of adjudication In *R v Sacco*[7] it was pointed out that a court may not decide a case in the light of inferences which arise only from selected facts considered in isolation (see also § 30 5 below). It is of paramount importance that the court should eschew piecemeal processes of reasoning.[8] Evidence must be weighed as a whole,[9] taking account of the probabilities (see § 30 2 2 below), the reliability and opportunity for observation of the respective witnesses (see § 30 11 2 below), the absence of interest or bias, the intrinsic merits or demerits of the testimony itself, and inconsistencies or contradictions, corroboration (see § 30 3 below) and all other relevant factors (for example demeanour, as discussed in § 30 4 below). "[I]t is axiomatic that the trier of fact must have regard to all the evidence and to all such considerations as reasonably invite clarification . . .."[10]

30 2 2 Inferences and probabilities to be distinguished from conjecture During the course of the evaluation of evidence inferences may be drawn and probabilities may be considered. Inferences and probabilities, however, must be distinguished from conjecture or speculation.[11] In *Caswell v Powell Duffryn Associated Collieries Ltd*[12] it was said that there can be no proper inference unless there are objective facts from which to infer the other facts which it is sought to establish.[13] If there are no positive proved facts from which the inference can be drawn, the method of inference fails and what is left is mere conjecture or speculation.[14] The court must stay "within the four corners of the proved facts . . . [I]t is not entitled to speculate as to the possible existence of other facts."[15]

    Probabilities must also be considered in the light of proved facts. It is, for example, possible to accept direct credible evidence even though this evidence conflicts with probabilities arising from human experience or expert opinion.[16]

---

[7] 1958 2 SA 349 (N) 353.

[8] *S v Sigwahla* 1967 4 SA 566 (A) 569H; *S v Snyman* 1968 2 SA 582 (A) 589; *S v Kubeka* 1982 1 SA 534 (W) 537H. But, obviously, where several accused are charged together the defence of each individual accused must be considered carefully. In *S v Jama & others* 1989 3 SA 427 (A) 439C–D Vivier JA said: "To adopt such a global view of the totality of the defence cases in order to reject the evidence of an individual accused is not permissible and constitutes a serious misdirection." See also *S v Mtsweni* 1985 1 SA 590 (A).

[9] *S v Civa* 1974 3 SA 844 (T) 846–7.

[10] *S v Zitha* 1993 1 SACR 718 (A) 720*i*–721*a*.

[11] *S v Mtsweni* 1985 1 SA 590 (A) 593D.

[12] 1939 3 All ER 722 733.

[13] *S v Essack & another* 1974 1 SA 1 (A) 16.

[14] *De Wet v President Versekeringsmaatskappy Bpk* 1978 3 SA 495 (C) 500.

[15] *S v Ndlovu* 1987 1 PH H37 (A) 68.

[16] *Motor Vehicle Assurance Fund v Kenny* 1984 4 SA 432 (E) 436H. See also § 8 6 2 above as regards the probative value of expert opinion evidence.

In *Mapota v Santamversekeringsmaatskappy Bpk*[17] the plaintiff had claimed damages for certain injuries which he had allegedly sustained when a bus had knocked him over and driven over his left foot. The plaintiff was the only person who could furnish direct evidence on how the accident occurred. His evidence was partially supported by two other witnesses who were present when the accident occurred, but who were not eye-witnesses of the actual manner in which the plaintiff had received his injuries. The bus driver and a medical practitioner testified on behalf of the defendant. These witnesses, however, were unable to give direct evidence of the manner in which the plaintiff's injuries were sustained. The medical expert expressed the opinion that it was improbable that the plaintiff had sustained the injuries in the manner alleged by the latter, but that he could not exclude the reasonable possibility that they were caused in that way. The medical expert was of the opinion that it was more probable that the injuries were sustained by somebody tramping on the plaintiff's foot. The plaintiff's claim was dismissed by the trial court. However, the Appellate Division took the view that the plaintiff's version of the accident was the only one which rested on direct evidence and his evidence, apart from the expert medical evidence, was not inherently improbable and was satisfactory in all respects. It was held that the scientific medical evidence could only refute the strong and otherwise acceptable and corroborated evidence of the plaintiff if that evidence unquestionably showed that the reasonable possibility that the accident could have taken place as described by the plaintiff did not exist. The Appellate Division concluded that the plaintiff had proved on a balance of probabilities that his injuries were sustained in the manner alleged by him because such reasonable possibility had not been excluded by the expert medical evidence.

30 3   CORROBORATION[18]

It stands to reason that whenever corroboration is present it would be easier to conclude that the required standard of proof has been satisfied. It is therefore understandable that the trier of fact will always look for corroboration even though corroboration is not formally required by law — except in the case of confessions, as discussed in § 30 3 3 below.

30 3 1 The rule against self-corroboration   Corroboration should in principle emanate from a source independent of the witness who stands to be corrobo-

---

[17] 1977 4 SA 515 (A).

[18] "Corroboration" ("stawing") is not a technical term. It is evidence which confirms or supports a fact of which other evidence is given. See *S v B* 1976 2 SA 54 (C) 59. In *Popovic v Derks* 1961 VR 413 it was said that corroboration is evidence which renders the *factum probandum* more probable by strengthening the proof of one or more *facta probantia*. Evidence which is merely consistent with facts which are *not* in dispute cannot be described as corroboration: corroborative evidence must have a bearing on facts which are in dispute. See *R v P* 1957 3 SA 444 (A) 454. See also generally Savage "What is Corroboration?" 1963 6 *Criminal Law Quarterly* 159.

rated.[19] Repetition of a story cannot furnish corroboration.[20] It can, at most, prove consistency — as is the case, for example, where a previous consistent statement of a witness is admitted in order to rebut an allegation of recent fabrication.[21] But proof of consistency is not the equivalent of corroboration.[22] In *Director of Public Prosecutions v Kilbourne* the rationale of the rule against self-corroboration was explained as follows:[23]

"There is nothing technical in the idea of corroboration. When in the ordinary affairs of life one is doubtful whether or not to believe a particular statement one naturally looks to see whether it fits in with other statements or circumstances relating to the particular matter; the better it fits in, the more one is inclined to believe it. The doubted statement is corroborated to a greater or lesser extent by the other statements or circumstances with which it fits in. In ordinary life we should be, and in law we are required to be, careful in applying this idea. We must be astute to see that the apparently corroborative statement is truly independent of the doubted statement. If there is any real chance that there has been collusion between the makers of the two statements we should not accept them as corroborative. *And the law says that a witness cannot corroborate himself.* In ordinary affairs we are often influenced by the fact that the maker of the doubted statement has consistently said the same thing ever since the event described happened. But the justification for the legal view must, I think, be that generally it would be too dangerous to take this into account and therefore it is best to have a universal rule."

30 3 2 Limitations on the rule against self-corroboration The injuries suffered by the victim of a violent offence may furnish corroboration of his or her testimony.[24] And so may emotional distress shortly after the incident.[25] But much will depend on the facts of the case and the nature of the defence advanced by the accused. The facts in issue may require the court to consider certain risks before accepting bodily and emotional condition as corroboration; for example: were the injuries self-inflicted? was the emotional distress genuine or simulated? And even if genuine, the court must still be satisfied that the emotional distress was indeed the result of the fact that the witness was the victim.[26]

The rule against self-corroboration is confined to oral or written communications of the witness concerned.

30 3 3 Corroboration of confessions Section 209 of the CPA provides that an accused may be convicted of any offence on the single evidence of a confession by such accused that he committed the offence in question, if such confession is

---

[19] In *R v Cross* 1970 1 CCC 216 217 Gale CJ said: "I have in mind the misdirection with respect to the fact that two buttons were missing from the complainant's coat when she appeared at the police station. While she stated that the two buttons were lost during her struggle with the accused there was no independent evidence that the buttons were on the coat prior to the struggle, and they were not found in the car. Hence any probative value of the evidence was dependent upon the veracity of the girl and it was, therefore, incapable of being viewed as corroboration." See further Van der Merwe 1980 *Obiter* 86 90–2.

[20] *R v Rose* 1937 AD 467 473.

[21] *S v Bergh* 1976 4 SA 857 (A) 869. See further § 9 6 5 above.

[22] *R v Whitehead* 1929 1 KB 99 102.

[23] 1973 1 All ER 440 456 (our emphasis).

[24] *R v Trigg* 1963 1 All ER 490.

[25] *R v Redpath* 1962 46 Cr App R 319; *R v Knight* 1966 1 WLR 230.

[26] See generally *S v Balhuber* 1987 1 PH H22 (A) 44.

confirmed in a material respect or, where the confession is not so confirmed, if the offence is proved by evidence, other than such confession, to have been actually committed. The purpose of s 209 is to prevent convictions on the basis of false confessions: "Experience in the administration of justice has shown that people occasionally do make false confessions for a variety of reasons."[27]

30 3 3 1   *Scope of s 209 of the CPA*   Section 217 of the CPA governs the admissibility of confessions,[28] whereas s 209 of the CPA relates to the sufficiency of a confession: in what circumstances will an admissible confession be sufficient for purposes of a conviction? In terms of s 209 there has to be either confirmation in a material respect (see § 30 3 3 3 below) or evidence *aliunde* (outside) the confession that the offence has been committed (see § 30 3 3 5 below). But even if the requirements of s 209 have been met, it does not mean that a conviction must necessarily follow: the court must in the ultimate analysis be convinced that the guilt of the accused has been proved beyond reasonable doubt.[29]

30 3 3 2   *Plea procedures and s 209 of the CPA*   A confession which is made in the course of plea proceedings need not satisfy the requirements of s 209 of the CPA.[30] But a confession or admissions made by an accused in the course of plea proceedings may for purposes of s 209 serve as confirmation of an extra-curial confession proved by the prosecution against the accused.[31] In *S v Rossouw*[32] parts

---

[27] *S v Kumalo* 1983 2 SA 379 (A) 383G–H.

[28] See ch 17 above.

[29] *S v Blom* 1992 1 SACR 649 (E) 657*i–j*; *S v Kearney* 1964 2 SA 495 (A) 501H; *S v Mbambo* 1975 2 SA 549 (A) 554D.

[30] *S v Talie* 1979 2 SA 1003 (C). Section 209 therefore does not relate to the *confessio in iudicio*: Bekker 1978 *THRHR* 207; Barton 1978 *SACC* 92; Klopper 1978 *SACC* 98.

[31] In *S v Mjoli* 1981 1 3 SA 1233 (A) it was held (Jansen JA dissenting) that an admission made by an accused during the explanation of plea in terms of s 115 of the CPA (see generally § 26 5 1 above) is capable in law of furnishing the confirmation as required by s 209 of the CPA even though the admission was never formally recorded as an admission in terms of s 220 of the CPA (as provided for by s 115(2)(*b*) of the CPA). It can be argued that this approach of the Appellate Division conflicts with the rule against self-corroboration (as discussed in § 30 3 1 above) and does not take proper account of the true meaning and effect of corroboration as discussed in § 30 3 above). In his dissenting judgment Jansen JA took the view that the reason for requiring confirmation is to reduce the risk of a false confession and that mere repetition of the confession cannot be said to reduce this risk. This argument was clearly based upon the rule against self-corroboration. However, Rumpff CJ said that the danger of convicting on a false confession was averted when a plea of not guilty was entered and the provisions of s 209 were satisfied. Paizes 1982 *SACC* 115 121 has submitted that this approach is not very helpful: to say that compliance with s 209 of the CPA is in these circumstances a safeguard is to beg the question of what s 209 actually requires by way of confirmation. "If the accused's own statement is sufficient corroboration, then such safeguard is illusory" (Paizes 1982 *SACC* 115 121). Viljoen JA adopted a more cautious approach than Rumpff CJ, although the former also stopped short of agreeing with Jansen JA. Viljoen JA proceeded from the premise that the inquiry was not from what source the confirmation emanated, but what the circumstances were under which the confirmatory statement was made: as long as the confirmation was such as to reduce the risk of a false confession it should suffice for purposes of s 209 of the CPA. He also added the *caveat* that if the source of information was the accused himself, then the court should be more cautious as the risk of a false confession would not be reduced to the same extent as it would if the confirmation emanated from an independent source. However, according to Viljoen JA this does not mean that such a confirmatory source is not permissible at all: everything must depend on the circumstances under which the statement was made. See further generally *S v Kumalo* 1983 2 SA 379 (A); *S v Erasmus* 1995 2 SACR 373 (E); *S v Rossouw* 1994 1 SACR 626 (E).

[32] 1994 1 SACR 626 (E).

of the accused's explanation of plea confirmed his extra-curial confession. But other parts contradicted the extra-curial confession. The court held that there was no proof of guilt beyond a reasonable doubt. The court came to this conclusion despite the fact that it was satisfied that there was — for purposes of s 209 — "sufficient confirmation in material respects".[33]

30 3 3 3 *Confirmation in a material respect*[34]   In *R v Blyth*[35] the accused had written a letter confessing to the murder of her husband by arsenical poisoning. The fact that his body contained some arsenic was found to be sufficient confirmation of her confession. The finding of arsenic in the body was found to be confirmation in a material respect even though this arsenic neither connected her to the murder nor amounted to evidence *aliunde* that her husband had indeed been murdered.[36] The requirement is only that a material aspect of the confession should be confirmed. However, it should also be pointed out that in this case the accused did not testify (see generally § 30 9 below). The Appellate Division rejected the argument of the defence that the hypothesis of suicide had not been disproved beyond a reasonable doubt. The Appellate Division also rejected the argument that the reference to arsenic in the confession could conceivably have been explained by the knowledge on the part of the accused that her husband had committed suicide by taking arsenical poison. The result of this case could have been different had the accused testified in her own defence.

30 3 3 4 *Confirmation in a material respect: other extra-curial confessions or admissions of the accused*   In *S v Erasmus*[37] the prosecution proved not only a confession which the accused had made to a magistrate but also an incriminating letter which was written by her to the investigating officer. The prosecution also proved various confessions which the accused had made to her daughter. But there was no evidence *aliunde* of the commission of the crime.

The circumstances relating to the death of the husband of the accused were consistent with suicide *and* murder — he was found shot. The court held that — before a conviction could be entered on the basis of any of the confessions — there had to be compliance with s 209 of the CPA *and* the standard of proof beyond reasonable doubt. The issue was whether the various confessions, or at least one of them, could be said to have been confirmed in a material respect. The prosecution submitted that the required confirmation for the confession made to the magistrate could be found in the other confessions made by the accused. Nepgen J held that there was no reason why the required confirmation could not come from another extra-curial confession made by the accused. He also held, however, that a high degree of confirmation of the confession to the

---

[33] At 632j.
[34] *R v Sephanyane* 1955 2 PH H223 (A): "The confirmation must relate to a material matter. It may further be assumed that the factor of materiality affects degree as well as kind, and that the confirmation must not be trivial or unsubstantial. But it need not go so far as to establish, independently, the accused's guilt."
[35] 1940 AD 355.
[36] Hoffmann & Zeffertt 568.
[37] 1995 2 SACR 373 (E).

magistrate was necessary because of certain unsatisfactory aspect of this confession. Nepgen J further held that the letter to the investigating officer was ambiguous and — in the absence of a clear indication of what the accused meant — the letter could not provide sufficient confirmation of the accused's confession. The confessions to the daughter of the accused, held Nepgen J, could, however, provide the required confirmation. These confessions to the daughter had been made in circumstances which indicated that they would not be false. It was held that the prosecution had proved beyond a reasonable doubt that the accused had killed her husband intentionally and in circumstances which were unlawful.

S v Blom[38] provides an example of a case where the accused — an unreliable witness — was acquitted because the two confessions proved against him both contained material untruths. The fact that a confession complies with s 209 of the CPA does not mean that the contents thereof must necessarily be accepted as the truth.

30 3 3 5 *Evidence* aliunde *the confession* Section 209 of the CPA can also be satisfied by evidence *aliunde* the confession that the offence to which the accused confessed had actually been committed (see § 30 3 3 above).[39] For example, if A confesses to the stabbing and murdering of B, it would be sufficient for the purpose of s 209 to prove that B died as a result of several stab wounds. In this instance the accused is not really protected against a false confession as the prosecution merely has to prove the commission of the crime.

30 4 CREDIBILITY:[40] THE IMPACT OF DEMEANOUR AND MENDACITY

The credibility ("geloofwaardigheid") of witnesses can be decisive to the outcome of a case. A wide variety of factors must be taken into account in assessing credibility:[41]

"Included in the factors which a court would look at in examining the credibility or veracity

---

[38] 1992 1 SACR 649 (E).

[39] Cf generally *S v Bengu* 1965 1 SA 298 (N).

[40] The problems which relate to credibility were set out by Lord Pearce in *Onassis v Vergottis* 1968 2 Lloyd's Rep 403 431: "Credibility covers the following problems. First, is the witness a truthful or untruthful person? Secondly, is he, though a truthful person, telling something less than the truth on this issue, or, though an untruthful person, telling the truth on this issue? Thirdly, though he is a truthful person telling the truth as he sees it, did he register the intentions of the conversation correctly and, if so, has his memory correctly retained them? Also, has his recollection been subsequently altered by unconscious bias or wishful thinking or by overmuch discussion of it with others? Witnesses, especially those who are emotional, who think that they are morally in the right, tend very easily and unconsciously to conjure up a legal right that did not exist. It is a truism, often used in accident cases, that with every day that passes the memory becomes fainter and the imagination becomes more active. For that reason a witness, however honest, rarely persuades a Judge that his present recollection is preferable to that which was taken down in writing immediately, after the accident occurred. Therefore, contemporary documents are always of the utmost importance. And lastly, although the honest witness believes he heard or saw this or that, is it so improbable that it is on balance more likely that he was mistaken? On this point it is essential that the balance of probability is put correctly into the scales in weighing the credibility of a witness. And motive is one aspect of probability. All these problems compendiously are entailed when a Judge assesses the credibility of a witness; they are all part of one judicial process. And in the process contemporary documents and admitted or incontrovertible facts and probabilities must play their proper part."

[41] Mohamed J in *Hees v Nel* 1994 1 PH F11 (T) 32.

of any witnesses, are matters such as the general quality of his testimony (which is often a relative condition to be compared with the quality of the evidence of the conflicting witnesses), his consistency both within the content and structure of his own evidence and with the objective facts, his integrity and candour, his age where this is relevant, his capacity and opportunities to be able to depose to the events he claims to have knowledge of, his personal interest in the outcome of the litigation, his temperament and personality, his intellect, his objectivity, his ability effectively to communicate what he intends to say, and the weight to be attached and the relevance of his version, against the background of the pleadings."

Some of the factors and issues considered below are: what is the impact of the demeanour of the witness upon credibility? must untruthful evidence given by a party — especially an accused — necessarily result in a verdict against this party?

The demeanour of witnesses includes "their manner of testifying, their behaviour in the witness-box, their character and personality, and the impression they create . . ."[42] It is considered real evidence in the sense that it is something that the trial court observes.[43] Was the witness "candid or evasive, ready or reluctant"[44] to give her account of events? Did she hesitate unnecessarily in responding to questions — especially under cross-examination? Was she too bold or too timid? Were there nervous fidgeting and facial twitches in response to straightforward relevant questions? In our law of evidence the demeanour of the witness can play a role in assessing her credibility. There is probably some remote historical link between this rule and the ancient and primitive ordeal known as the *corsnaed*, which was discussed in § 1 3 1 above.[45] However, it is most certainly quite rational to permit a trier of fact to make a finding on demeanour and to take such finding into account in assessing credibility. It is an inevitable consequence of a trial system based upon orality and confrontation. But the following principles govern the situation:

(a) Demeanour, in itself, is a fallible guide to credibility[46] and should be considered with all other factors: it is in the overall scrutiny of evidence that demeanour should be taken into account — and then only if there are sufficient indications thereof to be significant.[47]

(b) The limited value of a finding on demeanour becomes even less where an interpreter is used.[48]

(c) Ethnic differences between the trier of fact and the witness concerned can hamper the former's ability to assess demeanour as a factor affecting credibility.[49]

---

[42] Jones J in *Cloete v Birch* 1993 2 PH F17 (E) 51.

[43] Nokes *An Introduction to Evidence* 4 ed (1967) 449: "[T]he blush of a witness is as real as a dried blood-stain on a knife."

[44] *R v Mokwena* 1940 OPD 130.

[45] See generally Van der Merwe 1991 *Stell LR* 281 288.

[46] *R v Masemang* 1950 2 SA 488 (A).

[47] *S v Civa* 1974 3 SA 844 (T).

[48] Le Roux J in *S v Malepane* 1979 1 SA 1009 (W) 1016H–1017A: "Demeanour can be a false indication in this particular case. It must be remembered that all the accomplices are Black men testifying through an interpreter and however excellent the interpreter is (and I must say in this particular case he was one of the best I have come across) it is almost impossible to judge from demeanour alone whether a man is telling the truth or not as would be the case with a witness who is cross-examined directly by counsel." See also *R v Dhlumayo* 1948 2 SA 677 (A) 697.

[49] *Patel v Patel* 1946 CPD 46.

(d) Demeanour can hardly ever be decisive in determining the outcome of a case. Demeanour is merely *one* factor to be taken into account: "In addition to the demeanour of the witness", said Krause J in *R v Momekela & Commandant*,[50] "one should be guided by the probability of his story, the reasonableness of his conduct, the manner in which he emerges from the test of his memory, the consistency of his statements and the interest he may have in the matter under enquiry." Jones J has also noted that the "risk of accepting possibly incorrect evidence because it is given by a witness of good demeanour is reduced if that evidence accords with the inherent probabilities, or if it is corroborated, or if its only contradiction is by evidence of poor quality given by a witness of poor demeanour."[51]

(e) A trial court is obviously in a better position than the court of appeal to make a finding on demeanour; and the court of appeal "must attach weight, but not excessive weight"[52] to the trial court's finding. It is as a general rule important that a trial court should record its impression of the demeanour of a material witness.[53]

The maxims *semel mentitus, semper mentitur* (once untruthful, always untruthful) and *falsum in uno, falsum in omnibus* (false in one thing, false in all) do not apply in our law of evidence.[54] It is permissible either to accept or reject the evidence of a witness who has lied before or who has lied only with regard to a particular fact: everything depends upon the particular circumstances of the case. In *S v Oosthuizen* it was said:[55]

> "All that can be said is that where a witness has been shown to be deliberately lying on one point, the trier of fact *may* (not *must*) conclude that his evidence on another point cannot safely be relied upon . . . The circumstances may be such that there is no room for honest mistake in regard to a particular piece of evidence: either it is true or it has been deliberately fabricated. In such a case the fact that the witness has been guilty of deliberate falsehood in other parts of his evidence is relevant to show that he may have fabricated the piece of evidence in question. But in this context the fact that he has been honestly mistaken in other parts of his evidence is irrelevant, because the fact that his evidence in regard to one point is honestly mistaken cannot support an inference that his evidence on another point is a deliberate fabrication."

The court's rejection of the testimony of a witness does not necessarily establish the truth of the contrary. In *R v Weinberg*[56] it was pointed out that the disbelief of the statement of a witness merely removes an obstacle to the acceptance of *evidence* tending to prove the contrary. This does not mean that

---

[50] 1936 OPD 24.

[51] *Cloete v Birch* 1993 2 PH F17 (E).

[52] *Koekemoer v Marais* 1934 1 PH J27 (C). The court of appeal is *not* obliged to accept the trial court's finding on demeanour as conclusive. But "[b]earing in mind the advantage which a trial court has of seeing, hearing and appraising a witness, it is only in exceptional circumstances that [a court] will be entitled to interfere with a trial court's evaluation of oral testimony . . ." (Smalberger JA in *S v Francis* 1991 1 SACR 198 (A) 204*e*).

[53] *S v Mwanyekanga* 1993 2 PH H54 (C) 143. In the absence of findings on demeanour the court of appeal is in as good a position as the trial court to assess credibility: *S v Jochems* 1991 1 SACR 208 (A).

[54] *R v Gumede* 1949 3 SA 749 (A).

[55] 1982 3 SA 571 (T) (emphasis in the original).

[56] 1939 AD 71 80.

mendacity is irrelevant. For example, a false statement by an accused can be used in drawing an inference of guilt from other reliable evidence.[57]

In *Goodrich v Goodrich*[58] it was also emphasized that a court should carefully guard against the acceptance of the fallacious principle that a party should lose its case as a penalty for its perjury or lies under affirmation. It was pointed out that the specific circumstances of each case should be considered and that in each case the court should ask itself whether the fact that a party has attempted to strengthen or support its case with lies proves or tends to prove the belief of a party that its case is ill-founded: as a general rule a carefully considered and prepared false statement (and *a fortiori* a conspiracy with others that they should give false evidence in support of the case of the party concerned) would more likely be an indication of a party's awareness of the weakness of its case than a story contrived on the spur of the moment.[59]

30 5 CIRCUMSTANTIAL EVIDENCE

The difference between direct and circumstantial evidence was dealt with earlier in § 2 9 above. Circumstantial evidence is not necessarily weaker than direct evidence.[60] In some instances it may even be of more value than direct evidence.[61] Inferences are drawn from circumstantial evidence. In this process certain rules of logic must be followed (see §§ 30 5 2 and 30 5 3 below) and the difference between the standards of proof in criminal and civil cases may not be discarded (see § 30 5 3 below).

30 5 1 Cumulative effect The court should always consider the cumulative effect of all the items of circumstantial evidence. In *R v De Villiers*[62] it was pointed

---

[57] *R v Blom* 1939 AD 188 198; *R v Nel* 1946 WLD 406. In *S v Mtsweni* 1985 1 SA 590 (A) the Appellate Division considered the effect of a finding that the accused had given false evidence. The headnote in this case reads as follows: "Although the untruthful evidence or denial of an accused is of importance when it comes to the drawing of conclusions and the determination of guilt, caution must be exercised against attaching too much weight thereto. The conclusion that, because an accused is untruthful, he therefore is probably guilty must especially be guarded against. Untruthful evidence or a false statement does not always justify the most extreme conclusion. The weight to be attached thereto must be related to the circumstances of each case. In considering false testimony by an accused, the following matters should, inter alia, be taken into account: *(a)* the nature, extent and materiality of the lies and whether they necessarily point to a realization of guilt; *(b)* the accused's age, level of development and cultural and social background and standing in so far as they might provide an explanation for his lies; *(c)* possible reasons why people might turn to lying, e g because in a given case, a lie might sound more acceptable than the truth; *(d)* the tendency which might arise in some people to deny the truth out of fear of being held to be involved in a crime, or because they fear that an admission of their involvement in an incident or crime, however trivial the involvement, would lead to the danger of an inference of participation and guilt out of proportion in the truth."

[58] 1946 AD 390 396–7.

[59] See also further the discussion of *Goodrich v Goodrich* supra and *R v Mlambo* 1957 4 SA 727 (A) in *S v Steynberg* 1983 3 SA 140 (A).

[60] *Cloete v Birch* 1993 2 PH F17 (E). In *S v Reddy & others* 1996 2 SACR 1 (A) 8*i* Zulman AJA quoted *Best on Evidence* 10 ed para 297: "[E]ven two articles of circumstantial evidence, though each taken by itself weigh but as a feather, join them together, you will find them pressing on a delinquent with the weight of a mill-stone . . .."

[61] *S v Shabalala* 1966 2 SA 297 (A) 299.

[62] 1944 AD 493 508–9. See also *S v Reddy* supra 8*e–g*.

out that the court should not consider each circumstance in isolation and then give the accused the benefit of any reasonable doubt as to the inference to be drawn from each single circumstance.[63] This approach can also be put differently: the state must satisfy the court, not that each separate item of evidence is inconsistent with the innocence of the accused, but only that the evidence taken as a whole is beyond reasonable doubt inconsistent with such innocence.[64]

30 5 2 Inferences in criminal proceedings In *R v Blom*[65] it was said that in reasoning by inference in a criminal case there are two cardinal rules of logic which cannot be ignored. The *first* rule is that the inference sought to be drawn must be consistent with all the proved facts: if it is not, the inference cannot be drawn. The *second* rule is that the proved facts should be such that they exclude every reasonable inference from them save the one sought to be drawn: if these proved facts do not exclude all other reasonable inferences, then there must be a doubt whether the inference sought to be drawn is correct.[66] This second rule takes account of the fact that in a criminal case the state should furnish proof beyond reasonable doubt (see generally chapter 31 below). The rules as set out in *R v Blom* supra are not applicable when an application for a discharge in terms of s 174 of the CPA is considered.[67]

30 5 3 Inferences in civil proceedings In civil proceedings the inference sought to be drawn must also be consistent with all the proved facts, but it need not be the only reasonable inference: it is sufficient if it is the most probable inference.[68] For example, in *AA Onderlinge Assuransie Bpk v De Beer*[69] it was held that a plaintiff who relies on circumstantial evidence does not have to prove that the inference which he asks the court to draw is the only reasonable inference: he will discharge his burden of proof if he can convince the court that the inference he advocates is the most readily apparent and acceptable inference from a number of possible inferences.

The second rule as set out in § 30 5 2 above, and which applies to criminal proceedings, does not apply to civil proceedings because of the lesser standard of proof applicable in civil proceedings, namely, proof on a balance of probability

---

[63] *R v Hlongwane* 1959 3 SA 337 (A); *S v Ressel* 1968 4 SA 224 (A).

[64] *S v Mtembu* 1950 1 SA 670 (A); *R v De Villiers* supra 508–9; *S v Reddy* supra 8*c*.

[65] 1939 AD 188 202–3.

[66] *S v Sesetse* 1981 3 SA 353 (A) 369–70. *R v Blom* supra has been approved in many cases: *S v Steynberg* 1983 3 SA 140 (A); *S v Van As* 1991 2 SACR 75 (A) 102*e–f; S v Nango* 1990 2 SACR 450 (A) 457*b; S v Morgan* 1993 2 SACR 134 (A) 172*h–i.* In *S v Reddy* supra 8*c–d* Zulman AJA held: "In assessing circumstantial evidence one needs to be careful not to approach such evidence upon a piece-meal basis and to subject each individual piece of evidence to a consideration of whether it excludes the reasonable possibility that the explanation given by an accused is true. The evidence needs to be considered in its totality. It is only then that one can apply the oft-quoted dictum in *R v Blom* 1939 AD 188 at 202–3 where reference is made to two cardinal rules of logic which cannot be ignored."

[67] *S v Cooper & others* 1976 2 SA 875 (T). See further § 31 5 below.

[68] *Govan v Skidmore* 1952 1 SA 732 (N) 734.

[69] 1982 2 SA 603 (A).

[70] Thayer *A Preliminary Treatise on Evidence at the Common Law* (1898) 341.

(see chapter 32 below), as opposed to the stricter standard applicable in criminal proceedings, namely, proof beyond reasonable doubt (see chapter 31 below).

30 5 4 The so-called presumptions of fact The so-called presumptions of fact are not rules of law. The term "presumption of fact" is really only another way of indicating that the specific circumstances of a case are such that inferential reasoning is permissible. The presumption of fact has been described as a " . . . *praesumptio hominis . . .* which has no place in the law, and is merely in *arbitrio judicis . . .* addressing itself only to be the rational faculty . . .".[70] In *S v Sigwahla*[71] it was also pointed out that it is simpler to speak of inferences of fact than of presumptions of fact. In the absence of direct evidence the true enquiry is whether the court can from the totality of evidence draw inferences in accordance with the rules of logic mentioned in §§ 30 5 2 and 30 5 3 above.[72] The so-called presumption of fact is also discussed in § 28 3 above.

In *Arthur v Bezuidenhout*[73] it was accepted that the maxim *res ipsa loquitur* (the matter speaks for itself) gives rise to an inference rather than a presumption.[74] "It is really", said Innes CJ in *Van Wyk v Lewis,*[75] "a question of inference." It has been held that the maxim *res ipsa loquitur* also applies in criminal cases.[76] But in *S v Maqashalala* two judges did not agree on this point.[77] *Res ipsa loquitur* is also discussed in § 28 5 7 above.

It is submitted that the use of presumptions of fact is singularly unhelpful in the evaluation of evidence: it is not conducive to sound reasoning and may easily lead to a piecemeal approach (see § 30 2 1 above) and disregard for the rules of logic pertaining to inferences drawn from circumstantial evidence (see §§ 30 5 2 and 30 5 3 above). However, the law of precedent has seen to it that certain presumptions of fact still stalk the evidential terrain. In terms of the presumption of continuance (which exists *eo nomine*) the existence of a certain state of affairs in the past gives rise to an inference of its continued existence.[78] Each case, however, must be considered on its own merits.[79] There is also a presumption of fact that a defamatory statement in a telegram or on a postcard was read by a third person.[80]

---

[71] 1967 4 SA 566 (A) 569.

[72] *R v Sacco* 1958 2 SA 349 (N) 352.

[73] 1962 2 SA 566 (A) 575.

[74] See also *Sardi & others v Standard and General Insurance Co Ltd* 1977 3 SA 776 (A).

[75] 1924 AD 438 445.

[76] *S v Mudoti* 1986 4 SA 278 (ZS) 279J. Cf *R v Jass* 1939 EDL 249 and see Zeffertt 1986 *ASSAL* 476.

[77] 1992 1 SACR 620 (Tk). At 622 White J pointed out that the "basis for the application of the maxim in civil as well as criminal cases differs so materially that to do so in both fields can only lead to confusion and uncertainty. It seems preferable that its application be restricted to civil cases, where it had its origin and where it is regularly invoked, and that in criminal cases reference be made to the rules enunciated in *R v Blom* 1939 AD 188." At 623j Hancke J said "that as long as the correct standard of proof is applied according to whether it is a criminal or civil case, I can see no objection in applying the maxim *res ipsa loquitur* in both proceedings".

[78] *Salisbury Bottling Co (Pty) Ltd v Arista Bakery (Pty) Ltd* 1973 3 SA 132 (RA).

[79] *R v Fourie* 1937 AD 31.

[80] *Pretorius v Niehaus* 1960 3 SA 109 (O) 112.

In theft cases the prosecution frequently relies on the so-called "doctrine of recent possession" in terms of which the possessor of recently stolen goods is presumed to have been the thief.[81] In *S v Parrow* Holmes JA made it clear that there is no magic meaning in the doctrine of recent possession and that it is really a matter of inferential reasoning in the light of all the facts of the case.[82] It has been held that a mere caretaker cannot be regarded, for the purposes of the presumption of fact arising from the doctrine of recent possession, to be in possession of goods which he temporarily has in his care.[83] It is submitted that this is just another way of saying that, having regard to all the proved facts, no inference of guilt could be inferred.

A so-called presumption of fact cannot affect the incidence of the burden of proof.[84] It does, at most, give rise to an evidential burden.[85]

30 6   CREDIBILITY OF A WITNESS: PREVIOUS EXPERIENCE OF COURT[86]

Part of the headnote in *S v Sinam* reads as follows:[87]

> "The Court found that the magistrate had misdirected himself in several respects, inter alia by relying on his previous experience of a witness (a municipal constable who had testified before him on several occasions in the past) to make a favourable credibility finding as regards that witness, whose testimony he had relied on to justify his finding on the facts. The Court remarked in this respect that the previous experience an adjudicator of facts may have of a witness *qua* witness was of limited value and operate very unfairly and lead to an injustice being perpetrated — the accused had no way of testing the court's opinions and usually had no prior knowledge of the fact that the court would take its own view of the witness into consideration. Where the court does rely on its own knowledge of the witness, it must at least indicate that it is doing so with circumspection and that it is fully aware of the dangers inherent in such an approach; furthermore, the acceptance of the credibility of a State witness did not necessarily mean the rejection of the accused's version of the case. The magistrate in the instant case did not adhere to these principles

---

[81] See generally *S v Skweyiya* 1984 4 SA 712 (A) 716C.

[82] 1973 1 SA 603 (A) 604C (our emphasis): "On proof of possession by the accused of recently stolen property, the court may (not must) convict him of theft in the absence of an innocent explanation which might reasonably be true. This is an *epigrammatic* way of saying that the court should think its way through the totality of the facts of each particular case, *and must acquit the accused unless it can infer, as the only reasonable inference, that he stole the property*".

[83] *S v Letoba* 1993 2 SACR 615 (O).

[84] Schmidt 43.

[85] See §§ 31 2 and 32 2 below as regards the distinction between the burden of proof ("bewyslas") and evidential burden ("weerleggingslas").

[86] It may happen (especially with regard to police witnesses in small towns) that the presiding officer may form a general impression of the reliability of a particular witness as a result of having heard the latter testify in many previous trials. In the evaluation of evidence the court is not required to disregard such experience completely (*R v Mukuma* 1934 TPD 134). In *R v L* 1955 1 SA 575 (T) 577 it was said, e g, that it is inevitable that a court should form a general impression of the reliability of a witness who appears frequently before it and that it is impossible for that impression to be disregarded when the witness give evidence. However, the important proviso is that the evidence should still be weighed impartially (*R v Van Heerden* 1960 2 SA 405 (T)) in that the court should constantly bear in mind that there is no justification for basing a conviction solely on the improbability that a false story would emanate from an apparently responsible and trustworthy person who has frequently given what has seemed to the court to be fair and honest evidence (*R v P* 1955 2 SA 561 (A) 564). An objective approach is essential.

[87] 1990 2 SACR 308 (E).

and the Court held that in the circumstances of the case the magistrate's previous experience of the witness was insufficient justification for his credibility findings."

30 7 PRESENCE IN COURT BEFORE TESTIFYING

In § 22 2 1 above it was pointed out earlier that non-expert witnesses should as a rule wait outside the courtroom until they are called upon to testify. This is done to ensure that a witness is not influenced by what he hears from other witnesses who testify in his presence. The presence of a witness in court prior to his testifying does not make him an incompetent witness, but may have a detrimental effect on his credibility.[88] In *S v Ntanjana* it was said that a finding relating to the weight of such evidence would depend very much on the circumstances of the case and a proper assessment can really only be made after all the evidence has been heard.[89] In *S v Williams & others* Farlam J remarked and held as follows:[90]

> "While it is not the practice for witnesses to sit in court before they testify in criminal trials, they do so in civil cases without it being suggested that their evidence should on that ground be rejected. From the fact that a witness in a criminal trial has sat in court before giving evidence, it does not follow automatically that the witness is to be disbelieved. What is important is to consider what the witness heard before testifying and whether he or she is able to tailor his or her evidence so as to fit in with what he or she has heard."

In § 23 4 2 above it was pointed out that an accused has a right to be present at his trial[91] and that s 151(1)(b) of the CPA seeks to ensure that an accused who wishes to testify should do so before calling his defence witnesses.[92] Section 151(1)(b) provides as follows:

> "The court shall also ask the accused whether he himself intends giving evidence on behalf of the defence, and
> (i) if the accused answers in the affirmative, he shall, except where the court on good cause shown allow otherwise, be called as a witness before any other witness for the defence; or
> (ii) if the accused answers in the negative but decides, after other evidence has been given on behalf of the defence, to give evidence himself, the court may draw such inference from the accused's conduct as may be reasonable in the circumstances."

It is submitted that several important principles should be taken into account before a court can really draw an *adverse* inference which is "reasonable in the circumstances."[93] First, at the end of the prosecution's case the undefended accused should be warned that an inference which is reasonable in the circum-

---

[88] *R v Keller* 1915 AD 98 99.

[89] 1972 4 SA 635 (E) 636.

[90] 1991 1 SACR 1 (C) 16*j*–17*a*.

[91] See s 158 (as read with s 159) of the CPA.

[92] See generally Van der Merwe 1994 *Stell LR* 243 for a discussion of the history, purpose and constitutionality of s 151(1)(b) of the CPA.

[93] Much will indeed depend upon the circumstances of the case. The position of an accused who has legal representation and who testifies after having listened to four defence witness who had testified in support of his alibi differs materially from the position of an undefended accused who elects not to testify and is then unexpectedly let down by a defence witness who turns out to be a hostile defence witness, i e a witness "not desirous of telling the truth at the instance of the party calling him" (see generally § 25 3 3 above for a discussion of the hostile witness).

stances *may* be drawn from the fact that he, after having declined to testify and after having listened to one or more defence witnesses, does decide to testify.[94] Secondly, no inference adverse to the accused may be drawn from the *mere* fact that he gives evidence after having listened to one or more defence witnesses.[95] Thirdly, it would be in conflict with the constitutional and common-law presumption of innocence to proceed from the premise that an accused's evidence is suspect simply because he was not the first witness for the defence.[96]

30 8   FAILURE TO CROSS-EXAMINE

The nature and purpose of cross-examination was dealt with in § 18 6 1 above. A failure to cross-examine is generally considered to be an indication that the party who had the opportunity to cross-examine did not wish to dispute the version or aspects of the version of the particular witness who was, during the course of the trial, available for cross-examination. However, a failure to cross-examine is not a fatal factor, but merely a consideration to be weighed up with all the other factors in the case.[97] In *S v Gobozi*[98] it was said that a prosecutor's failure to cross-examine may often be of decisive importance in deciding whether the guilt of the accused has been established beyond all reasonable doubt: the accused's version, if not manifestly false, ought to be tested before it is rejected

---

[94] In *S v Makubo* 1990 2 SACR 320 (O) 321*e–f* the duplicated form used by the magistrate to explain the rights of the accused at the end of the prosecution's case merely contained the following concerning s 151(1)(*b*): "Artikel 151 vereis dat u eerste getuig en daarna u getuies dog indien u gegronde redes aanvoer waarom u na u getuies moet getuig, kan die hof dit toelaat." It is submitted that this warning is inadequate in the sense that it does not enable the undefended accused to make an informed consent. This matter, however, was not decided in *S v Makhubo* supra.

[95] Cf generally the following remarks made in *Zebediah v R* 1962 1 PH F6 (SR) 11 13 (emphasis added): "The considerations to which I have referred in relation to the calling of witnesses by counsel apply in essence to an unrepresented accused though with very much less emphasis. *Equally too no inference adverse to the accused should be drawn from the mere fact that he elects to give evidence last. If the prosecutor wishes to contend that the accused has done this in order to be able to mould his evidence and has so moulded his evidence, it is his duty to cross-examine on these points.* The reason why the accused called his witnesses first is relatively unimportant. The important point is whether the accused has in fact moulded his evidence to accord with that of the witnesses who have already given evidence. The question whether or not he decided to give evidence last in order to be able to mould his evidence is of course relevant to the question whether he has in fact moulded his evidence. I do not think the point can be taken further than that." See further Tansley 1964 *SALJ* 109 for a discussion of this case.

[96] Cf generally the following remarks made in the pre-Charter Canadian case of *R v Smuk* 1971 3 CCC (2d) 457 462 (emphasis added): "It is to be remembered that until the accused is found guilty at the conclusion of the trial . . . there is a presumption in our law that he is innocent and when he testifies presumably he testifies as a witness of truth and his evidence like that of any other witness must be carefully weighed and considered after the evidence has been given in Court. His evidence cannot be prejudged and no advantage or disadvantage is to be attributed to his evidence in advance because he testifies after defence witnesses have testified for and on his behalf . . . The credibility of one who testifies, whether he is an accused person or not, cannot under any circumstances be prejudged by any Court. His credibility like that of any other witness can only be assessed after he has testified and his credibility as a witness must be assessed upon a multiplicity of considerations, *perhaps even including the fact that he did not testify until after he had called all of his witnesses, if that fact is germane to the assessment of his credibility, but to state in advance that an accused person must be called first to testify and failing that, that his evidence must be suspect is a monstrous theory and completely and entirely foreign to our jurisprudence and is a practice that should not, under any circumstances, be encouraged.*"

[97] *R v M* 1946 AD 1023.

[98] 1975 3 SA 88 (E) 89.

since the process of testing a suspect story may reinforce it or even demonstrate its truthfulness or authenticity.

Failure to cross-examine may not be held against an illiterate and unrepresented accused.

30 9 FAILURE OF A PARTY TO TESTIFY (AND THE CONSTITUTIONAL RIGHT OF AN ACCUSED TO REFUSE TO TESTIFY)

In civil cases a party's failure to give gainsaying testimony under oath or affirmation may have an adverse effect on his case. However, the effect of such a failure would depend upon all the circumstances of the case.[99]

As far as criminal cases are concerned, Holmes JA held as follows in *S v Mthetwa*,[100] which was decided in 1972:

"Where the state case against an accused is based upon circumstantial evidence and depends upon the drawing of inferences therefrom, the extent to which his failure to give evidence may strengthen the inferences against him usually depends upon various considerations. These include the cogency or otherwise of the state case, after it is closed, the case with which the accused could meet it if innocent, or the possibility that the reason for his failure to testify may be explicable upon some hypothesis unrelated to his guilt . . . Where, however, there is direct *prima facie* evidence implicating the accused in the commission of the offence, his failure to give evidence, *whatever his reason may be* for such failure, in general *ipso facto* tends to strengthen the state case, because there is then nothing to gainsay it, and therefore less reason for doubting its credibility or reliability . . .."

The above rules (hereafter referred to as the "rules in *Mthetwa*") were based on several pre-1972 Appellate Division decisions[101] and have been quoted and relied upon on numerous occasions since 1972.[102] Constitutionalization in 1994 has given rise to the following issues: are the rules in *Mthetwa* compatible with an accused's constitutionally guaranteed right not only to be a non-compellable witness against himself but also to refuse to testify at his own trial? To put the matter differently: is there a measure of inconsistency or insincerity or even deviousness in a criminal justice system which, on the one hand, grants an accused a constitutional right to refuse to testify, but which, on the other hand, also takes the view that in certain circumstances an accused's refusal to testify in the face of a *prima facie* case against him can become a factor in assessing guilt?

It is submitted, largely on the basis of a judgment by Buys J in *S v Brown en andere*,[103] that there is a five-part answer to the above questions:

---

[99] *Brand v Minister of Justice* 1959 4 SA 712 (A) 715.

[100] 1972 3 SA 766 (A) 769A–E (emphasis in original).

[101] See generally *S v Snyman* 1968 2 SA 582 (A) 588F; *S v Letsoko & others* 1964 4 SA 768 (A) 776A–F; *R v Ismail* 1952 1 SA 204 (A).

[102] *S v Van Wyk* 1992 1 SACR 147 (Nm) 154; *S v Francis* 1991 1 SACR 198 (A).

[103] 1996 2 SACR 49 (NC). On this issue, see also generally *Attorney-General v Moagi* 1981 Botswana LR 1; *S v Scholtz* 1996 2 SACR 40 (NC); *S v Sidziya en ander* 1995 12 BCLR 1626 (Tk); *R v Boss* 1988 46 CCC (3d) 523. See further the discussion of *Griffin v California* 380 US 609 (1965) by Van der Merwe in 1994 *Obiter* 1.

(a) No adverse inference can be drawn against an accused merely by virtue of the fact that he has exercised his constitutional right to refuse to testify.[104] The rules in *Mthetwa*, in so far as they are inconsistent with this proposition,[105] must therefore be adjusted. It is submitted that it can no longer be argued or held that silence *ipso facto* strengthens a *prima facie* state case based on direct evidence.

(b) If an accused exercises his constitutional right to silence, the court is left with nothing but the uncontroverted *prima facie* case presented by the state: the silence of the accused has no probative value ("geen bewyswaarde").[106] In so far as the rules in *Mthetwa* seek to consider or identify the silence of the accused as a "fact"[107] that has some independent probative value, it must be rejected.

(c) It follows that the court is really only called upon to decide whether the uncontradicted *prima facie* case of the prosecution must harden into prove beyond reasonable doubt:[108]

> "Prakties beteken dit dat die probleem dus benader moet word uit die hoek van die onweerspreekte getuienis van die Staat en nie uit die hoek van die stilswye van die beskuldigde nie. Die vraag wat beslis moet word, is of die onweerspreekte Staatsgetuienis sterk genoeg om die *facta probanda* bo redelike twyfel te bewys en nie of die beskuldigde se stilswye die een of ander bewyswaarde het nie. Sy stilswye het volgens my oordeel geen bewyswaarde nie, maar gewone logika sê dat sy stilswye nadelige gevolge vir hom kan inhou."

(d) The accused's constitutional right to silence cannot prevent logical inferences:[109] the circumstances of a case may be such that a *prima facie* case, if left uncontradicted, must become proof beyond reasonable doubt. This happens not because the silence of the accused is considered an extra piece of evidence ("'n ekstra stukkie getuienis"),[110] but simply because the *prima facie* case in a particular case is in the absence of contradictory evidence on logical grounds strong enough to become proof beyond reasonable doubt. It has been said:[111]

> "The absence of gainsaying testimony from the accused merely means that the *prima facie* proof furnished by the state must be assessed as it stands. And the fact that the absence of gainsaying testimony must be attributed to the exercise of a constitutional right cannot prevent those logical inferences which irresistibly must be drawn from

---

[104] *S v Brown en andere* supra 60*f–g*. See also Geldenhuys & Joubert (eds) *Criminal Procedure Handbook* (1996) 6–8 and § 10 2 3 2 above.

[105] In *S v Brown en andere* supra 63*b–c* Buys J thought that they were not: "Alhoewel Holmes AR [in the rules in *Mthetwa*] sê dat die beskuldigde se swye die Staatsaak 'versterk', is dit duidelik dat die geleerde Regter eintlik niks meer sê nie, as dat die direkte getuienis van die Staat onweerspreek staan en dat daar gevolglik minder rede is om daardie getuienis te betwyfel. Ek lees nie hierdie uitspraak as synde gesag dat die Appèlhof die beskuldigde se stilswye as 'n ekstra stukkie getuienis teen hom in aanmerking geneem het nie."

[106] *S v Brown en andere* supra 63*h-i*.

[107] Cf, e g, *S v Snyman* 1968 2 SA 582 (A) 588H.

[108] *S v Brown en andere* supra 61*h–i*.

[109] In his dissenting judgment in *Griffin v California* supra 623 Stewart J said: "No constitution can prevent the operation of the human mind."

[110] *S v Brown en andere* supra 61*i–63c*.

[111] Van der Merwe 1994 *Obiter* 1 18.

what the state has proved within the limits and constraints of a constitutionalized criminal justice system. Surely, logical inferences which inevitably flow from uncontroverted *prima facie* proof cannot violate the constitutional passive defence right of the accused."

(e) If the accused's silence is, in the assessment of the prosecution's uncontroverted *prima facie* case, neither treated as "evidence" nor as a "factor", then it can hardly be argued that the drawing of logical inferences indirectly compels an accused to testify or amounts to a situation where an accused is being penalized for having exercised his constitutional right to refuse to testify.[112] Evidential pressure which stems from the sheer strength of the case presented by the prosecution cannot be described or identified as compulsion violating an accused's constitutional right to be a non-compellable witness and to refuse to testify.[113]

In the light of the principles set out in *(a)–(e)* above, an undefended accused should no longer at the end of the case for the prosecution be informed by the court that "failure to give evidence is a factor which can be taken into account together with other factors to make an inference of guilt".[114] Such a warning might very well lead an accused to believe that he must testify.[115] The correct warning that a court must give to an accused in our constitutionalized system was formulated by Buys J in *S v Brown en andere* supra[116] and is discussed in § 23 4 2 above.

30 10 FAILURE TO CALL AVAILABLE WITNESSES[117]

A party's failure to call *available*[118] witnesses may in exceptional circumstances lead to an adverse inference being drawn from such failure against the party concerned.[119] The extent to which such an inference can be drawn will depend on the circumstances of the case.[120] The court should, inter alia, consider the following: Was the party concerned perhaps under the erroneous but *bona fide* impression that he had proved his case and that there was therefore no need to have called the witness?[121] Is there a possibility that the party concerned believed that the potential witness was biased, hostile or unreliable?[122]

---

[112] *S v Brown en andere* supra 64*i*–65*g*.

[113] Van der Merwe 1994 *Obiter* 1 19.

[114] This quotation is from the headnote in *S v Makhubo* 1990 2 SACR 320 (O) and is an accurate translation of the phrase which appears at 322*g* of the report.

[115] See generally *S v Hlongwane* 1992 2 SACR 484 (N) 487*h*–*i*.

[116] At 65*f*–*g*: "Volgens my oordeel moet die beskuldigde ten opsigte van sy swygreg in 'n saak soos die onderhawige dus ingelig word dat hy 'n grondwetlike reg het om stil te bly en dat geen nadelige afleiding bloot uit sy stilswye gemaak kan word nie. Die gevolg egter van sy stilswye is dat die Staat se *prima facie* saak dat hy die misdaad gepleeg het, onweerspreek staan. Die saak moet dus beslis word op die Staat se weergawe alleen in die afwesigheid van sy weergawe van die gebeure en dit kan vir hom nadelig wees."

[117] See Chinner 1993 *SACJ* 255 264–6 for an in-depth discussion of this matter.

[118] *Elgin Fireclays Ltd v Webb* 1947 4 SA 744 (A); *R v Phiri* 1958 3 SA 161 (A) 165.

[119] *S v Texeira* 1980 3 SA 755 (A) 764; *Durban City Council v SA Board Mills* 1961 3 SA 397 (A). Application of the rule must not be such that it amounts to requiring a party to call all available witnesses.

[120] See *R v Bezuidenhout* 1954 3 SA 188 (A) 197C–D as followed in *S v Ramroop* 1991 1 SACR 555 (W) 559*e*–*g*.

[121] *Rand Cold Storage and Supply Co Ltd v Alligianes* 1968 2 SA 122 (T).

[122] *R v Juva* 1931 TPD 89 92–3; *S v Beahan* 1990 3 SA 18 (ZS) 22.

30 11 THE CAUTIONARY RULE: FUNCTION AND SCOPE

The cautionary rule is a rule of practice and must be followed whenever the evidence of *certain* witnesses is evaluated (see §§ 30 11 1–30 11 5 below). It serves as a constant reminder to courts that the facile acceptance of the credibility of certain witnesses may prove dangerous.

The cautionary rule requires, first, that the court should consciously remind itself to be careful in considering evidence which practice has taught should be viewed with suspicion and, secondly, that the court should seek some or other safeguard reducing the risk of a wrong finding based on the suspect evidence.[123]

It has often been stressed, however, that the exercise of caution should not be allowed to displace the exercise of common sense.[124] The application of the cautionary rule does not affect the standard of proof.[125] Corroboration is not the only manner in which the cautionary rule can be satisfied.[126] Any factor which can in the ordinary course of human experience reduce the risk of a wrong finding will suffice, for example, mendacity, a failure to cross-examine, the absence of gainsaying testimony, etc. It has been held that the fact that an accomplice gives evidence and, in addition to the accused, implicates a relative against whom he bears no ill will, can reduce the risk of a wrong conviction.[127] These circumstances constitute a factor in favour of the truth of such ordinarily suspect evidence emanating from an accomplice.

30 11 1 Instances of suspected deliberate false evidence The accumulated experience of courts of law has taught that certain witnesses may have special motives to give false evidence. For example, it has been accepted that an accomplice might have special reasons to incriminate an accused falsely. In *S v Masuku*[128] the following elaborate exposition of the basic principles relating to the evidence of an accomplice was given:

"(1) Caution in dealing with the evidence of an accomplice is imperative . . . (2) An accomplice is a witness with a possible motive to tell lies about an innocent accused; for example, to shield some other person, or to obtain immunity for himself. (3) Corroboration, not implicating the accused but merely in regard to the details of the crime, not implicating the accused, is not conclusive of the truthfulness of the accomplice. The very fact of his being an accomplice enables him to furnish the court with details of the crime which is apt to give the court the impression that he is in all respects a satisfactory witness, or, as has been described 'to convince the unwary that his lies are the truth'. (4) Accordingly, to satisfy the cautionary rule, if corroboration is sought it must be corroboration directly implicating the accused in the commission of the offence. (5) Such corroboration may, however, be found in the evidence of another accomplice provided that the latter is a reliable witness. (6) Where there is no such corroboration, there must be some other assurance that the evidence of the accomplice is reliable. (7) That assurance may be found

---

[123] Schmidt 111.

[124] *S v Snyman* 1968 2 SA 582 (A) 585.

[125] *S v J* 1966 1 SA 88 (RA) 90.

[126] *R v Ncanana* 1948 4 SA 399 (A).

[127] *R v Gumede* 1949 3 SA 749 (A).

[128] 1969 2 SA 375 (N) 375–7. See also *S v Hlapezula & others* 1965 4 SA 439 (A); *S v Hlongwa* 1991 1 SACR 583 (A); *S v Francis* 1991 SACR 198 (A).

where the accused is a lying witness, or where he does not give evidence. (8) The risk of false incrimination will also, I think, be reduced in a proper case where the accomplice is a friend of the accused. (9) In the absence of any of the aforementioned features, it is competent for a court to convict on the evidence of an accomplice only where the court understands the peculiar danger inherent in accomplice evidence and appreciates that acceptance of the accomplice and rejection of the accused is only permissible where the merits of the accomplice as a witness, and the demerits of the accused as a witnesses, are beyond question. (10) Where the corroboration of an accomplice is offered by the evidence of another accomplice, the latter remains an accomplice and the court is not relieved of its duty to examine his evidence also with caution. He, like the other accomplice, still has a possible motive to tell lies. He, like the other accomplice, because he is an accomplice, is in a position to furnish the court with details of the crime which is apt to give the court, if unwary, the impression that he is a satisfactory witness in all respects."

The evidence of an accessory after the fact also falls within the ambit of the cautionary rule.[129]

In *S v Dladla*[130] it was pointed out that circumstances may be such that the risk in acting upon the evidence of one accused — who had testified in his own defence and had implicated his co-accused — can be of an exceptionally high degree, especially where there are actual indications of attempts by, or of a tendency in, an accused to take advantage of the opportunity which the situation granted him, namely to try and save his own skin at the cost of his co-accused. The cautionary rule is therefore applied to the evidence of such an accused.[131]

The following witnesses are also suspected of having an ulterior motive for giving false evidence: police traps;[132] male and female complainants in sexual offences (see § 30 11 5 below); the plaintiff in paternity and seduction cases;[133] the private detective;[134] and persons who claim against the estates of deceased persons.[135] This list is not exhaustive.[136]

30 11 2 Evidence of identification[137] Evidence of identification must be approached with caution. Experience has shown that it is for various reasons very easy for the identifying witness to be mistaken. In *S v Mthetwa* it was said:[138]

"Because of the fallibility of human observation, evidence of identification is approached by the courts with some caution. It is not enough for the identifying witness to be honest: the reliability of his observation must also be tested. This depends on various factors, such as lighting, visibility, and eyesight; the proximity of the witness; the opportunity for observation, both as to time and situation; the extent of his prior knowledge of the accused; the mobility of the scene; corroboration; suggestibility; the accused's face, voice, build, gait and dress; the result of identification parades, if any; and, of course the evidence by or on

---

[129] *R v Nhleko* 1960 4 SA 712 (A).

[130] 1980 1 SA 526 (A) 529.

[131] See also *S v Johannes* 1980 1 SA 531 (A).

[132] *S v Mabaso* 1978 3 SA 5 (O); *S v Ramproop* 1991 1 SACR 555 (N).

[133] *Mayer v Williams* 1981 3 SA 348 (A).

[134] *Preen v Preen* 1935 NPD 138.

[135] *Borcherds v Estate Naidoo* 1955 3 SA 78 (A).

[136] See generally *S v Letsedi* 1963 2 SA 471 (A); *S v Malinga & others* 1963 1 SA 692 (A) 693–4; *S v Chouhan* 1987 2 SA 315 (ZS) 317I–J.

[137] See generally Stone *Proof of Fact in Criminal Trials* (1984) 190–213; Gooderson *Alibi* (1977) 186; *S v Ngcobo* 1986 1 SA 905 (N); *S v Zitha* 1993 1 SACR 718 (A).

[138] 1972 3 SA 766 (A) 768.

behalf of the accused. The list is not exhaustive. These factors, or such of them as are applicable in a particular case, are not individually decisive, but must be weighed one against the other, in the light of the totality of the evidence, and the probabilities . . .."

30 11 3 Children[139] In *R v Manda*[140] it was said that the imaginativeness and suggestibility of children are only two of a number of reasons why the evidence of children should be "scrutinized with care amounting, perhaps, to suspicion". In *S v S*[141] Ebrahim J examined this issue very carefully because he felt that a "new and more specific approach to cases involving children" was necessary.

30 11 4 The single witness[142] Section 208 of the CPA provides that an accused may be convicted of any offence on the single evidence of any competent witness. In civil cases judgment may also be given on the evidence of a single witness.[143] In *S v Sauls*[144] it was said that there is no rule-of-thumb test or formula to apply when it comes to the consideration of the credibility of a single witness. The trial court should weigh the evidence of the single witness and should consider its merits and demerits and, having done so, should decide whether it is satisfied that the truth has been told despite shortcomings or defects or contradictions in the evidence. In *S v Webber*[145] it was decided that the evidence of a single witness should be approached with caution and such evidence ought not necessarily be rejected merely because the single witness happens to have an interest or bias to the accused. The correct approach is to assess the intensity of the bias and to determine the importance thereof in the light of the evidence as a whole.

30 11 5 The cautionary rule in sexual offences[146] The cautionary rule applies to the evidence of female as well as male[147] complainants in sexual cases. "It is not only the risk of conscious fabrication that must be guarded against", said Schreiner JA in *R v Rautenbach*,[148] "[but] also the danger that a frightened woman, especially if inclined to hysteria, may imagine that things have happened which did not happen at all." There are also other reasons which have been advanced in support of the cautionary rule in sexual offences.[149]

---

[139] See generally *Woji v Santam Insurance Co Ltd* 1981 1 SA 1020 (A); *R v S* 1984 4 SA 419 (GW); *R v W* 1949 3 SA 772 (A).
[140] 1951 3 SA 158 (A) 163.
[141] 1995 1 SACR 50 (ZS). See especially 54*g*–60*c*, where Ebrahim J refers to and relies upon Spencer & Flin *The Evidence of Children* (1990) 238. For a discussion of *S v S* supra, see Watney 1995 *THRHR* 715.
[142] See *R v Mokoena* 1932 OPD 79 80; *R v Bellingham* 1955 2 SA 566 (A) 569G–H.
[143] Section 16 of the CPEA.
[144] 1981 3 SA 172 (A) 180.
[145] 1971 3 SA 754 (A).
[146] See generally *R v W* 1949 3 SA 772 (A); *R v M* 1947 4 SA 489 (N); *S v S* 1990 1 SACR 5 (A) 8; *S v De Graaff* 1992 1 PH H23 (A); *R v Rautenbach* 1949 1 SA 135 (A) 143; *S v F* 1989 3 SA; *S v Balhuber* 1987 1 PH H22 (A).
[147] *R v O* 1964 4 SA 245 (SR) 248H; *S v C* 1965 3 SA 105 (N) 108.
[148] Supra 143.
[149] In para 3 55 of the SA Law Commission's *Project 45: Report on Women and Sexual Offences* (April 1985) it was said: "A cautionary rule is applied to evidence of rape (and other sexual misconduct) because experience has shown that it is dangerous to rely on the uncorroborated evidence of the complainant in such circumstances. The reasons for this are that as rape usually takes place in secret and the complainant was involved, it is easy to lay a false charge and difficult to refute it. Furthermore a complaint could be

In *S v D & another*[150] the Namibian Supreme Court took a critical view of the cautionary rule under discussion and pointed out that "[w]hile it is true that different motives may exist for laying false charges, this surely applies to any offence and not only to offences of a sexual nature". In *S v D* supra Frank J also pointed out that the cautionary rule applies to male complainants as well. But he noted that in most cases of this nature the complainant is female. He came to the conclusion that the rule has no other purpose than to discriminate against women and that the rule is "probably also . . . contrary to art 10 of the Namibian Constitution, which provides for the equality of all persons before the law regardless of sex".[151] *S v D* supra was criticized in *S v M*,[152] where it was held that the cautionary approach in sexual offences does not discriminate and is not a legal rule but an admonition for the cautious application of common sense.[153] According to Paizes, caution is necessary not because the court is dealing "with the evidence of a woman, but because the *complaint* is of a particularly emotive and sensitive nature".[154] Schwikkard, however, argues that the cautionary rule under discussion "was moulded by the prejudices of another age, and that it is clearly influenced by a discredited conception of female psychology".[155]

30 12 THE RULE IN *VALACHIA*

In *R v Valachia & another*[156] it was decided that if part of a statement is proved against a party on the basis that it contains admissions, then the party is entitled to have the rest received as well if the two components comprise a single statement. However, in terms of the rule in *Valachia* the court is entitled to attach less weight to those parts of the statement favourable to its maker.[157] In *S v Ndluli & others* Nienaber J, relying on the rule in *Valachia*, said:[158]

> "A statement made by a man against his own interests generally speaking has the intrinsic ring of truth; but his exculpatory explanations and excuses may well strike a false note and should be treated with a measure of distrust as being unsworn, unconfirmed, untested and self-serving."

Rejecting exculpatory parts and accepting incriminating parts should only

---

motivated by an emotional reaction or spite, an innocent man might be falsely accused because of his wealth, the complainant might be forced by circumstances to admit that she had intercourse and represent willing intercourse as rape." The SA Law Commission recommended retention of the cautionary rule in sexual offences. But according to Schwikkard 1993 *SALJ* 46 47, the British Law Commission has recommended the scrapping of the caution to the jury in sexual offences.

[150] 1992 1 SACR 143 (Nm) 146*b*.

[151] At 146*f–g*.

[152] 1992 2 SACR 188 (W).

[153] At 194*h* Flemming DJP said: "Die waaksaamheid teen foutiewe oortuiging berus op normale en gesonde logika. Gesonde verstand sou 'n gebalanseerde mens wat die strafregtelike bewyslas reg toepas, tot dieselfde resultaat lei as versigtigheidsreëls."

[154] Paizes in Du Toit et al *Commentary* 24-7 (emphasis added).

[155] 1993 *SALJ* 46 49. For further discussion of *S v D* supra, see Wilmot 1992 *SACJ* 211 and Viljoen 1992 *TSAR* 543.

[156] 1945 AD 826 835. See also *S v Felix & another* 1980 4 SA 604 (A) 609H–610A; *S v Khoza* 1982 3 SA 1019 (A) 1039A–B.

[157] See also *R v Vather* 1961 1 SA 350 (A).

[158] 1993 2 SACR 501 (A) 505*g*.

take place on consideration of the evidence as a whole[159] and then only if there are sound reasons for such rejection and acceptance.

The rule in *Valachia*[160] is not confined to extra-curial statements which are proved against a party in court but also applies to an explanation of plea given by an accused in terms of s 115 of the CPA.[161] This matter is dealt with in detail in § 16 7 2 above.

---

[159] *S v Yelani* 1989 2 SA 43 (A) 50.
[160] *S v Motloba* 1992 2 SACR 634 (BA) 639*d–e*.
[161] *S v Cloete* 1994 1 SACR 420 (A).

CHAPTER 31

THE STANDARD AND BURDEN OF PROOF AND EVIDENTIAL DUTIES IN CRIMINAL TRIALS

PJ Schwikkard and S E van der Merwe

31 1 INTRODUCTION

The burden of proof has been described as "the duty which is cast on the particular litigant in order to be successful, of finally satisfying the court that he is entitled to succeed on his claim or defence, as the case may be".[1] Before a matter is brought before a court it is always necessary to consider who will bear the burden of proof and what standard needs to be met in order to discharge that burden. But before considering these issues it is necessary to distinguish between the burden of proof (or onus) and an evidentiary burden.

31 2 THE ONUS ("BEWYSLAS") AND EVIDENTIARY BURDEN ("WEERLEGGINGS-LAS")

The burden of proof or true onus "refers to the duty of a party to persuade the trier of facts by the end of the case of the truth of certain propositions".[2] But the evidentiary burden "refers to one party's duty of producing sufficient evidence for a judge to call on the other party to answer"[3] and it also encompasses "the duty cast upon a litigant to adduce evidence in order to combat a *prima facie* case made by his opponent".[4]

---

[1] *Pillay v Krishna* 1946 AD 946 952. This case is discussed more fully in § 32 1 below.
[2] Heydon *Evidence: Cases & Materials* 3 ed (1991) 15, where it is also noted that "[w]hat these propositions are depends on the substantive rules of law and pleadings".
[3] Heydon *Evidence* 15.
[4] *South Cape Corporation (Pty) Ltd v Engineering Management Services (Pty) Ltd* 1977 3 SA 534 (A) 548. See also *Pillay v Krishna* 1946 AD 946 952–3; *S v Ndlovu* 1986 1 SA 510 (N); *S v De Blom* 1977 3 SA 513 (A) 532.

It is fundamental principle of our law that in a criminal trial the burden of proof rests on the prosecution to prove the accused's guilt beyond a reasonable doubt. This burden will rest on the prosecution throughout the trial. At the outset of the trial, in tandem with the burden of proof, the state must also discharge an evidential burden. It will do this by establishing a *prima facie* case against the accused. Once a *prima facie* case is established the evidential burden will *shift* to the accused to adduce evidence in order to escape conviction. However, the burden of proof will *remain* with the prosecution. It is possible that even if the accused does not adduce evidence, he will not be convicted if the court is satisfied that the prosecution has not proved guilt beyond a reasonable doubt.[5]

In *S v Alex Carriers (Pty) Ltd* the court contrasted the burden of proof resting on the prosecution and the accused's "evidentiary" burden in the following terms:[6]

> "Conviction beyond reasonable doubt is what the State must achieve before it succeeds in making 'the wall of guilt fall on the accused'; it is unnecessary for the accused to push any part of that wall over onto the side of the State. An accused will accordingly be discharged if the State's case is not strong enough and, according to principle, it will sometimes be sufficient if the accused does nothing at all and sometimes it will be sufficient if he relies on pointing out the weaknesses in the State case (by, e g, cross-examination which exposes the unreliability of a witness). The practical effect of the State producing a stronger case might well be that such limited counters to the State case might transpire to be insufficient and that active rebuttal of the State case is necessary to counter the strength of that case. Even then there is no onus of proof on the accused. (As there still appears to be confusion, it might promote clarity to say that an accused experiences a necessity of rebuttal ["weer-leggingsnoodsaak"] rather than he bears a burden of rebuttal.) The quantity and strength of the rebutting considerations required by the accused to prevent the State producing a convincing case depends, in the nature of things, on the strength of the State case. The accused has to do nothing more than to cause the court, when reaching its decision, to have a reasonable doubt concerning the guilt of the accused."

31 3   THE INCIDENCE OF THE ONUS OF PROOF

The constitutional and common-law presumption of innocence and the principle that the burden of proof rests on a person making a positive averment cast on the state the burden of proving every element of the crime.[7] The *status quo* is that all persons are presumed innocent. The state seeks to prove the contrary. It therefore bears the burden of proof.

In order to discharge the burden of proof the state must prove that the accused is the criminal,[8] the commission of the act charged,[9] and its unlawfulness.[10] The state is also required to prove the absence of any defence raised by the accused,

---

[5] See generally Heydon *Evidence* 15.

[6] 1985 3 SA 79 (T), headnote; see 88I–89D for original text.

[7] *R v Ndlovu* 1945 AD 369. In *S v Kubeka* 1982 1 SA 534 (W) 538G Slomowitz AJ noted: "The rule that the State is required to prove guilt beyond a reasonable doubt has on occasion been criticized as being anomalous. On the other hand, the vast majority of lawyers (myself included) subscribe to the view that in the search for truth it is better that guilty men should go free than that an innocent man should be punished."

[8] *R v Blom* 1939 AD 188 at 210; *R v Hlongwane* 1959 3 SA 337 (A).

[9] *R v Nhleko* 1960 4 SA 712 (A) 721.

[10] *R v Ndlovu* supra.

for example, the absence of compulsion,[11] private defence,[12] consent, sane automatism,[13] the right to chastise or necessity.[14] The incidence of the onus of proof with regard to *mens rea* and *actus reus* is also in no way altered by a defence of voluntary or involuntary intoxication.[15] Where an alibi is raised the state bears the onus of proving that it was the accused who committed the crime.[16] In *S v Mhlongo*[17] the court held that an acquittal was not dependent on the court believing the accused's alibi, but whether such alibi is reasonably possibly true.

31 4   EXCEPTIONS TO THE GENERAL RULE

There are several exceptions to the general rule that the burden of proof rests on the state to prove guilt beyond reasonable doubt. These exceptions are obviously an infringement of the constitutional presumption of innocence. Since the coming into operation of the interim Constitution[18] it is clear that an infringement of the presumption of innocence will be tolerated only if it meets the requirements of the limitations clause.[19] Consequently, in considering these exceptions it is necessary to have regard to their constitutionality. The constitutionality of statutory presumptions that have the effect of placing a burden of proof on the accused is considered in chapter 29 above.[20]

31 4 1   The common-law exception   In terms of the common law everyone is presumed to be of sound mind until the contrary is proved.[21] As a result of this presumption an accused bears the onus of proof with regard to a defence of criminal non-responsibility on account of mental illness or mental defect.[22] The accused is required to discharge this onus on a balance of probabilities.[23]

Whether this common-law presumption is constitutionally tenable remains an open question. The Canadian Supreme Court in *R v Chaulk*[24] held that although

---

[11] *S v Mltetwa* 1977 3 SA 628 (E).

[12] *R v Ndhlovu* supra; *S v Ngomane* 1979 3 SA 859 (A).

[13] *S v Van Rensburg* 1987 3 SA 35 (T); *S v Viljoen* 1992 1 SACR 601 (T); *S v Potgieter* 1994 1 SACR 61 (A). See also § 31 4 1 below.

[14] *S v Adams* 1981 1 SA 187 (A).

[15] *S v Chretien* 1981 1 SA 1097 (A). Note that in terms of s 1 of the Criminal Law Amendment Act 1 of 1988 persons will be guilty of an offence if they consume or use any substance: *(a)* which impairs their faculties to appreciate the wrongfulness of their acts or ability to act in accordance with such appreciation; *(b)* knowing that such substance has that effect; and *(c)*, while their faculties are so impaired, commit an act prohibited by law (for which they would not be liable because of the impairment to their faculties).

[16] *R v Hlongwane* 1959 3 SA 337 (A).

[17] 1991 2 SACR 207 (A).

[18] Section 25(3)*(c)* provides that every accused has the right to be presumed innocent and to remain silent.

[19] *S v Zuma* 1995 1 SACR 568 (CC). See generally ch 29 above.

[20] The interim Constitution and s 60(11) of the CPA (inserted by virtue of the Criminal Procedure Second Amendment Act 75 of 1995) have given rise to a great deal of debate concerning the question of onus in bail proceedings. See, e g, *S v Mbele* 1996 1 SACR 212 (W); *S v Vermaas* 1996 1 SACR 528 (T); *S v Shezi* 1996 1 SACR 715 (T).

[21] *R v M'Naghten* 1843 10 Cl & Fin 200. See generally Hoffmann & Zeffertt 543–55.

[22] See also s 78 of the CPA.

[23] *R v Kaukakani* 1947 2 SA 807 (A); *S v Van Zyl* 1964 2 SA 113 (A) 121; *S v Mahlinza* 1967 1 SA 408 (A) 419; *S v Adams* 1986 4 SA 882 (A).

[24] 1991 1 CRR (2d) 1.

the presumption of sanity infringed the constitutional right to be presumed innocent, it was a reasonable limitation. The underlying rationale of this conclusion was that to require the state to prove sanity would place an almost impossible burden on the prosecution. In a minority judgment Wilson J held that the presumption of sanity could not be viewed as a reasonable limitation in that it did not impair as little as possible the accused's right to be presumed innocent as the same objectives could be met by merely placing an evidentiary burden ("weerleggingslas") on the accused. (It should be noted that in Canadian law there appear to be no provisions in terms of which the court can order an investigation into the accused's mental state.)[25] Burchell[26] argues that the difficulty of disproving insanity is an anomalous justification in the South African context as there is no similar shift in the burden in proof in respect of other defences which are equally difficult to prove. For example, where the defence of non-pathological incapacity is raised the onus rests on the state to rebut it and if there is a reasonable doubt that the accused lacked the requisite criminal capacity at the time of the offence, he or she must be acquitted.[27] This, he argues, might also lead to the conclusion that the presumption of sanity infringes the constitutional right to equality:

> "An accused who simply adduces evidence of non-pathological incapacity can receive a complete acquittal if a reasonable doubt exists in his or her favour, but the accused who raises insanity (pathological incapacity) must prove this condition on a preponderance of probabilities . . .."

The infringement of the presumption of innocence can also be viewed from another perspective: "[I]nsanity excludes the element of capacity which is a fundamental aspect of liability. Placing an onus of proving insanity would relieve the prosecution of establishing this element of liability and would, therefore, infringe the presumption of innocence."[28] Burchell's solution is to restrict the effect of the presumption of sanity to the creation of an evidentiary burden.[29] Although this distinction between the burden of proof and the evidentiary burden does not necessarily cure the *prima facie* unconstitutionality of the presumption of sanity,[30] it certainly strengthens the argument that it meets the

---

[25] In contrast the South African courts are obliged to order such an investigation in terms of ss 78 and 79 of the CPA. See *S v Mokie* 1992 1 SACR 430 (T); *S v Mphela* 1994 1 SACR 488 (A).

[26] Burchell & Milton *Principles of Criminal Law* 2 ed (forthcoming) ch 24.

[27] *S v Campher* 1987 1 SA 940 (A); *S v Laubscher* 1988 1 SA 163 (A); *S v Calitz* 1990 1 SACR 119 (A); *S v Wiid* 1990 1 SACR 561 (A); *S v Cunningham* 1996 1 SACR 631 (A); *S v Moses* 1996 1 SACR 701 (C). It is clear from these decisions that when the defence of criminal incapacity is not based on mental illness or mental defect the onus rests on the state to prove criminal capacity beyond a reasonable doubt. However, the accused must lay a foundation for the raising of the defence. See § 31 4 2 below. Cf *S v Shivute* 1991 1 SACR 656 (Nm) 660*h*. Burchell *Principles of Criminal Law* argues that the presumption of sanity cannot be justified on the basis that the accused's mental state is peculiarly within the sphere of knowledge of the accused because logic would dictate that the burden must also shift when a defence of intoxication or provocation is raised.

[28] Burchell *Principles of Criminal Law*.

[29] *Principles of Criminal Law*. He also notes that "the presumption of sanity has its origins in a system of law in which a clear distinction was not often drawn between a presumption which casts a burden of proof on a balance of probabilities onto the accused and a presumption which casts merely an evidential burden onto the accused". See Morton & Hutchison *The Presumption of Innocence* (1987) 69.

[30] See chs 28 and 29 above.

requirements of the limitations clause.[31] It is submitted that neither policy nor logic justifies distinguishing between defences based on pathological or non-pathological criminal incapacity. An approach which would be consistent with the provisions of the Constitution would be one that merely places a duty on the accused to lay a foundation for the defence of insanity. But it is unlikely that our courts would opt for such an approach.

It should be noted that if an accused *raises a defence of non-triability* on account of mental illness or mental defect, then the burden of proof rests upon the state to show beyond reasonable doubt that the accused is triable.[32]

31 4 2 Procedural duty to introduce a defence An accused has a duty to introduce his defence. This should be done by putting his defence to state witnesses who are being cross-examined.[33] The defence may also be introduced during the explanation of plea in terms of s 115 of the CPA. *The duty to introduce a defence does not mean that there is an onus of proof upon the accused.* It merely means that the accused has a procedural duty to raise the issue during the trial so that the state is able to concentrate upon the real issue. Lansdown & Campbell observe as follows:[34]

"Apart from this special case of allegations of insanity, where the onus of proof is upon the State it must disprove any defence raised by the accused. This does not mean that the prosecution must lead evidence on all possible issues to negative in advance all possible defences. The prosecution witnesses are not required to recite in every case that the accused acted without provocation, not in self-defence, under no mistake or duress, and so forth. Rather, if the defence wishes to rely on such a defence and put the prosecution to the disproof thereof, it must raise the particular issue."

An accused should, for example, lay a foundation for a defence of sane automatism.[35] In *S v Trickett*[36] it was held that although the prosecution has a burden of disproving a defence of automatism not caused by mental illness or mental defect, this burden does not operate until the defence has been put in issue. Similarly, in *S v Delport*[37] it was said that the state need not negative provocation unless the evidence indicates that it is a possible factor in the case.

In *S v Kalagoropoulos*[38] the court stated: "[A]n accused person who relies on non-pathological causes in support of a defence of criminal incapacity is required in evidence to lay a factual foundation for it, sufficient at least to create a reasonable doubt on the point."[39] Does this imply that the duty to introduce a

---

[31] See *R v Chaulk* supra.
[32] *S v Ebrahim* 1973 1 SA 686 (A). An accused is non-triable if by reason of mental illness or mental defect he is incapable of understanding the procedure so as to make a proper defence at his trial. See generally s 78 of the CPA; *S v Morake* 1979 1 SA 121 (B); Kruger 1979 *SACC* 169; Kruger *Mental Health Law* (1980) 179–84.
[33] *S v Nkomo* 1975 3 SA 598 (N). See § 18 6 4 above.
[34] At 910.
[35] See generally Schmidt 1973 *SALJ* 329; *S v Potgieter* 1994 1 SACR 61 (A).
[36] 1973 3 SA 526 (T) 532.
[37] 1968 1 PH H172 (A).
[38] 1993 1 SACR 12 (A). See also *S v Cunningham* supra 635 *a–c*.
[39] At 21*j*. See also *S v Potgieter* supra; *S v Els* 1993 1 SACR 723 (O); *S v Kensley* 1995 1 SACR 646 (A); *S v Nursingh* 1995 2 SACR 331 (D).

defence can in certain circumstances place an evidential burden on the accused? It is submitted not. Read in context, it is clear that the above quotation was made to qualify earlier decisions in which it was held that psychiatric evidence is not indispensable when criminal incapacity is attributed to non-pathological causes.[40] It is submitted that the better approach is that whilst the accused has a duty to introduce a defence of pathological incapacity, an evidentiary burden will arise only once the state has established a *prima facie* case of criminal capacity.

31 5   APPLICATION FOR DISCHARGE

Section 174 of the CPA provides that the court may return a verdict of not guilty if at the conclusion of the case for the state it is of the opinion that there is no evidence that the accused committed the offence referred to in the charge or any offence of which he may be convicted on the charge. The test which is applied is whether there is insufficient evidence for a reasonable man to convict.[41] However, the court has a discretion not to discharge the accused at the close of the state's case, even where no *prima facie* case has been established to shift the evidential burden onto the defence, if there is a reasonable possibility that the defence evidence might supplement the state's case.[42] Hoffmann & Zeffertt provide the following justification of this discretion:[43]

> " . . . [A] criminal trial is not a game, and its end is to achieve justice by convicting the guilty as well as freeing the innocent . . . [A] wish to be fair to the accused should not defeat obvious indications that may lead to a guilty accused's being convicted rather than set free".

However, it is unlikely that such an approach will survive constitutional scrutiny as it may well be argued that it contravenes the right to a fair trial guaranteed in s 25(3) of the interim Constitution. The Canadian courts have held that the presumption of innocence incorporates the principle of fairness,[44] and demands that the prosecution establish a *prima facie* case before the accused can be called upon to respond.[45] In the light of this reasoning it is submitted that the discretion conferred on the courts to refuse discharge if there is a reasonable possibility that the defence might supplement the state's case is unconstitutional.[46]

---

[40] See 21*i*.

[41] *S v Khanyapa* 1979 1 SA 824 (A). Assessors (see generally § 1 6 above) do not participate in this decision. See *S v Magxwalisa* 1984 2 SA 314 (N). Credibility is normally not considered, unless it is of very poor quality. See generally *S v Mpetha* 1983 4 SA 262 (C) 265D–G and *S v Cooper* 1976 2 SA 875 (T).

[42] *R v Mall (1)* 1960 2 SA 340 (N); *S v Ostilly* 1979 2 SA 104 (D); *S v Mpetha* supra; *S v Amerika* 1990 2 SACR 480 (C). See also the dual approach adopted in *S v Shuping* 1983 2 SA 119 (B).

[43] Hoffmann & Zeffertt 506.

[44] *R v Oakes* 1986 26 DLR (4th) 200.

[45] *Dubois v R* 1985 23 DLR (4th) 503.

[46] See Skeen in Du Toit et al Commentary 22-32E; Skeen 1993 *SAJHR* 525–38. See also *S v Gqozo (2)* 1994 (1) BCLR 10 (Ck).

31 6   THE CRIMINAL STANDARD OF PROOF

In *S v Glegg*[47] it was said that proof beyond reasonable doubt cannot be put on the same level as proof beyond the slightest doubt, because the burden of adducing proof as high as that would in practice lead to defeating the ends of criminal justice. It was also held that the words "reasonable doubt" in the phrase "proof beyond reasonable doubt" cannot be precisely defined, but it can well be said that it is a doubt which exists because of probabilities or possibilities which can be regarded as reasonable on the ground of generally accepted human knowledge and experience. Where there are no probabilities either way and it cannot be said that the innocent version of the accused is not reasonably true, then the evidence does not constitute proof beyond reasonable doubt.[48] In *R v M*[49] it was said that it is not a prerequisite for an acquittal that the court should believe the innocent account of the accused: it is sufficient that it might be substantially true. But fanciful possibilities should not be allowed to deflect the course of justice.[50] In *R v Difford*[51] the following remarks of the trial court were approved by the Appellate Division:[52]

"It is not disputed on behalf of the defence that in the absence of some explanation the Court would be entitled to convict the accused. It is not a question of throwing any onus on the accused, but in these circumstances it would be a conclusion which the Court could draw if no explanation were given. It is equally clear that no onus rests on the accused to convince the Court of the truth of any explanation he gives. If he gives an explanation, even if the explanation is improbable, the Court is not entitled to convict unless it is satisfied, not only that the explanation is improbable, but that beyond any reasonable doubt it is false. If there is any reasonable possibility of his explanation being true, then he is entitled to his acquittal . . .."

In *S v Magano*[53] the court set aside a conviction on the basis that the trial magistrate had misunderstood the required standard of proof in criminal cases when he found that "the evidence of the State was reasonably possibly true against that of the defence".

The standard of proof is not affected by the serious or trivial nature of the charge.[54] In those exceptional circumstances where statutes place the burden of proof on the accused the civil standard of proof applies. If a statute merely places an evidentiary burden on the accused, the state will still carry the burden of proving its case beyond reasonable doubt.[55]

---

[47] 1973 1 SA 34 (A).
[48] *S v Molautsi* 1980 3 SA 1041 (B).
[49] 1946 AD 1023.
[50] *Miller v Minister of Pensions* 1947 2 All ER 372 373.
[51] 1937 AD 370 272.
[52] See also *S v Alex Carriers (Pty) Ltd* supra, where the court noted that a court is not required to consider every conceivable possibility when these are not suggested by the facts.
[53] 1990 2 PH H135 (B).
[54] *S v Sinkanka* 1963 2 SA 531 (A).
[55] See also §§ 28 4 and 28 5 2 above.

CHAPTER 32

The Standard and Burden of Proof and Evidential Duties in Civil Trials

A St Q Skeen

32 1 INTRODUCTION

The general rule is that he who asserts must prove. The leading case of *Pillay v Krishna*[1] clearly sets out the law in this respect:

"The first principle in regard to the burden of proof is . . . the burden of proof always lies on him who takes action. If one person claims something from another in a court of law then he has to satisfy the court that he is entitled to it. But there is a second principle which must always be read with it . . . he who avails himself of an exception is considered a plaintiff; for in respect of his exception a defendant is a plaintiff. Where a person against whom the claim is made is not content with a mere denial, but sets up a special defence then he is regarded *quoad* that defence, as being the claimant: for his defence to be upheld he must satisfy the court that he is entitled to succeed upon it . . . In my opinion the only correct use of the word 'onus' is that which I believe to be in its true and original sense namely the duty which is cast on the particular litigant, in order to be successful, of finally satisfying the court that he is entitled to succeed on his claim or defence, as the case may be, and not in the sense merely of his duty to adduce evidence to combat a *prima facie* case made out by his opponent . . . The onus in the sense which I use the word can never shift from the party upon whom it originally rested."

This case emphatically illustrates the fact that the overall legal onus (burden of proof, "bewyslas") is fixed by the pleadings and never changes. Likewise, in *Klaassen v Benjamin*[2] it was said that the burden of proof is fixed by the pleadings and never shifts. The burden of proof lies with him who asserts, but if a party sets up a special defence, the onus of proving that defence is on the party who raises

---

[1] 1946 AD 946 951–3.
[2] 1941 TPD 80.

it. In *Tregea v Godart*[3] it was held that the determination of the overall onus of proof is a matter of substantive law. In this case it was decided that the rules determining which party had to prove the sanity or insanity of a testator had to be ascertained by reference to the law of succession (see § 4 3 above).

The incidence of the burden of proof decides which party will fail on a given issue if, after hearing all the evidence, the court is left in doubt. The overall onus is sometimes also referred to as "the risk of non-persuasion".

32 2 THE ONUS AND EVIDENTIARY BURDEN DISTINGUISHED

It is necessary to distinguish between the overall onus and the evidential burden ("weerleggingslas").[4] It was mentioned in § 32 1 above that the overall onus ("bewyslas") is fixed by the pleadings and never shifts during the trial. The evidential burden arises as soon as the evidence or a presumption of law or an inference creates the risk that a litigant may fail, for example, because a *prima facie* case has been made out against him (see § 32 6 below). The evidentiary burden may shift from one litigant to another during the course of the trial.[5]

In respect of certain defences to defamation (namely, qualified privilege, fair comment, and truth in the public benefit) the defendant is, according to the Appellate Division, encumbered with a full onus and not a mere evidentiary burden.[6] But the constitutional right to freedom of speech and expression — particularly in so far as this right relates to free and fair political activity — requires a different approach.[7]

---

[3] 1939 AD 16.

[4] The word "weerleggingslas" may be misleading and it has been suggested in *S v Alex Carriers (Pty) Ltd* 1985 3 SA 79 (T) that the word "weerleggingsnoodsaak", roughly translated as "necessity of rebuttal", may be more appropriate. See § 31 2 above.

[5] *Klaassen v Benjamin* 1941 TPD 80; *Pillay v Krishna* 1946 AD 946; *South Cape Corporation (Pty) Ltd v Engineering Management Services (Pty) Ltd* 1977 3 SA 534 (A).

[6] *Neethling v Du Preez & others* 1994 1 SA 708 (A), in which it was said that nothing stated in *SAUK v O'Malley* 1977 3 SA 394 (A) represents authority to the contrary.

[7] Part of the headnote in *Holomisa v Argus Newspapers Ltd* 1996 2 SA 588 (W) 591–2 reads as follows: "The court proceeded to assess the following propositions in *Neethling v Du Preez*: that the defendant bore the full burden of proving the truth of a defamatory statement, and that there was no general public policy defence for the publication of defamatory statements... *Held*, that neither proposition was compatible with the scheme of government and the structure of values and principles the new Constitution created. It was at odds with the Constitution to impose the onus to prove constitutional protection on the defendant publisher in the field of 'free and fair political activity', in regard to which a limitation on free speech and expression had to be 'necessary'. On the contrary, the emphasis the Constitution placed on free speech and expression in the context of free and fair political activity required that some greater protection be given to those who made false defamatory statements in the field. The plaintiff who sought to inhibit speech in the area of free and fair political activity should bear the onus of proving that the defendant has forfeited entitlement to constitutional protection. As to the rejection of a public policy defence, the Constitution necessitated asking the question whether the constitutional guarantee of the right to freedom of speech and expression justified the defendant's publication and required that it be found lawful. By corollary, the question was whether any limitation on that right was compatible with the requirement of s 33(1) that it be reasonable and justifiable in an open and democratic society based on freedom and equality, and, in the case of limitations on that right in so far as its exercise bears on free and fair political activity, that it also be necessary... *Held*, accordingly, that the common-law rules of defamation liability as enunciated in *Neethling v Du Preez* constituted a limitation on the right to freedom of expression and speech, particularly in so far as that right related to free and fair political activity, which was not warrantable under the Constitution's limitation section... The court then considered the argument on behalf of the

In *Mabaso v Felix*[8] it was held that in actions for damages in respect of delicts affecting the plaintiff's personality and bodily integrity the defendant ordinarily bears the onus of proving the excuse or justification which he raises. Sometimes, however, the nature of the pleadings may be such that the onus is placed on the plaintiff to negative the excuse or justification.

32 3   THE DUTY TO BEGIN IN TERMS OF SUPREME COURT RULE 39

Supreme Court rule 39(13) provides that where the onus of adducing evidence on one or more of the issues is on the plaintiff, and that of adducing evidence on any other issue is on the defendant, the plaintiff shall first call his evidence on any issue in respect of which the onus is upon him, and may then close his case. The defendant, if absolution from the instance is not granted, shall, if he does not close his case, thereupon call his evidence on all issues in respect of which such onus is on him.

Normally, where the plaintiff bears the overall onus of proof he will have the right or duty to lead his evidence first, but there may be circumstances where the pleadings place an evidentiary burden on the defendant; where this is so the defendant will have the duty to begin.[9]

32 4   THE DUTY TO BEGIN IN TERMS OF MAGISTRATES' COURTS RULE 29

Magistrates' courts rule 29(7)(a) provides that if the burden of proof is on the plaintiff, he shall first adduce his evidence. Rule 29(8) provides that where the burden of proof is on the defendant he shall first adduce his evidence. It appears

---

defendant that the Constitution required the importation of the 'actual malice' test set out in *New York Times Co v Sullivan* 376 US 254 (1964) into the South African law of defamation. The court took the view that this test was inappropriate and undesirable, favouring instead the approach of the Australian High Court in *Theophanous v Herald & Weekly Times Ltd & another* 1994 124 ALR 1 (HC) which adopted a standard of reasonableness as a justification for publishing false defamatory statements . . . *Held*, that the constitutional structure sought to nurture open and accountable democracy. Partly to that end, it encouraged and protected free speech and expression, including that practised by the media. If the protection the Constitution afforded was to have substance, there had to be some protection for erroneous statements of defamatory fact, at least in the area of 'free and fair political activity'. Constitutional protection should therefore be afforded to one who exercised his or her right of free speech by publishing even false defamatory statements in the area of 'free and fair political activity', unless the plaintiff showed that the publisher acted unreasonably. In such a case, the publisher would forfeit entitlement to constitutional protection . . . *Held*, accordingly that a defamatory statement which related to free and fair political activity was constitutionally protected, even if false, unless the plaintiff showed that, in all the circumstances of its publication, it was unreasonably made. The court then considered the question of the application of the defence set out above to the present dispute."

[8] 1981 3 SA 865 (A). See generally Visser 1982 *THRHR* 81.

[9] Hoffman & Zeffertt 502; *Topaz Kitchens (Pty) Ltd v Naboom Spa (Edms) Bpk* 1976 3 SA 470 (A); *Smith's Trustee v Smith* 1927 AD 482. But parties should not plead in a manner aimed at avoiding the burden of proof. In *Nieuwoudt v Joubert* 1988 3 SA 84 (SE) 91B–D Mullins J said: "A litigant is not entitled to conceal material allegations in order to obtain the advantage of placing the onus on his opponent. The onus must be determined on genuine and not artificial allegations in the pleadings, and if the onus should be on a particular party, he must accept it. Litigation is not a game where a party may seek tactical advantages by concealing facts from his opponents and thereby occasioning unnecessary costs. Nor in my view is a party entitled to plead in such a manner as to place the onus on his opponent, if the facts as known to such party place the onus on him. If he has to bear the onus of proof, he must accept it, and not seek by devious pleadings to obtain an advantage to which he is not entitled."

from *HA Millard and Son (Pty) Ltd v Enzenhofer*[10] that the words "burden of proof" refer to the evidentiary burden and not the overall onus.

32 5   INCIDENCE OF THE BURDEN OF PROOF

As was indicated in § 32 1 above, the general rule is that he who asserts must prove: as a consequence the plaintiff normally bears the burden of proof. A rough and ready test, which is not invariably applied, is that he who makes the positive assertion must prove the facts he asserts. This test, however, is not always applied. Where proof of a negative assertion is an essential element of a party's claim or defence the onus of proving the negative rests on the party who asserts the negative.[11] In *Topaz Kitchens (Pty) Ltd v Naboom Spa (Edms) Bpk*[12] it was confirmed that where the plaintiff wishes to enforce a contract, and the onus is on him to prove terms of the contract, then the onus remains with him even if he has to prove a negative.

What happens where the facts are within the peculiar and intimate knowledge of one of the parties? It is not a principle of our law that the onus should, for the sole reason of such knowledge, rest on him.[13] The ordinary principles must be applied, but less evidence will suffice to establish a *prima facie* case.[14]

Where the defendant raises a special defence (such as confession and avoidance) then in respect of that defence he bears the burden of proof.[15] A person who alleges negligence bears the onus of proof,[16] as does a person who challenges the validity of a will which, on the face of it, is regular.[17] Where the incidence of the burden of proof is not settled by precedent the principles enunciated in *Pillay v Krishna* (set out in § 32 1 above) assist in determining who bears the burden of proof.

32 6   THE TERM "*PRIMA FACIE* CASE"

The term "*prima facie* case" means that the party who had first adduced evidence has led enough evidence upon which a reasonable man might find for him when he closes his case. The leading case of *Gascoyne v Paul and Hunter*[18] deals extensively with the term "*prima facie* case". This case was followed in *Supreme Service Station (1969) (Pvt) Ltd v Fox and Goodridge (Pvt) Ltd,*[19] where it was held

---

[10] 1968 1 SA 330 (T); Hoffmann & Zeffertt 502.
[11] *Kriegler v Minitzer* 1949 4 SA 821 (A) 828.
[12] 1976 3 SA 470 (A).
[13] *Gericke v Sack* 1978 1 SA 821 (A). It was re-affirmed in *Eskom v First National Bank of Southern African Ltd* 1995 2 SA 386 (A) that it is not a principle of our law that the onus of proof of a fact lies on the party who has peculiar or intimate knowledge of that fact. The incidence of the onus of proof is determined by law. This does not, however, mean that a court, where the incidence of the onus of proof is uncertain and has to be determined, may not have regard, inter alia, to matters of practical convenience and fairness such as the sources of knowledge available to the rival parties.
[14] *Union Government v Sykes* 1913 AD 156.
[15] *Pillay v Krishna* 1946 AD 946.
[16] *Administrator, Natal v Stanley Motors* 1960 1 SA 690 (A).
[17] *Kunz v Swart* 1924 AD 618; *Tregea v Godart* 1939 AD 16.
[18] 1917 TPD 170.
[19] 1971 4 SA 90 (RA).

that the test whether a *prima facie* case has been established after only one party has led evidence should be "what might a reasonable court do" in the absence of any contrary evidence and not "what ought a reasonable court to do". In other words, the party who has not yet led any evidence runs the risk of judgment being given against him if he leads no evidence to combat the *prima facie* case. It does not mean that judgment will automatically be given in favour of the party who has established the *prima facie* case if no contrary evidence is led.

32 7   ABSOLUTION FROM THE INSTANCE

Absolution from the instance is possible at the conclusion of the plaintiff's case. If a plaintiff bears the onus of proof, he must lead sufficient evidence on which a reasonable man *might* or *could* find in his favour at the conclusion of his case without the leading, at that stage, of any evidence by the defendant.[20] This means that the plaintiff must establish a *prima facie* case before the defendant is put to his defence. After the plaintiff has closed his case the defendant may apply for absolution from the instance on the grounds that no reasonable court might find for the plaintiff on his evidence. If the application is successful, the defendant will not be called on to present his case. The court does not usually consider the credibility of the plaintiff's witnesses in deciding whether a *prima facie* case has been made out, except in instances where the evidence is too vague and contradictory to prove the facts in issue or where the evidence is highly improbable.[21]

Absolution from the instance is also possible at the conclusion of the whole case. At the conclusion of the whole case the court may give outright judgment in favour of one or other of the parties or it may grant absolution from the instance. Such a judgment means, in effect, that the defendant is absolved from liability. It is, however, open to the plaintiff to institute fresh proceedings if new evidence comes to light.

The test to be applied in deciding whether to grant absolution after the evidence of both parties has been led is whether there is evidence upon which the court *ought* to give judgment in favour of the plaintiff.[22] It may happen that absolution from the instance at the conclusion of the plaintiff's case is refused but is later granted at the end of the case even if the plaintiff leads no evidence.[23]

32 8   CIVIL STANDARD OF PROOF

The degree of proof required before a case may be decided in favour of the party who asserts is usually expressed as proof on a balance (or preponderance) of probabilities. In *Miller v Minister of Pensions*[24] Lord Denning described the

---

[20] *Gascoyne v Paul and Hunter* 1917 TPD 170; *Supreme Service Station (1969 (Pvt) Ltd v Fox and Goodridge (Pvt) Ltd* 1971 4 SA 80 (RA).

[21] *Katz v Bloomfield* 1914 TPD; *Shenker Bros v Bester* 1952 3 SA 664 (A).

[22] *Gascoyne v Paul and Hunter* 1917 TPD 170; *Ruto Flour Mills v Adelson* 1958 4 SA 307 (T).

[23] *Myburgh v Kelly* 1942 EDL 206.

[24] 1947 2 All ER 372 374.

standard of proof in civil cases as follows: "It must carry a reasonable degree of probability but not so high as is required in a criminal case. If the evidence is such that the tribunal can say 'we think it is more probable than not' the burden is discharged, but if the probabilities are equal it is not." This description was accepted in this country in *Ocean Accident and Guarantee Corporation Ltd v Koch.*[25]

In allegations of crime and dishonesty in civil cases the standard of proof remains the same.[26] The same applies to the proof of paternity or seduction in a civil case.[27] In certain applications (such as those for a temporary interdict or an attachment to found jurisdiction) the applicant need only establish a *prima facie* case.[28] In the case of a final interdict the normal civil standard of proof applies.

Proof on a balance of probality is a lesser standard of proof than proof beyond reasonable doubt. The latter standard applies to the prosecution in criminal cases and was discussed in § 31 6 above.

---

[25] 1963 4 SA 147 (A) 157.

[26] *Gates v Gates* 1939 AD 150: *Erasmus v Erasmus* 1940 TPD 377; *Goodrich v Goodrich* 1946 AD 390; *Maritime and General Insurance Co v Sky Unit Engineering (Pty) Ltd* 1989 1 SA 867 (T).

[27] *Mayer v Williams* 1981 3 SA 348 (A).

[28] *Webster v Mitchell* 1948 1 SA 1186 (W); *Gool v Minister of Justice* 1955 2 SA 682 (C) 688; *Yorigami Maritime Construction Co Ltd v Nissho-Iwai Co Ltd* 1977 4 SA 682 (C) 687.

CONSTITUTION OF THE REPUBLIC OF SOUTH AFRICA, ACT 108 OF 1996

Chapter 2

Bill of Rights

7 Rights

(1) This Bill of Rights is a cornerstone of democracy in South Africa. It enshrines the rights of all people in our country and affirms the democratic values of human dignity, equality and freedom.

(2) The state must respect, protect, promote and fulfil the rights in the Bill of Rights.

(3) The rights in the Bill of Rights are subject to the limitations contained or referred to in section 36, or elsewhere in the Bill.

8 Application

(1) The Bill of Rights applies to all law, and binds the legislature, the executive, the judiciary and all organs of state.

(2) A provision of the Bill of Rights binds a natural or a juristic person if, and to the extent that, it is applicable, taking into account the nature of the right and the nature of any duty imposed by the right.

(3) When applying a provision of the Bill of Rights to a natural or juristic person in terms of subsection (2), a court —

(a) in order to give effect to a right in the Bill, must apply, or if necessary develop, the common law to the extent that legislation does not give effect to that right; and

(b) may develop rules of the common law to limit the right, provided that the limitation is in accordance with section 36(1).

(4) A juristic person is entitled to the rights in the Bill of Rights to the extent required by the nature of the rights and the nature of that juristic person.

9 Equality

(1) Everyone is equal before the law and has the right to equal protection and benefit of the law.

(2) Equality includes the full and equal enjoyment of all rights and freedoms. To promote the achievement of equality, legislative and other measures designed to protect or advance persons, or categories of persons, disadvantaged by unfair discrimination may be taken.

(3) The state may not unfairly discriminate directly or indirectly against anyone on one or more grounds, including race, gender, sex, pregnancy, marital status, ethnic or social origin, colour, sexual orientation, age, disability, religion, conscience, belief, culture, language and birth.

(4) No person may unfairly discriminate directly or indirectly against anyone on one or more grounds in terms of subsection (3). National legislation must be enacted to prevent or prohibit unfair discrimination.

(5) Discrimination on one or more of the grounds listed in subsection (3) is unfair unless it is established that the discrimination is fair.

10 Human dignity

Everyone has inherent dignity and the right to have their dignity respected and protected.

11 Life

Everyone has the right to life.

12 Freedom and security of the person

(1) Everyone has the right to freedom and security of the person, which includes the right—

(a)   not to be deprived of freedom arbitrarily or without just cause;

(b)   not to be detained without trial;

(c)   to be free from all forms of violence from either public or private sources;

(d)   not to be tortured in any way; and

(e)   not to be treated or punished in a cruel, inhuman or degrading way.

(2) Everyone has the right to bodily and psychological integrity, which includes the right—

(a)   to make decisions concerning reproduction;

(b)   to security in and control over their body; and

(c)   not to be subjected to medical or scientific experiments without their informed consent.

13 Slavery, servitude and forced labour

No one may be subjected to slavery, servitude or forced labour.

14 Privacy

Everyone has the right to privacy, which includes the right not to have —

(a)   their person or home searched;

(b)   their property searched;

(c)   their possessions seized; or

(d)   the privacy of their communications infringed.

15 Freedom of religion, belief ond opinion

(1) Everyone has the right to freedom of conscience, religion, thought, belief and opinion.

(2) Religious observances may be conducted at state or state-aided institutions, provided that —

(a)   those observances follow rules made by the appropriate public authorities;

(b)   they are conducted on an equitable basis; and

(c)   attendance at them is free and voluntary.

(3) *(a)* This section does not prevent legislation recognising —

 (i)   marriages concluded under any tradition, or a system of religious, personal or family law; or

(ii)   systems of personal and family law under any tradition, or adhered to by persons professing a particular religion.

(b) Recognition in terms of paragraph *(a)* must be consistent with this section and the other provisions of the Constitution.

16 Freedom of expression

(1) Everyone has the right to freedom of expression, which includes —

(a)   freedom of the press and other media;

(b)   freedom to receive or impart information or ideas;

(c)   freedom of artistic creativity; and

(d)   academic freedom and freedom of scientific research.

(2) The right in subsection (1) does not extend to —

(a)   propaganda for war;

(b)   incitement of imminent violence; or

(c)   advocacy of hatred that is based on race, ethnicity, gender or religion, and that constitutes incitement to cause harm.

17 Assembly, demonstration, picket and petition

Everyone has the right, peacefully and unarmed, to assemble, to demonstrate, to picket and to present petitions.

18 Freedom of association

Everyone has the right to freedom of association.

19 Political rights

(1) Every citizen is free to make political choices, which includes the right —
(a)   to form a political party;
(b)   to participate in the activities of, or recruit members for, a political party; and
(c)   to campaign for a political party or cause.
(2) Every citizen has the right to free, fair and regular elections for any legislative body established in terms of the Constitution.
(3) Every adult citizen has the right —
(a)   to vote in elections for any legislative body established in terms of the Constitution, and to do so in secret; and
(b)   to stand for public office and, if elected, to hold office.

20 Citizenship

No citizen may be deprived of citizenship.

21 Freedom of movement and residence

(1) Everyone has the right to freedom of movement.
(2) Everyone has the right to leave the Republic.
(3) Every citizen has the right to enter, to remain in and to reside anywhere in, the Republic.
(4) Every citizen has the right to a passport.

22 Freedom of trade, occupation and profession

Every citizen has the right to choose their trade, occupation or profession freely. The practice of a trade, occupation or profession may be regulated by law.

23 Labour relations

(1) Everyone has the right to fair labour practices.
(2) Every worker has the right —
(a)   to form and join a trade union;
(b)   to participate in the activities and programmes of a trade union; and
(c)   to strike.
(3) Every employer has the right —
(a)   to form and join an employers' organisation; and
(b)   to participate in the activities and programmes of an employers' organisation.
(4) Every trade union and every employers' organisation has the right —
(a)   to determine its own administration, programmes and activities;
(b)   to organise; and
(c)   to form and join a federation.
(5) Every trade union, employers' organisation and employer has the right to engage in collective bargaining. National legislation may be enacted to regulate collective bargaining. To the extent that the legislation may limit a right in this Chapter, the limitation must comply with section 36(1).
(6) National legislation may recognise union security arrangements contained in collective

agreements. To the extent that the legislation may limit a right in this Chapter the limitation must comply with section 36(1).

24 Environment

Everyone has the right

(a) to an environment that is not harmful to their health or well-being; and

(b) to have the environment protected, for the benefit of present and future generations, through reasonable legislative and other measures that
   (i) prevent pollution and ecological degradation;
   (ii) promote conservation; and
   (iii) secure ecologically sustainable development and use of natural resources while promoting justifiable economic and social development.

25 Property

(1) No one may be deprived of property except in terms of law of general application, and no law may permit arbitrary deprivation of property.

(2) Property may be expropriated only in terms of law of general application —

(a) for a public purpose or in the public interest; and

(b) subject to compensation, the amount of which and the time and manner of payment of which have either been agreed to by those affected or decided or approved by a court.

(3) The amount of the compensation and the time and manner of payment must be just and equitable, reflecting an equitable balance between the public interest and the interests of those affected, having regard to all relevant circumstances, including —

(a) the current use of the property;

(b) the history of the acquisition and use of the property;

(c) the market value of the property;

(d) the extent of direct state investment and subsidy in the acquisition and beneficial capital improvement of the property; and

(e) the purpose of the expropriation.

(4) For the purposes of this section —

(a) the public interest includes the nation's commitment to land reform, and to reforms to bring about equitable access to all South Africa's natural resources; and

(b) property is not limited to land.

(5) The state must take reasonable legislative and other measures, within its available resources, to foster conditions which enable citizens to gain access to land on an equitable basis.

(6) A person or community whose tenure of land is legally insecure as a result of past racially discriminatory laws or practices is entitled, to the extent provided by an Act of Parliament, either to tenure which is legally secure or to comparable redress.

(7) A person or community dispossessed of property after 19 June 1913 as a result of past racially discriminatory laws or practices is entitled, to the extent provided by an Act of Parliament, either to restitution of that property or to equitable redress.

(8) No provision of this section may impede the state from taking legislative and other measures to achieve land, water and related reform, in order to redress the results of past racial discrimination, provided that any departure from the provisions of this section is in accordance with the provisions of section 36(1).

(9) Parliament must enact the legislation referred to in subsection (6).

26 Housing

(1) Everyone has the right to have access to adequate housing.

(2) The state must take reasonable legislative and other measures, within its available resources, to achieve the progressive realisation of this right.

(3) No one may be evicted from their home, or have their home demolished, without an

order of court made after considering all the relevant circumstances. No legislation may permit arbitrary evictions.

27 Health care, food, water and social security

(1) Everyone has the right to have access to —

(a) health care services, including reproductive health care;

(b) sufficient food and water; and

(c) social security, including, if they are unable to support themselves and their dependents, appropriate social assistance.

(2) The state must take reasonable legislative and other measures, within its available resources, to achieve the progressive realisation of each of these rights.

(3) No one may be refused emergency medical treatment.

28 Children

(1) Every child has the right —

(a) to a name and a nationality from birth;

(b) to family care or parental care, or to appropriate alternative care when removed from the family environment;

(c) to basic nutrition, shelter, basic health care services and social services;

(d) to be protected from maltreatment, neglect, abuse or degradation;

(e) to be protected from exploitative labour practices;

(f) not to be required or permitted to perform work or provide services that
   (i) are inappropriate for a person of that child's age; or
   (ii) place at risk the child's well-being, education, physical or mental health or spiritual, moral or social development;

(g) not to be detained except as a measure of last resort, in which case, in addition to the rights a child enjoys under sections 12 and 35, the child may be detained only for the shortest appropriate period of time, and has the right to be —
   (i) kept separately from detained persons over the age of 18 years; and
   (ii) treated in a manner, and kept in conditions, that take account of the child's age;

(h) to have a legal practitioner assigned to the child by the state, and at state expense, in civil proceedings affecting the child, if substantial injustice would otherwise result; and

(i) not to be used directly in armed conflict, and to be protected in times of armed conflict.

(2) A child's best interests are of paramount importance in every matter concerning the child.

(3) In this section "child" means a person under the age of 18 years.

29 Education

(1) Everyone has the right —

(a) to a basic education, including adult basic education; and

(b) to further education, which the state, through reasonable measures, must make progressively available and accessible.

(2) Everyone has the right to receive education in the official language or languages of their choice in public educational institutions where that education is reasonably practicable. In order to ensure the effective access to, and implementation of, this right, the state must consider all reasonable educational alternatives, including single medium institutions, taking into account —

(a) equity;

(b) practicability; and

(c) the need to redress the results of past racially discriminatory laws and practices.

(3) Everyone has the right to establish and maintain, at their own expense, independent educational institutions that —

(a) do not discriminate on the basis of race;

(b) are registered with the state; and

(c) maintain standards that are not inferior to standards at comparable public educational institutions.

(4) Subsection (3) does not preclude state subsidies for independent educational institutions.

30 Language and culture

Everyone has the right to use the language and to participate in the cultural life of their choice, but no one exercising these rights may do so in a manner inconsistent with any provision of the Bill of Rights.

31 Cultural, religious and linguistic communities

(1) Persons belonging to a cultural, religious or linguistic community may not be denied the right, with other members of that community —
(a) to enjoy their culture, practise their religion and use their language; and
(b) to form, join and maintain cultural, religious and linguistic associations and other organs of civil society.
(2) The rights in subsection (1) may not be exercised in a manner inconsistent with any provision of the Bill of Rights.

32 Access to information

(1) Everyone has the right of access to —
(a) any information held by the state; and
(b) any information that is held by another person and that is required for the exercise or protection of any rights.
(2) National legislation must be enacted to give effect to this right, and may provide for reasonable measures to alleviate the administrative and financial burden on the state.

33 Just administrative action

(1) Everyone has the right to administrative action that is lawful, reasonable and procedurally fair.
(2) Everyone whose rights have been adversely affected by administrative action has the right to be given written reasons.
(3) National legislation must be enacted to give effect to these rights, and must —
(a) provide for the review of administrative action by a court or, where appropriate, an independent and impartial tribunal;
(b) impose a duty on the state to give effect to the rights in subsections (1) and (2); and
(c) promote an efficient administration.

34 Access to courts

Everyone has the right to have any dispute that can be resolved by the application of law decided in a fair public hearing before a court or, where appropriate, another independent and impartial tribunal or forum.

35 Arrested, detained and accused persons

(1) Everyone who is arrested for allegedly committing an offence has the right —
(a) to remain silent;
(b) to be informed promptly
  (i) of the right to remain silent; and
  (ii) of the consequences of not remaining silent;
(c) not to be compelled to make any confession or admission that could be used in evidence against that person;
(d) to be brought before a court as soon as reasonably possible, but not later than
  (i) 48 hours after the arrest; or
  (ii) the end of the first court day after the expiry of the 48 hours, if the 48 hours expire outside ordinary court hours or on a day which is not an ordinary court day;
(e) at the first court appearance after being arrested, to be charged or to be informed of the reason for the detention to continue, or to be released; and

412

(f) to be released from detention if the interests of justice permit, subject to reasonable conditions.

(2) Everyone who is detained, including every sentenced prisoner, has the right —

(a) to be informed promptly of the reason for being detained;
(b) to choose, and to consult with, a legal practitioner, and to be informed of this right promptly;
(c) to have a legal practitioner assigned to the detained person by the state and at state expense, if substantial injustice would otherwise result, and to be informed of this right promptly;
(d) to challenge the lawfulness of the detention in person before a court and, if the detention is unlawful, to be released;
(e) to conditions of detention that are consistent with human dignity, including at least exercise and the provision, at state expense, of adequate accommodation, nutrition, reading material and medical treatment; and
(f) to communicate with, and be visited by, that person's —
    (i) spouse or partner;
    (ii) next of kin;
    (iii) chosen religious counsellor; and
    (iv) chosen medical practitioner.

(3) Every accused person has a right to a fair trial, which includes the right —

(a) to be informed of the charge with sufficient detail to answer it;
(b) to have adequate time and facilities to prepare a defence;
(c) to a public trial before an ordinary court;
(d) to have their trial begin and conclude without unreasonable delay;
(e) to be present when being tried;
(f) to choose, and be represented by, a legal practitioner, and to be informed of this right promptly;
(g) to have a legal practitioner assigned to the accused person by the state and at state expense, if substantial injustice would otherwise result, and to be informed of this right promptly;
(h) to be presumed innocent, to remain silent, and not to testify during the proceedings;
(i) to adduce and challenge evidence;
(j) not to be compelled to give self-incriminating evidence;
(k) to be tried in a language that the accused person understands or, if that is not practicable, to have the proceedings interpreted in that language;
(l) not to be convicted for an act or omission that was not an offence under either national or international law at the time it was committed or omitted;
(m) not to be tried for an offence in respect of an act or omission for which that person has previously been either acquitted or convicted;
(n) to the benefit of the least severe of the prescribed punishments if the prescribed punishment for the offence has been changed between the time that the offence was committed and the time of sentencing; and
(o) of appeal to, or review by, a higher court.

(4) Whenever this section requires information to be given to a person, that information must be given a language that the person understands.

(5) Evidence obtained in a manner that violates any right in the Bill of Rights must be excluded if the admission of that evidence would render the trial unfair or otherwise be detrimental to the administration of justice.

36 Limitation of rights

(1) The rights in the Bill of Rights may be limited only in terms of law of general application to the extent that the limitation is reasonable and justifiable in an open and democratic society based on human dignity, equality and freedom, taking into account all relevant factors, including —

(a) the nature of the right;
(b) the importance of the purpose of the limitation;

(c) the nature and extent of the limitation;

(d) the relation between the limitation and its purpose; and

(e) less restrictive means to achieve the purpose.

(2) Except as provided in subsection (1) or in any other provision of the Constitution, no law may limit any right entrenched in the Bill of Rights.

37 States of emergency

(1) A state of emergency may be declared only in terms of an Act of Parliament, and only when —

(a) the life of the nation is threatened by war, invasion, general insurrection, disorder, natural disaster or other public emergency; and

(b) the declaration is necessary to restore peace and order.

(2) A declaration of a state of emergency, and any legislation enacted or other action taken in consequence of that declaration, may be effective only —

(a) prospectively; and

(b) for no more than 21 days from the date of the declaration, unless the National Assembly resolves to extend the declaration. The Assembly may extend a declaration of a state of emergency for no more than three months at a time. The first extension of the state of emergency must be by a resolution adopted with a supporting vote of a majority of the members of the Assembly. Any subsequent extension must be by a resolution adopted with a supporting vote of at least 60 per cent of the members of the Assembly. A resolution in terms of this paragraph may be adopted only following a public debate in the Assembly.

(3) Any competent court may decide on the validity of —

(a) a declaration of a state of emergency;

(b) any extension of a declaration of a state of emergency; or

(c) any legislation enacted, or other action taken, in consequence of a declaration of a state of emergency.

(4) Any legislation enacted in consequence of a declaration of a state of emergency may derogate from the Bill of Rights only to the extent that —

(a) the derogation is strictly required by the emergency; and

(b) the legislation —

  (i) is consistent with the Republic's obligations under international law applicable to states of emergency;

  (ii) conforms to subsection (5); and

  (iii) is published in the national *Government Gazette* as soon as reasonably possible after being enacted.

(5) No Act of Parliament that authorises a declaration of a state of emergency, and no legislation enacted or other action taken in consequence of a declaration, may permit or authorise —

(a) indemnifying the state, or any person, in respect of any unlawful act;

(b) any derogation from this section; or

(c) any derogation from a section mentioned in column 1 of the Table of Non-Derogable Rights, to the extent indicated opposite that section in column 3 of the Table.

Table of Non-Derogable Rights

1 Section number	2 Section title	3 Extent to which the right is non-derogable
9	Equality	With respect to unfair discrimination solely on the grounds of race, colour, ethnic or social origin, sex, religion or language
10	Human dignity	Entirely

Table of Non-Derogable Rights

1 Section number	2 Section title	3 Extent to which the right is non-derogable
11	Life	Entirely
12	Freedom and security of the person	With respect to subsections (1)*(d)* and *(e)* and (2)*(c)*.
13	Slavery, servitude and forced labour	With respect to slavery and servitude
28	Children	With respect to: — subsection (1)*(d)* and *(e)*; — the rights in subparagraphs (i) and (ii) of subsection (1)*(g)*; and — subsection *(l)*(i) in respect of children of 15 years and younger
35	Arrested, detained and accused persons	With respect to: — subsections (1)*(a)*, *(b)* and *(c)* and (2)*(d)*; — the rights in paragraphs *(a)* to *(o)* of subsection (3), excluding paragraph *(d)*; — subsection (4); and — subsection (5) with respect to the exclusion of evidence if the admission of that evidence would render the trial unfair.

(6) Whenever anyone is detained without trial in consequence of a derogation of rights resulting from a declaration of a state of emergency, the following conditions must be observed:

(a) An adult family member or friend of the detainee must be contacted as soon as reasonably possible, and informed that the person has been detained.

(b) A notice must be published in the national *Government Gazette* within five days of the person being detained, stating the detainee's name and place of detention and referring to the emergency measure in terms of which that person has been detained.

(c) The detainee must be allowed to choose, and be visited at any reasonable time by, a medical practitioner.

(d) The detainee must be allowed to choose, and be visited at any reasonable time by, a legal representative.

(e) A court must review the detention as soon as reasonably possible, but no later than 10 days after the date the person was detained, and the court must release the detainee unless it is necessary to continue the detention to restore peace and order.

(f) A detainee who is not released in terms of a review under paragraph *(e)*, or who is not released in terms of a review under this paragraph, may apply to a court for a further review of the detention at any time after 10 days have passed since the previous review, and the court must release the detainee unless it is still necessary to continue the detention to restore peace and order.

(g) The detainee must be allowed to appear in person before any court considering the detention, to be represented by a legal practitioner at those hearings, and to make representations against continued detention.

(h) The state must present written reasons to the court to justify the continued detention of

the detainee, and must give a copy of those reasons to the detainee at least two days before the court reviews the detention.

(7) If a court releases a detainee, that person may not be detained again on the same grounds unless the state first shows a court good cause for re-detaining that person.

(8) Subsections (6) and (7) do not apply to persons who are not South African citizens and who are detained in consequence of an international armed conflict. Instead, the state must comply with the standards binding on the Republic under international humanitarian law in respect of the detention of such persons.

38 Enforcement of rights

Anyone listed in this section has the right to approach a competent court, alleging that a right in the Bill of Rights has been infringed or threatened, and the court may grant appropriate relief, including a declaration of rights. The persons who may approach a court are —

(a) anyone acting in their own interest;

(b) anyone acting on behalf of another person who cannot act in their own name;

(c) anyone acting as a member of, or in the interest of, a group or class of persons;

(d) anyone acting in the public interest; and

(e) an association acting in the interest of its members.

39 Interpretation of Bill of Rights

(1) When interpreting the Bill of Rights, a court, tribunal or forum —

(a) must promote the values that underlie an open and democratic society based on human dignity, equality and freedom;

(b) must consider international law; and

(c) may consider foreign law.

(2) When interpreting any legislation, and when developing the common law or customary law, every court, tribunal or forum must promote the spirit, purport and objects of the Bill of Rights.

(3) The Bill of Rights does not deny the existence of any other rights or freedoms that are recognised or conferred by common law, customary law or legislation, to the extent that they are consistent with the Bill.

Constitution of the Republic of South Africa, Act 200 of 1993

CHAPTER 3
Fundamental Rights

7 Application

(1) This Chapter shall bind all legislative and executive organs of state at all levels of government.

(2) This Chapter shall apply to all law in force and all administrative decisions taken and acts performed during the period of operation of this Constitution.

(3) Juristic persons shall be entitled to the rights contained in this Chapter where, and to the extent that, the nature of the rights permits.

(4) *(a)* When an infringement of or threat to any right entrenched in this Chapter is alleged, any person referred to in paragraph *(b)* shall be entitled to apply to a competent court of law for appropriate relief, which may include a declaration of rights.

(b) The relief referred to in paragraph *(a)* may be sought by —

 (i) a person acting in his or her own interest;

 (ii) an association acting in the interest of its members;

(iii) a person acting on behalf of another person who is not in a position to seek such relief in his or her own name;

(iv) a person acting as a member of or in the interest of a group or class of persons; or

 (v) a person acting in the public interest.

8 Equality

(1) Every person shall have the right to equality before the law and to equal protection of the law.

(2) No person shall be unfairly discriminated against, directly or indirectly, and, without derogating from the generality of this provision, on one or more of the following grounds in particular: race, gender, sex, ethnic or social origin, colour, sexual orientation, age, disability, religion, conscience, belief, culture or language.

(3) *(a)* This section shall not preclude measures designed to achieve the adequate protection and advancement of persons or groups or categories of persons disadvantaged by unfair discrimination, in order to enable their full and equal enjoyment of all rights and freedoms.

(b) Every person or community dispossessed of rights in land before the commencement of this Constitution under any law which would have been inconsistent with subsection (2) had that subsection been in operation at the time of the dispossession, shall be entitled to claim restitution of such rights subject to and in accordance with sections 121, 122 and 123.

(4) *Prima facie* proof of discrimination on any of the grounds specified in subsection (2) shall be presumed to be sufficient proof of unfair discrimination as contemplated in that subsection, until the contrary is established.

9 Life

Every person shall have the right to life.

10 Human dignity

Every person shall have the right to respect for and protection of his or her dignity.

11 Freedom and security of the person

(1) Every person shall have the right to freedom and security of the person, which shall include the right not to be detained without trial.

(2) No person shall be subject to torture of any kind, whether physical, mental or emotional, nor shall any person be subject to cruel, inhuman or degrading treatment or punishment.

12 Servitude and forced labour

No person shall be subject to servitude or forced labour.

13 Privacy

Every person shall have the right to his or her personal privacy, which shall include the right not to be subject to searches of his or her person, home or property, the seizure of private possessions or the violation of private communications.

14 Religion, belief and opinion

(1) Every person shall have the right to freedom of conscience, religion, thought, belief and opinion, which shall include academic freedom in institutions of higher learning.

(2) Without derogating from the generality of subsection (1), religious observances may be conducted at state or state-aided institutions under rules established by an appropriate authority for that purpose, provided that such religious observances are conducted on an equitable basis and attendance at them is free and voluntary.

(3) Nothing in this Chapter shall preclude legislation recognising —

(a) a system of personal and family law adhered to by persons professing a particular religion; and

(b) the validity of marriages concluded under a system of religious law subject to specified procedures.

15 Freedom of expression

(1) Every person shall have the right to freedom of speech and expression, which shall include freedom of the press and other media, and the freedom of artistic creativity and scientific research.

(2) All media financed by or under the control of the state shall be regulated in a manner which ensures impartiality and the expression of a diversity of opinion.

16 Assembly, demonstration and petition

Every person shall have the right to assemble and demonstrate with others peacefully and unarmed, and to present petitions.

17 Freedom of association

Every person shall have the right to freedom of association.

18 Freedom of movement

Every person shall have the right to freedom of movement anywhere within the national territory.

19 Residence

Every person shall have the right freely to choose his or her place of residence anywhere in the national territory.

20 Citizens' rights

Every citizen shall have the right to enter, remain in and leave the Republic, and no citizen shall without justification be deprived of his or her citizenship.

21 Political rights

(1) Every citizen shall have the right —
(a) to form, to participate in the activities of and to recruit members for a political party;
(b) to campaign for a political party or cause; and
(c) freely to make political choices.

(2) Every citizen shall have the right to vote, to do so in secret and to stand for election to public office.

22 Access to court

Every person shall have the right to have justiciable disputes settled by a court of law or, where appropriate, another independent and impartial forum.

23 Access to information

Every person shall have the right of access to all information held by the state or any of its organs at any level of government in so far as such information is required for the exercise or protection of any of his or her rights.

24 Administrative justice

Every person shall have the right to —
(a) lawful administrative action where any of his or her rights or interests is affected or threatened;
(b) procedurally fair administrative action where any of his or her rights or legitimate expectations is affected or threatened;
(c) be furnished with reasons in writing for administrative action which affects any of his or her rights or interests unless the reasons for such action have been made public; and
(d) administrative action which is justifiable in relation to the reasons given for it where any of his or her rights is affected or threatened.

25 Detained, arrested and accused persons

(1) Every person who is detained, including every sentenced prisoner, shall have the right—
(a) to be informed promptly in a language which he or she understands of the reason for his or her detention;
(b) to be detained under conditions consonant with human dignity, which shall include at least the provision of adequate nutrition, reading material and medical treatment at state expense;
(c) to consult with a legal practitioner of his or her choice, to be informed of this right promptly and, where substantial injustice would otherwise result, to be provided with the services of a legal practitioner by the state;
(d) to be given the opportunity to communicate with, and to be visited by, his or her spouse or partner, next-of-kin, religious counsellor and a medical practitioner of his or her choice; and
(e) to challenge the lawfulness of his or her detention in person before a court of law and to be released if such detention is unlawful.

(2) Every person arrested for the alleged commission of an offence shall, in addition to the rights which he or she has as a detained person, have the right —
(a) promptly to be informed, in a language which he or she understands, that he or she has the right to remain silent and to be warned of the consequences of making any statement;
(b) as soon as it is reasonably possible, but not later than 48 hours after the arrest or, if the said period of 48 hours expires outside ordinary court hours or on a day which is not a court day, the first court day after such expiry, to be brought before an ordinary court of law and to be charged or to be informed of the reason for his or her further detention, failing which he or she shall be entitled to be released;

419

(c) not to be compelled to make a confession or admission which could be used in evidence against him or her; and

(d) to be released from detention with or without bail, unless the interests of justice require otherwise.

(3) Every accused person shall have the right to a fair trial, which shall include the right—

(a) to a public trial before an ordinary court of law within a reasonable time after having been charged;

(b) to be informed with sufficient particularity of the charge;

(c) to be presumed innocent and to remain silent during plea proceedings or trial and not to testify during trial;

(d) to adduce and challenge evidence, and not to be a compellable witness against himself or herself;

(e) to be represented by a legal practitioner of his or her choice or, where substantial injustice would otherwise result, to be provided with legal representation at state expense, and to be informed of these rights;

(f) not to be convicted of an offence in respect of any act or omission which was not an offence at the time it was committed, and not to be sentenced to a more severe punishment than that which was applicable when the offence was committed;

(g) not to be tried again for any offence of which he or she has previously been convicted or acquitted;

(h) to have recourse by way of appeal or review to a higher court than the court of first instance;

(i) to be tried in a language which he or she understands or, failing this, to have the proceedings interpreted to him or her; and

(j) to be sentenced within a reasonable time after conviction.

26 Economic activity

(1) Every person shall have the right freely to engage in economic activity and to pursue a livelihood anywhere in the national territory.

(2) Subsection (1) shall not preclude measures designed to promote the protection or the improvement of the quality of life, economic growth, human development, social justice, basic conditions of employment, fair labour practices or equal opportunity for all, provided such measures are justifiable in an open and democratic society based on freedom and equality.

27 Labour relations

(1) Every person shall have the right to fair labour practices.

(2) Workers shall have the right to form and join trade unions, and employers shall have the right to form and join employers' organisations.

(3) Workers and employers shall have the right to organise and bargain collectively.

(4) Workers shall have the right to strike for the purpose of collective bargaining.

(5) Employers' recourse to the lock-out for the purpose of collective bargaining shall not be impaired, subject to section 33 (1).

28 Property

(1) Every person shall have the right to acquire and hold rights in property and, to the extent that the nature of the rights permits, to dispose of such rights.

(2) No deprivation of any rights in property shall be permitted otherwise than in accordance with a law.

(3) Where any rights in property are expropriated pursuant to a law referred to in subsection (2), such expropriation shall be permissible for public purposes only and shall be subject to the payment of agreed compensation or, failing agreement, to the payment of such compensation and within such period as may be determined by a court of law as just and equitable, taking into account all relevant factors, including, in the case of the determination of compensation, the use to which the property is being put, the history of its acquisition, its

market value, the value of the investments in it by those affected and the interests of those affected.

29 Environment

Every person shall have the right to an environment which is not detrimental to his or her health or well-being.

30 Children

(1) Every child shall have the right —
(a) to a name and nationality as from birth;
(b) to parental care;
(c) to security, basic nutrition and basic health and social services;
(d) not to be subject to neglect or abuse; and
(e) not to be subject to exploitative labour practices nor to be required or permitted to perform work which is hazardous or harmful to his or her education, health or well-being.

(2) Every child who is in detention shall, in addition to the rights which he or she has in terms of section 25, have the right to be detained under conditions and to be treated in a manner that takes account of his or her age.

(3) For the purpose of this section a child shall mean a person under the age of 18 years and in all matters concerning such child his or her best interest shall be paramount.

31 Language and culture

Every person shall have the right to use the language and to participate in the cultural life of his or her choice.

32 Education

Every person shall have the right —
(a) to basic education and to equal access to educational institutions;
(b) to instruction in the language of his or her choice where this is reasonably practicable; and
(c) to establish, where practicable, educational institutions based on a common culture, language or religion, provided that there shall be no discrimination on the ground of race.

33 Limitation

(1) The rights entrenched in this Chapter may be limited by law of general application, provided that such limitation —
(a) shall be permissible only to the extent that it is —
   (i) reasonable; and
   (ii) justifiable in an open and democratic society based on freedom and equality; and
(b) shall not negate the essential content of the right in question,
and provided further that any limitation to —
(aa) a right entrenched in section 10, 11, 12, 14 (1), 21, 25 or 30 (1) (d) or (e) or (2); or
(bb) a right entrenched in section 15, 16, 17, 18, 23 or 24, in so far as such right relates to free and fair political activity,
shall, in addition to being reasonable as required in paragraph (a) (i), also be necessary.

(2) Save as provided for in subsection (1) or any other provision of this Constitution, no law, whether a rule of the common law, customary law or legislation, shall limit any right entrenched in this Chapter.

(3) The entrenchment of the rights in terms of this Chapter shall not be construed as denying the existence of any other rights or freedoms recognised or conferred by common law, customary law or legislation to the extent that they are not inconsistent with this Chapter.

(4) This Chapter shall not preclude measures designed to prohibit unfair discrimination by bodies and persons other than those bound in terms of section 7 (1).

(5) *(a)* The provisions of a law in force at the commencement of this Constitution promoting fair employment practices, orderly and equitable collective bargaining and the regulation of industrial action shall remain of full force and effect until repealed or amended by the legislature.

(b) If a proposed enactment amending or repealing a law referred to in paragraph *(a)* deals with a matter in respect of which the National Manpower Commission, referred to in section 2A of the Labour Relations Act, 1956 (Act 28 of 1956), or any other similar body which may replace the Commission, is competent in terms of a law then in force to consider and make recommendations, such proposed enactment shall not be introduced in Parliament unless the said Commission or such other body has been given an opportunity to consider the proposed enactment and to make recommendations with regard thereto.

34 State of emergency and suspension

(1) A state of emergency shall be proclaimed prospectively under an Act of Parliament, and shall be declared only where the security of the Republic is threatened by war, invasion, general insurrection or disorder or at a time of national disaster, and if the declaration of a state of emergency is necessary to restore peace or order.

(2) The declaration of a state of emergency and any action taken, including any regulation enacted, in consequence thereof, shall be of force for a period of not more than 21 days, unless it is extended for a period of not longer than three months, or consecutive periods of not longer than three months at a time, by resolution of the National Assembly adopted by a majority of at least two-thirds of all its members.

(3) Any superior court shall be competent to enquire into the validity of a declaration of a state of emergency, any extension thereof, and any action taken, including any regulation enacted, under such declaration.

(4) The rights entrenched in this Chapter may be suspended only in consequence of the declaration of a state of emergency, and only to the extent necessary to restore peace or order.

(5) Neither any law which provides for the declaration of a state of emergency, nor any action taken, including any regulation enacted, in consequence thereof, shall permit or authorise —

(a) the creation of retrospective crimes;

(b) the indemnification of the state or of persons acting under its authority for unlawful actions during the state of emergency; or

(c) the suspension of this section, and sections 7, 8 (2), 9, 10, 11 (2), 12, 14, 27 (1) and (2), 30 (1) *(d)* and *(e)* and (2) and 33 (1) and (2).

(6) Where a person is detained under a state of emergency the detention shall be subject to the following conditions:

(a) An adult family member or friend of the detainee shall be notified of the detention as soon as is reasonably possible;

(b) the names of all detainees and a reference to the measures in terms of which they are being detained shall be published in the *Gazette* within five days of their detention;

(c) when rights entrenched in section 11 or 25 have been suspended —

   (i) the detention of a detainee shall, as soon as it is reasonably possible but not later than 10 days after his or her detention, be reviewed by a court of law, and the court shall order the release of the detainee if it is satisfied that the detention is not necessary to restore peace or order;

   (ii) a detainee shall at any stage after the expiry of a period of 10 days after a review in terms of subparagraph (i) be entitled to apply to a court of law for a further review of his or her detention, and the court shall order the release of the detainee if it is satisfied that the detention is no longer necessary to restore peace or order;

(d) the detainee shall be entitled to appear before the court in person, to be represented by legal counsel, and to make representations against his or her continued detention;

(e) the detainee shall be entitled at all reasonable times to have access to a legal representative of his or her choice;

(f) the detainee shall be entitled at all times to have access to a medical practitioner of his or her choice; and

(g) the state shall for the purpose of a review referred to in paragraph *(c)*(i) or (ii) submit written reasons to justify the detention or further detention of the detainee to the court, and shall furnish the detainee with such reasons not later than two days before the review.

(7) If a court of law, having found the grounds for a detainee's detention unjustified, orders his or her release, such a person shall not be detained again on the same grounds unless the state shows good cause to a court of law prior to such re-detention.

35 Interpretation

(1) In interpreting the provisions of this Chapter a court of law shall promote the values which underlie an open and democratic society based on freedom and equality and shall, where applicable, have regard to public international law applicable to the protection of the rights entrenched in this Chapter, and may have regard to comparable foreign case law.

(2) No law which limits any of the rights entrenched in this Chapter, shall be constitutionally invalid solely by reason of the fact that the wording used *prima facie* exceeds the limits imposed in this Chapter, provided such a law is reasonably capable of a more restricted interpretation which does not exceed such limits, in which event such law shall be construed as having a meaning in accordance with the said more restricted interpretation.

(3) In the interpretation of any law and the application and development of the common law and customary law, a court shall have due regard to the spirit, purport and objects of this Chapter.

INDEX

425

WITNESSES *(cont)*
    oath by — *see* OATH
    presence in court prior to testifying, 383
    recalled by court in criminal cases, 291–2
    religious belief, no, 233
    state witnesses, calling of, 288–9
    witness statement privilege, 126, 139